THE GENOCIDE
OF THE
OTTOMAN GREEKS

Studies on the State–Sponsored Campaign of Extermination of the Christians of Asia Minor 1912-1922 and Its Aftermath: History, Law, Memory

Turkish troops standing beside their hanged victim,
a decapitated and mutilated Greek woman, in Nazili (Aydin).
Photograph by N. Rigopoulos, taken 15 June 1920.
(courtesy Nikolaos Hlamides)

THE GENOCIDE OF THE OTTOMAN GREEKS

Studies on the State–Sponsored Campaign of Extermination of the Christians of Asia Minor, 1912-1922 and Its Aftermath: History, Law, Memory

Edited by

Tessa Hofmann

Matthias Bjørnlund

Vasileios Meichanetsidis

ΕΝΘΑ ΤΙΘΑΙΒΩΣΣΟΥΣΙ ΜΕΛΙΣΣΑΙ

Published by Aristide D. Caratzas

New York & Athens

The Genocide of the Ottoman Greeks
Studies in State-Sponsored Campaign of Extermination of the Christians of Asia Minor, 1912-1922 and Its Aftermath: History, Law, Memory

Published by
Aristide D. Caratzas, Publisher
An Imprint of
MELISSA INTERNATIONAL LTD.
P. O Box 344H • Scarsdale, NY 10583 • USA

Web Site: www.caratzas.com
Email: contact@caratzas.com

ISBN [13]: 978-0-89241-615-8
ISBN [10]: 0-89241-615-7

Table of Contents

Memory is everything to mankind.
Loss of memory is insanity.
Yet people often force themselves to forget events
and regard failure to remember them
as an achievement and a joy.

Forgetting injuries that were inflicted upon us
is sometimes a sign of maturity and wisdom.
This should not be applied, however,
when we consider instances
in which we have caused harm to others.
It is undeniable that, as time goes by,
our ability to recall a particular event fades,
leaving behind a dim and unclear picture.
This state of affairs helps us, to a certain extent,
to forget our pains and sufferings.

It is wrong to apply the same criteria on issues
that concern the masses.
There are epics, heroic deeds,
disasters and sufferings in every nation's history
that cannot be erased from the collective memory.
These events belong to history;
in this way new generations have the chance
to learn from good and evil deed of their forefathers,
to draw lessons and to avoid making the same mistakes themselves.

(Faik Ökte: Preface to *The Tragedy of the Turkish Capital Tax*, 1987)

Publisher's Note

OVER THE LAST TWO DECADES SCHOLARSHIP relating to the transition from the Ottoman Empire to the Republic of Turkey (1912-1923) has begun to focus more on the deliberate and violent physical elimination or forced expulsion ("ethnic cleansing," to use an anachronistic term) during that period, of the Christian populations of Asia Minor and eastern Thrace.

The efforts to eliminate the Greeks, the Armenians and the Assyrians, peoples whose biological presence in that geographic space goes back millennia before recorded history, are integral to the process that led to the creation of what became the modern Turkish Republic. The predatory methods used, and indeed what may be called a policy of effective physical elimination of populations, as well as of the cultural traces of their presence in areas they inhabited, bespeak of planning at the highest levels of government and its systematic implementation.

The population numbers are stark in terms of order of magnitude. An extensive bibliography on late Ottoman demographics attests to this fact: In 1912 the Christians of Asia Minor and Thrace numbered in the millions; by 1923 these numbers were reduced probably to less than 300,000.

Studies of mass murder and genocide in mid-twentieth century have been extensive, most notably those carried out by the Soviets in the thirties and by the German National Socialists during the Second World War.

On the other hand, studies relating to the genocide of the Christians of the Ottoman Empire until recently had been swept into the dustbin of history. Due to shifting geopolitical configurations western democratic governments were all too cautious in their diplomatic relations to raise the subject with a succession of Turkish regimes, whose sensitivity on the subject drew from the fact that their Kemalist foundation was built on this genocide.

Democratic values only touch the surface of the political process in Turkey even today, while its basic assumptions derive from an amalgam of Ottoman, Kemalist and Islamic precepts. Thus Turkish regimes developed a policy of denial of genocide and elaborate strategies and tactics to implement it. Some elements of this policy include, (a) control of the language used to describe crimes perpetrated by the government (George Orwell's phrase is apt in this instance, "[p]olitical language. . . is designed to make lies sound truthful and murder respectable..."); (b) legal prosecution of those referring to the genocide in the press (the charge generally is "insulting Turkishness"); (c) impeding study of the subject by limiting access to archival and other evidentiary material to all but a few professionals (mostly Turks and some Americans scholars) who have been enlisted to legitimate denial; and, (d) international diplomatic and lobbying operations actively promoting denial.

Ironically, the lawyer Raphael Lemkin, who provided the basic conceptual underpinning for defining and prosecuting war criminals in Nürnberg (he coined the very term "genocide"), had studied the persecutions of the Christians in the Ottoman Empire and the early Turkish Republic. The article on the Lemkin papers included in this volume reveals that it is not a stretch to conclude that his study of these events contributed to his later formulation.

Much of the serious scholarly work on the genocide of the Asia Minor Christians produced since the 1990s deals with the extermination of the Armenian populations; in this context, the publication by this house in 1989 of a significant primary source, (U.S. Consul) Leslie Davis' *The Slaughterhouse Province: An American Diplomat's Report on the Armenian Genocide*, has been widely used and cited by scholars. It should be noted that the publication prompted *inter alia*, vandalism in this publisher's office in New Rochelle, NY.

Greek scholars, with some significant exceptions, have been less active in researching the subject of the violent elimination of the the Greek presence in Asia Minor and eastern Thrace, which spanned at least three millennia. The avoidance of the subject of the genocide by many mainline academics in Greece is the result of a convergence of factors, which range from governmental reticence to criticize Turkey spilling over into the academic world, to ideological currents promoting a diffuse internationalism cultivated by a network of NGOs, often supported by western governments and Turkish interests. As a result certain circles will suggest that even a reference to the genocide committed by the Turks is motivated by "nationalism," or even go so far as to deny it.

This volume represents a kind of scholarly opening statement to an international audience on the subject of the extermination or expulsion of the Ottoman Greeks, as part of the genocide of the Christians of Asia Minor. The editors and contributors have chosen a number of levels of approach that include a historical overview, documentation and analysis; reference to international law; genocide education (at least as approached in the United States); memorialization, i.e. formal efforts and projects of remembrance of the crimes and their victims; and conceptualization of the phenomenon of genocide, on the one hand, from the point of view of state formation, and on the other, relating to the question of the critical use of (pictorial) sources. It is hoped that these different directions may stimulate further study into this phenomenon that, at the very least, appears to have played a determinative role in the development of Greek, Balkan and Turkish societies and, increasingly, in the relations between the European states and Turkey.

19 May 2011

The Editors

MATTHIAS BJØRNLUND is a Danish archival historian who has specialized in the Armenian genocide and related issues. He has published articles and book chapters on aspects of the Armenian, Greek, and Rwandan genocides, as well as on genocide as a legal and historical concept; he also is co-editor of the website, www.armenocide.de. Bjørnlund currently is an external lecturer at Danish Institute for Study Abroad (DIS), and teaches a Holocaust and Genocide course.

TESSA HOFMANN (Dr. Phil) is a German scholar of Armenian studies and sociology whose interests include Armenian history, culture and diaspora, the Ottoman genocide of the Christians of Asia Minor (Armenians, Arameans/Assyrians, Greeks) and the minorities in Turkey and the South Caucasus, and has written and/or edited numerous books and articles on these subjects. As a scholar of genocide, she focuses on the comparative study of the genocides committed during the last decade of Ottoman rule 1912-1922. Dr. Hofmann has been employed at the Institute for Eastern European Studies at the Freie Universität Berlin since 1983 and has been a research associate at the Chair for Eastern European Sociology since 2006.

VASILEIOS MEICHANETSIDIS has studied Humanities, Religion, Law, Byzantine and Oriental Studies and Peace Building Management in various European Universities. He has taught for a number of years at the European Schools of Brussels and served as Special Advisor to the Cyprus Ambassador to the Holy See and the UN Agencies in Rome. Meichanetsidis has always been interested in his heritage, as descendant of Pontic Greek survivors, and has concentrated for a number of years on the study of the genocide of the Greeks of Asia Minor.

A Note on Transliteration

The publisher approaches the problem of transliteration of modern Greek into English by maintaining a consistent correspondence between the Greek letters or diphthongs and their Latin equivalents, loosely using the U.S. Library of Congress conventions as a guide. In this volume however long marks are not used — as in ē for η (eta) or ō for ω (omega).

Thus, names of people, toponyms and various terms used are transliterated according to these terms, with the following exceptions:

(a) Greek names that have been used and incorporated into English literature: hence Athens not Athenai (or the abominable Athina), Corinth not Korinthos, Thessalonica not Thessalonike (or Thessaloniki), etc.

(b) Names of individuals well-known to English-speaking audiences, and whose names have appeared in print in the Anglicized form, are rendered accordingly: hence, John Capodistria is preferred to Ioannes Kapodistrias, [Kings] George, Constantine and Alexander, not Georgios, Konstantinos and Alexandros.

This category also includes scholars, journalists and others, whose names have commonly appeared in print transliterated in a form that may not conform to the publisher's rules.

For non-Greek names (especially Turkish), an effort has been made to restore the form of the original language, in the Latin alphabet.

Introduction

MATTHIAS BJØRNLUND, TESSA HOFMANN
AND VASILEIOS MEICHANETSIDIS

TO OUR KNOWLEDGE THIS COLLECTIVE, multi-disciplinary monograph is the first publication of academic documentation and analysis on the genocide conducted against the Greek Orthodox population — *rumlar* in Turkish — in the Ottoman Empire. We, like many contemporary observers,[1] consider this destruction of the Greek ethno-religious group an integral part of the annihilation of indigenous Christians during the last decade of Ottoman rule, which constitutes the first massive destruction of citizens by their own government in the modern period. During two consecutive chauvinist regimes, the Ottoman Greeks suffered at the same time and for the same reasons as did their Armenian compatriots. Serving as a template for further and more massive crimes, the early deportations from the Aegean littoral and Thrace in 1913–14 and from the capital Constantinople, where about 200 members of the Greek Orthodox intellectual, political, and economic elite had been arrested and deported on 8 March 1915, preceded the deportations and "decapitation" of the Armenian ethnic group from parts of Cilicia (Kilikia (Gr.), Çukurova (Tur.)) and from Constantinople that followed in March 1915 and from 24 April 1915, respectively.

The crimes committed by the Ottoman state against Christians and other Non-Muslim minorities such as Yezidis (Yazdis), together with the subsequent destruction of the European Jewry (*Shoah*) during World War II, shaped the internationally recognized legal understanding of genocide, the crimes that were committed against the Ottoman Greeks. However, the Greek genocide in particular remains lesser known to the general public and is still under-researched if compared with the numerous contributions on the Armenian genocide and even with the case of the Syriacs.[2] And without

[1] E.g., Bjørnlund, this volume; Vahagn Avedian, "The Armenian Genocide 1915 From a Neutral Small State's Perspective: Sweden," unpublished MA thesis, Uppsala University 2008, 42; Ara Sarafian and Eric Avebury, eds., *British Parliamentary Debates on the Armenian Genocide, 1915–1918* (Princeton and London: Gomidas Institute, 2003), 19.

[2] A comprehensive analysis of primary sources is to be found in David Gaunt's authoritative monograph *Massacres, Resistance, Protectors: Muslim-Christian Relations in Eastern Anatolia during World War I* (Piscataway, New Jersey: Gorgias Press, 2006), 317–26. For

consideration and analysis of the destruction of the Greeks, the full dimension of the Ottoman genocide cannot be determined. Any case study must remain incomplete or even misleading, if it does not take into consideration the empirical data from the Greek experience. It should be noted that the recent resolution by the *International Association of Genocide Scholars* recognizing the Greek and Syriac genocides (see Charny, this volume), as well as publications like the 2008 Special Issue of *Journal of Genocide Research* on late Ottoman genocides, suggest an increased focus on a wider range of victim groups, including the complex and equally under-researched case of the Ottoman Kurds, and an awareness that the fate of these groups cannot be treated in isolation if one aims to fully understand the dynamics of destruction in the final decades of the Ottoman Empire.[3] Still, the aforementioned deficit in the research on the Greek genocide persists for numerous, although not always obvious reasons.

Consequences of Historical Peculiarities

As a result of the existence of a Hellenic national state, the Ottoman citizens of Greek Orthodox belief were generally seen as protégées of that state. Against the overall background of the rise in popular ethnic nationalism, Turkish nationalists as well as their European and American contemporaries even perceived the Ottoman Greeks more as "agents" of the Greek state rather than as Ottoman citizens,[4] while representatives of the *rumlar* reinforced this perception by their support of Pan-Hellenic self-designation and irredentist concepts. Subsequently, issues of Greece's foreign relations, in particular Greek neutrality or alliance with the war-faring Entente during and after World War I, immediately influenced the fate of the Ottoman

---

further bibliographical information see the Tessa Hofmann article, footnote 4, in this volume.

[3] *Journal of Genocide Research* 10, no. 1 (2008); especially Dominik J. Schaller and Jürgen Zimmerer, "Introduction," 7–14. See also Apo Torosyan's 2007 documentary *Voices* that features interviews with one Greek and three Armenian genocide survivors. This special issue of *JGR* has recently been published as a book, *Late Ottoman Genocides: The dissolution of the Ottoman Empire and Young Turkish population and extermination policies*, Dominik J. Schaller and Jürgen Zimmerer, eds. (London and New York: Routledge, 2009).

[4] Many Westerners would furthermore hold racist stereotypes of Greeks and other non-Muslim or non-Turkish Ottomans. As Margaret Lavinia Anderson puts it, the most common such stereotype, that of Greeks, Armenians, and Jews (besides from, e.g., disloyal) as greedy and cunning, was often "proved" by trotting out a "proverb" beloved by all self-proclaimed experts on the Orient from London to Petersburg: "One Greek is able to cheat two Jews, but one Armenian can cheat two Greeks." Cf. Wilhelmine Germany, "'Down in Turkey, far away': Human Rights, the Armenian Massacres, and Orientalism," *The Journal of Modern History* 79 (March 2007): 100. For a similar trotting out of that proverb by a Turkish nationalist, see K. Ziya Müfti-Zada Bey, *Speaking of the Turks* (New York: Duffield, 1922), 114 and passim.

Greeks. These determinants of political action depended also on crucial domestic conflicts such as the *Εθνικός Διχασμός* (*Ethnikos Dichasmos*, i.e., "National Discord") (1915–1920). Whether seen from the angle of foreign or domestic politics, or from their close interdependency, Greek policies proved fatal for the remaining *rumlar* once the Greek military intervention in Asia Minor had lost the support or even approval of the Allies in late 1920. A similar no win-situation existed during the first years of World War I, when Greek "benign" or "benevolent neutrality" toward Germany became an obstacle for Allied support. Neither Greek neutrality (1914–1917), nor the subsequent alliance with the Entente (1917–1922) saved the *rumlar* from genocidal strategies of the CUP and Kemalist regimes.

The popular perception of Ottoman Greeks as agents of the Greek state, as "internal tumors," as some Young Turk hardliners (*Committee of Union and Progress*, also known by its acronym CUP) would put it,[5] is likely to have contributed to the related perception, analyzed below, that the fate the Ottoman Greeks met was somehow deserved or at least not worthy of consideration as an act of genocide. Even in today's Turkey, a country virtually without Greeks or other Christian minorities,[6] a country in the NATO alli-

---

[5] Uğur Ü. Üngör, "'A Reign of Terror': CUP Rule in Diyarbekir Province, 1913–1918" (Master's thesis, Department of History, University of Amsterdam, June 2005), 18.

[6] Around 1900, some 25 percent of the Ottoman population was Christian. The Christian community of present-day Turkey is estimated at 120,000, the approximately 280,000 Christian migrants not included. Only 20 of Turkey's 81 administrative units possess a church that offers services. Numerically as well as socially the figure of about 400,000 Christians in Turkey represents a *quantité négligeable* of 0.53 % of the country's overall population of 76 million. Among the Christians with foreign citizenship, nationals of Armenia and Georgia form the largest segment, most of them labor migrants. Estimates of Armenian nationals in Turkey vary from 12,000 to 83,000, and it is believed furthermore that there are 200,000 Georgian Orthodox Christians in Turkey, who unlike Armenian nationals do not need a visa. Armenian labor migrants in Turkey must be considered the most vulnerable group of foreign Christian residents, since as a result of Turkey's refusal to establish diplomatic relations with Armenia, Armenian migrants have difficulties in getting visa and are frequently illegal residents in Turkey, in permanent fear of the authorities.

Among the indigenous Christians, Armenians form the "largest" group, with some 65,000 Apostolic Armenians, 2,000 Armenian Uniates (1999) and 500 Protestant Armenians, followed by 16,000 Syriac Orthodox, 1,200 Syriac Catholics, and 6,000 members of the Chaldean Catholic Church (2005). The first independent demographic survey by Byron Kotzamanis from the University of Thessaly (2006) revealed that there were 2,800 households, or 5,249 *Romioi* or *rumlar* (Greek Orthodox, *rum ortodoks*) living in İstanbul. This figure, however, includes 600 Arabic speaking Syriac Orthodox as well as members of the East Syriac Chaldean Catholic Church who attend Greek schools in İstanbul. Though this survey revealed that the overall figure of Greek Orthodox in İstanbul was higher than generally believed, the population of this Christian denomination diminishing at fastest rate, with forty-five percent of İstanbul's Greek Orthodox population older than sixty-five ance with Greece, strong remembrance of such fears are present. As Fatma Müge Göçek expresses it, "the prevailing Turkish foreign policy of deterrence toward Greece is based on a suspicion that since its inception, Greece, inspired by the *Megale Idea* of a Greater Greece including the former lands of the Byzantine Empire, has been pursuing a policy of constant territorial expansion against Turkey."[7]

Modes of Perception: "Total Innocence," "Retributive Genocide" and "Equidistance"

Greece's increasing international isolation resulted in a perception of the Greek genocide as a mere consequence of Greek military actions during the Balkan Wars[8] and/or the Greek military intervention in Asia Minor (1919–1922), thus ignoring such events as the ethnic cleansing of Ottoman Greeks

---

years. There are/were Greek Orthodox on the islands of Imbros (Gökçeada (Tur.)) (about 240 mostly elderly) and forty on Tenedos (Bozcaada (Tur.)). At the end of the nineteenth century, among the 9,456 residents of Imbros only 200 were ethnic Turks or Muslims.

The most vulnerable group among the indigenous Christians of Turkey are the converts, deriving from the Muslim or ethnic Turkish communities. Most of the approximately 2,500 Turkish Protestants belong to Evangelical communities, in particular to Pentecostal Churches, organized in about 100 parishes (2007) that in turn are part of the *Alliance of Protestant Churches*. Three members of this community — the Turkish nationals Turan Topal and Hakan Taştan and the German national Tilman Geske — were murdered in Malatya (Melitene (Gr.)) on 18 April 2007, by five young Muslims, who had tortured them for hours in a semi-ritualized way before cutting their throats. The motives of the perpetrators, a blend of chauvinism and religious zeal, reflect the typical the perception of Christians in republican Turkey: despite their low numbers, Christians, and in particular evangelicals (proselytizing), are seen as a threat to Turkish identity, even though in 2005 only 385 Turkish citizens had officially converted from Islam to Christianity. Official and public statements by the country's most influential institutions such as the National Security Council (2006) confirm this perception, cf. Tessa Hofmann, "'Wer in der Türkei Christ ist, zahlt einen Preis dafür ...:' Christliche Minderheiten in der Republic Turkey," in *Märtyrer 2007: Das Jahrbuch zur Christenverfolgung heute*, Max Klingberg, Thomas Schirrmacher and Ron Kubsch, eds. (Bonn: Verlag für Kultur und Wissenschaft, 2007), 156–84; Tessa Hofmann, "Armenians in Turkey today: a critical assessment of the situation of the Armenian minority in the Turkish Republic," Nicolas Tavitian, ed. (Brussels: EU Office of Armenian Associations of Europe 2002), http://www.armenian.ch/asa/Docs/faae02.pdf.

[7] Fatma Müge Göçek, "Through a Glass Darkly: Consequences of a Politicized Past in Contemporary Turkey," *The Annals of the American Academy of Political and Social Science* 617 (May 2008): 99.

[8] The Balkan Wars offer yet another example of an under-researched subject, especially when it comes to the crimes committed by the warring parties. According to Alan Kramer, "in the seldom studied period 1911 to 1914 many of the ideas of a militant, sometimes racist, nationalism, were not only developed in theory but tried out in practice, starting with Italy's invasion of Libya and ending with the mass atrocities committed by all sides in the Balkan Wars," cf. *Dynamic of Destruction: Culture and Mass Killing in the First World War* (Oxford: Oxford University Press, 2007), 4.

1913–14, the deportations and massacres during World War I, or that there are indications that the genocidal intent of Turkish nationalists emerged already during the pre-war period of 1909–1911. More important than the chronological order, however, is the understanding of the very nature of genocide. There is a dominant belief that "genuine" genocide victims must be "innocent," i.e. non-combatants that are not involved in any militant action. Applied to ethno-religious minority groups, the construct of "innocence" holds that all members of "innocent" groups are loyal to the nominal or majority population under all circumstances and abstain from any irredentist or separatist sentiments, movements, or violent actions, including even cases of armed self-defence. This is an ethically highly questionable position in that it accepts the rule of one nation over another and ignores the circumstances under which such rule is established or carried out. In science and in politics such a position occurs as an obstacle to genocide recognition and awareness, as it is frequently the case with the resistance against foreign oppression, such as in the colonies of German Southwest[9] (1883–1915; present-day Namibia) and German East Africa[10] (1885–1918; present-day Tanzania, Burundi, and Rwanda), or the cases of local or regional Armenian self-defence in Van, Şebin-Karahişar, Urfa (Edessa (Gr.), Şanlıurfa (Tur.)), or Musa Ler (Dağ).

---

[9] After earlier struggles against German military and settlers, the Herero-led uprising of 12 January 1904 developed into four years of unequal fighting between the German *Schutztruppe* (Protection troops), joined by a Naval expedition corps in February 1904, and the native Herero peoples, joined as of October 1904, by the Nama, and other non-combatant ethnic groups such as the indigenous San; see Jürgen Zimmerer and Joachim Zeller, eds., *Völkermord in Deutsch-Südwestafrika: Der Kolonialkrieg (1904–1908) in Namibia und seine Folgen* (Berlin: Chr. Links Verlag, 2003).

[10] Increased repression, taxes, and compulsory labor on cotton plantations provoked the 1905–1907 Maji-Maji uprising, which was suppressed by armed German colonial forces. The latter implemented a strategy in 1906 of destroying the resources of the about 20 native peoples involved in the uprising; they set villages ablaze, destroyed crops and wells, and arrested the relatives of the leadership. As could be expected, this resulted in starvation and the depopulation of entire areas, profoundly changing the social structures of those African societies. The death toll is estimated to be as high 100–300,000, while European losses were 15 persons and 389 pro-colonial African soldiers. This was followed by hundreds of thousands more victims from among the East African population, during and after hostilities between German and British forces 1916–17, when civilians were forced by European troops to carry their supplies; additional losses were due to a famine that broke out in 1917, and to the influenza pandemic of 1918–20, which particularly affected the already weakened African population. Although the number of victims is much higher than in the case of the German Southwest colony, the fate of the German East African colony remains a case of forgotten genocidal repression, and has to date not received the same attention as the simultaneous events in the German South West colony, cf. Felicitas Becker and Jigal Beez, eds., *Der Maji-Maji-Krieg in Deutsch-Ostafrika 1905–1907* (Berlin: Ch. Links Verlag 2005).

A typical statement of this expectation is that of the former Turkish Ambassador Gündüz Aktan. Regarding the genocide of the Armenians Aktan stated in an interview:

> The Turkish people believe that what happened to the Armenians was not genocide. It was relocation to another part of the Ottoman Empire of only eastern Anatolian Armenians with an aim of creating an independent state of their own in areas where they were only in minority by ethnically cleansing the majority Turks. Many Armenians perished as well. The crucial question is why the Armenians are not content with the words tragedy, or catastrophe or disaster, but insist on genocide. What determines genocide is not necessarily the number of casualties or the cruelty of the persecution, but the intent to destroy a group. Turks have never harboured any anti-Armenianism. *The victims of genocide must be totally innocent* [Italics added by the editors].[11]

We suspect that the late Gündüz Aktan, who was a member of the Turkish think-tank International Strategic Research Organization, knew better, but preferred purposely to blend criteria of the United Nations Convention on the Prevention and Punishment of Genocide (1948) with his own distorted and simplistic interpretation, because this served his denialist mission well. Given the reality of genocidal settings, the rather naïve expectation of the "totally innocent," loyal ethnic collective can easily be dismissed as unrealistic, but is nevertheless widespread among scholars, including historians and scholars of genocide, who are not familiar with the details of legal genocide definitions and even less acquainted with the jurisdiction and rulings by the *International Court of Justice*.[12] They therefore accept "total innocence" of the victim group as a serious criterion of genocide.

Scored against the Greek experience the "innocence" criterion leads to misleading conclusions, the more if it is combined with the idea of genocide as reaction to provocative acts, the so-called provocation thesis,[13] and with the

---

[11] Aktan in the documentary film by Andrew Goldberg *The Armenian Genocide* (Two Cats Production with Oregon Public Broadcasting, New York, NY, 2006), quoted from Lane H. Montgomery, *Never again, again, again... Genocide: Armenia, The Holocaust, Cambodia, Rwanda, Bosnia and Herzegovina, Darfur* (New York: Ruder Finn Press, 2007), 23.

[12] In its rulings on Serbian war crimes in Bosnia, the ICJ ruled that the deliberate mass killings of Muslim men in Srebrenica constitute a crime of genocide, despite the fact that there were Muslim combatants among the victims. Applied to previous and current cases such as Shoah and Darfur, the invalidity of the "innocence" argument becomes obvious: The fact that about one million Jews served in different armies and paramilitary units during World War II was never seriously considered as an explanation, let alone excuse, for the massive destruction of the Jewish population in European countries occupied by Nazi Germany. The existence of armed fighters among the Fur population of West Sudan (Darfur) did not prevent the ICJ from declaring the crimes committed in Darfur as genocide.

[13] Cf., Robert F. Melson, *Revolution and Genocide: On the Origins of the Armenian Genocide and the Holocaust* (Chicago: University of Chicago Press, 1992), passim.

methodical approach of equidistance. Neither the Μεγάλη Ιδέα (*Megale Idea*, i.e., "the Great Idea") frequently quoted in this context, the Balkan Wars or the Greek military intervention in Asia Minor justifies the massacres and deportations to which Ottoman Greeks were exposed in increasing numbers since 1912. Nor do they fully explain the historic and political context of such crimes, which were directed not just against one particular ethnic group, but against all indigenous Christians and beyond. The adherents of the "innocence" criterion usually also ignore co-responsibilities, an aspect important for any genocide study. In the case of the Greek genocide this relates to the roles of the Entente and Central Powers during and after World War I, including Russia, which under Soviet rule became a key supporter and supplier of weapons of Kemalist Turkey.

Adhering to the principle of equidistance, on the other hand, is certainly a necessary precondition in conflict and area studies. In foreign relations "equidistance" applies to the principle of maintaining an equal distance from the policies of other nations, while as a research principle it would roughly mean keeping an equal scholarly distance from various subjects of research. This principle often fails however if applied to events such as genocide because, as a state crime, genocide is defined by legal and normative criteria only. This does not exclude the possibility that a victimized group can simultaneously or rather subsequently generate perpetrators of their own, as it happened in the Balkans during World War II and during the collapse of Yugoslavia, where ethnic groups consecutively or simultaneously were victimized and committed massive crimes against humanity, including genocide. But the "equidistant" belief that all actors in the human drama of genocide are equally "innocent" and "guilty" results in relativism that is neither historically, nor legally precise.[14]

In 1922, British historian and philosopher Arnold J. Toynbee (1889–1975) delivered an example of "equidistance" in the analysis of genocidal events when representing crimes that the Kemalist nationalist movement committed against the Pontus Greeks as mere "retaliation" for Greek crimes, putting the co-responsibility on British policies of 1919 as well: "[...] The Greeks of 'Pontus' and the Turks of the Greek occupied territories were in some degree victims of Mr. Venizelos' and Mr. Lloyd George's original miscalculations at Paris."[15] Therefore Toynbee believed that the Greek landings in

---

[14] On the uses of the concept of "equidistance" in relation to the Bosnian genocide as a means of relativization of mass crimes to justify political or military inaction, see Daniele Conversi, "Moral Relativism and Equidistance in British Attitudes to the War in the Former Yugoslavia," in *This Time We Knew: Western Responses to Genocide in Bosnia*, Thomas Cushman and Stjepan G. Mestrovic, eds. (New York: NYU Press, 1996), 244–81.

[15] Arnold J. Toynbee, *The Western Question in Greece and Turkey: A Study in the Contact of Civilizations* (Boston: Houghton Mifflin, 1922), 312–13.

Ionia created the Turkish nationalist movement led by Mustafa Kemal and was subsequently a reason for the mutual massacres that occurred during the Greco–Turkish War of 1919–22.

Seen from another angle, relativism must also be rejected if applied to the perpetrators of genocide. No mitigating circumstances for their crimes can be accepted. Massacres, death marches, compulsory labor under conditions that make the survival of the laborers virtually impossible cannot be held against the victim groups real or alleged political "disloyalty," their aspiration for autonomy or even separatism, or their attempted armed resistance against genocidal methods. Nor can the victim group be held responsible for the real or alleged crimes of a third state. One should of course always seek to understand the dynamics of historical events, but understanding does not or should not equal acceptance. This precaution seems the more necessary since we believe that there seems to be a deficit in the research of the conduct of the Greek forces in Asia Minor during 1919–1922. Obscured by the fact that this conduct became a matter of debate and of anti–Greek propaganda from the very beginning the events and victim figures demand further and more profound research and re–evaluation.[16]

Among the numerous under–researched aspects in this context is the role of the abovementioned Arnold Toynbee, who during World War I worked in the Intelligence Department of the British Foreign Office and since May 1915, together with Lewis Namier, as consultant for the *British War Propaganda Bureau* ("Wellington House," August 1914–1917),[17] whose task it was to influence American public opinion on the war. In the latter non–academic

---

[16] For a recent treatment of what is described as the relatively benign Greek administration in Smyrna under the rule of governor Aristeides Stergiades, 1919–22, and of atrocities committed in the course of the Greco–Turkish war during this period, see Giles Milton, *Paradise Lost. Smyrna 1922: The Destruction of Islam's City of Tolerance* (New York: Basic Books, 2008), passim.
For contemporary Turkish/Muslim nationalist views on the Greek administration and military campaign, see *Rigsarkivet* (*Danish National Archives*), *Udenrigsministeriets Arkiver* (*Foreign Ministry Archives*), 2–0355, "Konstantinopel/ Istanbul, diplomatisk repræsentation," "Noter og indberetninger om den politiske udvikling 1914–1922," "Græsk–Tyrkisk Konflikt. Officielle Noter 1919." This file contains a large number of notes, mainly in French, sent from various parts of Anatolia in 1919, protesting against Greek atrocities and war crimes. Most of the notes have characteristics in common that makes it plausible that they were written and sent as part of an organized campaign, but more research would be needed to determine whether this is actually the case. See also the forthcoming publication, Hervé Georgelin, "Exactions against the Turkish population between 1919 and 1922 under Greek occupying forces," *Online Encyclopedia of Mass Violence*, http://www.massviolence.org/+-Fall-of-the-Ottoman-Empire-+?id_ rubrique=6.

[17] See Jonathan A. Epstein, "German and English Propaganda in World War I" (paper presented at the New York Military Affairs Symposium [NYMAS], 1 December 2000). http://libraryautomation.com/nymas/propagandapaper.html.

capacity, Toynbee became sort of a specialist on war atrocities against civilians and published anti-German[18] and anti-Ottoman polemical writings. He was also a professor of Modern Greek and Byzantine History at the King's College in London. A discrepancy could be detected between Toynbee's position toward the Armenian genocide[19] and his stance of 1921/22, when he heavily criticised the Hellenic Army for "a ruthless warfare against the Turkish population, not omitting the commission of atrocities in the worst Near Eastern manner,"[20] reporting that he and his wife witnessed atrocities perpetrated by Greeks in the Yalova (Elenopolis (Gr.) Drepanon (Gr.)), Gemlik (Kios (Gr.)), and İzmit (Nikomedeia (Gr.) Kocaeli (Tur.)) areas during 1921.[21]

Toynbee seems genuinely horrified by what he saw and heard in 1921, even if, given his close association with the British government, this discrepancy could perhaps also be a reflection of the change in Allied policies towards Armenians and Greeks. U.S. war correspondent E. Alexander Powell, by no means pro-Greek or pro-Armenian, would explain the new situation as follows in 1920: "Neither England nor France have any desire to stir up this hornet's nest, which would probably result in grave disorders among their own Moslem subjects and which would almost certainly precipitate widespread massacres of the Christians in Asia Minor, for the sake of dismembering Turkey and ousting the Sultan."[22] Toynbee had helped arouse the American public opinion against the neutrality of the U.S. as editor of the comprehensive British "Blue Book" (1916) that was based predominantly on American accounts, incorporating additional and surprisingly precise British intelligence reports, and focused on the plight of women and children.[23] Brit-

---

[18] Toynbee wrote several pamphlets or books on atrocities, *The Destruction of Poland: A Study in German Efficiency* (1916); *The Belgian Deportations* (1917); *The German Terror in Belgium* (1917); *The German Terror in France* (1917). For a recent thorough documentation and discussion of the widespread German war crimes during World War I, see John Horne and Alan Kramer, *German Atrocities, 1914: A History of Denial* (New Haven and London: Yale University Press, 2001).

[19] E.g., Arnold J. Toynbee, "The Extermination of the Armenians," *The Times History of the War* 8, part 101, chapter 133 (London: *The Times*, 1916). See especially page 392, with a characterization of German co-responsibility for the Armenian genocide that reflects an excellent combination of precise analysis with propagandist side interests, which seems the more effective as Toynbee argues in an academically differentiated way.

[20] Arnold J. Toynbee and Kenneth P. Kirkwood, *Turkey* (London: Ernest Benn, 1926), 92.

[21] Toynbee, *The Western Question in Greece and Turkey*, 260.

[22] E. Alexander Powell, *The New Frontiers of Freedom: From the Alps to the Ægean* (New York: Charles Scribner's Sons, 1920), 197.

[23] For the most recent and complete edition of this valuable collection of sources, James Bryce and Arnold Toynbee, *The Treatment of Armenians in the Ottoman Empire, 1915–1916. Documents Presented to Viscount Grey of Falloden by Viscount Bryce* [uncensored edition], Ara Sarafian, ed. (Princeton: Gomidas Institute, 2000 [reprint of 1916 edition]).

ish foreign policy priorities were becoming entirely different around the time of the Greek defeat in Asia Minor. As a "crown witness" of Hellenic/Greek atrocities, Toynbee helped to politically condemn and internationally isolate Greece and thus supported the approach of the United Kingdom to Kemalist Turkey at the expense of the Ottoman *rumlar*.

The Primacy of Domestic Policies and Foreign Relations and Selectivity in Genocide Awareness

Lewis Einstein, U.S. diplomat at Constantinople, wrote on 28 July 1915 that,

> The persecution of the Greeks is assuming unexpected proportions. Only a fortnight ago they were reassured and told that the measures taken against the Greek villages in the Marmora were temporary and not comparable with those against the Armenians. Now it looks as if there is to be equality in suffering, and the intention existed to uproot and destroy both peaceful communities. The poor Greeks are obliged to leave their homes, often without any notice compelled to march night and day without food or water, and when they cry for this, their Turkish guards point to the mosque and tell them the highroad to the comforts of life lies in Islam. Their cattle, too, is requisitioned, and they are obliged to nourish it when they themselves starve. And by a refinement of cruelty the Greek community here is forbidden to give them relief. At the Patriarchate they are desperate and know not where to turn, for the Gounaris Cabinet at Athens seems more interested in thwarting Venizelos than in the welfare of its nationals here, and is said to have suppressed all the reports from Turkey about Greek persecution.[24]

One interesting thing to note here is that, while more research on the subject is needed, it appears as if Greek domestic policies could take the primacy over humanitarian considerations or such notions as ethnic or religious solidarity when it came to the ongoing destruction of Ottoman Greeks. But the primacy of foreign relations seems to have been the more important factor in determining how to officially remember and categorize the destruction of the Ottoman Greeks in Greece. As opposed to Armenian genocide survivors, who would generally come to refuse to accept circumscriptions of their experience such as "tragedy," "catastrophe," or "disaster," the Greek state chose to adopt the perception of the events in Asia Minor during 1919–1922 as a καταστροφή, i.e., a "catastrophe," thus avoiding any legal qualification of the death of more than one million Ottoman citizens of Greek

---

See also Ara Sarafian, "The Archival Trail: Authentication of The Treatment of Armenians in the Ottoman Empire, 1915–1916," in *Remembrance and Denial: The Case of the Armenian Genocide*, Richard G. Hovannisian, ed. (Detroit: Wayne State University Press, 1998), 51–65; "An Interview with Ara Sarafian," *Virgül* [Turkish review] 95 (May 2006) http://www.armeniandiaspora.com/forum/archive/index.php/t-52013.html.

24 Lewis Einstein, *Inside Constantinople: A Diplomatist's Diary During the Dardanelles Expedition, April–September 1915* (London: John Murray, 1917), 202–203.

ethnicity or Greek Orthodox belief. This approach is perhaps more or less appropriate or understandable considering the Greek domestic and foreign policies during that period, and such an approach dictated by *realpolitik* was in fact shared by the Turkish Republic:

> In March 1922, Mustafa Kemal denounced the "atrocities" of the "Greek princes and generals, who take particular pleasure in having women raped." [...] But after the establishment of the Republic, the tide turned and the accusatory tone of moral indignation was dropped. [...] Throughout the interbellum, the Turkish and Greek nations were portrayed as having coexisted perennially in mutual respect and eternal peace. Friendly inter-state relations in the service of Turkey's acceptance and stabilization into the nation-state system had gained precedence over old griefs, without any serious process of closure or reconciliation in between.[25]

However, the approach by the Greek state has done no justice to the experience of the Ottoman Greek victims and those survivors of genocide who had to adapt to official Greek positions as newcomers and refugees to Greece. The reasons for the official decision not to insist on genocide recognition and not even to forward compensation claims lay in the binding obligations of bilateral and multilateral treaties, signed between Turkey and Greece in 1923 and 1930, and in the genuine wish of Greece to escape by all means further complications in her relations with Turkey.

This stance persisted throughout the twentieth century, which after the "catastrophe" of Asia Minor resulted in continued persecution of the remaining Greeks in Turkey — manifested in, for instance, İstanbul Greeks "going on vacation" to avoid becoming scapegoats in the charged atmosphere in the early Kemalist republic,[26] in the 1942-44 "wealth tax" or "capital levy" that was imposed predominantly on non-Muslims and led to the internment of Greeks, Armenians, and Jews in the Aşkale labor camp near Erzurum (Theodosiopolis (Gr.)),[27] and in the pogrom of 1955.[28] The past century also

---

[25] Uğur Ü. Üngör, "Organizing Oblivion in the Aftermath of Mass Violence," *The Armenian Weekly: Special Issue Commemorating Genocide* (26 April 2008): 24.

[26] J. A. Spender, *Life, Journalism and Politics* (London: Cassell, 1927), 2: 112, "My principal object in going to Turkey, in December 1925, was to be at Angora when the decision of the League of Nations on the Mosul dispute was delivered. There was something like a panic on that subject, and a large number of those who professed to be best informed were convinced that if Mosul were awarded to us, the Turks would seize it — for it was then practically undefended — and defy us to turn them out. On reaching Athens I found that Greek residents in Constantinople were coming in large numbers by every ship 'to spend Christmas in Athens,' having the not unreasonable apprehension that, if there were trouble, it would fall first upon them."

[27] E.g., Leyla Neyzi, "Strong as Steel, Fragile as a Rose: A Turkish Jewish Witness to the Twentieth Century," *Jewish Social Studies* 12 no. 1 (Fall 2005): 172-73; C. L. Sulzberger, "Turkish Tax Kills Foreign Business," *New York Times*, 11 September 1943; Ayhan Aktar, *Varlik Vergisi ve 'Türklestirme' Politikalari* (İstanbul: Iletisim, 2000); Faik Ökte, *The Trage-*

brought the Κατοχή (Occupation) by the Axis states Italy, Germany, and Bulgaria (October 1940–October 1944).[29] The occupation was a likewise traumatic ordeal for the small country whose population of more than 7 million was exposed to oppression, starvation, the destruction of the Greek Jews, and massacres in brutal retaliation for armed resistance, causing the death of hundreds of thousands, among them 300,000 from starvation. War crimes and foreign oppression were immediately followed by a long and disastrous civil war which split the Greek society into irreconciled "left" and "right" factions, as was earlier the case with the Εθνικός Διχασμός (National Discord) between Greek liberals (Venizelists) and royalists. Another reason why Greek politicians have preferred not to integrate genocide awareness into their agendas or in the school curricula derives from the conditions of nation state building, as the awareness of having been victimized was perhaps not seen as compatible with such imperatives as developing a capable national army.[30]

Only during the 1990s did non-governmental organizations of the Pontic and Ionian Greeks Μικρασιάτες (*Mikrasiates,* i.e., Asia Minor Greeks) — the refugees and survivors from Ottoman Asia Minor and their descendants — succeed in changing the public opinion and bringing their claim for genocide awareness and recognition to a legislative level: On 8 March 1994 and 13 October 1998 the Greek Parliament issued resolutions in which it recognized 19 May (1919) and 14 September (1922) as days of commemoration of the genocide respectively of the Greeks of Pontus and of Asia Minor as a whole. The very fact that it took two parliamentary resolutions indicates that not even among the advocacy groups was the Greek genocide perceived as a common fate. In particular NGO advocates of the Pontus Greeks, who

---

dy of the Turkish Capital Tax (London: Croom Helm, 1987). The latter author was *dcft erdar* (head of finance) in İstanbul at the time of the implementation of the discriminatory Capital Tax. With a remarkable sense of justice he concludes his book with the words, "The Capital Tax was marked by chauvinist und racist concepts. [...] The most unforgivable aspect of the Capital Levy was the degradation, which it brought to the sovereignty, and dignity of Turkey. [...] For my part, I am still astonished that we were not all, with the Prime Minister at our head, indicted before the High Council for this blow struck at the honor and the dignity of the state." 94–95.

[28] Speros Vryonis, Jr., *The Mechanism of Catastrophe: The Turkish Pogrom of September 6–7, 1955* (New York: greekworks.com, 2005). See also Orhan Pamuk, chapter 19, "Conquest or Decline? The Turkification of Constantinople," in *Istanbul: Memories and the City* (London: Faber & Faber, 2006), 155–59.

[29] In German occupied Crete until the end of World War II in May 1945.

[30] On the related recent "textbook controversy" in Greece, see e.g. "Changes to Controversial 6th-Grade History Textbook Completed," *Athens News Agency*, 3 August 2007; George Gilson, "Battle Royal over History Book," *Athens News*, 23 March 2007 (both may be accessed on http://www.helleniccomserve.com/).

were more active in raising genocide recognition claims after the model of Armenian Diaspora organizations, limited themselves to the native Black Sea region of their ancestors, thus generating a regionalism in genocide awareness. In genocide studies, this concept of the "Pontus Genocide" resulted in a narrow focus that virtually excluded any focus on the destruction of Ottoman Greeks in other areas, with even more misleading consequences than the exclusive focus on the genocide of the Ottoman Armenians.

The Language Factor

Together with Latin, ancient Greek serves as the *reservoir language* for all modern Western languages. However, only few non-Greeks have a sufficient command of Modern Greek that would allow them to read and study primary archival sources, including the many survivor testimonies that had been collected and published in Greece and her Diaspora. Nor have the already existing publications in Greek language been made available for the international *academia* by translations into English. On a related note: even if one would assume that the relevant Ottoman archives were now in fact open to serious scholars, few inside or outside Turkey are today able to read Ottoman Turkish. This means that a large body of potentially important source material concerning the Greek genocide remains inaccessible to the vast majority of researchers, the editors of this volume included.

Nevertheless, it is our hope that this book will help to satisfy a long-felt need for documenting, analyzing, and interpreting the genocide against the Ottoman Greeks, and that it will at the same time inspire and encourage future publications, including translations from Greek publications into English, studies based on Greek and Turkish archival sources, analyses of the CUP and Kemalist decision-making processes regarding the destruction of the Ottoman Greeks, regional studies that focus on the varieties of the Greek experience, etc. For all the aforementioned reasons, we are very much aware that ours is only a modest step toward the aim of increasing the knowledge of the Ottoman genocide as the first massive genocidal state crime of the twentieth century.

* * * *

The anthology opens with a prologue by Israel W. Charny, widely recognized as a pioneer of genocide studies.[31] In line with his lifelong battle for the recognition and against the denial of genocide, against victim exclusivity, distortion of history, and moral relativism, he recounts his experiences with a host of challenges to, among other things, the recognition of the Greek

[31] E.g., Israel W. Charny, "A Passion for Life and Rage at the Wasting of Life," in *Pioneers of Genocide Studies*, Samuel Totten and Steven L. Jacobs, eds. (New Brunswick: Transaction Publishers, 2002), 429–478.

genocide by fellow genocide scholars. It is a strong reminder of the need to recognize the sufferings of all peoples, regardless of creed, color, or persuasion, as well as of the need to always be aware of the destructive potential in us all.

Tessa Hofmann gives a comprehensive overview of the Greek genocide, and offers a framework for understanding this event. It is an account of what she dubs "cumulative destruction with shifting focus," of the socio-political exclusion and dehumanization of the Greek and other minorities in the Ottoman Empire, over the increased radicalization that marked the period of the Balkan Wars, to the policies of violent persecution, deportations, large-scale massacres, and population exchange from 1914 onward. She compares the Armenian and Greek genocides, noting that while the former event generally differed from the latter in being of a more condensed and seemingly radical nature, they proved to be equally fateful.

In a revised version of his 1985 article, John Mourelos surveys the aborted attempts in 1914 at an exchange of Ottoman Greeks and Turks/Muslims from Greece. These attempts were initiated by the Ottoman government in the midst of severe persecution of the Ionian Greeks that would have disastrous consequences, not least for the refugees who would often have to live for years under miserable conditions on nearby Greek Aegean islands.[32] The main question he raises here is whether these persecutions were meant to force the Greek state to accept the exchange, or if the exchange negotiations were rather a cover up of the persecutions. He concludes that the latter answer is the most likely, i.e., that the objective of the Ottoman Government was to rid whole provinces of their Greek element. This policy was to be achieved by force, not by signing a convention on a voluntary exchange of minorities that would entail making concessions to the Greek state.

In his account of the destruction of the Ottoman Greeks in Danish sources, Matthias Bjørnlund takes as a starting point the abovementioned attempted ethnic cleansing of the Ionian Greeks in 1914, what Henry Beaumont, British diplomat at Constantinople in 1914, reported as the "partial elimination of the Greek population"[33] that took place in the period between the end of the Balkan Wars

---

[32] Major A. Winsor Weld, *Relief Work among the Aegean Islands* (Athens: American Red Cross Commission to Greece, 1919).

[33] Telegram No. 464, Mr. Beaumont to Sir Edward Grey, 31 July 1914, in *The Outbreak of War: Foreign Office Documents June 28th–August 4th 1914*, vol. 9 of *British Documents on the Origins of the War 1898–1914*, eds. G. P. Gooch and Harold Temperley (London: His Majesty's Stationery Office, 1926), 238.
See also Anglo-Hellenic League, "Letters on the Expulsion of Greeks from Asia Minor and in reply to allegations of ill-treatment inflicted on Turks in Greek Macedonia," 13 (30 May/12 June 1914); Milton, *Paradise Lost*, 48–53; Wolfgang Gust, "Verständnislose Aus-

and the outbreak of World War I. He describes how neutral observers such as Danish diplomats at Constantinople and Smyrna had good reasons to perceive the persecution and genocide of Greeks and Armenians during the period 1914–1916 as interconnected parts of CUP policies of violent Turkification with the aim of creating a "Turkey for the Turks." In other words, he contends that such policies, which continued well into the Kemalist era, were deliberately aimed at the ethnic and religious homogenization of Ionia and Anatolia.

Racho Donef focuses on the role of the Special Organization (*Teşkilât-ı Mahsusa*) in the destruction of Greeks, Armenians, and Syriacs before and during World War I. Drawing on a wide variety of sources, including documents from the Ottoman archives, he traces the history of the organization from its much debated genesis in the wake of the CUP takeover to the aftermath of the World War. Turkish historiography has generally celebrated those involved with the Special Organization as heroes and their victims as traitors, although this position has come to be challenged by a number of liberal Turkish scholars.[34] But the documentation provided here points to the fact that the organization, with its gangs of, as they were called, "murderers and thieves," was a particularly vital and brutal instrument in the CUP policies of ethnic cleansing and genocide.

Moving to the final stages of the destruction of the Ottoman Greeks, Nikolaos Hlamides surveys events leading up to the September 1922 Kemalist destruction of Smyrna before discussing the cataclysmic destruction itself. Using first and foremost British diplomatic reports and eyewitness testimonies by Western and Turkish observers, illustrated by photographs from his own collection, he gives a detailed account of the killings, looting, and fire, of Western indifference, and of the immediate aftermath that brought deportation, massacre, or exile to the survivors. One conclusion he draws is that the Smyrna Holocaust, as it was known, was no isolated or random incident: "The destruction of Smyrna and the annihilation of its Christian inhabitants, both Greek and Armenian, remain a haunting chapter in the genocide of Turkey's Greek and Armenian population."

In his article on the Smyrna catastrophe and its immediate context, Matthew Stewart presents a survey of a series of events that not only led up to the destruction of Smyrna and the virtual disappearance of Greeks from Asia Minor, but were crucial for the establishment of the Kemalist movement and

---

wüchse des Militarismus" [Incomprehensible excesses of militarism], *Historicum: Zeitschrift für Geschichte* (Vienna) (Fall 2007): www.historicum.net.

[34] E.g., Bedross Der Matossian, "Venturing into the Minefield: Turkish Liberal Historiography and the Armenian Genocide," *The Armenian Genocide: Cultural and Ethical Legacies*, Richard Hovannisian, ed. (New Brunswick and London: Transaction Publishers, 2007), 381.

the Turkish Republic as well. The Sèvres and Lausanne treaties, Great Power diplomacy and duplicity, and the Greek military incursion into Ionia and Anatolia, all impacted on that final outcome. The 1919–22 Greco–Turkish war was seen by nationalist Turks in particular as a war of liberation, and the often brutal conduct of the war by both sides in a sense culminated in the massive crime that was the burning of Smyrna by the Kemalists.

Harry J. Psomiades covers important aspects of the aftermath of the destruction of Smyrna in a slightly revised version of his scarce article in *Journal of Modern Hellenism.* He analyzes the crucial operations by the American Near East Relief (NER) that provided relief to and organized the evacuation of tens of thousands of surviving Greeks and Armenians before and after the Smyrna catastrophe, many of whom would arguably have perished, had it not been for the NER. It is argued here that in doing so, the NER and similar organizations were unwittingly aiding or encouraging the Kemalist objective of cleansing what was now to become Turkish soil from its Christian element. This is an ever–present dilemma for nations and humanitarian organizations: will the aid to or intervention in societies, torn by strife, aggravate rather than alleviate problems? Will evacuation of the persecuted become a de facto instrument of ethnic cleansing? Will food for the needy fall into the hands of warring parties and prolong rather than shorten the suffering?[35] In this case, as in so many others, these are perhaps moot points. As the author notes, the alternative to providing assistance to Greeks and Armenians in Asia Minor was no less ghastly.[36]

During the final phase of the Greek genocide, the International Red Cross (IRC/ICRC) was commissioned by the Allied powers to conduct an investigation into reports from American NER relief workers that large numbers of Ottoman Greeks were being deported from Pontus to the interior of Anatolia. Although such reports met with counter–claims and were vehemently denied by the Kemalist government, it was widely acknowledged that the deportations were part a systematic policy and that they often amounted to a death sentence, much like the death marches of 1915 during the Armenian genocide. In *New York Times*, 7 June 1922, this was called a "deliberate campaign of extermination." Stavros Stavridis contributes a chapter on the aborted IRC investigation, on how Allied and Turkish procrastination, inac-

[35] E.g., "African Dilemma: Food Aid May Prolong War and Famine," *New York Times*, 12 May 1991; "AU warning over Sudan 'charges'," 12 July 2008, http://news.bbc.co.uk/2/hi/africa/7503803.stm.

[36] The Greek government at the time appears to have clearly agreed with such an assumption when they awarded the War Cross to five American NER workers who had died while working to evacuate Greeks and Armenians from Asia Minor, cf. *New Near East* (July 1923): 12.

tion, or outright obstruction ensured that it was indeed as the title suggests a mission to nowhere.

A *New York Times* article dated 5 January 1947 contains the following sentence: "If the members of the United Nations pass appropriate legislation such incidents as the pogroms of Czarish [sic] Russia and the massacres of Armenians and Greeks by Turkey would be punishable as genocide."[37] The "appropriate legislation" mentioned here is of course The United Nations Convention on the Prevention and Punishment of the Crime of Genocide (UNGC), which was adopted in 1948. The subject of Steven Leonard Jacobs' thorough analysis is Raphael Lemkin — the Polish-Jewish lawyer who coined the legal-historical term "genocide" and who is recognized as the father of the UNGC — and his lengthy, detailed, unpublished writings on the Greek genocide, "an historical excursus as well as an evaluative judgment of those responsible for the genocide."

In the tradition of Lemkin, Alfred de Zayas surveys the genocide against the Ottoman Greeks and other Christian minorities from a legal point of view. One lesson to be learned from the Ottoman genocide(s) and their aftermath is that the consequences of denying justice for the victims and accountability for the perpetrators can be dire, not least because of the message it sends to past, present, and future perpetrators: it is possible to not only get away with genocide, but to profit from it.[38] Furthermore, as Henry Theriault puts it, the magnitude of genocide's "total destructive consequences compounds with each passing day that the original devastation remains unrepaired (at least to the extent that some reparation is possible), as initial losses of what would have been the bases of the victim group's future resource increases, political security, cultural and identity stability and other social, political, cultural, and economic gains as well as individual familial, economic, and other aspects of well-being, mean losses of all those gains."[39] But Alfred de Zayas contends that justice delayed may not necessarily be justice denied, i.e., that the present-day Turkish Republic remains liable for the crimes committed by the Ottoman Empire. The UNGC can be applied retroactively, and the international community can and must take measures to ensure reparation to the victims and refrain from giving recognition to the consequences of genocide and other crimes against humanity.

---

[37] See also "Genocide," *New York Times*, 26 August 1946.

[38] E.g., Vahakn N. Dadrian, "Genocide as a Problem of National and International Law: The World War I Armenian Case and its Contemporary Legal Ramifications," *Yale Journal of International Law* 14, no. 2 (Summer 1989): 332–33.

[39] Henry Theriault, "Post-Genocide Imperial Domination," Armenian Genocide Insert of the *Armenian Weekly* 73, no. 16 (21 April 2007), see http://www.hairenik.com/armenianweekly/gin042107_05.htm.

Such legal measures can be seen as necessary to establish an international rule of law and to address issues of rectification and reparation, as well as to prevent future genocides.[40] Education — studying historical instances of genocide, learning to recognize the dangers of prejudice, unquestioning obedience, or indifference to suffering — is a no less crucial way of working toward prevention.[41] Ronald Levitsky, drawing on his own experience with teaching the Pontian Greek genocide, discusses the challenges to genocide education, as well as its rewards. It is no easy task for students, or for anyone else, for that matter, to comprehend the ultimate horror that is genocide. Other problems include government pressure, indifference, or outright denial. The rewards, however, are many. Teaching about genocide can be a path to critical and ethical thinking, an inspiration to become "upstanders" rather than bystanders or perpetrators.

Michel Bruneau and Kiriakos Papoulidis look at genocide's aftermath from the perspective of memorialization and commemoration, more precisely the erection of commemorative monuments in Greece. Greek refugees who came to Greece in the wake of the genocide and the "population exchange" of 1923 would early on feel the need to build genocide monuments, but for a variety of reasons — practical, psychological, political — most projects were only realized between the 1960s and today. Despite such obstacles a host of monuments with a variety of themes have been erected. What they have in common is that all are embodying "the right to remember as well as the duty of remembrance." All have styles and shapes that impart narratives and information — of loss of lives and of homeland,[42] of resistance and heroism; thus, they all have a message to future generations.

Taking the destruction of the Greeks, Armenians, and Syriacs in the Ottoman Empire/Turkey as an example, Akis Kalaitzidis and Donald Wallace ask the question: what makes states kill their own citizens? Their answer lies in offering a theoretical framework for identifying and understanding a number of conditions that are conducive to genocide. One crucial condition is ethno-nationalism, as opposed to categories such as civic nationalism. It is the longing for homogeneity or purity, for security, for territorial independence and control. Once the decision is made for moving toward the creation

---

40 On legal justice/the rule of law and rectificatory justice, see Rama Mani, *Beyond Retribution: Seeking Justice in the Shadows of War* (Cambridge and Boston: Polity, 2002), passim.

41 E.g., Adam Strom, "Teaching about the Armenian Genocide," in Hovannisian, *The Armenian Genocide: Cultural and Ethical Legacies*, 239–44.

42 See also the comprehensive analysis of "war memorials as foci of the rituals, rhetoric, and ceremonies of bereavement," Jay Winter, "War memorials and the mourning process," in *Sites of Memory, Sites of Mourning: The Great War in European Cultural History* (Cambridge and New York: Cambridge University Press, 2004), 78–116. The quote is found on page 78.

of a single nation-state by employing the ideology of ethno-nationalism, expulsion or extermination of undesired groups is likely to follow. In the poem *Motherland* (*Vatan*), influential Young Turk and Kemalist ideologue Ziya Gökalp (1876–1924) presents his vision of an ideal Turkish nation-state: "A country that nobody plots against/Each individual being united in ideal, language, tradition, religion/Its parliament clean, without Boşo's speaking/Its children happily sacrificing their lives at its borders/Hey Turks, that is what your motherland should be!" "Boşo" refers to Yorgo Boşo/Georgios Boussios, a Greek member of the Ottoman Parliament opposed to the Turkification policies of the CUP.[43] The poem is a clear, condensed expression of the ethno-national ideology that created or magnified ethno-political cleavages, cleavages that would ultimately lead to genocide.

Finally, Abraham D. Krikorian and Eugene L. Taylor offer a comprehensive analysis of the pitfalls and promises of the attestation and attribution of genocide photographs. Visual documentation of human rights violations has taken on new dimensions with the advent of groundbreaking innovations like the internet, cell-phone videos, and Google Earth.[44] But it has long been recognized that photographs are important as historical documentation, as well as a particularly powerful and immediate means of, for instance, creating awareness of ongoing atrocities. "Photographs have a compelling and disturbing immediacy that the written word lacks," as it has been aptly put.[45]

On the other hand, photographic illustration in the context of genocide offers vast possibilities of controversy, misinformation, even manipulation, because only in rare cases are photographs truly self-evident. The majority demand captions with explanations, which in the case of the Ottoman genocide(s) are not always reliable. It therefore takes on a special urgency to affirm the accuracy of what such photographs represent, to identify such

---

[43] Üngör, "A Reign of Terror," 17–18. For the full text of the poem, published in 1918 see Fevziye A. Tansel, ed., *Ziya Gökalp Külliyatı 1: Şiirler ve Halk Masalları* (Ankara: Türk Tarih Kurumu Yayınları, 1989), 113. On the protests by Boussios and other Christian and Muslim minority members of the Ottoman Parliament against the Turkification policies imposed shortly after the CUP takeover see Erol Ülker, "Empires and Nation Building: Russification and Turkification Compared," (Master's thesis, Central European University, Budapest, 2004), chapter 4, "The National Policy of the Young Turks: From Dominant Nationality to Turkification," 84–99, http://web.ceu.hu/nation/theses/ukler0304.pdf. See also Vangelis Kechriotis, "Greek Orthodox, Ottoman Greeks or just Greeks? Theories of Coexistence in the Aftermath of the Young Turk Revolution," *Études Balkaniques* 1 (2005): 51–72

[44] For interesting examples: www.witness.org; http://blogs.ushmm.org/worldiswitness.

[45] Editor's "Introduction," in *Crimes of War: Guilt and Denial in the Twentieth Century*, Omer Bartov, Atina Grossmann and Mary Nolan, eds. (New York: The New Press, 2002), xxii.

photographs with persons, places, and times. With their minutely detailed analyses of a number of photographs depicting the destruction of Ottoman Greeks and Armenians the authors have come a long way toward reaching the goal of precision in attestation and attribution of genocide photographs.

* * * *

The editors would like to express their heartfelt gratitude to all contributors. In particular we feel indebted to Nikolaos Hlamides, who, in addition to his contribution, provided photographs and translations that added much value to this book. We also thank our publisher, Aristide Caratzas, for his courage to publish this book and to take on the substantial work that was necessary to bring the manuscript to print.

The Integrity and Courage to Recognize All the Victims of a Genocide

ISRAEL W. CHARNY

IT IS NO SECRET THAT I AM JEWISH, IN FACT PROUDLY SO. This includes the fact that although born in the U.S., and having reached an age where I was fully accredited in my profession as a clinical psychologist and enjoyed a thriving practice and academic career, I chose to make my life in Israel where I have now lived some 35 years.

It is also no secret that I feel deeply the horror of the Holocaust to my people. It was my encounter with this horror that led me as far back as in the 1960's, when I was still living and working in the U.S., to cry out in a dream that I, a trained psychologist having just then earned my certification also as an advanced specialist, understood *nothing* about how the Nazis and their collaborators did what they did to my people in the Holocaust. I literally cried out one night in response to a dream, "How could *human* beings smash infants against walls, kill children gleefully in the face of their parents, beat people sadistically to death with their own hands, or round up fellow human beings in naked herds and send them to their choking deaths in gas chambers?" I woke up in the morning with the realization that, although I had been trained at an outstanding American university and had been working in a first-class psychiatric hospital, I had literally received no training whatsoever in understanding human cruelty, evil, destructive aggression, and worse the homicidal readiness of people to destroy masses of other human beings. I then knew that I would devote the rest of my life, along with the clinical practice, which I conduct and love to this day, to learning about and advancing knowledge of this aspect of our human natures. My first professional presentation on the subject in those early years was at a college for Jewish Studies (Gratz College, Philadelphia), and became my first publication which was entitled, "Teaching the Violence of the Holocaust: A Challenge to Educating Potential Future Oppressors, and Victims to Nonviolence," and was published in 1968 in a journal for Jewish educators.[1]

[1] Israel W. Charny, "Teaching the violence of the Holocaust: A challenge to educating potential future oppressors and victims for nonviolence," *Jewish Education* 38, no. 2 (March, 1968): 15–24.

In my judgment to this day, it is a good and sensitive piece, but it was never honored or referred to very much in the developing professional literature of the Holocaust, including in works specifically about the ever important area of teaching children about the Holocaust. Why the lack of interest in the article? I think this was because I referred to *all of us* human beings as cut from the same cloth; and that we *all* have serious work to do not simply mourning and overcoming our peoples' experiences as victims; but in developing ourselves as strong decent human beings who will do our utmost neither to be victims (we have to fight back against those who seek to murder us), but *also* not to be oppressors who kill others if and when we find ourselves in historical–societal circumstances that call on us and enable us to have the power and the opportunity to be the ones who commit genocide against others.

Acknowledging Any Genocidal Violence to Others by Victim Peoples

I think that the victims of past genocides of many peoples "like" being spoken about (sympathized with) as victims and celebrated for overcoming the traumatic losses of the genocides of their people, but don't like any discussions of past or possible future destructiveness by their people to others. Once, when we were preparing the memorable first encyclopedia of genocide,[2] the Serbian ambassador to Israel came to me. He proved an affable, attractive man; indeed the two of us were fellow tennis players and had an immediate sense of sharing with one another an attitude of enjoying life along with our serious professional activities. Moreover, the ambassador told me that one of his parents was Jewish and had been in Auschwitz, and of course that bonded us on a more personal level too. But his basic intention in coming to see me was to present to me for the encyclopedia the (quite serious and important) information on genocidal murders of Serbs by Croats (who, of course, had been the vicious killers of Serbs and Jews in World War II) and Muslims in the war and genocidal events of the early 1990's. I replied to the ambassador that his data were very welcome, but that we could only accept the data if they were part of — accompanied by — the fuller picture that included the genocidal murders perpetrated by the Serbs against the other ethnic groups in the former Yugoslavia, like the genocide of six or more thousand Bosnians at Srebrenica, for in the 1990's round of ugly genocidal destructiveness in the Balkans it was the Serbian murders of others that were the predominant though not the exclusive story of evil. The ambassador stormed out of my office and home.

---

[2] See the forewords by Bishop Desmond Tutu and Simon Wiesenthal in the chapter "Why Is It Important to Learn about the Holocaust and the Genocides of *All* Peoples?" in *Encyclopedia of Genocide,* Israel W. Charny, ed. (Santa Barbara and Denver: ABC–Clio Publishers, 1999).

"Well," the reader may say, "you are obviously right that we are all human beings with whatever tendencies and potential for being mass murderers that apparently our whole human race will need to face in itself, if we are to make any progress in stopping genocide on this planet. But you are asking a lot from people to recognize this part of themselves, especially when they are legitimately concerned with their own painful losses to the evils of others. Apparently this is a delicate educational and spiritual task that is going to need a lot of talent to get across to people and is going to take a lot of time."

Indeed, returning to my own Jewishness, together with my colleague, Daphna Fromer, I have been the author of a study of the attitudes that we Jews and Israelis harbor towards a past genocidal massacre that we indeed committed,[3] and the author of studies of the attitudes of us Jews/Israelis towards fictional scripts of what we could conceivably do in future scenarios.[4] In a larger perspective, I am quite proud of the fact that, overall, while being beleaguered and threatened by extinction by an overwhelmingly larger Arab force surrounding us, we Israelis have maintained a remarkable record of decency and humanistic values in our military actions. But there have been some small but clearly vicious and obviously *genocidal massacres* — the term the great Leo Kuper created for smaller scale events of mass murder[5] for which we must take responsibility; and like all people we need to become aware of our potential for doing such things.

The first of the above studies that Fromer and I did in this series that we ended up calling *A Series of Studies of the Psychology of Evil* was of the attitudes of Israelis to the murder of 49 defenseless Arab men, women and children in Kfar Kassem, at the time a village outside of Tel Aviv, on the day of the outbreak of the Sinai War in 1956. We wanted to show what number of

---

[3] Israel W. Charny and Daphna Fromer, "A Study of Attitudes of Viewers of the Film *Shoah* towards an Incident of Mass Murder by Israeli Soldiers (Kfar Kassem, 1956)," *Journal of Traumatic Stress* 5, no. 2 (1992): 303–18. See also Israel W. Charny, "Research out of Commitment to Face the Potential for Evil in All of Us," *Journal of Traumatic Stress 7*, no. 3 (1994): 479–83.

[4] Israel W. Charny and Daphna Fromer, "A Study of the Readiness of Jewish/Israeli Students in the Health Professions to Authorize and Execute Involuntary Mass Euthanasia of 'Severely Handicapped' Patients," *Holocaust and Genocide Studies* 5, no. 3 (1990): 313–35. Reprinted in electronic form, with a new introduction, in *IDEA: A Journal of Social Issues* 9, no. 1 (25 September 2004): http://www.ideajournal.com/articles.php?type=1.
Israel W. Charny and Daphna Fromer, "The Readiness of Health Profession Students to Comply with a Hypothetical Program of 'Forced Migration' of a Minority Population," *American Journal of Orthopsychiatry* 60, no. 4 (1990): 486–95.

[5] Leo Kuper, *Genocide: Its Political Use in the Twentieth Century* (London: Penguin Books, 1981).

Jews/Israelis who otherwise evidently go to great lengths to pursue their concerns about the Holocaust will approve or condone or "understand" the murders done of unarmed Arab civilians. Did I get hell from my colleagues at Tel Aviv University for that study? Of course, they couldn't exactly say I was a traitor, so they said the study was "unscientific" — what may well be the most hurtful or serious criticism in the world of academia, I say with wry humor, and therefore inadmissible, although the study subsequently passed the more rigorous tests of the editors of a significant journal and was properly published as legitimate science.[6]

Other studies Fromer and I did were of students in the three helping health professions of medicine, psychology and social work, and how far these Jewish–Israeli students of ours could and would go in the simulations we created towards doing harm to other human beings. Would you believe it? Here too the results show a regrettable readiness to do harm to others (overall, about a third of the subjects attested that they were ready to do harm to the stated objects in the studies). These studies resulted in a series of publications in fine American journals. However, they were never published in Hebrew. One Israeli journal (*Sichot* by name) in fact had first accepted an article, but then succumbed to a reader's report that said, unhesitatingly and unambiguously, that our reported results were "fraudulent lies," and canceled its intention to publish. Our efforts to discuss the judgment with them were to no avail; they would no longer speak with us.

I purposely bring up instances of doing harm to others and genocidal massacres by my own people in order to make the point that we always need to consider the historical facts and learn whether a known victim people *also* has a history of destroying others. For the facts of life seem to be that genocidal destruction is a serious potential of every people, and we are not going to gct vcry far for our common humanity on this planct by dividing simply and naively into victims and perpetrators. Thus, as noted, the Serbs are today implicated as the main perpetrators of genocide in the former Yugoslavia in the early 1990's, but they were not alone in committing genocidal crimes, and they too were the victims of genocidal killing by others. Moreover, the history of the area shows a ping-pong over the years, and that in World War II it was the Croats who served as allies of the Nazis - there were many who said they surpassed the Nazis in their viciousness - and executed genocide of both the Jews and the Serbs. Historian Nicholas Robins has shown that Peruvian Indians in the eighteenth century were *both* victims of genocide by the Spanish as well as perpetrators of genocide against the Spanish. To the best of my knowledge, Robins is the first scholar to make the

[6] See also Israel W. Charny, "To Commit or Not Commit to Human Life: Children of Victims and Victimizers - All," *Contemporary Family Therapy* 12, no. 5 (1990): 407–26.

firm theoretical point that has been missing from the literature of genocide, and is singularly missing from the public minds of victim peoples who are understandably concerned with mourning their losses, that victims of genocide can also be perpetrators — in the same historical period or at other times in history.[7]

"OK," may say the perturbed reader, "we got the point. Victims don't like to admit that they have been perpetrators or could be perpetrators. So we have our work cut out for us in education about genocide. But surely we have to recognize first and foremost the grief and anguish and rage of people at being victims. That's also sound psychology and pedagogy. Join with people in their suffering first of all, and then go on to work with them on their own ethics towards others."

The Sorry Recurrences of Denial of Genocides

Presumably when it comes to identifying the known victims of a given genocide, once the historical information is all in to the satisfaction of most serious scholars, there is not going to be very much ignoring or distortion of the facts. Unfortunately, this too turns out not entirely true, for as is well known we have serious cases of denials of most genocides, to the point where denial has been identified by many scholars of genocide as "the last stage of a genocide." Thus, we have serious deniers of the facts of the Holocaust such as the David Irvings[8] and Ahmadinejads[9] of this world who make anti-

---

[7] Nicholas A. Robins, *Genocide and Millennialism in Upper Peru: The Great Rebellion of 1780–1782* (Westport: Praeger, 2002).

[8] David Irving became one of the notorious deniers of the Holocaust of our era after enjoying at one point a certain amount of success and public prominence for his originality as a scholar of the Nazi regime (he is not academically trained and has no research degree, but his work was impressive and interesting). However, overall, Irving emerged as a manipulator of information and specifically as a virulent anti-semite and Holocaust denier. It was Irving who brought his status in the western world to a head when he sued Deborah Lipstadt in London for having identified him as a denier. There followed a landmark decision by the British court in which Mr. Justice Gray ruled, "Irving is an active Holocaust denier; he is anti-Semitic and racist and he associates with right-wing extremists who promote neo-Nazism." *BBC News*, 20 July 2001, online:
http://news.bbc.co.uk/2/hi/uk_news/1448417.stm.

[9] Even more serious than his denials of the Holocaust — Ahmadinejad even devoted a government-sponsored "conference," accompanied by a public cartoon contest, to denying the Holocaust — are Ahmadinejad's continuous statements of commitment to the destruction of the State of Israel. On Israel's 60th birthday in May 2008, Ahmadinejad gave a speech, in which, according to the official IRNA news agency, he stated, "Those who think they can revive the stinking corpse of the usurping and fake Israeli regime by throwing a birthday party are seriously mistaken. Today the reason for the Zionist regime's existence is questioned, and this regime is on its way to annihilation."

semitic mockeries of the facts; and we have the Bernard Lewises[10] and Turkish governments[11] who devote major energies to denials of the Armenian

---

Ahmedinejad brands Israel a "stinking corpse," see *Khaleej Times Online*, May 8, 2008: http://www.khaleejtimes.com/DisplayArticle.asp?xfile=data/middleeast/2008/May/middleeast_May162.xml&section=middleeast.

Ahmadinejad's denials of the Holocaust then add a further fuel to the fire of his hatred and flagrant anti-Semitism and thereby bolster the assessments of the dangerousness of his threats to see Israel destroyed. Needless to say, the accompanying nuclear-arms race by Iran under his direction is then the more ominous and terrifying.

[10] Bernard Lewis is a very eminent scholar of Turkish history, who had written about "holocaust of a million to a million and a half Armenians" in his book, *The Emergence of Modern Turkey* (New York: Oxford University Press, 1962). However, in a subsequent edition he removed this statement, and in various professional and public appearances clearly took on the mantle of a denier of the Armenian Genocide. After he gave an interview in Paris, he was sued by the Armenian community and found guilty — intriguingly — of dereliction as a scholar, for failing to cite the considerable body of opinion contrary to his denial position. The *Encyclopedia of Genocide* reported this case as follows:

Professor Bernard Lewis Found Guilty of Denial of Armenian Genocide

In June 1995, Professor Bernard Lewis of Princeton University was found guilty by a court in Paris on civil charges that had been brought against him, as per the headline in *Le Monde*, "for denying the reality of the Armenian Genocide." This court, which was hearing a second civil case against Lewis following an earlier criminal case, found Lewis guilty of a "fault" and causing damage to another party because of his dereliction of responsibility as a scholar. The court ruled that in his denials of the genocide, Lewis calculatedly ignored and did not relate to major evidences and judgments by serious bodies, such as the UN Whitaker Commission in 1985 and the European Parliament in 1987, which have attested to the Armenian Genocide. Lewis was therefore convicted for "hiding elements which go against his thesis ... [that] the reality of the Armenian Genocide results from nothing more than the imagination of the Armenian people." He was ordered to pay a fine of 10,000 francs, punitive damages of one franc and all court costs. *Le Monde*, in which Lewis had denied the Armenian Genocide, was ordered by the court to report the sentence. — Press Reports Source: Charny, Israel W. (1999). Encyclopedia of Genocide [online] (Santa Barbara: ABC-CLIO). Available from:
http://www.ebooks.abc-clio.com/?bookid=9781576074466&loc=177&format=page
Page 177. [Accessed 20th May 2008].

[11] The Turkish government is notorious for conducting over seemingly endless years a huge worldwide campaign to censor and cancel any reference to the Armenian Genocide on the part of other governments as well as in cultural products — books, art, museum exhibits, movies, etc. See for example Helen Fein, "Changing Minds at Microsoft: Armenian Genocide Denial Checked," in the online *ISG Newsletter*, 25:

[11] The Turkish government is notorious for conducting over seemingly endless years a huge worldwide campaign to censor and cancel any reference to the Armenian Genocide on the part of other governments as well as in cultural products — books, art, museum exhibits, movies, etc. See for example Helen Fein, "Changing Minds at Microsoft: Armenian Genocide Denial Checked," in the online *ISG Newsletter*, 25:
http://www.instituteforthestudyofgenocide.org/oldsite/newsletters/25/microsoft.html.

Genocide. Denials of known genocides have emerged as a major subject worthy of grave consideration in the scholarship of genocide.[12]

But then after dealing with the problematic people and governments who make denials of a known genocide their paths to being aggrandizing nationalists, or heroes of bigotry, or exhibitionistic troublemakers, surely we can finally relax that there are not going to be any more serious sources of denials among the majority of fair-minded people.

It is hard enough that we have peoples who were victims of genocide denying when their people too are or have been perpetrators in history; it is provocative and seriously aggravating that we have professional deniers who say that a genocide didn't take place or who warp the facts of a given genocide, such as minimizing the numbers of dead, denying the intentionality of the murders, or denying the facts and revising how the murder process was executed, such as in the use of gas chambers by the Nazis. But surely the large majority of decent people in this world will not be drawn to ignoring, bypassing, concealing or denying information about who were the victims of a given genocide. Most of all, we expect unhesitatingly that *we will be able to rely on the many peoples who themselves have been victims of genocides to spell out accurately the full information of what transpired in their genocidal event.*

Again we have an unhappy surprise, for it is not that way at all. First, we find that there are large numbers of people who are drawn to some measure of belief, support or allowance of denials as a possible alternative point of view of history. Second, to add grievous insult to injury, we find that some victim peoples not only don't want to know about genocides to other peoples other than their own, but that they actively seek to remove, reduce or ignore knowledge of other victims who were killed alongside them, by the same perpetrator, in the genocidal event they suffered!

I have given the name "innocent denials" to the first of the above regrettable phenomena, a term that I use for the many people, in many cultures, who are available to be seduced by the extreme propaganda of the deniers, including in a democratic culture by the notion that "there are two sides to the story," and that whenever this is the case a truly free and democratic person will give full opportunity to both sides to be heard.[13]

---

[12] For an encompassing classification of many different types of denials of genocides, see Israel W. Charny, "A Classification of Denials of the Holocaust and Other Genocides," *Journal Genocide Research* 5, no. 1 (2003): 11–34.

[13] Israel W. Charny, "Innocent Denials of Known Genocides: A Further Contribution to a Psychology of Denial of Genocide," *Human Rights Review* 1, no. 3 (2000): 15–39.

I am reminded of an amazing scene on American radio that was described to me by a wonderful Jewish survivor of the Holocaust, Lili Kopecky, who had been forced by the Nazis to go into the "old crematorium" at Auschwitz to collect the ashes of non-Jewish prisoners in urns for their families who had paid the Nazi government to receive them. In her capacity, Kopecky saw first hand the *sonderkommando*, who were responsible for pulling bodies out of the gas chambers and moving them to the crematoria. Kopecky, who lived in Israel where she ably headed one organization of Auschwitz survivors, was a capable intellectual who also devoted some of her time to lecturing in the United States, including in particular at Emory University in Atlanta which published several of her lectures.[14] One radio show on a cable news network sought to pitch Kopecky against a known denier of the Holocaust, Arthur Butz, a professor of engineering at Northwestern University who was an arch American denier of the Holocaust and its gas chambers.[15] In a dramatic scene that ensued in their live radio telephone debate, Kopecky, a small, dainty but fearless woman who had seen it all, confronted Butz with her totally personal testimony that she had been there![16] After bearing the brunt of Kopecky's relentless first-hand rebuttals, Butz broke off the conversation, "I don't want to hear any more," and hung up.[17] Butz was hardly an "innocent denier," but an obvious anti-semite and bigot. But beyond their need to create radio entertainment because that was their job, the radio station programmers who naively sought a "debate" between a denier and a witness, and the countless listening audience members who sincerely wanted to weigh the "opposing viewpoints," were engaging in innocent denial by supporting the public appearance and notoriety of a vicious denier of the Holocaust. Giving deniers a public platform as if they deserve to have their "viewpoint" heard isn't simply an exercise in free speech and an interesting public debate, it constitutes a kind of respect for the denial. In effect, it allows for further circulation of the denial as a possibly legitimate notion and thereby supports the meta-messages of denials of known genocides, which

---

[14] Lili Kopecky, *In the Shadow of the Flames: Six Lectures on the Holocaust* (Atlanta: Emory University Witness to the Holocaust Project, 1982).

[15] Arthur R. Butz, *The Hoax of the Twentieth Century* (Richmond: Historical Review Press, 1975).

[16] The radio show was entitled *Freeman Reports* and it was broadcast on Cable News Network to an audience of several hundred thousand listeners. The program with Butz and Kopecky was broadcast on 30 April 1981.

[17] Over a period of several years, Kopecky wrote a column for the international newsletter published by our *Institute on the Holocaust and Genocide* in Jerusalem. The aforesaid story appeared in one of her columns. Lili Kopecky, "Voice of an Auschwitz Survivor: A survivor fights denials including a media debate with Arthur Butz and an account of this survivor's work in the Auschwitz crematorium" *Internet on the Holocaust and Genocide* 48 (April, 1994): 5–6.

are a combination of celebration of the past genocide being denied and a paving of an approving way for future genocides.[18]

It turns out that there is a variety of motives and needs that lead people, who are not bigots, to be interested, approve or actively support the rabid denials of a known genocide even though they themselves consciously do not really want to be racists or bigots, but we shall not explore this subject in depth here. Our purpose at this time has been to assemble a knowledge of several forms of denials of valid historical information about genocides as a background for our encountering still another largely unrecognized form of denial, which in this essay we want to introduce into the literature of genocide, namely, how strong efforts are made by several survivor or constituency groups to obscure, ignore, conceal or at least minimize awareness of other victims who died alongside "their," "preferred" victim group in a given genocide.

The Courage to Name Other People as Victims of Genocide Alongside One's Own

It turns out that several victim peoples have shown intense tendencies to drown out, ignore, and even question the veracity of the facts about other peoples who were exterminated right alongside of them.

My first experience of this sad phenomenon was, again, with my own Jewish people. Slowly and uncertainly word came out that there were other peoples who suffered and died alongside of ours, including notably the Roma (Gypsies), Soviet, and in particular Russian POWs — as hated Slavs, homosexuals, and to a lesser and less lethal extent, Jehovah's Witnesses. It should also be noted that some of these victims found their deaths in "our" gas chambers. The historical and human bonds between the different victims of the Nazis should be a strong one, but they are not. I know that for the Jewish people, the profound ethnic-nationalistic experience of identifying with the Jewish victims does not easily admit awareness of other "stranger" victims alongside them, so that these other victims were only rarely recognized at Holocaust commemoration events. And if they were brought up by someone, the reactions of many Jewish leaders were distinctly negative. Rarely were there invitations to these other peoples to participate with Holocaust survivors in shared memorial events; and there was also considerable resistance even to intellectual recognition and public mention of these other victims. Regrettably, these negative reactions often were also expressed in revealing state-

---

[18] Israel W. Charny, "The psychology of denial of known genocides," in *Genocide: A Critical Bibliographic Review,* Volume 2, Israel W. Charny, ed. (London: Mansell, 1991), 3–37.

ments as well as nonverbal gestures that conveyed the clear superiority, let alone greater significance, of the Jewish victims over these other hapless and obviously less significant populations.

It is not that the factual record was censored as it routinely is in totalitarian societies, or for that matter as various information about genocide, especially about perpetrating genocide, is denied even in some otherwise free societies such as Japan, which denies its genocidal acts against the Chinese in Manchuria in the 1930's. In the academic record, the information about other victims of the Holocaust was available, but it was not incorporated into the popular or cultural record where it was largely ignored. Thus, an outstanding Holocaust professional, who served as the second in command in the creation of the excellent U.S. Holocaust Museum, Prof. Michael Berenbaum, personally authored a very valuable book on the non-Jewish victims in the Holocaust.[19] The authority of this work is unquestioned in the literature of the Holocaust, and yet the influence of this work and of its author nonetheless has been circumscribed in the real politics of Jewish communal life. Thus, when the United States Holocaust Museum came into being, a fierce battle erupted among the directors with regard to excluding the participation of any representative of the Roma on the board. It was only after some years that a spokesman of this community, Prof. Ian Hancock, was reluctantly voted in as a member of the board of directors.

The same Hancock has continued to write with deep feeling about Jews' predominant attitude of superiority and exclusivity as victims of the Holocaust. In an interesting literary piece that summarized a prevailing emotional–political attitude of the Jewish community towards recognizing the Gypsies as victims, Hancock wrote:

> In a play by Sydney Schiffer, *The Far Side of Enough*, the representative of a fictitious international Gypsy organization offers to give a talk on the Romani Holocaust at an equally fictitious Jewish Holocaust memorial center, but is told that while such a talk would be possible, even welcome, the wording would first need to be changed. The rabbi explains that "we believe the Nazis singled us out for extermination in a way that justifies our applying the term 'The Holocaust' to us and us alone [...] I would feel honored to have you speak, if you would only agree to substitute the term 'Genocide.'" The Gypsy becomes angry, and the discussion after his departure centers on how any trouble he could make might be "neutralized." Someone else says, "Let the Gypsy speak. We'll ask our friends in the media to bury it — so deep no one will notice." We are left wondering at the end of the play whether the address is ever given.

---

[19] Michael Berenbaum, *A Mosaic of Victims: Non-Jews Persecuted and Murdered by the Nazis* (New York: New York University Press, 1990).

> While insistence on the uniqueness of the Jewish tragedy has taught the world that the racial persecution of the Jews was a destructive and vile disease, has it really learned that racial hatred against all humanity is equally destructive and vile? Is society really sensitized to the dangers of its happening again, but to another people next time?[20]

To my great disappointment, but not surprise, for all our peoples after all share a single common humanity and each of our peoples repeat and mirror our common human traits, I have seen the same phenomenon in the Armenian community — for whatever reason especially among American Armenians, but not only among them.

It turns out that many of us were not at all sufficiently aware that alongside of the Armenian victims of what we rightly know as the "Armenian Genocide," other peoples were also victims at the hands of the same Ottoman Turks, in a good number of cases literally alongside the Armenians in shared geographical areas. These victims included other Christian peoples, the Aramaeans/Assyrians and the Greeks of Ottoman citizenship, and as this information has been brought more and more to the fore in recent years there are some who have even proposed renaming the Armenian Genocide, or at least giving it the alternate name of the "Christian Genocide."

In truth, even the title, "The Christian Genocide," is not the best choice insofar as it could seem to remove from the Armenian community their hard-won gains for recognition of the genocide of their people. It would be similar to renaming the Holocaust to not focus on the Jewish victims, because in fact, as we noted, there were also *millions* of non-Jewish victims at the hands of the Nazis, such as the Roma (Gypsies), Soviet/Russian POWs (as hated Slavs whom Hitler had in his sights for mass extermination as well), homosexuals, and others. We would never want to remove or attenuate the identification of the Holocaust as an overwhelming persecution of the Jewish people, but at the same time we do need to develop clear identifiers for recognizing the other non-Jewish victims of the Holocaust, and of the Nazi regime in general, as well. Besides, the name "Christian Genocide" for the

---

[20] Ian Hancock, "Uniqueness, Gypsies and Jews," Charny, ed., *Encyclopedia of Genocide*, 501.

The late beloved Simon Wiesenthal was a very strong exception in the Jewish community. He wrote personally and passionately of remembering Roma nearby him in the concentration camp and bemoaned Jewish opposition to recognition of the Roma as fellow victims, but even his voice was not welcomed or honored on this subject.

Another prominent Jewish example was the French liberal parliamentarian and Holocaust survivor Simone Weil, who as the chairperson of the European Parliament actively supported the official recognition of the genocide against the European Roma and Sinti by the Federal Republic of Germany.

period of the Armenian Genocide also would not even do full justice to the facts because there were also still other victims of the Turks, the Yazidis (also: Yezidis), sometimes referred to as a pagan people because they are not Christians (although they incorporate some themes from Christianity in their religious practice). Our western world was rudely reacquainted with the Yazidis just a few months ago when a mega suicide-bomber terrorist attack was directed at the Yazidis in northern Iraq, and there were write-ups in our western press describing the unique religious identity of this people. The point for the Turks during the period beginning in 1915 was to advance a pan-Turkism, that non-Turks were to be destroyed, and insofar as Turkish national identity was closely entwined with an Islamic religious identity, the genocide was a jihad against non-Moslems.

Thus, a report in the *Atlantic Monthly*, in November 1916, recorded:

> The extermination of the Armenians is well under way. Thousands of Nestorians [of the Assyrian Church of the East] and Syrians [of the Syriac Orthodox Church] have vanished from the face of the earth. More than 300,000 Greeks have been deported from the Ottoman Empire, and many more sent to the interior. The fate that awaits the surviving Christians and Jews — in fact, of all the non-Turkish elements — depends on the term of the fratricidal war and its fortunes. The Young Turks are watchfully waiting to carry out their program: "Turkey for the Turks."

Clearly there were additional victims, and the job of every decent and responsible person is to recognize, name, and honor each and all of the victims. How to do so, including what names to apply to the interlocking genocides of different peoples, is important and interesting, but reasonable people will not want to dispute or conceal or omit the facts of these additional genocidal murders.

Yet I have had the experience a few years ago of participating in a seminar in Yerevan of outstanding intellectuals from around the world, a great majority of them Armenians but not only, when a world-renowned Armenian scholar from the United States, who was chairing a session of the seminar, proposed that the seminar recognize officially the Aramaean/Assyrian, Greek and Yazidi victims of the genocide along with the Armenians, and again this was a scene where all hell broke loose. I confess that *part* of me was laughing, though of course only silently inside of me, as I pictured the who knows how many times that I had witnessed angry Jewish faces around tables of counsel in our Jewish institutions barking at "traitorous" proposals to recognize some non-Jewish victims of the Holocaust. The proposal was defeated that day in Yerevan, not by an actual vote which as far as I could see would have turned out at least equal and maybe even in favor of the proposal, but by dint of the rage and vehemence of the protestors and, as I characterized

Jewish life, insinuations that those who would propose such recognition were traitors to their real Armenian cause.

Fast forward to 2007 and a proposal to recognize Assyrians and Greeks as victims of genocide by the Ottoman government alongside the Armenians comes up before the honorable leadership of the *International Association of Genocide Scholars (IAGS)* as a resolution to be brought to a vote by the membership which read as follows:

> RESOLUTION – IAGS 2007
>
> WHEREAS the denial of genocide is widely recognized as the final stage of genocide, enshrining impunity for the perpetrators of genocide, and demonstrably paving the way for future genocides;
>
> WHEREAS the Ottoman genocide against minority populations during and following the First World War is usually depicted as a genocide against Armenians alone, with little recognition of the qualitatively similar genocides against other Christian minorities of the Ottoman Empire;
>
> BE IT RESOLVED that it is the conviction of the International Association of Genocide Scholars that the Ottoman campaign against Christian minorities of the Empire between 1914 and 1923 constituted a genocide against Armenians, Assyrians, and Pontian and Anatolian Greeks.
>
> BE IT FURTHER RESOLVED that the Association calls upon the government of Turkey to acknowledge the genocides against these populations, to issue a formal apology, and to take prompt and meaningful steps toward restitution.

Historically, the IAGS — when it was named simply the *Association for Genocide Scholars* — had played an important role in recognizing and ratifying the historical validity of the Armenian Genocide. At its second biennial international conference in Montreal in June 1997, the association had approved, unanimously, the following resolution:

> That this assembly of the Association of Genocide Scholars in its conference held in Montreal, June 11–13, 1997, reaffirms that the mass murder of Armenians in Turkey in 1915 is a case of genocide which conforms to the statutes of the United Nations Convention on the Prevention and Punishment of Genocide. It further condemns the denial of the Armenian Genocide by the Turkish government and its official and unofficial agents and supporters.

Through the years this resolution has been cited over and over again in many historical and political forums, and very much in battles against efforts to deny the Armenian Genocide; and it also became an important facilitating base for a next milestone in intellectual politics in 2000 when at the Thirtieth Anniversary of the Scholars' Conference on the Holocaust and the Churches, convening at St. Joseph University, Philadelphia, Pennsylvania, 126 Holocaust scholars, signed a statement affirming that the World War I Armenian Genocide is an incontestable historical fact and urged the governments of Western Democracies to recognize it as such. The petitioners, among whom was Nobel Laureate for Peace Elie Wiesel who was the keynote speaker at the conference, eminent Holocaust scholar Yehuda Bauer from Jerusalem, and Elizabeth Maxwell from the UK, also asked the Western Democracies to urge the Government and Parliament of Turkey to finally come to terms with a dark chapter of Ottoman–Turkish history and to recognize the Armenian Genocide as "an invaluable impetus to the process of the democratization of Turkey."

So it is in the perspective of the history of significant resolutions that IAGS now faced this new proposal to recognize additional victims of and alongside the Armenian Genocide. Again here madness erupted! What now happened was amazing and deeply disappointing to me. First came tedious demands for additional scholarly documentation of the victimization of these groups that in effect were calculated to stall and derail the resolution process, although here I also say fair enough: Even though the demands were disingenuous efforts to block the resolution, IAGS is an organization of scholars and it is fair game for opponents of any process in the organization to express and anchor the politics of their position in demands for scholarly evidences. Led by Thea Halo, author of a moving book on her mother's experience of the Greek Genocide,[21] and Adam Jones, a professor at University of British Columbia and recent author of the first issues–oriented comprehensive textbook on genocide studies for college and graduate school instruction,[22] the resolution was now buttressed with heavy reference sources. For example, they pointed out that the Aramaean/Assyrian Genocide had just recently been studied extensively in an article published in IAGS' own influential journal, *Genocide Studies and Prevention:* "Native Christians Massacred: The Ottoman Genocide of the Assyrians during World War I."[23]

---

[21] Thea Halo, *Not Even My Name* (New York: Picador, 2000).

[22] Adam Jones, *Genocide: A Comprehensive Introduction* (Oxford and New York: Routledge and Taylor & Francis, 2006).

[23] Hannibal Travis, "Native Christians massacred: The Ottoman Genocide of the Assyrians during World War I," *Genocide Studies and Prevention* 1, no. 3 (2006): 327–71.

> Abstract: "The Ottoman Empire's widespread persecution of Assyrian civilians during World War I constituted a form of genocide, the present–day term for an attempt to destroy a national, ethnic, or religious group, in whole or in part. Ottoman soldiers and their Kurdish and Persian militia partners subjected hundreds of thousands of Assyrians to a deliberate and systematic campaign of massacre, torture, abduction, deportation, impoverishment, and cultural and ethnic destruction. Established principles of international law outlawed this war of extermination against Ottoman Christian civilians before it was embarked upon, and ample evidence of genocidal intent has surfaced in the form of admissions by Ottoman officials. Nevertheless, the international community has been hesitant to recognize the Assyrian experience as a form of genocide. The Assyrian genocide is indistinguishable in principle from its Armenian counterpart, however, and its re-

In truth, in the heated back-and-forth public discussion of the resolution that took place on the association's blog and in many other e-mail communications, the genocide of the Aramaeans/Assyrians seemed to me to be accorded greater consensual validation, but there was more pressing opposition to the subject of the genocide of the Greeks. The authors of the resolution also produced additional documentations of the murders of the Greeks both in the early period of 1916 and later towards the end of the genocidal process in 1922. In the present essay, we already saw earlier the example of a report from the *Atlantic Monthly* in 1916. Additional sources were cited such as Frank W. Jackson, Chairman of the Relief Committee for Greeks of Asia Minor, who wrote on 17 October 1917:

> Along with the Armenians most of the Greeks of the Marmora regions and Thrace have been deported on the pretext that they gave information to the enemy. Along the Aegean coast, Aivalik stands out as the worst sufferer. According to one report, some 70,000 Greeks have been deported towards Konia and beyond. At least 7000 have been slaughtered. The Greek Bishop of Aivalik committed suicide in despair.

Also quoted was American Ambassador, Henry Morgenthau, who had fought energetically with the Turkish leadership to stop the Armenian Genocide, and who wrote in 1919 in his famous book, *Ambassador Morgenthau's Story*, "The story which I have told about the Armenians I could also tell with certain modifications about the Greeks and the Syrians."[24]

In their memo of supporting evidences, Halo and Jones[25] also cite the American Consul at Aleppo, Jesse B. Jackson who filed a report on 5 April 1922 from Dr. Mark H. Ward and Dr. F. D. Yowell, Directors of the Near East Relief unit at Harput. In it Ward and Yowell testified to the tens of thousands of Greeks from the Black Sea region — two-thirds of whom were women and children — being marched south, with medical attention, food and shelter

---

cognition by scholars and the international community may assist in the resettlement and relief of the Assyrian remnant currently fleeing by the thousands from its homelands in Iraq" (page 327).

[24] Henry Morgenthau, Sr., *Ambassador Morgenthau's Story* (New York: Doubleday Page & Company, 1919). See Chapter 24, "The Murder of a Nation."

[25] Thea Halo and Adam Jones, "Notes on the Genocides of Christian Populations of the Ottoman Empire: Submitted in support of a resolution recognizing the Armenian, Assyrian, and Pontic and Anatolian Greek Genocides of 1914–23," presented to the membership of the International Association of Genocide Scholars (IAGS), 2007, Sarajevo, Bosnia and Herzegovina, July 2007. Circulated to membership of IAGS in March 2007, presented at the IAGS conference in Sarajevo in July, 2007, then circulated again on 17 September 2007, with a cover letter from Gregory Stanton, who was now the president of IAGS, calling on the membership to vote by 16 November 2007.

denied to them, causing many thousands to perish from "starvation, exposure, typhus, and dysentery." Yowell and Ward reported that the road was strewn with thousands of dead bodies along the way, and that armed guards had prodded the "deportees" on. Yowell wrote on 5 May 1922 as follows:

> Conditions of Greek minorities are even worse than those of the Armenians. Sufferings of the Greeks deported from districts behind the battlefront are terrible and still continue. These deportees began to reach Harpoot before my arrival last October. Of thirty thousand Greek refugees who left Sivas five thousand died on the way before reaching Harpoot. One American relief worker saw and counted fifteen hundred bodies on the road east of Harpoot.
>
> In Harpoot district our relief has been to give these needy people in opposition to the wishes of the Turks who did everything in their power to prevent our doing so. We were not allowed to employ any Greeks in our work or to take any orphan children, left by dying Greek deportees, into our orphanages. Sick Greeks could not be received into our hospital except on the written order of the Turkish Commissioner.
>
> Two thirds of the Greek deportees are women and children. All along the route where these deportees have traveled Turks are permitted to visit refugee groups and select women and girls whom they desire for any purpose.... Their whole route today strewn with bodies of their dead, which are consumed by dogs, wolves, vultures. The Turks make no effort to bury these dead and the deportees are not permitted to do so. The chief causes of death are starvation, dysentery, typhus. Turkish authorities frankly state that it is their deliberate intention to exterminate the Greeks, and all their actions support this statement.

Nonetheless, notwithstanding the considerable references that were marshaled by the authors of the resolution, there continued an amazing degree of intense protest against the resolution, including by some outstanding scholars in IAGS — although it can also be proffered for the record that the resolution was fully supported by *all* the members of the then-presiding and incoming Executive Boards of the association. A major political attempt now followed to prevent the resolution being brought before the membership for a vote. This big push to derail the resolution took place at a meeting, which combined several IAGS leadership boards, which had been convened in the course of the association's biennial conference in Sarajevo, Bosnia in July 2007. This meeting was held prior to the association business meeting scheduled for later in the week, and the opponents of the resolution were hoping to get a decision that would stop the voting on the resolution at the business meeting.

As noted, the opponents of the resolution included distinguished scholars whom we all respected and appreciated for their contributions over the years. Intriguingly, a majority of them were clustered at a single institution and obviously had come to a joint policy decision among themselves, so that there were some who questioned whether there was a specific funding source involved in their work whom they were appeasing, but this was without any information available to support such a conjecture, and to me it was inconceivable that such noteworthy scholars would be susceptible to economic realpolitik. One other leading member of the opposition was an internationally famous and beloved Armenian scholar who, in fact, in the past had written explicitly about the genocide of the Aramaeans/Assyrians and Greeks as well as the Armenians.[26]

What was this madness? For myself — and I was then the presiding president of IAGS — I was heartbroken. In the brouhaha that followed, I did my best to tell a very amusing and I felt convincing story of an experience that had taken place when I had been in Armenia not that long before, when I had actually been asked by the Director of the Armenian Genocide Memorial and Museum on the Tsitsernakaberd Hill of Yerevan to go and greet a large crowd that had gathered at the Memorial to celebrate the commemoration of the Pontus Greek Genocide on May 19. The Armenians in Yerevan had no questions. Greek flags flew unfurled in Yerevan at the Genocide Memorial! They recognized the Greek Genocide and event and honored it! I told the Director of the Armenian Genocide Memorial and Museum that (long before the IAGS resolution) I had encountered many questions and much resistance to recognizing any other victims of the genocide other than the Armenians, and he laughed at the notion of victim exclusivity. "Oh, you know how those Americans are," the Director laughed with characteristic gusto, naturally addressing me as the Israeli I am and ignoring my also being an American-born citizen of the U.S. (I hold my citizenships in both beloved countries).

I myself cannot subscribe to any scurrilous interpretations of our colleagues' opposition, and I can only understand their positions as expressions of a dynamic of insistence on an exclusive victim status of a given victim people to whom they are devoted, and to whose memorial they make huge contributions. There may also have been some honest intellectual skepticism and caution by some of these scholars who really want a clearer intellectual record than we have amassed in our western world for some of the other genocides or some aspects of them. But I was shocked and disappointed. The unpleasant IAGS battle caused me to lose some friendships that were dear to me for years, not because of any honest questioning or differences of

---

[26] "While the death toll in the trenches of Western Europe was close to 2 million by the summer of 1915, the extermination of innocent civilians in Turkey (the Armenians, but also Syrian and Assyrian Christians and large portions of the Greek population, especially the Greeks of Pontus, or Black Sea region) was reaching 1 million." Peter Balakian, *The Burning Tigris: The Armenian Genocide and America's Response* (New York and London: Harper Collins, 2003), 285–86.

opinion, but because of the adamancy and political strong-arming of the opposition, and in some cases even threats of resignation from the organization (since when do we insist on 100% representation of all our ideas by a major professional organization to which we belong?). I simply could not understand the readiness of some of the opponents to rupture longstanding personal relationships or to leave the organization we had worked so hard to build because they disagreed about this resolution.

All of the above is no different than the opposition we frequently encounter to recognizing other victims of the Holocaust among my own people, as well as among some of the non-Jews who are brilliantly active in the remembrance of the Holocaust. As a resident of Israel — where of course I do most of my work and interact socially in the professional community of the country in which I live — I have spent so much of my adult life in a sea of reserved feelings and silent critique of me for my insistence on recognizing *all* the victims of any given genocide including the Holocaust; more largely for my insistence on recognizing the genocides of *all* victim peoples and not staying focused exclusively on the uniqueness of the Holocaust; let alone my insistence on recognizing several instances of our Israeli lapses into being perpetrators of genocidal massacres. I have come to a deep conviction that a crucial intellectual and spiritual task for *all* of us is to inventory our own selves and identify our quite natural participation in various prejudiced thinking and involuntary emotions towards various peoples who are different than ours. I feel convinced that the only way that makes sense in genocide studies, and in life on this planet in its entirety, is to honor and support unambiguously the right to life of *all* peoples, and this to me is the larger meaning of scholarship to recognize all victims of each genocidal event.

Now I am happy to write that as far as IAGS is concerned, this will also be a happy-end-story. The resolution indeed did not *go to a vote at the business meeting. To this extent the opponents had won, but what was decided was that more time would be given to the members to study the pros and cons of the resolution and then vote by electronic ballot on the resolution a few months later. The result was now to prove salutary, for a large number of members voted and the resolution was accepted conclusively and resoundingly. The resolution thus becomes another constructive step towards a worldview of recognizing all victims of all genocides. And the whole story has also become an opportunity for us all to learn more about ourselves and our own participations in our flawed human race.*

Jerusalem
April 2008

Γενοκτονία εν Ροή — Cumulative Genocide

The Massacres and Deportations of the Greek Population of the Ottoman Empire (1912–1923)

TESSA HOFMANN

I. *Time Frames for the Decision on Genocide*

AT THE TURN OF THE NINETEENTH CENTURY, the collapsing multi-ethnic and multi-religious Ottoman Empire was a state torn by internal and external crisis, by national independence movements as well as by the imperialist appetite of competing European powers. Ethnic homogenization, achieved by assimilation, ethnic dispersion, expulsion or even destruction was seen as a counter-measure against destabilization.

The indigenous Christians of the Ottoman Empire — more than five million within the boundaries of Asia Minor or present-day Turkey — had developed a firm ethno-religious identity already during the early Middle Ages and had ever since proven resistant to attempts of assimilation. Excluded from the military and at most times from higher and decision-making ranks in the civil service, Ottoman non-Muslims, and in particular Armenians and Greeks, had to limit themselves to trade, commerce and entrepreneurship, similar to the situation of Jews in Medieval Europe. The reforms of the *Tanzimat* era (1829–1876) helped the Ottoman Christians, and in particular the Greeks and Armenians, economically to prosper. But their visible wealth and simultaneous legal inferiority as *dhimmis* (*zimmi* (Tur.)) *or raya(h)* (*reaya* (Tur.))[1] made them vulnerable minorities. This vulnerability increased, when Muslim suspicion of Christian disloyalty added to social envy and traditional religious antipathy. Massacres of Christians more frequently occurred during the reign of the reactionary Sultan Abdülhamit II (1878–1908). They were directed mainly against the *ermeni millet-ı* (Armenian-Apostolic Christians), who unlike the Ottoman Orthodox Greeks, or *rum millet-ı*[2] lacked a foreign protector or a national state outside the Ottoman

[1] *Raya(h)* or *reaya*, i.e. "cattle" or "flock;" in Ottoman Turkish a member of the tax-paying lower class of Ottoman society, in contrast to the elite class (*askeri*), to which the nobility, the military and the religious clergy belonged. Although the term originally included Muslim taxpayers as well, it was, in its later use, reduced to non-Muslim taxpayers.

[2] In this contribution, I refer to Greeks, or Ottoman Greeks as the community of Orthodox Christians of the Byzantine tradition. Most of them would be of Greek ethnicity, although by far not all were Greek-speakers; the most common self-identifier was *Romiosyne*, or

realm, these massacres however were never limited to Armenians. In some areas, the regional or local authorities allowed that violence was extended to other Christian denominations. Gustave Meyrier, the French Vice-consul at Diyarbakır (Amida (Gr.)), explained in his second report of 9 February 1895, the anti-Christian atrocities in this province as being driven by religious hatred: "The state of affairs affects all Christians regardless of race, be they Armenian, Chaldaean, Syrian or Greek. It is the result of religious hatred that is all the more implacable in that it is based on the strength of some and the weakness of others."[3] A similar pattern appears during World War I, when the deportations and massacres in the Diyarbakır province developed into the general destruction of Christians, affecting in particular the Aramaic-speaking population in that region.[4] The "spill-over effect"

---

an identity linked to a sense of belonging to Orthodox Christianity and heir to the world of the Later Roman (Byzantine) Empire. The rum [Roman] millet-ı, however, included also groups of other than Greek ethnicity. To differentiate the (Ottoman) Greeks from those, who were nationals of Greece, I designate the latter Hellenes when necessary.

[3] Sébastien de Courtois, *The Forgotten Genocide: Eastern Christians, the Last Aramaeans.* (Piscataway, New Jersey: Gorgias Press, 2004), 101.

[4] Ibid.; Two of three collections of accounts on the massacres during 1914–1916 in Southwest Anatolia gathered by representatives of the Syriac Orthodox and Catholic churches were published in Germany and the Netherlands, where Syriac Orthodox communities of refugees had emerged:
a) The Aramaean writer and scholar Abed Mshiho (Abdulmesih in Arabic) Na'man Karabashi (from Karabaş/Qarabash) was an eyewitness to the genocide. In 1918, 15 years old and a pupil (*malfono*) at the Mor Gabriel (Za'afaran) Monastery, he gathered survivor accounts of the atrocities committed by Ottoman regulars and Kurdish irregulars in the Tur Abdin region. German editions of the report by Abed Msiho Na'man from Qarabash, *Vergossenes Blut* [*Shed Blood*] (Augsburg: ADO Publikationen, 1997 and Glane/Losser, Netherlands: Bar Hebräus Verlag 1999); and *Vergossenes Blut: Geschichten der Greuel, die an den Christen in der Türkei verübt, und der Leiden, die ihnen 1895 und 1914–1918 zugefügt wurden* [*Bloodshed: Tales of the Atrocities, Committed against the Christians in Turkey, and of the Sufferings They Underwent in 1895 and During 1914–1918*], translated and edited by George Toro und Amill Gorgis (Glane/Losser: Bar-Hebräus Verlag, 2002).
b) A collection of accounts, gathered by the archpriest Sleman (Shlimon/Salomon) d'Beth Henno (Hannah, or Hinno in Turkish) from Arkah of survivors in his parish, was published first in Aramaic in 1977, *Gunhe d-suryoye d-Tur'Abdin da-šnath 1915* [*Reversals of fortune against the Syriac Christians of Tur Abdin in 1915*], and since 1987 in two German translations, the most recent being *Die Verfolgung und Vernichtung der Syro-Aramäer im Tur Abdin 1915* [*The Persecution and Extermination of the Syro-Aramaeans in Tur Abdin 1915*]: *gesammelt vom Erzpriester Sleman Henno aus Arkah, Tur Abdin,* translated from Syro-Aramean by Amill Gorgis und Georg Toro (Glane/Losser: Bar Hebräus-Verlag, 2005). A Turkish edition also has appeared: Hori Süleyman Hinno, *Farman. Tur'Abdinli süryanilerin 1914–1915 katliamı* (Athens, 1993). An edition also has appeared in the United States.
c) A collection by the Catholic monk Ishaq/Ishoq (Bar) Armalto appeared in Arabic and French in 1919: Isaac Armalet (Fr.), *Les Calamités des Chrétiens/Al-Qusara fi Nakabat an-Nasara* (Beirut, 1919). It focuses on events in Mardin (Maride (Gr.)) in 1895 and 1914–

showed itself also during a conservative counter-revolution in April 1909, when anti-Armenian massacres occurred in the Adana province:

> The slaughter was unsparing. Greeks and Syrians were struck down with the Armenians. Entire families were burned to death in their homes. Hundreds of girls and women were maltreated and carried off to the harems, where the women were separated from the men.[5]

The frequent use of fire in the destruction of the Ottoman Christians is noteworthy. The term "holocaust" as a synonym for genocidal destruction was first applied by the American missionary Corinna Shattuck, who witnessed the "great holocaust" in Urfa (Edessa (Gr.), Şanlıurfa (Tur.)), when 3,000 Armenians were burnt alive in their cathedral in late 1895.[6] The term was then continuously used by Europeans to describe the annihilation of Ottoman Christians: In 1898 the French-Jewish Journalist Bernard Lazare called the nationwide slaughters of Armenians and other Christians during 1895 and 1896 a holocaust, while the Englishman Frederick Zaccheus Duckett Ferriman (1856–1934) titled his book on the Adana slaughter *The Young Turks and the Truth About the Holocaust in Asia Minor During April 1909* (London 1913). With the disappearance of the Christian population in Asia Minor, the historic context of "holocaust" as a synonym for anti-Christian destructive events sank into oblivion. During and after World War II, it was increasingly applied to the destruction of the European Jews, although Elie Wiesel believed, that he had invented it in 1958.[7]

The question about the beginning of genocidal schemes among the Ottoman political elite interrelates with the question, whether the Young Turkish revolution marked a change of paradigms in the ideology and nationality policies of the ruling elite. There exist opposing views:

1918. A fourth collection of eyewitness accounts by Syriac Orthodox clerics and lay persons was published in German translation under the title *Seyfe* [*Sword*] in the Netherlands; it mainly contains descriptions of the atrocities in poetic verse: *Seyfe: Das Christen-Massaker in der Türkei, 1714–1914* [*Seyfe: The Massacre of Christians in Turkey, 1714–1914*] (Glane/Losser: Bar Hebräus-Verlag, 1981). See also Courtois, *The Forgotten Genocide*; David Gaunt, *Massacres, Resistance, Protectors: Muslim-Christian Relations in Eastern Anatolia during World War I* (Piscataway, New Jersey: Gorgias Press 2006). For a contemporary publication see Joseph Naayem, *Shall this Nation Die?*, Preface by Lord Bryce (New York: Chaldean Rescue, 1920), http://www.aina.org/books/stnd.htm.

[5] "Details of Slaughter Received," *The New York Times*, 5 May 1909.

[6] Hans-Lukas Kieser and Dominick J. Schaller, "Völkermord im historischen Raum 1895–1945" [Genocide in historical context, 1895–1945], in *Der Völkermord an den Armeniern und die Shoah* [*The Armenian Genocide and the Shoah*], Hans-Lukas Kieser and Dominick J. Schaller, eds. (Zürich: Chronos Verlag, 2002), 41.

[7] Gunnar Heinsohn, *Lexikon der Völkermorde* [*Encyclopedia of Genocides*] (Reinbek: Rowohlt, 1998), 174.

> Now [Turkish and European scholars] tend to accept that the Muslims' original anti-imperialistic self-defensive nationalism which culminated in the Pan-Islamism of Abdülhamid II was replaced by an aggressive linguistic and ethnic nationalism under the CUP[8] and that the latter is partly responsible for the partial disintegration of the Ottoman State – though it was called to life to hinder, not to promote this process.[9]

Erik Jan Zürcher, on the other hand, suggests the gradual evolution of Muslim nationalism into an "Ottoman nationalism," which was predominantly, but not exclusively Turkish, but exclusively Muslim:

> The [...] question, which often occupied the same Young Turk authors, was that of the communal basis of any future Ottoman state, whether it should be based on a single nationality, on a voluntary union of nationalities or perhaps on religion. By the early twentieth century sincere belief in a 'Union of [ethnic] Elements' (*İttihadı Anasır*) was probably limited to some Greek, Arab and Albanian intellectuals and the 'Liberal' group led by Prince Sabahattin. The vast majority, certainly of the Unionists, already before the 1908 revolution subscribed to a kind of Ottoman Muslim nationalism in which the dominant position of the Turks was taken for granted. There was a growing awareness of Turkishness, but for most Young Turks this was one facet of a complex identity in which being an Ottoman and a Muslim played equally important parts. From the start the organizers of the 1908 revolution opened up their ranks to non-Turkish Muslims, but not (or at least not automatically) to non-Muslims.[10]

Since the military coup d'état of 1908, the nationalist elite's journey to genocide was a gradual evolution, triggered by foreign and domestic events, in particular those of the year 1913 which saw the Second Balkan War, expulsions of the Muslim population from Bosnia and Macedonia, but also the reform scheme for the six Armenian provinces according to the Berlin Treaty (1878). On various occasions and even in the early stages of their movement the nationalists had articulated their intention to defend against alleged threats of Christian separatism.

Such a feeling emerged among Turkish or Muslim Ottoman nationalists, years before they gained power. The issues of debates on political principles and orientation of the early twentieth century resemble in many aspects the recent discussion of anti- or pro-European attitudes in Turkey. An exponent of the controversial positions was exiled liberal Ahmed Rıza (1859–1930), editor of the journal *Meşveret* (*Consultation*), in which he set out ideas of

---

[8] Committee of Union and Progress (*İttihat ve Terakki Cemiyeti*), better known in Europe as the Young Turks.

[9] Gábor Demeter, "The Views of the Young Turks and the Conservatives about Foreign and Domestic Politics before the Balkan Wars," in *Europe and the World in European Historiography*, C. Lévai, ed. (Pisa: Pisa University Press, 2006), 197.

[10] Erik Jan Zürcher, "From Empire to Republic: Problems of Transition, Continuity and Change," http://www.let.leidenuniv.nl/tcimo/tulp/Research/Fromtorep.htm.

reform, strongly flavoured by Auguste Comte's philosophy of positivism, with whom he shared anti-imperialist positions. In the late nineteenth century Rıza had written that one of the main faults of the Ottoman system was its tolerance of non-Muslim minorities; enforced conversion would have pre-empted any secessionist difficulties. For him, separatism was high treason.[11] His advocacy of a strong central government within the Ottoman Empire and the exclusion of foreign influence led in February 1902 to a major split within the Young Turk exiles at the First Congress of Ottoman Liberals in Paris. There, Ahmed Rıza clashed with Prince Sabaheddin, who, with Armenian support, favoured administrative decentralization and European assistance to promote reform.[12]

Two relevant preparatory steps in the development towards genocide are socio-political exclusion and dehumanization. Exclusion was articulated already in August 1910 and September 1911, at the occasion of the Third and Fourth annual CUP meeting at Thessalonica (Θεσσαλονίκη, also known as Salonika, and Selânik in Turkish). Ziya Gökalp (1876–1924), a member of the CUP Central Committee since 1910 and leading ideologist of Turkism, who became the deputy of Home Minister Talât Paşa and responsible for minority issues in the CUP's Central Committee, exempted the non-Muslims from the ethnic definition of a Turkish nation: "Greeks, Armenians and Jews who lived in Turkey were Turks only in respect of citizenship but not of nationality [...] they would remain a foreign body in the national Turkish state."[13]

On 25 June 1909 the *Ottoman Lloyd,* No. 146 reported a visit of the Ecumenical Patriarch Joachim III (the Magnificent) to the Ottoman Commander in Chief Mahmut Şevket in order to protest against "murders and violence"[14]

---

[11] Donald Bloxham, *The Great Game of Genocide: Imperialism, Nationalism, and the Destruction of the Ottoman Empire* (Oxford/New York: Oxford University Press, 2005), 62.

[12] *Encyclopaedia Britannica*, quoted in http://mertebe.org/English/Turkmenistan/history/ot_1807_1920.html;
Cf. also Feroz Ahmad, "Young Turk-Armenian Relations during the Second Constitutional Period, 1908–1914" (paper presented at the First International Social Studies Symposium on *The Art of Living Together in Ottoman Society: The Case of Turkish-Armenian Relations*, Erciyes University, 20–22 April 2006).
http://armenians-1915.blogspot.com/2007/01/1349-young-turk-armenian-relations.html.

[13] Quoted from Robert Melson, "Provocation or Nationalism: A Critical Inquiry into the Armenian Genocide of 1915," in *The Armenian Genocide in Perspective*, Richard G. Hovannisian, ed. (New Brunswick: Transaction Publishers, 1986), 77.

[14] According to a report dated 24 June 1909 by the German Ambassador Wangenheim to the German Chancellor von Bülow, cf. Konstantinos Fotiadis, *Der Genozid an den Pontosgriechen. Band 12: Unveröffentlichte Dokumente aus den Archiven der Außenministerien Deutschlands, Österreichs, Italiens und des Vatikans* [*The Genocide of the Greeks of Pontus.*

against Greeks in the Ionian town of Kydonies (Κυδωνίες, also the more archaic Κυδωνίαι, Kydoniai/Cydoniae; Ayvalık in Turkish). The *generalissimo* used the opportunity to articulate his discontent with the irredentist development at Crete that he linked to the activities of Greek associations (σύλλογοι, *syllogoi*) in Asia Minor: "All agree about this. I speak about the societies and *syllogoi*. No, we cannot stand this situation any longer. We will break your heads; we shall annihilate all of you. Either we shall be lost or you!"[15] The Greek daily *Εμπρός* [*Empros*] (Athens) of 24 June 1909 concluded:

> Neither the conduct of Şevket towards the Patriarch nor the murders and violence in Kydonia, nor the despotism in Xanthis is as such of significance. These are events, deriving all from the same reason. The Turks have decided to lead a war of annihilation against the Christians of the Empire, and of course they started, where they face the strongest enemy inside Turkey and the smallest resistance outside the country.[16]

As early as September 1910, the German Ambassador described violence as a seemingly unavoidable tool of "Ottomanization,"[17] as the merger of the numerous ethno-religious groups in the Ottoman Empire was then called:

> In many parts of the country the disappointment of the non-Turks has already become evident, and there is every appearance, that a peaceful solution of this task [i.e., of Ottomanization; T.H.], based on joint efforts, cannot be achieved. That leaves the only question, whether the Turks will gradually carry out the merger by force, similar to the way in which Russia had russified the foreign citizens. The Sublime Porte, supported by the chauvinist Committee [CUP] does not seem to recoil from the difficulties of this program, even if these appear to be insuperable. It prefers the Turks in every way when appointing staff to posts and tends to minimize the rights of the other nationalities in a reading of the treaties as restrictive as possible. [...] In par-

---

Volume 12: Unpublished Documents from the Archives of the Foreign Offices of Germany, Austria, Italy and the Vatican] (Thessalonica: Herodotos, 2003), 54.

15 According to an informant of the German Ambassador Miguel, commander Şevket offended the Patriarchate in a slightly different version: "Listen, Patriarch, eventually we reach a point, where either we have to oppress you or you have to annihilate us!" Compare PA/AA, Türkei No. 168, Vol. 6, 7, letter of 26 June 1909; cf. Fotiadis, ibid., 56–57.

16 Fotiadis, ibid., 54.

17 A term used synonymously for Turkification, in order to mislead foreign opinion. It had been Talât's and his followers' suggestion after the Fourth CUP meeting (September 1911) to follow, for tactical reasons the previous policy of voluntary "osmanization" (ottomanization) and cooperation with Armenian political parties until the external circumstances would be more appropriate for the realization of the extermination program. Arsen Avakyan, *Genocid 1915 g.: mechanizmy prinyatiya i ispolneniya rešeniy* [*The Genocide of the Year 1915: The Mechanisms of Decision-Making and Implementation of the Decisions*] (Erevan, 1999), 25.

ticular, the struggle is directed against the Ottomans of Greek origin and against the Ecumenical Patriarchate [...][18]

Italy's seizure of the Ottoman provinces of Tripolitania and Cyrenaica (Libya today), as well as of the Dodecanesian archipelago that was inhabited by Greeks, had led to the Italo-Turkish War (September 1911–October 1912), which accelerated the anti-Christian and anti-minority sentiments. It is against this background of war and territorial losses, that the annual *İttihat* (CUP) party meeting at Thessalonica was held in autumn 1911. The *London Times* of 3 October 1911, summarizing the proceedings of the Committee of Union and Progress, reported a decision by the meeting that the Ottomanization of all Turkish citizens must be accomplished by force of arms, since persuasion had failed. The same information can be found in Turkish sources and also was cited by the German Protestant theologian, missionary and recorder of the Armenian genocide Dr. Johannes Lepsius:

> The congress confirms that sooner or later the Ottomanization of all peoples of the Empire must follow, and if this cannot be achieved by peaceful means one must not shrink from violent or even military means. [...] The non-Turkish peoples should lose the right to found organizations based on ethnicity, for decentralization threatens the unity of the Ottoman state. Ethnic minorities can be disregarded. They may preserve their religion. But instead of their native tongue they should use the official language of the Empire, Turkish.[19]

Assimilation was to be achieved by geographical dispersion — mainly by resettlement and deportations, which

> [...] were planned, ordered, and coordinated by the Ottoman Ministry of the Interior's "Directorate for the Settlement of Tribes and Immigrants" at Constantinople. At times, however, the directorate's officials joined those of the ministry's "Directorate for Public Security" on the spot in the provinces when

[18] Letter by German Ambassador Miguel to Chancellor von Bethmann Hollweg of September 6, 1910; Berlin, Political Archives of the German Foreign Office (PA/AA), File Türkei Nr. 175 b, Vol. 8ff., Vol. 9. Translated from Fotiadis, *Der Genozid an den Pontosgriechen*, 67–68.

[19] *İttihat ve Terakki kongreleri*, "Memleket," 16/12/1947. Quoted from Avakyan, *Genocid 1915 g.*, 16. — Lepsius summarized the 1911 CUP meeting as the intended "complete Ottomanization of all Turkish subjects [...] however, it is clear, that this can never be achieved by persuasion, but that one has to take refuge to the use of arms. The Empire's nature has to remain Muslim, and Muslim institutions and traditions have to be respected. Other nationalities should be refused the right of organization, for decentralization and self-administration is treason against the Turkish Empire. The nationalities would be a *quantité négligeable*. They may preserve their religion, but not their language. The development of the Turkish language will be one of the main means in order to secure the Muslim predominance and to assimilate the other elements." Johannes Lepsius, *Bericht über die Lage des armenischen Volkes in der Türkei* [*Report on the Situation of the Armenian People in Turkey*] (Potsdam: Tempelverlag, 1916), 221–22.

> the situation demanded. Thus, a relatively small number of high-ranking administrators oversaw and engineered the deportations and extermination of virtually millions of Ottoman citizens. Most of them must be regarded as experts in crimes against humanity. In the course of their careers they repeatedly committed atrocities against the various groups targeted by the Ottoman government and after World War I, the governments of the Turkish Republic.[20]

Retaliation became another motif for the destruction of the indigenous Christians in the Ottoman Empire. In such schemes, the Christians were considered hostages against expected European interventions. Months before the first Balkan War started in late autumn 1912, the *İttihat* Central Committee member Abdül Reşit threatened in his speech in the Rumeli Hisar *İttihat* club in March of the same year:

> If Europe attacks in order to wipe us out, then we will be forced to carry out such a plan of revenge against our subject Christian peoples, that the Europeans will be stupefied and unable to take even a single step against us.[21]

The Balkan Wars of 1912–13 completed this radicalization, as the actions against the Greek population of Eastern Thrace and the littorals of Asia Minor prove. According to the Turkish writer, feminist and leading CUP member Halide Edip (Adıvar; 1884–1964), who expressed the average nationalist's opinion in her memoirs (1926), it was then that the Ottoman elite was overcome by the sense that "the Turks must exterminate others" in order "to avoid being exterminated."[22] The two reasons, given by Edip for this conclusion, were the "massacre of three thousand Macedonian Turks and Moslems," which the nationalist author chose to characterize[23] as "one of the greatest massacres of the last hundred years" and Europe's alleged ethical double standard, i.e.,

> [...] the massacres did not arouse one quarter of the indignation which the Armenian massacres had done. These facts spoke bitterly in Turkey against Europe, and in the Islamic worlds in Asia.[24]

---

[20] Hilmar Kaiser, "The Ottoman Government and the End of the Ottoman Social Formation, 1915–1917," http://www.hist.net/kieser/aghet/Essays/EssayKaiser.html (Posted August 2001).

[21] Grigoris Balakian, *Armenian Golgotha: A Memoir of the Armenian Genocide, 1915–1918* (New York: Alfred J. Knopf, 2009), 246.

[22] Halide Edip (Adıvar), *Memoirs* (London: Murray, 1926; reprint, Piscataway: Gorgias Press, 2005), 333.

[23] Edip's selection ignored the earlier massacres of 1822 in Chios, when it is estimated that out of about 117,000 Greek islanders approximately 25,000–52,000 had been killed; it also ignored the massacres of Armenians in 1894–96 (estimates vary between 100,000 and 300,000 killed) and of 1909 in the Ottoman Adana province (estimated 20,000–30,000 victims).

[24] Edip, *Memoirs*, 333.

The situation described by Halide Edip fully corresponds with the Thomas theorem: *If men define situations as real, they are real in their consequences.*[25] Being a construct in the first place, the Turkish nationalists' perception of the Ottoman Christians as potential traitors nevertheless caused the real destruction of the Ottoman Christians.

The genocide of the Armenians, Greeks or Aramaeans/Assyrians should therefore be understood not as a direct response to alleged Christian provocations, but as a stage in the Turkish nationalist movement, which as a reaction to the continuing disintegration of the empire settled on a narrow nationalism and excluded the indigenous Christians of Asia Minor from the moral universe of the state. That being so, bringing up the much discredited myth of Christian disloyalty in the context of the deportations and massacres before, during and after World War I is as offensive to the victims and the historic truth as bringing up the Nazi rationalization of an alleged international Jewish conspiracy would be in the context of the Nazi Holocaust. Because both the Christians under Ottoman rule and the Jews in Nazi-occupied Europe perished not for something they actually did or failed to do, but for who they were and how they were perceived by the perpetrators.[26] It appears psychologically crucial for genocide perpetrators to convince themselves of the necessity of self-defensive action.

The Balkan Wars also increased the relevance of Islam and a Muslim alliance in the political rhetoric and practice of the Young Turks, something which lasted not only through World War I, but also right until the end of the Turkish "liberation struggle" 1919–1922:

> [...] with the outbreak of the Balkan War, theoretical questions paled into insignificance. There was a national emergency and the most important issue now seemed to be the mobilization of all national resources. What was national was no longer in doubt by the end of 1912: [...] When the Young Turks organized the war effort through countless political, social, economic and cultural organizations which all carried the title *milli* [national] it was no longer in doubt what was meant by this term. It meant by and for the Ottoman Muslims. This tendency continued throughout the years of World War I (which was also officially declared a *Jihad* and which was partly fought out as a brutal ethnic/religious conflict in Anatolia and beyond). The proclamations of the national resistance movement in Anatolia after 1918 make it abundantly clear that the movement fought for continued independence and unity of the Ottoman Mus-

---

[25] William Isaac Thomas and Dorothy Swaine Thomas, *The Child in America* (New York: Knopf, 1928), 572.

[26] See also Robert Melson, *Revolution and Genocide: On the Origins of the Armenian Genocide and the Holocaust* (Chicago: University of Chicago Press, 1992).

> lims. The religious character of the movement was often remarked upon at the time.[27]

Main target groups of the CUP assimilation and dispersion policy were non-Muslims and Muslim refugees (*muhacirler*) from the Balkans, most of which would be Slavic in origin and language. As the Circassian refugees before them, the Muslims from the Balkans were purposely resettled in Armenian and Greek areas of Asia Minor and received the land and properties of previously deported Christians. Similar to the Circassians, who supported the Turkish nationalists hoping for their own autonomy, the Balkan *muhacirler* took an active part in the persecution and annihilation of the indigenous Christians.

Dr. Martin Niepage (1886–1963), who taught at a German secondary school in Aleppo, had become a compassionate eyewitness of the genocide against the Armenians. Together with his colleagues Dr. Graeter and Marie Spiecker and the school's director Huber he signed an appeal to the German lawmakers, asking — in vain — for German intervention. However, despite military censorship he succeeded in publishing and disseminating his petition in Christian circles during World War I. In this booklet, Niepage explained the reasons for the CUP's self-destructive genocide against Ottoman Christians as part of the party's intention to profoundly change the ethnic composition of the Ottoman Empire by creating a Turkish national state:

> If anyone enquires into the motives, which induced the Young Turkish Government to decree and carry out these frightful measures against the Armenians, one might give the following explanation:
>
> The Young Turk has always floating before his eyes the European ideal of a united national state. He hopes to Turkify the non-Turkish Mohammedan races — Kurds, Persians, Arabs, and so on — by administrative methods and through Turkish education, and he reinforces these by an appeal to their common interests as Mohammedans. The Christian nations — Armenians, Syrians, Greeks — alarm him by their cultural and economic superiority, and he sees their religion as an obstacle to their turkification by peaceful means. They have, therefore, to be either exterminated or converted to Mohammedanism by force. The Turks do not suspect that, in doing this, they are sawing off the branch on which they are sitting themselves. Who is to bring progress to Turkey if not the Greeks, Armenians and Syrians, who constitute more than a quarter of the population of the Empire?[28]

---

[27] Zürcher, "From Empire to Republic."

[28] Martin Niepage, *The Horrors of Aleppo, Seen by a German Eyewitness* (London: T. Fisher Unwin, 1917 [reprinted 1975]), 20. The German original was published under the title *Ein Wort an die berufenen Vertreter des deutschen Volkes: Eindrücke eines deutschen Oberlehrers aus der Türkei* [*A Word to the Elected Representatives of the German People: Impressions of a German Teacher in Turkey*] (Werningerode, 1916), 11–12. The English translation omitted some of the cruellest episodes in the German original.

In early June 1915 Talât, member of the CUP triumvirate, informed the German Embassy at Pera (Constantinople) about his government's intention

> [t]o use the opportunity of the World War thoroughly to eliminate [*gründlich aufzuräumen*] their internal enemies — *the indigenous Christians of all denominations* — without being disturbed by diplomatic interventions from abroad. [Italics added][29]

II. *Chronology of a Genocide*

As in later phases of the annihilation of the Ottoman Empire's Christian population, the persecution of the Ottoman Greeks started with the destruction of the elite and the confiscation of arms. Between 1909 and 1911 Christian leaders — Greeks, Bulgarians, Serbs — in Ottoman ruled Macedonia "mysteriously disappeared or were found murdered."[30] The U.S. Consul at Thessalonica, George Horton, who was an eyewitness, noted what he called the "Turkification" of Macedonia:

> From the extermination of notables, the program extended to people of less importance. Bevies of despairing peasant women who had come to visit the *vali* [governor] and demand news of their husbands, sons, or brothers appeared on the streets of Salonika. The answers were usually sardonic: "He has probably run away and left you," or, "He has probably gone to America" were favourite replies. The truth, however, could not long be hidden as shepherds and others were soon reporting corpses found in ravines and gullies in the mountains and woods [...] The next step was the so-called disarming. This meant, as always, the disarming of the Christian element and the furnishing of weapons to the Turks. That the object was not so much to collect hidden arms as to terrorize the inhabitants was soon made evident from the tortures inflicted during the search.[31]

Retreating from Eastern Thrace during the First Balkan War, the Ottoman Army plundered the Greek villages in the Didymotichon (Διδυμότοιχον) and Adrianople (Αδριανούπολις, Adrianoupolis, Edirne (Tur.)) districts and torched those of the districts Malkara and Kessani (Keşan (Tur.)). Numerous killings and murders occurred during the Balkan Wars, in particular at the

---

[29] Letter of 6 June 1915, of the German Embassy, *Politisches Archiv des Auswärtigen Amtes* (PA/AA), Botschaft Konstantinopel, Vol. 169, A53a, 3451. Cited from Wolfgang Gust, "Verständnislose Auswüche des Militarismus" [Incomprehensible Excesses of Militarism], *Historicum: Zeitschrift für Geschichte* (Vienna) (Fall 2007): 19.

[30] Marjorie Housepian, *The Smyrna Affair: The First Comprehensive Account of the Burning of the City and the Expulsion of the Christians from Turkey in 1922* (New York: Harcourt Brace Jovanovich, 1971), 19–20.

[31] George Horton, *The Blight of Asia: An Account of the Systematic Extermination of Christian Populations by Mohammedans and of the Culpability of Certain Great Powers; with the True Story of the Burning of Smyrna* (Indianapolis: The Bobbs-Merrill Company, 1926): http://www.hri.org/docs/Horton/hb-3.html.

time, when the Ottoman army reoccupied Eastern Thrace in February 1913. However, the persecutions in Thrace exceeded the usual slaughters of Christians. For the first time thousands of Greeks were systematically driven away from their villages and purposely exposed to exhaustion and starvation during death marches, which were officially called relocations. Konstantinos Vakalopoulos, the Greek historian who concentrated on Thrace, summarized the situation during and after the Balkan Wars:

> The conditions, under which the Greek population was expelled from their villages and towns and exiled by the Young Turks, were brutal and inhuman. They were expelled from the urban centres at the coast of the Propontis[32] and the Black Sea under threat and panic as well as continuous terror and murder. Not one day passed without casualties [...] The expulsion was carried out without earlier notice or limitations. The properties of the East Thracians were rapidly assigned to the *muhacirs*, Muslim refugees from Epirus, Bosnia and most of all Macedonia. The expelled Greeks were not allowed to take anything with them, and numerous old people died from exhaustion, starvation and as a result of the atrocities, committed during these marches of misery towards the coasts.[33]

According to Vakalopoulos, the Greek population of Eastern Thrace numbered more than 350,000 before the Balkan Wars. Of those, 100,000 had been deported into the interior of Asia Minor or Central Anatolia. Only 54,000 of the deportees returned after the Ottoman capitulation of October 30, 1918. Vakalopoulos concludes that the other deportees had died as result of forced labor and diseases.[34] According to the Central Commission of the Ecumenical Patriarchate at Constantinople, which supervised the reintegration of Greek Orthodox refugees after World War I, 232,000 more Greeks from Eastern Thrace had been compelled to immigrate into Greece. Most of these exiles (193,403 persons) were inhabitants of the province of Adrianople; more than the half of them returned to their home province between 1918 and 1920, while only 86,910 of those who had been exiled to Greece stayed there after World War I.[35]

---

32 The littoral between Constantinople and Rodosto (in Greek, Rhaedestos, in Turkish Tekir Dağ).

33 Konstantinos A. Vakalopoulos, "Vertreibung und Genozid an den Griechen Ost-Thrakiens" [Expulsion and genocide against the Greeks of Eastern Thrace], in *Verfolgung, Vertreibung und Vernichtung der Christen im Osmanischen Reich 1912–1922* [*Persecution, Expulsion and Annihilation of the Christians in the Ottoman Empire 1912–1922*], Tessa Hofmann, ed. (Münster: Lit-Verlag, 2004), 129. For further reading see the same author's monograph *Διωγμοί και Γενοκτονία του Θρακικού Ελληνισμού: Ο Πρώτος Ξεριζωμός (1908 –1917)* [*Persecutions and Genocide of Thracian Hellenism: The First Uprooting (1908–1917)*] (Thessalonica: Herodotos, 1998).

34 Vakalopoulos, ibid., 132.

35 Ibid.

While in Thrace the "pressure on the Greek population to emigrate" was cancelled in spring 1914, in order "not to provoke Greece,"[36] the CUP policy of deporting Greeks continued in 1914 in Asia Minor, first in Ionia, then in the Pontus (Black Sea) region. Months before the Ottoman Empire entered the theatre of war, the Home Minister Talât ordered on 14 May 1914:

> It is urgent for political reasons the Greek residents of the Asia Minor Coast to be forced to vacate their villages and to be settled in the vilayets of Erzurum and Chaldea. Should they refuse to be settled in the determined places, please give oral instructions to brother Muslims, for the purpose of forcing the Greeks, by every kind of actions, is to be voluntarily expatriated. Do not forget, in this case, to take from the migrants certificates that they abandon their homes by their own initiative.[37]

A report of 19 June 1914 by the Danish consulate in Smyrna (see Annex II) about "disorders in the Vilayet of Aydin"[38] to Denmark's Legation at Constantinople describes in detail the mechanism of terrorizing and expelling the Greek inhabitants who had been compelled to accommodate Muslim refugees from Thrace and Macedonia in their own homes, by providing one room out of every three. At a later stage, armed Muslim bands openly attacked Greek settlements and towns: "[...] women were seduced, girls were ravished, some of them dying from the ill-treatment received, children at the breast were shot or cut down with their mothers."[39]

In May 1914 the Ottoman head of government (Grand Vizier) Ğalib Bey confided to the German Ambassador that he negotiated with his Greek colleague Eleutherios Venizelos about

> [...] a population exchange of the Greeks from Aydin for the Turks from Macedonia. For the future he intends the cleansing of the entire Asia Minor littoral from the Greeks, in order to replace them by Tartars [sic]. [...] Because of his approval of the Greek emigration by Venizelos the Patriarchate is angry with the latter.[40]

---

36 According to a telegram by German Ambassador Hans von Wangenheim dated 20 May 1914 (translated from Fotiadis, *Der Genozid an den Pontosgriechen*, 82).

37 Cf. Harry Tsirkinidis, *"At last we uprooted them...": The Genocide of Greeks of Pontos, Thrace and Asia Minor, through the French Archives.* (Thessalonica: Kyriakides Brothers, 1999),107.

38 The town of the same name, Aydın, was the Greek Τράλλεις (Tralleis) in ancient times.

39 Rigsarkivet [the Danish National Archives], Udenrigsministeriets Arkiver [the Foreign Ministry Archives] (UM), 2-0355, "Konstantinopel/Istanbul, diplomatisk repræsentation," "Noter og indberetninger om den politiske udvikling, 1914–1922," "Verdenskrigen. Rapporter fra Smyrna. Nov. 1914–Marts 1916," Alfred Van der Zee til [to] Carl Ellis Wandel, 19/6 1914.

40 PA/AA, Türkei Nr. 175 b, Vol. 9, Nr. 232, A. 994a: Telegram by Ambassador Hans von Wangenheim, 20 May 1914 [translated from Fotiadis, *Der Genozid an den Pontosgriechen*, 81–82].

Although the population "exchange" did not materialize at that time, the *kaymakam* of Bergama (Πέργαμος, Pergamos) and Rahmi, the vali of Smyrna,[41] both refugees from Thessalonica, nevertheless increased the pressure on the Greeks of the Aydın province, in particular on those from the Kydonies (Ayvalık) region; after Smyrna, Kydonies was the largest Greek city in the region. By order of the *kaymakam*, the olive groves that formed the base of the existence of Kydonies, were expropriated and assigned to Muslim refugees from the Balkans. Although they no longer possessed them, the Greeks of Kydonies were taxed on these groves. Because of the alleged danger of espionage the Greeks were no longer allowed to work as skippers or pilots.

The massacre, looting and burning of the town of Φώκαια (Phocaea; in Turkish, Foça), northwest of Smyrna, in June 1914, which was committed by armed irregulars or *muhacirler,* in collaboration with the local police, was obviously part of the strategy to terrorize the Ionian Greeks.[42] It left 100 dead and caused the flight of thousands. Abduction of girls and women, rape, mutilation and killings were reported from other places during June 1914.[43] *The Manchester Guardian* of 29 June 1914 summarizes the casualties in Aydın province based on "letters received from an Englishman recently in one of the Aegean Islands:"

> It will be seen that the writer, who is in a position to know the truth confirms the charges made by Greece against Turkey of ill-using and expelling the Hellenes settled on the Asiatic coast. The letter-writer says:
> The state of the Christian villages on the coast is very terrible — all the horrors of war in peace, and these are inoffensive villagers not even accused of any offence against the Government. At Mytilene the churches are full, and

---

[41] There exist conflicting descriptions of the role and position of Governor Rahmi during the terror and expulsion of Greek residents from Ionia (Spring-Summer 1914). Whereas the contemporary to these events, the Second *Dragoman* of the German Embassy, Dr. Schwörbel, described Rahmi as the initiator of anti-Greek activities in 1914, Giles Milton, following the positive description by George Horton, describes Rahmi as a high ranking and influential CUP member of Jewish ancestry from Thessalonica, who ruled in his realm like an autocrat, but for the benefit of the non-Muslims there: "Ever since the Young Turk revolution of 1908 and his subsequent appointment as governor of Smyrna, he had found himself increasingly disenchanted with central government in Constantinople. The triumvirate in control had once been his confidants. Now [in 1914], the relationship was severely undermined by their decision to enter the war on the German side." Giles Milton, *Paradise Lost: Smyrna 1922: The Destruction of Islam's City of Tolerance* (New York: Basic Books, 2008), 65. About the 1914 events in Ionia see also Annex II of this contribution.

[42] "Massacre of Greeks charged to the Turks: Priest, old men and children are reported slain, bodies are thrown into well," *Atlanta Constitution*, 17 June 1914, front page: http://www.greek-genocide.org/press/17061914.html.

[43] "Turkish atrocities against Greeks: Massacres in Asia Minor," *The Scotsman* (Edinburgh), 19 June 1914, 7: http://www.greek-genocide.org/press/19061914.html.

> there is no further accommodation, and I believe about 10,000 in all have left Chesme. A number of women and children embarked at Chesme on our steamer. They wished to get out at Smyrna, but were not allowed, and were therefore brought on here.
>
> The *moharjis* (Turkish emigrants) from Europe who were brought to Chesme to expropriate the Christians were not from Macedonia, but nearly all Albanians of Gheg tribe, from Serbian territory. So the excuse of retaliation for such a supposed expropriation by the Greek Government from Macedonia cannot be offered. The whole thing (in which the Turkish Government, of course, professes ignorance and innocence) is undoubtedly a perfectly ruthless and carefully organized plot of the Committee for getting rid of the Christian population along the Anatolian coast. This is shown by the similarity of method throughout. The smaller outlying villages are first attacked, and the expropriation is there carried out by force. The larger communities are then threatened with the same dispossession by violence. The inhabitants do not, of course, await execution, but having seen it at their doors, anticipate it by leaving. It is then represented to the consuls that they left of their own accord, and had no cause for fear. If what has happened is condoned the larger communities, such as Aivali [Ayvalık] and even Smyrna will no doubt be dealt with.
>
> The Christian villages in the environs of Aivali having now been completely, village by village, cleared of their inhabitants, proceedings against Aivali itself (it contained about 30,000 inhabitants, nearly all Christian) have commenced, and the first fugitives arrived yesterday. The Kaimakam of Aivali told the inhabitants that they must go. He said, "This is no longer your country; if you don't go to-day you will be compelled to go to-morrow."
>
> Stories of cruelty and outrage in the expulsion of the inhabitants from the villages — features which it was impossible indeed should be lacking — are simply confirmed. A good many girls are in the hospitals at Aivali in consequence of their treatment by the moharjis * * *
>
> "I live in a sort of hope that the progress southward may be arrested. It surely would not be too much of an irregularity for British ships to go to certain points on the coast for this purpose."
>
> Achramythium and the villages of the district, where the Christian population was large are now completely emptied of their inhabitants. I suppose the same is now the case as regards Chesme district.[44]

Already before the war Said Halim, the Ottoman head of government, informed the German Ambassador about the "total removal of the Greek population from the littoral of Asia Minor."[45] On 5 March 1915, Grand Vezir Said

---

[44] "Why the Greeks fled: Organized Persecution in Asia Minor," *The Manchester Guardian*, 29 June 1914. A German diplomatic report of 1915 mentions a population of 36,000 inhabitants for Ayvalık "in normal times," which had been reduced to 22,000, cf. German Foreign Office, Political Archives (PA/AA), Berlin, File Türkei No. 168, Vol. 14 f. No. 552, A. 26689, quoted in Fotiadis, *Der Genozid an den Pontosgriechen*, 90.

[45] German Embassy of Constantinople, 16 July 1914, PA/AA, R1913, A14975, cited in Gust, "Verständnislose Auswüche des Militarismus," 19.

Halim proudly announced that, "the littoral of Asia Minor has more or less lost its Greek population."[46]

According to a report of 4 September 1915 by Dr. Schwörbel, the Second *Dragoman* (interpreter) at the German embassy, there was a pre-war population of 36,000 residents in the almost exclusively Greek town of Kydonies. A third of the population had escaped to the near island Mytilene after the onslaught of 1914. In his report, Schwörbel mentioned a remaining population of "only about 22,000 exclusively Greek inhabitants,"[47] which was twice deported, in July 1915[48] and in April 1917.

Schwörbel, who travelled twice in official missions to Ionia during summer 1915, reported also the presence of concentration camps[49] along the Soma-

---

[46] German Embassy of Constantinople, 5 March 1915, PA/AA, R1915, A8112, cited in Gust, "Verständnislose Auswüche des Militarismus," 19.

[47] The ancient town of Kydoniai/Kydonies is now a village, situated opposite of the island Lesvos, not far from Ayvalık, which was built as the chief seaport in northwest Asia Minor in the third decade of the nineteenth century.

[48] According to information by the Hellenic consul at Smyrna, quoted in a telegram of 31 July 1915 of the German Embassy. PA/AA, Türkei, No. 168, Vol. 14, 15, p. 88, quoted from Fotiadis, ibid., 88. The German Ambassador Mirbach at Athens telegraphed on 19 July 1915 that the Hellenic Ambassador at Constantinople had been ordered officially to protest against the deportation of the Greek population of Ayvalık into the interior. PA/AA, Türkei, No. 168, Vol 14, 15, quoted from Fotiadis, *Der Genozid an den Pontosgriechen*, 87. — The German Ambassador at Constantinople, Metternich mentioned in a dispatch to the German Chancellor dated 31 January 1916 that the expulsion of "thousands of Greeks" from the Aegean and Marmara littorals had ceased, although it previously had been justified as militarily necessary. "In Eregli at the Marmara Sea the population was even allowed to return to their previous residences, which, according to the view of the [Ecumenical] Patriarch must be first of all explained by my intervention." PA/AA, Türkei, No. 168, Vol. 14, 15, quoted from Fotiadis *Der Genozid an den Pontosgriechen*, 102.

[49] A term originating in African history and being in common European and American usage during World War I, albeit with the connotation of destruction and not only internment. During the Second War of Independence of the *Boerevolk* (1899–1902), Britain killed 27,000 Boer women and children, of whom 24,000 in concentration camps (http://www.boer.co.za/boerwar/hellkamp.htm), which in the commemoration of Boers survives as a "holocaust." All functions of modern concentration camps can be observed in the genocide of the tribes of Herero and Nama during the German Colonial genocide (1904–1908) in the former German colony Deutsch Südwest (today Namibia): forced labor (Arbeitslager), sexual abuse and torture of women of the target group, medical experiments on and genetic "research" of the many babies, born after such rapes, notably by the German physician and anthropologist Eugen Fischer (1874–1967), physical destruction by starvation, disease and exhaustion. It should be noted that Adolf Hitler was inspired by Fischer's book *Grundriß der menschlichen Erblichkeitslehre und Rassenhygiene (Eugenik)* [*Outline of Human Heredity and Race Hygiene (Eugenics)*] co-authored in 1921 with Erwin Baur and Fritz Lenz. During the Nama uprising, half the tribe (over 10,000) were killed, while the remaining 9,000 or so survivors were confined in concentration camps: http://www.ppu.org.uk/genocide/g_namibia1.html.

Bandırma (Panormos (Gr.)) railways with Greek women, children and old people; they were deportees from the Marmara coast, entirely left to themselves without food and accommodation:

> Because the government does not care at all about feeding these masses and because under the recent conditions the possibilities for the deportees to find work or to earn any money are scarce, the daily casualties are high, as the railway physician of the Soma–Pandarma line confirmed.

Schwörbel concluded:

> With the exception of Aivali and Smyrna with its environs the entire Greek civilization, which flourished until recently at the west coast of Asia Minor is destroyed. The reason lies in the Islamist movement in Asia Minor, initiated in the beginning of May last year by the recently immigrated refugees from Macedonia and Mytilene and stirred up by the general governor of Smyrna, Rahmi Bey, with the aim to expel the Christian populations from Asia Minor and to replace them with Muslims.[50]

An earlier German eyewitness in Ionia, Dr. Harry Stürmer, worked in Constantinople as foreign correspondent for the *Kölnische Zeitung* (Cologne). In his memoirs, published in 1917 in neutral Switzerland, he recalled the situation at the beginning of World War I in 1914:

The impact of these prototypes in South Africa on the Ottoman genocide during World War I and the German genocide during World War II are still under-researched, but the German experience, gained in Namibia may have influenced their Ottoman allies. In this respect, the biography of the Protestant theologian Paul Carl Albert Rohrbach (1869–1956) seems important; he was a prominent publisher and representative of a liberal imperialism, author of travelogues as well as an official of the German colonial administration in Namibia (1903 until Spring, 1907). As Commissioner for Settlement and economic expert Rohrbach criticised the annihilation policies of von Trotha, the German supreme commander in Namibia, and recommended instead to use the aboriginal population of Southwest Africa as servants, with the exception of the "Hottentots" (Nama), because they were "economically useless, and for that reason there exists no interest to maintain that 'race': In order to secure the peaceful settlement of whites against the culturally disabled, predatory indigenous tribe their actual annihilation can be mandatory" (1907). Although sympathetic with the Armenians, whose culture and abilities Rohrbach admired and had praised in his book published in 1903, *Vom Kaukasus zum Mittelmeer: Eine Hochzeits- und Studienreise durch Armenien* [*From the Caucasus to the Mediterranean Sea: A honeymoon and journey of study through Armenia*], the Armenian Patriarch of Constantinople, as well as by Henry Morgenthau and the French author René Pinon, believed that Rohrbach was responsible for providing the Young Turks with the idea of deportation. In 1913 Rohrbach had presented the idea of relocating the Armenians to Mesopotamia in a lecture to the Deutsche Gesellschaft für Erdkunde [German Geographic Society]. See also Vahakn N. Dadrian, *German Responsibility in the Armenian Genocide: Review of the Historical Evidence of German Complicity* (Watertown, Massachusetts: Blue Crane Books, 1996), 114.

[50] German Foreign Office, Political Archives (PA/AA), Berlin, File Türkei No. 168, Vol. 14 f. No. 552, A. 26689. Quoted from Fotiadis, *Der Genozid an den Pontosgriechen*, 96–97.

> At the time of the Sarayevo murder I happened to be in the Aydin vilayet, in Smyrna and its hinterland. There I have witnessed with my own eyes vile deeds which must make everybody blush in anger against the Turkish government, which tolerates and supports these crimes, starting with old women, raped one after the other by a dozen of *muhacirs* and wayward soldiers, up to the smouldering ruins of Phokaia.[51]

On 11 April 1916, nearly a year after the Armenian elite in Constantinople and other Ottoman cities had been wiped out by massive arrests, imprisonment and deportation, atrocities against Greeks were reported from various parts of the Ottoman Empire, in particular from Adrianople and near-by Demotika (also Dimotica, mediaeval, and present-day Διδυμότειχο, Didymoticho), where Turks and Bulgarians joined in a massacre of the local Greeks, killing 400 and wounding 300 more after

> [p]illaging their houses. In the Smyrna district several Greek villages were raided. 200 persons being killed and many wounded. Constantinople was likewise the scene of serious massacres, no figures pertaining to which are available.[52]

Carl Werth, the Secretary of the German consulate at Sivas (Sevasteia (Gr.)), reported on 28 June 1916, that Armenians of a labor battalion together with "all Greeks" had been detained at Karahişar and were kept prisoner in the local Armenian church in Sivas:

> The Greeks and those Armenians who converted to Islam were set free today after a heavy bastinado, while the remaining Armenians had been advised by the authorities to convert. Otherwise they would be deported with unknown destination. The Armenians fear for a fourth slaughter.[53]

In 1916, the deportation of Greeks from the Aegean and Marmara coasts ceased temporarily, and in Ereğli the population was even allowed to return. However, at the same time repression started in the Pontus region. As early as 27 August 1915, the German consul at Trebizond (Τραπεζούντα Trapezounta; Trabzon (Tur.)), Heinrich Bergfeld had cabled to Chancellor von Bethmann Hollweg at the occasion of the arrest and massacre of the last remaining Armenians, expressing his fear that the regional CUP members might repeat the treatment they applied to the Armenians against the Greeks, if they went unpunished.[54] Less than a year later, in June 1916 all

---

[51] Harry Stürmer, *Zwei Kriegsjahre in Konstantinopel: Skizzen deutsch-jungtürkischer Moral und Politik* [*Two War Years in Constantinople: Sketches of German and Young Turkish Ethics and Politics*] (Lausanne: Payot, 1917), 150–51.

[52] "Massacres of Greeks in Turkey Reported," *The New York Times*, 20 April 1916, 6.

[53] Political Archives of the German Foreign office (PA/AA), Berlin, quoted from: http://www.armenocide.de/armenocide/armgende.nsf/WebStart_De?OpenFrameset.

[54] Political Archives of the German Foreign office (PA/AA), Berlin, File Embassy Constantinople (Botschaft Konstantinopel), No. 170, quoted from: http://www.armenocide.de/armenocide/armgende.nsf/WebStart_De?OpenFrameset.

Greeks from the village of Taderesi in the Angora (Ankara) province and all Greeks of the littoral in the Kastamonu (Kastamone (Gr.)) district were deported into the interior, followed by the Greek population of Sinope (Sinop (Tur.)), where Greeks were given only four hours notice. Consul M. Kuckhoff telegraphed on 16 July 1916 from Samsun (Amisos (Gr.)):

> [...] In Turkish the terms deportation and destruction have the same meaning, for in most cases those who are not killed fall victim to deceases or starvation. Probably these [i.e., the deportations] are fanatic activities of the *vali* of Castamuni, who uses the flight of Greek conscripts over the sea and the prevention of espionage as a pretext to annihilate the entire people.[55]

In a special cable the *New York Times* of 21 August 1916 reported that Turkish authorities in the Black Sea regions

> [...] are rounding up civilians in a considerable number of villages and sending them off in batches to concentration camps in the interior. This means practically a sentence to death, for in large numbers they are forced to go afoot, absolutely without food. En route these pitiful caravans are attacked by Turks, who rob them of whatever they have in their possession, unhappy mothers being deprived of their children. The deportations are on a considerable scale.[56]

In a letter of 1918 Germanos (born Στυλιανός Καραβαγγέλης, Stylianos Karavangeles, 1866–1953), the Greek Orthodox Metropolitan Bishop of Amaseia (Αμάσεια, Amasya (Tur.)) and Samsun (ancient Αμισός, known in more modern Greek as Σαμψούντα)[57] described the systematic destruction of agriculture of the Greek Pontus and emphasised the calculated climate factor for killing the female population:

> First, the army reduced to ashes the entire surrounding region. Nearly all the villages, rich in tobacco plantations, civilized friends of progress and possessing a lively national sentiment, were pillaged and then set on fire. A large number of women and children were killed, the young girls outraged and immediately afterward driven into the interior. Where? Into the vilayet of Angora, to Tchoroum, to Soungourlou, and still further. The winter was of the

---

[55] Telegramm Nr. 129, 15 July 1916 by Heinrich Bergfeld, Consulate Samsun, per Fotiadis, *Der Genozid an den Pontosgriechen*, 114.

[56] "Turks deporting Greeks: Civilian concentration camps victims attacked and despoiled," *The New York Times*, 21 August 1916, 2:
http://www.greek-genocide.org/press/21081916.html.

[57] Germanos of Amaseia (Pontus) had been a leading figure in the struggle to assert Greek national claims in the Ottoman province of Macedonia in the early twentieth century. At the behest of the Ottoman authorities, the Holy Synod removed him from Kastoria in 1907 and named him metropolitan of Amaseia in 1908, where he defended the rights of the local Greek and Armenian population against increasing Turkish nationalism. He fled Turkey in 1923 after having been sentenced to death. See *Encyclopedia of Modern Christian Politics*, Roy Palmer Domenico and Mark Y. Henly, eds. (Santa Barbara, California: Greenwood Press/ABC-Clio, 2006), 298.

most severe kind; these girls had to march thirty or forty days across snow-covered mountains and sleep by night in the open. For several days they were without food, for they were not even allowed to use money to buy bread; they were continually beaten by the gendarmes and stripped of any money they might have on them, and when they got to the towns they were brutally pushed into the hot public baths, on the pretext of hygiene and cleanliness, and just as quickly dragged out. Thus, an easy prey to the rigors of the cold, they were driven on further. The majority, of course, died on the road, and none of the dead being buried at all, vultures and hogs feasted on human flesh.[58]

In Ionia, the intervention of the German General of Cavalry, Otto Liman von Sanders, supported by the German Foreign Office, saved the Greeks from wholesale deportation in 1916[59] and the Greeks of Smyrna in late 1917,[60] although in April 1917 Liman had ordered the "evacuation" of the Greek population of Ayvalık and its surroundings,[61] which at that time was estimated to be 12,000 to 20,000.[62] The reason given for Liman's order was "persistent treason and espionage communication" of the Ayvalık residents with the Entente military;[63] Greece's entry into the war was obviously no decisive criterion for Liman's decision on or against deportation. But as both the German and the Austrian ambassador mentioned, it aroused criticism by Talât, now head of government, whose newly created cabinet found Liman's deportation order difficult to support, "after they had pledged to moderation

---

[58] "Turkish Cruelty Bared by Greeks," *The New York Times*, 16 June 1918, 42.

[59] It had been ordered by the provincial governor (*vali*) Rahmi Bey.

[60] Telegram of the German Ambassador Bernstorff, 11 December 1917. PA/AA, Türkei, No. 168, Vol. 16, cf. Fotiadis, *Der Genozid an den Pontosgriechen*, 181.

[61] In his memoirs Liman von Sanders did not mention the deportation of 1917, but wrote in the context of his inspection tour to Ayvalık in summer 1915 that Germans in Turkey were exposed to "truly unfounded attacks: During summer of the same year, at the time of the Dardanelles fights, I received a letter of the German Ambassador, by which King Constantine of Greece inquired whether I really had said to the mayor of Edremid that 'all Greeks deserved to be thrown into the sea.' But during my brief stay in that town I had neither met with or talked to the mayor of Edremid, nor to a similar personality, and of course I did not make any remarks about Greeks, with whom I had nothing to do there. I was able to reject with few words this shameless invention. [...] Being a Turkish general, I was a stumbling block to several fanatic Greeks." Otto Liman von Sanders, *Fünf Jahre in der Türkei* [*Five Years in Turkey*] (Berlin: Verlag August Scherl, 1920), 70.

[62] "10,000 to 15,000 persons of Greek ethnicity," according to a telegram of 3 April 1917 by the Austrian Ambassador Count Trautmannsdorf. Vienna, HHStA, Türkei XII, Liasse 467 LIV, "Griechenverfolgungen in der Türkei 1916–1918" [Persecutions of Greeks 1916–1918], cf. Fotiadis, *Der Genozid an den Pontosgriechen*, 312–13.

[63] Telegram of April 7, 1917 from the Embassy at Constantinople, forwarded by State Secretary Arthur Zimmermann, Berlin, on 8 April 1917, PA/AA, Türkei, No. 168, Vol. 15, 16. Quoted in Fotiadis, *Der Genozid an den Pontosgriechen*, 150–51.

and tolerance."[64] A similar deportation order was signed by another German, General Fritz Bronsart von Schellendorf, who was the second strongman in the Ottoman Army and Chief Commander at Constantinople, detached to War Minister Enver.[65]

Earlier in 1916, the wholesale deportation of all Greeks from the Ottoman littorals was already planned, as Home Minister Talât confirmed in October 1916 during a talk with the German Ambassador Radowitz; but Enver himself ordered to stop the execution of such plans in order not to provoke Greece, which was then still neutral. The same policy of avoiding a provocation of Greece was followed by the political German leadership and the German diplomatic corps.

As a result of such priorities the deportation was carried out in a partial way. On 3 October 1916, Ambassador Radowitz reported to Berlin that the "cleansing" was partly accomplished, by "the expulsion of the Syriac Christians from the Eastern borderlands and of the Greeks from certain districts of Asia Minor und Rumelia."[66]

Obviously there were also plans to carry out a deportation of prominent Greeks from the Ottoman capital Constantinople similar to the earlier massive arrest and deportation of the Armenian elite in spring 1915. On 5 October 1916, Radowitz reported to Berlin that the Turks had already composed a deportation list of 38,000 Greeks from Constantinople. On 13 October Radowitz announced that the danger of "a massive expulsion with all the known consequences is approaching," because Talât in person went to Smyrna supposedly in order to instruct the *vali* there.[67] The British Legation at Berne (Switzerland) wrote in a "Memorandum concerning the abominable ill-treatment of the Greeks in Turkey," dated 11 December 1917:

> Greeks are being daily cleared out of Constantinople and its surroundings and taken to the interior of the country. Their property is seized and their belongings sold by auction. The women and girls are distributed between the German officials and the Moslems of importance. [...] It is estimated that in Constantinople over 300 Greeks have been enslaved. But in Asiatic Turkey it is said that over 100,000 have been killed, or died of hunger, since the beginning of August last.[68]

For allegedly "strictly military reasons," War Minister Enver ordered in December 1916 the deportation of the Greek population from the Black Sea

---

64 Ambassador Trautmannsdorf in his telegram of 3 April 1917. Vienna, HHStA, Türkei XII, Liasse 467 LIV. Fotiadis, *Der Genozid an den Pontosgriechen*, 312, cf. footnote 47.

65 Fotiadis, *Der Genozid an den Pontosgriechen*, 115.

66 PA/AA, IA Türkei 183, Armenien Vol. 44, No. 7155 R 14093.

67 Fotiadis, *Der Genozid an den Pontosgriechen*, 131–32.

68 Public Record Office, London, Foreign Office, Reference FO 286/677.

littoral in an area of 50 kilometres. According to official information, given to the German diplomats this regulation should have been carried out "milder" than in the Armenians' case. However, the German diplomats soon understood that not only the winter season and the "failure to organize provisions" would lead to high casualties, but that there was also a lack of intention to keep the promises of humanitarian treatment. Despite earlier promises, the Greeks of Giresun (Κερασούς or Κερασούντα, Kerasounta) were not allowed to stay in nearby Kulakkaya, only 50 kilometres south of Giresun. Against all previous announcements they were driven in mid-winter over the mountains towards Sivas.[69] Based on information from Austrian sources, the German diplomats understood in early February 1917, that the "ban of the Greek population of Samsun," which had been conducted under the pretext of pursuing Greek bands in reality was nothing else but a "large scale" persecution of Greeks. A report from the Austrian Foreign Office gives the details of the extremely cruel expulsion from the villages Aylasköy and Kadıköy near Samsun:

> On the same day the villages, which belong to Samsun [...] were occupied by military forces and the inhabitants (3–4,000) summoned under the pretext that the *mutessarif* wished to talk to them, and then they were driven at night-time into the interior, without any clothing and provisions. Considering the present rough time of the year, the lack of accommodation and food many of these unfortunate will soon meet their death.[70]

In the late 1920s the Danish railway engineer and ardent admirer of Mustafa Kemal, Olaf A. Rygaard conversed with several Turks who had been engaged in the killings of Greeks and Armenians during the World War and the so-called Liberation Wars (1919–1922). Rygaard, who qualified the Ottoman Turks as *herskerfolk* (*Herrenvolk* in German, i.e. literally "ruling people" or "master people") and ascribed the massive and brutal killings of Greek and Armenian civilians to the CUP and the "lawlessness" of the "Liberation Wars," includes in his memoirs, published in 1935, the confessions and information that he then received. About Giresun and the holocaust committed there we read:

> I spend the waiting period taking rides in the surroundings and taking a closer look at the city, which was greatly damaged by the bombardments of the Russian warships during the world war. The shattered Armenian stone houses have only been repaired by the Turks by putting a wooden storey on top of them. The churches are in ruins and are used as stables and prisons. Per [Rygaard's horse] stands up against a wall that is still decorated with murals depicting the Virgin Mary. Gruesome massacres of Greek and Armenian women and children have taken place in these churches where these unfor-

[69] Fotiadis, *Der Genozid an den Pontosgriechen*, 139.

[70] Ibid., 142.

> tunates, according to what the Turks themselves told me, were burnt. These atrocities have partly taken place during the reign of the Triumvirate *Enver–*, *Cemal–*, and *Talaat Pasha,* before Kemal Pasha took control, and partly during the completely lawless times during the Wars of Liberation.
>
> These three men have irreparably damaged Turkey. Enver threw the country into the World War, Talaat ordered the extermination of the Armenians in 1915, and Cemal ravaged wildly in Syria, raging about the Arabs' natural defection when the Holy War was declared.[71]

Such retrospective condemnation notwithstanding, contemporaries did want to believe that the appointment of Talât as head of government in mid-February 1917 could be a turning point in the CUP policies towards the Christians of the Ottoman Empire. The German Ambassador (at that time Kühlmann) reported to Berlin:

> [...] I believe that as a result of all this the extermination policy has profoundly harmed the Turkish Empire. For a long time the atrocities of the Armenian campaign will overshadow the Turkish reputation and provide poisonous weapons to those who deny Turkey the recognition as a civilised state and who demand the expulsion of the Turks from Europe. Seen from a domestic view, the country had been significantly weakened by the peril and the ban of a physically strong, industrious and economical population, in particular, because the shortage in people is one of the major obstacles for a more rapid development of Turkey's resources.
>
> In confidential talks with Talaat Pasha I never concealed my opinion towards these issues from the beginning of my official mission here. That he mentions the equality of Ottoman nationalities in his first programmatic speech after he gained power has to be welcomed. As I confidentially learn one can definitely count on the end of the expulsion of Armenians and on the ceasing of the locally committed persecution of Greeks. According to this, the Armenians will be allowed to return to their old settlements (after some time), provided that these are not situated in areas of war.
>
> Of course, the wild chauvinist orientation is not finished yet. The capable and inconsiderate minds, that had represented it, will not be pacified due to their temporary defeat. Nor can one now count with the rapid and complete end of complaints on oppressions and persecutions by individual administrators in various provinces. But experiences teaches that the orders given in Constantinople are more or less conducted in the provinces — the more, if the order is not the result of foreign repression on the central government, but corresponds with the free decision of the Turkish rulers. And that is the case, this time.[72]

---

[71] Olaf A. Rygaard, *Mellem Tyrker og Kurder. En Dansk Ingeniørs Oplevelser i Lilleasien* [*Between Turks and Kurds. The Experiences of a Danish Engineer in Asia Minor*] (Copenhagen: Gyldendal, 1935), 172. (Translated from Danish by Matthias Bjørnlund).

[72] Report of Ambassador Kühlmann, 16 February 1917, PA/AA, quoted from: http://www.armenocide.de/armenocide/armgende.nsf/WebStart_De?OpenFramest.

The deportation order hit the areas of Rize (Rizous (Gr.)) and Platanu (Platanous (Gr.)) most of all. Of the 16,750 inhabitants of the Elevi and Tripolis (Tirebolu (Tur.)) area only 550 survived. In Trebizond, which came temporarily under Russian occupation in 1917 the Greek population was, as a result of deportations and flight, reduced from 49,520 to 20,300. On 23 February 1918, the German centrist MP Matthias Erzberger (1875–1921) forwarded an appeal to the German Foreign Office, which Erzberger had received from a compatriot in Constantinople. This appeal, dated 17 February 1918, ended with observations on the Pontus Greeks:

> At this occasion I would like to draw your attention to the Turkish actions against the Greeks residing at the Black Sea. The Turks proceed in the same way as against the Armenians. Killings and deportation on land over distances of hundreds of kilometres [...] In Eskişehir such convoys had to camp for days in the most grim coldness. It is the most genuine Christian genocide [Völkermord.][73] In the case of the Greeks, every political or strategic necessi-

[73] Synonyms to the term of genocide were used in European and in particular in Germanic languages already during World War I and before Raphael Lemkin introduced a Greco-Latin neologism in 1944. For instance, and according to the Swedish genocide scholar David Gaunt, the Swedish Social Democrat leader and minister of state Hjalmar Branting (1920–25) coined the Swedish word for genocide, *folkmord*, with regards to the Armenian genocide still in 1917: http://www.levandehistoria.se/default.php?id=1266. Branting said in a speech in Stockholm on March 28, 1917: "Dokumenten säga klart ifrån, att här ej är tal om övergrepp av underordnande, utan det är frågan om ett organiserat och systematiskt folkmord, värre än vad vi någonsin sett maken till i Europa. Det har gällt att hela stora områdes befolkning, att massakrera dem, driva de överlevande i öknen under förhoppning att de ej skola uthärda utan att deras ben skola vittra i ökensanden. Detta folkmord står bland krigets alla ohyggligheter beträffande offrens antal och den systematiska vildheten i dess utförande utan motstycke. När vi läsa därom har det isat våra hjärtan, verkligen på allvar isat våra hjärtan." See Bertil Bengtsson, *Svärdets År: Om folkmordet på de kristna i Tyrkiet 1894–1922* [*Year of the Sword: The Genocide of the Christians in Turkey 1894–1922*] (Södertalje: Syrianska Riksförbundet, 2004), 124.

According to a German television history documentary by Guido Knopp, in the same year of 1917 the German Emperor Wilhelm II articulated the idea to isolate Russian POWs on the *Kurische Nehrung*, a waterless sand bar on the East Prussian coast. One of his advisors protested, "Your Majesty, but such a step would be genocide!" (*Majestät, das wäre Völkermord!*). The Danish scholar and chairman of the *Danish Friends of Armenians*, Aage Meyer Benedictsen, used the term *Folkemord* to describe the Armenian genocide; cf. Åge Meyer Benedictsen, *Armenien: Et Folks Liv og Kamp Gennem To Aartusinder* [*Armenia: The Life and Struggle of a People Over the Course of Two Millenia*] (Copenhagen: De Danske Armeniervenner 1925), 242. Although the terms *folkmord*, *Völkermord* and *Folkemord* had not yet gained the precise legal definition as given by Raphael Lemkin in his early law project of 1934 or his later draft for the United Nations convention, the semantic connotation already was that of the intentional killing (murder, or *mord* in Swedish, German and Danish) of a people (*folk*, *Volk*). In this definition, it comes close to the term "democide," as introduced by the genocide scholar Rudolph Joseph Rummel in 1992, for the killing of a people or citizens by their own state or government. In Rummel's definition, democide includes all "intentionally or consciously negligently committed human or, respectively ty is invalid since the peace treaty[74] with the once hostile inhabitants of the Black Sea.[75]

Deportations of Greeks were also conducted outside the Pontus region. In 1917, the deportation in Ionia restarted. On 17 October 1917 Frank W. Jackson, the chairman of the U.S. Relief Committee for Greeks of Asia Minor announced in New York, that:

> [...] more than 700,000 Greeks have fallen victim to persecution in the form of death, suffering, or deportation. The story of the Greek deportations is not yet generally known. [...] Quietly and gradually the same treatment is being meted out to the Greeks as to the Armenians and Syrians. [...] There were some two or three million Greeks in Asia Minor at the outbreak of the war in 1914 subject to Turkish rule. According to the latest reliable and authoritative accounts, some seven to eight hundred thousand have been deported, mainly from the coast regions into the interior of Asia Minor. [...] Along with the Armenians most of the Greeks of the Marmora regions and Thrace have been deported on the pretext that they gave information to the enemy. Along the Aegean coast, Aivalik stands out as the worst sufferer. According to one report, some 70,000 Greeks have been deported towards Konya and beyond. At least 7,000 have been slaughtered. The Greek Bishop of Aivalik committed suicide in despair.[76]

The German Military Pastor Dr. David wrote on 17 March 1918 about the intention of deputy corps commander Osmanlı Bey to deport all remaining Christians of the Ankara province, namely 2,000 Greeks, 3,000 Catholics as well as several hundreds of Protestants and Armenian-Apostolic Christians. According to David, the intention was to deport them into the interior and disperse them over Muslim villages. However, the deportation did not take

---

governmental massive killings with the exception of war;" cf. Gunnar Heinsohn, *Lexikon der Völkermorde* (Reinbek/Hamburg: Rowohlt, 1998). In this sense, the Ottoman genocide against Christian subjects was the first massive democide or *folkmord* of modern history.

Finally, in Greek the now official synonym for genocide, γενοκτονία (*genoktonia*) has been used since medieval times to mean "killing of a nation."

[74] The German-Russian Peace Treaty of Brest-Litovsk, was concluded after several rounds of negotiations following the armistice of 22 November 1917. The treaty was signed in Brest-Litovsk on 3 March 1918, and ratified by Soviet Russia on 15 March 1918. As one result of this treaty Soviet Russia ceded the previously Russian ruled Armenian territories of Kars and Ardahan and the Georgian territories of Adjara (Batumi) for "new regulations," de facto to the rule of Ottoman Turkey, thus exposing the Christian population of these territories to renewed atrocities.

[75] Translated from Wardges Mikayelyan, *Die Armenische Frage und der Genozid an den Armeniern in der Türkei (1913–1919): Dokumente aus dem Politischen Archiv des Deutschen Auswartigen Amts* [*The Armenian Question and the Genocide of the Armenians in Turkey (1913–1919): Documents of Political Archives of Ministry of Foreign Affairs of Germany*] (Yerevan: Academy of Sciences of the Republic of Armenia, 2004), 479. Online edition: http://www.aga-online.org/de/akten/deutscheAktenStuecke.pdf.

[76] "Greek persecution in Turkey," *The Scotsman*, 6 November 1917, 7.

place, due to resistance of the Angora *vali*.[77] In April 1918, some 8,000 Greek families were deported from Asia Minor. Two months later, the German Ambassador Metternich wrote in a report of 30 June 1918 to the German Foreign Office that after the annihilation of the Armenians that of the Greeks was to be expected as soon as Greece would turn against Turkey.[78]

Already in July and August 1914 Greek Orthodox men in the age groups of 18 to 48 years had been drafted into the notorious *amele taburları* or labor battalions of the Ottoman army. Many of them did not survive the hardships of compulsory labor, malnutrition and poor accommodation or the lack of it altogether. In a German cable of 12 May 1918 to the Foreign office in Berlin, the statements of Ottoman prisoners of war were repeated, who spoke of a "methodical annihilation of the Greeks," due to the general mobilization, the confiscation of property and the deportations. These captives mentioned a number of more than 200,000 Greek draftees until the end of 1917, of which many had been slaughtered or committed suicide in order to escape the hardships, ill-treatment, diseases, starvation and cold weather. The confiscated property of Greeks was of a value of more than 5 million Turkish gold pounds. The Turkish officers had met previous Greek millionaires from Ayvalık, deported to the provinces of Mosul or Konya, now in rags and begging or occupied with roadwork. A daily rate of 40 to 50 Greek deportees would die from diseases.[79] In its public announcement of 8 June 1918, based on the aforementioned reports by Ottoman POWs at Thessalonica, the American Committee of Armenian and Syrian Relief added:

---

[77] German Foreign Office, Political Archives (PA/AA), Botschaft Konstantinopel, Armenien [Embassy Constantinople, Armenia] No. 102, Microfiche No. 7225.

[78] Dr Johannes Lepsius quoted from this report at the occasion of the trial of Soghomon Tehlirian (Teilirian in the court proceedings) in Berlin, 3 June 1921: "Count Metternich, who was German Ambassador in Constantinople in 1918, wrote in a report of 30 June: 'The Armenians are finished. The Young Turkish pack now prepares with impatience for the moment, when Greece will turn against Turkey. The Greekhood [Griechentum] forms the cultural element of Turkey. In that case, it will be annihilated, as was the Armenian [element].' That was the view of Count Metternich." Cf. *Der Völkermord an den Armeniern vor Gericht: Der Prozess Talaat Pascha [The Genocide of the Armenians on Trial: The Talât Paşa Court Proceedings]*, third edition, Tessa Hofmann, ed. (Göttingen: Gesellschaft für bedrohte Völker, 1985), 61. This work was first published in Berlin, 1921; the second expanded edition in 1980, and the third revised and expanded edition in 1985; the last two editions were produced by this writer. The English online edition of the court proceedings differs at parts from the German original. The quotation from the Metternich report is slightly shortened and not precise: "Yes, Count Metternich, who was the German Ambassador in Constantinople in 1918, wrote in a report dated 30 July as follows: The Armenian Question is finished. The gang of Young Turks is eagerly preparing itself for the moment when Greece will turn against Turkey so that the Greeks can be annihilated as well, just like the Armenians:"
http://www.armeniapedia.org/index.php?title=Trial_of_Soghomon_Tehlirian-First_Afternoon.

[79] Fotiadis, *Der Genozid an den Pontosgriechen*, 185–86.

> The streets in the larger cities are full of Greek orphans, half-naked and begging for bread because the Turkish authorities have torn them from the bosom of their parents.[80]

The issue of the Ottoman Christian labor conscripts was raised during a parliamentary debate by Emmanuel Emmanouelides, member of the Ottoman Parliament from Pontus, who on 4 November 1918 set before his colleagues in that body eight issues, of which the seventh had to do with the labor battalions:

> On the occasion of the conscription there were created the labor battalions. They [the state authorities] destroyed through starvation and through general deprivations 250,000 from the men thus [...] We ask: What does the new government know of the perpetrators? What does it think on this matter? And, when will it initiate the measures that it is able to undertake?[81]

The end of the World War stopped the persecution and destruction of the Ottoman Greeks only temporarily. As predicted by knowledgeable European authors such as René Puaux, the chances for a secure existence of the remaining Christians under Ottoman rule were doubtful, to say the least. The government at Constantinople was weak and ambivalent in its attitude towards the Christian Ottomans, and the rebel Nationalist government at Sivas (later in Ankara) contested the Sultan's government with the reproach of treason of vital national interests. Following immediately the Armistice of Mudros (30 October 1918), there broke out spontaneous resistance against the victorious Allies. In many regions so called "Committees in Defence of National Rights" (*Müdafaai Hukuk Milliye Cemiyetler*) or "Resistance against Division" (*Redd-i-Ilhak*), founded by direct order of Talât, Enver or by initiative of the *Karakol* (High Commissioner),[82] called on the Muslim population to resist the Allied occupation and any division of Ottoman territories as well as the repatriation of Christian refugees and surviving deportees. Since many Muslims had been engaged in crimes against Armenians, Greeks or Syriacs, they now feared to be held legally responsible. Furthermore, numerous Muslims anticipated the same fate of expulsion and expropriation as the Armenians and Greeks had done before. Therefore armed anti-Allied partisan groups sprang up, joined by deserters from the Ottoman Army.

---

[80] "Atrocities: Turks slaughter Greeks, sell women to slavery," *Los Angeles Times*, 9 June 1918, 11.

[81] Speros Vryonis, "Greek Labor Battalions in Asia Minor," in *The Armenian Genocide: Cultural and Ethnical Legacies*, Richard G. Hovannisian, ed. (New Brunswick and London: Transaction Publishers, 2007), 286.

[82] Literally "guard." Another task of *Karakol* was to organize the escape of all suspects who were investigated for their involvement in the genocide against the Armenians. cf. Taner Akçam, "Die Türkei und der Völkermord an den Armeniern: Retter des Vaterlandes" ["Turkey and the Genocide against the Armenians: Saviors of the Fatherland"], *Die Tageszeitung*, 13 July 2001 (German translation from *Le Monde Diplomatique*).

From its beginning, anti-Allied and anti-Christian resistance was received as identical aspects of this movement. The resistance movement gained momentum, when the Sultan sent General Mustafa Kemal to Samsun on 19 May 1919 in order to dissolve the irregular resistance movement. Instead of accomplishing this order of the Ottoman head of state, Mustafa became the head of the movement. Refugees from the officially banned CUP and the Special Organization found refuge and support in his realms.

Already in late 1918 the news read that:

> [...] the Turkish authorities, despite Turkey's defeat, are pursuing a brutal attitude towards the Christian populations of the empire and are inciting the Ottoman people to fanatical outrages against the non-Moslems. [...] Many signs of organizing among the Turks for new massacres of Christians, and particularly Greeks, are noted.[83]

In March 1919 the Greek Prime Minister Eleutherios Venizelos communicated Turkish police instructions from the Aydın province to the Council of the Great Powers, according to which

> [...] the police are instructed to prepare for the extermination of the Greek population. A number of known *komitadjis* [irregulars] have been concentrated in the neighbourhood of Aydin and supplied with money and arms. The police are therefore unobstructed to "spare no efforts for the public safety" and to start a general massacre on the slightest pretext. Each member of the police force is commanded to kill four or five Greeks. These instructions have been given in writing, but they announce that oral instructions as to the exact method of conducting the massacre will follow.[84]

The British Admiral of the Fleet John de Robeck, then commander-in-chief of the Mediterranean Fleet (1919–1922) and subsequently until his death Allied High Commissioner at İstanbul, reported on 11 November 1919:

> [...] the Christians are now bewildered and terrified [...] Every district has its band of brigands now posing as patriots and even in the vicinity of Constantinople robbery under arms is of daily occurrence, the principal victims being naturally the unprotected Christian villagers. Behind all these elements of disorder stands Mustapha Kemal [...] The government cannot and will not move a finger to help the Christians.[85]

Turkish authorities even imposed taxes on the Greek population of Asia Minor to be paid to the *çeteler*, "which notwithstanding, continue to plunder the Greeks and commit numerous atrocities."[86]

---

[83] "Turks Organizing New Massacres," *The New York Times*, 8 December 1918, 6.

[84] "Extermination of Greeks: A Turkish Plot Revealed," *The Times* [London], March 21, 1919, 9.

[85] "Memorandum by Mr. Rendel on Turkish Massacres and Persecutions of Minorities since the Armistice," 20 March 1922, British Foreign Office Archives, FO 371/7876, 1.

[86] "Reported Turkish atrocities in Asia Minor," *The Scotsman*, 22 September 1919, 5.

The Allies had promised the remaining Ottoman Christians,

a) to hold legally accountable those responsible for the massacres during the World War; b) to safeguard the return of Christian women and children, which had been abducted by Muslims and were held in Muslim households after the war; and c) to protect the life and property of Ottoman Christians. However, given a background of increasing violence, the threat for new massacres and their general reluctance to become involved in new military actions, the Allies decided that Greece should send its own forces into Ionia in order to protect the Christians of that region.

A wealth of substantiated, detailed information about the third and last phase of the destruction of indigenous Christians in Asia Minor in general and the Greeks in particular comes from the minutes taken during the 87 meetings of the so called Armenian-Greek Section (A.G.S.) at the British representation at Constantinople, covering the period between March 1919 to March 1922. During these sessions, information on the situation of Ottoman Greeks was given by the two representatives of the Ecumenical Patriarchate, Dr. Théotokas and Mr. Calvocoressi. Edited and published in 2007 by the Armenian-American lawyer Vartkes Yeghiayan, these protocols, which were all sent to Lord Curzon, the British Foreign Secretary in London among others, impressively testify to the Allied ineptitude in preventing the ongoing systematic and massive crimes against the Ottoman Christians.[87]

In his conclusive 1922 memorandum *On Turkish Massacres and Persecution of Minorities since the Armistice* the British diplomat George William Rendel (1889–1979) mentioned that "as early as May 1919 reports of renewed persecutions of Armenians and Greeks all over Anatolia and Pontus began to come in."[88] In Aydın, more than 3,000 Greek men, women and children were massacred in June 1919, when the Greek army of occupation retreated from that town,[89] which was nearly completely destroyed by fire,

> [a]nd the greater part of its inhabitants were killed, some being shot, others pierced with red hot irons, others cut to pieces and others put to death with the cruellest tortures. The inhabitants' property was plundered, virgins were carried off to the mountains, and now Aydin is a vast cemetery. After the destruction of Aydin 800 women and children were sent off by railway to Nazli and Denizli on June 18th and 19th, 1919.[90]

---

[87] *British Reports on Ethnic Cleansing in Anatolia, 1919–1922: The Armenian-Greek Section*, Vartkes Yeghiayan, ed. (Glendale, California: Armenian Remembrance Center, 2007).

[88] Rendel, "Memorandum," 1.

[89] Ecumenical Patriarchate, *The Black Book of the Sufferings of the Greek People in Turkey, from the Armistice to the End of 1920* (Constantinople: Press of the Patriarchate, 1920), 46.

[90] Ibid., 52.

In the Greek Orthodox diocese of Angora the repressions and atrocities of the Armenian genocide seemed to repeat themselves, including hostage taking and tormenting of children and the demand on the Christian victims to buy weapons, which could be used as "proof" of an alleged Christian threat:

> The Christian communities were terrorized. The male Christians of Eski Shehir were deported from the town, after being imprisoned and heavily taxed. [...] Children 10 to 12 years of age were mercilessly beaten as they were conducted to the military headquarters to be questioned if their fathers, uncles or brothers were hiding and to disclose where they could be found. [...] The town of Kutahia was the scene of indescribable atrocities, from the day on which the fanatical Kemalists Tserkess Edhem Bey [Çerkes Ethem][91] and Major Ismail Hakky Bey [İsmail Hakkı Paşa] arrived there. The latter, followed by 150 chosen Albanians found no great difficulty in obtaining the assistance of the Turks of Kutahia. After consulting with them, he planned the annihilation of the Greek and the other Christian elements, himself presiding in all acts of horror. He ordered that all Greeks be disarmed. [...] Some people in the district of Kutahia were called to enlist and the Greek community of that town was asked to deliver 245 military rifles with proportionate quanti-

---

[91] Ethem's reign of terror eventually ended, after his brother Tevfik denounced him in a letter of 27 November 1920 to Mustafa Kemal and the commander of the Western Front, İsmet İnönü, for "disobedience." According to official Turkish historiography, he initiated a revolt in Kütahya on 27 December 1920 and was declared a rebel by the Turkish Grand National Assembly (Ankara) on 17 January 1921. His units were completely defeated by 22 January 1921, and he was sentenced to death on 9 May 1921:

http://goturkey.turizm.gov.tr/BelgeGoster.aspx?17A16AE30572D3130239EEA0FCDF038B786 5257CB2BC6B19.

http://goturkey.turizm.gov.tr/BelgeGoster.aspx?17A16AE30572D3130239EEA0FCDF038BE0 2233C478ECCCA1.

In 1920, Christians also fell victim to clashes between the various ethnic Muslim groups, in particular in connection with the so-called Circassian rebellion, as the A.G.S. minutes of 1 September 1920 demonstrate:

"On the 11th August [1920] a teacher from the village of Codja Dagh was killed by two Lazes from Kiossli. Two days later seven Lazes carried off two Greeks from the village of Chrissi and murdered them in the forest and a day later an Armenian was killed by soldiers at Yagli Keriz.

The town of Bolou [Bolu in Turkish; Βιθύνιον, Bithynion in Greek] was occupied by the Circassians after the departure of Kemalist officials and on the 23rd August 200 Nationalist Kurds attacked the town and killed the Circassians. The Kurds then surrounded the Armenian quarter in which there were 20 Greek families. They pillaged the houses, shut up the men in the Armenian church, killed the women and then set fire to the church and the whole town. Very few escaped." Yeghiayan, *British Reports on Ethnic Cleansing in Anatolia*, 167. The A.G.S. minutes of 1 September 1920 conclude: "With the exception of 13 Armenians who arrived in Constantinople via Zonguldak, the 600 Armenians and 80 Greeks of Bolu were massacred," ibid., 169.

ties of ammunition, for their exemption from military service. But the Greeks of that town had no rifles and had to purchase them.[92]

Since spring 1920, reports about massacres of Greek non-combatants in all parts Asia Minor increased. In Yozgat on 21 May 1920, Circassian Kemalist troops under the command of Ethem killed nearly all Greeks and Armenians;[93] the Christian remnants of that town were killed — 60 Greeks and 20 Armenians — when Kemalist troops occupied the town again on 9 July 1920 and pillaged the houses of Greeks.[94] The Bithynian districts of Bursa (Προύσα or Προύσσα, Prous[s]a (Gr.)) and İznik (Νίκαια, Nicaea (Gr.)), and the peninsula and town of İzmit (Νικομήδεια, Nicomedia (Gr.))[95] were terrorized by a group of Kemalist irregulars under the command of a certain officer Cemil Bey. On 8 September 1920 Cemil and his men entered the Greek village of Otsoglou in the vicinity of Yozgat and

> [...] caused all the villagers, 280 in number and all Greek, to gather in the church. Then, after violating beastly all the women and girls in the presence of their fathers, husbands and brothers, he killed them. Then he killed all males, not excepting small babies. One baby was found killed, sucking his slain mother. From this terrible slaughter only 24 people could escape, having run away before the arrival of the troops. As the Kemalist army had the intention to invade and massacre all the surrounding villages, the poor inhabitants were obliged to leave their homes and to go to the mountains, where many of them perished.[96]

The same Cemil was also responsible for massacres of 14–15 August 1920, which took place in the town of İznik/Nicaea, just a few kilometres from Constantinople on the Asia Minor side. A British officer, quoted in the Rendel memorandum, reported on 7 October 1920 about İznik:

> From information in the hands of the Smyrna Division, which is confirmed by previous reports, the whole Greek population of Iznik has been massacred. Apparently the majority of the massacres took place at the end of August —

---

92 Ecumenical Patriarchate, *The Black Book*, 40.

93 Ibid., 37.

94 Yeghiayan, *British Reports on Ethnic Cleansing in Anatolia*, 161

95 An Inter-Allied Commission was sent in May 1921 to investigate the alleged *Greek* atrocities against Turks of March and April 1921 in the Yalova-Gemlik and İzmit areas. The Yalova Commission confirmed the destruction of Greeks by Kemalists in the previous year 1920 (namely in Nicaea, Ortakeni, Elmalık, Fulacık and in several Armenian villages of the same district); the İzmit Commission mentions that attacks on Christians "increased in numbers and ferocity — more particularly with regards to the Greeks — in March 1920, and even more so in June and July 1920 (when preparations were being made for Greek offensives). The Greek authorities have submitted a list of thirty-two villages looted or burnt, with more than 12,000 persons massacred, 2,500 missing, and the remainder of the population (more than 15,000) living as refugees in Izmit." Cf. Rendel, "Memorandum," 4.

96 Ecumenical Patriarchate, *The Black Book*, 38.

> the remainder of the population were killed before the Greeks took the town, i.e. at the end of September. — The number of killed is said to be about 130 families, or about 400–500 men, women and children. [...] All the bodies I saw had been mutilated, apparently they had first had their hands and feet cut off, after they were either burnt alive in the cave or had their throats cut [...] Djemal Bey is said to be responsible for these massacres. [...] The ancient Greek church of Iznik, which dates from 332 A. D. has been thoroughly smashed up, only the walls remaining. [...] It is said that a number of people were massacred inside the church. The Greek soldiers, who have every opportunity of visiting these places, are not unnaturally bitterly enraged about it.[97]

In Ionia, massacres, committed by Kemalist forces and local bands had begun on 22 June 1920. These were described in a telegram of 11 August 1920, sent to the French Prime Minister by a committee of residents from towns of the Aydın province, i.e. from Nazili, Saraköy, Denizli and Khonesi:[98]

> [...] Kemal's forces operating in the Nazli region in conjunction with criminals who came from Sokia [Söke][99] and from Peran of Meandros, belonging to Sokiali Ali sub-command on the pretext of the advance of Greek army looted Christian houses at Nazli carrying off spoils. They burnt the city with explosive shells excluding Muslim neighbourhood and ended their mission with massacres and tortures against Christian population. Eye witnesses tell the story with terror that under smouldering ruins were found many charred innocent beings. According to calculations the number of the savagely massacred and dead under the ruins of Nazli exceeds 500 persons.
>
> The rest, more than 3,000 of whom were women, children completely stripped were driven by force to the interior in a deplorable condition, while the Turkish population with loot were transported by train.
>
> Weak old people unable to follow caravan were savagely killed en route. Their corpses remain unburied.
>
> On the road between Eazei Kouyoudjak only, a distance of 12 kilometres, 53 corpses found. It is estimated others, who were massacred were thrown in the Meandros River.
>
> The fate of those, who survived is unknown. According to information some survivors dispersed in various inhabited areas of interior in lamentable condition.
>
> Fate of residents of Saraköy totally unknown. Town looted, remains uninhabited. In Denizli where 20,000 Greeks were concentrated suffered the same fate.
>
> Male population indiscriminately led to deserted island of Lake Egirdir,[100] Turks applied themselves to looting and orgies against women and children.

---

[97] Rendel, "Memorandum," 3.

[98] Important towns on the road connecting Smyrna and Konya.

[99] A quarter of Scala Nova (Kuşadası (Tur.)) in Southwest Turkey, which was at that time occupied by Italian forces.

[100] The Greek place name was Ακροτήρι (Akroteri), situated near the ancient Ionian town of Sparta; in 1980 it was renamed Eğridir Gölü (Lake Eğridir).

> Leaders of Kemal's followers fight for distribution of spoils. Scared population abandons town. Fate of Khonesi residents remains unknown.[101]

A year later, in June 1921, "terrible massacres" were reported from the Pontus seaports of Samsun and Trebizond: "The streets are strewn with bodies of Greeks. Many shops have been ransacked. An American destroyer has arrived at Samsun to protect American subjects there."[102] Many of the new horrors in the Pontus region were caused by the irregulars under the command of Osman Ağa Feridunoğlu, alias Topal Osman ("the lame" Osman, 1894 - April 2, 1923),[103] Mayor of Giresun and a commandant of the Kemalist army,[104] as Rendel described him:

> [...] American travellers and others just arriving from Samsun, said a dispatch from Constantinople, report horrible details of the persecution of Christian populations in that region. The notorious murderous chief, Osman Agha, arrived at Samsun the second day of Bairam [...], inaugurating his entry by the murder of ten Greeks. Then, surrounding the stores of the American Tobacco Company, he arrested all Greek clerks, numbering about 800, and had them transported to an unknown destination. The Greek quarter was then surrounded and 1,500 other Greeks arrested and deported to the interior.
>
> The population of thirty other villages of the Samsun region were massacred while they were being transported to the place of exile. [...] Other villages, having refused to comply with the deportation order, were set on fire by the Turks, and the inhabitants, regardless of age and sex, were killed.
>
> The American commission, which went to this place reported these crimes and brought back burned bones, which were shown to the Turkish Governor.[105]

Mustafa Kemal personally welcomed the deportation of the Greek residents of Samsun as a well-deserved reaction to atrocities committed by the Hellenic army. In his telegraph response to 70 Turkish notables from Samsun, who had intervened on behalf of their Greek compatriots, Kemal argued that

> [...] he [Mustafa Kemal] had just returned from the front, where he had seen the crimes committed by the Greeks; that the exile of these people was a merciful act and he regretted that there existed wicked Turks who sided with the enemy. Nevertheless the notables obtained a "Fetva" (a religious decision) from the Moufti of Samsun that the massacre of these people could not be permitted and Osman Agha was recalled.[106]

---

101 Quoted from Tsirkinidis, *"At last we uprooted them...,"* 168–69 (translation from French by Harry Tsirkinidis [toponyms by Tessa Hofmann]).

102 "Reported Massacre of Greeks," *The Argus* (Melbourne), 6 June 1921.

103 Osman, who was of Laz or Circassian ethnicity, had his first meeting with Mustafa Kemal as early as 29 May 1919 in Havza.

104 Rendel, "Memorandum," 4.

105 "700,000 Greeks Victims of Turks," *The New York Times*, 10 July 1921, 4.

106 Yeghiayan, *British Reports on Ethnic Cleansing in Anatolia*, 221.

After the deportation of the Samsun Greeks, atrocities and deportations continued in the 394 Greek villages of the adjacent districts during the following three months.

> The presence of Topal Osman and his brigands was decisive. He killed, raped and threw many victims alive into the flames of their burning houses. He daily ordered the arrest of entire groups, accompanied by plunder, rape and murder. He ordered to hold the arrested in schools and churches, which he set ablaze. Mustafa Hakyemez, who saw Topal Osman as the liberator of Giresun, reports how he replaced the Pontian flag in Taşkışla by the Turkish one: "He saved us from the Greek partisans. The main guilty among the Greeks he ordered to put into sacks, burdened by stones, and to throw them into the sea."[107]

Greek refugees from Samsun, who had escaped to Constantinople, reported there that the Kemalists had burnt 3,000 Greek villagers alive.[108] A semi-official statement, issued in Athens on 8 September 1921, reads among others:

> At Bafra the male population were strangled in the church and schools. Osman Agha has burned 18 villages in the region of Zara, and ordered a general massacre in Charki Karahissa. At Arbaya friends of Osman Agha strangled 44 persons in one house alone, and set fire to 42 villages. At Osman Agha's orders, ten families were strangled in Landik.[109]

A month after the Samsun massacre and deportation had started, the Greek Legation at Washington summarized the casualties of "700,000 Greeks [who] have been massacred, deported or have died of famine since the war with Turkey began."[110]

The deportation of Greeks from the Pontus region is also recalled in the memoirs of the Armenian survivor Varteres Mikael Garougian, who watched them arrive in Harput, probably in 1921, before the few surviving Armenians were deported again, together with the Greeks:

> From the shores of the Black Sea caravans of deported Greeks began to reach Kharpert [Harput]. Even though they were wretched and sick, the Government was only concerned with driving them on. To furnish them food? Don't ask! Their attitude was: 'They're a part of your own race. You help them!' You'd think that the deported Armenians were the ones to have initiated the deportation of the Greeks! Yet, even from what they didn't have, the Kharpert

---

[107] Konstantinos Fotiadis, "Der Völkermord an den Griechen des Pontos" ["The Genocide of the Greeks of Pontus"], in Hofmann, *Verfolgung, Vertreibung und Vernichtung der Christen im Osmanischen Reich*, 197; M. Hakyemez is quoted from Cemal Şener, *Topal Osman Olayı*. (İstanbul: Ant Yayınevi, 1992 [originally published in Ankara, 1968]), 119.

[108] "Villages fired by Kemalists – Inhabitants reported to have been burnt alive," *The Scotsman* (Edinburgh), 18 August 1921, 5.

[109] "Alleged Turkish atrocities," *The Scotsman*, 12 September 1921, 7.

[110] "700,000 Greeks Victims of Turks," *The New York Times*, 10 July 1921, 4.

> Armenians dug in to share with these refugees. Apparently, the Government intended to push these people toward Van, but changed its mind and later settled them into Armenian villages in Kharpert. You'd think that the numbers of the two groups of emigrants totalled only a few! Behold the '*mal*' of being displaced! From Konya, they were of mixed blood — Armenian and Greek. Fortunately, Near East Relief, seeing their plight, stretched out its helping hands. Among this group of emigrants was the ailing Professor Bezazian, whose condition worsened. When he died, his body was buried in Kharpert with much sorrow. However, not believing that he had died, the Turkish Government had his body exhumed after which the Government was satisfied.[111]

In October 1921, being marched to prison and presumably execution, Garougian and other Armenians passed through Hanköy in the Harput region, when he discovered the corpses of Greek deportees:

> The Euphrates River flowed a short distance away, and south of Keumar Khan there was an inn, nestled in the bosom of two mountains, where travellers would descend to spend the night. From the owner of the inn we purchased some *lavash* bread and a bit of *khavurma* (toast), which the *gendarmes* and I ate before retiring for the night. Arising early in the morning, we continued our descent to the guardhouse named Isoli. As we walked along the *yol* (path), we encountered decaying corpses of men and women. The stench was terrible. I asked my guards who these dead bodies were and where they came from. They informed me, truthfully, that these bodies were Greek emigrants who had been deported from the edge of the Black Sea. Because they were unable to survive the travel and hunger, they became ill and died. Since the moving caravans did not have time to bury the dead bodies, they left them on the path and departed. Although I had been aware that this caravan had come to Kharpert, where the Armenians had helped the Greeks, up to that time I had been unaware that there had been victims from the journey. As we continued on our journey, we encountered more corpses, large and small, being devoured by ravenous vultures. These people who became food for the birds had descended from the ancient, mighty Greek and Roman empires which at one time reigned over an extensive area from this region up to the faraway Armenian principalities of Kars. How much can change through the ages! The descendants of yesterday's rulers have now become slaves, dying of hunger, driven along these same paths.[112]

Already on 2 March 1921, the National Assembly at Ankara ordered the reintroduction of labor battalions for Ottoman non-Muslims. According to Turkish scholar Leyla Neyzi of the Sabancı University, "one of the main reasons for the formation of these units was to ensure that local non-Muslims (particularly local Greeks) would leave their regions of origin and not join

---

[111] Varteres Mikael Garougian, *Destiny of the Dzidzernag* (Princeton and London: Gomidas Institute 2005), 134–35. Garougian completed his memoirs in 1957, the year before his death.

[112] Ibid, 142–43.

the forces fighting the Turks."[113] Interestingly, the subscription into the labor battalions was also imposed on oppositional or otherwise "unreliable" Muslims, according to Garougian. Being meanwhile sentenced to compulsory labor himself, he joined a labor unit that "was composed of mostly young Greek men, gathered after the massacres from the area of Samsun and now driven to this location. Another portion of the group was from Konya, composed of anti-Kemalist *sheikhs* and *mullahs* (religious leaders). It was almost evening when we reached Zara, located on the tableland of the Armenian mountains."[114] Like in previous years, living and working conditions were deliberately inhuman and unbearable, as Garougian remembered:

> The number of men in our *tabur*, called *Emelia Tabur* [*amele taburu;* Pl. *amele taburları*], was increasing by the day. All the soldier-laborers had been specifically sent to this area [Kurucuk, near Erzurum] so that the hunger, thirst, and cold would precipitate our deaths. Why use bullets to kill? Later on the Turks would be labelled as murderers! Instead, let the soldier-workers die off because of their inability to withstand the lack of proper clothing, hunger, and never-ending lice! [...] Every day we were given shovels, taken out as a group to shovel the train tracks. In the evening we'd fill the water storage tanks. Many times we'd board the train, going to Hasan Kala or toward the area of Kars to clear off the snow. All along the entire line, there had been established stopping places where the *Emelia Tabur* laborers would meet to clear off the virtually invincible snows on the train lines in the mountains. It was in these groups of workers that I met an older Greek named Barbera who'd been working in conditions like this for two to three years. He came from a village called Horopel, which was situated between Erzerum and Kighi. The Greek told me that during the battles between Armenians and Turks most of the Armenian laborer-soldiers in the Turkish Army were slaughtered on the Plain of Pasin, near the Kurujuk village. Barely a few hundred of them survived to be exchanged as prisoners later during the Armistice.[115]

At the same time Mustafa Kemal established special tribunals (courts of independence), which issued arbitrary death sentences against Greek Or-

---

[113] http://en.wikipedia.org/wiki/Labor_battalion_(Turkey).

[114] Garougian, *Destiny of the Dzidzernag,* 169. According to Zürcher, however, the labor battalions were manned predominantly by Christians throughout World War I, "By and large the labor battalions were composed of Christian recruits. This should not come as a surprise. Ethnically homogeneous units were the rule rather than the exception in the Ottoman army and there was a distinct hierarchy among the different ethnicities, with Arab units being considered second rate and Kurdish ones utterly unreliable. Armenians and Greeks, whose loyalty was doubtful in the eyes of the Ottoman leaders, were obvious candidates for recruitment into the labor battalions which were held in low esteem. In the first instance, the units were formed from the age groups (over forty-five years old), from which, in the case of Muslims, the Mustahfiz (territorial reserve) were recruited." Eric Jan Zürcher, "Ottoman labor battalions in World War I," Internet essay, 4 (8 February 2008): http://www.arts.yorku.ca/hist/tgallant/documents/zurcherottomanlaborbattalions.pdf.

[115] Garougian, *Destiny of the Dzidzernag,* 178–79.

thodox Ottoman subjects. In all areas under control of the Nationalist government hundreds of Greeks were executed by hanging — or massacred, in particular during the initial phase — among them many publishers, entrepreneurs, the mayors of towns and villages and previous members of the Ottoman parliament. Thus the intellectual and political elite of the Asia Minor Greeks was destroyed in the course of a few months. In Alaçam in the district of Sinope, the entire male Christian population above the age of 12 had been imprisoned in May 1921 and subsequently massacred.[116] In June 1921 seven Orthodox priests from Alaçam, Bafra "and outlying districts were arrested and after being publicly tortured, were crucified in the market-place of Guioz-Keuy [Gözköy]."[117] In the Pontus region alone the daily rate of hanging was 60 during September 1921. In his telegram to the League of Nations the Ecumenical Patriarch of Constantinople quoted the Turkish newspapers of Samsun, the *Ehâle* and the *Helâl* of 18, 19 and 25 September 1921, giving a list of three Armenians and 168 Greeks, including two naturalised Americans, one missionary and the other professor at the American College at Merzivan (Marzovan (arm.), Merzifon (Tur.)), who were condemned to death and executed.[118] In the vicinity of Kavak (Pontus), 1,300 Greeks were shot on 15 or 16 August 1921 in about two and a half hours.[119] During the meeting of the Armenian Greek Section of 31 August 1921, Dr. Théotokas read the Ecumenical's Patriarchate's report of 24 August 1921, which also covered the

> [q]uestion of Ottoman Greeks who were being tried by the Turkish Courts for supposed acts of brigandage; and said that the prisoners were being ill-treated and subjected to severe humiliation, and that, through fear of worse treatment, they made no complaint to Captain Wilson, when he interrogated them on the round of inspection.[120]

In the A.G.S. meeting of 12 October 1921,

> [...] Dr. Théotokas said, that a Greek lady who had escaped from Samsoun had furnished the Patriarchate with a reliable and vivid account of the recent executions in that town. The victims were given three days notice of their fate; they were hanged naked and in batches, all the condemned having to undergo the terrible ordeal of standing by and witnessing the executions until their turn arrived. In one case a father and son were given the option of choosing which should be hanged first.[121]

---

[116] Yeghiayan, *British Reports on Ethnic Cleansing in Anatolia*, 236.

[117] Ibid.

[118] "Alleged Turkish crime - Appeal to the League of Nations," *The Scotsman*, 7 October 1921, 3.

[119] Rendel, "Memorandum," 5.

[120] Yeghiayan, *British Reports on Ethnic Cleansing in Anatolia*, 220.

[121] Ibid., 228.

A fortnight later, the representative of the Ecumenical Patriarchate added information on massive executions by hanging in Amasya. The A.G.S. minutes of 26 October 1921 concluded:

> These additional details show with what deliberation and studied cruelty, these sentences have been carried out; the victims were alleged to have been hanged in batches, the first victim being the aged Abbé Platon, Metropolitan Vicar of Samsoun [Samsun]. After these executions, the bodies of the victims were stripped of their clothes and valuables, and the gold teeth of the executed extracted by the Turks.[122]

Commenting on the numerous incidents of the year 1921, G. W. Rendel admitted indirectly that he had lost track:

> The persecutions of 1921 were on a larger scale and more atrocious than those of 1920. The area affected is so great, and the atrocities are so varied and continuous, that it is difficult to select special cases for mention. Moreover, the mass of documentary evidence at our disposal is now so enormous that any compression of the information contained in it into suitable limits become well-nigh impossible.

However, Rendel singled out the well documented massacre at Merzivan at the end of July 1921, which had been subject of a memorandum by the Armenian Greek Section of the British High Commission at Constantinople, transmitted by the British High Commissioner Horace Rumbold (1920–24) on 22 October 1921, and also of a much fuller and entirely independent first-hand account by the agent of the U.S. Near East Relief at Merzivan, Donald M. Hosford.

The Merzivan massacre had been conducted by Topal Osman and his brigands, who had announced their "visit" to the town in advance and obviously in accordance with Sadık, the Kemalist commissioner for the area, who used the opportunity to have murdered two wealthy Armenians, to whom he owed money. The Kemalist government promised an enquiry but never took any action against Osman and his gangs.[123] According to newspaper accounts and British diplomatic correspondence, the Christians of Merzivan were gathered in three large buildings:

> Those gathered in the red house were mostly young girls, who were all violated. The houses were subsequently set on fire, but after much difficulty most of the occupants were let out. The next day, Mr. Hosford says, Miss Anthony, of the American Near East Relief, was able to watch, the hauling out of wagon-loads of dead bodies and the burying of these bodies in pits across the valley from our house. She feels very certain that some of those thus buried were not entirely dead. Mr. Hosford summarises the results of the massacres as follows: "In no way was there any distinction in the treatment as between

---

[122] Ibid., 230.

[123] "The Turk at Work," *The Times*, 26 October 1921, 11.

> Greeks and Armenians [...] From a Christian population of 2,000 to 2,500, almost all of the men were killed, many of them our employees and men formerly connected with the college. Women and children were also killed, in all upwards of 700. All Greeks were deported. About 700 Armenians were left in the city, including only 20 or 30 men at most. Every Christian house was looted and 400 houses were burnt. [...] Repeated tales of the utmost cruelty were borne to us, such as the burning of churches with Greeks inside, the use of priests, with their robes soaked in kerosene, as torches, &c. It is not difficult [...] for an eye-witness of the work of these men in Merzivan to believe such tales, and there is ample supporting evidence of the general truth of the statements."[124]

Torching and burning Christians in their houses or churches had become common practice since the late nineteenth century. Winston Churchill called the World War I annihilation of the Ottoman Armenians "one administrative holocaust."[125] Alone in the Syrian village of Shaddadeh near the Habur River, 80,000 Armenian deportees had been burnt alive or suffocated in an oil-rich cave system in 1916.[126] Eytan Belkind, member of the Zionist *Nili* espionage group and officer in the Ottoman army, observed in Deir al-Zor, how 5,000 Armenians were grouped around a huge stake of thistles and thorns, which was then set ablaze:

> You could hear the screams of the unfortunate victims, which were burnt to death in the huge fire, in a distance of miles.[127]

Torching and burning alive was so common a practice that for Armenians a key episode in their genocidal trauma became *The Dance* (1909), as described in the poem of Siamanto (killed 1915): "During the Adana massacre, Armenian women were compelled to dance while burning."[128]

In Pontus and other northern parts of Asia Minor, the destruction of the elite and the massacres were followed since June 1921 by death marches, unsuccessfully camouflaged as deportation and reaching their climax between 15 April and 15 May 1922.

---

124 Cf. Rendel, "Memorandum," 4–5.

125 Winston Churchill, *The World Crisis, 1911–1918: The Aftermath* (New York, 1927), 5: 157; quoted by Harut Sassounian: http://www.armeniangenocide.com/section3/first.html and by Robert Fisk, "Dead Reckoning: Holocaust vs Holocausts," *Independent*, 5 August 2000.

126 Robert Jébéjian, *Routs* [read *Routes*] *and Centers of Annihilation of Armenian Deportees in 1915 within the Boundaries of Syria* (Aleppo: Violette Jébéjian Library, 1994), 65.

127 Quoted from a letter to the editor of correspondent Hannes Stein (Jerusalem), published in *Frankfurter Allgemeine Zeitung*, 4 August 1998; compare also the memoirs of E. Belkind, *Kakh zeh haya... Sippuro shel Ish Nili* [*It was this way... The Story of a Nili Member*] (Tel Aviv, 1979).

128 An American translation *Bloody News from My Friend: Poems by Siamanto* was edited by Peter Balakian and Nevart Yaghilian (Detroit, MI: Wayne State University Press, 1996).

> After having executed a large number of notables in the bigger towns, Samsoun, Amasia, &c., they proceeded to the deportation of practically the whole Greek population. In the early autumn [1921] the number of deportees was alleged to have reached 35,000. The accounts of these deportations received from Greek and other survivors are as ghastly as any of the accounts of the Armenian atrocities during or after the war. They are nearly all confirmed by the letters of the Near East Relief agents and of other eye-witnesses which we have received from the American Embassy and through private sources.[129]

At the A.G.S. meeting of 9 November 1921, the representative of the Armenian Apostolic Patriarchate, Dr. Davidian[130] [Tavitian in Western Armenian] read from a traveller's report about the situation at Sivas; the informant mentioned among others a convoy of about 4,000 Greeks,

> [...] who were being deported from Samsoun to Tokat and other smaller batches of 25 to 30 persons, who were chained to one another. These poor wretches, to avoid starving had been forced to pay 10 Piastres for a glass of water and 30 Piastres for a loaf of bread, the correct price of which being 8 Piastres.[131]

Alternatively to deportation, disarmament of residents and destruction of settlements was another method, as applied in the case of Christian villages

> [o]f Bafra, Hafsa [Havza; district of Samsun], Marsovan [Merzifon], Ladik and Vizier Keupru [Vezir Köprü; district of Samsun] in the following manner: [...] The Turkish Military Authorities then received orders to burn all the mountain villages, and Bakir–Tchaj Maden [Bakir Çay Maden] (between Marsovan and Vizier Keupru) containing 120 houses, was the first to be totally destroyed, all its inhabitants perishing in the flames. The Christian inhabitants of the surrounding districts fearing that a similar fate awaited them, took refuge to the mountains and their villages were in turn destroyed. In this way about forty villages in the district of Tavshan Dagh [Tavşan Dağ] were burnt.
> The villages in the plain were then attacked, but thanks to a certain Turk who warned the Christians of their coming fate, a great number succeeded in escaping to the mountains. Turkish Troops then surrounded 67 villages, and with the exception of a few old men and a number who declared that they would embrace Islam and who paid large sums of money, all the men were killed.

---

129 Rendel, "Memorandum," 5.

130 Representative of the National Administration of the Armenian–Apostolic Patriarchate of Constantinople. The survivor and prelate Grigoris Palakian (Balakian in Western Armenian) called him in his memoirs (published in Armenian original 1922 and 1956) a "dictator, having held his authority for all four years of the Armenian massacres [1915–18], during which he had been a mere spectator of the annihilation — and had not dared to resign his absolutely nominal post." Balakian, *Armenian Golgotha,* 431.

131 Yeghiayan, *British Reports on Ethnic Cleansing in Anatolia*, 234.

> With the exception of girls of 14 and 15, and young married women who were sorted out for retention in Harems, all the women and children were deported to the interior of Asia Minor.[132]

Throughout the autumn and winter of 1921–22, agents of the Near East Relief (NER) witnessed more or less helplessly how Christian deportees, predominantly Greeks, were driven in guarded convoys of thousands and under the harshest conditions into the interior.

> On the 26th July, Mr. Fuller of the American Near East Relief met about 3,000 women and children being driven towards the interior by Turkish guards. On the 1st September, Mr Hopkins of the same organization met 12,000 being driven southwards between Harput and Malatia. They were being robbed and ill-treated by their guards. Mr. Hopkins saw "many corpses of Greeks lying by the roadside where they had died from exposure. Many of them were the corpses of women and girls." About the 1st October he and two other relief workers passed about 10,000 Greeks. He says: "I remember one group of about 2,000 being women alone, most of them with no shoes, many carrying babies [...] A driving cold rain was falling [...] they had no protection whatever and their only place to sleep was the wet ground." Mr. Hopkins continues: "The deportation of Greeks is not limited to the Black Sea Coast, but is being carried out throughout the whole country governed by the Nationalists. The Greek villages are deported entire, the few Turks or Armenian inhabitants are forced to leave, and the villages are burned. The purpose is unquestionably to destroy all Greeks in that territory and to leave Turkey for the Turks. These deportations are, of course, accompanied by cruelties of every form just as was true in the case of the Armenian deportations five and six years ago."[133]

News about the death marches filtered through relatively slowly, for the NER agents "were forced by the Nationalist authorities to send false telegrams, and were not allowed to relieve the Greeks, and caravans were apparently diverted so that they might not witness what was being done."[134]

Based on a lengthy interview with NER chief surgeon Dr. Mark H. Ward, who was compelled by the Turkish authorities to leave Harput (now Elaziğ) on 15 March 1922,[135] the British High Commissioner Rumbold telegraphed on 10 May 1922 to his government; together with an earlier report in *The Times* of 5 May 1922, the Rumbold telegrams of 25 April and 10 May prompted a debate in the House of Commons on 15 May 1922 during which

---

132 Ibid., 236–37.

133 Rendel, "Memorandum," 6.

134 Ibid.

135 "Kemalist War on Christians: hostility to American relief work," *The Times*, 8 June 1922, 7: http://www.greek-genocide.org/press/08061922.html.

Arthur Neville Chamberlain confirmed the assessment of the situation,[136] as given by High Commissioner Rumbold:

> The Turks appear to be working on a deliberate plan to get rid of minorities. Their method has been to collect at Amasia, Ottoman Greeks from region between Samsoun and Trebizond. These Greeks are marched from Amasia via Tokat and Sivas as far as Caesarea, and then back again until they are eventually sent through Kharput to the east. In this manner a large number of deportees die in the road from hardship and exposure. The Turks can say that they did not actually kill these refugees, but a comparison may be instituted with the way in which the Turks formerly got rid of dogs at Constantinople by landing them on an island where they died of hunger and thirst. [137]
>
> Large numbers of deportees who were being sent to Van and Bitlis passed through Kharput between June and December last year. Now that spring has come, these deportations have begun again. Once these gangs have passed Diarbekir, which is the last American relief station, Americans loose all track of them, but Dr. Ward has little doubt that many deportees die in the mountains east of that place [...] American Near East Relief was not allowed to shelter children whose parents had died on the road. These children are driven forward with other deportees [...] Two thirds of Greek deportees are women and children. At present fresh deportations and outrages are starting in all parts of Asia Minor, from the Northern Seaports to the South Eastern district [...][138]

In his earlier telegram of 25 April 1922 Rumbold mentioned that "the whole Greek population from the age of 15 upwards, of the Trebizond area and the hinterland was being deported, apparently to labor battalions at Erzerouni [Erzurum] and other places."[139] On his way back to the U.S., Dr. Ward met in London on 7 June 1922 with Foreign Office representative Lancelot Oliphant, to whom he summarized the deportation that he had witnessed as an intended extermination, calculated by the Nationalist Turkish government:

---

[136] "Turkish Deportations — Confirmation of the Times telegram," *The Times*, 16 May 1922, 21.

[137] The initiative to get rid of the street dogs came from Dr. Bahattin Şakir, then a prominent member of the Medical Faculty, who used the dogs in experiments. According to the French writer Philippe Videlier, the Institut Pasteur in Paris had been first asked to elaborate a plan for annihilating the dogs and worked out a project of killing them with gas and make industrial use of the bones and fat of the animals. Fearing that the foreigners might demand a too high share in profits, the Young Turks, however, "decided for the traditional method, which was less expensive, although more evident" Philippe Videlier, "Türkische Nacht: Die Geschichte vom Sultan und den drei Paschas" [Turkish Night: The Tale about the Sultan and the Three Pashas], *Lettre International*, no. 68 (April 2005): 5: http://www.aga-online.org/de/tuerkischeNacht/tuerkischeNacht.pdf.

[138] Telegram Nr. 201 by Sir H. Rumbold, 10 May 1922; quoted in Tsirkinidis, *"At last we uprooted them...,"* 241–42; cf. also "'Unspeakable Turk:' Atrocities in Asia Minor, roads strewn with dead; Britain's strong action," *The Irish Times*, 16 May 1922, 5.

[139] "Unspeakable Turk," ibid.

> From May, 1921, to March last, when I left, thirty thousand deportees, of whom six thousand were Armenians and the rest Greeks, were collected at Sivas and deported through Kharput to Bitlis and Van. Of these thirty thousand, ten thousand perished last winter and ten thousand escaped to have been protected by the Americans. The fate of the other ten thousand is not known. The deportations are continuing: every week's delay means death to hundreds of these poor people. The Turkish policy is extermination of these Christian minorities.[140]

Major Forrest D. Yowell, prior director of the NER Harput branch, had been arrested on 5 March 1922 for reasons "which the Turkish authorities refused to divulge, and was forcibly deported."[141] In spring 1922 he wrote in his report the U.S. Secretary of State, Charles E. Hughes:

> The attitude of the Vilayet Government toward the Greeks who were being (and who are still) deported through Sivas–Harpoot–Diarbekir from the Black Sea Coast and the Konia district, seems to be one of extermination. From statistics obtained from American sources — persons who have come into contact with the deportees in the course of their work of relief — we have accounted for at least 30,000 who reached Sivas. Of this number 8,000 died on the route to Harpoot and 2,000 remained in Malatia (March). After many obstacles thrown in our way by Turkish officials to prevent the N. E. R. from assisting these refugees were overcome, we were able to save thousands of lives by giving food, clothing and medical care.
>
> However, 2,000 refugees died in Harpoot, Mezra, and scattered in villages near by. The remaining 20,000 were sent on toward Diarbekir, and it was not merely a coincidence, in my opinion, that days when terrible snowstorms were in progress were selected to send these people, three fourths of whom were women and children, out over almost impassable mountains, without food or covering of any kind, and where no shelter can be found. In all cases these people have been robbed of everything that can be taken from them before they have progressed but few days on their journey, and the most attractive girls taken into Moslem homes.
>
> Of the 15,000 sent toward Diarbekir 3,000 died on the route and 1,000 died in Diarbekir. About 1,000 (all men) were taken by the Government to work on the roads between Harpoot and Diarbekir. They were given no pay, and their entire food allowance consisted of 200 grs. of bread per day and a little thin soup once a day. They had no shelter and were compelled to sleep out of doors in bitterly cold weather, without bedding or covering, and when they are too ill to work their food allowance is discontinued and they are allowed to die without medical care.
>
> Of the 9,000 Greeks known to have been sent on toward Bitlis, nothing further is known on their fate, as all efforts of the Americans to get there or send

---

140 "Kemalist war on Christians, Says 22,000 Greeks Died on the March," *New York Times*, 7 June 1922, 3.

141 "Turks' Insane Savagery," *The Times*, 5 May 1922, 10: http://www.hellenic-genocide.com/press/05051922.html.

> relief has met with failure. This we do know, Bitlis is almost totally destroyed and is not capable of supporting more than a few thousand of people. As it is also located in high mountains, reached by passes only through which vehicles cannot now travel, it can be safely assumed that few of the deportees sent toward Bitlis reached there.
>
> In the Vilayet of Mamouret-ul-Aziz the Near East Relief was not permitted to employ any Greek, for or without compensation; it was not allowed to take in any Greek children, orphans or destitute, and in many cases Greek men were forcibly taken by Moslems to work for them without compensation, and it was necessary for the Near East Relief to give them bread to prevent them from starving.
>
> We were not allowed to take any Greek into our hospital or to give medical aid without a written permit from the Director of Sanitation, and the patient was compelled to call in person for the permit. In many cases the patient died before he succeeded in getting a permit and in the majority of cases they failed to get permits at all.
>
> Cases are on record in Harpoot where money was paid to Turkish officials for such permits. Convalescents from our hospital were invariably taken by the Government and sent out over the mountains before they had regained near normal strength. In effect the authorities admitted to myself and other Americans that the Greeks were enemies of the Government and that they should be killed, and that those who assisted them were enemies of the Governor.[142]

While in Constantinople in early May 1922, Major Yowell stated in an interview:

> [t]hat Christian men are thrown into gaol for no reason except to extort ransom from relatives. Women are forced into Moslem houses as slaves without the right to appeal to any tribunal. Turkish officials frankly state that the only way they can get money is by blackmailing Christians.[143]

The accusation of intended extermination was repeated in numerous reports of other NER workers, published since May 1922. The NER workers who preferred to remain anonymous described various restrictions of their humanitarian work, forced labor of the deportees and extremely unhygienic circumstances as the result of restrictions that were another mean of destruction. The latter was obviously the result of orders by Dr. Cevdet Bey, the Ankara Commissioner for Deportees, and his colleague Dr. Şerifeddin

---

142 Quoted from Herbert Adams Gibbons, "Near East Relief prevented from helping Greeks," *Christian Science Monitor*, 13 July 1922, 1: http://www.umd.umich.edu/dept/armenian/bts/JULY06_7-13-1922_CSM_NearEastReliefPreventedFromHelpingGreeks.pdf; see also, Letter from Mark H. Ward and Forrest D. Yowell to the American Consul at Aleppo, Jesse B. Jackson, 5 April 1922, 2: http://www.greek-genocide.org/docs/adp/ward_yowell_5_april_1922.pdf.

143 "Turks' Insane Savagery," *The Times*, 5 May 1922, 10: http://www.hellenic-genocide.com/press/05051922.html.

Bey, who benefited personally from the complete dependence of their female victims:

> An American who was in Sivas from October, 1921, to May, 1922 says that the deportees began to pass through there in the autumn, supposedly on their way to Harput, coming not only from the region of Samsun, but from all the villages and cities of northern Asia Minor. Throughout the winter they came, in an indescribable condition of dirt and distress. The Americans were refused point-blank, permission to do anything for the Greeks. Finally Vali Haidar Bey agreed to let the Americans minister to women and children and to boys under fifteen, but not to older boys and men who were sent to Erzerum to work on the roads. This was a pretext. The snow was deep. They were without shelter, and most of them perished of the cold. Outside Sivas is a *sevkiat*[144] — deportation camp — where sheds without roofs or windows or doors — just palisades — are the only shelter. No Near East Relief worker was allowed to approach this camp. The sick were brought in to town and thrown into the Armenian church, which one of the American workers calls "the Black Hole of Calcutta." Only she thinks that the original Black Hole could not have been as bad. For into this church, whose windows are boarded up and where it is dark and damp, are carried and dumped pell-mell cases of all kinds of the horrible diseases. The Americans are not allowed to do anything for these people. They all perish. None can possibly be saved. Their bodies are not removed.
>
> And yet this "Hospital" is under the charge of the Angora Commissioner of Deportees, Dr. Djevdet Bey, who with his assistant, Dr. Sherifeddin Bey, are examples of the fiends educated Orientals are capable of becoming. Dr. Djevdet was always debonair, and jested with the American women when they begged to be allowed to separate the cases and pay men to go in to remove the bodies. Dr. Djevdet refused permission to open orphanages or hotels for the girl children and their mothers. Finally, the Near East Relief did get eight houses, but all sorts of difficulties were made for the exiles who would enter them. They had to have papers, and it took two or three days of going from bureau to bureau to get these. As the women were already in an exhausted state, very many of them perished in this last effort to get to the asylum of unnecessary cruelty — the way we should never treat a suffering dog or horse. Dr. Djevdet and his assistant took forcibly from the Near East homes certain picked girls to serve suppers in their house and kept them till morning. Those, who refused to come received orders the next day to leave Sivas — an awful fate. These horrors reached their climax in May. On May 14th the Americans received the order to give up all boys over fourteen, and these were taken from the orphanages.[145]

Edith Wood, who had worked for the NER in Malatya since the end of November 1921 until early spring 1922 was convinced that the conditions there were even:

---

[144] *Sevkiyat* means "deportation" or "relocation" in Turkish.

[145] Gibbons, "Near East Relief prevented from helping Greeks."

> [...] more horrible than in Harput, although she was permitted to take in and attempt to care for the Greek orphans, which had been forbidden at Harput. Housing the children only prolonged their agony, however, as only half of those under 12 were temporarily saved. From four to seven of those who passed the initial test of being able to stand food and washing passed away each day Miss Wood thought that they might be pulled through. Their constitution was too greatly undermined by the journey from the coast. "It was like an endless chain," said Miss Wood. "The children would often be gone before I had taken their names. Forty to fifty of the older women passed on each day also. You see, starvation, exposure, exhaustion did their work before these deportees arrived at Malatia. They came to me in the last stages.
>
> Food and medicine were no good, although I tried my best. The Turks were doing nothing at all for them. In Malatia bodies lay around in the streets and fields. No attempt was made to bury them. Deportation is worse than a sentence of execution. Unless one sees these things, it is difficult to believe that such monstrous cruelty and barbarity exist in this world. Making women and children suffer that way until they drop and expire seems incredible. But that is Malatia, and they receive us coldly in Constantinople when we want to tell what we know for the benefit of our Government, and let it appear very clearly that my story is unwelcome and that I am a hysterical woman exaggerating or falsifying — that is the way it is.
>
> It took me fourteen days' constant travel to get from Malatia to Samsun on the Black Sea coast [...] All the way it was a heartrending journey, passing women and little children on their long road to Calvary. [...] I hardly pitied those who had given up en route. Bodies lay along the roadside and in the fields everywhere. There was no hope for the Greeks from Malatia to Samsun, and the most fortunate were those who perished at the start."[146]

Smyrna, the Cosmopolitan "Little Paris of the Orient" was the last stage of what is called "the Asia Minor tragedy" in the official modern history of Greece. Defeated by the Turkish nationalist forces, deserted by the Allies, the retreat of Greek forces from Asia Minor in late summer 1922 became a massive flight, joined by tens of thousands of Ottoman Christian civilians.

By the size of its population, Smyrna was the second largest city of the Ottoman Empire. It was at the same time a predominantly non-Muslim city, called "gâvur [infidel] Smyrna" for that reason by Muslims. According to U.S. Consul George Horton,

> [...] it is probable that (at the time of its destruction) the inhabitants exceeded five hundred thousand in numbers. The latest official statistics give the figure as four hundred thousand, of whom one hundred and sixty-five thousand were Turks, one hundred and fifty thousand Greeks, twenty-five thousand Jews, twenty-five thousand Armenians, and twenty thousand foreigners: ten

---

[146] Ibid.

> thousand Italians, three thousand French, two thousand British and three hundred Americans.[147]

Based on the official Ottoman *salname* (statistical yearbook), the German consulate estimated that at the beginning of the 20th century the population was 300,000 with a relative Greek Orthodox majority of 140,000 and a minority of 90,000 Muslims.[148] Of course, it is highly difficult to ascertain precise demographic statistics in times of war, massive flight, multiple migration and deportation. But as the only and last remaining Christian stronghold, one may assume that Smyrna had been the refuge for many Christians from adjacent and even distant provinces. The population was ethnically fragmented, for the inhabitants of Smyrna did not form an integrated community. Each group lived on its own ethno-religious island with its own educational, cultural and other institutions.

The Hellenic forces and administration withdrew on 26 August/8 September 1922.[149] In the early hours of 27 August/9 September regular and irregular Kemalist cavalry under the command of Nurettin Paşa occupied the completely undefended city, and first looted and then destroyed the Armenian quarter Haynots in the north of Smyrna, before setting it on fire in the night of 31 August/13–14 September. The Armenian eyewitness and survivor Garabed (Karapet) Hatcherian noted in his diary:

> Wednesday, the 13th: [...] After traversing a few districts, I enter Chalgidji Bashi where there is very little activity. I see a Turkish soldier on patrol. It is obvious that the Haynots and the surroundings are under siege. [...] I continue my path towards Chalgidji Bashi, but on the passage leading from Katirdji Oglou to Chalgidji Bashi, I see a Turk who approaches me saying, "We did what was due; you turn back." The Turk, who obviously had assumed an active role in the arson, takes me obviously for his compatriot and accomplice and advises me not to advance, but to turn back. I answer, "Very well," with the attitude of someone who understands the situation [...] The crackle of burning materials and the transformation of explosives into flaming clouds produce an infernal sight the likes of which I have never seen before. In Istanbul and other cities, I have seen huge fires. During the battles in the Dardanelles and in Romania, I have witnessed the burning of so many cities and

---

147 Horton, *Blight of Asia*.

148 Report of 18 November 1909 by the Imperial consul Mordtmann (Smyrna): German diplomatic documents; Annual commercial reports of the Imperial Consulate of Smyrna. Quoted from Hervé Georgelin, "Smyrne, septembre 1922 : une cité grecque-orthodoxe et arménienne non assimilable par le nationalisme turc," *Yevrobatsi*, 3 December 2005, footnote 2: http://www.yevrobatsi.org/st/item.php?r=0&id=1086 (last accessed in May 2008). It should be noted that Ottoman statistics were based on the *millet* system, giving figures for ethno-religious groups (Muslims, Christian denominations, Jews) only.

149 A difference of 13 days is caused by the different calendar systems used, i.e. the Julian and Gregorian (Old and New Style).

villages, but none of those fires has made such a strong impression on me. The fire in Smyrna is indescribable and unimaginable.[150]

Lasting four days, the obviously controlled and manipulated fire of Smyrna destroyed the lower parts of the city, which were Christian (European), starting with the Armenian and the Greek quarter adjacent to Haynots. Many Christians died in their burning houses or were killed by collapsing walls.

> The larger part of the European quarter of Smyrna is burning. According to an American eye-witness, Miss Mills, headmistress of the American College, the fire was started by a sergeant of Turkish regulars, who entered a house carrying tins of petroleum. Estimates of the damage caused by the fire up to last evening amount to £15,000,000 [...] It is reported here that up to the outbreak of the fire about one thousand persons had been massacred, but it is feared here that the number is now much greater.
>
> (From our correspondent in the Near East, Constantinople, September 14th)
>
> Fire broke out in the Armenian quarter of Smyrna and spread to the European quarter, where several consulates and other houses have been destroyed. United States and Allied contingents were landed, but have been unable to prevent the extension of the fire, which now threatens the whole European quarter.
>
> Athens, Sept. 13. — According to a Greek journalist who escaped from Smyrna on board the Messageries steamer Lamartine, Mgr. Chrysostomos, the Orthodox Metropolitan of Smyrna and the Gregorian Armenian Archbishop have been murdered. — (Reuters.)[151]

One of the prominent victims of the massacres was the martyred and posthumously canonized Greek Orthodox Metropolitan of Smyrna Chrysostomos (Kalafatis; 1867–1922), who had become a hate-figure for Turkish nationalists since 1914, when he invited European diplomats from Constantinople to inspect the atrocities committed in Ionia. Although Chrysostomos had been offered a passage from Smyrna by the Catholic Archbishop of the city already on 25 August 1922, he declined the safe escape with the words: "It is the tradition of the Greek Church and the obligation of a priest to stay with his parish!" The American Consul Horton described his death:

> The tales vary as to the manner of Chrysostom's death, but the evidence is conclusive that he met his end at the hands of the Ottoman populace. A Turkish officer and two soldiers went to the offices of the cathedral and took him to Nureddin Pasha, the Turkish commander-in-chief, who is said to have adopted the medieval plan of turning him over to the fanatical mob to work its will upon him. There is not sufficient proof of the veracity of this state-

---

150 Dora Sakayan, ed., *An Armenian Doctor in Turkey: Garabed Hatcherian: My Smyrna Ordeal of 1922* (Montreal: Arod Books, 1997), 14–15.

151 "Smyrna Burning," *The Times*, 15 September 1922, 10: http://www.greek-genocide.org/press/15091922.html.

ment, but it is certain that he was killed by the mob. He was spit upon, his beard torn out by the roots, beaten, stabbed to death and then dragged about the streets. His only sin was that he was a patriotic and eloquent Greek who believed in the expansion of his race and worked to that end [...] He died a martyr and deserves the highest honours in the bestowal of the Greek Church and government. He merits the respect of all men and women to whom courage in the face of horrible death makes an appeal.[152]

A few days before his death, on 31 August Chrysostomos, as the Metropolitan of Smyrna sent a letter to Meletios, the Ecumenical Patriarch at Constantinople, in which he blamed the Allied High Commissionership for the destruction of the Ottoman Greeks because of its order to disarm them and in which he predicted the massacre of the undefended Christian population in Smyrna:

> [...] Everybody feels that the greatest dangers and sufferings hang upon the unfortunate Christian population of the interior and of Smyrna, [wrote the Archbishop,] because it is very well known that the Turkish populations, civic and agricultural, without any exception, are armed to the teeth, [...] because of the last three years' negligence and good-will of the High Commissionership, and the other Greek military and police authorities.
>
> A victorious entry of the Turkish Army in the cities of the interior, and most especially in the capital city of Smyrna, when to this army shall be added all the armed Turkish populations, which until now were living in full security under the cover of the Greek administration and the protection of the Greek Army, will be marked by excitements of rage and hate and by terrible slaughters. Needless to insist upon this point here, because we all have a very bitter and bloody experience of the continuous and inevitable slaughters and massacres, which everywhere are marking the passage of Turks, whether they are victorious or defeated.
>
> Unfortunately, the whole Greek population, that of the cities and of the villages, is armless, thanks to the very stern measures of the High Commissioner, who has not allowed even the Committee for the Defence of Asia Minor to buy and bear arms and to give arms to civil guards, which would greatly contribute to the rising of the morale of the Greeks for the protection of the lives of the citizens from the armed bands and the Turkish masses.
>
> Thus, Greeks will be delivered to massacre and destruction. Hundreds of thousands of Greeks will perish without the possibility of the slightest defence, not even for its preservation for a few days and hours, until a European intervention may be affected to save the situation."[153]

However, this intervention never happened. Numerous Christians drowned in the harbour of Smyrna, when trying to escape to the Allied navy of 27

---

152 Horton, *Blight of Asia.*

153 "Slain Archbishop Foresaw Massacre: Chrysostomos Sent Letters to Foreign Officials Predicting Smyrna Disaster," *The New York Times*, 24 September 1922, 35: http://www.greek-genocide.org/press/24091922.html.

battle ships, among them three American destroyers. It added to the horrors of the people of Smyrna that the Allies watched, more or less indifferently, how their Christian co-religionists were burnt, slaughtered, raped, shot down by machine guns or drowned:

> [...] What happened on the night of 31 August, on the waterfront of Smyrna, towards which the crowds of the Smyrniots were heading, continuously trapped by the fiery torrents of the burning city and the crowds of Nureddin, is related by the French historian Driault:
>
> "Thousands of unfortunate people crowding along the waterfront fell into the sea. A great part of the port has been filled with hundreds of corpses that one could walk on them. Those floating on water were finished off by the Turks with swords and woods [clubs] [...]" And the same writer adds: "Who will describe the atrocious scenes? ... Countless lives, mostly women, children and old people have been massacred amidst ignominious savagery [...]"
>
> The most terrible of all is that this orgy of blood, disaster and various other crimes took place under the eyes, frequently the spiteful smiles and even the cheers of the crews of the foreign war ships, or the official representatives of the Christian powers [...]
>
> The same (French) consul himself invited to dinner, [...] excused himself for his delay of a few minutes with these terrible words: *"Because," he said, "the motor-launch in which I was on my way from the French war ship hit continuously upon the floating corpses of Greek women."* And the American consul [George Horton] listening to this cynical excuse, spited himself for being a human being. [...]
>
> In the French *Revue de Paris* these terrible things are cited among others concerning the Christian population: "The cries of the massacred reached from the beach and the corpses of the drowned floated around the ships. Amidst this savagery sounds of music have been heard from a British war ship to the satisfaction of its passengers." And the correspondent of *The Times* in Constantinople adds himself in his 3/16 September telegram: "A British party that was guarding the gas factory witnessed atrocious crimes at the expense of Greek women in the street without intervening, as they had the command to not intervene, except in an event concerning the security of the factory."[154]

On 3/16 September 1922 Nurettin ordered a proclamation, according to which all Greek and Armenian men of 18 until 45 years of age would be treated as prisoners of war "until the termination of hostilities."[155] All others, residents of Smyrna or refugees from outside, were ordered to leave the

---

[154] Quoted from Χρήστος Εμ. Αγγελομάτης, *Χρονικόν Μεγάλης Τραγωδίας: Το Έπος της Μικράς Ασίας* [*The Chronicle of the Great Tragedy: The Epic of Asia Minor*] (Athens: Βιβλιοπωλείον της Εστίας [Hestia Bookshop], 1963), 243–44, 248–49: http://www2.fhw.gr/chronos/13/en/foreign_policy/sources/12.html.

[155] Ibid., 254. Cf. an English translation of the proclamation: http://www2.fhw.gr/chronos/13/en/foreign_policy/sources/14.html for more details on the deportation order by Nurettin see also footnotes 88 and 89 in the contribution of Nikolaos Hlamides in this volume.

country until 30 September 1922. Men and women were then separated, the men led away and shot in groups.[156] Dr. Esther Lovejoy of the American Red Cross was eyewitness to the fate of the approximately 200,000 remaining Christian women:

> "I was the first American Red Cross woman in France," she said, "but what I saw there during the Great War seems a love feast beside the horrors of Smyrna. When I arrived at Smyrna there was massed on the quays 250,000 people — wretched, suffering and screaming — with women beaten and with their clothes torn off them, families separated and everybody robbed.
>
> Knowing their lives depended on escape before Sept. 30, the crowds remained packed along the waterfront — so massed that there was no room to lie down. The sanitary conditions were unspeakable.
>
> Three-quarters of the crowd were women and children, and never have I seen so many women carry children. It seemed that every other woman was an expectant mother. The flight and the conditions brought on many premature births, and on the quay with scarcely room to lie down and without aid most of the children were born. In the five days I was there more than 200 such confinements occurred.
>
> Even more heartrending were the cries of children who had lost their mothers or mothers who had lost their children. They were herded along through the great guarded enclosure, and there was no turning back for lost ones. Mothers in the strength of madness climbed the steel fences fifteen feet high and in the face of blows from the butts of guns sought the children, who ran about screaming like animals.
>
> The condition in which these people reached the ships causes one to wonder if escape were better than Turkish deportation. Never has there been such systematic robbery. The Turkish soldiers searched and robbed every refugee. Even clothing and shoes of any value were stripped from their bodies.
>
> To rob the men another method was used; men of military age were permitted to pass through all the barriers till the last by giving bribes. At the last barrier they were turned back to be deported. The robbery was not only committed by soldiers, but also by officers. I witnessed two flagrant cases committed by officers who would be classed as gentlemen.
>
> On Sept. 28 the Turks drove the crowds from the quays, where the searchlights of the allied warships played on them, into the side streets. All that night the screams of women and girls were heard, and it was declared next day that many were taken for slaves.
>
> The Smyrna horror is beyond the conception of the imagination and the power of words. It is a crime for which the whole world is responsible in not having through the civilized ages built up some means to prevent such orders as that of the evacuation of a city and the means with which it was carried out. It is a crime for the world to stand by through a sense of neutrality and permit this outrage against 200,000 women.

---

[156] Housepian, *The Smyrna Affair*, 172–73.

> Under the order to remain neutral I saw the launch of an American warship pick up two male refugees who were trying to swim to a merchant ship under the Turkish rifle fire and return them to the hands of the waiting Turk soldiers on the beach for what must have been certain death. And under orders to remain neutral I saw soldiers and officers of all nationalities stand by while Turk soldiers beat with their rifles women trying to reach children who were crying just beyond the fence."[157]

Consul Horton wrote about the fate of the Greek Orthodox men, deported from Smyrna and its vicinities after 30 September 1922:

> This last scene on the Smyrna quay reveals the whole diabolical and methodically carried-out plan of the Turks. The soldiers were allowed to glut their lust for blood and plunder and rape by falling first on the Armenians, butchering and burning them and making free with their women and girls. But the Greeks, for whom a deeper hatred existed, were reserved for a slower and more leisurely death. The few that have been coming back tell terrible tales. Some were shot down or killed off in squads. All were starved and thousands died of disease, fatigue and exposure. Authentic reports of American relief workers tell of small bands far inland that started out thousands strong.
>
> The Turks allege that they carried off the male population of Smyrna and its hinterland to rebuild the villages destroyed by the Greek army on its retreat. This has a ring of justice and will appeal to any American unacquainted with the actual circumstances. The Greek peasants of Asia Minor were Ottoman subjects, in nowise responsible for the acts of the Hellenic government. Very few enlisted voluntarily in its armies and they used every influence and subterfuge imaginable to avoid fighting. Had the Greeks of Asia Minor been a stout warlike race and had they cooperated strongly with the Greeks of the mainland they could have kept the Turks at bay.
>
> The object of Khemal, as we have seen, was one of simple extermination. The reason alleged was one of those shrewd subterfuges used by the Turks to fool Europeans. But not all the unfortunates carried away by the Turks were Greek men. Many thousands of Christian women and girls still remain in their hands to satisfy their lusts or to work as slaves. A report submitted to the League of Nations gives the number as "upward of fifty thousand," but this seems a very conservative estimate. The United States should sign no treaty with Turkey until these people are given up.[158]

In 1923, the French author René Puaux pointed out to the distinct European dimension in the responsibility for the Smyrna disaster:

> Perhaps the immensity of the tragedy of Smyrna could have been avoided or at least diminished, had there not existed a twofold illusion: the trust of the

---

[157] "Woman pictures Smyrna horrors: Dr. Esther Lovejoy, an eyewitness, tells of terrible scenes on the Quay; she assails neutrality; declares it a crime for the world to lack the means to prevent such outrages," *The New York Times*, 9 October 1922, 3.

[158] Horton, *Blight of Asia.*

> Great Powers in the Turks, and the trust of the Christians of Asia Minor in the Great Powers.[159]

Puaux estimated the number of Greeks deported into the interior of Anatolia as high as 150,000.[160] Most of these captives were massacred outside Smyrna or other Greek towns of Ionia/West Anatolia. The remainder was kept in a state of slavery[161] and treated with genocidal intent. One survivor, the writer Elias Venezis (pen name, born Mellos, 1904–1973) wrote down his experience and memories as early as 1924, soon after the massive Greek–Turkish exchange of populations. A Greek youth of just 18 years from Ayvalık, Venezis was conscripted into a slave labor battalion and "remained a slave without any rights and even without any official recognition of existence for fourteen months."[162] In his memoirs, Venezis tells how the Ayvalık conscripts were kept in the local prison several nights, during which 15 were selected to march outside the town to be bayoneted to death, while the remaining 43 were marched to the various labor camps of Western Anatolia. His group was the fourth such recruited group from Ayvalık, but in difference to the first three groups, numbering in hundreds his was determined to die in a slower way.[163]

After various death marches since 1915, disguised as deportations and after the previous conscriptions of 1914 and 1921 Turkish militaries and paramilitaries had achieved a rich experience in ways of physical destruction by indirect ways. Despite the time of the year and the already cold nights - it was the end of October 1922 — the Ayvalık conscripts had to undress with the exception of their underwear, and were marched in this semi-denuded state and without proper footwear to the town of Manisa (Magnesia (Gr.)). En route, they were not allowed to drink anything else but infectious swamp-water, with the clear calculation that typhus and other epidemics would decimate the undernourished, exhausted men. Deliberately they were kept under catastrophic conditions of lacking hygiene. These details in the account of Venezis let one doubt in the assumption of Erik Jan Zürcher that "the mistreatment of Armenian recruits in the labor battalions [or of Ottoman Greeks] [...] is but an extreme case of what was going on throughout the army."[164]

---

159 René Puaux, *Les derniers jours de Smyrne.* Paris 1923, quoted from Sakayan, *An Armenian Doctor in Turkey*, vi.

160 Puaux, ibid., compte d'auteur, 30–31.

161 Elias Venezis, *Το Νούμερο 31328* [*Number 31328*] (Athens: Εστία, 1956 [reprinted 1995]), 161.

162 Vryonis, "Greek Labor Battalions in Asia Minor," 276.

163 Ibid., 278.

164 Zürcher, "Ottoman Labor Battalions in World War I," 4.

One of the first tasks of E. Venezis' *taburu* in Manisa was to clear the area of the corpses of 40,000 Christian men, women and children from Manisa and Smyrna, which had been tied to one another with wire, before they were killed and dumped in a huge ravine of Mount Sipylo (Kırtıdere (Tur.)). The corpses already had begun to disintegrate, and the water drove them to the ravine's edge, "where they reached the road and railroad tracks."[165] The Turkish authorities feared that the floating remnants of massive killings of Christians might be seen by the Spanish official Dallara, who was "appointed to examine the conditions of the prisoners and the 'care' that the Turkish government was providing them."[166]

Under such fatal conditions, the mortality rate of the Greek slave laborers from Western Anatolia was extremely high. Out of the roughly 3,000 male labor conscripts from Ayvalık, only 23 survived — less than one percent![167] The inhuman treatment of Ottoman nationals by their own state could already be observed during the World War. In his report of 7 March 1917, the Hellenic consul of Konya (Ikonion (Gr.)) described the situation at a time, when Greece was still neutral:

> These unfortunate men, on being drafted into these battalions, are distributed throughout the interior of the Empire, from the coasts of Asia Minor and the Black Sea to Bagdad, the Caucasus, Mesopotamia, and Egypt, some to construct military roads, others to make tunnels for the Bagdad Railroad, and others to cultivate the fields. Receiving absolutely no pay, badly nourished and clothed, exposed to changes in the weather, to the blazing sun of Bagdad and the intolerable cold of the Caucasus, assailed by sickness, fever, eruptive typhoid, and cholera, they are perishing by thousands. For a while those able to pay the exemption fees were released from service; and thus those who were relatively well off were rescued from ruin and sure death, but for the last five months these, too, have been compelled to serve in these labor battalions. While visiting the hospitals of the city of Iconium, I have seen these unfortunates stretched out on their beds or on the ground like living skeletons, waiting in agony for death as their deliverer from this life of misery and privation. There is a total lack of drugs and food, and the only attention and sick receive is a visit from the doctor twice a day. Those who are able to stand go about the streets of the city begging a piece of bread. In order to give a faithful picture of this grievous situation it is enough to state that the cemetery of Iconium [Konya], as a result of the great mortality of the Greeks working in these labor battalions, has been filled to overflowing with graves in which not one corpse, as is the usual custom, is buried, but into which are cast, like dogs, as many as four, five, or even six dead.
>
> As for the "deserters," they were not only treated with the harshest cruelty, but their alleged existence in a given village was often the excuse for tortures

---

[165] Venezis, quoted from Vryonis, "Greek Labor Battalions in Asia Minor," 284.

[166] Ibid.

[167] Ibid., 288.

> of the other inhabitants to make them disclose their whereabouts, accompanied by confiscation, plundering, massacre, and other excesses.[168]

At the time of the second draft of Greek labor conscripts and during the final stage of genocide, a Greek physician noticed a death toll of 80 percent in Islahiye:

> During my stay in Islahiye, I saw labor battalions conscripted exclusively of 5,000 Greeks from Denizli. They were decimated in a very few months. Starvation, forced labor of a daily work schedule of twelve hours uninterrupted hard labor, sunstroke, illness and deprivation of all necessities brought conditions in which barely 1,000 managed to survive. There would enter the hospital daily 100 sick persons, the majority of whom would die the following day.[169]

In a period of only two months after the destruction of Smyrna the Turkish National Assembly at Ankara issued on 1 November 1922 its decision to expel all the remaining Christian population from Asia Minor, estimated by the Near East Relief to be still about half a million of people.[170] In late 1922 the League of Nations High Commissioner on Refugees, the Norwegian scholar Dr. Fridtjof Nansen, came to the conclusion that the remaining Greeks of Asia Minor were doomed if they were not evacuated. Even among those who escaped to Greece or other countries however, the mortality rate was high, because the refugees or "exchanged" Ottoman Greeks had undergone great hardships. Nansen himself had to admit that. In his statement before the Council of the League he informed that body that from September 1922 until July 1923 alone "up to 70,000 [refugees] died of disease and weakness owing to malnutrition."[171] During the last months of 1923 the mortality rate among the refugee population was 45 per cent; 70 per cent of the deaths were due to malaria; 25 per cent to typhoid, paratyphoid and dysentery and 5 per cent to other various diseases.[172]

In fact, after the destruction of Smyrna nobody on the international arena was ready to fight for the right of Greeks to exist in Asia Minor. In their bilateral treaty of January 1923 Turkey and Greece decided the mutual compulsory expulsion and termination of citizenship of their ethno-religious minorities. This was followed by the multilateral Lausanne Treaty of 24 July 1923, which in retrospective acknowledged the

---

168 Cf. "Turkish Cruelty Bared by Greeks," *The New York Times*, 16 June 1918, 42.

169 Vryonis, "Greek Labor Battalions in Asia Minor," 288.

170 "Expulsion of Christians," *The Times*, 3 November 1922, 13.

171 League of Nations, *Official Journal*, 4th Year, No. 8 (August 1923), Annex 534, "Greek Loan for Refugees," 1014.

172 League of Nations, *Greek Refugee Settlement* (Geneva: Publications of the League of Nations, 1926), 93.

[...] expulsion and liquidation of millions of people in the name of a dubious "national rebirth," conducted by a dominant elite at the expense of minorities. There was no longer any talk about the return of Armenian refugees and the establishment of justice. Furthermore the treaty contained a Greek-Turkish population exchange, which in its large scale was the first one of that kind, thus legalising an already established "ethnic cleansing." With regards to talks about Kurdish, Armenian and Greek minorities in his country Dr. Rıza Nur, the general secretary of the Turkish delegation to the conference, noted, that "these alien elements are a bother and microbes and that one has to cleanse the Kurds by means of an assimilation program from the alien language and race."[173]

On 13 August 1923 Mustafa Kemal delivered a long speech to the Grand National Assembly in which he said with relief and joy:

At last we uprooted the Greeks from Pontus.[174]

However, deportations did not end with the uprooting of Christian minorities and the foundation of the Turkish Republic (October 1923), but remained a well-established instrument in nationality and minority politics. The Deportation Law of 1934 was designed as an assimilatory tool "to disseminate the Turkish culture," in particular in areas determined by the Home Ministry for the settlement of non-Turkish or heterodox Muslim deportees, who subsequently had to be Turkified, as was the intention for "the areas in the West, in particular the Mediterranean and the Aegean Seas, the Marmara Sea and Thrace."[175] Other areas in the East and Southeast of Anatolia and/or the Armenian Highland such as Ağri (near Mount Ararat), Sason (Sassun in Armenian), Tunceli (previously Dersim), Van, Kars, the South of Diyarbakır, Bitlis, Bingöl and Muş were intended to be "depopulated" for "health, economic, cultural, military and security reasons." No further settlement would be allowed on these once Kurdish and/or Armenian/Christian areas. The result of continued massive deportation and dissemination of hundreds of thousands of people since the Balkan Wars was a truly uprooted population.

The Treaty of Lausanne permitted 90,000 Greeks of Turkish nationality to stay on in the previous Ottoman capital of Constantinople, officially renamed İstanbul after the Kemalist conquest in 1922. A further 60,000 İstan-

---

173 Rıza Nur, *Hayat ve Hatıratım* (İstanbul, 1992) 2: 260; quoted in Hans-Lukas Kieser, "Armeniermord und Diplomatie: Von der Lästigkeit vertuschter Geschichte," *Traverse: Zeitschrift für Geschichte* (2002) 2: 131-42:
http://www.hist.net/kieser/mak4/TraverseDebatte.html#fn7.

174 Quoted from a report by the French colonel Mougin, reproduced by Tsirkinidis, *"At last we uprooted them...,"* 300.

175 Quoted from Fikret Aslan, Kemal Bozay, et al., *Graue Wölfe heulen wieder: Türkische Faschisten und ihre Vernetzung in der BRD* [*Grey Wolves Howl Again: Turkish Fascists and Their Networks in the Federal Republic of Germany*] third ed. (Münster: Unrast, 2000), 38.

bul born Greeks of Hellenic nationality received the same right.[176] However, in 1946 the Social Democrat *Cumhuriyet Halk Partisi* (Republican People's Party, CHP), founded by Mustafa Kemal and in terms of personal and ideological continuity a direct successor of the *İttihat ve Terakki Cemiyeti*, issued a Minority Report (*Azınlıklar Raporu*), in which CHP set up the following goals, as far as the remaining Greeks in Turkey were concerned:

> The number of Greeks in Anatolia is insignificant. In future there will be no threat anywhere. Therefore our attention has to be focused on the Greeks [*Rumlar*] of Istanbul. Because of their closeness to Greece and because of their high percentage in the population effective precautions must be taken seriously. In this case the only thing that can be said is that Istanbul must be cleared from all Greeks until the 500th anniversary of its conquest.[177]

This report was written just two years after the notorious Capital Tax (*Varlık Vergisi*)[178] that was exclusively applied to non-Muslims (Jews and Christians). The Anti-Greek pogroms of 6-7 September 1955 became the next relevant step to purge İstanbul from its indigenous Greek population.

III. *Comparing Genocides*

Since the years of the World War, the destruction of the Ottoman Greeks was compared by contemporaries to that of the Armenians. In his memoirs (1919), the U.S. Ambassador Henry Morgenthau [Sr.] described the Armenians as main targets of the CUP policy of mono-ethnization, but by far not as its only victims:

> The Armenians are not the only subject people in Turkey which have suffered from this policy of making Turkey exclusively the country of the Turks. The story which I have told about the Armenians I could also tell with certain modifications about the Greeks and the Syrians. Indeed the Greeks were the first victims of this nationalizing idea.[179]

In a similar spirit Pailadzo Captanian, a surviving Armenian deportee from Samsun wrote in her memoirs that were published on the occasion of the Paris Peace Conference (1919) and hence did not include the experience of the years to follow:

---

176 Hans Lamer, *Wörterbuch der Antike*, 6th ed. (Stuttgart, 1963), 296-97.

177 Quoted from Faik Bulut, Kürt Sorununa Çözüm Arayışları, *Devlet ve Parti Raporları Yerli ve Yabancı Öneriler 1920-1997* [*Search for a Solution of the Kurdish Question*] (İstanbul: Ozan Yayıncılık, 1998), 178. Also Rıdvan Akar, "Bir Resmi Metinden Planlı Türkleştirme Dönemi" [Planned phase of Turkification, as given in an official document], *Birikim* Sayi 110 (1998): 68-75.

178 See Faik Ökte, *The Tragedy of the Turkish Capital Tax* (London: Croom Helm, 1987).

179 Henry Morgenthau, *Ambassador Morgenthau's Story* (New York: Doubleday Page, 1918), reprinted as Memorial Edition (New York: New Age Publishers, 1975), 323.

> Before the deportations the Turks conducted a general census. From the figures, produced by the commission in charge, one can gather that the approximately four and a half million Armenians, Greeks, Syriacs and Nestorians were to be included into a scheme of annihilation that aimed at the destruction of the Christian element in the East. As the largest Christian population group of the Ottoman Empire the Armenians, however, were persecuted and exterminated in the cruellest way. The rage of the murderers was directed against them.[180]

A more prominent Armenian survivor, the Tokat (Evdokia (Gr.)) born cleric and previous prelate of Kastamone, Grigoris Palakian (Balakian; ca. 1876–1934) commented in his memoirs, published 1922:

> There were [...] two ancient nations rivaling the Germans in Asia Minor, as true heirs to these historic lands: the Armenian and the Greek, the former in the interior provinces, the latter in the coastal cities. Hence the Germans found it necessary, if not by active assistance then at least by passive and silent compliance, to allow the Turks to do away with these two races, in particular with the Armenians, since the king of Greece was the son-in-law of the German emperor.[181]

Although deportations of Ottoman Greeks had begun in the aftermath of the Balkan Wars and months before the Ottoman Empire entered the Great War, it was the nationwide massive World War I massacres and death marches of the Ottoman Armenians that became the embodiment of atrocities and threat, which were measured after them. According to a survey-based estimate of the German embassy on 4 October 1916, two million out of an Armenian pre-war population of 2.5 million in the Ottoman Empire had been deported.[182] Of these, 1.5 million had perished during massacres and deportations, as the German Ambassador wrote to Chancellor von Bethmann Hollweg. There were certain specifics in the Armenian genocide that impressed and frightened the European and North American contemporaries:

---

180 Pailadzo Captanian, *Neunzehnhundertfünfzehn (1915). Der Völkermord an den Armeniern; eine Zeugin berichtet*, Meliné Pehlivanian, ed. (Leipzig: Kiepenheuer, 1993), 132. Captanian's memoirs were published first in French (Paris: M. Flinikowski, 1919), followed by the edition of the Armenian original (New York, 1922).

181 Balakian, *Armenian Golgotha*, 48.

182 Conducted by Beatrix Rohner, an Aleppo based German sister of the "German Charity Alliance for Christian Relief in the Orient" (*Deutscher Hilfsbund für Christliches Liebeswerk im Orient*). She counted all Armenian deportation convoys arriving at Aleppo, enquiring about the number of deportees at the time and when the convoys left their hometowns. In her care were 720 Armenians of an original number of 3,336 persons. The German embassy Constantinople projected this proportion, roughly 1 in 5, to the number of deportees that survived vs. those that were lost. Online edition of the document and the English translation:
http://www.armenocide.de/armenocide/armgende.nsf/WebStart_De?OpenFrameset;

a) The rapidity of destruction that began in March 1915 with the deportation of Armenians in the Adana province and largely completed in autumn 1916, after only twenty months. As W. Peter, a Swiss national serving as U.S. consular official in Samsun put it:

> Turkey may not be in the front ranks as regards organization and talent, but [...] when [...] a question of massacres, robbery etc. [...] it has shown well planned and very quick action. Only the Turk is capable of dispatching hundreds of thousands people to another world in a very short time.[183]

b) The sadistic modes of destruction. Henry Morgenthau wrote about this particular aspect:

> One day I was discussing these proceedings with a responsible Turkish official, who was describing the tortures inflicted. He made no secret of the fact that the Government had instigated them, and, like all Turks of the official classes, he enthusiastically approved this treatment of the detested race. This official told me that all these details were matters of nightly discussion at the headquarters of the Union and Progress Committee. Each new method of inflicting pain was hailed as a splendid discovery, and the regular attendants were constantly ransacking their brains in the effort to devise some new torment. He told me that they even delved into the records of the Spanish Inquisition and other historic institutions of torture and adopted all the suggestions found there. He did not tell me who carried off the prize in this gruesome competition, but common reputation through Armenia gave a preeminent infamy to Djevdet Bey,[184] the Vali of Van, whose activities in that section I have already described. All through this country Djevdet was generally known as the "horseshoer of Bashkale" for this connoisseur in torture had invented what was perhaps the masterpiece of all — that of nailing horseshoes to the feet of his Armenian victims.[185]

Atrocities — sexual humiliation, molestation and torture, repeated rape, mutilations and killings — against unarmed Armenian civilians and in particular children and pregnant women or newborn babies, occurred regularly during the deportations from the Eastern provinces, where the highest percentage of Armenians lived. In comparison, Greek Orthodox deportees seemed less harassed during the World War, again perhaps with the exception of East Anatolian areas such as Pontus. Nevertheless the contemporary eyewitnesses and commentators had no doubt that the deportations of Greeks in general were equally fatal.

---

183 Quoted from Mark Levene, "The experience of genocide: Armenia 1915–16 and Romania 1941–42," in Kieser and Schaller, eds., *Der Völkermord an den Armeniern und die Shoah* (Zürich: Chronos Verlag 2002), 438.

184 Cevdet in modern Turkish spelling; the brother-in-law of War Minister İsmail Enver and responsible for the destruction of the Assyrian population both in Ottoman occupied Iran (1914–15) and the Ottoman province of Van.

185 Morgenthau, *Ambassador Morgenthau's Story*, 307.

As early as February 1916 Kuckhoff, the German consul of Samsun, warned that the Orthodox Greeks might meet the same fate as the Armenians, should Greece abandon neutrality.[186] Many European and North American observers expressed similar fears. These fears materialized at the time of the Greco–Turkish War and beyond. As in the case of the Armenians, priests were frequently targets of the sadism both of their guards that led the deportation conveys, and of the Turkish/Muslim civilian population. In a highly brutalized society, even children would occasionally participate in the killing of entirely defenceless victims. Eyewitness and labor battalion conscript Elias Venezis recalled a group of thirty Greek Orthodox priests who were joined to his labor caravan; among them was an old man, who soon gave out and could no longer walk:

> The soldiers dragged him to the side of the road and they released him face down and then began to beat him with their rifle butts. He did not even give a groan, only his tongue began to lick the earth to see if it were dry or bitter.
>
> From the heights of Attalus, a few meters from where we were, the Turkish children were playing, and they ran downhill to the scene. The soldiers withdrew in order to continue our march and the children began at once to stone the body which was in its death throes. For some time we could hear the dull thud of the stones as they began to accumulate atop the priest.[187]

Christian women and even infant girls were another victim group.[188] "Rape was to become a daily exercise to the point that female prisoners were turned to prostitution[189] to sate the appetites of the Turkish soldiers as well

---

186 Fotiadis, *Der Genozid an den Pontosgriechen*, 104–105.

187 Quoted from Vryonis, "Greek Labor Battalions in Asia Minor," 282.

188 In his report from Aleppo, Martin Niepage quoted a German traveller, Mr Greif, who had seen the corpses of naked, raped Armenian women at the railway of Tel Abiad and Raz-ul-Ain, many of them with sticks driven into their anuses. Niepage, *Ein Wort an die berufenen Vertreter des deutschen Volkes*, 7. This detail was not included in the English translation of 1917.

189 On the distribution of women among officials and population see Viscount Bryce and Arnold Toynbee, *The Treatment of the Armenians in the Ottoman Empire, 1915–1916* (Beirut: G. Donigian & Sons, 1972), 225, 238, 347–48, 475; *United States Official Documents*, Ara Sarafian, ed., 5 vols. (Watertown, Mass: Armenian Review, 1993), 1: 7, 26, 31, 36, 49; 2: 27. On police violence, see Bryce, *The Treatment of the Armenians*, 426, 475. On forced prostitution, ibid., 91; Tessa Hofmann and Meliné Pehlivanian, "Malatia 1915: Carrefour des convois de déportés d'après le journal du missionaire allemand Hans Bauernfeind," in *L'extermination des déportés arméniens ottomans dans les camps de concentration de Syrie–Mésopotamie (1915–1916): La deuxième phase du genocide,* ed. Raymond H. Kévorkian (Paris: Revue d'histoire arménienne contemporaine, 1998), 2: 318–19. The original German text was published online under the title "'Der schlimmsten Orte einer…': Malatia 1915–1918:" http://www.aga-online.org/de/texte/malatia/index.php; Vahakn N. Dadrian, "Children as victims of genocide: the Armenian case," *Journal of Genocide Research* 5, no. 3 (September 2003): 421–27: http://www.crag.org.uk/articles/article11.html.

as local Turkish villagers. Many of them died from sexual abuse, while others became ill and shamed."[190] Venezis' memoirs contain the fate of two young Greek girls that the soldiers had taken

> [f]or their sexual satisfaction. Finally, the commander of the guards realized that the young fifteen-year-old girl had been so brutally and frequently raped that she could no longer walk. As she lay down on the ground from exhaustion, dying, the officer kicked her with his booted foot and she fell from a height of some 10 meters and rolled into the rapidly flowing river below. So he ordered the death caravan to march on until midnight. The young girl could no longer service his needs.[191]

In retrospective comparison, the genocide of Ottoman Armenians and Greeks reveals a magnitude of equal or similar patterns, which at the same time appear as general components of modern genocide: in preparatory phases, the massive arrest and destruction of the intellectual and political elite, the destruction of potential resistance by disarmament, forced labor of male adults and even adolescents in special "army" units; during the advanced phases of genocide local or regional massacre and the death marches of the remainders of the Christian population; abduction of infants and their compulsory Islamization and Turkification.

Forcibly transferring children of one group to another group (Art. II, e) "with intent to destroy, in whole or in part, a national, ethnical, racial or religious group, as such" is one of five criminal acts that are defined as genocide in the UN Convention on the Prevention and Punishment of the Crime of Genocide (1948). An early eyewitness account, published in *The New York Times* of 16 June 1918, focuses on the state organized dimension of assimilation policies, including compulsory child transfer during the World War:

> [...] The first step in the persecutions of the Greeks was the attack on the ecclesiastical, legal, and educational rights which had always been possessed within the Turkish Empire by the Greek ecclesiastical authorities and which had gone far toward mitigating the distress of the Turkish regime. The Turkish language was introduced into Greek schools; geography and history had to be taught in Turkish. Greek priests were arrested and imprisoned without warning or reason and without notification of the ecclesiastical authorities. Forcible conversions to Mohammedanism, long forbidden by law, began to appear again, particularly in the case of Greek girls carried off to Turkish harems without the usual right of intervention which the Greek Patriarch and Metropolitans had always possessed [...]
>
> One of the most diabolical methods was the institution of the so-called orphan asylums at Panormo.
>
> These orphan institutions have in appearance a charitable object, but if one considers that their inmates are Greek boys who became orphans because

[190] Vryonis, "Greek Labor Battalions in Asia Minor," 280.

[191] Ibid., 282–83.

> their parents were murdered, or who were snatched away from their mothers, or left in the streets for want of nourishment, (of which they were deprived by the Turks) and that these Greek children receive there a purely Turkish education, it will be at once seen that under the cloak of charity there lurks the 'child collecting' system instituted in the past by the Turkish conquerors and a new effort to revive the janissary system. The Greek boys were treated in this manner. What happens to the Greek girls? If we review the Consular reports about the persecutions from the year 1915 to 1917 we shall find hardly one of them which does not speak of forcible abductions and conversions to Mohammedanism. And it could not have been otherwise, since it is well known that this action, as has been stated above, was decided upon in June, 1915, in order to effect the Turkification of the Hellenic element. This plan was carried out methodically and in a diabolical manner, through the 'mixed settlements' of Greeks and Turks, always with a predominance of Mohammedan males and of Greek females in order to compel mixed marriages.[192]

In this article, I have quoted numerous reports on atrocities committed against the Greek Orthodox population. The difference between the genocide(s) against the two largest Christian ethnic groups of the Ottoman Empire, the Armenians and the Greeks, consists therefore less in quality, than in quantities such as the degree of applied methods and the speed, in which state crimes were carried out. In all, the difference was mainly that of a nation-wide, full-scale genocide and a cumulative destruction with shifting regional focus. At the end of the day, both approaches proved to be equally fatal for Ottoman Armenians and Greeks.

The Greek genocide was conducted over a period of a decade in three phases: before, during, and after World War I, and by the two subsequent regimes of the Committee of Union and Progress (*İttihat ve Terakki Cemiyeti*) and the rebel Kemalist government at Samsun and Ankara. During World War I, high-ranking Germans such as Generals Otto Liman von Sanders, head of the Imperial German Mission to the Ottoman Empire, and Fritz Bronsart von Schellendorf bore some co-responsibility of the deportation orders of Christians, despite their full awareness of the fatal consequences of such orders. German diplomats tried to save the Greek Orthodox population of Asia Minor from the atrocities and hardships of the Armenian deportations at least while Greece had remained neutral in the war. They did not achieve very much and had to admit that they were deceived by their Young Turk Allies. As in the Armenian case, German and Austrian diplomatic correspondence covers the main genocidal events and many details of the consequences of deportation orders during the World War.

---

192 "Turkish Cruelty Bared by Greeks," *The New York Times*, 16 June 1918, 42: http://www.greek-genocide.org/press/16061918.html.

In general, the speed and intensity of the genocide against Greek Orthodox Ottomans and sometimes also Hellenic subjects varied, depending on the foreign and domestic politics of Greece, whose neutrality during the World War to a certain extend prevented the full range destruction of the Ottoman Greeks, although this consideration never completely stopped the ongoing genocide. The year 1915, when the Armenian, Pontus and Aramaean-Assyrian genocide started, coincided with the *Ethnikos Dichasmos*, the "National Schism," between the parliament and the king of Greece. Domestic affairs of Greece started to overshadow the Greek relations with the Entente states again, when Prime Minister Venizelos and his pro-Entente government lost the elections in November 1920 and the pro-German King of the Hellenes Konstantinos I von Schleswig-Holstein-Sonderburg-Glücks-burg (1913–1917, 1920–1922) after a plebiscite returned on 19 December 1920, regaining political power. Encouraged by her Allies and the Paris Peace Conference, Greece had landed troops in Asia Minor in May 1919 in order to protect the Christian population of Ionia. But when the military occupation transformed into a war with the Kemalist irregulars — the Liberation Army according to Turkish narrative, the Allies were all too ready to distance themselves from their unreliable and, more important at the time, politically less relevant Greek partners. The Ottoman Greeks immediately felt the repercussions in the form of increased massacres and persecution. Their fate was a cumulative genocide, which was repeated until the terrified Greeks of Asia Minor either had perished or fled or were expelled in the asymmetric Lausanne "population exchange."

By cumulative genocide I mean specifically serialized destruction, conducted in phases and with subsequently changing "crime scenes" in various areas of East Thrace and Asia Minor[193] (as opposed to the coherent, nationwide genocide of the Armenians, carried out in 1915–16). The genocide against the Ottoman Greeks was slowed down or accelerated by external conditions, in particular the neutrality or hostility of Greece as the protector state of the Ottoman Greeks. While "cumulative genocide" is characterized by extreme, massive violence and full genocidal intent, its scope depends on considerations of opportunity etc. "Cumulative genocide" is not to be confused with "cumulative radicalization" of genocidal intents. Destructive intent, as noted by the German diplomacy, did exist as early as 1909 and entered its phase of radicalization already in 1910 to 1913.

A comparison of victim tolls illustrates that the cumulative genocide against the Ottoman Greeks was equally fatal as that of the Armenians. The popula-

---

[193] The term Asia Minor is used in this study not only for Ionia (west Anatolia today), but also for the entire peninsula, stretching from the Ionian coast to the Armenian highlands, including Pontus and Cappadocia.

tion of both ethnic groups numbered more than two million each, with a probable estimate of a pre-war population of 2.5 million Armenians and 2.5–3 million Greeks.

According to the survey-based estimate of 4 October 1916 by the German Embassy at Constantinople cited above, three fifths, or about 1.5 million, of the Armenian population in the Ottoman Empire had perished. The total figure of Ottoman Greeks, deported during World War I from Thrace and Asia Minor into the Ottoman interior or to Greece varies considerably. The Ecumenical Patriarchate gives the figure of 490,063; the Central Relief Commission for Deported Greeks (founded in November 1918)[194] gives 503,229; the American Committee for Armenian and Syrian Relief estimated "more than 500,000,"[195] while René Puaux (1919), based on statistics of the Ecumenical Patriarchate, gives the figure of 773,915 deportees in Thrace, Asia Minor and Pontus;[196] finally, the Greek Ministry of Foreign Affairs gives an estimate of 1.5 million deported Ottoman Greeks.[197] According to a telegram from Athens to the Greek Legation at Washington, as published by the American Committee for Armenian and Syrian Relief on 8 June 1918, half of the deportees perished "from torture and illness."[198] Metropolitan Germanos estimated the Pontus Greek casualties even as high as 80 or 90 percent of the deportees:

> Believe me that out of 160,000 people of Pontus deported, only a tenth and in some places a twentieth have survived. In a village, for example, that counted 100 inhabitants, five only will ever return; the others are dead. Rare, indeed are those happy villages where a tenth of the deported population has been saved.[199]

During the debates in the Ottoman parliament, which commenced on 4 November 1918, Greek and Armenian MPs referred to 550,000 Greeks and one million Armenians murdered, while Turkish parliamentarians declared these figures to be exaggerated, admitting overall losses of 500,000 to 600,000

---

194 Cf. René Puaux, *La déportation et rapatriement des Grecs en Turquie* (Paris: Éditions du Bulletin Hellenique, 1919), 18–19:
http://www.greek-genocide.org/docs/rene_puaux_ deportation.pdf.

195 Ibid.

196 Ibid., 8.

197 "Turkish Cruelty Bared by Greeks," *The New York Times*, 16 June 1918, 42.

198 "1,000,000 Greeks Killed?," *The New York Times*, 1 January 1918, 15:
http://www.hellenic-genocide.com/press/01011918.html;
"Atrocities: Turks slaughter Greeks, Sell Women to Slavery," Los Angeles Times, 9 June 1918, 11: http://www.hellenic-genocide.com/press/09061918.html.

199 "Turkish cruelty bared by Greeks," *The New York Times.*

victims.[200] At the occasion of the Paris Peace Conference, the Greek head of government mentioned in February 1919 one million Armenian and 300,000 Greek victims. In his report of 20 March 1922, G. W. Rendel writes about the World War I period during which "over 500,000 Greeks were deported, of whom comparatively few survived."[201]

There are at least two methodological problems when victim estimations of the period 1918–1923 are discussed:

1) At the time of the Paris Peace Conference, the representatives of Ottoman Christians had ambiguous interests. On the one hand they certainly wished to emphasize the quantitative extent of their losses. On the other hand they avoided high figures that might become an obstacle for their claims to repatriate refugees or to achieve a national homeland in parts of the Ottoman state territory; they felt obliged to prove that there were, for example, enough Armenians left to populate the territories, claimed by the Joint Armenian Delegation to the Paris Peace Conference.

2) There was and is no generally agreed definition of victims and losses. A narrow definition counted only the victims of massacres and other atrocities, excluding the victims of "white massacres," as Armenian and Greek contemporaries called the more indirect methods of annihilation, such as the death marches and famine, dehydration, exhaustion and epidemics, to which the victims were purposely exposed.[202] Such discrepancies in definition may explain the discrepancies in victim numbers, ranging in the case of the Armenians from 600,000 (House of Commons, October 1915), 800,000 (Mustafa Kemal to General Harbord, head of the American delegation, in

---

[200] Taner Akçam, *Armenien und der Völkermord: Die Istanbuler Prozesse und die türkische Nationalbewegung* [*Armenia and the Genocide: The Istanbul Trials and the Turkish National Movement*] (Hamburg: Hamburger Edition, 1996), 87.

[201] Rendel, "Memorandum," 1.

[202] The distinction between "white" and "red" massacres may transform into disputes on inclusiveness versa uniqueness of genocide, as Anson Rabinbach summarized: "In the American context there is a polarization between an 'exclusive' notion of 'uniqueness' represented by scholars like Steven Katz, who claims that 'the concept of genocide applies only when there is an actualized intent to physically destroy an entire group' (and refers only to the Holocaust) and 'inclusivists' like David E. Stannard and Ward Churchill, who include disease and depredation, as well as enslavement and massacre of native Americans, in the term. Churchill goes still further, charging that uniqueness is itself 'a form of denial.' These debates, whose ferocity comes in no small degree from the competitive victimhood inherent in American multicultural politics, have generated more confusion than clarity." Anson Rabinbach, "Raphael Lemkin's Concept of Genocide; Comment," *Internationale Politik* (Spring 2005): http://www.ip-global.org/archiv/2005/spring2005/raphael-lemkin---s-concept-of-genocide.html.

October 1919)[203] and 1.5 million (German embassy, based on polls among deportation convoys in Aleppo, 4 October 1916); the German estimate explicitly relates to victims of massacres as well as of indirect modes of killing.

Some recent Greek historians present a total of 1.4 or 1.5 million victims of massacres, deportation, compulsory labor, or flight under extreme weather conditions for the decade 1912–1922. This assumption is based on a figure of 1,221,000 refuges and expatriates from the Ottoman Empire that arrived in Greece according to the statistics of League of Nations refugee service, and subtracted from an estimated Ottoman Greek population of 2.7 million. Tsirkinidis explains the balance of 1,479,000 persons with roughly 353,000 victims in Pontus, 230,000 in East Thrace and 900,000 in Asia Minor. "Of those, 250,000 died in a few days in the city of Smyrna[204] and its vicinity, and a further 300,000 men died during mass executions after 8 September 1922."[205] However, given the numerous flaws of Ottoman statistics[206] and massive migration processes, combined with expulsion and flight during the last decade of Ottoman rule, it seems extremely difficult to establish genuinely hard figures both of the Greek pre-War population and its losses caused by genocide.

Much lower estimations are given by Rudolph Rummel, who calculated a mean value of 1,888,000 Armenians, Greeks, Nestorians and other Christians as victims of the CUP and 703,000 Greeks and Armenians, murdered

---

[203] Akçam, *Armenien und der Völkermord*, 124.

[204] The *London Daily Chronicle* of 18 September 1922, gives a figure of "at least 120,000" victims in Smyrna.

[205] Harry Tsirkinidis, "Der Völkermord an den Griechen Kleinasiens (1914–1923)," in Hofmann, *Verfolgung, Vertreibung und Vernichtung der Christen im Osmanischen Reich*, 173. Cf. the critical comment by N. Hlamides in this volume, footnote 120.

[206] The background for the divergence of estimates and the relatively low figures given by most other sources derives from the politicization of Ottoman figures as a result of Article 61 in the Berlin Treaty that stipulated administrative reforms in the six Ottoman provinces inhabited by Armenians. Besides the Ottoman interest in understating the figures of the Armenian, or any other Christian populations, there were inherent methodological flaws in the Ottoman census, such as, counting the male population only; the Christian avoidance to register the birth of male children as a result of exposure to a widespread tax and the risk of being drafted (after 1908); the merger of predominantly Muslim areas with Christian areas into administrative units for the purpose of marginalizing Christians (akin to gerrymandering). Cf. Gerayer Koutcharian, "Der Siedlungsraum der Armenier unter dem Einfluss der historisch-politischen Ereignisse seit dem Berliner Kongress 1878: eine politisch-geographische Analyse und Dokumentation" [The Armenian area of settlement under the impact of historical-political events since the Berlin Congress 1878: a political-geographical documentation], *Abhandlungen des geographischen Instituts/ Anthropogeographie* 43 (1989): 77–86.

by the Nationalist Turks (1919–1922), among them 264,000 Greek victims.[207]

Taking into account the flaws of Ottoman statistics, as well as difficulties with the accuracy of demographic estimates under complex conditions of war and massive flight, it does not seem unlikely that 3.5 million of the indigenous Christian population of the Ottoman Empire perished in the period 1912–1922, among them 1.5 million Armenians, 1.5 million Greeks and half a million Aramaic speaking Christians (Aramaeans, Assyrians, Chaldaeans and other denominations). Rummel, who has discussed the statistics of "Turkey's Genocidal Purges" at length on pages 78–88 of his *Statistics of Democide*, wrote in conclusion:

> Democide had preceded the Young Turks' rule and with their collapse at the end of World War I, the successor Nationalist government carried out its own democide against the Greeks and remaining or returning Armenians. From 1900 to 1923, various Turkish regimes killed from 3,500,000 to over 4,300,000 Armenians, Greeks, Nestorians, and other Christians.

Rummel's total of 3.5 to 4.3 million Ottoman Christian victims coincides with Mustafa Kemal's revelation that the CUP ordered murder of "millions of our Christian subjects" in an interview, published on 1 August 1926, in which the Turkish head of state argued for the justification of the execution of 60 leading CUP functionaries:

> These leftovers from the former Young Turkey Party, who should have been made to account for the lives of millions of our Christian subjects who were ruthlessly driven en masse from their homes and massacred, have been restive under the Republican rule. They have hitherto lived on plunder, robbery and bribery [...][208]

IV. *Legal Assessment*

In their joint declaration of 24 May 1915 Great Britain, France and Russia had designated the current massacres against the Armenians as "crimes against humanity and civilization," for which "the Allied governments announce publicly to the Sublime Porte that they will hold personally responsible [for] these crimes all members of the Ottoman government and those of their agents who are implicated in such massacres."[209] Under the existing International Law, the massacres of Ottoman Christian subjects appeared as

---

[207] Rudolph J. Rummel, *Statistics of Democide: Genocide and Mass Murder Since 1900* (Charlottesville: Center for National Security Law, University of Virginia, 1997), 83, 85.

[208] Emile Hilderbrand, "Kemal promises more hangings of political antagonists in Turkey" [Interview with Mustapha Kemal], *Los Angeles Examiner* (Sunday edition), 1 August 1926.

[209] See the full text in an online edition: http://www.armenian-genocide.org/ Affirmation. 160/current_category.7/affirmation_detail.html.

a "crime against humanity," as introduced into International Law by The Hague Convention, adopted at the First and Second Peace Conference at The Hague (1899 and 1907); the relevant passages for a prevention of genocide are in articles 22–28 and 46 in the *II Convention Regarding the Laws and Customs of War by Land* of 29 July 1899.

However, the Hague Conventions were, first of all, meant to civilize warfare between states. There was no appropriate legal tool for the punishment and prevention of massive violence caused by a state and directed against its own citizens until the United Nations adopted the Convention on the Prevention and Punishment of the Crime of Genocide on 9 December 1948 (entry into force, 12 January 1951). For the author of the Convention's draft, Raphael Lemkin (1900–1959), the genocide against the Ottoman Armenians and the massacre of Assyrians in Iraq 1933 formed prototypes of genocide. In his autobiography Lemkin told how during his studies of law at the university of Lemberg[210] (then Poland and Lwów in Polish, now L'viv in Ukraine) his attention was caught by the Armenian genocide after World War I and at the time of the Berlin court proceedings (1921) against the Armenian assassin of the one-time Ottoman Home Minister Talât[211] as well as of Binbud Khan Jivanshir, Ex-Home Minister of Azerbaijan (Constantinople 1921):[212]

> The truth came out only after the war. In Turkey, more than 1,200,000 Armenians were put to death for no other reason than they were Christians [...] After the end of the war, some 150 Turkish war criminals were arrested and interned by the British Government on the Island of Malta. The Armenians sent a delegation to the peace conference in Versailles. They were demanding justice. Then one day, the delegation read in the newspapers that all Turkish war criminals were released. I was shocked. A nation was killed and the guilty persons were set free. Why is a man punished when he kills another man?

---

210 Now the capital of West Ukraine, Lemberg/L'viv/Lwòw had been inhabited predominantly by Poles in the early twentieth century, being at the same time a traditionally multi-ethnic town with a German, Jewish (one third of a total population of 361,000 in 1918) and even an Armenian community. It had been under Austrian rule until 1918, when it became part of Poland after Ukrainian-Polish clashes. Polish soldiers, irregulars and civilians killed up to 1,100 Jews in revenge for their neutrality during the fight and stopped the killing only after the Jews of Lemberg pledged their loyalty to the Polish republic.

211 See Raphael Lemkin: "Outrage! Facing History and Ourselves:" http://www.facinghistory.org/campus/reslib.nsf/sub/onlinecampus/publications/readings/lemkin_outrage#5; Harut Sassounian, "Lemkin Discusses Armenian Genocide in Newly-Found 1949 CBS Interview," *The California Courier*, 8 December 2005.

212 Assassinated by Misak Torlakian outside the Pera Palace Hotel on 18 July 1921. Torlakian, an Armenian Ottoman subject, was tried on the charges of murder by the British military court, on 11 August 1921; Vartkes Yeghiayan, *The Trial of Misak Torlakian* (Glendale, California: Center for Armenian Remembrance, 2006).

> Why is the killing of a million a lesser crime than the killing of a single individual?
>
> [...] A bold plan was formulated in my mind. This consisted [of] obtaining the ratification by Turkey [of the proposed UN Convention on Genocide] among the first twenty founding nations. This would be an atonement for [the] genocide of the Armenians.[213]

As early as 1933 at the League of Nations Fifth International Conference for the Standardization of Penal Law, Lemkin tried to introduce an international convention against "the destruction of national, religious and racial groups." He proposed a ban on mass slaughter, but could not persuade the League to vote on it, with the Nazi delegation making a mockery of such a proposal. The presentation of his project at the League of Nations proved to be detrimental to his career as lead prosecutor, and being Jewish in Poland added to his career decline. Shortly after the Madrid meeting, he was admonished by the Polish Foreign Minister and under pressure, resigned his position in 1934, going into private practice until 1939.[214]

In 1946, Lemkin proposed a law against genocide to the United Nations, which was adopted on 9 December 1948, with only few changes. Each of the five crimes,[215] qualified as genocide in the UN convention, are based on Lemkin's empirical knowledge about the massive state crimes and killings of millions of people during both World Wars, in particular the annihilation of the Armenians and of the European Jewry. Lemkin defined genocide as,

> [t]he systematic destruction of whole national, racial or religious groups. The sort of thing Hitler did to the Jews and the Turks did to the Armenians.

Although Lemkin saw the Jews as main targets of the Nazi annihilation policy in Europe, he did not separate their fate completely from that of his homeland Poland and believed that the Nazi elite intended the destruction of the Poles as well:

> Lemkin understood the "biological" dimension of the destruction of Jews and emphasised at the same time and in a paradox way that the Jewish catastrophe had just started earlier and reached a larger extent than the intended annihilation of "Slavic" peoples. In this aspect the National Socialist genocide

---

213 *Encyclopaedia of Genocide*, Israel W. Charny, ed. (Santa Barbara: ABC–Clio, 1999), 79.

214 Tanya Elder, "Guide to the Raphael Lemkin (1900–1959) Collection," undated, [1763]–2002, (bulk 1941–1951). 2003, P–154:
http://www.cjh.org/academic/findingaids/ajhs/nhprc/Lemkin02-03.html.

215 Cf. Article II: "In the present Convention, genocide means any of the following acts committed with intent to destroy, in whole or in part, a national, ethnical, racial or religious group, as such: (a) Killing members of the group; (b) Causing serious bodily or mental harm to members of the group; (c) Deliberately inflicting on the group conditions of life calculated to bring about its physical destruction in whole or in part; (d) Imposing measures intended to prevent births within the group; (e) Forcibly transferring children of the group to another group."

> corresponded with the crimes, committed previously against ethnic minorities, such as the Kazakh of Central Asia, the Armenians in Turkey or the expulsion of the Greek Orthodox population in Asia Minor by the Turks in 1922.[216]

Newspaper reports of the years 1946 and 1947 on the debate of international penalization of genocide indicate that Lemkin was, in a similar way, well aware of Greek co-victims in the Armenian genocide during World War I; at lectures titled "Armenian and Greek massacres by Turkey" he gave these as examples of state crimes that could have been prevented with appropriate laws.[217]

The reasons for why this knowledge about the genocide of the Greeks, the Armenians' co-victims, was forgotten in later years are manifold and are worthy of research on their own right.

---

[216] Anson Rabinbach, "Lemkins Schöpfung: Wie Völkermord zum juristischen und politischen Begriff wurde; Die Entstehung der Völkermordkonvention" [Lemkin's creation: How genocide became a legal and political term; the emergence of the Genocide convention], *Internationale Politik: The Journal of the German Council on Foreign Relations–Global edition* (February 2005): 27.

[217] "Genocide under the Law of Nations," *The New York Times*, 5 January 1947; "Genocide," *The New York Times*, 26 August 1946.

ANNEX 1

Table: A Comparison of the Christian Genocides in the Ottoman Empire

Key elements of genocide	Armenians	Syriacs	Greeks
Duration	Spring 1915–autumn 1916.	October 1914–March 1918.	1912/13 - 1922/23 (cumulative genocide).
Location	Nationwide (Exceptions: Constantinople/İstanbul, Adrianople/Edirne, Smyrna/İzmir).	1) Nationwide (Ottoman provinces Diyarbakır and Van/Hakkâri). 2) NW Iran (province Azerbaijan, districts Urmia, Khoi, Salmas).	1) 1912/13: East Thrace. 2) 1913–15: Ionia (West Anatolia), Marmara Coast. 3) 1916–17: Pontus. 4) 1919–1922: Nationwide.
Means of annihilation	Destruction of elite; compulsory labor; deportation; massacres.	Destruction of elite; compulsory labor; deportation; massacres (in a particular high degree).	Destruction of elite; compulsory labor; deportation; massacres.
Deportation ordered by	Home Minister (Talât, May 1915).	"Spill over" effect of Armenian deportations, in particular in Diyarbakır province. Responsibilities: a) In Diyarbakır province 1915: Governor Reşid; in Van province 1915: Cevdet Bey; central government. b) In Iran 1914/15, 1918: Ottoman military authorities; Cevdet Bey.	Home Minister (Talât; May 1914, Ionia), War Minister (İsmail Enver; Dec 1916); German commander Liman von Sanders (April 1917, Ayvalık/Ionia); regional Kemalist authorities (Pontus, June 1922); Kemalist authorities (Smyrna, September 1922).
Perpetrators	Gendarmes; paramilitaries; parts of Muslim population; at places regular army involved.	Regular army; paramilitaries (high involvement of Kurdish irregulars); parts of Muslim population (high involvement of tribal Kurds).	Ottoman regular army and Muslim paramilitaries; 1919–1922: paramilitary "liberation units;" parts of Muslim population.
Name	*Mets yerern* (great crime).	*Sayfo* (sword, relating to massacres and attempted self defence 1915).	*Sphagi* (massacre) and *xerizomos* (uprooting); *Megale Katastrophe* (great catastrophe).
Number killed	1.5 million (German embassy, October 1916).	365,000 (= 90,000 Syriac Orthodox + 275,000 Assyrians and Chaldaeans); every 5th or 6th Assyrian systematically massacred during occupation of Iran.	550,000 (until 1918); in all, over one million.

ANNEX 2

Danish Consul Alfred Van der Zee til [to] Carl Ellis Wandel, 19/6 1914.

Rigsarkivet [the Danish National Archives], Udenrigsministeriets Arkiver [the Archives of the Foreign Ministry] (UM), 2-0355, "Konstantinopel/ Istanbul, diplomatisk repræsentation," "Noter og indberetninger om den politiske udvikling, 1914–1922," "Verdenskrigen. Rapporter fra Smyrna. Nov. 1914–Marts 1916."

About three months ago the Governor General of Smyrna, acting as I understand on instructions from the Ministry made an inspection in the small towns situated at the coast of this province. It would appear that in the course of this *tournée administrative* he gave semi official orders to the sub governors to force the Greek population resident therein to evacuate these towns. No order of expulsion was decreed but the Turkish officials were to make use of the tortuous and vexatious measures so well-known to them.

The like instructions were, I understand, given by the Governors of the other maritime provinces. The reason for this measure was, from what I gather, the belief that so long as the Greeks were in possession of Chios & Mytilene, the presence of a kindred population on the opposite littoral constituted a source of danger to the Empire. As a result of these instructions a severe boycott was shortly after proclaimed and measures, many and different, were adopted to compel this population out to quit their hearths and homes.

As the rayah Greeks clung however to their fields it was decided to take more active steps. The immigration of Thracian & Macedonian refugees gave the local authorities the opportunity for more harassing measures.

A proclamation was issued that in order to house the mohadjirs, one room out of every three in the dwellings belonging to the rayah Greeks was to be given to them: further the local authorities were to see to the execution of this order.

The results are easily comprehensible. Unable to live with their guests, the Greek rayah began to emigrate, selling their property for what they could get for it and seeking new lands for their exertions, but the process was naturally a slow one as in a land where the peasant has little money it was naturally difficult to realise property from one day to another.

The local authorities then determined to activate matters and more imperious orders were sent from head quarters.

As a direct consequence of these orders trouble broke out at Adramyt, on the coast just opposite the northern part of Mytilene.

After open hints that it would be advisable for them to leave the place, menaces that they would be done to death were resorted to, and finally the threats began to take shape in the murder of villagers returning from their fields and the waylaying of townsmen. A reign of terror was instituted and the panic-stricken Greeks fled as fast as they could to the neighbouring island of Mytilene.

Soon the movement spread to Kemer, Kiliseköy, Kinick, Pergamos and Soma. Armed bands of *bashibozuks* attacked the people residing therein, lifted their cattle, drove them from their farms and took forcible possession thereof.

The details of what took place harrowing, women were seduced, girls were ravished, some of them dying from the ill-treatment received, children at the breast were shot or cut down with their mothers.

Not content with driving the rayahs out, these blood-thirsty emissaries of a "so called Constitutional Government" then attacked the property of foreigners driving out their employees lifting their cattle and looting their farms. In answer to complaints made to the authorities the reply was: "Let foreigners go and buy farms in their own lands!"

From Pergamos the bands advanced to Dikilli driving out the people and looting the town, then, dividing forces, some bands took the direction of Menemen and others went south towards Phocea.

In the Menemen district the villages of Ali-Agha and Gerenköy were partly sacked after having been looted, the affrighted inhabitants fleeing in all directions.

At Serenköy, a village in the same district, the people determined to resist and a fierce fight took place lasting from 8 ½ at night till about one o'clock in the morning, when the villagers' ammunition having failed, a hand to hand struggle was sternly fought in which most of the defenders, who were by far the minority, fell, after having heroically fought for their lives and for the honour of their women.

The few survivors who escaped sought refuge in Menemen which the bands then threatened, but as this town is one of some 20,000 inhabitants they dared not openly attack it, but satisfied themselves with shooting the inhabitants who strayed out of its near neighbourhood.

The inhabitants thereupon decided to leave it but before doing so & perhaps hoping against hope, they determined to send away their wives and daughters.

On the 18th Inst. some 700 women and about 300 to 400 children came to the railway station with the intention of taking train for Smyrna but by orders of Government no tickets would be given them & and the train passed without stopping.

[...]

A few miles further down at the village of Ouloujak the bashibozouks drove away all the cattle belonging to Greeks and ordered inhabitants, on threat of death, to leave the place. The unfortunate villagers were only too ready to comply with these arbitrary orders, but once again, by order of the Vali, the stationmaster was forbidden to deliver tickets & trains passed without stopping.

Afraid to return they lay huddled for two days and nights in the neighbourhood of the station, vainly calling to the passengers in the through trains to get assistance sent them.

The Persecutions in Thrace and Ionia in 1914

and the First Attempt at an Exchange of Minorities between Greece and Turkey[1]

JOHN MOURELOS

IN THE AFTERMATH OF THE 1912–1913 WARS, the situation in the Balkans and the Eastern Mediterranean was particularly fragile: the *status quo* in the area was profoundly upset by the collapse of the European part of the Ottoman Empire, and both winners and losers of the wars were forming new alliances while the Great Powers were engaged in a common effort to prevent the upheaval from spreading to Europe.[2] While these new alignments were changing the political identity of the Balkans, migrations and massive expulsions of large populations were affecting the ethnic composition of the peninsula. It is estimated that in the years 1912–1914 about 890,000 people of various ethnicities crossed the borders of the Balkan countries, including those of the Ottoman Empire.[3]

These migrations were prompted by various events: a) as soon as the hostilities had started, civilian populations spontaneously fled the battlefields and contested areas; b) the new political map of the area drawn by the treaties of London and Bucharest prompted ethnic minorities to migrate to their countries of origin or protector states; c) finally, minorities were forcefully expelled for political and strategic reasons at the end of 1913 and during

[1] This paper is a slightly revised version of the paper entitled "The 1914 Persecutions and the First Attempt at an Exchange of Minorities between Greece and Turkey," *Balkan Studies* 26, no. 2 (1985): 389–413. It is mainly based on documents at the Archives of the Greek Ministry, quoted as *A.Y.E.* (Αρχείον Υπουργείου Εξωτερικών — Archives of the [Greek] Foreign Ministry). *A.Y.E./K.Y.* denotes the records of the Central Service in Athens and *A.Y.E./P.K.* refers to the records of the Greek Legation in Constantinople. Translations of quotations, in the French language in the original version of the paper, are by Vasileios Meichanetsidis.

[2] E. C. Helmreich, *The Diplomacy of the Balkan Wars, 1912–1913* (New York: Russell and Russell, 1969 [third edition]), *passim*; Douglas Dakin, "The Diplomacy of the Great Powers and the Balkan States, 1908–1914," *Balkan Studies* 3, no. 2 (1962): 327–374; George B. Leon, *Greece and the Great Powers, 1914–1917* (Thessalonica: Institute for Balkan Studies, 1974), 11–15.

[3] Stephen P. Ladas, *The Exchange of Minorities: Bulgaria, Greece and Turkey* (New York: Macmillan, 1932), 15–16.

1914. It is to this kind of deportation that the phenomenon of population exchange is related.[4]

The authority of the idea of population exchange belongs undoubtedly to the Sublime Porte. The doctrine of Ottomanization (Turkification or Islamization) of the Empire[5] dates back to the years of Abdülhamit II and the ancient regime, the Armenian massacres of 1894–96 being a clear example of this.[6] The idea was later seized upon by the Young Turks and included in their program for the modernization of the Empire.[7]

The successive defeats of 1911 and 1912–1913 and the almost total loss of the Ottoman territories in North Africa and Europe had a direct impact on the ideology of the Young Turks: the alteration and change of the ethnic composition of the Empire to achieve a clear numerical predominance of the Turkish population, resulting in the concept of ethnic homogenization that was achieved by policies of population exchange, but also forced assimilation and physical annihilation. The latter occurred in Anatolia and Northern Mesopotamia during World War I, the first in Europe even before that period, where the Empire's losses caused strong nationalist tendencies, not least among the Muslims who would conceptualize or carry out the program of ethnic homogenization in the remaining parts of the Empire. To be sure, the three components of the movement's ideology (Ottomanism, Islamism,[8] Nationalism) remained the same but the emphasis was primarily shifted toward the Asian heartland of the Empire, but also the areas around Con-

---

[4] Ladas, *The Exchange of Minorities,* 15–16.

[5] On the Ottomanization of the Christian minorities see Roderick Davison, "Turkish Attitudes Concerning Christian-Muslim Equality in the Nineteenth Century," *The American Historical Review* 54 (1954): 844–64; Vahakn N. Dadrian, *The History of the Armenian Genocide: Ethnic Conflict from the Balkans to Anatolia to the Caucasus* (Providence and Oxford: Berghahn Books, 1997), 113–84; Lord Kinross, *The Ottoman Centuries: The Rise and Fall of the Turkish Empire* (New York: William Morrow, 1979), 559–60.

[6] On the Armenian massacres see Dadrian, *The History of the Armenian Genocide*, 155, 182, 225, 233 n.44. On the Armenian massacres and Greek attitudes, see Ioannis K. Hassiotis, "The Greeks and the Armenian Massacres (1890–1896)," *Neo-Hellenika* 4 (1981): 69–109.

[7] Doğu Ergil, "A Reassessment: The Young Turks, their Politics and anti-Colonial Struggle," *Balkan Studies* 16, no. 2 (1975): 34–35, 40–41, 59–65.

[8] On the religious dimension of the movement of the Young Turks (Islamism) see A. Servier, *Islam and the Psychology of the Musulman*, A. S. Moss-Blundell, trans. (London, Chapman & Hall, 1924), 241–42; Vahakn N. Dadrian, "The Armenian Question and the Wartime Fate of the Armenians as Documented by the Officials of the Ottoman Empire's World War I Allies: Germany and Austria-Hungary," *International Journal of Middle Eastern Studies* 32 (2002): 59–85, esp. 61–62, with specific primary source documentation 79 n. 15; Dadrian, *The History of the Armenian Genocide*, 113–84; Roderick Davison, "The Armenian Crisis, 1912–1914," *The American Historical Review* 53 (1948): 482–83.

stantinople, namely Thrace and the Sea of Marmara. The Young Turks' original ideals concerning the multinational character of the Ottoman Empire (Ottomanism) and the federative role of the parliament, and their plans to establish a liberal constitution with room for political parties of differing persuasions, were pushed aside by the emergence of an implacable nationalism.[9]

The Congress of the Committee of Union and Progress (CUP) held in Constantinople in September 1913 affirmed the new ideological position of the Young Turks,[10] and the general elections held in early 1914, in which the CUP was the only participating political party, registered a shrinking of Christian representation in the Ottoman Parliament.[11] This transformation of attitude toward the various ethnic minorities, once viewed as an integral part of the Turkish economy and now seen as a threat to the survival of Turkish national identity, contributed to the adoption of a policy of ethnic purification and cleansing which was to be implemented in principle by an exchange of populations, but not always and exclusively so.

Such an exchange was first carried out at the end of 1913 and involved the Ottoman Empire and Bulgaria. The two defeated parties of the Balkan Wars concluded a convention to that effect and set up a mixed commission charged with carrying out the exchange of populations and properties. In effect, the convention only recognized a *de facto* situation, created by the wars, since the populations involved had already fled or been expulsed. Furthermore, the exchange concerned only a limited zone whose width covered fifteen kilometers on either side of the border.[12]

---

[9] Feroz Ahmad, *The Young Turks: The Committee of Union and Progress in Turkish Politics, 1908–1914* (Oxford: Clarendon Press, 1969), 152–55; Alexis Alexandris, *The Greek Minority of Istanbul and Greek–Turkish Relations 1918–1974* (Athens: Centre for Asia Minor Studies, 1983), 42–43; Ergil, "A Reassessment," 40–48.

[10] Ahmad, *Young Turks*, 140–42.

[11] Ibid., 143, 155; Katerina Boura, "General elections in the Ottoman Empire: The Greek members of Parliament, 1908–1918," (in Greek), *Δελτίο Κέντρου Μικρασιατικών Σπουδών* [*Bulletin of the Centre for Asia Minor Studies*] 4, (1983): 80–81.

[12] Ladas, *The Exchange of Minorities*, 18–20. Dimitri Pentzopoulos, *The Balkan Exchange of Minorities and its Impact upon Greece* (Paris and The Hague: Mouton, 1962), 54–55. The Mixed Bulgarian–Turkish Commission drew up a list of 48,570 Muslims living in Bulgaria and 46,764 Bulgarians living in Ottoman Thrace, whose properties were to be exchanged. The work of the Mixed Commission started in June 1914 and was discontinued in October of that year. The appraisal and liquidation of the properties of these persons was never carried out. The exercise was, nevertheless, highly important, since it was the first attempt to condone, through official negotiations, an ethnic transfer caused by the upheaval of war.

The case with Greece was different, due to the peculiar state of Greek-Turkish relations. The uncertainty concerning sovereignty over the Aegean islands, a problem that under the terms of the Treaty of London was to be solved by the Great Powers, persisted even after the conclusion of the Hellenic-Ottoman Convention of Athens (1/14 November 1913), straining the relations between the two governments and causing a naval arms race in the spring of 1914. An outright military confrontation was averted only through the intervention of the Great Powers, mainly that of Germany.[13]

In this charged atmosphere, and while Greece and Turkey were on the brink of war, a wave of persecution broke out against the Greeks in Eastern Thrace, laying waste Greek villages in the area.[14] The persecution usually followed this pattern: various forms of psychological and physical intimidation,[15] including obstruction of agricultural activities, raids, arsons, killings, forced evacuation of whole villages within a few hours, forced expatriation, massacres, deportations into the Asian heartland and obligatory conscription in labor battalions (*Amele Taburları*). Furthermore, refugees were attacked and robbed on their way to the boats that were to take them to Kavala and to Thessalonica.[16] In the period from January 1914 to July 1915, 15,572 families numbering 60,926 people were thus forced to flee Eastern Thrace.[17] To the repeated demarches of the Greek Government, the Sublime

---

[13] A. F. Frangulis, *La Grèce et la crise mondiale* (Paris: F. Alcan, 1926), I: 109–10; Helmreich, *The Diplomacy of the Balkan Wars,* 414–15, 431–42; Leon, *Greece and the Great Powers,* 12–15; Y. Mourelos, *Les rapports greco-turcs de 1908 a 1923* (Paris, 1975), 68–72.

[14] *A.Y.E./K.Y./1915/A 21 z:* "Memorandum on the general statistics of refugees in Macedonia," 1–2. The first wave of Greek refugees arriving in Macedonia did not originate in Eastern Thrace but in the regions that had been ceded to Bulgaria in conformity with the Treaty of Bucharest, and evacuated by the Hellenic Army at the end of 1913. The emigration of the Greek inhabitants of those regions (31,112 persons as of December 1914) amounted to a refugee flight in face of the arrival of the Bulgarian administration. On the persecutions of the Greek population in Eastern Thrace see A. Papadopoulos, *Persecutions of the Greeks in Turkey Before the European War,* Caroll N. Brown, trans. (New York 1919); T. Kiakidis, "History of Samakovo and the neighbouring Greek Communities," [in Greek] in *Θρακικά* 24 (1962): 280–90; Konstantinos A. Vakalopoulos, *Persecutions and Genocide of Thracian Hellenism: The First Uprooting (1908–1917)* [in Greek] (Thessalonica: Herodotos, 1998); Konstantinos A. Vakalopoulos, "Vertreibung und Genozid an den Griechen Ost-Thrakiens (1908–1922)" [Expulsion and genocide of the Greeks of Eastern Thrace, 1908–1922], in *Verfolgung, Vertreibung und Vernichtung der Christen im Osmanischen Reich 1912–1922* [*Persecution, Expulsion and Annihilation of the Christians in the Ottoman Empire 1912–1922*], Tessa Hofmann, ed. (Münster: Lit-Verlag, 2004).

[15] The forms of intimidation basically were implemented by paramilitary units, called "The Special Organization." On the "Special Organization" see also Erik J. Zürcher, *Turkey: A Modern History* (London and New York: I. B. Tauris, 2003), 114–15, 121.

[16] *A.Y.E./K.Y./1915/A 21 z:* "Memorandum," Table A.

[17] *A.Y.E./K.Y./1915/A 21 z:* "Memorandum," 2.

Porte replied to the effect that it was indeed Greece that fostered among the inhabitants of Eastern Thrace the impulse to emigrate.[18] At the same time the Porte deliberately downplayed the magnitude of the expulsions, presenting them as natural, if uncontrollable, outbursts of retaliation for the expulsions of Muslims from the newly acquired Greek provinces (Macedonia and Epirus).[19] It is not accidental that those who carried out the persecution of the Eastern Thrace Greeks were Muslim refugees along with local CUP chapters.[20]

This policy of persecution however was not outside the control of the Ottoman authorities or merely reactive. Rather, it deliberately aimed at the transformation of Eastern Thrace into a purely Muslim province, which the Sublime Porte considered necessary for the protection of Constantinople. In this the Porte had the support of Germany, especially after the arrival at the Ottoman capital of the military mission under the General Liman von Sanders at the end of 1913.[21] In the spring of 1914, Germany undertook to mediate the Greek–Turkish differences and to bring together the two rivals under her aegis, but her initiative was frustrated by the Ottoman Government's refusal to contemplate any concessions concerning the question of the Aegean islands.[22]

---

[18] *A.Y.E/K.Y./1914/A 21 e:* Panas to Streit, Report No. 5,480, 26 February/11 March 1914, No. 7,018, 11/24 March 1914, No 9,272–9,274, 1/14 April 1914, No 1,595, 3/16 April 1914, No. 1,609, 4/17 April 1914, No. 1,895, 17/30 April 1914, No. 1,976, 29 April/12 May 1914. Ğalib Kemal to Streit, Note 12/25 March 1914. *A.Y.E/K.Y./1914/St 3:* Capsambelis to Panas, No. 1,328, 13/26 April 1914. Panas to Streit, No. 1,900 17/30 April 1914.

[19] On a Greek response to the Turkish allegations of ill-treatment of Muslims in the Greek provinces of Macedonia see *Letters on the Expulsion of Greeks in Asia Minor, and in Reply to Allegations of Ill-treatment Inflicted on Turks in Greek Macedonia* (London: Anglo-Hellenic League, 1914).

[20] A. Pallis, "Ethnic Emigrations in the Balkans and Persecutions of Greeks (1912–1914)," [in Greek] *Δελτίο Κέντρου Μικρασιατικών Σπουδών* [*Bulletin of the Center for Asia Minor Studies*] 1 (1977): 86. During the period 1912–1920, 143,189 Muslims left Greece. Problems between the Muslims of Macedonia and the Greek administration arose immediately after the signature of the Treaty of Bucharest, when the first complaints were registered concerning abuse of power, see *Report of the International Commission to Inquire into the Causes and Conduct of the Balkan Wars* (Washington D.C.: Carnegie Endowment for International Peace, 1914), 201.

[21] *A.Y.E./K.Y./1914/A 21 e:* Dragoumis to Streit, No. 643, 7/20 April 1914; Papadopoulos, *Persecutions of the Greeks in Turkey*, pp. VII–XI. Typical of the German attitude was the statement of the German Foreign Secretary, Gottlieb von Jagow, to the Greek chargé d'affaires in Berlin, Ion Dragoumis, that the underlying cause for the persecutions in Eastern Thrace was the fact that "every Greek in Turkey is an apostle of Panhellenism." On the Liman von Sanders mission, see Harry Howard, *The Partition of Turkey (1913–1923)* (New York: Howard Fertig, 1966) 39–47.

[22] Frangulis, *La Grèce et la crise mondiale,* I: 110–11; Leon, *Greece and the Great Powers,* 13; Mourelos, *Les rapports greco-turcs,* 71.

The Turkish intransigence was coupled, in early May, by a new wave of violent persecutions whose victims were the Greek inhabitants of the western coast of Asia Minor.[23] In a general climate of fanaticism, cultivated by the press, a new series of arrests and expulsions were launched, without the Greek consulates and vice consulates being officially notified.[24] The situation was closely followed by the Greek side. On 3/16 May, the Greek Minister at Constantinople, Demetrios Panas, cabled the following to Foreign Minister George Streit:

> Even in the improbable case that the question of the islands would have been resolved in a manner giving satisfaction to Turkey, she would never depart from the plan she conceived, that of annihilating the Greek element in Turkey.[25]

On 4/17 May, the Greek Government denounced to the European capitals the high-handedness of these recent Turkish actions. However, the Greek legation at Constantinople acted in a very restrained manner for fear of further jeopardizing Greek interests within the Ottoman Empire.[26] It even went so far as to propose to the Sublime Porte that a Greek-Turkish commission be dispatched to Eastern Thrace and to Macedonia in order to ascertain in place the behavior of the respective Ottoman and Greek authorities.[27] The Turks rejected the proposal and chose instead to send the minister of the interior, Talât Paşa, on a tour of Thrace, at the end of which it was announced that all appropriate measures had been taken to put an end to the persecutions.[28]

On 7/20 May the Ottoman ambassador to Athens, Ğalib Kemal Bey, met with Prime Minister Eleutherios Venizelos and proposed — for the first time —

---

23 For further information see Henry Morgenthau, *Ambassador Morgenthau's Story* (Detroit: Wayne State University Press, 2003 [reprint the 1918 edition]), 222–23; Taner Akçam, *From Empire to Republic: Turkish Nationalism and the Armenian Genocide* (London and New York: Zed Books, 2004), 147; Matthias Bjørnlund, "The 1914 Cleansing of Aegean Greeks as a Case of Violent Turkification," *Journal of Genocide Research* 10, no. 1 (March, 2008): 41–57.

24 *A.Y.E./K.Y./1914/A 21 e:* Panas to Streit, No. 2,287, 3/16 May 1914.

25 *A.Y.E/K.Y./1914/A 21 e:* Panas to Streit, No. 2,310, 3/16 May 1914. ("... Même dans le cas improbable où question des îles aurait été résolue d'une façon donnant satisfaction à la Turquie, celle-ci ne se départirait jamais du plan qu'elle a conçu de l'anéantissement de l'element Grec en Turquie ..."

26 *A.Y.E./K.Y./1914/A 21 e:* Panas to Streit, No. 2,287, 3/16 May 1914. Streit to Greek Legations in Paris, London, Berlin, Vienna, Petersburg, Rome, No. 12,831, 4/17 May 1914.

27 The Sublime Porte had explained away the new outburst of persecutions in Asia Minor as a natural consequence of what it claimed to be maltreatment of the Macedonia Muslims by the Greek administration.

28 *A.Y.E./K.Y./1914/A 21 e:* Panas to Streit, No. 1,895, 17/30 April 1914. Dragoumis to Streit, No. 830, 5/18 May 1914.

the exchange of the Greek inhabitants of the Aydın Vilayet with the Muslims of Macedonia and Epirus, claiming that his proposal was part of a more general effort to diffuse the crisis in the relations between the two countries. On 8/21 May, he submitted his proposal in writing, and he received a positive reply the next day. Venizelos' letter of 9/22 May[29] stated as necessary preconditions for carrying out the proposed exchange that it should be done on a voluntary basis, that it should also include the Greeks of Eastern Thrace, and that a mixed Greek–Turkish commission should arrange for the exchange of the properties of the populations involved.[30]

On 10/23 May, the Greek foreign ministry further clarified the Greek position in a *note verbale* to the Imperial Ottoman legation: a) the Greek inhabitants of Eastern Thrace and of the Aydın Vilayet would be exchanged simultaneously with the Muslim inhabitants of Macedonia and Epirus after their desire to emigrate had been ascertained; b) the exchange would be carried out with the full agreement, and under the protection, of the two governments; c) a mixed commission comprised of four members would be entrusted with the duty of assessing the value of the movable and immovable properties of the populations to be exchanged and of supervising the exchange. Furthermore it would determine the modalities of the exchange, concerning in particular the time periods within which the emigrants would depart as well as the regions affected by this measure; d) the commission would establish its headquarters in Smyrna (İzmir (Tur.)) or Thessalonica and would have the right to create any necessary sub-commissions; e) in addition to the duties mentioned above, the commission would also undertake to assess the value of properties of those Greeks and Muslims who had already left their homes.

The Greek Government pointed out orally that the conclusion and the implementation of the agreement was conditional upon the termination of the forced emigration of Greeks in Asia Minor and in Thrace.[31] Foreign Minister Streit justified his government's agreement to an arrangement that meant, in effect, the uprooting of peaceful peasants who were now suffering the direct consequences of the Balkan Wars without having been directly involved in them, in the following terms:

> The need, on the one hand, to cease the forced emigration in Thrace and in Asia Minor, where the systematic persecution of the Greek element is known to you, and, on the other hand, the preoccupation to save in the largest possible measure these populations which abandon their homes to seek refuge in Greece by canalising this movement and by linking it usefully with the voluntary emigration of the Muslims of Macedonia at the expense of an exchange of

---

[29] See Appendix.

[30] Frangulis, *La Grèce et la crise mondiale*, I: 111–12

[31] *A.Y.E./K.Y./1914/A 21:* Greek Foreign Ministry to Imperial Ottoman Legation, *note verbale*, 10/23 May 1914.

the abandoned properties from both parts, this is the object pursued by the royal government at the moment when it accepted the proposal made by Turkey.[32]

On 14/27 May, the Ottoman Government announced its willingness to extend the measure to include the inhabitants of Eastern Thrace. It added, however, that it deemed it a matter of urgency to see the measure applied in the Aydın Vilayet because of the increasing influx there of Muslim emigrants from Macedonia.[33] On 20 May/2 June it announced the appointment of Şükrü Bey, civil inspector in Eastern Thrace, known for his anti-Greek feelings, as the first member of the Ottoman representation on the mixed commission. The Greek Government pointed out that before any appointments were made the rules of procedure of the commission should be clarified.[34] Five days later it reiterated its requirement that an end be put to the persecutions as a *conditio sine qua non* for the beginning of negotiations.[35]

Indeed, starting in mid-May, the persecutions of Greeks on the western littoral of Asia Minor had reached alarming proportions.[36] Thousands of refugees had been gathering at the coast, trying to escape to Greece, and many had already arrived on the islands of Mytilene and Chios. The Ecumenical Patriarchate declared, on 25 May/7 June, the Orthodox Church in a state of persecution and suspended all church and school activities.[37] Faced with these developments, the Greek Government instructed its ambassador in Constantinople to file a strong protest with the Ottoman Government making it clear that unless the wave of persecutions abated, not only would the planned exchange of minorities become impossible to implement, but

[32] *A.Y.E./K.Y./1914/A 21*: Streit to Dragoumis, No 14, 710, 23 May/5 June 1914: "Le besoin, d'un côté, d'enrayer le mouvement de l'émigration forcée en Thrace et en Asie Mineure, où la persécution systématique de l'élément hellène vous est connue, de l'autre la préoccupation de sauver dans la plus large mesure possible ces populations qui quittaient leurs foyers pour aller se réfugier en Grèce, en canalisant ce mouvement et en le combinant utilement à l'émigration volontaire des Musulmans de la Macédoine aux frais d'un échange des propriétés délaissées de part et d'autre, voilà quel était l'objectif poursuivi par le Gouvernement Royal au moment où il accepta la proposition qui lui fat faite par la Turquie ..."

[33] *A.Y.E./K.Y./1914/A 21:* Streit to Panas, No. 13,666, 14/27 May 1914.

[34] *A.Y.E./K.Y./1914/A 21:* Streit to Panas, No. 15,038, 20 May/2 June 1914.

[35] *A.Y.E./K.Y./1914/A 21:* Greek Foreign Ministry to Imperial Ottoman Legation, *note verbale*, 25 May/7 June 1914.

[36] Félix Sartiaux, "Le sac de Phocée et l'expulsion des Grecs d'Asie Mineure en juin 1914," *Revue des deux mondes* 24, no. 6 (November–December 1914): 654–86.

[37] *A.Y.E./K.Y./1914/A 21 e:* Streit to Panas, No. 15,726, 24 May/6 June 1914. Panas to Streit, No. 2,876, 25 May/7 June 1914, Frangulis, *La Grèce et la crise mondiale*, 112.

Greece would be forced to resettle the large numbers of recent refugees on the lands previously owned by Muslims who had left Greece.[38]

The reaction of the Sublime Porte was typical: first create *faits accomplis* and then cover them up with gestures of "good will." On 24 May/6 June, the grand vizier declared that he had no knowledge of the incidents denounced by Greece, and promised to monitor the situation closely and take any measures that might be necessary.[39] On 27 May/9 June and on 29 May/11 June, acting as if nothing extraordinary had happened, the Ottoman legation in Athens reiterated the need for the mixed commission to start its work without further delay. An examination of the situation in Eastern Thrace had revealed nothing to be alarmed about, it added, and, as for the Asia Minor coast, an investigation conducted there under the supervision of Talât himself had resulted in the dismissal of certain public servants found to be insufficient in discharging their duties.[40]

Realizing that the long-term objective of Ottoman policy was the extermination of the Greek element in the Ottoman provinces neighboring Greece, the Greek Government concluded it had to examine the possibility of armed confrontation. To that end, it decided to sound out the intentions of its ally Serbia, on 30 May/12 June.[41] The tone of the instructions sent to the Greek minister in Belgrade was clearly dramatic:

> The situation has become intolerable, Greece no longer finds a way to remain inactive; the systematic extermination of its kin can only worsen if she lets herself be intimidated by the incessant provocations. As you know, we have — by diplomatic notes — requested the immediate cessation of persecutions and the reintegration of the refugees in their homes. If satisfaction is not given we shall be obliged to pose an ultimatum and to demand full satisfaction; in case of failure, we shall be obliged to break off relations and we shall not retreat even from extreme consequences. Please convey confidentially what preceded to the Serbian Government. We appeal to a friendly and Allied Government in order to request its benevolent attitude and moral support. In case Bulgaria should participate in the war or should refuse to defend its neutrality we will invoke *casus foederis*. For the moment, Greece does not intend to mobilize land forces in the hope that the war will not go beyond na-

---

[38] *A.Y.E./K.Y./1914/A 21 e:* Streit to Panas, No. 15,726, 24 May/6 June 1914.

[39] *A.Y.E./K.Y./1914/A 21 e:* Panas to Streit, No. 2,840, 24 May/6 June 1914, No. 2,869, 26 May/8 June 1914.

[40] *A.Y.E./K.Y./1914/A 21:* Imperial Ottoman Legation to Greek Foreign Ministry, *note verbale*, 27 May/9 June 1914. Necip Bey to Streit, Note 29 May/11 June 1914.

[41] On the breakup of the Balkan League and the conclusion of the Greek-Serbian Treaty, see Helmreich, *The Diplomacy of the Balkan Wars*, 341–67.

> val operations.[42] She will do it only if Turkey concentrates in Adrianople in order to traverse Bulgaria or if Bulgaria mobilises. Our action, due to intolerable provocations, has no other aim but to secure a durable peace and the *status quo* in the Balkans. I request you to telegraph me the answer given to you.[43]

This text shows Greece resolved to declare war on the Ottoman Empire if she could ensure Serbia's assistance against possible Bulgarian aggression. To the disappointment of Greece, the answer was negative. Absorbed by her differences with Austria–Hungary, Serbia viewed her alliance with Greece primarily in terms of her own protection against the Bulgarian threat. Certainly she had no intention of getting involved in a Greek–Turkish war over the future of the Aegean Islands or the fate of the Greek minority in the Ottoman Empire. Minister Alexandropoulos' cable from Belgrade, dated 31 May/13 June, read in part:

> [Serbian Prime Minister] M. Passitch personally fears that if we end up in a war in which Bulgaria will certainly take part, the consequences, because of the situation in the Balkans, will be disastrous for Greece and Serbia, the latter being unprepared.[44]

The official reply of the Serbian Government, received on 4/17 June, was even clearer: while considering it of the utmost importance to observe faith-

---

[42] As a result of the 1913 arrangements, Greece and Turkey had no common land boundaries. The Greek General Staff therefore assumed that the next confrontation between the two countries would take place exclusively at sea.

[43] *A.Y.E./K.Y./1914/A 21 e:* Streit to Alexandropoulos, No. 16,530, 30 May/12 June 1914: "... La situation étant devenue intolérable, la Grèce ne saurait plus rester impassible; l'extermination systématique de ses congénères ne peut qu'empirer si elle se laisse intimider par les provocations incessantes. Par notes que vous connaissez, nous avons demandé cessation immédiate persécutions et réintégration réfugiés dans leurs foyers. Si satisfaction n'est pas donnée, nous serons obligés poser ultimatum et exiger pleine satisfaction; à défaut, serons obligés rompre et ne reculerons pas devant extrêmes conséquences. Veuillez porter confidentiellement ce qui précède connaissance gouvernement serbe. Nous nous adressons au gouvernement ami et allié pour demander attitude bienveillante et son appui moral. Dans le cas où Bulgarie participerait guerre ou se refuserait défendre sa neutralité nous invoquerions *casus foederis*. Pour le moment, Grèce ne compte pas mobiliser forces de terre espérant que guerre ne dépassera pas operations maritimes. Elle ne le fera que si Turquie concentre troupes à Adrinople pour traverser Bulgarie ou si Bulgarie mobilise. Notre action, due à provocations intolérables, n'a que le but d'assurer paix durable et *statu quo* dans Balkans. Je vous prie me télégraphier réponse que vous sera donnée ..."; Frangulis, *La Grèce et la crise mondiale*, 112.

[44] *A.Y.E./K.Y./1914/A 21 e:* Alexandropoulos to Streit, No. 547, 31 May/13 June 1914. *A.Y.E./K.Y./1914/A 21 st:* Alexandropoulos to Streit, No. 613, 2/15 June 1914: "M. Passitch personnellement craint que si on arrive à une guerre à laquelle Bulgarie sûrement prendra part, les suites, à cause de la situation dans les Balkans, en seront désastreuses pour Grèce et Serbie, cette dernière n'étant pas preparée."

fully all the provisions of her treaty with Greece, Serbia found herself in a position of having to point out that the Greek Government was pushing things to a dangerously explosive point without having exhausted all peaceful alternatives. In the event of a Greek–Turkish conflict Bulgarian involvement should be taken for granted, and that would result in a general mobilization in Greece since the war would no longer be limited to the Aegean. Under the terms of Article 5 of the Greek–Serbian Military Convention, Serbia would also have to proceed to general mobilization in order to go to the assistance of her ally. But the Balkan Wars had already exhausted the Serbian Army, and Bulgaria was better armed. Besides, the state of her economy did not allow Serbia any military adventures. Furthermore, Romania had not made clear her intentions in the event of a third Balkan War. Finally, the restless Muslim population in Albania was likely to attack both Greeks and Serbs, if Albania were occupied by Bulgaria and the Ottomans. Therefore, all that Serbia could offer Greece was her unqualified diplomatic support to the Greek Government's denunciations of the persecutions.[45]

Similar advice for a peaceful settlement of the Greek–Turkish crisis also came from Bucharest:

> [Romanian Prime Minister] M. Bratiano told me that he was surprised by the brusque change of attitude by the Royal Government which, without exhausting the means of conciliation and entente, appears to provoke the war. As you know, he told me, I have declared on many occasions and I repeat it again, that Romania would not let the Turks make a land war against Greece and thus injuring the Treaty of Bucharest. But now it is Greece which provokes and which will cause trouble to peace, which all the world relies on, and this changes the situation; my latest news is that the Turks appear conciliatory; by consequence Greece must do as much to reach a peaceful solution, otherwise there will be complications whose consequences she will have to bear.[46]

Unable to secure international support, Greece had no other choice but to accept Ottoman terms. Discussing the situation with the Romanian Minister,

---

[45] *A.Y.E./K.Y./1914/A 21 st:* Alexandropoulos to Streit, No. 614, 3/16 June 1914. Panas to Streit, No. 3,262, 4/17 June 1914. Frangulis, *La Grèce et la crise mondiale*, 112–13.

[46] *A.Y.E./K.Y./1914/A 21 st:* Papadiamantopoulos to Streit, No. 601, 3/16 June 1914: "M. Bratiano m'a dit qu'il est etonne du brusque changement de 1'attitude du Gouvernement Royal qui, sans epuiser les moyens de conciliation et d'entente, parait provoquer la guerre. Comme vous le savez, m'a–t–il dit, j'ai declare a plusieurs reprises et je le repete encore, que la Roumanie ne laisserait pas les Turcs faire une guerre par terre contre la Grece et porter ainsi atteinte au traite de Bucharest. Mais maintenant c'est la Grece qui provoque et qui va troubler la paix a laquelle tout le monde tient et cela change la situation; mes dernieres nouvelles sont que les Turcs se montrent conciliants, par consequent Grece en doit faire autant et arriver a une solution pacifique, autrement il y aura des complications dont elle aura a supporter les consequences."

Streit concluded with the following discouraging assessment of Greece's position:

> I have added not being able to dissimulate that the declaration of Romania makes our position *vis-à-vis* Turkey, difficult enough by itself, even more difficult, following [...] incredible vexatious acts which these [Greek] populations suffer.[47]

The prevailing impression in Athens was that Greece, having failed to launch a first attack on the Ottoman Empire, was in danger of finding herself in a disadvantageous position. Everything seemed to point to the eventuality that the Ottoman Empire would decide, at the appropriate moment, to settle its disputes with Greece by force of arms.[48] Meanwhile, the Ottomans were largely successful, on an international level, in their public relations effort since they appeared to have offered a peaceful way out of the crisis through negotiations and had thus reassured those who viewed with fear the possibility of a third conflagration in the Balkans.

On 7/20 June, the Turks, who were not unaware of the Greek Government's moves, reiterated their proposal that the mixed commission be set up and start its work immediately. At the same time they officially announced that the process of reinstatement of refugees in their homes had started.[49] Indeed the persecutions had by then lost some of their initial impetus. Reluctantly and with great circumspection, Greece embarked on the road to negotiations. Turning to the Great Powers, she promoted the idea of offering the commission chairmanship to an official from a neutral country; it was the least she could ask for under the circumstances. The response of the European capitals was favorable.[50]

Rendered slightly more optimistic by that response, Greece announced to the Sublime Porte, on 13/26 June, the appointment of the Greek representa-

---

[47] *A.Y.E./K.Y./1914/A 21 st:* Streit to Papadiamantopoulos, No. 17,220, 4/17 June 1914: "... J'ai ajouté ne pouvoir dissimuler que déclaration Roumanie rend plus difficile encore notre position vis-à-vis Turquie, assez difficile par elle-même par suite [...] vexations innouies que ces populations (grecques) subissent."

[48] *A.Y.E./K.Y/1914/A 21 st:* Panas to Streit, No. 17,280, 4/17 June 1914, No. 3,417, 6/19 June 1914. Streit to Papadiamantopoulos, No. 17,302, 5/18 June 1914. Dragoumis to Streit, No. 1,146, 8/21 June 1914.

[49] *A.Y.E./K.Y./1914/A 21:* Ğalib Kemal to Streit, 8/21 June 1914. *A.Y.E./K.Y./1914JA 21 st:* Streit to Greek Legations in Constantinople, Paris, London, Petersburg, Vienna, Rome, Bucharest, Belgrade, No. 17,777, 7/20 June 1914.

[50] *A.Y.E/K.Y./1914/A 21:* Streit to Greek Legations in Paris, London, Vienna, Petersburg, Rome, Berlin, No. 17,783, 8/21 June 1914. Romanos to Streit, No. 1,966, 10/23 June 1914, No. 2,007, 11/24 June 1914. Theotokes to Streit, No. 1,182, 11/24 June 1914, No. 1,234, 14/27 June 1914. Psychas to Streit, No. 946, 12/25 June 1914. Gryparis to Streit, No. 1,132, 17/30 June 1914.

tives to the commission (Consuls Constantine Dimaras and George Tsorbatzoglou) as well as her proposal concerning neutral arbitration in the event that the commission should be unable to reach a decision by majority vote.[51] Meeting with Ğalib Kemal Bey at the foreign ministry on 16/29 June, Streit announced to the Porte's envoy that the two Greek commissioners had already been instructed to go to Smyrna, the commission seat, and asked the Porte to name its second representative on the commission. At the same he also reiterated the Greek proposal concerning arbitration, to which the Porte's minister replied by expressing his skepticism on the grounds that the search for an appropriate arbitrator would entail the loss of valuable time.[52]

The next day Ğalib Kemal spelled out his positions in a letter addressed to Streit: a) the choice of arbitrator should be made by the two governments; b) the arbitrator should not be present at the deliberations of the commission, but should step in only in the event of irreconcilable differences between the two parties; c) the arbitrator's jurisdiction should be clearly defined by the two governments before his arrival in Smyrna.[53] The Greek positions on the question of arbitration had by then been spelled out as follows: a) the arbitrator should be chosen by the Great Powers; b) he should be a citizen of a neutral country (Switzerland and Sweden were the most appropriate); c) he should be neither a soldier nor a diplomat, but a senior civil servant. Thus, the question of arbitration was still open to discussion.[54]

On 17/30 June, the Ottoman legation communicated to the Greek Government that the second Turkish delegate on the commission was to be Muhtar Bey, former cabinet member, who would also assume the chairmanship of the Ottoman delegation. The same communication stated that the measure of population exchange would also include Greek villages in the zone of the

---

[51] *A.Y.E./K.Y./1914/A 21:* Streit to Ğalib Kemal, Notes 13/26 June 1914 and 15/28 June 1914. Streit to Panas, No. 18,739, 14/27 June 1914. Constantine Dimaras started his career as court assessor at Smyrna. Subsequently he became consul at Monastir, consul-general at Jannina, Adrianople, Odessa and Constantinople. On 24 June/6 July, when the seat of the Mixed Commission had been announced, he was also named Consul-General at Smyrna. George Tsorbatzoglou had served at the consulates of Serres, Smyrna, Plovdiv, and at the Legation in Constantinople. He had also been Consul-General in Jerusalem, and, starting in November 1912, he had been holding the office of Secretary General with the General Administration of Macedonia.

[52] *A.Y.E/K.Y./1914/A 21:* Streit to Panas, No. 18,940, 16/29 June 1914.

[53] *A.Y.E/K.Y./1914/A 21:* Ğalib Kemal to Streit, Note 17/30 June 1914. Panas to Streit, No. 3,612, 16/29 June 1914.

[54] *A.Y.E./K.Y/1914/A 21:* Theotokes to Streit, No. 1,232, 15/28 June 1914. Streit to Theotokes, No. 18,939, 16/29 June 1914.

Straits, but contained no information concerning the question of arbitration.[55] The Greek Government then brought up the question of arbitration directly to the Porte through the Greek ambassador in Constantinople.[56] On 22 June/5 July, the grand vizier agreed, in principle, to the presence of an arbitrator in the deliberations of the commission provided that he did not act as its chairman. The Greek Government had no objections and on 24 June/7 July, acting on behalf of both sides, requested the Swiss Government to name a person of its choice to the position of arbitrator.[57]

The first session of the commission was convened at the governor's mansion, in Smyrna, on 28 June/11 July. From the beginning, the talks revolved around three fundamental questions: a) the conditions of emigration; b) the bases for the appraisal of properties of the exchangeable persons and the modalities of payment of indemnities; c) the terms of seeking arbitration.

Conditions of Emigration

From the beginning of the negotiations the concerted effort of the Greek representatives aimed at limiting the wave of forced migrations. The instructions from Athens were clear: the concept of exchange required, in principle, numerical equality between the Greeks and Muslims to be exchanged; furthermore, the measure would affect only rural populations as distinct from the inhabitants of cities and their suburbs. The voluntary character of the emigration and the safety of the emigrants could only be guaranteed if, in the text of the convention to be drawn up, these two terms were stated in such a way as to prevent any use of force.

The desire of people to emigrate would be ascertained by the commission, which could, for that purpose, create sub-commissions charged with the task of assessing the situation in the regions subject to the exchange. Each regional sub-commission would be composed of a local civil servant and of the consul, vice-consul or consular agent of the other country. The duties of the sub-commissions would also include the supervision of the whole operation, which should be carried out within time limits fixed by the commission.

The Greek Government would also prefer the principle of voluntary emigration to have a retroactive effect, which would allow those who had already

[55] *A.Y.E./K.Y./1914/A 21:* Imperial Ottoman Legation to Greek Foreign Ministry, Note verbale, 17/30 June 1914.

[56] *A.Y.E./K.Y./1914/A 21:* Ğalib Kemal to Streit, Note 20 June/3 July 1914. Streit to Ğalib Kemal, Note 21 June/4 July 1914, Streit to Panas, No. 19,776, 21 June/4 July 1914.

[57] *A.Y.E./K.Y./1914/A 21:* Panas to Streit, No 3,769 22 June/5 July 1914, No. 3,837, 23 June/6 July 1914. Streit to Panas, No. 19,975, 24 June/7 July 1914. Streit to Ğalib Kemal, Note 24 June/7 July 1914. Streit to Romanos, No. 20,166, 24 June/7 July 1914.

emigrated under pressure to return to their homes. Finally, the instructions to the Greek members of the commission called for the inclusion in the convention under consideration of a special clause settling the question of the emigrants' citizenship.[58] This approach was dictated by the Greek Government's desire to see an end put to the Ottoman authorities' practice of exerting pressure on the Greek populations to emigrate. At the same time it was hoped that this would bring relief to the Greek element by helping to contain the outbursts of persecution.

The Greek proposals were rejected. At the meeting of 10/23 July the Ottoman representatives declared that, on instructions from the Sublime Porte, the voluntary character of the emigrations could be ascertained beyond doubt by a simple statement to that effect of the persons concerned to the authorities of their place of residence, without any involvement on the part of the mixed commission. Behind this statement one could clearly see the Porte's designs for a new round of forced Greek emigration.[59] The Greek representatives countered the Turkish objections by claiming that the mixed commission was the only body able to offer guarantees in that matter.[60] Their arguments were based on the three principles of "échange de populations," "échange spontané," "échange simultané," thus reviving a terminology that had been used repeatedly in the letters exchanged by the two parties before the start of the negotiations.[61]

A new disagreement developed when the Greek side tried to link the principle of voluntary emigration with that of simultaneous implementation and numerical balance of the persons to be exchanged. The commission's mandate was, according to the Ottoman representatives, to appraise and exchange the properties of the emigrants, not to determine their number. Any restraining measures, such as insistence on numerical balance and on simultaneous departure, were likely not only to delay the whole process of emigration, but also, and more importantly, to jeopardize the very concept of exchange. The Turks believed that they could send to Greece and receive from her those inhabitants of the regions included in the measure of exchange who wished to emigrate, regardless of numbers.[62] The Greek representatives countered that the waves of emigration first had to be contained if the two countries wanted to be in a position to incorporate a significant number of refugees in their territories. Unproven speculations and prepos-

---

[58] *A.Y.E./K.Y./1914/A 21:* Instructions to the Greek members of the Mixed Commission, 1/14 July 1914.

[59] *A.Y.E./K.Y./1914/A 21:* Dimaras to Streit, unnumbered, 10/23 July 1914 and 19 July/2 August 1914. Tsobatzoglou to Venizelos, unnumbered, 5/18 December 1914.

[60] *A.Y.E./K.Y./1914/A 21:* Streit to Dimaras, No. 22,371, 11/24 July 1914.

[61] *A.Y.E./K.Y./1914/A 21:* Minutes of the 7/20 July 1914 meeting of the Mixed Commission.

[62] *A.Y.E/K.Y./1914/A 21:* Dimaras to Streit, No. 2,699, 8/21 July 1914.

terous guesses of people's desire to emigrate could not form the foundations to support such an important contract.[63]

The Turks reacted with similar intransigence to the idea of repatriation of those Greeks who had fled the Ottoman territory under persecution. The Sublime Porte made it clear that these refugees, regardless of their rural or urban identity, were completely covered by the exchange agreement. Under the terms of the agreement, a distinction between rural and urban populations would be applicable only in the future. Therefore, all those Greeks who had already fled to Greece were subject to the measure of exchange even if they came from cities or suburbs.[64]

On 19 July/2 August, the Turks announced that they rejected any further discussion of the subject and that they would interrupt the talks until the Greek side relented. The Greek Government, which from the very beginning had no illusions concerning the repatriation of the refugees,[65] had no choice but to give in.[66]

The question of the refugees' nationality gave rise to another disagreement. Under article 4 of the Athens Convention (1/14 November 1913), the Muslims of the newly acquired provinces of Greece (Macedonia, Epirus, Crete) could choose a nationality within a period of three years. Those who opted for the Ottoman nationality would have to leave Greece. Those who, although having opted for the Greek nationality, still wished to leave Greece would reacquire Ottoman nationality but would keep title to their immovable property in Greece, which they could lease or entrust to a third party for management.

---

[63] *A.Y.E/K.Y./1914/A 21:* Dimaras to Streit, No 3,042, 27 July/10 August 1914.

[64] *A.Y.E/K.Y./1914/A 21:* Dimaras to Streit, unnumbered, 7/20 July 1914.

[65] This can be clearly seen in the instructions to the Greek delegates: "If it is possible to give to the principle of the freedom of emigration a kind of retro-active effect, it would be desirable that the treaty stipulates that the individuals, who — from both sides — have already emigrated, will have the faculty, by means of a declaration made following the procedure described in the preceding paragraphs, to return to their homes. Even in case not much hope of the success of such a demand could ever be sustained, you should take the opportunity to formulate it, or eventually to abandon it against concessions on other points." ("S'il est possible de donner au principe de la liberté d'émigration une sorte d'effet rétroactif, il serait desirable que la convention stipulât que les individus qui, de part et d'autre, ont déjà émigré, auront la faculté, moyennant une déclaration faite suivant la procédure prévue dans les paragraphes précédents, de réintégrer leurs foyers. Encore qu'il n'y ait pas lieu de fonder beaucoup d'espoir sur le succès de pareille demande, vous saisirez l'occasion de la formuler, sauf à l'abandonner contre des concessions sur d'autres points"): *A.Y.E./K.Y./1914/A 21:* Instructions to the Greek members of the Mixed Commission, 1/14 July 1914.

[66] *A.Y.E./K.Y./1914/A 21:* Dimaras to Streit, unnumbered, 19 July/2 August 1914.

At the meeting of 5/18 July the Greek representatives presented a draft text which, based on the Athens Convention, provided that the Greeks who had already arrived in Greece or would do so in the future, should automatically become Greek citizens, but keep the right, if they so wished, to reacquire Ottoman citizenship by stating their wish to the competent Greek authorities within one year. By doing so they would be under the obligation to return to their place of origin.[67]

The Turks rejected the Greek draft claiming that it jeopardized the very concept of exchange, a natural consequence of which was that the settlement of a refugee in a foreign territory would imply in itself the change of his nationality. Thus they frustrated all hope for a reinstatement of Greek refugees in their homes.[68] Furthermore, invoking the general provisions of Ottoman law concerning the change of Ottoman nationality, under which those inhabitants of the Empire who opted for another nationality had to leave its territory, the Turks made sure to have Greek refugees sign prepared statements to the effect that they would not return to the empire. The only concession the Greek representatives managed to wrest from their interlocutors in this matter was the agreement that, by reciprocity, Muslim refugees leaving Greece would in turn forfeit their right to return to the country.[69]

The talks concerning the conditions of emigration (determination of desire to emigrate, numerical balance, questions of nationality) made no progress until the end of the negotiations. Nor should one have expected otherwise, considering the disarmingly frank statement by the Ottomans to the effect that the long-term purpose of the exercise should be the gradual uprooting of Greeks and Muslims from mutually selected regions to the benefit of both countries.[70]

---

[67] *A.Y.E./K.Y./1914/A 21:* Minutes of the 75/18 July 1914 meeting of the Mixed Commission.

[68] *A.Y.E./K.Y./1914/A 21:* Minutes of the 7/20 July 1914 meeting of the Mixed Commission. Dimaras to Streit, Report No. 3,042, 27 July/10 August 1914.

[69] *A.Y.E./K.Y/1914/A 21:* Minutes of the 12/25 July 1914 meeting of the Mixed Commission. Dimaras to Streit, No. 2,699, 8/21 July 1914, No. 3,075, 29 July/12 August 1914. The Turks had unofficially suggested setting a two-month time limit for the return to Greece of those Muslim emigrants who wished to do so, but the Greek reaction made them withdraw the proposal. Then they claimed that the Convention on the Exchange should in no way affect the provisions of the Athens Convention, so that those Muslims living in Greece who did not wish to exchange their property could leave the country under the terms of articles 4 and 6 of the Athens Convention. The Greek delegation countered that only those provisions of the Athens Convention would remain valid, which were not modified by the letter or the spirit of the new Convention on Exchange.

[70] *A.Y.E./K.Y/1914/A 21:* Dimaras to Streit, No. 2,699, 8/21 July 1914. Tsorbatzoglou to Venizelos, unnumbered, 31 October/13 November 1914.

Appraisal of Properties

The problem of property appraisal was at the center of the negotiations. The striking imbalance in the numbers of refugees up until that time (150,000 Greeks against 52,000 Muslims) made it imperative for the Greek side to try to establish clear distinctions among the various categories of "refugees" (*de facto* expatriated persons) and of the various categories of their properties.[71] The first category of refugees included those who had fled their homes but had not left the Ottoman Empire. Since the Sublime Porte was already committed to their reinstatement, they should be excluded from the measure of exchange, and the Ecumenical Patriarchate would see to it that they received compensation for possible loss of property.[72]

A large dispute arose concerning the second category of refugees, those who, alarmed by the persecutions, had already fled to Greece leaving rural and urban properties behind them (many of them came from towns on the western littoral of Asia Minor). The Turks first stated clearly that there was no hope of those refugees returning to their homes and then proceeded to exclude them from the measure of compensation as well, on the grounds that since the mixed commission's mandate was to arrange for the exchange of rural populations and rural properties, claims of urban property owners could not be considered by the commission.

The Greek side stated that it would be inconceivable that those who had fled their homes because of the persecutions be excluded from compensation, regardless of the nature of their immovable properties. To support their argument, the Greeks pointed to the fact that the Muslims who had emigrated freely under the terms of the Athens Convention had kept title to their immovable properties in Greece. Surely then the Greek refugees who kept arriving in Greece in such a miserable psychological state, after having been forced out of their homes, should not be deprived of their properties either. In other words, the Hellenes were trying to convince their interlocutors that the Ottoman Government was under an obligation to pay compensation for every kind of property left by the Greek refugees in their flight, property still in existence or already lost.[73]

The initial Turkish attitude to the question of appraisal of lost or damaged properties was that such an undertaking was extremely difficult if not impossible. They became more forthcoming later, when the Greeks dropped *ad*

---

[71] *A.Y.E./K.Y./1914/A 21:* Streit to Panas, No. 18,287, 11/24 June 1914. *A.Y.E./K.Y./1914/A 21 st:* Panas to Streit, No. 3,482, 10/23 June 1914.

[72] *A.Y.E./K.Y./1914/A 21:* Dimaras to Streit, unnumbered, 28 June/11 July 1914, No. 2,559, 30 June/13 July 1914.

[73] *A.Y.E./K.Y./1914/A 21:* Streit to Panas, No. 18,287, 11/24 June 1914. Dimaras to Streit, No. 2,559, 30 June/13 July 1914, No. 2,699, 8/21 July 1914.

referendum their demand that the refugees be allowed to return to their homes, but finally no substantial progress was made in this matter either.[74]

The third category included those who would emigrate in the future under the provisions of the Convention on Exchange. The two parties agreed that the appraisal of refugees' immovable properties would be based on land registers, tax records, and the administration of the Ottoman public department. As for the appraisal of movable properties, which was a far more difficult task, it was agreed that each refugee's statement would be compared with the taxes he had been paying on the property concerned.[75] The Greek representatives refused to include religious and educational institutions in the exchange, as those were under the jurisdiction of the Ecumenical Patriarchate, which was recognized by the Ottoman Government itself as the highest spiritual authority over the communal properties of the Greeks in the empire. In return they had to accept complete reciprocity concerning the fate of similar Muslim institutions in Greece.[76]

Concerning large landed estates *(çiftlikler),* the Ottoman representatives promoted the idea of having contracts drawn up between individual landowners from each side, it being understood that the value of the *çiftlikler* included in such individual arrangements would be deducted from the total value of rural properties of the respective appraised villages. Without objecting to the general idea the Hellenes insisted on the need for a better method to be found permitting not only the total appraisal of the rural properties of each village, but also the distinction between big and small landowners.[77]

Finally, since the total value of property left behind by the refugees in one country would exceed that left in the other, the commission took up the question of how the resulting surplus would be paid to the state concerned. The Greek delegation suggested that calculations be made to determine the amount payable every six months. It should be pointed out that, by the above arrangement, Greece was to receive money, particularly after the

---

[74] *A.Y.E/K.Y./1914/A 21:* Dimaras to Streit, unnumbered, 6/19 July 1914. Streit to Dimaras, No. 21,816, 9/22 July 1914. Dimaras to Streit, unnumbered 10/23 July 1914. Streit to Dimaras, No. 22,371, 11/24 July 1914. Dimaras to Streit, unnumbered, 13/26 July 1914. Minutes of the 23 October/5 November 1914 meeting of the Mixed Commission. Venizelos to Panas, No. 39,158, 29 October/11 November 1914. Tsorbatzoglou to Venizelos, unnumbered, 31 October/12 November 1914.

[75] *A.Y.E./K.Y/1914/A 21:* Instructions to the Greek members of the Mixed Commission, 1/14 July 1914.

[76] *A.Y.E./K.Y./1914/A 21:* Dimaras to Streit, No. 2,559, 30 June/13 July 1914. Tsorbatzoglou to Venizelos, unnumbered, 31 October/13 November 1914.

[77] *A.Y.E./K.Y./1914/A 21:* Tsorbatzoglou to Venizelos, unnumbered, 31 October/13 November 1914.

return of Greek refugees to their homes had been ruled out. It was finally agreed, as a compromise, that the question should be approached in two steps, the first concerning the value of property of those refugees who had left before the signature of the Convention on Exchange, and the second dealing with future refugees. Even this compromise, however, was a clear success for the Greek delegation since it guaranteed officially that those Greeks who had been persecuted would receive compensation.[78]

Arbitration Procedures

Greek proposals concerning arbitration, made before the mixed commission started its work, had been received favorably by the Turks. At the first meetings the Greek representatives presented a draft agreement outlining the arbitrator's jurisdiction.[79] Under that agreement the arbitrator's decisions would be definitive and binding for both sides without delay or access to appeal. The two governments would ask the Federal Government of Switzerland to appoint an arbitrator who would be entitled to be present, without participating, at the commission's meetings and would be empowered to summon witnesses and to conduct investigations in place, having at his disposal every means likely to facilitate his task. His expenses would be covered in common by the two states. The Swiss Government's initial response to the joint Greek–Turkish request[80] was positive, but it asked for more details regarding the arbitrator's jurisdiction before giving a definitive answer.[81]

The work of the mixed commission was suspended suddenly after the meeting of 25 July/8 August 1914. The interruption was attributed first to the observance of the religious holiday of Bayram, and later to the second Ottoman delegate's sickness. In reality, however, it was a deliberate move on the part of the Sublime Porte, which was awaiting the results of the Greek–Turkish negotiations about the future of the Aegean islands going on at the same time in Bucharest. When those talks collapsed, the Greek Government tried to get the mixed commission to resume its functions, especially since the persecutions of the Greek population had not abated.[82] On 11/24 September, the Sublime Porte suggested that the mixed commission's seat be

---

[78] *A.Y.E./K.Y./1914/A 21:* Dimaras to Streit, No. 2,699 8/21 July 1914.

[79] *A.Y.E./KY./1914/A 21:* Instructions to the Greek members of the Mixed Commission., 1/14 July 1914.

[80] See above.

[81] *A.Y.E./K.Y./1914/A 21:* Sicilianos to Streit, No. 2,360, 6/19 July 1914.

[82] *A.Y.E./K.Y./1914/A 21:* Dimaras to Streit, No. 3,459, 18/31 August 1914. Venizelos to Panas, No. 28,729, 9/22 September 1914. Panas to Venizelos, No. 5,966, 3/16 September, No 6,108, 7/20 September 1914.

transferred to Constantinople. The Greek Government agreed, but despite its efforts for an early resumption of the commission's work, the latter did not start its meetings before the 24 October/6 November.[83]

The second round of the Mixed Commission's work (24 October/6 November–1/14 December) was even more disappointing. At its very first meeting disagreements arose on the major issues (appraisal of scattered property, determination of people's desire to emigrate, numerical balance of exchangeable persons). The whole attitude of the Ottoman delegates left no room for optimism: declaring the points of disagreement minor, they made concessions on the question of ascertaining people's wish to emigrate, but demanded in return that the Greek side stop insisting on the simultaneous departure and numerical balancing of the emigrants. The Greek Government found some merit in this Turkish proposal.[84] It suggested that the emigration of big rural landowners be excluded from the rule of numerical balance and that their landed estates be exchanged with equal-sized land of rural settlements.

The Turks were not content. On 27 November/10 December, they stated that they accepted the idea of ascertaining people's desire to emigrate, but added that it should be carried out by the lowest-ranking members of the various sub-commissions. They also stated that they agreed to the principle of appraisal of scattered properties on condition that it was extended to include the properties abandoned by Muslims who left Macedonia and Epi-

[83] *A.Y.E./K.Y./1914/A 21:* Panas to Venizelos, No. 6,375,15/28 September 1914. Venizelos to Panas, No. 32,175, 16/29 September 1914. Panas to Venizelos, No. 6,424, 17/30 September 1914, No. 6,459, 19 September/2 October 1914. Venizelos to Panas, No. 32,808, 19 September/2 October 1914. Panas to Venizelos, No 6,569, 22 September/5 October 1914, No. 6,702, 27 September/10 October 1914, No. 6,771, 1/14 October 1914. Venizelos to Panas, No. 36,119, 9/22 October 1914. Panas to Venizelos, No. 7,101, 15/28 October 1914, No. 7,369, 24 October/6 November 1914. In the Greek delegation Constantine Dimaras was replaced by the first *dragoman* of the Greek Legation in Constantinople, Ioannis Papas.

[84] Venizelos' instructions read as follows: "We consider that we could profit from eventual conciliatory dispositions of the Ottoman Government upon two points: by not insisting upon the questions of strict equality in the number of individuals to be exchanged and upon the simultaneity of their departure. Besides, verification that is duly carried into effect of the spontaneous desire of the populations to emigrate removes much of the importance from the issue of the simultaneity of departure." ("Nous considérons que nous pourrions profiter des dispositions conciliantes éventuelles du Gouvernement Ottoman sur ces deux points, en n'insistant pas sur les questions de l'égalite stricte du nombre des individus à échanger et de la simultanéité de leur départ. La constatation dûment effectuée du désir spontané des populations à émigrer ôte d'ailleurs à la simultanéité du depart beaucoup de son importance"): *A.Y.E./K.Y./1914/A 21:* Venizelos to Panas, No. 42,479, 24 November/7 December 1914.

rus when the Greek Army arrived there. The Hellenes considered the first solution proposed by the Turks insufficient, since in effect it placed no control on local administration, and asked for more details concerning the appraisal of scattered properties.[85]

On 1/14 December 1914, the Ottoman delegates suspended the talks once more with the excuse that they had to inform the Sublime Porte on the points of disagreement. They claimed in particular that the Greek Government's interpretation of the question of ascertaining people's desire to emigrate differed from that of the Ottoman side.[86] The meeting of 1/14 December was to be the last one for the mixed commission. The obstructionist tactics of the Ottoman delegates did not allow the talks to make substantial progress. Neither did the general climate.

During the second round of negotiations, the persecutions in Asia Minor followed this pattern: each time the Greek Government denounced incidents of mass expatriation, the Sublime Porte would claim ignorance, but when, subsequently, masses of refugees arrived in Greece, it would then admit the fact, while giving assurances that nothing of the sort would be allowed to happen again.[87]

Upon the Ottoman Empire's entry into the First World War, a method used by the Turks to scare people out of the country consisted in drafting into the Ottoman Army ethnic Greek of Ottoman nationality. When a number of Greeks, under the threat of death penalty for draft evasion, gathered in Smyrna to try to make their way to Greece, the Turkish authorities offered to let them go on the condition that this would not be considered as a form of forced emigration. Finally, at the Church's mediation, a deal was worked out whereby draft evaders could subsequently join the Ottoman Army without fear of punishment. This solution, however, which was expected to contain emigration, had the exact opposite result since, by making draft possible, it therefore made it all the more imperative for draft evaders to flee the country on their own and join the swelling numbers of refugees arriving in Greece.[88]

Concluding Remarks

The attempted 1914 exchange, as well as the Greek–Bulgarian exchange of 1919, differs from the Greek–Turkish exchange of 1923. The 1914 exchange

---

[85] *A.Y.E./K.Y./1914/A 21:* Panas to Venizelos, No. 8,233, 28 November/11 December 1914.

[86] *A.Y.E./K.Y./1914/A 21:* Panas to Venizelos, No. 8,289, 1/14 December 1914.

[87] *A.Y.E./K.Y./1914/A 21 st:* Venizelos to Panas, No. 41,974, 16/29 November 1914.

[88] *A.Y.E./K.Y./1914/A 21 st:* Dimaras to Venizelos, No. 9,185, 12/25 December 1914.

was an attempt at facilitating mutual and voluntary emigrations, whereas by 1923 we are dealing with a compulsory measure. In 1914 and 1919 a relatively limited number of people were affected, while in 1923 the exchange resulted in a generalized expatriation.

In 1923 the measure was imposed by the winner of a war, Kemalist Turkey, on the loser, Greece, as a consequence of the Asia Minor debacle and because of Turkish refusal to accept that Ottoman Greeks remain in new Turkey and the *de facto* refusal of the international community to safeguard the Greek population of Asia Minor from further destruction. In 1914, however, it was forced on the winner of the war, Greece, by the loser, Ottoman Turkey; then, as in 1923, as the end result of a series of violent persecutions.

To be sure, the principle of exchange of minorities for the purpose of national purification remains the same, and one could not in good faith deny that the attempt of 1914 is a precursor of the Treaties of Neuilly and Lausanne. Nevertheless, in 1914 the chances of a "successful" exchange were minimal. Both the obstructionist tactics of the Turkish representatives on the mixed commission and the unabated impetus of the persecutions after the beginning of the negotiations make one wonder whether the failure of the talks had been planned.

In other words, the question is the following: were the persecutions launched in order to force the Greeks to accept the exchange, or were the exchange talks the smokescreen behind which to cover the persecution? Certainly, the reasons that led the Sublime Porte to propose this measure to Athens were political and strategic rather than the claimed humanitarian ones. The real objective of the Turkish Government was to rid whole Ottoman provinces of the Greek element, and this it could achieve by following a policy of force, not by signing a convention on a voluntary exchange of minorities, in which it would of course have to make concessions to the Greek side. The Turkish filibuster on the two most critical points of the talks (determination of wish to emigrate, numerical balance of the exchanged) seems to corroborate the hypothesis that in reality they were but a cover for the persecutions.

Why, then, did Greece accept a proposal that was in effect a blow to the *Megale Idea*, especially after her spectacular gains in the Balkan Wars, which had brought her most cherished irredentist dream closer than ever to realization? In the spring and summer of 1914, as Europe was following its irreversible course to war, the Greek Government, lacking international support, could ill afford a new armed confrontation with Turkey. Taking advantage of this state of affairs, the Turks, although defeated on the battlefield, managed to impose their own terms, since they were in a position to present the Greek Government with the choice of either accepting their proposals or abandoning to their fate the Greek populations in Eastern Thrace and on the Asia Minor coast. The Greek Government was fully aware of the situation. In a characteristic comment, the Greek minister in Constantinople called the resumption of the mixed commission's deliberations "pure comédie."[89] These tactics, employed by Turkey time and again, which consist of covering up *faits accomplis* by launching spectacular public relations events, take on special significance today. To neutralize these tactics one must first identify the underlying reasons that make them possible.

---

[89] *A.Y.E./K.Y./1914/A 21 st:* Panas to Venizelos, No. 8,118, 27 November/10 December 1914.

Danish Sources on the Destruction of the Ottoman Greeks, 1914–1916[1]

MATTHIAS BJØRNLUND

THE YEARS SPANNING THE FINAL PHASE OF THE OTTOMAN EMPIRE and the creation of the Turkish Republic were marked by the persecution and destruction by the CUP ("Young Turk") and Kemalist regimes of non-Turkish, particularly Christian, Ottoman groups. The ethnic and religious make-up in the area that comprises present-day Turkey changed dramatically in the years 1914–24, partly as a result of deliberate policies aimed at securing complete dominance of the ruling Turkish elites in particular, and of ethnic Turks in general.[2] These policies ranged from linguistic and economic measures to ethnic cleansing and genocide achieved by violent Turkification — a combination of deportations and death marches, forced assimilation, "confiscation" of property, cultural and material destruction, general deprivations, and large-scale massacres.[3] There was a number of Danish eyewitnesses to

[1] This study is a revised and expanded version of my article "The 1914 Cleansing of Aegean Greeks as a Case of Violent Turkification," originally published in the *Journal of Genocide Research* 10, no. 1 (March 2008): 41–58.

[2] For recent scholarly works on the subject (mainly, but not exclusively on the Armenian genocide): e.g., Uğur Ü. Üngör, "When Persecution Bleeds into Mass Murder: The Processive Nature of Genocide," in *Genocide Studies & Prevention (GSP)* 1, no. 2 (Fall 2006): 173–95; Taner Akçam, "The Ottoman Documents and the Genocidal Policies of the Committee of Union and Progress (*İttihat ve Terakki Cemiyeti*) toward the Armenians in 1915," ibid., 127–48; Matthias Bjørnlund, "'When the Cannons Talk, the Diplomats Must Be Silent:' A Danish Diplomat in Constantinople during the Armenian Genocide," ibid., 197–223, especially 206–209. Recent monographs on the Armenian and Assyrian genocides include Donald Bloxham, *The Great Game of Genocide: Imperialism, Nationalism, and the Destruction of the Ottoman Armenians* (Oxford and New York: Oxford University Press, 2005); Taner Akçam, *A Shameful Act: The Armenian Genocide and the Question of Turkish Responsibility* (New York: Metropolitan Books, 2006); David Gaunt, *Massacres, Resistance, Protectors: Muslim-Christian Relations in Eastern Anatolia During World War I* (Piscataway, New Jersey: Gorgias Press 2006).

[3] On the use of "ethnic cleansing" and "genocide" in this context: Some scholars view these terms as anachronistic, in that they were not coined at the time of the actual events. In "Notes on Terminology and Orthography," *Crossing the Aegean: An Appraisal of the 1923 Compulsory Population Exchange between Greece and Turkey*, Renée Hirschon, ed. (New York and Oxford: Berghahn Books 2003), xi, it is stated that "[c]ontributors [to the volume] use the terms 'population transfer,' 'population exchange,' 'population expulsion' interchangeably, while 'ethnic cleansing,' a term coined in the 1990s for events in the

former Yugoslavia for what in effect took place in 1923, constitutes an anachronism." Stéphane Audoin-Rouzeau and Annette Becker, *1914–1918: Understanding the Great War* (London: Profile Books, 2002), 64, call the destruction of the Ottoman Armenians "this most important mass slaughter of the Great War," but believe that the use of the term "genocide" in this context is anachronistic. For various reasons I disagree with such assertions.

First, I believe scholars should apply the most exact terms to describe events, whether or not these terms are believed by some to be "controversial" or "inconvenient," and whether or not they were coined at the time of the events or to describe these events. "Anachronistic" terms are constantly being used quite unproblematically by scholars to describe events, and Hirschon herself uses the term "ethnic cleansing" (in quotation marks) to denote the forced displacement of peoples in the Asia Minor region 1922–23 when she compares "this early attempt at 'ethnic cleansing' to the situation in the former Yugoslavia..." See "Preface," in Hirschon, ed., *Crossing the Aegean*, xvi. Also, in the same volume Michael Barutciski, "Lausanne Revisited: Population Exchanges in International Law and Policy," 24, uses the term (without quotation marks) to describe events of the early 1920s: "Following the defeat of the Greek army in Asia Minor in 1922, the victorious Turks imposed this treaty which effectively legalized the ethnic cleansing of 'enemy' populations in both Greece and the emerging Turkish state." Comparing events, which are deemed to have important characteristics in common, demands a common terminology. I agree with Renée Hirschon when she calls the term "ethnic cleansing" a "distasteful euphemism" ("Preface," in *Crossing the Aegean*, xv), but at the same time the term — defined as violent policies aiming at expelling ethnic groups with the purpose of creating homogenous areas — quite accurately describes the mindset and intention of, e.g., CUP and Kemalist decision makers when it comes to certain parts of the policy of Turkification, ca. 1914–24, of Serb decision makers in Bosnia in the 1990s, or of Bulgarian, Greek, Serb, and Turkish decision makers during and after the Balkan Wars. In addition, if one wants to point out "distasteful euphemisms," one could mention Hirschon's own description (Hirschon, "'Unmixing Peoples' in the Aegean Region," in *Crossing the Aegean*, 3) of the CUP policy of, e.g., genocide, when, according to Hirschon, "the non-Muslim residents in strategic areas were relocated to the interior of Anatolia, some later moving back, others migrating elsewhere." Second, it is questionable if terms such as "ethnic cleansing" and "genocide" are anachronistic when used to describe group destruction in the Ottoman Empire/Turkey. For instance, in 1925 the Danish MP H. F. Ulrichsen used the term "cleansing policy" to describe CUP and Kemalist policies (see below), and the term "genocide" was coined by Raphael Lemkin to describe not only the Holocaust, but also aspects of these same policies. Hans-Lukas Kieser, "Armenians, Turks, and Europe in the Shadow of World War I: Recent Historiographical Developments," in *Der Völkermord an den Armeniern, die Türkei und Europa* [*The Armenian Genocide, Turkey and Europe*] Hans-Lukas Kieser and Elmar Plozza, eds. (Zürich: Chronos Verlag, 2006), 52–53, contends: "As historians, we can abandon the use of the term genocide and convey its content in other words. An important reason, however, to use this neologism as a historical (not in the first place legal or even militant political) term is its precise meaning in the context of contemporary history; it stands for the intended total or partial destruction of an ethnic group, be it by killing or other violent measures. Beyond the evidence that the Armenian case accords with the definition in the UN Convention, there is another powerful argument for using the term genocide for 1915 — the simple fact that the pioneers of genocide studies, first of all Lemkin himself, started out from this experience." And, I will add, in the case of Lemkin from the Greek experience as well: see Jacobs, in this volume. On the definitions of aspects of these policies, including diplomats, missionaries, and relief workers. In this paper I will examine witnesses to the persecution of the Ottoman Greeks 1914–16, and how these events were interpreted by observers from a neutral country, mainly as seen from the major harbor city of Smyrna (İzmir (Tur.)), and from Constantinople, the Ottoman capital. The reasons for this chronological and geographical delimitation are that it was in these cities that the diplomats Alfred van der Zee and Carl Ellis Wandel, the two most important Danish observers to the events, were placed, and it was during these years that their most substantial reports on the subject were written.

For various reasons, most contemporary Western observers concentrated on reporting on the specific aspect of CUP (and to a large extent also Kemalist) policies that was the destruction of the Ottoman Armenians[4] — a fact which has subsequently been reflected by scholarly accounts of the period that likewise tend to focus on the Armenian genocide rather than on the persecution of other groups. I believe that two main reasons that Western observers reported primarily on the Armenian genocide were: 1) that before, during, and after the 1914–24 period most such observers (the missionaries and the rescue workers) worked among Armenians rather than among, e.g., Greeks or Syriacs (Assyrians/Aramaeans);[5] and 2) that these observers were therefore generally more receptive to the suffering of the particular group they had often literally built their lives around, and were placed at geographical locations where they could mainly observe the de-

---

the concepts "genocide," "ethnic cleansing," and "crimes against humanity" relating to the Armenian and other genocides: William A. Schabas, "The 'Odious Scourge:' Evolving Interpretations of the Crime of Genocide," *GSP* 1, no. 2 (Fall 2006). On "ethnic cleansing" as a historical concept: e.g., T. Hunt Tooley, "World War I and the Emergence of Ethnic Cleansing in Europe," Steven Béla Várdy and T. Hunt Tooley, eds., *Ethnic Cleansing in Twentieth Century Europe* (Boulder: East European Monographs, 2003), 63–98.

[4] On such Danish observers: Matthias Bjørnlund, "'A fate worse than dying': sexual violence during the Armenian genocide," *Brutality and Desire: War and Sexuality in Europe's Twentieth Century,* ed. Dagmar Herzog (Basingstoke: Palgrave Macmillan, 2009); Matthias Bjørnlund, "Karen Jeppe, Aage Meyer Benedictsen, and the Ottoman Armenians: National survival in imperial and colonial settings," *Haigazian Armenological Review,* forthcoming; Maria Jacobsen, *Diaries of a Danish Missionary: Harpoot, 1907–1919,* Ara Sarafian, ed. (Princeton and London: Gomidas Institute Books, 2001).

[5] There may be no Danish sources to the Syriac genocide (*Seyfo*), but scholar and chairman of the relief organization *Danish Friends of Armenians,* Aage Meyer Benedictsen, *Armenien: Et Folks Liv og Kamp Gennem To Aartusinder* (Copenhagen: De Danske Armeniervenner 1925), 260, briefly mentions the destruction of the Syriacs as being comparable to the Armenian genocide. On Benedictsen, see Bjørnlund, "Karen Jeppe;" Matthias Bjørnlund, "En excentrisk komet," *Goldberg: Magasin om jødisk kunst, kultur, religion, samfund* 1, no. 4 (October 2007): 12–14.

struction of the Armenians. A third reason is that many saw the Armenian genocide, with its widespread, large-scale, and systematic massacres and death marches, as more condensed in time and more radical in its intent and execution than, e.g., the Greek genocide. But at the same time a number of these observers shared the view that the goals of the CUP and the Kemalists, as well as the end results of their policies, were largely similar: the disappearance from Asia Minor of what were viewed by Turkish nationalists as (potentially) troublesome minorities. For instance, H. F. Ulrichsen, a Danish lawyer, conservative MP, and leading member of the organization *Danish Friends of Armenians*, contended that during CUP and Kemalist rule, "the 'cleansing policy' [*Udrensningspolitik*] [...] had as its aim the removal of all the foreign bodies — Christians and Jews — which were influencing Turkey to such a large degree."[6]

1914: Background and Ideology

The main "Danish" witness to early CUP attempts at cleansing Greeks from Ottoman soil, Alfred van der Zee, was in fact Dutch. He had been the Danish, as well as the Swedish, consul in Smyrna, *vilayet* of Aydın (Smyrna) since November 1910.[7] A Dutch citizen, born in the Netherlands May 9, 1872, he

[6] H. F. Ulrichsen, "Tyrkerne og det græske Patriarkat," [The Turks and the Greek Patriarchate] *Armeniervennen* 5, nos. 1–2 (January–February 1925): 5. See also Bjørnlund, "The 1914 Cleansing;" J. C. Willesen, *Guds Folk og Martyrfolket* [*God's People and the Martyred People*] (Copenhagen 1922), 6. Between 1914–16 Ulrichsen was consular secretary to Carl Ellis Wandel, Danish diplomatic minister at Constantinople, and had observed aspects of the CUP policy of destruction: e.g., *Danish National Archives, Archives of the Foreign Ministry* (hereafter: UM), 3. G. 53a, "Wandel, Carl Ellis," pk. 1; *Kraks Blaa Bog* (Copenhagen: Kraks Legat, 1931), 1066. Ulrichsen later visited the Ottoman Empire/Turkey for substantial periods of time in 1919 and 1924: UM, 2-0355, "Konstantinopel/Istanbul, diplomatisk repræsentation, 1914–1921," "Kopibog 1914–1921, 1916 03 06 - 1919 09 22," telegram nr. 13, 7/4 1919; *Armeniervennen* 5, nos. 1–2 (January–February 1925), 4–5. Regarding the 1924 visit (ibid., 5), he wrote that, "Thousands of wealthy Greeks had left Constantinople in a hurry when they heard about the fate of their compatriots in Smyrna. Other thousands had been left without work, simply because they were Christians. The Young Turks demand, that all citizens were equal in the eyes of the law, had been dropped even by the Young Turks long before that. The same Kemalists, who abolished the Caliphate, and whose leading men declared themselves to be religiously indifferent, now demanded that only Muslims work for the state and for the licensed companies. Brussa, which the student fraternity visited in July this year, had already been cleansed of Greeks as well as of Armenians. The wealthiest neighborhood was empty, churches and schools were abandoned, the windows were broken, the furniture more or less destroyed." Except where otherwise noted, all translations are mine.

[7] UM, 2-0355, "Konstantinopel/Istanbul, diplomatisk repræsentation. 1822–1920. Korrespondencesager vedr. Danske konsulater i Levanten 1864–1918," pk. 27, "Upplysningar om danska konsulstjänstmän och om d. vicekonsulars [illegible] 1911," Van der Zee to

was a highly qualified businessman who ran the offices of the family business *W. H. van der Zee*, and who spoke English, French, Italian, German, Greek, and Turkish as foreign languages.[8] He was also a shipbroker and an agent for the major Danish shipping company *DFDS*.[9] Van der Zee replaced the deceased Danish Consul F. J. C. Clemm, who had died in the spring of 1910, and he remained at this post until 1922.[10] The vice-consul at the Danish consulate in Smyrna at the time was Dutch Levantine insurance agent John Atkinson de Jongh, born 1854, who had held that position since 1877.[11]

Thus, Van der Zee was in a crucial position to witness the early efforts by the CUP to force the violent homogenization of the ethnic and religious make-up of Anatolia before the policies of extermination during World War I. Attempts at removing non-Turkish influences from the Ottoman economy had been reintroduced almost immediately by the radical faction of the CUP that had taken control of the empire in 1913, and in the spring and summer of 1914 this policy was supplemented with the cleansing of more than 100,000 Greeks from Ionia (the Ottoman Aegean littoral) and Ottoman Thrace.[12] As is

---

Swedish ambassador d'Anckarsvärd [who represented Denmark in the Ottoman Empire until 1914], 12/1 1911.

[8] UM, 2-0355, "Konstantinopel/Istanbul, diplomatisk repræsentation. 1822-1920. Korrespondencesager vedr. Danske konsulater i Levanten 1864-1918," pk. 27, "Upplysningar om danska konsulstjänstmän och om d. vicekonsulars [illegible] 1911," questionnaire filled out by Van der Zee, 12/1 1911.

[9] UM, 2-0355, "Konstantinopel/Istanbul, diplomatisk repræsentation. 1822-1920. Korrespondencesager vedr. Danske konsulater i Levanten 1864-1918," pk. 27, "Cons. de Danemark, Smyrne," UM to d'Anckarsvärd, 31/3 1910.

[10] UM, 2-0355, "Konstantinopel/Istanbul, diplomatisk repræsentation. 1822-1920. Korrespondencesager vedr. Danske konsulater i Levanten 1864-1918," pk. 27, "Cons. de Danemark, Smyrne," 12/3 1910.

[11] UM, 2-0355, "Konstantinopel/Istanbul, diplomatisk repræsentation. 1822-1920. Korrespondencesager vedr. Danske konsulater i Levanten 1864-1918," pk. 27, "Upplysningar om danska konsulstjänstmän och om d. vicekonsulars [illegible] 1911," questionnaire filled out by De Jongh, 2/11 1911. Members of the De Jongh family, merchant Oscar de Jongh and his wife, were killed by Turkish cavalry 9 September 1922, on the first day of the destruction of Smyrna: *Daily Telegraph*, 29 September 1922, quoted in Lysimachos Oeconomos, *The Tragedy of the Christian Near East* (London: The Anglo-Hellenic League 1923), 7-8. See also George Horton, *The Blight of Asia: An Account of the Systematic Extermination of Christian Populations by Mohammedans and of the Culpability of Certain Great Powers; with the True Story of the Burning of Smyrna* (London: Sterndale Classics 2003 [reprint of the 1926 edition]), 85.

[12] Henry Morgenthau, *Ambassador Morgenthau's Story* (Detroit: Wayne State University Press, 2003 [reprint of the 1918 edition]), 222-23; Taner Akçam, *From Empire to Republic: Turkish Nationalism and the Armenian Genocide* (London and New York: Zed Books, 2004), 147. According to Van der Zee, 70-80,000 Ionian Greeks had been expelled before June 1914: UM, 5. L. 15., "Grækenland-Tyrkiet: Politiske Forhold," pk. 1, nr. 41, 27/6 1914. According to Michael Llewellyn Smith, *Ionian Vision: Greece in Asia Minor 1919-*

always the case with ethnic cleansing, there was nothing "clean" about the operation when seen from the perspective of victims and bystanders. Papers reported how thousands of Greeks in Thrace were forced by the authorities to embark for Greece by ship. Others had to choose between either fleeing the empire or converting to Islam.[13] Greeks from the Rodosto region were reported to be suffering on the fields and roads while Turkish-speaking Albanians and Muslim Cretans were being settled in their houses.[14] Apparently this policy was the result of careful deliberation and preliminary research made by the CUP, although it was decided to conceal the connection between, on the one hand, the CUP and government agencies like the ministry of war, and, on the other hand, the Special Organization (SO) that carried out the operation.[15] The reason for the authorities to act behind the scenes in this manner was to avoid foreign intervention.[16] But according to a June 1914 report from Van der Zee to his superior, Carl Ellis Wandel, Danish diplomatic minister at Constantinople, it appeared that the large-scale, systematic and violent expulsion of what was described as the generally peaceful and hard-working Greek population was in fact carried out on the orders of the central government.[17]

This policy was to some extent dictated by perceived security concerns. The CUP believed the Ottoman Greeks to be suspect on account of their alleged ties to the Greek state, and more specifically, they wanted to prevent the Greeks living along the coastline from becoming a fifth column. This danger was believed to be imminent as Greece had recently come to control the nearby islands of Chios and Mytilene (Lesbos) through the intervention of the European Powers. These islands, it was stated, could be used to launch

---

1922 (London: Allen Lane, 1973), 31, the 1914 events were "not a 'massacre' in the sense of the Armenian or Bulgarian massacres, though numerous incidents of murder, destruction and rape took place. It was what the Greeks call a *diogmos* – persecution." Roger W. Smith, "Introduction," in Morgenthau, *Ambassador Morgenthau's Story*, xxxiv, and Halil Berktay, "A Genocide, Three Constituencies, Thoughts for the Future (Part I)," *Armenian Weekly* 73, no. 16 (21 April 2007), call the events "ethnic cleansing."

13 *Nationaltidende*, 19 April 1914, 26 April 1914, 19 May 1914; *Jyllandsposten*, 19 April 1914.

14 *Nationaltidende*, 30 April 1914.

15 Akçam, *From Empire to Republic*, 144–49. On the SO, see also Erik J. Zürcher, *Turkey: A Modern History* (London and New York: I. B. Tauris, 2003), 114–15, 121.

16 Nesim Şeker, "Demographic Engineering in the Late Ottoman Empire and the Armenians," *Middle Eastern Studies* 43, no. 3 (May 2007): 465.

17 UM, 2-0355, "Konstantinopel/Istanbul, diplomatisk repræsentation," "Noter og indberetninger om den politiske udvikling, 1914–1922," "Verdenskrigen. Rapporter fra Smyrna. Nov. 1914–Marts 1916," 25/6 1914. See also Horton, *Blight of Asia*, 28–34.

attacks.[18] In addition, the persecution of Greeks could serve to put pressure on the Greek Government to solve the overall dispute regarding the Aegean islands in a manner beneficial to the Ottoman Government.[19] But the islands dispute, security concerns, or revenge for the ongoing cleansing of Balkan Muslims (see below) were apparently not the only reasons, as economic, political, and ethno-religious concerns seem to have made the cleansing policy part of a larger project of Turkification. According to Taner Akçam, the CUP had prior to World War I "formulated a policy that they began to execute in the Aegean region against the Greeks and, during the war years, expanded to include the Assyrians, the Chaldeans, the Syrians, and especially the Armenians, a policy that eventually became genocidal. [...] Detailed reports were prepared [by the SO] outlining the elimination of the Christian population. These measures were implemented in the Aegean region in the spring of 1914."[20] Under the heading "Disorders in the Vilayet of Aidin," Van der Zee reported that in March 1914, the *valis (vali)* of Smyrna and the nearby regions had made inspection tours to the coastal towns and villages of the *vilayets*, "advising" the local civil servants to force the Greeks to leave:

> About three months ago the Governor General of Smyrna [*vali* Evranoszade Rahmi Bey], acting, as I understand, on instructions from the Ministry, made an inspection in the small towns situated on the coast of this province. It would appear that in the course of this *tournée administrative* he gave semi-official orders to the sub-governors to force the Greek population resident therein to evacuate these towns. No order of expulsion was decreed, but the Turkish officials were to make use of tortuous and vexatious measures so well-known to them. Similar instructions were, I understand, given by the Governors of the other maritime provinces.[21]

---

[18] UM, 2-0355, "Konstantinopel/Istanbul, diplomatisk repræsentation," "Noter og indberetninger om den politiske udvikling, 1914–1922," "Verdenskrigen. Rapporter fra Smyrna. Nov. 1914–Marts 1916," 19/6 1914; UM, 5. L. 15., "Grækenland-Tyrkiet: Politiske Forhold," pk. 1, nr. 31, 23/6 1914. On the importance to the CUP of regaining islands in Greek possession: Ahmed Djemal Pascha, *Erinnerungen eines Türkischen Staatsmannes* (München: Drei Masken Verlag, 1922), 17, 55, 111–12; William Peter Kaldis, "Background for Conflict: Greece, Turkey, and the Aegean Islands, 1912–1914," *Journal of Modern History* 51, no. 2 (June 1979): 1119–46; Henry Morgenthau, *United States Diplomacy on the Bosphorus: The Diaries of Ambassador Morgenthau, 1913–1916*, comp. and intro. by Ara Sarafian (Princeton and London: Gomidas, 2004), 19–20; *Vort Land*, 10 January 1914.

[19] Llewellyn Smith, *Ionian Vision*, 32; *Jyllands-Posten*, 10 January 1914.

[20] Akçam, "Ottoman Documents and the Genocidal Policies," 133–34.

[21] UM, 2-0355, "Konstantinopel/Istanbul, diplomatisk repræsentation," "Noter og indberetninger om den politiske udvikling, 1914–1922," "Verdenskrigen. Rapporter fra Smyrna. Nov. 1914–Marts 1916," 19/6 1914. Quotes by Van der Zee, taken from reports written in English, have been silently edited.

This general interpretation is supported by Hans-Lukas Kieser, who quotes the memoirs of Mahmut Celal Bey (Bayar), head of the Smyrna cell of the CUP in 1914 and later to become Turkey's third president for saying that the CUP and the Ministry of War, run by Enver Paşa since 3 January 1914 "were, parallel to the regular activities of the government, working towards the liquidation of the 'concentrations of non-Muslims' in the Aegean region..."[22] According to Wandel, it was Dr. Nazım Bey, leading member of the radical inner circle of the CUP that would later orchestrate the Armenian genocide,[23] who during the Balkan Wars 1912-13 had developed a plan to settle Muslims, who had themselves been violently cleansed from Macedonia, at various places in the empire from where non-Muslims would be deported.[24] The Turkish diplomatic minister at Athens at the time, Ğalib Kemal (Söylemezoğlu), even proposed to the Greek authorities that the Muslims of the Greek administrative provinces of Macedonia and Epirus should be exchanged with the rural Greek population of the Smyrna province and of Ottoman Thrace, a plan based on a similar 1913 Turkish-Bulgarian agreement. Greek Prime Minister Eleutherios Venizelos seems to have approved of such an exchange in 1914, on condition that it would be a voluntary emigration and that the persecution and forced emigration of Greeks would cease.[25]

---

22 Hans-Lukas Kieser, "Dr. Mehmed Reshid (1873-1919): A Political Doctor," in *Der Völkermord an den Armeniern und die Shoah* [*The Armenian Genocide and the Shoah*] Hans-Lukas Kieser and Dominik J. Schaller, eds. (Zürich: Chronos Verlag, 2002), 257. On Celal, see also Fatma Müge Göcek, "Turkish Historiography and the Unbearable Weight of 1915," *The Armenian Genocide: Cultural and Ethical Legacies*, Richard Hovannisian, ed. (New Brunswick and London: Transaction Publishers, 2007), 358-59. After a conversation with Bedri Bey, chief of police of Constantinople, Morgenthau wrote in his diary on 25 May 1914 that he believed that the CUP aimed to expel the Greeks as well as the Bulgarians, the Serbs, and the Albanians, cf. Morgenthau, *United States Diplomacy on the Bosphorus*, 60-61. On 2 July 1914, he had a conversation with Talât who had seemed "determined to have Greeks of the country, not cities, leave their country," ibid., 74.

23 See, e.g., Üngör, "When Persecution Bleeds into Mass Murder," 173. When Nazım became minister of education in 1918, Wandel wrote about this "energetic and efficient man" that he was among the most radical members of the CUP, and, referring also to radical CUP member and former Minister of Education Şükrü Bey, that it was seemingly now a rule that such persons were appointed to that post: UM, 2-0355, "Konstantinopel/Istanbul, diplomatisk repræsentation. 1914-1922. Noter og indberetninger om den politiske udvikling," "Verdenskrigen. Politiske Indberetninger om Tyrkiets Stilling, Juni 1917- Aug. 1918," 24/7 1918, nr. LXVII.

24 Ibid.

25 Yannis G. Mourelos, "The 1914 Persecutions and the First Attempt at an Exchange of Minorities Between Greece and Turkey," *Balkan Studies* 26, no. 2 (1985); Ayhan Aktar, "Homogenizing the Nation, Turkifying the Economy: The Turkish Experience of the Population Exchange Reconsidered," in Hirschon, ed., *Crossing the Aegean*, 83; Llewellyn Smith,

The outbreak of World War I prevented the exchange, as it would also prevent a final settlement of the islands dispute. But before that, the authorities, represented by the ministry of interior's Office of Tribal and Refugee Settlement, had decided not to wait for the consent of the Greek Government.[26] So, in the spring and summer of 1914, it was initiated in earnest in a decidedly violent and compulsory manner that has been compared to the Nazi policy of "Aryanization" — defined as the "reorganization of economic resources in favor of 'ethnically-desirable' citizens and therefore of the ethnically-defined state itself."[27] For the CUP, to be "ethnically-desirable" meant to be Turkish as well as Muslim, since non-Turkish Muslims (e.g., Kurds), who were deported to areas previously occupied by Christians from 1914 onward, were expected to assimilate (i.e., Turkify) by giving up their ethnic identity.[28] Discriminatory policies had already been directed against Christians; the electoral system, for instance, was designed to discriminate heavily against Christians, and the authorities, despite their promises, did not return Anatolian land to Armenians driven away during or after the Abdülhamit II massacres.[29]

Immediately after its 1913 coup d'état, the new, more radical CUP leadership tried to give the appearance that they continued efforts to "Ottomanize" and centralize the empire in a peaceful and democratic manner. But, as Wandel and other observers noted, if this had ever in reality been CUP policy it was no longer the case.[30] Rather, as Feroz Ahmad puts it, repression

---

Ionian Vision, 32–33. See also Norman M. Naimark, *Fires of Hatred: Ethnic Cleansing in Twentieth Century Europe* (Cambridge: Harvard University Press, 2001), 43.

[26] Akçam, "Ottoman Documents and the Genocidal Policies," 133.

[27] Donald Bloxham, "Determinants of the Armenian Genocide," *Looking Backward, Moving Forward: Confronting the Armenian Genocide*, Richard G. Hovannisian, ed. (New Brunswick: Transaction Publishers 2003), 29–30.

[28] Akçam, "Ottoman Documents and the Genocidal Policies," 134–35. See also Bjørnlund, "When the Cannons Talk, the Diplomats Must Be Silent," 206–209; Hans-Lukas Kieser, "Muslim Heterodoxy and Protestant Utopia: The Interaction between Alevis and Missionaries in Ottoman Anatolia," *Die Welt des Islams* 41, no. 1 (March 2001): especially 100ff. On the continued Turkification of Kurds and other non-Turkish groups in the 1920s and 1930s cf. Soner Çagaptay, *Islam, Secularism, and Nationalism in Modern Turkey* (London and New York: Routledge, 2006).

[29] UM, 139. D. 1., "Tyrkiet - Indre Forhold," pk. 1, nr. II, 24/7 1914. See also Bloxham, "Determinants of the Armenian Genocide," 28; Anahide Ter Minassian, *"Van 1915," Armenian Van/Vaspurakan*, Richard G. Hovannisian, ed. (Costa Mesa: Mazda Publishers, 2000) 211; Alexis Alexandris, *The Greek Minority of Istanbul and Greek-Turkish Relations 1918–1974* (Athens: Centre for Asia Minor Studies, 1992), 42ff.

[30] See, e.g., Hugh Poulton, *Top Hat, Grey Wolf and Crescent: Turkish Nationalism and the Turkish Republic* (London: Hurst, 1997), 80–81; Christopher J. Walker, *Armenia: The Survival of a Nation* (New York: St. Martin's Press, 1981), 188–95; Akçam, *From Empire to*

and violence became the order of the day.[31] Although Wandel acknowledged that the extent of the radicalization was partly caused by events outside CUP control, he emphasized that it was not simply the result of defensive *ad hoc* measures against, say, Western imperialism, but an integral part of an active, deliberate policy rooted in Turkist supremacist beliefs that basically had as its goal to preserve power. Since it was not, or no longer, believed that this could be reached by a multiethnic, multi-religious, Turkish-dominated empire, it would be reached by somehow creating a "Turkey for the Turks," economically, politically, linguistically, and ethnically, increasingly combined with an expansionist Pan-Turkist vision of a Turkish Empire uniting ethnic Turks from Asia and Russia.[32]

Wandel accordingly described the nature of the CUP by describing its members not as great idealists or statesmen, but as organizers using every means to further their organization, fighting for power rather than ideals: "For some there is no doubt about their integrity, but it is the general understanding that [the CUP] will continue to pursue the policy it has already initiated, a policy which has led to so many conflicts." He believed that this policy would eventually lead to "national suicide."[33] In fact, though the costs were immense, it was a price that was deemed worth paying for the creation of the relatively homogeneous (if unstable) nation that is the modern Turkish Republic.[34] But, as Wandel also emphasized, although many Young Turks were not "great idealists," they did share some broad ideals that, if nothing else, served to legitimize their power monopoly in particular, and of ethnic Turks in general, as well as to prevent the disintegration of the empire through centralization and homogenization.[35]

Republic, 65; Hervé Georgelin, "Smyrne à la fin de l'empire ottoman: un cosmopolitisme si voyant," *Cahiers de la Méditerranée* 67 (2003), http://cdlm.revues.org/document127.html#ftn1

31 Feroz Ahmad, *The Young Turks: The Committee of Union and Progress in Turkish politics, 1908–1914* (Oxford: Clarendon Press, 1969), 163.

32 See, e.g., Zürcher, *Turkey: A Modern History,* 132–37; Hülya Adak, "Identifying the 'Internal Tumors' of World War I: *Talât Paşa'nin Hatiraları* [*Talât Paşa's Memoirs*] or the Travels of a Unionist Apologia into 'History'," *Räume des Selbst: Selbstzeugnisforschung transkulturell*, Andreas Baehr, Peter Burschel and Gabriele Jancke, eds. (Cologne, Weimar and Vienna: Böhlau Verlag 2007), 158ff.

33 UM, 139. D. 1., "Tyrkiet – Indre Forhold," pk. 1, nr. CLX, 22/9 1915. See also Sarafian, comp., in Morgenthau, *United States Diplomacy on the Bosphorus*, 52.

34 Uğur Ü. Üngör, "A Reign of Terror: CUP Rule in Diyarbekir Province, 1913–1918," (Master's thesis, Department of History, University of Amsterdam, June 2005), 6.

35 Ronald Grigor Suny, "The Holocaust before the Holocaust: Reflections on the Armenian Genocide," in Kieser and Schaller, eds., *Der Völkermord an den Armeniern und die Shoah*, 94–98; Bloxham, "Determinants of the Armenian Genocide," 24–34; Üngör, "A Reign of Terror," 13–15, 17ff.

The nation, beginning with the spheres of trade and language, was to be cleansed of "foreign elements" in order to establish an ethnic culture and economy.[36] It was ethnic nation-building through marginalization, forced assimilation, or destruction of the non-Turkish components of first and foremost the age-old Anatolian multicultural make-up, a process that required the rewriting of history and the definition of non-Turks as the Other.[37] According to Wandel, though not all non-Turks were "loyal," and Christians were generally opposed to the CUP system of centralization and to the principle "Turkey for the Turks," they saw it as necessary to work with the CUP rather than to break with it when it came to improving their living conditions.[38] This was despite the fact that Christians of the empire were subjected to what he described as a repressive and xenophobic regime which systematically discriminated against them.[39]

From Boycott to Violent Persecution

As noted, the 1914 cleansing was initially attempted by the reintroduction of economic boycott[40] and by other intimidating measures.[41] As Van der Zee

---

[36] Üngör, "A Reign of Terror," 20–21; Akçam, *From Empire to Republic*, 138–39; Ayla Göl, "Imagining the Turkish nation through 'othering' Armenians," *Nations and Nationalism* 11, no. 1 (2005): 129–30. On the connection between CUP linguistic policies and the subsequent genocide: Hilmar Kaiser, *Imperialism, Racism, and Development Theories: The Construction of a Dominant Paradigm on the Ottoman Armenians* (Ann Arbor: Gomidas, 1998), 28.

[37] Akçam, *From Empire to Republic*, x; Robert Melson, "Provocation or Nationalism: A Critical Inquiry into the Armenian Genocide of 1915," *The Armenian Genocide in Perspective*, Richard G. Hovannisian, ed. (New Brunswick: Transaction Publishers, 1986), 77.

[38] UM, 139. D. 1., "Tyrkiet – Indre Forhold," pk. 1, no. II, 24/7 1914.

[39] Ibid.

[40] On the 1909–11 economic boycotts of Ottoman Greeks: Elena Frangakis-Syrett, "The Economic Activities of the Greek Community of Izmir in the Second Half of the Nineteenth and Early Twentieth Centuries," in *Ottoman Greeks in the Age of Nationalism: Politics, Economy, and Society in the Nineteenth Century*, Dimitri Gondicas and Charles Issawi, eds. (Princeton: The Darwin Press, 1999), 26, 28; Haris Exertzoglou, "The Development of a Greek Ottoman Bourgeoisie: Investment Patterns in the Ottoman Empire, 1850–1914," ibid., 100; Richard Clogg, "The Greek *Millet* in the Ottoman Empire," in *Christians and Jews in the Ottoman Empire: The Functioning of a Plural Society: The Central Lands*, Benjamin Braude and Bernard Lewis, eds. (New York and London: Holmes & Meier Publishers, 1982), 1: 199. On economic boycotts in the Ottoman Empire: *An Economic and Social History of the Ottoman Empire, 1300–1914*, Halil İnalçik, ed. (Cambridge: Cambridge University Press, 1994), 840–41.

[41] A consequence of the boycott was that Turks were not allowed to work for Christians: Morgenthau, *United States Diplomacy on the Bosphorus*, 68, 70. On the closing of Orthodox Greek churches and schools as a protest against boycott and persecutions: ibid., 70; UM, 2-0355, "Konstantinopel/Istanbul, diplomatisk repræsentation," "Noter og indberetninger om den politiske udvikling, 1914–1922," "Verdenskrigen. Rapporter fra Smyrna.

saw it, the Ionian region was already sparsely populated and had plenty of arable soil, with ample room for Muslim settlers even if the authorities had chosen not to expel the Greeks.[42] So in the sense that the cleansing was part of an economic project, it was carried out as a means of creating a national economy dominated by Turks/Muslims — political logic overtook economic concerns during the 1910s, as it has been put.[43] The aim of economic Turkification was to create a class dominated by Turks or Turkified Muslims who were perceived by the CUP (and later by the Kemalists) as loyal, not only because of their ethno-religious traits, but because they owed their position to those who had "removed the competition," i.e., removed Christian entrepreneurs who were seen as dominating the empire's economy at the expense of Muslims. These Christian entrepreneurs had gained a degree of independence and had become a perceived obstacle, not just because of their ethnicity and religion, but also because of their perceived membership of an economic class that was seen as having a limited allegiance to the state.[44] Wandel stated that "the Turks attempted, in connection with the boycott movement, to create a Turkish business class that could substitute the Greek (or, as it was later said, the Christian) one, and the newly founded Turkish trade association announced that it had in a few weeks managed to replace the closed Greek businesses with 600 Turkish retail businesses with a capital of some 100,000 Turkish Pounds."[45]

Nov. 1914–Marts 1916," 19/6 1914; *Berlingske Tidende*, 9 June 1914; Philip Mansel, *Constantinople: City of the World's Desire, 1453–1924* (London: John Murray, 1995), 369.

[42] UM, 2-0355, "Konstantinopel/Istanbul, diplomatisk repræsentation," "Noter og indberetninger om den politiske udvikling, 1914–1922," "Verdenskrigen. Rapporter fra Smyrna. Nov. 1914–Marts 1916," 25/6 1914. Most of the *muhadjirs* who settled in the Aegean region were not familiar with the climate or agricultural conditions (many did not even speak Turkish), which, according to local governor of Çeşme, Hilmi Uran, quickly resulted in a significant deterioration of living standards: Aktar, "Homogenizing the Nation," in Hirschon, ed., *Crossing the Aegean*, 84. Such elements of poor planning of resettlement of refugees from rural areas seem to have been a recurrent issue in both Greece and the Ottoman Empire/Turkey, although a significantly larger percentage of Muslim refugees were peasants, cf. ibid., 88–89.

[43] Çağlar Keyder, "The Consequences of the Exchange of Populations for Turkey," in Hirschon, ed., *Crossing the Aegean*, 45. For a Marxist interpretation: Doğu Ergil, "A Reassessment: The Young Turks, their Politics and Anti-Colonial Struggle," *Balkan Studies*, 16, no. 2 (1975), especially the section "Breaking the Power of the Foreign and Minority Compradore Bourgeoisie: Armenian and Greek Operations of the Union and Progress," 59ff.

[44] Keyder, "The Consequences of the Exchange," in Hirschon, ed., *Crossing the Aegean*. 51; Aktar, "Homogenizing the Nation," ibid., 91.

[45] UM, 2-0355, "Konstantinopel/Istanbul, diplomatisk repræsentation," "1888–1920. Indberetninger om Handelsforhold," "Økonomiske Forhold, Handel og Søfart i Tyrkiet 1914," 3/9 1914, p. 2. The announcement by the Turkish trade association seems to have

Inga Nalbandian, a Danish writer and newspaper correspondent who was married to Mardiros Nalbandian, an Armenian scholar from Galata, reported from Constantinople that those she refers to as "agents" would walk into the ladies' compartment on the Bosphorus ferry to warn the Muslim women not to buy from Christians. She also reported that this was just a small part of a large, chauvinist campaign that drove many Christians to ruin. For instance, at the Constantinople university, all three Greek professors, together with three out of five Armenian professors, had been fired without warning or cause. Nalbandian stated on this policy:

> It is a whole wave that comes and goes, the reason for the boycott is two-sided. The adoption of "the reforms in Asia Minor" [i.e., the recent reforms imposed by the Western powers affecting the Armenian *vilayets* in Eastern Anatolia, MB] - the red cape dangling in front of the eyes of the Turkish bull - must be punished, and punished severely, and since it is considered too dangerous to initiate an unconcealed massacre, the Armenians must be struck in a pecuniary manner. And regarding the Greeks — the Ottoman Greeks, that is — the still unsolved island question plays a large role; furthermore, one must add the bitter grudge held by the Turks, and not least by the all powerful Enver Pasha and through him the whole government, against the Ottoman Greeks, as there are among these to be found a number of rich men who have given and still give large sums to the Greek navy.[46]

In a lengthy report, Wandel described how it was only after the CUP dictatorship had come to power that Turkish shops in Constantinople would advertize that "This is a Muslim Business."[47] In another report, on the state of the economy in the empire in 1914, he wrote how numerous Greek merchants and shop owners went bankrupt in Constantinople, Smyrna, and other cities because of the boycott.[48] At the same time, Muslim preachers supported the boycott through their sermons.[49] But when the boycott did not have the desired overall effect — "[as] the *rayah* ['herd'] Greeks clung, however, to their fields," as Van der Zee expressed it[50] — the cleansing of

---

been overly optimistic: ibid., p. 3. On this trade organization, see also telegram from Constantinople under the heading "Turkey for the Turks": *Berlingske Tidende*, 5 May 1914.

46 *Nationaltidende*, 29 April 1914. See also *Nationaltidende*, 20 June 1914. On Nalbandian, see Inga Nalbandian, *Your Brother's Blood Cries Out*, Victoria Rowe, ed. and transl. (London: Gomidas Institute, 2007).

47 UM, 139. D. 1., "Politiske Begivenheder i Tyrkiet i 1914," 26/1 1915.

48 UM, 2-0355, "Konstantinopel/Istanbul, diplomatisk repræsentation," "1888–1920. Indberetninger om Handelsforhold," "Økonomiske Forhold, Handel og Søfart i Tyrkiet 1914," 3/9 1914, p. 2.

49 Ergil, "A Reassessment," 63.

50 UM, 2-0355, "Konstantinopel/Istanbul, diplomatisk repræsentation," "Noter og indberetninger om den politiske udvikling, 1914–1922," "Verdenskrigen. Rapporter fra Smyrna. Nov. 1914–Marts 1916," 19/6 1914.

Ottoman Greeks outside the major cities was attempted by violent persecution. As the consul reported 19 June:

> After open hints that it would be advisable for them to leave the place [Adramyt], menaces that they would be done to death were resorted to, and finally the threats began to take shape in the murder of villagers returning from their fields and the waylaying of townsmen. A reign of terror was instituted and the panic-stricken Greeks fled as fast as they could to the neighbouring island of Mytilene. Soon the movement spread to Kemer, Kilissekeuy, Kinick, Pergamos and Soma. Armed *bashibozuks* [Turkish irregular troops] attacked the people residing therein, lifted the cattle, drove them from their farms and took forcible possession thereof. The details of what took place [are] harrowing, women were seduced, girls were ravished, some of them dying from the ill-treatment received, children at the breast were shot or cut down with their mothers.[51]

These *bashibozuks*, alternatively called "Turkish gangs" or *chettés* (or *chetes, shotas;* in Turkish *çeteler* – irregulars) in the reports, numbered 8–10,000 in the *vilayet* of Aydın alone, and were according to Van der Zee's reports financed and run by the state.[52] Many of these gangs consisted of members of the SO and/or radicalized Muslim refugees from the Balkans or the Caucasus, the so-called *muhadjirs* (in Turkish, *muhacirler*),[53] who according to

---

[51] Ibid. On the sexual violence connected to the 1914 persecutions, see also Horton, *Blight of Asia*, 32.

[52] UM, 2-0355, "Konstantinopel/Istanbul, diplomatisk repræsentation," "Noter og indberetninger om den politiske udvikling, 1914–1922," "Verdenskrigen. Rapporter fra Smyrna. Nov. 1914–Marts 1916," 19/6 1914. See also Llewellyn Smith, *Ionian Vision*, 31; Toynbee wrote: "The procedure bore evidence of being systematic. The terror attacked one district after another, and was carried on by 'chetté' bands, enrolled from the Roumele refugees as well as from the local population and nominally attached as reinforcements to the regular Ottoman gendarmerie." See Arnold J. Toynbee, *The Western Question in Greece and Turkey: A Study in the Contact of Civilisations* (London: Constable, 1922 [reprint, New York: Howard Fertig, 1970]), 140.

[53] On the hundreds of thousands of *muhadjirs* and their harrowing experiences in the Balkan Wars or the Russian Empire: *Report of the International Commission to Inquire into the Causes and Conduct of the Balkan War* (Washington, D.C.: Carnegie Endowment for International Peace, 1914); Aktar, "Homogenizing the Nation," in Hirschon, ed., *Crossing the Aegean*, 82; Toynbee, *The Western Question in Greece and Turkey*, 138–40; Çagaptay, *Islam, Secularism, and Nationalism*, 6–7; Alan Kramer, *Dynamic of Destruction: Culture and Mass Killing in the First World War* (Oxford: Oxford University Press, 2007), 132ff; Peter Mentzel, "'Ethnic Cleansing,' Emigration, and Identity: The Case of Habsburg Bosnia-Herzegovina," in Várdy and Tooley, eds., *Ethnic Cleansing in Twentieth Century Europe*. 99–112; Dennis P. Hupchick, "Bulgaria's 'Turks': A Muslim Minority in a Christian Nation-State," ibid., 133–156; Stephen D. Shenfield, "The Circassians: A Forgotten Genocide?," in *The Massacre in History*, Mark Levene and Penny Roberts, eds. (Herndon VA: Berghahn Books, 1999), 149–62. For a Danish witness to atrocities committed by Bulgarians against

Wandel carried out the persecutions, plundering and murdering "as many of the hated Greeks as possible."[54] Subsequently, these gangs also attacked non-Ottoman Greek citizens and their property in a systematic fashion, and the justification given by the authorities for this particular part of the campaign could indicate that the operation was not simply meant as a security measure, but had an ideological, not to say xenophobic, rationale: "let foreigners go and buy farms in their own lands."[55] Hans-Lukas Kieser contends that to the CUP, the cleansing operation was also "retaliation for the evil which, according to them, the Muslims under Greek domination had been suffering since the Balkan Wars."[56] For instance, the Danish newspaper *København*, 17 June 1914, reported that after these wars, Greek "administrative harassment" had caused tens of thousands of Muslims to leave their homes. And *Nationaltidende*, 2 April 1914, quoted a telegram on how Muslims had recently been expelled via Thessalonica. Both the CUP and at least a sizeable number of the *muhadjirs* had in the wake of the 1912-13 wars become radicalized to the point of becoming anti-Christian, and even though these Christians belonged to groups that had lived in Anatolia and surrounding areas for thousands of years, they were now not only designated as "infidel," but also as "foreigners."[57]

Muslim and Greek civilians in 1912 see Franz von Jessen, *Mænd og Kampe paa Balkan* [*Men and Battles in the Balkans*] (Copenhagen: Gyldendal, 1913), 236-40.

[54] UM, 139. D. 1., "Politiske Begivenheder i Tyrkiet i 1914," 26/1 1915, p. 17. For the estimated number of *bashibozuks*: UM, 5. L. 15., "Grækenland-Tyrkiet: Politiske Forhold," pk. 1, nr. 31, 23/6 1914. On "Turkish hatred of Greeks," see also Morgenthau, *United States Diplomacy on the Bosphorus*, 68; Harry Stürmer, *Two War Years in Constantinople: Sketches of German and Young Turkish Ethics and Politics*, rev. ed., annotated and introduction by Hilmar Kaiser (London: Sterndale Classics, 2004 [reprint of the 1917 edition]), 69. Vahram Dadrian relates that in November 1914, on the day of the declaration of Jihad, a meeting was held in Çorum "to which the city's Greek and Armenian dignitaries were also invited. Those who spoke there insisted that there was no difference among Christians, regardless of their nationalities: they were all malicious enemies of the Turks," cf. Vahram Dadrian, *To the Desert: Pages from My Diary* (Princeton and London: Gomidas Institute 2003), 8. On Greeks as "aliens" to Turks, see Otto Liman von Sanders, *Fünf Jahre in der Türkei* [*Five Years in Turkey*] (Berlin: Verlag August Scherl, 1920), 50.

[55] UM, 2-0355, "Konstantinopel/Istanbul, diplomatisk repræsentation," "Noter og indberetninger om den politiske udvikling, 1914-1922," "Verdenskrigen. Rapporter fra Smyrna. Nov. 1914-Marts 1916," 19/6 1914. Over the last decades, a sizeable number of Greek citizens had migrated to Western Anatolia, e.g., to benefit from the opening of trade in the region, and these Greeks were now being targeted alongside Ottoman Greeks, see Llewellyn Smith, *Ionian Vision*, 24-25.

[56] Kieser, "Dr. Mehmed Reshid," in Kieser and Schaller, eds., *Der Völkermord an den Armeniern und die Shoah*, 257. See also Smith, *Ionian Vision*, 51.

[57] Kieser, "Dr. Mehmed Reshid," in Kieser and Schaller, eds., *Der Völkermord an den Armeniern und die Shoah*, 257. Rahmi and other high-ranking radical nationalists like Talât

Ayhan Aktar describes the events in Ionia as "tension manifesting itself in hostile mob behavior and a more nationalistic state bureaucracy,"[58] but fails to see a connection between these manifestations. But according to Kusçubaşı Eşref Sencer, an SO leader, the cleansing was indeed a planned event. He quoted Enver Paşa as saying on 23 February 1914 that non-Muslims had to be got rid of as they had proved that they did not support the continued existence of the state, and that the salvation of the state was linked to stern measures against them.[59] And Russian Consul-General at Smyrna, Andrew (Andrey) D. Kalmykow, recalled a talk he had around this time with Interior Minister Talât Paşa in the presence of *vali* Rahmi Bey. According to Kalmykow, the following exchange took place between Rahmi and Talât: "'What can I do?' asked the vali with a smile. 'We have sent Turkish farmers to colonize the coast, but the Greek peasants simply won't stay with them and move away of their own free will.' 'No, Rahmi,' said Talât Paşa, 'the Greeks cannot remain. They are forced to leave. They must go.'"[60]

The 1914 Smyrna Persecutions

The massacre of some 100 Greeks[61] at Phocaea (Foça (Tur.)) that began on the night of 12 June was one of the worst attacks of the campaign. After having looted the villages south of Menemen, causing the Greeks to flee, the *bashibozuks* attacked the town of Phocaea from three sides — according to Van der Zee, they were "ably assisted by the Cretans who work at the salt depots," referring to Muslim Cretans who had previously migrated or been expelled.[62] On 25 June the consul quoted an eyewitness to the destruction:

---

and Mustafa Kemal (Atatürk) hailed originally from the Balkans. They had been radicalized by the loss of homeland and family members and were among the Young Turks most adamant on creating a new, ethnically homogenous homeland in Anatolia.
For an introduction, see Erik-Jan Zürcher, "Greek and Turkish refugees and deportees 1912-1924," 2003, http://www.let.leidenuniv.nl/tcimo/tulp/Research/ejz18.htm. See also Akçam, *A Shameful Act*, 85-87; Andrew D. Kalmykow, *Memoirs of a Russian Diplomat: Outposts of the Empire, 1893-1917*, ed. Alexandra Kalmykow (New Haven: Yale University Press 1971), 253; Çağaptay, *Islam, Secularism, and Nationalism*, 7. On how the Balkan Wars created what is described as "indignation at Christians" and caused difficulties for missionaries like Eva Elvers (Germany), Thora von Wedel-Jarlsberg (Norway), and Maria Jacobsen and Wilhelmine Grünhagen (Denmark) in Eastern Anatolia: *Rigsarkivet, Private Institutioner*: *Kvindelige Missions Arbejdere* (*Women Missionary Workers; KMA*), 10,360, Pk. Nr. 42, protocol of meetings in KMA's Armenia Committee, 15 January 1913.

58 Aktar, "Homogenizing the Nation," in Hirschon, ed., *Crossing the Aegean*, 83.

59 Quoted in Akçam, "The Ottoman Documents and the Genocidal Policies," 133.

60 Kalmykow, *Memoirs of a Russian Diplomat*, 258.

61 June 16 cable from Athens in *New York Times*, 17 June 1914.

62 UM, 2-0355, "Konstantinopel/Istanbul, diplomatisk repræsentation," "Noter og indberetninger om den politiske udvikling, 1914-1922," "Verdenskrigen. Rapporter fra Smyrna.

> [W]ithin a quarter of an hour after the assault had begun every boat in the place was full of people trying to get away and when no more boats could be had the inhabitants sought refuge on the little peninsula on which the lighthouse stands. I saw eleven bodies of men and women lying dead on the shore. How many were killed I could not say, but trying to get into a house of which the door stood ajar I saw two other dead bodies lying in the entrance hall. Every shop in the place was looted and the goods that could not be carried away were wantonly destroyed.[63]

The authorities apparently tried to keep the destruction of Phocaea a secret, but after two days a French steam tugboat arriving at Smyrna on its way to Makaronia conveyed the news.[64] The crew had observed a large number of people on the promontory, and sailed some 700 "half starved wretches" to Mytilene. The authorities there sent boats to rescue the remaining 5–6,000 Phocaeans to the island.[65] According to French eyewitness Charles Manciet, the town of 8–9,000 Greeks and circa 400 Turks was methodically destroyed and plundered by well-armed bands, and although the Smyrna authorities sent regular troops to Phocaea, ostensibly to restore order, these soldiers continued to destroy the town. Manciet expressed the belief that the *bashibozuks* were organized and armed by the authorities to expel the Christians,[66] a notion shared by another French eyewitness, Félix Sartiaux, who

Nov. 1914–Marts 1916," 25/6 1914. On the persecution of Greek villagers in the vicinity of Phocaea prior to the attack on the city itself: Félix Sartiaux, "Le sac de Phocée et l'expulsion des Grecs d'Asie Mineure en juin 1914," *Revue des deux mondes* 24, no. 6 (November–December 1914): 657. On Muslim Cretans settling in the Ottoman Empire before World War I: Sophia Koufopoulou, "Muslim Cretans in Turkey: The Reformulation of Ethnic Identity in an Aegean Community," in Hirschon, ed., *Crossing the Aegean,* 211; Toynbee, *The Western Question in Greece and Turkey*, 139.

63 UM, 2-0355, "Konstantinopel/Istanbul, diplomatisk repræsentation," "Noter og indberetninger om den politiske udvikling, 1914–1922," "Verdenskrigen. Rapporter fra Smyrna. Nov. 1914–Marts 1916," 25/6 1914. See also Stürmer, *Two War Years in Constantinople,* 101; Llewellyn Smith, *Ionian Vision,* 31–32.

64 UM, 2-0355, "Konstantinopel/Istanbul, diplomatisk repræsentation," "Noter og indberetninger om den politiske udvikling, 1914–1922," "Verdenskrigen. Rapporter fra Smyrna. Nov. 1914–Marts 1916," 25/6 1914.

65 Ibid. On the evacuation of Greek refugees from Phocaea to Mytilene, see also Morgenthau, *United States Diplomacy on the Bosphorus*, 71. On previous persecutions of Muslims by Greek *chetes* on Mytilene: Bruce Clark, *Twice a Stranger: How Mass Expulsions Forged Modern Greece and Turkey* (London: Granta Books 2007), 38. According to Greek sources, 3800 refugees from Phocaea arrived at Thessalonica 16 June; many were wounded by bullets or bayonets and they related how they had been attacked by bands of robbers supported by gendarmes: *Berlingske Tidende*, 16 June 1914.

66 In Horton, *Blight of Asia,* 28–33. On Manciet, see also Sartiaux, "Le sac de Phocée et l'expulsion des Grecs d'Asie Mineure," 658ff. According to a Greek census, the number of Greeks in Phocaea was 10,825 ca. 1912: Alexis Alexandris, "The Greek Census of Anatolia (1910–1912): A Contribution to Ottoman Historical Demography," in Gondicas and Issawi, eds., *Ottoman Greeks in the Age of Nationalism,* 58.

would also identify two local CUP members as direct orchestrators of the methodical destruction of Phocaea.[67] The simultaneous attacks on the Greeks of the Kara Burnu Peninsula, which coincided with the landing of some 600 *muhadjir* families at Kato-Panagia (Aşari Çiftlik (Tur.)) and with the landing of a number of other such families at Çeşme (Chesmé, Tsesme) who were to replace the Greeks of Alacata (Myonessos (Gr.)), also indicate that a major, organized, and effective anti-Greek campaign took place.[68] Greeks fled the region in their tens of thousands to avoid looting and murder, while the *muhadjirs* were assisted by the local authorities in driving them out and taking over their properties.[69]

For instance, Ayhan Aktar describes how the Greeks of the coastal town of Çeşme, opposite the island of Chios, fled immediately after Hilmi Uran was appointed local governor of the town in May 1914. Although Uran (and Aktar) seem to downplay the organized aspects of the cleansing of the area, according to Aktar, Uran stated that "just a few days after [Uran's] arrival, the Greek community in and around Çeşme started to panic and arranged the means of transport to the nearest island, Chios. Nearly forty thousand Greeks migrated in two weeks."[70] According to Danish newspaper *Politiken*, 24 June 1914, most of these refugees had to live in the open on Chios, and the Greek authorities had great difficulties in providing for them. 4,000 refugees had fled to the deserted island of Hunil where they, according to the report, were dying of hunger. The timing of Uran's arrival with the departure of the Greeks could be a coincidence, but it seems more likely that it points to the organized nature of the cleansing, with local officials being appointed by the central authorities to carry out the project. This was seemingly also the case when in June 1913, radical Young Turk Mehmet Reşid Şahingiray, an ardent nationalist with a religiously and racially inspired hatred of Christians, was hastily installed as *mutesarif* of the northern Ottoman Aegean sub-province of Karesi (Balıkeşir (Tur.)) where he dedicated himself to the expulsion of Greeks.[71] As to Çeşme, the Greeks fled in such a haste that their homes and possessions were left largely intact. As local gov-

---

[67] Sartiaux, "Le sac de Phocée et l'expulsion des Grecs d'Asie Mineure," 663.

[68] UM, 2-0355, "Konstantinopel/Istanbul, diplomatisk repræsentation," "Noter og indberetninger om den politiske udvikling, 1914-1922," "Verdenskrigen. Rapporter fra Smyrna. Nov. 1914-Marts 1916," 25/6 1914. See also *Nationaltidende*, 8 June 1914.

[69] UM, 2-0355, "Konstantinopel/Istanbul, diplomatisk repræsentation," "Noter og indberetninger om den politiske udvikling, 1914-1922," "Verdenskrigen. Rapporter fra Smyrna. Nov. 1914-Marts 1916," 25/6 1914.

[70] Aktar, "Homogenizing the Nation," in Hirschon, ed., *Crossing the Aegean*, 83.

[71] Kieser, "Dr. Mehmed Reshid," in Kieser and Schaller, eds., *Der Völkermord an den Armeniern und die Shoah*, 257-61.

ernor, it was Uran's responsibility to arrange for the orderly redistribution of Greek property, but this was plundered by locals or by *muhadjirs* arriving from Thessalonica before he could fulfill his task.[72] This could be indicative of the general fact that even when an "orderly conduct" of ethnic cleansing or genocidal practices was attempted by the authorities, local mobs were not always easily controlled.

Generally, the *bashibozuks* seem to have met little resistance, but at the village of Saraköy in the Menemen district, Greeks formed an armed resistance resulting in fierce fighting lasting for four hours until the defenders ran out of ammunition. Then the villagers, outnumbered and outgunned, fought a hand-to-hand combat until they were killed. A few managed to escape to the nearby town of Menemen, but as this was a town of some 20,000 inhabitants, the *bashibozuks* shot any inhabitants who left the town, but did not dare to attempt an outright attack.[73] This could point to the fact that even though Turkification through persecution was CUP policy, it was a policy that, at this point at least, could not be followed too openly or with any widespread use of regular military forces. Stealth, "plausible denial," and political concerns outweighed the desire to cleanse the area completely. Still, it is estimated that some 150–200,000 Ottoman Greeks left their homes before the outbreak of World War I, either by direct force or, as it is put, "voluntarily," i.e., by threats of force.[74]

1914: Denial and Significance

Despite the attempts to keep the cleansing a secret and to deny both the existence of and the responsibility for it, the Ottoman Government soon had to change course under foreign pressure, especially from France. Also, the persecutions generated anger and bitterness in Greece. The country proceeded to mobilize its forces, as did the Ottoman Empire, but the CUP were aware that they were not ready for a war against Greece that many believed would break out if the persecutions did not stop.[75] For instance, in an inter-

---

[72] Aktar, "Homogenizing the Nation," in Hirschon, ed., *Crossing the Aegean* , 83–84.

[73] UM, 2-0355, "Konstantinopel/Istanbul, diplomatisk repræsentation," "Noter og indberetninger om den politiske udvikling, 1914–1922," "Verdenskrigen. Rapporter fra Smyrna. Nov. 1914–Marts 1916," 19/6 1914. However, according to "a Constantinople dispatch" quoted in *New York Times*, 16 June 1914, 40 inhabitants of Menemen were killed in what appears to be a successful defense of the city.

[74] Aktar, "Homogenizing the Nation," in Hirschon, ed., *Crossing the Aegean,* 83; UM, 3-0355, "Konstantinopel/Istanbul, diplomatisk repræsentation," "1888–1920. Indberetninger om Handelsforhold," "Commercial Report for the Year 1914" 27, no. 3 (1915), 2.

[75] UM, 139. D. 1., "Politiske Begivenheder i Tyrkiet i 1914," 26/1 1915, p. 17; UM, 5. L. 15., "Grækenland–Tyrkiet: Politiske Forhold," pk. 1, nr. 26, 19/6 1914; UM, 5. L. 15., "Grækenland–Tyrkiet: Politiske Forhold," pk. 1, nr. 28, 20/6 1914. See also Dimitri Pentzopoulos,

view with a Danish paper in June 1914, Greek King Constantine I stated that peace could not be upheld as long as the persecutions of the Greeks were continuing,[76] and Venizelos made similar remarks in the Greek parliament.[77] In the Danish newspaper *Nationaltidende*, 26 April 1914, it was reported that the Greek consul at Smyrna had tried to approach *vali* Rahmi Bey in order to clarify the matter of the expulsions, but had received the answer that he "had left for the countryside." After consultations with the Austro-Hungarian ambassador at Constantinople, Count Johann Pallavicini, Carl Ellis Wandel was convinced that although neither Greece nor the empire was ready for war, a war between these countries was inevitable in the near future, and he was also convinced that the Anatolian Greeks would then be worse off than ever before.[78] During World War I, even more violent persecutions of Greeks did in fact take place on a regular basis;[79] however, this development began well before June 1917 when Greece finally joined the war against the empire and her Allies.

Regarding a developing CUP policy of denial, the official reactions to the 1914 events point toward aspects of the contemporary official Ottoman (as well as the present Turkish) denial of, e.g., the Armenian genocide: the claim that the government, when it came to killings and persecution, had no control of local officials or of the designated killer gangs, and the attempts to apply damage control through cover ups, shifting of blame, and propaganda. Talât declared in June 1914 that the "regrettable incidents" in the Smyrna region happened because many local officials still believed that the orders they received from the government to protect the Greek population had been issued under pressure from the Great Powers, i.e., not issued in ear-

---

The Balkan Exchange of Minorities and Its Impact on Greece (London: Hurst, 2002 [reprint of 1962 edition]), 53–54; Morgenthau, *United States Diplomacy on the Bosphorus*, 67; *Politiken*, 10 February 1914; *Nationaltidende*, 15 June 1914; *New York Times*, 14 June 1914. According to Danish diplomatic ministers to Russia and Austria-Hungary, Harald Scavenius and Flemming Lerche, a reason why the Ottoman authorities discontinued the attempts at cleansing the Aegean Greeks was that the two Dreadnoughts that Great Britain had sold to the empire had not yet been delivered, and were not expected to be delivered for two months. Thus, Greece was still the superior naval power, and the Ottoman authorities were therefore careful not to give Greece cause to declare war: UM, 5. L. 15., "Grækenland-Tyrkiet: politiske forhold," pk. I, nr. XV, 18/6 1914, H. Scavenius to E. Scavenius; nr. XXVI, 18/6 1914, Lerche to E. Scavenius. See also *Nationaltidende*, 13 June 1914; 15 June 1914; 19 June 1914; *København*, 17 June 1914; Kaldis, "Background for Conflict," 1137ff.

[76] *Politiken*, 22 June 1914. See also *Berlingske Tidende*, 26 April 1914.

[77] *Berlingske Tidende*, 13 June 1914.

[78] UM, 5. L. 15., "Grækenland-Tyrkiet: Politiske Forhold," pk. 1, nr. 26, 19/6 1914.

[79] Akçam, *From Empire to Republic*, 146–47; UM, 139. N. 2., "Tyrkiet: Behandling af Grækere paa tyrkisk Omraade," nr. X, 14/1 1917.

nest. Thus, according to Talât, all responsibility for wrongdoings rested with Rahmi Bey.[80] The U.S. ambassador at Constantinople, Henry Morgenthau, related that Talât would not admit that government officials were entirely responsible for what was called "uprisings." This, incidentally, could be an implicit recognition of the fact that officials bore the main responsibility for these events.[81]

Talât even went on what Van der Zee called a "farcical tour" of the towns and cities in the Smyrna region, making speeches promising complete security while the local Greeks had to stay at home, day and night, to avoid being beaten up or shot.[82] According to a telegram from Talât to the Porte, sent during his stay in Smyrna, the court martial in the city had sentenced 47 persons to 3–5 year prison terms for plundering Greek property. This could indicate that the interior minister wanted to signal that the anti-Greek persecutions were, officially at least, not, or no longer, acceptable. At the same time it was reported that two Greeks were to stand trial since they allegedly had made Greeks leave the country by spreading rumors of Turkish massacres.[83] Talât also claimed that Greeks from the Çeşme region had left voluntarily and that they had not been attacked at any point.[84] It seems that by late June 1914 Talât had decided that the campaign inaugurated under his auspices had to be terminated, put on hold, or conducted in a less open and direct manner,[85] but Van der Zee saw no reason to trust the authorities:

> To add one more act to this pitiable farce the Imperial Government applied for the delegates [dragomans, i.e., interpreters representing the major foreign embassies, MB] to show civilised Europe that the work of the restitution is sincerely carried on and it is now promenading these gentlemen in motor cars & special trains, giving them good dinners and fine wines, while the victims of its atrocities are begged their bread or living on the charity eked out to them. What these representatives of the Great Powers will have to tell

---

[80] UM, 5. L. 15., "Grækenland-Tyrkiet: Politiske Forhold," pk. 1, nr. 13, 9/6 1914. In what appears to be a somewhat similar fashion, Talât had, according to an official Ottoman telegram, earlier travelled to Rodosto and Adrianople (Edirne (Tur.)) to "inquire about the reasons for the Greek migration." The CUP were allegedly strongly against expelling the Greeks of Ottoman Thrace, a policy that they claimed was organized by the son of *vali* of Adrianople, Hacı Adil Bey while the *vali* himself had failed to intervene: *Berlingske Tidende*, 26 April 1914. Apparently, the persecution continued in and around Adrianople: *Berlingske Tidende*, 27 April 1914; *Nationaltidende*, 19 May 1914.

[81] Morgenthau, *United States Diplomacy on the Bosphorus,* 75.

[82] UM, 5. L. 15., "Grækenland-Tyrkiet: Politiske Forhold," pk. 1, nr. 41, 27/6 1914. See also Akçam, *From Empire to Republic*, pp. 145–46.

[83] *Nationaltidende*, 19 June 1914.

[84] *Nationaltidende*, 23 June 1914.

[85] UM, 5. L. 15, "Grækenland-Tyrkiet: politiske forhold," pk. I, nr. 28, 20/6 1914. See also Kaldis, "Background for Conflict," 1139.

them I know not but, in any case, one thing is absolutely certain: that whatever their report is the tyrannous measures will not cease, though they may be carried on less openly, as the communication of the Grand Vizier to the American Companies here conclusively proves. In his communication to the Singer Co. at Smyrna the United [States] Consul General Horton says that "he is instructed by [his] Ambassador to inform it that he has obtained the promise of the Grand Vizier that for two months the Greek employees will not be molested but that at the expiration of that time they must be replaced.[86]

The consul's (perhaps incorrect) assessment of the dragomans' mission was shared by the British ambassador at Constantinople, Sir Louis Mallet, who told Morgenthau that the European powers were going to "whitewash" the empire as it did not suit them to have war now.[87]

While it was officially claimed that only 1,000 Greeks had left the empire and that they had done so of their own free will and against the wishes of the authorities,[88] the Ottoman press acknowledged that persecution, albeit allegedly of an unauthorized nature, was widespread. According to Wandel, *Tânin* reported that while a gang of 8,000–10,000 robbers were continuing their violent acts around Smyrna, the government had taken precautions that would undoubtedly restore order.[89] Another official paper, *Tercüman-i Hakikat*, claimed that the Powers, by not explicitly denouncing the empire's policies regarding Greece and the Ottoman Greeks, actually applauded the empire's attitude.[90] Whether or not this was true mattered perhaps less than the fact that Turkish nationalists felt somewhat encouraged by the lack of forceful outside intervention — after all, neither Greece nor any other nation turned out to be willing to enter a war against the empire to aid the Ottoman Greeks.

---

[86] UM, 2-0355, "Konstantinopel/Istanbul, diplomatisk repræsentation," "Noter og indberetninger om den politiske udvikling, 1914–1922," "Verdenskrigen. Rapporter fra Smyrna. Nov. 1914–Marts 1916," 25/6 1914. See also Morgenthau, *United States Diplomacy on the Bosphorus*, 67. Regarding the objectivity of U.S. Consul General Horton at Smyrna as a witness to the 1914 events, see Morgenthau, ibid., 69–71; the latter initially had some reservations, as Horton had a Greek wife and was regarded by Morgenthau as being pro-Greek, but other sources seem to confirm Horton's reports, e.g., Van der Zee who, if anything, was pro-Turkish rather than pro-Greek (see below).

[87] Morgenthau, at Smyrna, *United States Diplomacy on the Bosphorus*, 70. See also Kalmykow, *Memoirs of a Russian Diplomat*, 258. According to Hilmar Kaiser the dragomans' commission did in fact hold the government and the CUP responsible, helping to terminate the anti-Greek campaign, see "The Ottoman Government and the End of the Ottoman Social Formation, 1915–1917,"

http://www.hist.net/kieser/aghet/Essays/EssayKaiser.html, 2001.

[88] *Nationaltidende*, 14 June 1914.

[89] UM, 5. L. 15, "Grækenland-Tyrkiet: politiske forhold," pk. I, nr. 31, 23/6 1914.

[90] Ibid.

But Ottoman papers also tried to give the impression that Greece or Greeks in general were equally responsible for the "incidents," as when they reported on what they described as Greek bands of robbers that used Aegean islands as bases for raids. This claim may be exaggerated if one considers that *Stamboul* exemplified it by quoting a telegram relating an incident concerning a boat with three Greek robbers who had presumably shot at persons near Çeşme.[91] There is no evidence, however, that Wandel, anymore than Van der Zee, found the official propaganda trustworthy. Wandel was satisfied with the consul's reports on the cleansing of the Greeks, as was expressed in a letter to the consul. Here, Wandel mentioned the 19 and 25 June reports that, he emphasized, contrary to regular procedure had been sent directly to the Danish Foreign Ministry.[92]

In 1914, the aim of the Turkification policy was not to exterminate but to expel as many Greeks from Ionia and Ottoman Thrace as possible as not only a "security measure," but as an extension of the policy of economic and cultural Turkification, while at the same time accommodating the *muhadjirs* that had been driven out of their own homes under brutal circumstances.[93] This policy was to a large degree informed by a radically exclusionist political ideology that has been aptly defined by Aktar, albeit he seems to apply it to a post-World War I context:

> The turkification programme can [...] be defined in practice as a set of policies aimed at establishing the unconditional supremacy of Turkish ethnic identity in nearly all aspects of social and economic life.[94]

Wandel, a businessman by trade like Van der Zee, believed that the losses resulting from the persecutions were irreparable since an industrious class of people had been expelled despite that the Smyrna province was already thinly populated. He predicted that the province would suffer from the re-

---

[91] UM, 5. L. 15, "Grækenland-Tyrkiet: politiske forhold," pk. I, nr. 41, 27/6 1914. See also *Nationaltidende*, 18 June 1914.

[92] UM, 2-0355, "Konstantinopel/Istanbul, diplomatisk repræsentation," "Noter og indberetninger om den politiske udvikling, 1914-1922," "Verdenskrigen. Rapporter fra Smyrna. Nov. 1914-Marts 1916," Wandel to Van der Zee, no date, but attached to report from Van der Zee to Wandel, 15/6 1914. The report contains information on a *corps consulaire* meeting held on the initiative of the *doyen* of the corps, Kalmykow, to assess the Greek persecutions.

[93] Akçam, *From Empire to Republic*, 148.

[94] Aktar, "Homogenizing the Nation," in Hirschon, ed., *Crossing the Aegean*, 9. For an early report on how the Kemalists attempted to create a national movement to "liberate the Turkish trade from foreign middlemen," see report on "Le Congrés Economique de Smyrne," held 7 February 1923 under the leadership of Mustafa Kemal Paşa: UM, 52. Smyrna. 2. B., "Konsulatet i Smyrna's Repræsentation i 'Board of Commerce'," nr. 81, 23/3 1923.

sults of this policy for years to come.[95] Both he and Van der Zee elaborated on this in their annual reports regarding the state of the empire's economy in 1914. Wandel related that according to many businessmen, the anti-Greek boycott movement and persecutions damaged the empire's economy even more than had the Balkan Wars.[96] And in his lengthy *Commercial Report for the Year 1914*, Van der Zee described in details how devastating an impact the persecutions had on almost every aspect of the economy in the Smyrna region. To name one example, the expulsions caused, directly and indirectly, the loss of 40% of the estimated 1914 tobacco harvest.[97]

Such assessments of the consequences of the virtual disappearance of Christians from Asia Minor are still shared by scholars today: "Turkey lost its entrepreneurial class since finance, industry and commerce had largely been in the hands of the Christian populations — Greeks and Armenians."[98] But the possibilities created for Muslims to take over where they left by becoming entrepreneurs themselves; the practical experiences of ethnic cleansing; the general impunity of the perpetrators; and the relative political "success" of the cleansing — tens of thousands of Greeks fleeing, leaving their homes and possessions to be taken over by Muslim refugees[99] — meant that even more radical and violent measures could be seen as not only possible, but as yet another extension of a policy of "social engineering"

---

[95] UM, 5. L. 15., "Grækenland-Tyrkiet: Politiske Forhold," pk. 1, nr. 41, 27/6 1914.

[96] UM, 2-0355, "Konstantinopel/Istanbul, diplomatisk repræsentation," "1888-1920. Indberetninger om Handelsforhold," "Økonomiske Forhold, Handel og Søfart i Tyrkiet 1914," 3/9 1914, 1.

[97] UM, 3-0355, "Konstantinopel/Istanbul, diplomatisk repræsentation," "1888-1920. Indberetninger om Handelsforhold," "Commercial Report for the Year 1914," 27/3 1915, p. 11. On the remarkable decline in the Ottoman tobacco harvest from 1913-14 and 1914-15 (some of which can of course be explained by circumstances related to World War I), Zafer Toprak, *Türkiye'de "Milli Iktisat" (1908-1918)* (Ankara: Yurt, 1982), 315. I thank Uğur Ü. Üngör, University of Amsterdam, for pointing me to this volume and for providing the translation. According to a Danish member of the *Committee for the Exchange of the Greek and Turkish Populations* under the *League of Nations*, for Greece, a positive effect of the "population exchange" was that settlers brought with them experience that promoted tobacco cultivation, resulting in a growth in Greece's tobacco production from 23.5 million kilos in 1922 to 66 million kilos in 1925: J. V. Christensen, *Den Store Folkeflytning mellem Tyrkiet og Grækenland. En Indsats af folkenes Forbund* (Copenhagen: Gad, 1927), 62.

[98] Hirschon, "The Consequences of the Lausanne Convention: An Overview," in Hirschon, ed., *Crossing the Aegean*, 16. See also Keyder, "The Consequences of the Exchange," ibid., 46; Aktar, ibid., 81; Clark, *Twice a Stranger*, 13; Ergil, "A Reassessment," 64-66.

[99] UM, 5. L. 15., "Grækenland-Tyrkiet: Politiske Forhold," pk. 1, nr. 41, 27/6 1914.

through Turkification. Besides, as Talât told Morgenthau during the Armenian genocide, "We care nothing about the commercial loss."[100]

1915: War and Turkification

There is no doubt that, especially during World War I, there existed a general disregard within the Ottoman establishment for the needs and lives of the civilian population, whether Muslim, Jew, or Christian.[101] Wandel contended that "[w]artime conditions and the greed that has gripped the Ottoman rulers already in 1915 set mighty forces within Turkey's economical life in motion, and in 1916 these forces have to an even larger degree been used in the service of war and of the unwarranted need. Only a negligible part of the economic activity stemmed from the real societal needs, and therefore these needs were not met. Even the physical subsistence level required to keep individuals alive were not provided for large parts of the civilian population."[102] Wandel blamed the major speculators who amassed vast fortunes at the expense of the general population, and who were supported by the CUP and by the government in general where corruption was endemic. Commissions were created to deal with the problems and promises were made, but to little avail.[103]

But when it came to the treatment of non-Turkish groups in general, and Christian groups in particular, these atrocious conditions were not simply dictated by the general necessities and the brutalization of war, by defensive measures against real or potential outside intervention or internal dissent, or by the widespread corruption, diseases, and crisis. As mentioned above, pre-war ideological, economical, and political considerations played a large part in what the radical wing of the CUP achieved or attempted to achieve from their take-over in 1913 to their downfall in 1918, including the cleansing and genocide of Armenians, Greeks, and Syriacs. Through war and gen-

---

100 Morgenthau, *Ambassador Morgenthau's Story*, 232.

101 See, e.g., Maria Jacobsen, *Maria Jacobsens Diary 1907–1919: Harput* [in Armenian] (Antelias, Lebanon: Armenian Catholicosate, 1979), 122–23 (a facsimile of the original, handwritten Danish-language diaries is included); Henry H. Riggs, *Days of Tragedy in Armenia: Personal Experiences in Harpoot, 1915–1917* (Ann Arbor: Gomidas Institute, 1997), especially chapter 2.

102 UM, 2-0355, "Konstantinopel/Istanbul, diplomatisk repræsentation. 1914–1922. Noter og indberetninger om den politiske udvikling," "Verdenskrigen. Politiske Indberetninger om Tyrkiets Stilling, Juni 1917– Aug. 1918," 21/6 1917, p. 1.

103 UM, 2-0355, "Konstantinopel/Istanbul, diplomatisk repræsentation. 1914–1922. Noter og indberetninger om den politiske udvikling," "Verdenskrigen. Politiske Indberetninger om Tyrkiets Stilling, Juni 1917– Aug. 1918," nr. VI, 10/1 1918; UM, 2-0355, "Konstantinopel/Istanbul, diplomatisk repræsentation," "Kopibog 1914–1921, 1914 06 14 – 1916 03 06," nr. 22, 2/11 1915.

eral crisis, the CUP seems to have followed a path of radical modernization through Turkification and industrialization, etc., as consistently and effectively as possible. They were grabbing and creating opportunities to persecute, driven by what has in a slightly different context been called "goal-directed opportunism,"[104] and doing so with a dedication that was seemingly only strengthened and radicalized by the Balkan Wars and World War I. Wandel was quite clear on how he believed at least parts of the Turkification project to be both foolish, incoherent, and unrealistic, but he did not doubt the will, intention, and dedication of especially the leading members of the CUP to conduct such policies. He contended that wartime plans of anything from ethnic and religious homogeneity, over large-scale industrialization and national self-sufficiency,[105] to an initially European-inspired, but still truly Turkish fashion industry that would develop in "splendid isolation,"[106] could very well turn out to be wishful thinking. He also contended that these plans were nevertheless taken seriously by the ruling Turkish nationalists, and they had real consequences.

According to contemporary Danish sources, the most important and radical of CUP genocidal practices during 1915 was the destruction of the Ottoman Armenians. For example, Wandel analyzed in September 1915 how the CUP ideology had evolved from seemingly democratic Ottomanism to the current mix of xenophobia and extreme nationalism, an ideology that up to this point had led to severe persecution of Greeks and the extermination of Armenians:

> The CUP took the reins of power with a motto saying "equal rights for all Ottoman citizens." But to create the unity mentioned in the title of the Committee in the vast and ethnically diverse Empire, there had to be created both a sense of Ottoman solidarity that included all the peoples of the Empire, while simultaneously guarantees had to be created that this new "Ottomanism" would also in the future be led by Young Turk members of the Committee;

---

[104] Vahakn N. Dadrian, "The Agency of 'Triggering Mechanisms' as a Factor in the Organization of the Genocide Against the Armenians of Kayseri District," *Genocide Studies and Prevention* 1, no. 2 (Fall 2006): 107.

[105] UM, 2-0355, "Konstantinopel/Istanbul, diplomatisk repræsentation. 1914-1922. Noter og indberetninger om den politiske udvikling," "Verdenskrigen. Politiske Indberetninger om Tyrkiets Stilling, Juni 1917- Aug. 1918," 21/6 1917, p. 13. In 1917, the CUP and the Ottoman press announced that economic Turkification was an "economic *Jihad*," i.e., it was a national and a religious duty to work to achieve a Muslim Turkish dominated economy: UM, 2-0355, "Konstantinopel/Istanbul, diplomatisk repræsentation. 1914-1922. Noter og indberetninger om den politiske udvikling," "Verdenskrigen. Politiske Indberetninger om Tyrkiets Stilling, Juni 1917- Aug. 1918," 21/6 1917, p. 33.

[106] UM, 2-0355, "Konstantinopel/Istanbul, diplomatisk repræsentation. 1914-1922. Noter og indberetninger om den politiske udvikling," "Verdenskrigen. Politiske Indberetninger om Tyrkiets Stilling, Juni 1917- Aug. 1918," 21/6 1917, p. 14.

> i.e., at the same time create equal rights for all Ottoman citizens, without regards to ethnicity and religion (the idealistic demands of the revolution), and make sure that this new Ottomanism would still be a purely Turkish movement. The struggle between these two demands lasted a while, until the Committee immediately after the end of the Balkan Wars resolutely discarded the first demand (equal rights for all Ottomans), and decided to pursue the road of Turkification, the road characterized by the boycott in the spring of 1914 that struck Greeks who were Ottoman subjects as well as Greek subjects, the simultaneous persecutions of Greeks in Asia Minor and Thrace, and, later that year, favored by the World War and the subsequent annulment of the Capitulations [and] the declaration of Jihad - with German assistance - [this] finally led to the xenophobic and nationalist policy, the recent consequences thereof I have several times closely examined, and which at the moment has as its main purpose the extermination of the Armenian population in the Empire.[107]

But although Wandel contended that the Armenians were the primary target of CUP persecution, he had also come to believe that the process of Turkification through ethnic cleansing and genocide was meant to be total, that it was meant to sooner or later include not only Armenians, but also Greeks and Jews — the aim being to remove from Turkey all "foreign elements."[108]

---

[107] UM, 139. D. 1., "Tyrkiet - Indre Forhold," pk. 1, nr. CXXV, 23/9 1915. The view that Turkist ideology before World War I was radically exclusive is shared even by the well-known deniers of the Armenian genocide, Stanford J. Shaw and Ezel Kural Shaw, *History of the Ottoman Empire and Modern Turkey, Volume II: Reform, Revolution, and Republic: The Rise of Modern Turkey, 1808-1975* (Cambridge and New York: Cambridge University Press, 1977), 262: "Of course Turkish nationalism, if brought to its logical conclusion, contradicted both Ottomanism and Islamism. If the empire was made into a Turkish national state, there would be no room not only for most of the non-Muslims but also for the non-Turkish Muslims who supported the empire because of their position as Muslims."

[108] UM, 139. D. 1., "Tyrkiet - Indre Forhold," pk. 1, nr. CXXIV, 16/6 1916. On persecution of Ottoman Jews, see also UM, 139. D. 1., "Tyrkiet - Indre Forhold," pk. 1, nr. CXXV, 22/9 1915; UM, 139. D. 1., "Tyrkiet - Indre forhold," pk. 1, nr. CVIII, 8/5 1916; Yair Auron, *The Banality of Indifference: Zionism and the Armenian Genocide* (New Brunswick: Transaction Publishers 2000), 64–65; Yair Auron, "Zionist Attitudes toward the Armenian Genocide," in *In God's Name: Genocide and Religion in the Twentieth Century*, Omer Bartov and Phyllis Mack, eds. (New York: Berghahn Books, 2001), 273; *British Parliamentary Debates on the Armenian Genocide, 1915–1918*, Ara Sarafian and Eric Avebury, eds. (Princeton and London: Gomidas Institute, 2003), 19; Peter Balakian, *The Burning Tigris: The Armenian Genocide and America's Response* (New York and London: Harper Collins, 2003), 284. In November 1915, Wandel stated that the increasingly popular Pan-Islamic movement in the empire was at least partly responsible for the anti-Christian and anti-Jewish policies, resulting in a situation where the government would no longer negotiate or do business with neither Christians nor Jews, "[t]he only question that is being asked is: Muslim or not Muslim? And even the Jewish businessmen have been forced to get themselves a Muslim partner:" UM, 2-0355, "Konstantinopel/Istanbul, diplomatisk repræsentation," "Kopibog 1914-1921, 1914 06 14 - 1916 03 06," nr. 23, 4/11 1915.

According to the diplomat, the primary reason that Greeks were at the time generally not treated in the same way as Armenians was that the CUP and the empire's Allies wanted Greece to remain neutral. This is what he means when he, in the quote below, taken from an August 1915 report, states that the "rational completion" of the policy of violent Turkification would be impossible regarding the Ottoman Greeks. This report, however, was written at a point when Wandel was still hoping that the CUP would not remain what he considered to be so daring and irrational as to bring to its final conclusion the chauvinist and xenophobic policy — the massacres, death marches, expulsions, general persecution, forced conversions to Islam, etc., which it pursued, as Wandel stated, under the pretext of "military necessity:"[109]

> In my earlier reports, it has already been stated how the Young Turk Government, with the aim of strengthening its position internally, lately has made xenophobia and hatred toward Christians a leading principle in its policy [...] The aim of this policy is to force foreigners and Christians to leave the country by making their existence in Turkey unbearable, thereby at the same time satisfying the fanaticism that has become an asset for the government, but it is of course not possible to speak of the rational completion of this policy, at least not concerning the Greeks. [...] For Turkey's own sake it is probably about time that the persecutions are stopped. The fanatical Committee complains that there is no patriotism in Constantinople, which it wants to transform into a Turkish-Muslim capital, but it does not seem to realize that it makes a big mistake in driving out the foreigners and the Christians, even seen from an academic point of view, since it thereby drives out the entire intelligence of the country, the entire part of the population that is in possession of spirit, insight and means, the businessmen, the scientists and the financers, and that, if the principle of "Turkey for the Turks" is to be carried through, there will be nothing but civil servants and peasants in the country.[110]

1915: Greeks and Armenians in Smyrna

While Greeks living in the Dardanelles region and surrounding areas were being severely persecuted during 1915,[111] conditions were different in

---

109 The CUP's common use of the phrase "military necessity" to excuse or explain their exterminatory policies was just as commonly dismissed by witnesses: e.g., Martin Niepage, *Rædslerne i Aleppo. Sete af et Tysk Øjenvidne* [*The Horrors of Aleppo. Seen by a German Eyewitness*] (London, 1917), 3–4; Ara Sarafian, ed., *United States Official Records on the Armenian Genocide 1915–1917* (Princeton and London: Gomidas Institute, 2004), 51–52.

110 UM, 139. D. 1., "Tyrkiet - Indre Forhold," pk. 1, nr. XCVII, 14/8 1915. On the xenophobic policy of the CUP, see also UM, 139. D. 1., "Tyrkiet - Indre Forhold," pk. 1, nr. LXX, 3/7 1915.

111 See, e.g., Sarafian, ed., *United States Official Records*, 54; Çağaptay, *Islam, Secularism, and Nationalism*, 9; Ben Lieberman, "Ethnic Cleansing in the Greek-Turkish Conflicts from

Smyrna. The American Consul at Smyrna, George Horton, did report on 4 February that "lawless Turkish bands are appearing in increasing numbers in this district and are spreading a reign of terror among the Christians of all races."[112] At the time, Horton was not sure whether or not these *bashibozuks* (Horton actually uses the term comitajis, which was the common term used to denote Bulgarian irregulars) were controlled by the CUP, but mentioned it as a possibility in his report. In his report it can also be read how "[t]he Turkish students in the schools are being taught a song, the refrain of which is, roughly translated, 'Revenge! Revenge! Revenge! Let us kill, let us cut to pieces, Let us swim in blood up to our knees, Revenge! Revenge! Revenge! Let us wipe the stain from our clothes.'"[113]

But generally, persecution in the region was limited. Alongside Constantinople, Smyrna was a place where Christians were for the moment left relatively safe from the otherwise empire-wide massacres and deportations.[114]As the Armenian farmer Hoohannes Kölian stated about the conditions in the Smyrna region in 1915: "We continued to live in peace while almost our whole nation was homeless, wandering around in the desert."[115] In the case of Smyrna, this was perhaps particularly remarkable as the city was known by Muslims as "Infidel Smyrna" and has been described as "the heart of Hellenism in Asia Minor."[116] The relative calm can probably be ascribed to factors like German military resistance, personified by commander-in-chief of the Ottoman 5th Army, General Liman von Sanders, who despite direct and

---

the Balkan Wars through the Treaty of Lausanne: Identifying and Defining Ethnic Cleansing," in Várdy and Tooley, eds., *Ethnic Cleansing in Twentieth Century Europe*, 183. On how the 1915 persecutions of Ottoman Greeks were downplayed or denied in Greece by the Gounaris administration for pro-German and anti-Venizelos reasons: Lewis Einstein, *Inside Constantinople: A Diplomatist's Diary During the Dardanelles Expedition, April–September 1915* (London: John Murray 1917), 202–203, 232–33.

112 Sarafian, ed., *United States Official Records*, 1–2.

113 Ibid.

114 A number of Armenians were, however, being deported from Constantinople in 1915, even after the 24 April deportations: UM, 139. D. 1., "Tyrkiet – Indre Forhold," pk. 1, nr. CXIII, 4/9 1915.

115 H. L. Larsen, *Falden Blandt Røvere: Armenierne paa Apostelen Paulus' Veje. En Orientrejse 1924* [*Fallen Among Robbers: The Armenians in the Footsteps of the Apostle Paul. Travels in the Orient 1924*] (Industrimissionen i Armenien, 1924), 67. On Kölian's experiences during and after the 1922 destruction of Smyrna, ibid., 68–70. Names such as "Kölian" may be misspelled (as was often the case when Western observers attempted to spell out Ottoman names), but I follow the Danish original for lack of additional information.

116 Llewellyn Smith, *Ionian Vision*, 29. See also Kalmykow, *Memoirs of a Russian Diplomat*, 252–53; Biray Kolluoğlu Kırlı, "Forgetting the Smyrna Fire," *History Workshop Journal* 60, no. 1 (Autumn 2005): 25.

repeated orders from the Ottoman authorities managed to put a stop to the deportations of Armenians in late 1916;[117] to the fact that there were relatively few Armenians in the region; and perhaps also to the presence of a large amount of Western diplomats and other observers.[118] Based on the experience of the threat of Western intervention after the 1895 massacre of Armenians in Constantinople,[119] the Ottoman authorities may have feared a similar reaction here. But there were exceptions even in 1915, as testified by Armenian genocide survivor Hysni Nasarian. She was deported from Smyrna in the summer of that year and lost five of her six children and her husband on the death march.[120]

The only important "Danish" observer in any of the Ottoman provinces with a large Greek population, Alfred van der Zee, could therefore not report much on persecutions in the Smyrna region in 1915. He would have had to be careful in his reports anyway, with heavy censorship imposed by the authorities even on diplomatic correspondence, meaning that all consular reports had to be sent as unciphered letters.[121] But the consul almost exclusively ascribed the relative safety of Christians to the unwillingness of local high-level Turkish civilian and military authorities, particularly vali Rahmi Bey, to participate in the Armenian genocide, and does not mention the significance of Liman von Sanders at all. Like Van der Zee and George Hor-

---

[117] Wolfgang Gust, ed., *Der Völkermord an den Armeniern 1915/16. Dokumente aus dem Politischen Archiv des deutschen Auswärtigen Amts* (Springe: zu Klampen Verlag, 2005), 68, 90; Artem Ohandjanian, *1915: Irrefutable Evidence. The Austrian Documents on the Armenian Genocide* (Yerevan: National Academy of Sciences, 2004), 127–28; Vahakn N. Dadrian, "The Comparative Aspects of the Armenian and Jewish Cases of Genocide: A Sociohistorical Perspective," in *Is the Holocaust Unique? Perspectives on Comparative Genocide*, Alan S. Rosenbaum, ed. (Boulder: Westview Press, 1996), 109–10; note 17, 132–33. Von Sanders was, however, seemingly behind the deportation of Greeks from Ayvalık (Kydoniai (Gr.)) in April 1917: See Hofmann in this volume, also Toynbee, *The Western Question in Greece and Turkey*, 143–45. For the German general's own account of how he "countless times saved the Greeks in Smyrna and the whole of the Asia Minor littoral from Turkish injustices," see von Sanders, *Fünf Jahre Türkei*, 188.

[118] Benedictsen, *Armenien*, 255.

[119] See, e.g., Joseph L. Grabill, *Protestant Diplomacy and the Near East: Missionary Influence on American Policy, 1810–1927* (Minneapolis: University of Minnesota Press, 1971), 41ff; James Eldin Reed, "American Foreign Policy, The Politics of Missions and Josiah Strong, 1890–1900," *Church History* 41, no. 2 (June 1972): 236–37; Arman J. Kirakossian, ed., *The Armenian Massacres, 1894–1896: U.S. Media Testimony* (Detroit: Wayne State University Press, 2004), 23ff.

[120] *7 Gamle Koner* (Lemvig: Industrimissionen blandt Armenierne, 1927), 12–13.

[121] UM, 2-0355, "Konstantinopel/Istanbul, diplomatisk repræsentation," "Kopibog 1914–1921, 1916 03 06 – 1919 09 22," nr. 36, 2/5 1916.

ton,[122] British citizen Annie Marshall, who had come to Smyrna in September 1918 after having been interned in Anatolia since the beginning of the war, had gotten a similar impression of Rahmi. Marshall stated that "[w]ith regard to the native population the Vali was favorable to the Armenians, and comparatively few were deported," although she adds that wealthy Armenians had to pay enormous sums of "protection money."[123] There may be reasons to be somewhat skeptical toward these observers in this respect, as there seems to be conflicting evidence as to whether local Turkish officials actively opposed the Armenian genocide to any significant degree. These authorities, when talking to Western observers, may have seen an interest in downplaying German influence and in appearing to be moderate. This, however, is not because it is unlikely that such officials would resist CUP policies like the Armenian genocide, as this did happen on a number of occasions.

The question is whether Van der Zee in this case let himself be duped by his explicit admiration for the vali, and by his general sympathies for local Turkish military figures such as general Pertev Paşa of the 4th Army Corps, and Cemal Bey, commander of the Smyrna Forces, both of whose "good temper" Van der Zee reported to have enjoyed.[124] As it happened, Pertev had been the commanding officer of Cafer Tayyar Eğilmez Bey in 1914, when Tayyar alongside Rahmi and Celal were secretly acting as the leading forces behind the cleansing of the Greeks in the region.[125] Still, although Wandel could be closer to the mark in the case of Smyrna when he stated that "where the Germans do not reign, the Committee and terrorism reigns,"[126] it is perhaps possible that Rahmi initially resisted deportations of Armenians until 1916 when Liman von Sanders apparently decided to go up against the vali and the CUP. According to Van der Zee, reporting in September 1915, "[t]o add to the misery that prevails, bands of deserters are scouring the country and

---

[122] Sarafian, *United States Official Records*, Horton to U.S. Secretary of State Robert Lansing, 5 August 1915, 183. See also *The Times*, 8 October 1915: "Rahmi Bey, the bold Vali of Smyrna who has treated the interned British and French residents of the town right well, has repeatedly protested to the Porte against these crimes and has refused to hand over suspected Armenians for trial."

[123] Annie C. Marshall, "Impressions of Smyrna in War-Time," *The Contemporary Review* 115 (January-June 1919): 330. On blackmail of wealthy Armenians as a possible motive behind the 1916 deportations of Armenians in Smyrna, Ohandjanian, *1915: Irrefutable Evidence*, 127–28.

[124] UM, 2-0355, "Konstantinopel/Istanbul, diplomatisk repræsentation," "Noter og indberetninger om den politiske udvikling, 1914–1922," "Verdenskrigen. Rapporter fra Smyrna. Nov. 1914–Marts 1916," 12/3 1915.

[125] Akçam, *From Empire to Republic*, 145.

[126] UM, 2-0355, "Konstantinopel/Istanbul, diplomatisk repræsentation," "Kopibog 1914–1921, 1914 06 14 - 1916 03 06," nr. 18, 13/10 1915.

levying blackmail on the wretched inhabitants. [...] The only bright feature on this darkened horizon is the fact that there has been so far no persecution of the Armenians owing to the absolute refusal of Rahmy Bey, Governor General, to carry out the orders sent him."[127] Furthermore, the consul reported that Rahmi had been called to Constantinople on 3 September 1915, where he, the consul implies, had to defend his resistance to the Armenian deportations.[128] One possible explanation for this could be that, even at this relatively early point, Rahmi may have been preparing to negotiate with the Entente, and would thus, as noted above, want to at least appear to be a moderate, with or without the tacit consent of the CUP.[129] According to Wandel, Rahmi and Cemal Paşa were the two leading CUP members who were thought to be seeking contacts with the Entente.[130] But in light of German and Austrian sources, which describe Rahmi as working with the CUP and against Liman von Sanders to secure the deportations of Armenians and

[127] UM, 2-0355, "Konstantinopel/Istanbul, diplomatisk repræsentation," "Noter og indberetninger om den politiske udvikling, 1914–1922," "Verdenskrigen. Rapporter fra Smyrna. Nov. 1914–Marts 1916," 2/9 1915.

[128] UM, 2-0355, "Konstantinopel/Istanbul, diplomatisk repræsentation," "Noter og indberetninger om den politiske udvikling, 1914–1922," "Verdenskrigen. Rapporter fra Smyrna. Nov. 1914–Marts 1916," 3/9 1915. See also UM, 2-0355, "Konstantinopel/Istanbul, diplomatisk repræsentation," "Noter og indberetninger om den politiske udvikling, 1914–1922," "Verdenskrigen. Rapporter fra Smyrna. Nov. 1914–Marts 1916," 17/9 1915. Einstein, *Inside Constantinople,* 286, in a diary entry 11 September 1915, stated that "Rahmi, the only Union and Progress man who has distinguished himself honourably, is now here from Smyrna, where all appreciate him as Vali, to protest against the Armenian measures, and state his personal unwillingness to enforce them." According to Van der Zee, Rahmi returned to Smyrna on 16 September: UM, 2-0355, "Konstantinopel/Istanbul, diplomatisk repræsentation," "Noter og indberetninger om den politiske udvikling, 1914–1922," "Verdenskrigen. Rapporter fra Smyrna. Nov. 1914–Marts 1916," 17/9 1915.

[129] According to a later report by Wandel, it seemed that Rahmi had in fact several times secretly negotiated with the British on behalf of the CUP, much to the annoyance of the Germans who tried to have him removed from his post: UM, 2-0355, "Konstantinopel/Istanbul, diplomatisk repræsentation," "Verdenskrigen. Politiske Indberetninger om Tyrkiets Stilling, Juni 1917–Aug. 1918," nr. LXVIII, 25/7 1918.

[130] UM, 2-0355, "Konstantinopel/Istanbul, diplomatisk repræsentation," "Kopibog 1914–1921, 1916 03 06 – 1919 09 22," nr. 27, 22/3 1916. Marshall, "Impressions of Smyrna in War-Time," 328, states that Rahmi was "very friendly with the English" during the war, although she is uncertain whether this was sincere or based on self-interest. For a recent description of Rahmi as "humane" *vis-à-vis* Greeks and Armenians in the Smyrna region: Mark Mazower, *Salonica, City of Ghosts: Christians, Muslims and Jews 1430–1950* (London: Harper Perennial, 2005), 153.

Greeks in 1916 and 1917,[131] and of the *vali's* prior role in the persecution of Greeks in the region, this seems debatable.[132]

Van der Zee's apparent sympathies were also shown in May 1915, when he reported from Smyrna that "[p]erfect security reigns and no one is worried or annoyed in any way." This seems to be a remarkable statement concerning a population of a strategically and economically important city in a country at war, a population that did in fact at the time experience naval blockade, bombardments, the taking of Western hostages, and the general hardships and uncertainties at a time when not only Armenians, but also Greeks from the coast of Marmara and of some of the Ottoman Aegean islands were being deported. These events led Morgenthau to conclude that "[e]vidently Turkish nationalistic policy is aimed at all Christians and not confined to Armenians."[133] Also, as Van der Zee stated in the abovementioned May 1915 report, Ottoman citizens and citizens of belligerent countries were not allowed to leave for neutral Greece, but citizens of neutral countries were, and thousands of them did, so some people in and around Smyrna were clearly worried.[134] And they may have had good reason to be, as Talât as early as October 1914 had warned Morgenthau that if the Entente invaded the Smyrna region, the Ottoman authorities would have the city of Smyrna destroyed, with the further intent of having Turks replacing Christians, thus making "Infidel Smyrna" a Muslim, Turkish city.[135] Still, the CUP seem to have been too eager to ensure that Greece would uphold its neutrality to risk going after the Ottoman Greeks with full force.[136]

Despite the limited persecutions of Greeks and Armenians in Smyrna, there was a tense atmosphere in and around the city, with rigorous searches of

---

131 Gust, *Der Völkermord an den Armeniern*, 534–35; Hofmann, this volume.

132 Marshall states that "Rahmy Bey is said to hate the Greeks. He is a native of Salonika, and his dislike dates from the time when the city was handed over to Greece. The Greeks in the Province of Aidin were bitterly perscuted, and over half a million were killed, and their property confiscated," cf. "Impressions of Smyrna in War-Time, " 330.

133 Sarafian, *United States Official Records.* 54.

134 UM, 2-0355, "Konstantinopel/Istanbul, diplomatisk repræsentation," "Noter og indberetninger om den politiske udvikling, 1914–1922," "Verdenskrigen. Rapporter fra Smyrna. Nov. 1914–Marts 1916," 26/5 1915. On Greeks vainly seeking permission to leave Smyrna during a cholera epidemic in the summer of 1916: von Sanders, *Fünf Jahre Türkei*, 187.

135 Morgenthau, *United States Diplomacy on the Bosphorus*, 107.

136 UM, 2-0355, "Konstantinopel/Istanbul, diplomatisk repræsentation," "Kopibog 1914–1921, 1914 06 14 - 1916 03 06," nr. XIV, 12/2 1915; UM, 2-0355, "Konstantinopel/Istanbul, diplomatisk repræsentation," "Kopibog 1914-1921, 1914 06 14 - 1916 03 06," nr. XXV, 20/3 1915. See also Toynbee, *The Western Question in Greece and Turkey*, 141.

arms; keeping a sporting gun was enough to be court-martialed.[137] Ottoman Greek soldiers in Smyrna who had so far been employed doing road works in labor battalions were now being sent to an uncertain fate in Adrianople.[138] According to Wandel, the May 1915 declaration by Great Britain, France, and Russia that they would hold members of the Ottoman Government personally responsible for what was called "crimes against humanity and civilization," i.e., the Armenian genocide, only led, as he put it, to more anger, chauvinism, and fanaticism, and this was to some extent felt in Smyrna as well during the summer.[139] While 20 leading members of the Armenian Hunchak Party were being hanged publicly in Constantinople as a "reply" to the Allied declaration, 111 British and French citizens were arrested in Smyrna, and Wandel was certain that the declaration would serve the opposite of its intention.[140] Also, starvation began to be widespread around Smyrna; inside Smyrna people were beginning to run out of money to buy whatever food there was, and there were increasing fears of an Allied invasion.[141] The Danish mechanic and feldwebel (sergeant) Hans Rasmussen, who had volunteered for the German air force in 1914, and who had been sent on a mission from the Dardanelles front to Smyrna in the summer of 1915 to help defend the city, confirmed in a letter the Turkish and German

---

[137] UM, 2-0355, "Konstantinopel/Istanbul, diplomatisk repræsentation," "Noter og indberetninger om den politiske udvikling, 1914–1922," "Verdenskrigen. Rapporter fra Smyrna. Nov. 1914–Marts 1916," 17/7 1915.

[138] UM, 2-0355, "Konstantinopel/Istanbul, diplomatisk repræsentation," "Noter og indberetninger om den politiske udvikling, 1914–1922," "Verdenskrigen. Rapporter fra Smyrna. Nov. 1914–Marts 1916," 19/10 1915. On such labour batallions: Erik J. Zürcher, "Ottoman Labour Battalions in World War I," in Kieser and Schaller, eds., *Der Völkermord an den Armeniern und die Shoah*, 187–96; Speros Vryonis, Jr., "Greek Labor Battalions in Asia Minor," in Hovannisian, *The Armenian Genocide: Cultural and Ethical Legacies*, 275–90; Toynbee, *The Western Question in Greece and Turkey*, 142.

[139] On the Entente declaration, see also, e.g., Eberhard Wolffskeel von Reichenberg, *Zeitoun, Mousa Dagh, Ourfa: Letters on the Armenian Genocide*, Second Edition, ed. Hilmar Kaiser (Princeton and London: Gomidas Institute, 2004), ix; Sarafian and Avebury, eds., *British Parliamentary Debates*, 59–60.

[140] UM, 2-0355, "Konstantinopel/Istanbul, diplomatisk repræsentation," "Kopibog 1914–1921, 1914 06 14 - 1916 03 06," nr. LVII, 18/6 1915. On earlier imprisonments of French, British, Belgian, Montenegrin, and Serb nationals in Smyrna, ordered by Enver Paşa on 6 March 1915 following bombardments by an Anglo-French fleet, and on Rahmi's attempts at "moderating the orders received": UM, 2-0355, "Konstantinopel/Istanbul, diplomatisk repræsentation," "Noter og indberetninger om den politiske udvikling, 1914–1922," "Verdenskrigen. Rapporter fra Smyrna. Nov. 1914–Marts 1916," 12/3 1915.

[141] UM, 2-0355, "Konstantinopel/Istanbul, diplomatisk repræsentation," "Noter og indberetninger om den politiske udvikling, 1914–1922," "Verdenskrigen. Rapporter fra Smyrna. Nov. 1914–Marts 1916," 2/9 1915.

fear of an Allied invasion in the region, as well as the general poverty of the inhabitants of Smyrna.[142]

1916: Forced Starvation and the Expectation of Massacre

In February 1916, the deliberate and radical nature of the CUP nationalist ideology was expressed by the experienced diplomat Cevad Bey, Ottoman minister at Copenhagen and a *diplomate de carrière* with close connections to the CUP. In an interview given to leading Danish newspaper *Politiken*, he stated that, "We have now introduced the Turkish language in Turkey. This is the first result of a national awakening: Turkey for the Turks. [...]. When we change old signs and street names, our enemies claim that we tear down the European inscriptions out of hatred and malice. There is no truth in that. We only do what all nations have done before us. They call us chauvinists and rebels. I assure you, we only want one thing: our economical and political independence. This we all agree upon. There are no longer both old and young Turks. There are only Turks. And during the war we are all young."[143]

That same month, Allied airplanes dropped leaflets authored by former CUP leader İsmail Hakkı who was now leading a liberal opposition group based in Thessalonica, and who at one point wrote on CUP policies that "[t]he most horrible crimes are being committed against the Greeks and particularly the Armenians in the Ottoman Empire. [...] Their life, property and honor are constantly in danger."[144] The leaflets, titled *Beyan-el-Hak* (*Bejun-ul-Hakk*), accused the CUP of, among other things, tyranny, and opted for revolution.[145] Wandel commented in this connection on the general state of things in the empire, reiterating his belief that while the CUP and the Ottoman administration were generally too unrealistic, radical, ambitious, impatient, corrupt, and/or inept to truly succeed in the complete Turkification of the empire, the extreme policies carried out against the Armenians and Greeks were indeed part of an overall scheme:

> When it comes to tyranny, then it is true that even though the Young Turks have decided to follow another policy than the despot Abdul-Hamid, they use

---

[142] In J. Ravn-Jonsen, ed., *Danske Frivillige i Verdenskrigen: Soldaterbreve fra Fronterne* (Copenhagen and Kristiania: E. Jespersens Forlag, 1917), 143–44.

[143] UM, 4. F. 2, "Tyrkiet: Gesandtskabet her," "Djevad Bey," 22/2-15/12 1916. Private letter from Wandel to E. Scavenius. Konstantinopel, 5/11 1915. On Cevad, see also Einstein, *Inside Constantinople*, 12–13.

[144] Quoted in Ohandjanian, *1915: Irrefutable Evidence*, 109.

[145] A copy of one of Gümülcine's leaflets, in fact a 4-page journal written in Ottoman Turkish, can be found together with a translation into French in UM, 2-0355, "Konstantinopel/Istanbul, diplomatisk repræsentation. 1914–1922. Noter og indberetninger om den politiske udvikling," "Verdenskrigen. Indberetninger og Avisudklip, Juni 1914–Marts 1919." See also Ohandjanian, *1915: Irrefutable Evidence*, 109.

> the same means that he used: violence and robbery internally; tricks, schemes, protraction, and delays in relations with the outside world. The Committee have, though, instead of having used the rivalry between the Great Powers like Abdul-Hamid did, initiated a new national, political action, which it does not have the skills, the comprehensive plan, or the means to carry through. There are plenty of examples of this practice: the Armenians and the Greeks have during these last years been witnesses to the extermination and the boycottage, the Turkish population have witnessed exploitation, blackmail, and requisition. Even neutral foreigners are treated in an arbitrary and ruthless manner, and when the diplomatic missions are protesting, the only answer is that the Capitulations have been gotten rid of, and that Turkey is now a free country.[146]

In 1916, crisis and starvation throughout the empire was becoming even more widespread and serious, and Turkification played no small part in that. From Constantinople it was reported how the "sad situation" in the capital was partly caused by the continuing ideologically motivated expelling and boycott of thousands of Greek merchants.[147] There was a catastrophic lack of seed corn in the *vilayets* of Anatolia, and, according to Wandel, some Muslim peasants protested the removal of the Armenians, but seemingly to no avail. Although these peasants seem to have realized that their hardships were at least partly caused by the extermination of the Armenians, the CUP regarded the long term success of Turkification as more important than trying to, e.g., avert famine in the shorter term, even among the general Muslim population.[148] But Greeks and Armenians who had not (yet) been either massacred or deported were disproportionally, and often intentionally and systematically, affected by famine.[149] Around this time, Wandel complained to the Danish Foreign Ministry that, mainly because of censorship, he felt he

146 UM, 139. D. 1, "Tyrkiet - Indre Forhold," pk. 1, nr. XLIII, 29/2 1916.

147 *Vort Land*, 18 February 1916.

148 UM, 2-0355, "Konstantinopel/Istanbul, diplomatisk repræsentation," "Kopibog 1914–1921, 1916 03 06 - 1919 09 22," nr. 31, 5/4 1916. See also Clarence D. Ussher, *An American Physician in Turkey: A Narrative of Adventures in Peace and War* (Boston and New York: Houghton Mifflin, 1917), 329–30. During this period, Wandel had several meetings with, e.g., the Minister of Finance (who at the time was Talât) and various officials like Undersecretary Hasan Tahşin Bey, as well as with Foreign Minister Halil Bey and with officials of the Ministry of War, to enquire about the requisition of Danish steamer *Sally Mærsk:* e.g., UM, 2-0355, "Konstantinopel/Istanbul, diplomatisk repræsentation," "Kopibog 1914–1921, 1916 03 06 - 1919 09 22," 6/3 1916, "Rekvisition af *s/s Sally Mærsk*."

149 See, e.g., UM, 2-0355, "Konstantinopel/Istanbul, diplomatisk repræsentation," "Kopibog 1914–1921, 1916 03 06 - 1919 09 22," nr. 7, 19/12 1917; UM, 2-0355, "Konstantinopel/Istanbul, diplomatisk repræsentation," "Kopibog 1914–1921, 1916 03 06 - 1919 09 22," nr. 61, 15/4 1918 (on the disproportionate suffering in Constantinople of Jewish and Christian citizens).

knew too little about what was going on in the provinces,[150] but important information from outside of Constantinople did get through to him from time to time. For instance, in late March that year, a Danish workshop engineer employed at the cement factory *Arslan* (built by the Copenhagen-based Danish company *F. L. Smidth*) told Wandel about the conditions of the Christians in the area where the factory was located.[151] This was approximately 30 kilometers southeast of Constantinople, in the town of Daridje (Derince (Tur.)) on the Asian coast of the Sea of Marmara. The unnamed engineer related to Wandel that,

> When flour was brought to the two towns that were located near the factory, out of which one is a Muslim town of only about 1500 inhabitants, while the other one is Greek and has about 5000 inhabitants, one could always be sure that the small Turkish town would get 3-4 times as much flour as the relatively large Greek town. Because of the lack of bread, the Greek women had to risk their lives gathering herbs in the mountains. All the fields in the region were uncultivated—from lack of seed corn and manpower and out of fear of requisition; poultry and fruit, etc., had been taken by the numerous members of the territorial army that were quartered there, and whose officers overlooked and benefitted from all sorts of abuse, etc., etc. All Armenians in said town had been deported, but a couple of months ago there passed a convoy of Armenian women and children who, forced by starvation and crying, tried to beg a little bread. 2 Greeks, whose execution have been mentioned in the daily papers, had only been arrested because they had been found near the railway bridge that an officer from an English submarine had tried to blow up. They were two workers from the factory who probably had nothing to do with espionage.[152]

This report indicates that while Ottoman Christian subjects were systematically being mistreated, Armenians were, at this point and place at least, generally being subjected to more direct methods of destruction than were Greeks.[153] It also indicates that the end results of these policies were likely to be largely similar.

---

150 UM, 2-0355, "Konstantinopel/Istanbul, diplomatisk repræsentation," "Kopibog 1914-1921, 1916 03 06 - 1919 09 22," nr. 35, 24/4 1916. See also Morgenthau, *United States Diplomacy on the Bosphorus*, 429.

151 For a short description and a picture of the factory: Knudåge Riisager, *F. L. Smidth & Co. 1882-1922* (Copenhagen, 1921), 166-67.

152 UM, 2-0355, "Konstantinopel/Istanbul, diplomatisk repræsentation," "Kopibog 1914-1921, 1916 03 06 - 1919 09 22," nr. 29, 24/3 1916.

153 On Greeks as witnesses and rescuers *vis-à-vis* the Armenian genocide: Ioannis K. Hassiotis, "The Armenian Genocide and the Greeks: Response and Records (1915-23)," in *The Armenian Genocide: History, Politics, Ethics*, Richard G. Hovannisian, ed. (New York: Macmillan, 1992), 129-51; Sarafian, *United States Official Records*, e.g., 88, 141, 143, 180, 192-93, 414; James L. Barton, comp., *"Turkish atrocities": Statements of American Missionaries on the Destruction of Christian Communities in Ottoman Turkey, 1915-1917* (Ann

By 1916, reports from Van der Zee to Wandel were becoming few and uninformative due to the censorship,[154] while Danish observers — other than Wandel, mainly missionaries and relief workers such as Maria Jacobsen, Jenny Jensen, Karen Marie Petersen, Hansine Marcher, and Karen Jeppe — were still in a position to keep on gathering important information on the continued destruction of the Ottoman Armenians.[155] Wandel did get some information on the persecution of Greeks from other sources, like in March 1916 when he learned that the German diplomatic staff at Constantinople were worried about "the many political mistakes" made by the Ottoman Government, and that they found it "highly inopportune" that the empire at the moment provoked Greece by expelling the Greek population from Vurla (Vourla (Gr.)) in the Smyrna region.[156] In Constantinople Wandel also had several conversations with his Greek colleague Demetrios Panas, who related that Austrian Ambassador Pallavicini had told him to warn the Greek Government not to declare war on Bulgaria, as this would supposedly result in terrible reprisals taken by the Ottoman Government against the Ottoman Greeks. Although Pallavicini said that these reprisals would ensure that the Greeks were even worse off than the Armenians, according to Wandel, Panas claimed that he did not believe these threats were serious. He stated that the Germans and Austrians would protect the Greek civilians.[157] While some in Greece were assessing that warnings or threats such as Pallavicini's were to be taken seriously, and that any attempt at gaining territory in Asia Minor would be extremely difficult, if not impossible, in the long run, others were more outright cynical (and, in that respect, perhaps also more realistic) than Panas in admitting that increased persecution of the Ottoman Greeks was

---

Arbor: Gomidas Institute, 1998), e.g., 78–79; James Bryce and Arnold Toynbee, *The Treatment of Armenians in the Ottoman Empire, 1915–1916. Documents Presented to Viscount Grey of Falloden by Viscount Bryce* [uncensored edition], Ara Sarafian, ed. (Princeton: Gomidas Institute, 2000 [reprint of 1916 edition]), 388–96; Christopher J. Walker, "The End of Armenian Taron and Baghesh, 1914–1916," in *Armenian Baghesh/Bitlis and Taron/Mush*, Richard G. Hovannisian, ed. (Costa Mesa, CA: Mazda Publishers 2001), 198.

[154] UM, 2-0355, "Konstantinopel/Istanbul, diplomatisk repræsentation," "Kopibog 1914–1921, 1916 03 06 - 1919 09 22," nr. 132, 29/3 1916.

[155] See, e.g., note 4; *Rigsarkivet, Private Institutioner: Kvindelige Missions Arbejdere* (*KMA*), 10.360, Pk. Nr. 15, "Armenier-Missionen, Diverse Skildringer vedr. Arminierne [sic] 1906–1927;" *Armeniervennen*, 6/7–8 (July–August 1926): 27–29.

[156] UM, 2-0355, "Konstantinopel/Istanbul, diplomatisk repræsentation," "Kopibog 1914–1921, 1916 03 06 - 1919 09 22," nr. 25, 14/3 1916.

[157] UM, 3. G. 53b, "Wandel, Carl Ellis, 1912–26," nr. 44, 31/10 1916.

likely, if not inevitable, but that it was a price worth paying if it could lead to *enosis*.[158]

Conclusion

To the CUP, one of the major advantages of the destruction of the Armenians and Greeks was that the Powers would be presented with a *fait accompli*. The Christians would be gone who had served as an excuse for these powers to interfere with what the CUP regarded as the internal matters of the empire. The persecutions of the Greeks from 1914 onward therefore point toward an actual policy of extermination of Christian nationalities, if not in the sense that these policies were planned to be parts of a "grand scheme" of partial and total genocides,[159] then in the sense that both policies were connected in profound ways.[160] There is evidence to suggest that the anti-Greek and anti-Armenian policies to a large degree resulted from closely linked "rational" and xenophobic deliberations that were inherently genocidal.[161] There were institutional links, from the CUP over the Office of Tribal and Refugee Settlement to the SO. There were more or less rudimentary ideological links — "Turkey for the Turks"; the identification of the "internal ene-

---

[158] Llewellyn Smith, *Ionian Vision,* 33, 38–39, 50–53. On the apparent popularity of the *enosis* idea in Greece, cf. "Letter from Greece," feature article by Emil Rasmussen, *Politiken*, 5 July 1915.

[159] On "partial" and "total" genocides, Levene argues that although the Armenian genocide, like the Holocaust and the Rwandan genocide, was a rare instance of "total genocide" (which basically means that the scope, scale, and intensity of the killings is, if not unlimited, at least with few constraints and exceptions), other aspects of the "homogenization" of Anatolia can be characterized as "partial genocide," see Mark Levene "Creating a Modern 'Zone of Genocide': The Impact of Nation- and State-Formation on Eastern Anatolia, 1878–1923," *Holocaust & Genocide Studies* 12, no. 3 (Winter 1998): see especially 395–401. On "total" and "partial" genocide, see also Robert F. Melson, *Revolution and Genocide: On the Origins of the Armenian Genocide and the Holocaust* (Chicago: University of Chicago Press, 1992), especially 2–4, 247–57.

[160] Kieser, "Armenians, Turks, and Europe," in Kieser and Plozza, eds., *Der Völkermord an den Armeniern, die Türkei und Europa*, 48: "The fate of the Armenians in the context of total war does not appear as an isolated monolith: it is shown as a part of a puzzle - marking the tip of the iceberg - of state violence and coercion aiming at the construction of a Turkish ethno-nation in Anatolia, in opposition to other political projects. Thus the experiences of expelled or 'exchanged' Orthodox Ottomans (*Rum*) and massacred Assyrians/Syriac (*Süryani* and *Asuri*) as well as of resettled Muslims and *muhacir* (refugees of the Balkan and Caucasus as they were assimilated into the Turkish nation in Anatolia) are taken as parts of the broad picture."

[161] Akçam, *From Empire to Republic,* 149; Morgenthau, *Ambassador Morgenthau's Story,* 34–36; Hilmar Kaiser, "Armenian Property, Ottoman Law and Nationality Policies during the Armenian Genocide, 1915–1916," in *The First World War as Remembered in the Countries of the Eastern Mediterranean*, Olaf Farschid, Manfred Kropp, and Stephan Dähne, eds. (Beirut: Orient-Institut, 2006), 51–52.

my" (Greeks, Armenians) with the "external enemy" (Greece, Russia, Great Britain; the Entente). There were economic links, as the disappearance of Christian competition could presumably pave the way for a national (i.e., ethno-religiously monopolized) Turkish/Muslim economy. And there were individual links, strikingly personified by the abovementioned Mehmet Reşid. In 1914 he was involved with the cleansing of Greeks, while he directed the extermination of Armenians and Syriacs in the Diyarbakır region in 1915–16.[162]

Lewis Einstein, special agent at the U.S. Embassy in Constantinople, wrote in his diary 1 May 1915 that even when threatened militarily on every side during World War I, the Ottoman Government was bent on breaking the last remnants of an alleged political opposition: "They have crushed the Turkish opposition, they expelled the Greeks, and now is the Armenians' turn ..."[163] Wandel believed that the reason for the CUP for such acts was basically to preserve power by any means, for themselves in particular and for Turks in general.[164] But even in a time of crisis power can be gained or preserved through a number of means, and evidence suggests that the CUP rather consistently chose means that involved group persecution or destruction, leading to the perhaps most important link between the fates of Greeks and Armenians: their almost complete disappearance from Ottoman/Turkish territory.

The most important event that concerned the Greeks in the empire immediately after the 1914–16 period was arguably the Pontian genocide that was initiated in earnest in late 1916. But there seems to have been no Danish observers in that region at the time, and this is of course reflected in the sources, or rather lack thereof. There had been a Danish vice-consul at Trabzon (Trebizond, Trapezous (Gr.)) since 1882, the Austrian citizen Attilio

---

[162] Kieser, "Dr. Mehmed Reshid," in Kieser and Schaller, eds., *Der Völkermord an den Armeniern und die Shoah*, 245–80. Üngör, "When Persecution Bleeds into Mass Murder," 193 (note 86), mentions another CUP official involved with persecutions of Greeks in 1914 and with the Armenian genocide: "On 2 September 1914 Ibrahim Bedreddin (Bedri for short) became the postal clerk of Diyarbekir province. Previously he had held this office in Basra and Mosul. After the Balkan Wars 1912–1913, he had coordinated the CUP-sponsored deportation of the Ottoman Greeks of Biga (a town between Çanakkale and Bursa). On 12 September 1915 he was officially appointed district governor of Mardin, which he remained until 11 December 1916." On Sükrü Bey, director of the Directorate for the Settlement of Tribes and Immigrants, as another example of a "modern" (i.e., biological and eliminatory) racist Young Turk, cf. Gust, *Der Völkermord an den Armeniern*, 421.

[163] Einstein, *Inside Constantinople,* 11. On the expulsions of Christians and Jews from the Bosphorus area May 1915: ibid., e.g., 13, 19, 35, 44–45, 48, 58, 83–84, 171–72, 202–203, 210–11, 218, 220.

[164] UM, 139. D. 1., "Tyrkiet - Indre Forhold," pk. 1, nr. CLX, 22/9 1915.

Sassi, but he did not report on the fate of the Pontian Greeks. In fact, he hardly reported on anything at all, even during times when he was not cut off from communicating with Constantinople.[165] This does not mean that no Danish sources reported on anti-Greek measures from 1917 onward. For instance, Wandel did receive some information on the Pontian genocide, but this information seems to have come exclusively from other legations, and is therefore not too important as such. As a person he was likely to have been affected by this event, like he had been affected by the Armenian genocide, but in his capacity as a diplomat he adhered to strict neutrality. This was the case when, in January 1917, he was strongly urged by U.S. Ambassador Abram I. Elkus, Henry Morgenthau's successor, to protest against the continued persecution of the Pontian Greeks. Wandel simply noted this fact in his report to the Danish Foreign Ministry, and apparently neither he nor the ministry took any action.[166]

In the summer of 1917, Wandel was also encouraged by Panas to, as a representative of neutral Denmark, assume protection of Greek citizens in the empire at a time when Greece was entering World War I on the side of the Entente. While Wandel for a period of one day seems to have seriously considered this proposition, due to, as he expressed it, "the persuasive skills of my amiable Greek colleague," he quickly turned down the proposition, as had the representatives of other neutral countries like the Netherlands, Spain, and Sweden. The main reason for Wandel and other diplomats to reject Panas' proposition was, besides from the enormous added workload it would generate, that diplomats regarded the protection of Ottoman Greeks as impossible at this point. As Wandel put it, "[t]he inborn hatred that the Turks since old times have nurtured against the Greeks, something which they in times of peace only hide to some extent for political reasons, will surely also break out the day that a state of war is declared between the two countries, which will ensure that the efforts of a neutral legation to protect Greek interests here will be completely hopeless."[167] Shortly after-

---

165 UM, Gr. 2-0355, "Konstantinopel/Istanbul, diplomatisk repræsentation. 1822–1920. Korrespondencesager vedr. Danske konsulater i Levanten 1864–1918," pk. 27, "Upplysningar om danska konsulstjänstmän och om d. vicekonsulars [illegible] 1911."

166 UM, 139. N. 2., "Tyrkiet: Behandling af Grækere paa tyrkisk Omraade," nr. XVI, 24/1 1917. On Elkus and pre-1917 plans of deporting the Pontian Greeks "in a movement similar to the Armenian deportation," cf. Abram I. Elkus, *The Memoirs of Abram Elkus: Lawyer, Ambassador, Statesman*, with a commentary by Hilmar Kaiser (Princeton and London: Gomidas Institue, 2004), 80–81.

167 UM, 2-0355, "Konstantinopel/Istanbul, diplomatisk repræsentation," "Kopibog 1914–1921, 1916 03 06 - 1919 09 22," nr. 137, 7/7 1917. It seems that Panas was acting without the consent of his government, and his superiors in fact made him apologize to Wandel for making the proposition: UM, 2-0355, "Konstantinopel/Istanbul, diplomatisk repræsentation," "Kopibog 1914–1921, 1916 03 06 - 1919 09 22," nr. 148, 19/7 1917.

ward, the Danish diplomatic mission, consisting of Wandel, a secretary, and a dragoman, decided instead to take over the somewhat more manageable responsibility for the protection of Chinese citizens in the empire.[168]

[168] UM, 2-0355, "Konstantinopel/Istanbul, diplomatisk repræsentation," "Kopibog 1914-1921, 1916 03 06 - 1919 09 22," nr. 168, 1/9 1917.

The Role of *Teşkilât-ı Mahsusa* (Special Organization) in the Genocide of 1915

RACHO DONEF

A HIT MAN FOR MİT (*Milli İstihbarat Teşkilatı* or Turkish National Intelligence Agency) who went by the *nom de guerre* Yakup Cemil, claimed to a Turkish journalist, that it was he who murdered ASALA's (Armenian Secret Army for the Liberation of Armenia) leader Hagop Hagopian, in Athens, in 1988.[1] Yakup Cemil also narrated some of his exploits in Europe, while on assignment to eradicate ASALA. He recalls how MIT men would identify Armenian shop owners in Vienna and Paris who assisted ASALA financially, and paint the initials TM on their shops' roller shutters; TM stood for both *Türk Malı*, i.e. "Made in Turkey" and *Teşkilât-ı Mahsusa*,[2] in reference to the Special Organization which massacred Christians in the First World War. Yakup Cemil was clearly aware of the tradition in which he operated. Furthermore, Yakup Cemil claimed to be the proud grandson of *Teşkilât-ı Mahsusa* assassin Yakup Cemil who was responsible for the deaths of many Armenians.[3]

In the official Turkish historiography concerning *Teşkilât-ı Mahsusa*, its members are presented as heroes who helped the Ottoman Empire in the First World War, by instigating revolts in the Caucasus against the Russian Empire. In other words, while Armenians and Assyrians[4] are regarded as traitors who sided with the enemy against the Ottoman Empire and thereby deserved to be deported and massacred, the treachery of the Muslim peoples in the Russian Empire is deemed to be a glorious act. This kind of contradiction is the norm in the official Turkish historiography. Also, by empha-

[1] Soner Yalçın, *Teşkilatın iki silahşörü* (İstanbul: Doğan Kitabevi, 2001), 54; journalist Soner Yalçın interviewed Yakup Cemil extensively but his real identity is not revealed.

[2] Ibid., 41.

[3] Ibid., 211.

[4] The appellation Assyrian in this paper denotes people who belong to a number of religious denominations: the Syriacs (Orthodox, Catholic and Protestant), the Nestorians and the Chaldeans.

sizing the role of *Teşkilât-ı Mahsusa* in the Caucasus and in the Arab lands their involvement in the massacres of Christian people is omitted.[5]

Enver Paşa's[6] aide-de-camp, Arif Cemil, in his memoirs revealed that according to *Teşkilât-ı Mahsusa's* regulations (*nizamname*), the eastern front was to operate under the name of Caucasian Independence Society (*Kafkas İhtilal Cemiyeti*). Much care was taken for this regulation to circulate without falling into enemy hands. The first objective of the regulation stated in this document is the instigation of a universal rebellion in the Caucasus by arming the various ethnic groups and thereby causing problems to Russia's military effort. These armed ethnic groups were to assist the Ottoman Army when it was to invade the Caucasus region of Russia.[7]

David Gaunt suggests that Enver who "was fond of undercover operations and special task forces — death squads — outside ordinary military command ... founded in secret the *Teşkilât-ı Mahsusa* (Special Organization), which became a state organ on 15 October 1911.[8] According to Phillip Stoddard, *Teşkilât-ı Mahsusa* was officially founded later, "in 1913, or perhaps not until August 1914."[9] Arif Cemil reports that *Teşkilât-ı Mahsusa* was officially established after a meeting in early August 1914 and that once officially established, Süleyman Askeri Bey was appointed as the head of *Teşkilât-ı Mahsusa*.[10] Mustafa Balcıoğlu, who claims to have had access to Turkish Military History archives (ATAŞE), containing *Teşkilât-ı Mahsusa* documents, identifies 17 November 1913 as the establishment date.[11] Taner Akçam states "[t]he extant information leads us to conclude that in 1911 a group associated with Enver Paşa began to call itself the 'Special Organization.' This group was initially founded to organize a guerilla war in Libya

[5] For example see Mustafa Balcıoğlu, *Teşkilat-ı Mahsusa'dan Cumhuriyete* (İstanbul: Nobel Yayın Dağıtım, 2001), 8; Hikmet Çiçek, Dr Bahattin Şakir, *İttihat ve Terrakki'den Teşkilât-ı Mahsusa'ya bir Türk Jakobeni* (İstanbul: Kaynak Yayınları, 2004), *passim*.

[6] Enver, a member of the ruling triumvirate, was a military adventurist who pursued his dream of Pan-Islamism (*İttihad-i İslam*) even after his fall from power, in campaigns in the Caucasus and Central Asia.

[7] Arif Cemil, *Birinci Dünya Savaşında Teşkilât-ı Mahsusa* (İstanbul: Arma Yayınları, *n.d.* [original publication 1933]), 27-28.

[8] David Gaunt, Jan Beṯ Şawoce and Racho Donef, *Massacres, Resistance, Protectors: Muslim–Christian Relations in Eastern Anatolia during World War I* (Piscataway, NJ: Gorgias Press, 2006), 58.

[9] Phillip Henrick Stoddard, "The Ottoman Government & the Arabs, 1911-18: A Preliminary Study of the *Teşkilât-ı Mahsusa*" (Ph.D diss., Princeton University, 1963), 2.

[10] Cemil, *Birinci Dünya Savaşında Teşkilât-ı Mahsusa* , 13.

[11] Mustafa Balcıoğlu, "Kendi Belgeleriyle Teşkilât-ı Mahsusa," *Türk Dünyası Tarihi* (July 1992): 24.

against Italy at the end of 1911. It is probable that the Organization was formally established in 1913 under the leadership of Enver Paşa and played an important role in the Balkan Wars in the summer of 1913. It was reconstructed in January 1914, when Enver Paşa was the minister of war."[12]

Stoddard, who wrote a doctoral thesis on the *Teşkilât-ı Mahsusa* in the late 1950s, was granted unprecedented access by Turkish authorities to archival material and he extensively interviewed one of the leaders of *Teşkilât-ı Mahsusa*, Esref Kuşçubaşı, as well as Cemal Kutay. It can be assumed that, in return for this access, "Stoddard concentrates on the Organization's activities in the Arab lands and barely mentions either the economic program or the persecution of the Armenians."[13] Also, Stoddard's key informant Kuşçubaşı operated mainly in the Arab lands. Enver Paşa sent Eşref Kuşçubaşı to supply money and command to the army in Yemen, which was cut off after the rebellion of the governor of Mecca.[14]

It seems therefore acceptable to talk of two *Teşkilât-ı Mahsusas*; one which was officially established under the order of Enver Paşa on 5 August 1914 when it was reorganized and expanded, and one which operated already during 1913 and became instrumental in the establishment of the provisional government of Western Thrace. Cemal Paşa, one of the members of the governing triumvirate[15] during *İttihat*'s rule, admitted in his memoirs, that a semi-official *Teşkilât-ı Mahsusa* imposed on the military headquarters and the government the principle of turning a blind eye to its activities in Western Trace and acted as it wished, on the other side of Maritza River.[16] It can be surmised that *Teşkilât-ı Mahsusa* operated before 1914 in some clandestine capacity, and that its *modus operandi* was already established.

Even after its official establishment, *Teşkilât-ı Mahsusa* was only nominally under the tutelage of the war ministry, and not under the control of the

---

[12] Taner Akçam, *A Shameful Act: The Armenian Genocide and the Question of Turkish Responsibility* (New York: Metropolitan Books, 2006), 94.

[13] Erik Jan Zürcher, "Young Turks, Ottoman Muslims and Turkish Nationalist: Identity politics 1908-1938" in *Ottoman Past and Today's Turkey*, ed. Kemal Karpat (Leiden: Brill Academic Publishers, 2000), 159ff.

[14] Eşref Kuşcubaşı, *Hayber'de Türk cengi*, ed. Phillip H Stoddard and Basri Danışman (İstanbul: Arba Yayınları, 1997), 20.

[15] It should be noted here that although it is customary to refer to the ruling triumvirate comprising Enver, Talât and Cemal pashas, Halide Edip (Adıvar) noted that "[t]he General assumption that Turkey was ruled by a triumvirate is not correct. Of the three men... Djemal was never strong enough to impose his own ideas"; Halidé Edib, *Turkey Faces West* (New Haven: Yale University Press, 1930), 127.

[16] Cemal Paşa, *Hatırât*, ed. Ahmet Zeki İzgör (İstanbul: Nehir Yayınları, 2000), 53.

government but very much under the personal control of Enver Paşa.[17] This became evident at the trial of the Ittihadists in 1919 when leading members of the government were unable to provide information about *Teşkilât-ı Mahsusa*. Even Said Halim Paşa, a former grand vizier, during the court martial proceedings when he was asked by the judge whether or not he was informed about this Organization, he responded, "[o]nly when everything was over."[18] Stoddard notes that "Eşref Kuşçubaşı has said on several occasions that many of [the] cabinet ministers were not informed about the *Teşkilât-ı Mahsusa* because of what he termed of their 'inreliability.'"[19]

While Said Halim Paşa may have lied to protect himself, other members of *İttihat* knew and were appalled by what was happening. Muhittin Birgen, a left-wing member of *İttihat ve Terraki* (Union and Progress) and the chief editor of the newspaper *Tanin*, in his account about the period, remarked that in Enver's military circle there was a number of people who were adventurous and that "other than these people, there was an Organization which they called *Teşkilât-ı Mahsusa*: undercover politicians of foreign affairs. Among them there were different types. They used discretionary funds and supported Enver."[20]

Teşkilât-ı Mahsusa co-existed with the intelligence agencies of the interior ministry and the directorate of the general staff, in addition to Talât and Cemal Paşa's private spy networks.[21] According to Iliadis, having Cemal Paşa's intelligence agency working on conventional areas of internal security, the role of *Teşkilât-ı Mahsusa* was to resolve special problems with revolutionary and separatist ethnic movements within the Ottoman Empire boundaries. The main target was reportedly the Arab nationalist movements.[22]

---

[17] Emin Demirel notes that although Sadrazam (Prime Minister) Reşat approved the establishment of Teşkilât-ı Mahsusa, his link to the agency were in appearance only, as the agency reported to Enver; Emin Demirel, *Teşkilât-ı Mahsusadan günümüze gizli servisler* (İstanbul: IQ Kültür-Sanat Yayıncılık, 2005), 58.

[18] Osman Selim Kocahanoğlu, *Ittihat ve Terakki'nin Sorgulanması ve Yargılanması* (İstanbul, Temel Yayınları, 1998), 93.

[19] Stoddard, "The Ottoman Government & the Arabs," 48-49.

[20] Muhittin Birgen, *İttihat ve Terakki'de on sene*, Volume 1, ed. Zeki Arıkan (İstanbul: Kitap Yayınevi, 2006), 300. It is interesting to note, that despite his comments, Muhittin Birgen appears to have been a member of *Teşkilât-ı Mahsusa*. Eşref Kuşcubaşı dictated his narrative "Hayber'de Türk Cengi" while in Malta during 1917-18 to Birgen, a fellow prisoner, cf. Stoddard, "The Ottoman Government & the Arabs," 243.

[21] Μάνος Ηλιάδης, *Οι τούρκικες μυστικές υπηρεσίες και η MIT*, [Manos Eliades, *Turkish Intelligence Agencies and MIT*] (Athens: Λαβύρινθος, 1998), 45.

[22] Ibid., 73.

Yalçın Küçük argues that foreigners, especially the Germans, assisted in the establishment of *Teşkilât-ı Mahsusa* and contributed to its budget. According to Stoddard "at least partially money came from the discretionary funds of the war ministry which allowed Enver Paşa to keep a tight leash on the organizations of the *Teşkilât-ı Mahsusa*."[23] *Teşkilât-ı Mahsusa's* special budget was called *Teşkilât-ı Mesture* (Concealed Organization).

What were these activities of *Teşkilât-ı Mahsusa*, which needed to conceal even the budget? As already stated, officially *Teşkilât-ı Mahsusa* was established to fight the Russians and the Arabs in special operations, and as Stoddard claims, also to spread seeds of separatism in the colonies of the Allies.[24] Other evidence indicates that *Teşkilât-ı Mahsusa* was involved in special operations to attack and slaughter Christian populations.

Mevlanzadeh Rifat, a journalist and nationalist Kurd, eyewitness of the events of 1914-18, reported on a secret meeting in 1914 at Nuruosmaniye Street, close to Babiali [the Sublime Porte, the seat of Ottoman Government], to which Talât Bey had invited certain members of his party. The speakers talked of the necessity "of removing the Armenian people in the name of the salvation of the empire." Notably, Dr. Nazım (one of the most important members of *İttihat*) rejected half measures: "If this liquidation is not general and definitive... [it] will cause us troubles. It is necessary for the Armenian nation to be uprooted, that not a single Armenian remains in our soil." A provisional executive committee looking for the most adequate means for solving the problem swiftly was constituted by Dr. Bahattin Şakir, Ahmed Şükrü and Dr. Nazım. Sometime later, Dr. Şakir suggested calling this task force the *Teşkilât-ı Mahsusa*.[25]

Celal Bayar, a former president of the Turkish Republic, recalls in his memoirs a number of meetings that were held between May and July 1914 in which "the elimination of masses" was discussed. To further this aim, Enver Paşa decided to release convicts[26] and to train them. Celal Bayar, who was in

---

[23] Yalçın Küçük, *Türkiye üzerine tezler, 1908-1998*, Vol.5, (İstanbul: Tekin Yayınevi, 2002), 634.

[24] Stoddard, "The Ottoman Government & the Arabs," 4.

[25] Mevlanzadeh Rıfat, *Türkiye İnkilabının içyüzü*, Aleppo, 1929; quoted in Arthur Beylerian, *Le Grandes Puissances, L'Empire Ottoman et Les Armeniens dans les Archives Français* (Paris: Publications de la Sorbonne, 1983), xxx-xxxi.

[26] Mete Tuncay claims that while conducting research on Colonel Kasap Osman (Osman the Butcher) he saw a copy of the Provisory Law, dated 4 March 1915, which enabled the release of convicts; Mete Tuncay, 'Son Beş Yılda Ermeni Sorunu Nasıl Tartışıldı?', *BIA Haber Merkezi*, 12 March 2005, http://bianet.org/bianet/kategori/toplum/56180/asdasd [accessed 15 February 2008] (footnote 4).

charge of the nationalization campaign[27] in Smyrna (Izmir), quoted a report by a *Teşkilât-ı Mahsusa* agent describing the removal of "internal tumors."[28]

Fatih Rıfkı Atay, later a government official during the İttihat rule and journalist after the establishment of the republic, while still at military school when the war started, went to headquarters to volunteer his services as a civilian. Dr. Nazım, who listened to his wish, laughed and replied: "We are looking for people in prisons to set up gangs. That is not a place for a youngster like you." Leaving the headquarters, Fatih Rıfkı was perplexed by what he called an "army of murderers."[29]

Ahmet Refik Altınay, who was originally a member of İttihat and a senior official in the government, was disgusted with the policies of his party and wrote a book to condemn them:

> In the beginning of the war many gangs were sent to Anatolia from Istanbul. The gangs consisted of murderers and thieves, which had been taken out of prisons. These people were trained for one week in the Department of Interior and were sent to the Caucasus border through the efforts of the Special Organization [sic]. In the Armenian massacres these gangs committed the biggest murders.[30]

Professor Halil Berktay, a Turkish historian who does not subscribe to the official thesis, maintains that it was indeed the Special Organization that murdered the Armenians.[31] Nonetheless, *Teşkilât-ı Mahsusa* activities were not directed only against the Armenians; Greeks as well as Assyrians have also been victims of massacres perpetrated by it. David Gaunt provides numerous examples of murders carried out by *Teşkilât-ı Mahsusa* against the Assyrian population:

> In the market of Midyat there was a place named Shaqfo, near the house of the [West Syriac Protestant] Nateqo family, and there I saw how the Turkish forces killed the young Christian boys. They would throw [from the roof] young boys headlong from that high building to fall down and die at once. Many Christian caravans arrived at Midyat, and they were filled with women and children. They were taken to the mosque's yard. The yard would become overcrowded. To reduce the number of hostages, the Turkish forces gathered the boys, around 500–600. They told them to lie down, face down. Then they

---

[27] Celal Bayar was brought from Bursa to be in charge of the campaign to identify Turks to take over the property, which the Greeks were forced to leave behind after their deportation.

[28] Celal Bayar, *Ben de yazdım, Milli Mücadeleye Giriş*, Volume 5 (İstanbul, 1967), 1552-82.

[29] Fatih Rıfkı Atay, *Zeytindağı* (İstanbul: Pozitif Yayınları, 1981), 36.

[30] Ahmet Refik, *Two Committees Two Massacres*, trans. Racho Donef (London: Firodil Publishing House, 2006), 24.

[31] Halil Berktay, "Ermenileri özel örgüt öldürdü," *Radikal*, 9 October 2000.

took some thick sticks and beat them on the head. Then some 40 to 50 Turkish soldiers riding horses rode back and forth over the boys' heads until they died.

Bet̠ Şawoce notes that "the commander of the forces is identified as Sami Bey of the *Teşkilât-ı Mahsusa*, who was in Midyat with a contingent of 'mujahedin' recruited from released convicts."[32]

Other sources confirm the role of the convicts in the massacres. A German Officer, Colonel Stange, was in charge of a Turkish *Teşkilât-ı Mahsusa* detachment operating on the Russian border area. In his report Stange "refers to the employment of convicts (*Sträflinge*) in the enactment of the genocide. They were part of the "Special Organization" (*Teşkilât-ı Mahsusa*) which, after their more or less abortive guerilla campaign against Russia, was transferred to the command of the killer squads in the campaign of the extermination of the bulk of the Armenians of the Eastern provinces.[33]

One of the most notorious murderers of *Teşkilât-ı Mahsusa*, Topal Osman [Osman the Lame] from Giresun, acted against the Greeks, ostensibly to quash Greek rebellions in the Pontus region. In reality he was a plain murderer. In January 1916, Topal Osman caught a group of "Greek spies who allegedly worked for the Russians, and handed them to the 7th Division. Topal Osman's practices even displeased the authorities."[34] Balcıoğlu does not specify the type of activities that Topal Osman inflicted upon Greeks, but it can be speculated that Topal Osman's excesses were evidently widely known, to the point where even the government could not cover it up. Balcıoğlu tries to camouflage these activities by roundabout expressions so as not to tarnish the image of Topal Osman as a hero of the Turkish Independence War. He concludes that "Topal Osman crushed the Greek gangs with *rough* [my emphasis] methods."[35]

Evidently, Topal Osman's genocidal activities cannot be concealed even in the accounts of the most ardent official Turkish historiographers. Yet other historians, such as Sait Çetinoğlu, who are not constrained by the official thesis, draw the conclusion that Topal Osman "with the support of local

---

32 Jan Bet̠ Şawoce, "Oral Testimonies on Tur Abdin 1914-15" in Gaunt, *Massacres, Resistance, Protectors*, 342.

33 Vahakn N. Dadrian, "Documentation of the Armenian Genocide in German and Austrian Sources" in *The Widening Circle of Genocide (Genocide a Critical Bibliographic Review)*, Volume 3, ed. Israel W. Charny, (New Brunswick, NJ: Transaction Publishers, 1994), 110.

34 Mustafa Balcıoğlu, *Teşkilat-ı Mahsusa'dan Cumhuriyete* (İstanbul: Nobel Yayın, Dağıtım, 2001), 178.

35 Ibid., 179.

notables and authorities without having to face any hurdles, subjected the local Christian population to ethnic cleansing."[36]

I have been fortunate to examine a number of documents in the Ottoman archives consisting of a collection of reports concerning expenditure for prison restorations in 1914 and 1915 in the gaols of Mardin, Midyat, Cizre, Nsibin, Savur and Diyarbakır (all areas of the traditional Assyrian homeland). The documents discuss budgetary issues and detail the repair work undertaken. We learn that the prison budget was transferred from the finance ministry to the department of interior, which is perhaps more appropriate in time of war. Notably, the documents raise a pertinent question: Why would the *İttihat* Government embark upon restoration of prisons in 1915, while the war was in full force and expenditure was surely required elsewhere? It can be speculated with some degree of certainty, given the context described in this paper, that the prison restoration program created the pretext for emptying prisons and releasing convicts. It is the last document in the collection that is the most intriguing:[37]

> Province of Diyarbakır
> Secretariat
>
> To the Department of Interior
>
> Your Excellency
>
> A piece of inspection schedule of June 1915 has been presented through a memorandum from the General Court of Appeal [?] about Central Provincial Prison and to command belongs unto him to whom all command belongs.
>
> 21 August 1915 vali signature
>
> ...
>
> As shown in the detailed inventory above, during the month of June of the current year, eighty-three people were imprisoned because of treason and thirteen because of misdemeanors, in the Central Prison.
>
> July 1915
>
> ...
>
> In the prison inspection report that has been presented at this time, it has been understood that from the 174 prisoners at the 30th of June of the current year, eighty three were imprisoned because of treason and thirteen due to misdemeanours; three people sentenced in 1913 by the judge in Beşiri which is attached to the Central Province; from those sentenced in 1914, twenty eight are in the interrogation department and the remaining fourty seven in hand [or at hand, available, ready] ....

---

[36] Sait Çetinoğlu and Dara Cibran, "Pontus Sorunu," 2007, unpublished advance electronic copy, n.p.

[37] Documents located by David Gaunt and provided by Jan Bet Şawoce; transliteration anonymous; translation Racho Donef (document only partially reproduced); see Prime Ministerial Ottoman Archives BOA.DH.MB.HPS.M.21/64.1333.L27.

28 July 1915
Judge
New criminal court judge assistant functionary on behalf of court of appeal

The detailed inventory and discussion about the whereabouts of prisoners and their crimes, points to the possibility of prisoners from this region as well being used against the attacks on the Christians. While more than likely those charges with treason were Christians, the reports states that forty-seven prisoners are available.

As *İttihat*'s "secret army," as Zürcher puts it[38] the *Teşkilât-ı Mahsusa* recruited disparate elements, including soldiers, gendarmes, thugs, murderers, thieves and adventurers, as well as ideologues. These were organized in four types of groups:

> i) Current and former convicts; the able-bodied formed a military detachment (e.g. Yakup Cemil's detachment), the rest formed labor gangs;
>
> ii) Mevlevi and Bektashi religious order groups;
>
> iii) Volunteer groups, consisting of Kurds, Circassians, Druzes and Lazes;
>
> iv) Armed irregular groups (brigands / *çeteciler*): the gangs of Yakup, the gang of Topal Osman, the gang of Maksut, the gang of Veysel Bey and others.[39]

Teşkilât-ı Mahsusa started to execute parts of the *İttihat*'s plan to exterminate Christian masses before its official establishment day in August 1914. For example on 25 June 1914 the Danish consul in Smyrna reported to his government about "Disorders in the Vilayet of Aidın" in the Aegean region:

> The bands of bashibozouks, who had gone south of Menemen after looting all the villages on their way, attacked Phocea on the night of the 12th June on three sides and ably assisted by the Cretans [Muslim refugees from Crete] who work at the salt depots soon turned it into a shambles.
>
> Quoting from the words of an eyewitness 'within a quarter of an hour after the assault had begun every boat in the place was full of people trying to get away and when no more boats could be had the inhabitants sought refuge on the little peninsula on which the lighthouse stands. I saw eleven bodies of men and women lying dead on the shore. How many were killed I could not say but trying to get into a house of which the door stood ajar I saw two dead

[38] Zürcher, "Young Turks, Ottoman Muslims...," 159.

[39] Atilla Çeliktepe, *Teşkilat-ı Mahsusa'nın Siyasi Misyonu*, 2nd ed. (İstanbul: IQ Kültür Sanat Yayınları, 2003), 107.

bodies lying in the entrance hall. Every shop in the place was looted and the goods that could not be carried away were wantonly destroyed.[40]

It is evident that the gangs that the consul is referring to in his letters are those organized by the *Teşkilât-ı Mahsusa*. The consul calls these gangs "bashibozuks," being aware of the tradition of the *başıbozuks*[41] in the Ottoman Empire, and according to Matthias Bjørnlund the consul knew that these attacks "were financed and run by the state."[42]

Evidence from Greek sources indicates that these gangs already operated in 1913, attacking Greeks first in Western Thrace and then in Western Anatolia. The Greek consul of Smyrna, Kapsambeli, reports on 28 May 1914 that the cathedral was besieged by refugees from Soma who recounted the attacks on them by *başıbozuks*; by committing plunder and violence they forced Greeks to leave their homes.[43] The French newspaper *Le Temps* on 13 June 1914 also reported the attacks by *başıbozuks* in Pergama.[44]

The Black Book, published by the Ecumenical Patriarchate in 1919, provides a myriad of instances where Greeks were attacked by irregular groups, before the start of the war. In July 1913 in Adrianople (Edirne) irregular troops attacked the Greek population[45] and in İmam Pazar on 6 April 1914 *başıbozuks* attacked the village and killed two people, a third dying of fear.[46]

---

40 Rigsarkivet [the Danish National Archives], Udenrigsministeriets Arkiver [the Archives of the Foreign Ministry] (UM), 2-0355, "Konstantinopel/Istanbul, diplomatisk repræsentation", "Noter og indberetninger om den politiske udvikling, 1914-1922", "Verdenskrigen. Rapporter fra Smyrna. Nov. 1914-marts 1916", Alfred Van der Zee til [to] Carl Ellis Wandel, 25/6 1914; for full text and other documents see Racho Donef, 'The Hellenic Genocide in the Danish Archives," 2004, (Letter 2, paragraphs 2 and 3) http://www.greece.org:8080/opencms/opencms/HEC_Projects/Genocide/en/6_Archives/Official/Danish [accessed 23 April 2007].

41 *Bashibozuks* were irregular troops; it literally translates as "the head is *kaput*", which clearly indicates the nature of these irregular troops used by the Ottomans.

42 See Matthias Bjørnlund, "The Destruction of the Ottoman Greeks in Danish sources" in this anthology; I am indebted to Mr. Bjørnlund for reviewing the first draft of my paper and making a number of pertinent suggestions, including pointing to new sources. I am also indebted to Tessa Hofmann for reviewing a later draft.

43 Χάρης Τσιρκινίδης, *Έχω όπλο την αγχόνη: Το ντοκουμέντο της Μεγάλης Καταστροφής υπό το φως των ξένων απορρήτων αρχείων, 1908-1925*, [*I Have the Gallows as My Weapon: The Documentation of the Great Catastrophe in Light of Foreign Secret Archives, 1908-1925*] (Athens: Εκδόσεις Ερωδιός, 2005), 73.

44 Ibid., 74.

45 Οικουμενικό Πατριαρχείο, *Η Μαύρη Βίβλος διωγμών και μαρτυριών του εν Τουρκία Ελληνισμού 1914-1918*, [*The Black Book of the Persecution and Suffering of the Greeks in Turkey, 1914-1918*] (Constantinople: Ecumenical Patriarchate, 1919), 3-4; the Ecumenical Patriarchate published a second volume in 1920.

46 Ibid., 8.

In Babaeski, in the village of Kumburlu, four Greek men were killed by the ubiquitous *başıbozuks*.[47] These are only a handful of selected examples from a very detailed 413-page publication.

Many massacres were carried out in Eastern Anatolia as well, by the various gangs of *Teşkilât-ı Mahsusa*, one of which operated under the leadership of a brutal thug named Çerkez Ahmet (Ahmet the Circassian). Rafael de Nogales, a Venezuelan mercenary serving in the Ottoman army, who had first hand experience of massacres against Armenians and knew Çerkez Ahmet's modus operandi, recalled that:

> Djevded Paşa [governor of Van] ordered Tcherkez Ahmed to make a raid with his bandits upon the surrounding hamlets, wherein, let me say in passing, only women and children remained. I shall not go into detail as to what Tcherkess Ahmed did with those unhappy creatures. Suffice it to say that Djevded himself felt obliged to reprimand his agent, whether sincerely or not, and that the very Kurds were appalled by his fiendishness.[48]

Ali Fuat Ender, Cemal Paşa's chief of staff during the period when he was the commander of the Fourth Army, reported that "a telegram arrived from the provincial administration of Aleppo: 'Today the bandits Halil and [Çerkez] Ahmet Beys visited me, they told me that the *business of the killings in Diyarbakır were completed* and now they came to do the same in Syria. I arrested them." Ali Fuat Ender does not state the date of this occurrence. Cemal Paşa ordered the vali of Aleppo to free Halil and Ahmet. Ali Fuat Ender insisted that what he called these two "bloody *komitacıs*" be arrested and court-martialled. Ali Fuat's insistence had eventually paid off, but by the time Cemal Pasha reversed his orders, when the two murderers realized what was happening, they left for Istanbul. Finally, both Halil and Ahmet were sent to and were executed in Aleppo, when Talât Paşa gave the green light through a cipher to Cemal Paşa on 28 September 1915.[49]

No one was more enthusiastic in implementing the centrally taken decision to deport and eliminate Christians than the vali of Diyarbakır, Dr. Reşit Şahin Giranşiray. A Circassian member of *Teşkilât-ı Mahsusa*, Reşit was in charge of operations in the East and Iraq on behalf of the organization. Reşit "first worked with no official title but later became vali of Diyarbakır and carried out the task of deportation of Armenians."[50]

---

[47] Ibid., 7.

[48] Rafael de Nogales, *Four Years Beneath the Crescent* (New York: Charles Scribner's, 1926), 85.

[49] Ali Fuad Erden, *Birinci Dünya Savaşı'nda Suriye Hatıraları*, Türkiye (İstanbul: İş Bankası Kültür Yayınları, 2003), 225-27; [emphasis mine]

[50] Abidin Nesimi, *Yılların içinden* (İstanbul: Gözlem yayınları, 1977), 39.

Uğur Ü. Üngör notes that "[i]n the summer of 1915, all Christian communities of Diyarbekir were equally struck by the genocide, although the Armenians were often particularly singled out for immediate destruction."[51] As well as being responsible for massacres against the Armenians and Assyrians, Dr. Reşit Şahin Giranşiray also murdered a number of Turkish officials who refused to carry out his orders: "vali of Basra, Ferit, mutassarif of Müntefek, Bedi Nuri, kaymakam[52] of Lice, Hüseyin, deputy kaymakam of Beşiri, Sabit, journalist İsmail Mestan; all socialists and/or humanists."[53]

According to Abidin Nesimi, the son of the *kaymakam* of Lice, to carry out his activities Reşit, "established a mobile gendarme unit composed of Circassians as a strike force."[54] Nesimi's information is based on first hand account of Dr. Fahri Kutlar, member of *Teşkilât-ı Mahsusa* who worked in the cell of Obeidullah Effendi. Nesimi's research led him to conclude that that this group of people [*Teşkilât-ı Mahsusa* in Diyarbakır] consisted of pillagers and plunderers: "[t]hat is why this group could not carry out deportations but turned them into massacres."[55]

Jacques Rhetoré, a Dominican priest and eye witness to the events taking place in the Province of Diyarbakır, recalled that the vali preceding Reşit Bey "was a conciliatory man; Hamdi (Hamid) Bey was not prejudiced against the Christians. In February 1915 he was substituted by Rachid Paşa."[56] This appointment points to government culpability in massacres that took place in Diyarbakır. Indeed, the government appointed one of its own, whose disposition was one that suited the plans of İttihat. Reşit Bey amassed a fortune by robbing Armenians and Assyrians of their possessions and transferring them into his custody. "Rashid Paşa came to Diyarbakır with a very modest train, after one year left his post to Ankara, accompanied by twenty-four full cars of gold, precious objects, carpets, furniture of value which he had stolen from the Armenians."[57]

---

[51] Uğur Ü. Üngör, "A Reign of Terror" (Master's thesis, Department of History, University of Amsterdam, June 2005), 76.

[52] *Vali*: governor of a province; *Mutassarif*: governor of a *sancak* province; *Kaymakam*: governor of a district.

[53] Nesimi, *Yılların içinden*, 38-39.

[54] Ibid., 39.

[55] Ibid., 40.

[56] Marco Impagliazzo, *Una finestra sul Massacro, Documenti inediti sulla strage degli Armeni (1915-16)* (Milano: Guerini e Associati, 2000), 114.

[57] Ibid., 124.

During the court martial proceedings, on 12 December 1918, the former Education Minister Ahmet Şükrü Bey expressed the view that Dr. Reşit Bey's intention to purchase a house worth 9,000 liras in Ankara seemed to confirm suspicions about his wartime activities. [58]

After his fall from grace, Reşit penned a diatribe to defend himself against the charges — that he massacred Armenians and that he plundered their property and that he also arranged for the murders of the *kaymakams* of Lice and Beşiri who did not follow his orders — in which he concocted a story that Hüseyin Bey and Sabri Bey were murdered by Armenians.[59] This tradition of blaming the victims for their predicament is one that can be found in the official Turkish historiography over and over again.

As it has been documented in this paper, there is no shortage of first hand accounts concerning *Teşkilât-ı Mahsusa* activities. The lack of original documentation, as far as *Teşkilât-ı Mahsusa's* records are concerned, is not an impediment to tracing its toil. The presiding judge in the trial of the Young Turks pointed out that many original documents have been destroyed.[60] The judge was referring to *Teşkilât-ı Mahsusa* documents. However, this is also true for other documents produced during the period in question. In some instances the destruction of documents was requested by the headquarters. The following previously unpublished cipher from the Ottoman archives, only partly reproduced here, attests to the destruction of documents:

> Department of the Interior
> Directorate of Settlement of Tribes and Immigrants
> To the *Vilayets* [Provinces] of Adana, Halep, Diyarbakır, Erzurum, Bitlis, Van, Trabzon, Sivas, Hüdavendigar, Musul, Edirne / Mutasarrifates of İzmit, Canik, Kayseri, Mar'aş, Zor, Urfa
> (Cipher)
> Concerning the distribution of children who lost their guardians [parents] during the transportation of the Armenians .... *the destruction of this cipher after its requisite manifestation is being communicated by a circular.*
> 12 July 1915
> On behalf of the Minister
> Signature[61]

---

[58] Kocahanoğlu, *Ittihat ve Terakki'nin*, 195.

[59] Reşid Mülâhazat, "Doktor Reşidin Hatıraları-2," *Memleketim*, 4, quoted in Nejdet Bilgi, *Dr Mehmed Reşid Şahingıray'ın Hayatı ve Hâtıraları: İttihad dönemi ve Ermeni meselesi* (İzmir: Akademik Kitabevi, 1977), 34.

[60] Kocahanoğlu, *Ittihat ve Terakki'nin*, 516.

[61] Italics for emphasis mine; documents located by David Gaunt and provided by Jan Bet Şawoce; transliteration anonymous; translation Racho Donef; see Prime Ministerial Ottoman Archives, BOA, D.H.R. ŞFR.1333 C 17 - 51/411.

Ittihat leaders made further efforts to destroy any evidence of their atrocities: on 13 September 1915, Cemal Paşa ordered residents of Aleppo to return any "photographs which may have been taken by the engineers or other officers of the Bagdad Railway Construction Company relating to the convoys of Armenians ... together with the negatives, to the military commisssariat of the Bagdad Railway at Aleppo" and warned that "[a]ny contravention of this order will be punished by court martial."[62]

Despite the better efforts of the organization, some incriminating evidence still survived and was tendered as evidence in the 1919 trials. One of the most telling of these documents is a cipher sent by Dr. Behaettin Şakir of *Teşkilât-ı Mahsusa* to Dr. Nazım through Sabit Bey, governor of Harput: "Are the Armenians who were sent there being liquidated? Are the destructive people about whom you informed me that they have been driven out and plundered, being destroyed? Are they only being driven out? Let me know clearly my brother."[63]

The judge was particularly damning in his closing remarks at the court martial, expressing his view that... "[t]he participation in a tragedy brought into being by causing a tumult within the country and backing a number of gangs which set to deprive of liberty, life and property and dishonor" and that "much harm has been committed under the name of *Teşkilât-ı Mahsusa*." [64]

İttihat ve Terakki had a set goal of ethnic cleansing. Its plan was put into practice very early during their rule, perhaps as early as 1909, when the short-lived Young Turk spring ended. The ethnic cleansing campaign became in earnest when the semi-official *Teşkilât-ı Mahsusa* and bands of *başıbozuks* were allowed to operate alongside the army and intimidate the local Christians. The campaign became more systematic and massive with the official establishment of the *Teşkilât-ı Mahsusa* and its manning with released as well as former convicts, thugs and ordinary murderers such as Çerkez Ahmet.

Under the leadership of Enver Paşa, *Teşkilât-ı Mahsusa* massacred the local Christian population, Greek, Assyrians and Armenians alike. Topal Osman who later was recruited to Mustafa Kemal's campaign terrorized the Greek population in Pontus. The vali of Diyarbakır facilitated the massacres of

[62] Anonymous, *Germany, Turkey and Armenia: a selection of documentary evidence relating to the Armenian Atrocities from German and other sources* (London: J. J. Keliner & Co, 1917), 75-76

[63] Kocahanoğlu, *Ittihat ve Terakki'nin*, 518.

[64] Kocahanoğlu, *Ittihat ve Terakki'nin*, 92.

many Armenians and Assyrians as well as Greeks;[65] Çerkez Ahmet killed many Armenians and even bragged about it to Ahmet Refik who was appalled.[66] Ömer Naci Bey, a member of *Teşkilât-ı Mahsusa*, attacked Assyrians of Azakh with his death squad.[67]

The names of the Ottoman Turkish functionaries, officers and band-leaders who were involved in *Teşkilât-ı Mahsusa* are far too many to be enumerated in this paper;[68] only the most infamous ones have been superficially discussed. It is important to note, however, that today many of these people are treated as heroes in Turkey and their activities are still being concealed in Turkish historiography. At best, the extensive massacres are justified on the fallacious grounds that the Ottomans were defending themselves. This approach is just as vile and reprehensible as the crime of genocide itself.

---

[65] See for example Üngör, "A Reign of Terror," 75.

[66] Refik, *Two Committees Two Massacres,* 40-44..

[67] See Racho Donef, "The siege of the Assyrian village in Azakh in 1915," *Assyrian Star*: Seyfo, the forgotten genocide, 58 no. 2 (Summer 2006): 18-21; Donef, "Turkish Archival documents in deportation and sieges" and for a more detailed analysis, David Gaunt, "The Battle for Azakh," in Gaunt, *Massacres, Resistance, Protectors*, 273-294 and 446-494 respectively.

[68] For a list of names see Stoddard, "The Ottoman Government & the Arabs," 173-179; also Çeliktepe, *Teşkilat-ı Mahsusa'nın Siyasi Misyonu*, 167-173.

The Smyrna Holocaust: The Final Phase of the Greek Genocide*

NIKOLAOS HLAMIDES

This article provides a history of the September 1922 destruction of Smyrna (İzmir (*Tur.*)) *in the context of the Ottoman Empire's state orchestrated 1914–23 genocidal campaign against its Greek and other Christian minorities. Previously unpublished archival material, chiefly British, coupled with a variety of previously unpublished or rare eyewitness testimonies illustrate how fire, massacre, deportation and expulsion resulted in a holocaust that saw the city's Greek and Armenian inhabitants exterminated in one of the last phases of the Genocide.*

Introduction

BETWEEN 1914 AND 1923 THE OTTOMAN TURKISH GOVERNMENT ruled by *İttihat ve Terakki Cemiyeti* (the Committee of Union and Progress or CUP), also known as the Young Turks, and its successor, the Turkish Nationalist Movement under the command of Mustafa Kemal, carried out a systematic program of physical annihilation against the Ottoman Greeks and other Christian minorities of the Empire. Through massacre, conscription into labor battalions, deportation into the Interior, expulsion and other acts of violence, Turkish authorities achieved the collective extinction of more than two thousand Greek communities across the Empire. The destruction of Greek-inhabited towns and villages by means of fire was a widely employed practice which often followed or accompanied a massacre or deportation and would ensure that any survivors could not return. However, frequently fire was also used as a more direct method of extermination. Numerous archival reports record that Greeks would often be gathered and imprisoned in a large building, church or school, and the building then set alight causing death to all inside. Any escapees would be shot or massacred by Turkish gendarmes who were surrounding the building or village.[1]

During his stay of more than twenty-one months in Turkey, Donald M. Hosford, who had taken up a position at Anatolia College in Marsovan (Myrsy-

* *Two notes, on the title and the subtitle of this article, a map of Smyrna and an appendix of photographic documentation may be found at the end of this article.*

[1] See, e.g., the report on the burning of Greek villages by the General Staff in FO 286/833, British Foreign Office Archives, and "700,000 Greeks Victims of Turks," *The New York Times*, 10 July 1921, 4.

phon (Gr.), Merzifon (Tur.)), witnessed the annihilation of the Greek population.[2] Before his departure he noted that each night "the horizon at some point was lighted by a burning village."[3] In a report on conditions in Marsovan, Hosford described one particular event in some detail:

> Christian men, women and children were gradually gathered into three places, the city prison, the French Boys' School and a place described as a large red house. [...] Those gathered in the red house were for the most part young girls. All of them were violated and many of them were taken by the chetehs when they left the city. Those in the French School included several of our workers so that my knowledge is more complete regarding that group. There were in the group some men and many women and children. While they were in the building they were many times ordered to go from one room to another, marching in single file. As they went, any desirable girls were taken out of the line, and several men and boys were also taken out of the line and killed. Sunday noon fire broke out in the city. Several people affirm that they saw the fire start simultaneously at five different places. [...] The fire lasted for approximately twenty-four hours and 400 houses were burned. One of the first building[s] of these to burn was the French School in which one of these groups was gathered. The chetehs showed no disposition whatever to release the people from the building. Finally, after much protest by a group of leading Turks of the city, the people were let out after the building was already on fire.[4]

In Smyrna, known as *Gâvur İzmir* (Infidel Smyrna) by Turks during the Ottoman period owing to its large Christian population, May 1914 signified the start of arson, pillaging, massacre, deportation and expulsion against Greek-inhabited villages.[5] In 1914 alone an estimated 50,000 Greeks were deported from the Smyrna district into the Interior.[6] However, atrocities against Christians in the region of Smyrna were relatively sporadic in comparison with the systematic forced deportations and massacres being perpetrated against the Greeks elsewhere in the Empire. Arthur L. Frothingham writes in his volume *Handbook of War Facts and Peace Problems* (1919), "With the exception of the Greek populations of Constantinople, Smyrna,

---

[2] Donald M. Hosford of Cleveland, Ohio was born in Crete, Nebraska on 21 December 1896. When Anatolia College was shut down he chose to stay on in the country as a relief worker.

[3] "Recent Conditions and Events in Northern Anatolia, Particularly in Marsovan," United States National Archives, Files of the Department of State, NA 867.4016/441.

[4] Ibid.

[5] Oecumenical Patriarchate (Eastern Orthodox Church), *Persecution of the Greeks in Turkey 1914–1918* (London: Hesperia Press, 1919), 70–77. See also "Les persecutions contre les Grecs en Turquie [The persecutions against the Greeks in Turkey]," *Le Temps* (Paris), 29 July 1916, 2.

[6] *Documents on British Foreign Policy 1919–1939,* First Series (London: Her Majesty's Stationery Office, 1967), 15: 182–83.

and some other cities, all the Greeks of Turkey are suffering martyrdom through deportations, outrages on women, and starvation."[7] The same was largely true for the Armenians.[8] This is often believed to be due to the fact that foreign eyewitnesses were so plentiful in the port city of Smyrna and the Ottoman capital city of Constantinople. However, Armenian Genocide scholar Vahakn N. Dadrian presents a somewhat different perspective in his volume *The History of the Armenian Genocide: Ethnic Conflict from the Balkans to Anatolia to the Caucasus*: "Contrary to certain assertions, the fate of the Armenian populations of these two cities was not determined by the good will of the Ittihadist perpetrators sparing the destruction of these Armenians through deportation, but rather through a set of exigencies that constrained the Ittihadists. In Smyrna it was the local German military commander who, through his threat of forceful intervention, persuaded the Ittihadist governor-general of the province to cease and desist from resuming 'the massive deportation of the Armenians' of the region."[9] Although Dadrian deals here with the plight of the Armenians, his arguments are directly applicable to the Greek minority of the same region during the same period.[10]

Against the background of physical destruction of the Ottoman Greek population, Greece entered World War I in 1917 on the side of the Allies and, as arranged by the Allies, the Hellenic army arrived in Smyrna on May 15, 1919. "With a view to avoiding disorders and massacres of Christians in Smyrna and its environs, the occupation of the town and forts by Allied Forces has been decided upon by President [Wilson], Prime Minister [Lloyd George] and M. Clemenceau. Greek troops are on their way to Smyrna and Turks will be summoned to hand over forts to a landing party," declared Arthur James Balfour, British Secretary of State for Foreign Affairs, in a tele-

---

[7] Arthur L. Frothingham, *Handbook of War Facts and Peace Problems* (National Security League: New York, 1919), 74.

[8] So far as Smyrna, Tessa Hofmann writes, "Three hundred Armenians were deported from Smyrna on 13 August 1916. The deportation of the remaining Armenian community in Smyrna — variously put at between 6,000 and 20,000 (30,000 in the outlying region around the town) — was prevented by the German Supreme Commander, Marshal Liman von Sanders," see Gerard Libaridian, ed., *A Crime of Silence: The Armenian Genocide: Permanent Peoples' Tribunal* (London: Zed Books, 1985), 73. Both Greeks and Armenians were deported from Constantinople but on a smaller scale.

[9] Vahakn N. Dadrian, *The History of the Armenian Genocide: Ethnic Conflict from the Balkans to Anatolia to the Caucasus* (Oxford: Berghahn Books, 1995), xxvii. It is thought that German intervention was largely motivated by a concern that such action might prompt an end to Greece's stance of neutrality in the Great War.

[10] Isabel V. Hull, *Absolute Destruction: Military Culture and the Practices of War in Imperial Germany* (Ithaca, NY: Cornell University Press, 2005), 286. See also Tessa Hofmann's contribution, "Γενοκτονία εν Ροή — Cumulative Genocide," in this volume.

gram dated 11 May 1919.[11] The Greeks of Smyrna and other Christians greeted the Hellenic troops as liberators. Although there was minimal Turkish resistance to the Hellenic mandate over Smyrna, the landing of troops was deemed an invasion by the nationalist Turks and eventually formed the foundation of the Greco-Turkish War.[12] Smyrna was later assigned to Greece in August 1920 by the Treaty of Sèvres, to which Ottoman Turkey was a signatory. The treaty stipulated that "The Greek Government will be responsible for the administration of the city of Smyrna [...]" and "[...] shall be entitled to maintain in the city of Smyrna [...] the military forces required for the maintenance of order and public security."[13]

In 1919 Mustafa Kemal (1881–1938), initially a member of the Committee of Union and Progress and a commander in the Ottoman army, formed the Turkish Nationalist Movement and regrouped both the Ottoman army and Turkish irregulars under his command in a bid to attack the Allies. Simultaneously he was preserving the genocidal policy of the Young Turks towards the Christian minorities. The Hellenic army launched a series of offensives against the nationalist Kemalist-Turks, who rejected the Treaty of Sèvres as signed by Ottoman Turkey.[14] The Hellenic action was rooted in the ideology

---

[11] Secret telegram sent by A. J. Balfour from Paris dated 11 May 1919, Foreign Office, British National Archives, FO 141/580/1.

[12] "Probably no event in the history of modern Greece was more inopportune, ill-advised, and suicidal than its occupation of Smyrna on 15 May 1919." This was Peter Buzanski's analysis of the event as found in the opening line of his article "The Interallied Investigation of the Greek Invasion of Smyrna, 1919," *The Historian* 25 (May 1963): 325. The landing of Hellenic troops at Smyrna was indeed far from idyllic but perhaps not as disastrous as Buzanski would like to make out. An Interallied Commission was appointed to investigate the excesses reportedly committed by Greeks and subsequently found the Hellenic troops had indeed been guilty of atrocities. However, the report did not find the Turkish authorities entirely blameless either, despite the fact that criticism was largely reserved for the Greek authorities. George Horton, the U.S. Consul at Smyrna, made the following remark on the landing in his memoirs: "Much has been said of atrocities and massacres committed by the Greek troops at the time of their landing at Smyrna on 15 May 1919. In fact, the events that occurred on that and the few succeeding days have been magnified until they have taken on larger proportions in the public mind than the deliberate extermination of whole nations by the Turks, and no consideration seems to have been given to the prompt suppression of the disorders by the Hellenic authorities and the summary punishment of the principal offenders, several of them by death." George Horton, *The Blight of Asia: An Account of the Systematic Extermination of Christian Populations by Mohammedans and of the Culpability of Certain Great Powers; with a True Story of the Burning of Smyrna* (Indianapolis: Bobbs-Merrill, 1926), 72–73.

[13] Lawrence Martin, *The Treaties of Peace 1919–1923* (New York: Carnegie Endowment for International Peace, 1924), 2: 810.

[14] For a comprehensive account of the Greek army's expedition in Turkey see: *Η Εκστρατεία εις την Μικράν Ασίαν (1919–1922)* [*The Asia Minor Expedition (1919–1922)*], vols. 1–6 (Athens: Διεύθυνσις Ἱστορίας Στρατοῦ [Army History Directorate], 1957–1965).

of the *Μεγάλη Ιδέα* (*Megale Idea*, the Great Idea) of a Greater Greece, encompassing Greeks "unredeemed" from the Ottoman yoke by the territorial expansion of Greece over all regions of the Ottoman Empire that were inhabited by Greeks.[15] However, for the Kemalists the Greco-Turkish War set a new pretext to continue the destruction of the Greek element in Turkey. The secretary of the Relief Committee for Greeks of Asia Minor asserts that this policy of annihilation continued in regions hundreds of kilometres from the zone of war: "The Nationalists, taking advantage of the war with Greece, have been carrying out their program of extermination of the non-Turkish elements in Asia Minor. [...] Many regions in the interior of Asia Minor have been scenes of deportation, massacre, imprisonment and execution of innocent people after mock trial."[16]

Abandoned by the Allies who had originally supported and encouraged the Hellenic incursion, the Hellenic army found itself under attack. Kemalist forces defeated the advancing Hellenic army and forced them to retreat towards the shores of Western Anatolia.[17] In their wake they brought with them thousands of Ottoman Christian subjects who without the protection of the Hellenic army feared Turkish reprisals.

Archbishop Chrysostomos, the Orthodox Metropolitan of Smyrna, feared that with the Turks steadily advancing upon Smyrna the city's destruction would be imminent. In a letter dated 31 August 1922 and sent to Meletios, the Ecumenical Patriarch in Constantinople, Chrysostomos wrote, "[the] Greeks will be delivered to massacre and destruction. Hundreds of thousands of Greeks will perish [...]." Chrysostomos organized committees among the members of the two bodies under his chairmanship to inform the Hellenic High Commissioner and Commander-in-Chief, as well as the consul generals of Great Britain, France, Italy and America, of the disasters he anticipated would take place and to persuade them to take appropriate action to protect the city's civilian population.[18]

---

15 Dimitri Pentzopoulos, *The Balkan Exchange of Minorities and its Impact on Greece* (London: Hurst, 2002 [reprint of the 1962 edition]), 25.

16 John P. Xenides, *The Greeks in America* (New York: George H. Doran Company, 1922), 22. For more on the Greek Relief Committee see my paper "The Greek Relief Committee: America's Response to the Greek Genocide," in *Genocide Studies and Prevention* 3, no. 3 (December 2008).

17 There exist a significant number of reports attesting to various atrocities that the Greek army committed against Turkish inhabited towns during a disorderly retreat. The examination of such claims is worthy of a study in its own right. Sir H. Rumbold telegraphed the Foreign Office on 7 September 1922, "Allegations by nationalists that retreating Greeks are indulging in wanton destruction derive some confirmation from other sources."

18 "Slain Archbishop Foresaw Massacre," *The New York Times*, 24 September 1922, 35.

Greek and other Christian subjects of Anatolia now fled, converging in a terrified mob on the city of Smyrna, where they hoped either to find protection or to be evacuated.[19] Christians, from anywhere within 150 miles inland, flocked in great numbers towards Smyrna. The influx of refugees reached a figure of thirty thousand per day.[20] Smyrna's civilian population had grown to approximately 500,000 during Greece's Allied Powers-approved mandate over the Smyrna *Vilayet* (Province) and now 150,000 refugees were pouring into Smyrna.[21] In response to the humanitarian crisis unfolding, George Horton, the American Consul General, summoned the staff of the American College, together with local representatives of relief organizations and commercial firms and formed a relief unit, later known as the American Disaster Relief Committee, to distribute bread to refugees along the quay.[22]

On 2 September Sir Horace Rumbold (1869–1941), the British High Commissioner at Constantinople, received instructions from the British Government,

> [...] owing to inability of Greek army to defend town from invasion Great Powers should be informed in order that they may take urgent measures for protection of town and of interests of their subjects [...] you should concert with Commander-in-Chief Mediterranean for protection and possible evacuation of British colony.[23]

---

[19] C. A. Macartney, *Refugees: The Work of the League* (London: League of Nations Union, London, 1930), 79.

[20] Melville Chater, "History's Greatest Trek," *The National Geographic Magazine*, XLVIII, 5 (November, 1925): 534. *The Greek Refugees Settlement Scheme* published by the League of Nations in October 1923 referred to the number of fleeing Greeks as "hundreds of thousands of Greek inhabitants," FO 286/881, British Foreign Office Archives.

[21] The estimate of Smyrna's population provided in a testimony by Consul Horton at Immigration Hearings, George Horton Papers, is used here solely as an approximation for the population growth during Greece's Allied Powers-approved mandate in order to establish an approximate figure for the population just prior to September 1922. Horton referred to Smyrna's normal civilian population as 450,000, an estimate not terribly far off a 1912 figure of 416,494, but indicated that it had grown by 50,000 to 500,000 excluding Greek and Allied servicemen during the Allied occupation of 1919–22. The estimate of the refugee influx can be found in the Papers of Mark Lambert Bristol, The United States Library of Congress in Washington. See Marjorie Housepian, *The Smyrna Affair: The First Comprehensive Account of the Burning of the City and the Expulsion of the Christians from Turkey in 1922* (New York: Harcourt Brace Jovanovich, 1971), 258.

[22] Chater, "History's Greatest Trek," 534.

[23] Foreign Office to Sir H. Rumbold, Constantinople, 2 September 1922. Copies of telegrams exchanged between Sir H. Rumbold, Constantinople, and the Foreign Office, The Lloyd George Papers, British Parliamentary Archives, LG/F/208/1.

Also on September 2, Mr. Charles H. Bentinck, the British Chargé d'Affaires at Athens, telegraphed the British Foreign Office:

> [...] I venture to suggest that His Majesty's Government might on humanitarian grounds offer any available transports to help in removing Christian population and that warships might proceed to Smyrna to prevent entry of Turks before evacuation of Christians is completed. French Minister admitted to me two days ago that he considered massacres of Christian population inevitable [...].[24]

The next day Bentinck telegraphed the Foreign Office again,

> Two Greek warships and several transports have left for Smyrna to evacuate materials and troops as no defence of town is contemplated. I gather that no provision is being made for evacuation of civilians.[25]

On 3 September the first British warship, *H.M.S. Iron Duke*, reached Smyrna in order to protect British interests.[26] A detailed plan for the "evacuation of British colony at Smyrna" was drawn up on the *H.M.S. Iron Duke* the following day. Its purpose was "to afford British subjects desirous of leaving Smyrna an opportunity to do so under the protection of H.M. Ships."[27] British Royal Marines were landed on 5 September to supervise the evacuation of British subjects.[28] They were instructed "to keep order on the piers and assist in preventing any but British subjects from embarking."[29]

On the orders of Admiral Mark Lambert Bristol the American vessels *U.S.S. Litchfield* and *U.S.S. Simpson* were dispatched to Smyrna, shortly followed by the *U.S.S. Lawrence*, with relief workers, including the Director of the Near East Relief committee, a medical unit and emergency supplies onboard to assist the refugees.[30] By 6 September there were at least fourteen Allied and

---

[24] Mr. Bentinck, Athens, to Foreign Office, 2 September 1922: Copies of telegrams exchanged between Mr. Bentinck and Mr. Lindley, Athens, and the Foreign Office, The Lloyd George Papers, British Parliamentary Archives, LG/F/209/1.

[25] Mr. Bentinck, Athens, to Foreign Office, 3 September 1922, Ibid.

[26] "British Warship at Smyrna," *The Times*, 4 September 1922, 8.

[27] Papers of Commander S. L. Vereker, 75/87/1, Department of Documents, Imperial War Museum, London.

[28] Martin Gilbert, *Winston S. Churchill: Volume IV 1916–1922* (London: Heinemann, 1975), 820.

[29] Papers of Commander S. L. Vereker, 75/87/1, Department of Documents, Imperial War Museum, London.

[30] Henry P. Beers, "United States Naval Detachment in Turkish Waters, 1919–24," *Military Affairs* 7, no. 4 (Winter 1943): 218; and "Kemalist Victory Complete," *The Times*, 11 September 1922, 10. For information concerning Admiral Bristol see Marjorie Housepian, "George Horton and Mark L. Bristol: Opposing Forces in U.S. Foreign Policy 1919–1923," *Δελτίο Κέντρου Μικρασιατικών Σπουδών* [*Bulletin of the Centre for Asia Minor Studies*] 4 (Athens, 1983): 131–58.

American vessels at Smyrna; the *H.M.S. Iron Duke*, the *H.M.S. King George V* and four British destroyers, along with three French warships, two Italian, and three American.[31] American sailors were landed on 6 September to protect American lives and property.[32]

The last of the Hellenic troops, except for a few stragglers, had left Smyrna on Friday 8 September with all the Hellenic civil servants and police upon a convoy of Hellenic warships.[33] At approximately seven in the evening, the Hellenic High Commissioner in Smyrna, Aristeides Stergiades, the last Hellenic official to leave Smyrna, handed over the town to the Allied consuls and boarded the British vessel *H.M.S. Iron Duke*.[34] With that, the city's Hellenic occupation came to an official end. Smyrna was silent, its streets desolate, and the lives of its Christian inhabitants at the mercy of the arriving Turkish troops.

The Turkish Entry

Turkish Kemalist forces rode into Smyrna on the morning of Saturday 9 September. "They galloped in with drawn sabres and revolvers ready, presenting a most swashbuckling appearance" according to Mr. Wallace, a British resident of Smyrna.[35] They were met by Royal Navy Captain Bertram S. Thesiger (1875–1966) of the British warship *H.M.S King George V* who informed them that the Hellenic troops and civil servants had all gone and advised them to restore confidence by riding quietly along the quay. One British naval officer recorded the conversation conducted in French between Captain Thesiger and the unidentified Turkish commander as follows: "Who are you and why do you stop my army?" began the Turk. To this Captain Thesiger apparently replied,

> I am a Captain in his Majesty's navy and have been commissioned to assist in the surrender of this town to you, everything is peaceful, and you will meet with no resistance, but if you enter yelling and brandishing your scimitars you will undoubtedly be asking for trouble.[36]

---

[31] "British Troops in the Dardanelles — Ionian Greeks Panic Stricken," *The Times*, 8 September 1922, 10.

[32] Beers, "United States Naval Detachment," 218.

[33] Patrick Balfour Kinross, *Ataturk: The Rebirth of a Nation* (London: Weidenfeld and Nicolson, 1964), 320.

[34] Housepian, *The Smyrna Affair*, 100; "Greeks Hand Over Smyrna To Allies, Looting Reported," *The New York Times*, 9 September 1922, 1; "Kemalist Victory Complete," *The Times*, 11 September 1922, 10; Michael Llewellyn Smith, *Ionian Vision* (London: Allen Lane, 1973), 304.

[35] "Last Days of Smyrna," *The Times*, 19 September 1922, 10.

[36] Memoir of Charles J Howes, 86/14/1, Department of Documents, Imperial War Museum, London.

Mr. Wallace asserts that,

> [t]heir officer agreed, but a few minutes later he was wounded by a bomb thrown by a crazy Armenian. He made light of his injuries, and his troopers maintained perfect discipline.[37]

Smyrna's administration was assigned to General Nurettin Paşa (1873–1932), a Turkish military commander who had a reputation for fanaticism and cruelty.[38] Nurettin Paşa, infamous for his involvement in earlier massacres of Greeks, had apparently once suggested that all Greek and Armenian populations remaining in Anatolia should be deported and killed.[39]

Keen to protect their interests at Smyrna and rightly anticipating a catastrophe of some kind, Britain, France, Italy and America all had vessels anchored in the harbour facing the city.[40] This, however, did not deter the Turkish troops from immediately engaging in an orgy of slaughter, rape, arson and looting at the expense of Smyrna's Christian residents, who were seen as sympathisers of the Allies. The Armenian Quarter was the first to be pillaged. The plundering prompted the European consuls to intervene but Turkish General Nurettin Paşa assured them that the occupation would be peaceful. However, massacres continued and in the Armenian quarter alone 150 Armenians were killed and a large number of women and girls were taken by Turkish soldiers.[41] Turkish regulars rounded up Greeks and Armenians compromised by their support of the Greek administration, and executed large numbers of them.[42] After taking possession of the city the Turkish army set up camp on foothills a few miles away. Toward evening bandits and brigands entered Smyrna and commenced killing and looting in the Greek and Armenian quarters. Turkish civilians also began to participate in looting at the expense of Greeks and Armenians.[43]

On Sunday September 10 Mustafa Kemal entered Smyrna. He drove to the Konak, the government building on the quay, which had been the headquarters of the Greek occupation government for the past three years. Following the horrific behaviour of his soldiers the previous day and to silence the fears of the foreign consuls who were now very anxious for the safety of

---

37 "Last Days of Smyrna," *The Times*, 19 September 1922, 10.

38 Kinross, *Ataturk*, 324.

39 Taner Akçam, *A Shameful Act: The Armenian Genocide and the Question of Turkish Responsibility* (New York: Metropolitan Books, 2006), 363.

40 Housepian, *The Smyrna Affair*, 86.

41 René Puaux, *La Mort de Smyrne* (Paris: Edition de la Revue des Balkans, 1922), 6–7.

42 Macartney, *Refugees*, 79.

43 As described in the testimony of United States Captain John M. Walters of the steamship *Winona*. His account was published in "Eyewitness Tells of Smyrna Horror," *The New York Times*, 10 October 1922, 3.

their nationals, Kemal issued a proclamation sentencing to death any Turkish soldier who molested non-combatants.[44] Unfortunately, Kemal's proclamation did little to prevent further massacres or the fire that was soon to transpire and would ultimately put an end to Smyrna's existence.

The Fire

On the morning of Wednesday September 13 the Commander-in-chief of the British Mediterranean Fleet reported: "Situation in town is outwardly quiet but a great deal of looting and maltreatment is going on. Armenian quarter was rounded up last night with considerable slaughter."[45] The fire was started in the Armenian Quarter later that day.[46] Turkish regulars had started the fire according to the sworn testimony of American observers.[47] Miss Minnie Mills of the American Collegiate Institute said that she "could plainly see the Turks carrying tins of petroleum into the houses, from which, in each instance, fire burst forth immediately afterward. There was not an Armenian in sight, the only persons visible being the Turkish soldiers of the regular army."[48] Reverend Charles Dobson, the British Chaplain at Smyrna, noted, "It is most significant that the fire shot up in several places with very little intervals of time and pointed to a systematic incendiarism such as only a well coordinated movement could have effected. Also, that the city was fired immediately after the changing of a wind that for the previous three days was in the general direction of the Turkish quarter. Any fire, previous to the change, would have swept the Turkish quarters. Independent witnesses, who have been at Smyrna since the fire, speaking of the unsatisfac-

---

[44] Kinross, *Ataturk,* 321, 325.

[45] Commander-in-Chief, Mediterranean, to the Admiralty, 13 September 1922. Copies of telegrams exchanged between Sir H. Rumbold, Constantinople, and the Foreign Office, The Lloyd George Papers, British Parliamentary Archives, LG/F/208/1.

[46] Recent studies on the Smyrna fire support the general consensus that the fire was started in the Armenian Quarter on Wednesday, 13 September 1922, and the vast majority of eyewitness accounts validate this. It should be noted, however, that a few sporadic accounts record the fire as starting on Tuesday, 12 September 1922. This one-day error margin can perhaps be attributed to the chaos and confusion in Smyrna following the Kemalist entry. The testimony given by Edward M. Fisher, director of the YMCA at Smyrna, is one example where the fire was claimed to have been started on the Tuesday, 12 September. Even works of contrasting viewpoints such as Stanford J. Shaw's and Ezel Kural Shaw's *History of the Ottoman Empire and Modern Turkey, Volume II: Reform, Revolution, and Republic: The Rise of Modern Turkey, 1808–1975* (Cambridge and New York: Cambridge University Press, 1977), 363, state that the fire broke out on Wednesday, 13 September.

[47] Macartney, *Refugees,* 79.

[48] Housepian, *The Smyrna Affair,* 142.

tory and lame stories of the Turks, tend to confirm their guilt in this matter."[49]

In a telegram to the Foreign Office, Sir Rumbold remarked: "Although I did not say so to my colleagues I wish to point out the destruction of Smyrna by fire which Sir H. Lamb [British Consul General at Smyrna] considers as deliberate, seems to show that Mohammedan fanaticism is aroused. Mustapha Kemal will not be slow to take advantage of this fact."[50]

Thousands of Greek and Armenian citizens, driven from their quarters either by fire or fear of massacre, huddled along the narrow quay, were trapped between the waters and the approaching fire, which was steadily reducing the port city of Smyrna to ashes. Many hoped to save themselves by swimming out to the fleet of American and Allied ships anchored in the harbour, but were initially refused aboard since the ships would not compromise their stance of neutrality. They were left to drown. According to eyewitnesses, suicide by drowning also became commonplace. Crazed mothers entreated American bluejackets (sailors) to take their babies, so that they might be free to drown themselves. The bodies of hundreds of Christians who were slaughtered or who found death at their own hands on the night of the fire had come to the surface of the harbour. The Americans, French and Italians urged the Turks to remove the litter of bodies but no attention was paid to these requests.[51]

Turkish Eyewitness Accounts

Approximately eighty years after the fire, Gülfem İren, a Turkish eyewitness to the Smyrna Holocaust, was able vividly to recall the events despite being only six years old at the time of the fire:

> There was an ammunition depot near an Armenian church. The fire broke out from that depot. Was it the Armenians or the Turks that set fire to the depot? If I am to be asked, I believe the Turks set the fire there so it would be greatly efficient and clean. Also, later no one said 'The *kör olsun* [Turkish curse: may they be blind] Greeks and Armenians burnt [İzmir]' and so there is that to consider too. That means we are to be blamed. But I may be mistaken [...] A lot of filth [the Christians] had been got rid of, but were they right or wrong to do so? They were partly right because the Ottoman Empire had collapsed.

---

[49] Charles Dobson, *The Smyrna Holocaust* (London: The Anglo-Hellenic League, 1923), 28. See also Dobson's earlier report on Smyrna in British Foreign Office Archives, FO 371/7949.

[50] Sir H. Rumbold, Constantinople, to Foreign Office, 15 September 1922: Copies of telegrams exchanged between Sir H Rumbold, Constantinople, and the Foreign Office, The Lloyd George Papers, British Parliamentary Archives, LG/F/208/1.

[51] "200,000 in Smyrna Hopeless of Rescue," *The New York Times*, 19 September 1922, 1.

> It was easy for foreigners to break up a state that had just collapsed. The place of the Fair was the shelter for thousands of Armenians, Greeks, and Jews. They did that so they could do the cleansing. To empty out the houses, they were going from house to house, door to door, and then hiding to kill them. This cleansing was needed in order to build the Turkish Republic. In no other way could a republic have been formed. There cannot be such a cosmopolitan republic [...] I still think to myself, did such a thing have to happen. Just as much as these lands were ours, they were theirs too, from the time of their ancestors. We say this is our homeland, and indeed we are thankful, but as much as it is ours it is theirs as well [...] In the sea I saw their carcasses [...] For months that filth wouldn't leave Smyrna's bay. The waves would drag them back and forth, back and forth [...] We came home, but for months the Greeks were being gathered by our soldiers. And almost every night the Greek men were being taken in groups past our doorstep, with their hands tied, their hair sticking up, and their beards grown, they were in a miserable state. They were taken up to the mountains and shot.[52]

Falih Rıfkı Atay (1894–1971), a prominent Turkish author, journalist and close confidant of Mustafa Kemal, witnessed the burning of Smyrna. The following excerpt is from Atay's book *Çankaya*:

> It was the day of the great fire. As the fire spread through the [residential] districts people ran towards the quay [...] As my heart trembled I watched this unique tragedy [...] As İzmir was burning its *Rumluk* (Greekness) was flowing from the city, the people of the first civilization, the ones who spent the Middle Ages together with the Muslims, those who were living in their homes in comfort and had İzmir's and Western Anatolia's agriculture, trade and entire economy in their hands, spending a life time in palaces, mansions and farms, were now, in the twenty second year of the Twentieth Century, throwing themselves onto a boat to leave and never return again [...] Infidel İzmir with flames by night and smoke by day burnt to an end. Was it really just Armenian arsonists that were responsible for the fire as we were told at the time? Many were saying it was the work of the army general Nureddin Paşa [...] He was arrogant, narrow-minded and a person addicted to atrocity and having power [...] As I have decided to write the truth about what I know I would like to extract a page from my notes that I took at the time here: "Pillagers helped the fire to grow [...] Why were we burning İzmir? If the mansions along the waterfront, the hotels and the casinos were to stay, were we scared we would never be able to free ourselves of the minorities? During the First World War when the Armenians were being deported, again we had burnt every district and neighbourhood in the Anatolian cities and towns because of this very same fear. This wasn't something that solely derived from the urge for destruction. The feeling of inferiority played a part. A corner that looked like a piece of Europe, that looked Christian or foreign, was destined

---

52 Leyla Neyzi, *"Ben Kimim?": Türkiye'de Sözlü Tarih, Kimlik ve Öznellik* [*"Who Am I?": Oral History, Identity and Subjectivity in Turkey*] (İstanbul: İletişim Yayınları, 2004), 95, 97–98 [translation mine].

> not to be ours. If there was to be another war and we were defeated, was leaving İzmir as barren land sufficient enough to protect its Turkishness? If it wasn't for Nureddin Paşa, who I had known to be a strong fanatic and an enraged demagogue, I believe this tragedy would not have reached such proportions."[53]

İbrahim Gez, a Turkish war veteran from Söke (Sokia (Gr.)), Aydın, made the following statement on the Smyrna events in an interview first published in 1973:

> From *Kışla Square* [today's Konak Square] until *Alsancak* all that bay was full of infidel carcasses. Our soldiers had passed by them and killed them all with bayonets. There were seven fleets opposite the *Passeport* [the wharf located near the European district], English, French and Greek fleets. All of the infidel Greeks were throwing themselves into the sea, and crying out "save us." The fleets didn't save them either. The place of the Fair was a European graveyard. The Armenians and the infidels didn't surrender their houses. Raiders all burnt those houses. Bombs, guns were going off. Most of the infidels and Armenians burned alive.[54]

The three Turkish eyewitness accounts presented above are of particular significance because they undermine the traditional Turkish oral narrative of these events. Turkish academic Leyla Neyzi accepts there has been a reordering of events in order to exculpate the Turks:

> [...] Turkish forces entered İzmir on 9 September 1922 after having defeated the Greek army. But the İzmir fire started a few days after this (13 September), after the Turkish army had entered İzmir. However, in the collective memories of the Turks the date is so uncertain that some make the mistake of claiming that the fire started before the Greek army had left İzmir.[55]

Another Turkish academic Biray Kolluoğlu Kırlı who conducted interviews with Turkish eyewitnesses also noted this reordering of historical events:

> It was interesting to observe that in the memories of these interviewees the order of events was reversed. In response to my question 'whether they had heard any arguments about reports of the fire being started by the Turkish troops' they were saying that this was not possible because the army came after the fire. I must add that this reordering of the events is not exclusive to the elderly Izmirians who survived the Anatolian War. In the various settings where I have offered these observations, audiences from Turkey were taken aback by the actual chronology of the events.[56]

---

[53] Falih Rıfkı Atay, *Çankaya: Atatürk'ün Doğumundan Ölümüne Kadar Bütün Hayat Hikayesi* [*Çankaya: Ataturk's Entire Life Story from his Birth to His Death]* (İstanbul: Doğan Kardeş Matbaacılık Sanayii A.Ş. Basımevi, 1969), 322–25 [translation mine].

[54] Nail Ekici, Derman Bayladi and Mahmut Alptekin, *Cumhuriyete Kan Verenler* [*Those who gave blood to the Republic*] (İstanbul, 1973), 101 [translation mine].

[55] Neyzi, *"Ben Kimim?"* 80 [translation mine].

[56] Biray Kolluoğlu Kırlı, "Forgetting the Smyrna Fire," *History Workshop Journal* 60, no. 1 (Autumn 2005): 35–36.

It should be noted that the Turkish eyewitness accounts can be independently corroborated by those of foreign observers. For instance, Gülfem İren testifies that the fire broke out from an ammunition depot near an Armenian church. This is almost perfectly consistent with the account of events given by, say, (Assistant Professor) Oran Raber, a plant physiologist, who was in Smyrna as a tourist, who asserts that the fire broke out when the "Turks threw a bomb into the [Armenian] church, which set it on fire and exploded the stored munitions."[57]

British Eyewitness Accounts

On 18 September 1922 in an article headed "Deliberately Planned," *The Times*' Near East correspondent at Constantinople reported:

> Appalling stories of the Smyrna fire are told by British residents who have just arrived here. All whom I have seen say they believe that the fire was deliberately planned by the Turkish commanders with the object of making an end of "Giaur Izmir" [Infidel Smyrna].
>
> One of the arrivals asserts that the massacre occurred in the Armenian quarter, where he himself saw streets strewn with bodies of men and women. After this fire broke out at several points on one line within the quarter. It spread rapidly and troops in many cases formed a cordon and kept refugees within the burning area. Another British observer states that before the fire several Greek women were violated by Turkish soldiers within sight of a British naval detachment posted at the gasworks, which was unable to intervene, orders having been given that they were not to take charge of refugees. These orders were countermanded after the outbreak of fire.[58]

Despite the vast number of British eyewitnesses in Smyrna, apparently the only British foreign correspondent in Smyrna at the time was Mr. George Ward Price (1886–1961) of *The Daily Mail* newspaper. Aboard the anchored British flagship *H.M.S. Iron Duke*, he wrote:

> What I see as I stand on the deck of the *Iron Duke* is an unbroken wall of fire, two miles long, in which twenty distinct volcanoes of raging flames are throwing up jagged, writhing tongues to a height of a hundred feet. Against this curtain of fire, which blocks out the sky, are silhouetted the towers of the Greek churches, the domes of the mosques, and the flat square roofs of the houses. All Smyrna's warehouses, business buildings, and European residences, with others behind them, burned like furious torches. From this intensely glowing mass of yellow, orange and crimson fire pour up thick clotted coils of oily black smoke that hide the moon at its zenith. The sea glows a deep copper red, and, worst of all, from the densely packed mob of many thousands of refugees huddled on the narrow quay, between the advancing

---

[57] Oran Raber, "New Light on the Destruction of Smyrna," *Current History* (May 1923): 316.

[58] "Deliberately Planned," *The Times*, 18 September 1922, 10.

> fiery death behind and the deep water in front, comes continuously such frantic screaming of sheer terror as can be heard miles away [...] Picture a constant projection into a red-hot sky of gigantic incandescent balloons, burning oil spots in the Aegean, the air filled with nauseous smell while parching clouds, cinders and sparks drift across — and you can have but a glimmering of the scene of appalling and majestic destruction which we are watching. It started as an insignificant outbreak of black smoke fourteen hours ago — at 2 p.m. on Wednesday — in the Armenian quarter, which lies a mile and a half inshore.[59]

F. W. Bunter, a medical officer on the British Royal Navy Hospital Ship *H.M.S. Maine* present at Smyrna described some of the atrocities carried out against Greeks on the Quay as he observed from the *Maine*:

> It was not long after our stay in Constantinople with our fleet that we had a sudden call to sail to Smyrna where the Turks were raiding and devastating the city. The carnage and cruelty to the Greek civilians was indescribable. We saw from where we were just off the shore the Turks bayoneting bodies, men, women and children, through the windows of their home. Hundreds of Greeks, civilians as well as troops, hanging over the dock water-side and the Turkish soldiers coming along and deliberately severing the victims' arms resulting in hundreds of bodies falling to their deaths in the sea. Hundreds too were swimming towards us and eventually we rescued them, treated them and took them down to Malta.[60]

Mr. Hole, Vice-Consul at Smyrna, arrived in Constantinople on 16 September with the consulate archives. On 19 September Sir Horace Rumbold, the British High Commissioner in Constantinople, relayed Hole's account of events to the British Foreign Office by telegram:

> Evacuation of Greek troops in Smyrna was completed by September 8th. Something like 50,000 refugees had also arrived from the interior, of these no more than 5,000 were able to leave. On September 9th at 11 Turkish cavalry entered town which was formally surrendered by allied representatives. They were perfectly in hand and gave assurance regarding safety of persons and property. Turkish civil population who previous to evacuation had been pleading defenceless conditions appeared all over Smyrna armed to the teeth. There was some looting and murder but Turkish occupying officer explained as soon as he had sufficient forces at his disposal, city would be tranquilized. On arrival on September 10th of a division of regular infantry, incidents rather increased than diminished and army was responsible for much looting. Several British houses notably at Burnobad were forced and in the streets patrols held up and robbed civilians. On September 10th Italian consul general informed Mr. Hole confidentially that, that evening an important decision concerning deportation of Armenians was to be arrived at [the] Konak. The

---

59 "Smyrna Almost Wiped Out," *The Daily Mail*, 16 September 1922, 7.

60 Unpublished memoir of F. W. Bunter, 87/22/1, Department of Documents, Imperial War Museum, London.

> following day was first of Armenian massacre. Certain Armenians had furnished a pretext for adoption of vigorous measures by having bombs in their possession and a systematic hunt now took place. Men were killed in large numbers and parties were formed and driven off. Sir H. Lamb succeeded in partially penetrating into Armenian quarter and counted twenty bodies in fifty yards. On September 12th fires broke out at several points in Armenian quarter. Turks asserted that Armenians burnt down their houses to discredit them in the eyes of Europe. It may, however, be remarked that [the] first houses fired were all to windward of district and that in the evening when some of [the] fires had died down a new one was started half a mile to windward again. Whole quarter had been surrounded by a Turkish cordon since the previous day. Natural spread of fire was accelerated by new fires started in European quarter: this was particularly noticeable following morning when wind blowing now from European quarter half a dozen houses burst severally into flames half a mile to windward. Mr. Hole has no doubt that both massacre and fire including destruction of European quarter were deliberate work of Turks carried out by order of responsible authorities, object of former being vengeance against Armenians who had sided with Greeks and of latter to root out Christian and foreign influence generally. Plight of refugees is pitiable; they were herded together on narrow quay with such few possessions as they had been able to save with very little possibility of obtaining water or food and none of shelter. About 1,500 were, since a week, crowded into lighters against exterior of breakwater, shot if they attempted to escape. Evacuation of British colony was completed on September 12th. Possibly a dozen British elected to remain and a certain number of Maltese. One British subject, Mr. Murphy, was wounded in his house by looting regular soldiers and died September 12th. So far as Mr. Hole knows, there was no other loss of British life.[61]

In an account written at the time, Charles James Howes, Chief Petty Officer of the British destroyer depot ship *H.M.S. Diligence*, recorded the events in Smyrna:

> Rape and looting was now the order of the day in Smyrna and human life was not worth a farthing. Two young women were seized by the Turks and after being raped their breasts were cut off and they were laid in the roadway [...] Two Turks held a Greek while a third one ran his bayonet through the poor devil's stomach. Many bodies were hung by the neck to the trees and the harbour was littered with dead bodies. [...] With the approach of night the panic increased and so did the fire and by midnight 200,000 souls were between the blazing Hades and the deep sea. Turkish cavalry were stationed to each end of the front so that escape was an impossibility. The people were cut down right and left by the soulless devils, who had broken their promise, and the scene can only be described as worse than hell. Shrieking women calling

[61] Sir H. Rumbold, Constantinople, to Foreign Office, 19 September 1922: Copies of telegrams exchanged between Sir H. Rumbold, Constantinople, and the Foreign Office, The Lloyd George Papers, British Parliamentary Archives, LG/F/208/1.

to unresponsive children who were beyond answering, children of tender age calling for parents who [sic] hearts had left their bloodstains on Turkish swords, such were the horrible scenes witnessed. Now and again a cavalryman would take a fancy to a young girl of fifteen or sixteen, drag her away and then a ghastly scream would tell its own story. [...] Right along the sea front was a wall of unbroken fire with flames 100 feet high, casting a lurid glow in the sky. The night was rendered at intervals by loud explosions and all the while the people in the rear were being massacred. In the words of our Commander-in-Chief (Sir John de Brook), "the spectacle was magnificently terrible." The stench of human flesh burning was appalling and the streets were stacked with dead men, women, children and dogs. Bandits were in from the mountains behind and taking advantage of the panic started looting the shops which had not already been burnt carried [out] highway robbery on a large scale. Their ardent belief was that dead men tell no tales and after holding up anybody and obtaining their money, proceeded to stab them to death. Meanwhile the fire was roaring and raging fierce and its toll of victims increased. The heavens were lit by the flames and myriads of sparks flew skywards, the crackling of the wood and the collapsing of the houses, sounded like a salvo of guns. The whole of Smyrna, except the Turkish quarter, was now in the grip of the greedy fire. [...] As hard as our boats and sailors worked during the night in rescues we didn't seem to make much impression in diminishing the crowd. Old women of 80 and upwards had all the household goods they had managed to rescue on their humped backs, cripples were staggering along the burning beach and were dropping on the way, skeletons and remains of crutches testifying to their fate. Then came the blinded led by instinct mostly gasping and choking with fumes. And even, the Turkish murderers carried on their nefarious blood spilling. Feeding the flames were the bodies of tiny children and women alike. The shock brought on premature births and little bodies were actually born amidst this medley of fire, murder, and rape before we could get them aboard the ships allotted. If hell is only a fierce demotion it is heaven like to this inferno. We have just left Smyrna as I write this and we had many refugees aboard. Our doctor had the sick quarters full of different cases, one case is a doctor who was shot through both legs, his "crime" being that he attended the wounded on the beach, the remainder are women suffering from various injuries. One of the saddest cases I met was that of a little girl of nine who with her father and mother and baby in arms were making their way to the boats when their parents were shot dead. This little girl picked the baby up off the ground and dashing through the flames reached the boat. She was attended to for burnt legs. And still these continue their raping, arson, and murder unchecked. [...] I dote [sic] think the majority of English reading people will believe this narrative, and will say I exaggerate. Well here is the truth, think of the old time torture, add to them the modern appliances for the destruction of mankind, exaggerate it as much as you like and you will not realise half the horrors of the evacuation of Smyrna.[62]

---

[62] Smyrna September 1922 memoir of Charles J Howes, 86/14/1, Department of Documents, Imperial War Museum, London.

Reverend Charles Dobson, the British chaplain of Smyrna, wrote of the horrors at Smyrna. His account of the events first published in 1923 under the noteworthy title of *The Smyrna Holocaust* is repeated here in part:

> I was particularly struck with one group consisting of women and babies, and a young girl, almost nude, shot through the breast, and with clotted blood on her thighs and genital organs, that spoke only too clearly of her fate before death. These bodies were buried by Orthodox priests. [...] There was desultory shooting, looting and rape all over the place. [...] In the back streets even nationals of the Great Powers were held up and looted of their money and their valuables. [...] We heard at the back of our house, one day, a lot of cheering in which I recognised the Turkish word 'padishah' (Sultan, I think). On looking out, I saw about two hundred Greeks or Armenians kneeling and sitting on the road, guarded by Turkish soldiers. I afterwards learned from an absolutely unimpeachable source that these men were subsequently butchered. The method of killing, my informant told me, was by steel to avoid rifle fire. One could give a multitude of isolated incidents, which go to prove the absolute unleashing of lust and savagery among Kemalistic troops. [...] A child brought a message to me from the priests of an Orthodox Church, asking that I might come and spend the night with them in order to give them protection, because they had warning of a contemplated attack on the church, and they knew that on the previous night Turkish soldiers had burst into another church and there mutilated men and violated women. [...] There was constantly shooting in the back streets, followed by screams and panic-stricken running. The Turks were openly looting everywhere. One man was shot through both thighs, one of which was fractured, his screams were unheeded by the terror-stricken people. [...] I have met, recently, a nurse who left Smyrna ten days after the fire and who told me of her work in extracting bullets from bodies of wounded children, and who was a witness of the ravishing of Greek women. I mention this to show that the Turkish treatment of the Christian population was not a sudden excess, but a sustained policy. The Reverend Robert Ashe, now Chaplain at Carthagena (Spain) told me of the fate of the Greek priest of Boudjah; his informant was the brother of the Roumanian Consul. According to him, this priest was blinded and then crucified on the door of Mr. Gordon's house in Boudjah. The Turkish soldiers nailed horse shoes to his hands and feet; he was dead when the Consul's brother saw him, he kissed his hands and left him there.[63]

American Eyewitness Accounts

American eyewitness Dr. James L. Park, a staunch critic of Hellenic policy in the Near East, describes the events following the Turkish entry in a most graphic letter to his family in Indiana, sent in October 1922:

[63] Dobson, *The Smyrna Holocaust*, 24–29.

On September 9th, the Turks entered Smyrna by force of arms, following six hours in the rear of the retreating Greeks [...] I saw people being robbed and then shot, houses being torn open and the contents being strewn on the streets, the women carried off, the men shot or stabbed at their own door-steps, or driven out of the city in bands of from 100 to 200, to be killed, forced to hold up their hands and shout for Kemal while being clubbed and jabbed by the bayonet [...] On the 13th of September at 3:00 p.m. fire broke out in the Armenian quarter at various places, finally converging into two huge raging furnaces by 7 o'clock and sweeping rapidly toward the waterfront. The 100,000 refugees and 100,000 inhabitants of Smyrna were driven from their houses, finally all collecting on the quay, which became packed with a tremendous, terror-stricken throng, of such magnitude that I cannot yet take it in, or form a sufficient conception of the meaning of it. Early in the evening at 4:30, the sky was darkened with smoke. The air was charged with a concentrated fear. Until 7 o'clock I was on duty at the Smyrna Theatre, identifying American citizens who were taken off to the American destroyer *Litchfield*. At 10 p.m. our Consulate was swallowed up in the vast, roaring furnace. All through the night, the roaring of the fire that took in the greater part of the city or the entire European section, the continuous wail of the 200,000 people on the quay that seemed to be doomed to be swallowed up in the flames when the fire would finally break through to the water front, people throwing themselves into the sea to be drowned, to swim to the nearest ships, or to give up half way out from exhaustion, the crash of falling buildings, the shots on the quay, homicidal and suicidal, all combined to make the night one long, horrible fiendish nightmare. I saw it from on board the American destroyer. The glare of the fire was visible twenty miles out at sea. On the 14th killing of Armenians and Greeks continued. I saw a man beaten to death when I went ashore and thrown into the sea [...] I have not told half of the things I have seen. The disgusting aftermath, the bloated bodies of men, women and animals floating along the quay, the cart-loads of human bodies carried out of the city, the streets in the Armenian quarters strewn with bodies and household goods, the depressing forest of charred ruins, representing wealth and prosperity that is no more, and cannot soon be again, the awful scramble and moaning, crushing mobs of refugees trying to get on board the boats brought for them, the open and shameless robbery of refugees by the Turk soldiers that went through them systematically, to rob, beat and violate the women and girls, without any pretence of secrecy.[64]

Another American eyewitness was Edward M. Fisher, director of the YMCA at Smyrna, who was robbed and narrowly escaped death at the hands of Turkish irregulars a few days before making the following testimony on the events of the Smyrna conflagration:

The fire started Tuesday afternoon, and within ten hours had spread nearly two miles. The lamentations of the women and the piercing cries of the chil-

---

[64] "Indiana Man, Eye Witness To Smyrna Horrors, Tells Of Harrowing Experiences," *The Indiana Evening Gazette*, 3 November 1922, 1.

dren are still ringing in my ears. It seemed as if reason had fled and the fire and sword of the Turk had triumphed. In an incredibly short time the quay was a seething mass of horrified humanity. The Christian population had already lived through a nightmare of intimidation and slaughter by the Turks; it needed only the fire to complete their frenzy. Mobs of them surrounded the American sailors doing patrol duty and begged in the name of the Saviour and America that they be saved, but our bluejackets were helpless. The heat of the spreading flames was unendurable. The refugees dipped blankets into the water of the bay and wrapped them around their bodies. Others fled up side streets, goaded by the overpowering heat, only to find Turkish soldiers with machine guns ready to slay them. The harness of horses took fire and the infuriated animals dashed among the dense crowds on the pier, trampling many to death.[65]

Deportation and Evacuation

General Nurettin Paşa issued a proclamation on September 16 declaring that all Greek and Armenian men between the ages of 18 and 45 would be sent to the Interior and conscripted into labor battalions.[66] Nurettin repeated the order on September 24 in a revised proclamation.[67] Alfred E. Brady of the American Smyrna Disaster Committee reported that "Although the majority of Greek and Armenian civilian men in Asia Minor have been deported into Angora, into what is tantamount to slavery, and the majority of women and children exiled, the Turks' campaign of massacre and terror continues, as the last surviving Christian communities are wiped out one by one."[68] Greek sources estimate that the number of deportees exceeded 100,000.[69] U.S. Vice-Consul Maynard Barnes estimated that only 45,000 men were being held as prisoners of war but that those sent to the Interior were "dying off rapidly."[70] These deportations were but a continuation of those that had begun in 1914.

---

65 "200,000 in Smyrna Hopeless of Rescue," *The New York Times*, 19 September 1922, 1.

66 Χρήστος Εμ. Αγγελομάτης, *Χρονικόν Μεγάλης Τραγωδίας: Το Έπος της Μικράς Ασίας* [*The Chronicle of the Great Tragedy: The Epic of Asia Minor*] (Athens: Βιβλιοπωλείον της Εστίας [Hestia Bookshop], 1963), 254.

67 Sir H. Rumbold to the Marquess Curzon of Kedleston, 5 October 1922, Enclosure 2, British Foreign Office Archives, FO 141/580/1.

68 D. Caclamanos, "Dr. Rechad and the Greeks," Letters to the Editor, *The Times*, 17 October 1922, 8.

69 Estimate by the Greek representative to Allen Dulles, 10 October 1922, *Papers Relating to the Foreign Relations of the United States*, U.S. Department of State (Washington, D.C.: Government Printing Office, 1922), 2: 941. See Housepian, *The Smyrna Affair*, 258–59.

70 Barnes's estimate was reported to Admiral Mark L. Bristol on 18 October 1922, United States National Archives, Files of the Department of State, NA 767.68/114/40. See Housepian, *The Smyrna Affair*, 259.

The Turkish authorities also issued the Allies with a time limit for the evacuation of all Greeks and Armenians from Smyrna. British reports claim that Mustafa Kemal stated that, "no refugees will be allowed to leave after 30th September."[71] Those in Smyrna on 1 October were to be massacred or deported to the Interior, whether men, women or children. The British Rear Admiral Commanding 3rd Light Cruiser Squadron reported, "Noureddin [General Nurettin Paşa] stated that any refugees remaining after 30th September would be massacred."[72] Mustafa Kemal would not permit entry of Greek ships for evacuation purposes until permission had been granted by the Turkish National Assembly in Angora. The British government deemed this "reply returned by Mustafa Kemal [...] tantamount to condemnation of quarter million people to death by starvation."[73] Permission, however, was eventually given. The Turks stated that Greek ships would only be allowed to enter if operating directly and under control of Allied or American authorities. The Belgian consul appealed to the Turkish authorities at Smyrna to grant exemptions for a handful of indispensable Greeks employed at Smyrna's water works. Likewise, the American Relief Committee requested that Greeks employed in its refugee bakeries may be allowed to stay but in each case the response from the local authorities was: "No exceptions can be made."[74] Mark Prentiss, representative of the Near East Relief at Smyrna, appealed to America:

> We must evacuate the refugees quickly, preventing the extermination of women and children. Only four small ships here are available. There is urgent need of food and more food.[75]

General Nurettin Paşa advised:

> If the Allies wish to evacuate the Christians, they should send ships quickly.[76]

A conference of Allied admirals and consuls was held onboard the French battleship *Jean Bart* on Saturday the 17 in order to discuss the question of

---

[71] Commander-in-Chief, Mediterranean to Admiralty, 18 September 1922: Copies of telegrams exchanged between Sir H. Rumbold, Constantinople, and the Foreign Office, The Lloyd George Papers, British Parliamentary Archives, LG/F/208/1.

[72] Commander-in-Chief, Mediterranean, Constantinople, to Admiralty, 21 September 1922: Copies of telegrams exchanged between Sir H. Rumbold, Constantinople, and the Foreign Office, The Lloyd George Papers, British Parliamentary Archives, LG/F/208/1.

[73] Foreign Office to Lord Harding, Paris, 22 September 1922: Copies of telegrams exchanged between Lord Harding and Lord Curzon, Paris, and the Foreign Office, The Lloyd George Papers, British Parliamentary Archives, LG/F/208/3.

[74] "Turks to Give Smyrna Refugees More Time: So London Hears, but Evacuation From That Port Was Reported Stopped Monday," *The New York Times*, 4 October 1922, 3.

[75] "20,000 Greek Refugees in Smyrna Camps," *The New York Times*, 24 September 1922, 3.

[76] "Turks Whet Sabres to Terrify Smyrna," *The New York Times*, 21 September 1922, 3.

relief for the refugees. Resolutions were passed at the conference; the first of which stressed the need for prompt action,

> [...] immediate steps must be taken to prevent approximately 200,000 mostly Greeks from starvation or massacre.[77]

In a 18 September telegram the rear admiral of the 3rd Light Cruiser Squadron reported:

> Fire appears to have burnt out. I was able to see whole town from high roof.[78]

In a telegram received on 19 September, the British Commander-in-Chief informed Admiralty:

> Number of floating corpses increasing daily.[79]

On 20 September Sir H. Rumbold received an appeal by telegram from the vice consul at Mytilene:

> About 200,000 totally destitute Christians still lying on sea-shore at Smyrna awaiting help to leave. Turks issued proclamation that all Hellenic Raya [a non-Muslim Ottoman subject] males between 17 and 45 prisoners of war; others and women, also foreigners, can leave within fortnight provided obtain passports necessitating most vexatious formalities delay and expense. This means deliberately exposing Christians to die from hunger exposure and massacre, as all identification papers burnt. Unless pressure or drastic measures be immediately taken, none will survive. Please aid urgently before too late.[80]

The situation in Smyrna aroused great indignation in Britain. The Archbishop of Canterbury referred to it as "one of the most terrible catastrophes which modern civilization has known." The Save the Children Fund, which previously had been concerned with relief mostly in Russia, launched an emergency appeal to rescue "100,000 Homeless, Helpless, Hopeless Babes" in Smyrna.[81] The work of the Save the Children Fund in Smyrna was approved and authorised by Lord Curzon on behalf of the British government.[82] On 25 September in the Assembly of the League of Nations at Geneva, Lord Arthur James Balfour, Britain's representative on the Council of the League of Nations, spoke of the government's willingness to assist the Armenian and Greek refugees stranded in Smyrna. Balfour said,

---

77 Commander-in-Chief, Mediterranean to Admiralty, 17 September 1922: Copies of telegrams exchanged between Sir H. Rumbold, Constantinople, and the Foreign Office, The Lloyd George Papers, British Parliamentary Archives, LG/F/208/1.

78 Commander-in-Chief, Mediterranean to Admiralty, 18 September 1922, ibid.

79 Commander-in-Chief, Mediterranean, to Admiralty, 19 September 1922, ibid.

80 Sir H. Rumbold, Constantinople, to Foreign Office, 22 September 1922, ibid.

81 "100,000 Homeless, Helpless, Hopeless Babes," *The Times*, 7 October 1922, 15.

82 Ibid.

> I have received information from my Government according to which they fear that there is a real danger of some great calamity happening to a large number of refugees, Armenian and Greek, who are now without shelter and without food in Smyrna. I need hardly say that on such an occasion I am not going to touch in the remotest way on any question of political interest. I am concerned only with the question of humanity. I am sure that I can have all your sympathy in this matter, and I may say that my Government are prepared, if other Governments will collectively provide a similar amount, to give without delay £50,000 for this humanitarian object. I earnestly hope that their efforts will be seconded by representatives of other countries.[83]

However, British indifference to the refugees' plight at the start of the Smyrna calamity — due to an unwillingness to compromise their stance of neutrality — cost countless lives and as a consequence attracted strong criticism. A. P. Davidson, a retired British rear admiral, wrote to *The Times*:

> Admitting the Turks were in force at Smyrna why was not the Mediterranean Fleet given a free hand to protect not only British subjects but also, in the sacred cause of humanity, the defenceless Christian refugees? I submit that, had this been done, thousands of lives would have been saved, and Smyrna would have been spared devastation by fire and the sword. Surely, as our policy had encouraged the Greeks to undertake their incursion into Asia Minor, it was our duty, when we knew the Greek Army was on the run, to help the Greeks evacuate Smyrna, and I venture to state that had our Fleet been given a free hand, not only by words, but by being given discretion to use strong action, if necessary, and holding the Turkish commander responsible, massacres would have been reduced to a minimum and Smyrna itself would have been saved from destruction, pillage and loss of trade interests. Is it too late now to hope for action, not only for the freedom of the Straits, which goes without saying, but also for the protection of the unfortunate remnant in Smyrna, or have we cast overboard our old established principle of interest in and protection for defenceless Christian peoples who trusted us?[84]

The *Birmingham Post* published a letter from a resident of Smyrna who too expressed his disappointment at Allied indifference:

> No doubt you have heard of the great catastrophe that has befallen our beautiful city of Smyrna, which was totally burnt by the Turks, and more than 125,000 of its inhabitants, mostly Greeks and Armenians, were massacred and burnt alive. The scenes I have witnessed and the cruelty committed are beyond description [...] Unfortunately, all these events have happened whilst our famous Dreadnoughts and other ships, along with those of France and Italy, our Allies, were lying in the harbour of Smyrna, witnessing the spectacle,

[83] "Help for Smyrna Refugees — Big League Plan," *The Times*, 26 September 1922, 9.

[84] "Near East Crisis," *The Times*, 22 September 1922, 11.

which was of their own creation and the result of their famous diplomacy and their disagreement.[85]

Before the Turkish entry into Smyrna, British Chargé d'Affaires Bentinck telegraphed from Athens, "Feeling [here] is that as original landing at Smyrna was by mandate of allies Greeks may reasonably hope for assistance in saving refugees."[86] Although the British Government did complete a tremendous amount of relief work, it is apparent that Britain never fully comprehended its own obligations. Analysis of British archival material reveals an underlying unwillingness on the part of senior policy makers to fully partake in the relief efforts. In a telegram to Sir Rumbold the British Foreign Office made transparently clear its view:

> We consider generally that relief of Greeks, whether remaining in Turkey or transported to Greece, should come from private organizations.[87]

In a message sent by the Foreign Office to the British minister in Athens, Francis Oswald Lindley (1872–1950), this is still evident:

> We are anxious to help as much as we can but in view of heavy charge which will fall on British exchequer we must have your positive assurance that Greeks are themselves doing all they possibly can.[88]

In reply, Lindley wrote in no uncertain terms:

> It should be remembered that these refugees are not Greek subjects and very many thousands are not even Greek speaking. In fact they are Christian minorities whose protection has been subject of constant pledges on the part of His Majesty's Government; Greek government in agreeing to receive them has already done more than any other government [...] It should be realized that refugee question has not nearly reached its worst. Hundreds of thousands are still awaiting shipment from Asia Minor and everything points to enormous numbers leaving European Turkey.[89]

Eventually, however, the surviving refugees were successfully transported to Mytilene by Greek ships, flying no flag as per the request of Turkish au-

---

[85] Lysimachos Oeconomos, *The Martyrdom of Smyrna and Eastern Christendom: A File of Overwhelming Evidence, Denouncing the Misdeeds of the Turks in Asia Minor and showing their responsibility for the Horrors of Smyrna* (London: George Allen & Unwin, 1922), 84.

[86] Mr Bentinck, Athens, to Foreign Office, 8 September 1922: Copies of telegrams exchanged between Mr Bentinck and Mr Lindley, Athens, and the Foreign Office, The Lloyd George Papers, British Parliamentary Archives, LG/F/209/1.

[87] Foreign Office to Sir H. Rumbold, Constantinople, 22 September 1922: Copies of telegrams exchanged between Sir H. Rumbold, Constantinople, and the Foreign Office, The Lloyd George Papers, British Parliamentary Archives, LG/F/208/1.

[88] Foreign Office to Mr. Lindley, Athens, 24 September 1922: Copies of telegrams exchanged between Mr Bentinck and Mr Lindley, Athens, and the Foreign Office, The Lloyd George Papers, British Parliamentary Archives, LG/F/209/1.

[89] Mr. Lindley, Athens, to Foreign Office, 25 September 1922, ibid.

thorities, with the assistance of the American and British navies. On 29 September acting British Vice-Consul Robert W. Urquhart reported,

> It is estimated that over 180,000 have been evacuated under the supervision of *H.M.S. Cardiff* and *H.M.S. Curacoa* and of the American destroyers up to date, and this total is being added to at the average rate of 30,000 per day.[90]

On October 1, the senior officer of the 2nd Light Cruiser Squadron, British Mediterranean Fleet, reported:

> Approximate total number all nationalities so far evacuated 177,000 [...] Since Tuesday 26th September total numbers removed by British and American efforts 146,700 [...][91]

American estimates indicate that 213,480 of all nationalities were evacuated.[92] There are interesting but few accounts of at least one Japanese commercial vessel engaged in evacuation efforts. The *Boston Daily Globe* reported:

> In the harbor at that time was a Japanese freighter which had just arrived loaded to the decks with a valuable cargo of silks, laces and china representing many thousands of dollars. The Japanese captain, when he realized the situation did not hesitate. The whole cargo went overboard into the dirty waters of the harbor, and [the] freighter was loaded with several hundred refugees, who were taken to the Piraeus and landed in safety on Greek shores.[93]

Lieutenant Casper Silas Balfour Swinley of the *H.M.S. Curacoa* wrote of his experience of the evacuation in his naval diary:

> On the 26th the evacuation commenced. Every available hand in the ship was landed and arrangements were made for dealing with the situation. At the end of the jetty crowds of refugees assembled with their baggage and were sorted out by the Turkish Guard who kept back men of military age. The remainder were allowed through and had next to pass the American barrier and our own barrier. These barriers were necessary to prevent the crowds rushing the different ships alongside the jetty and to allow the officers to

---

[90] Acting Vice Consul Urquhart, Smyrna, to Sir H. Rumbold, 29 September 1922, British Foreign Office Archives, FO 141/580/1.

[91] Senior Officer, Second Light Cruiser Squadron (Mediterranean) to the Admiralty, 1 October 1922: Copies of telegrams exchanged between Sir H. Rumbold, Constantinople, and the Foreign Office, The Lloyd George Papers, British Parliamentary Archives, LG/F/208/2.

[92] Constantine G. Hatzidimitriou, ed., *American Accounts Documenting the Destruction of Smyrna by the Kemalist Turkish Forces, September 1922* (New York/Athens: Aristide D. Caratzas, 2005), 118.

[93] "Japanese at Smyrna," *Boston Daily Globe*, 3 December 1922, E4. See also Stavros Stavridis, "Unsung Heroes of Asia Minor: The Search for The Japanese Ship at Smyrna," *The National Herald* (New York), 7 September 2007, 1. It should be noted that photographic documentation coupled with eyewitness survivor testimonies confirm that at least on 8 September 1922 a Japanese commercial vessel picked up Greeks from the Smyrna quay.

> keep control of traffic. Many of these unfortunate refugees, chiefly Greeks and Armenians, were in a pitiable state and several died on board or fell exhausted on reaching the gangways. Nothing but sheer will power could have got some of them on board, especially with the very heavy boys which the majority of women carried, as well as babies only a few days, and in some cases a matter of hours, old. Families became separated, and the shrieking and crying of women and children whose husbands and fathers had been seized by the Turks at the barriers was truly pitiful. Each ship was crammed and there was hardly room to move on deck. The sailors, both British and American, worked well and cheerfully, especially the former, and water parties were organized to relieve some of the many who were dying for want of food and drink. This state of things went on for four and a half days and the discomforts of working on a dirty, fly-infested jetty on particularly hot days can be imagined. On the Saturday morning, after 5,000 had been embarked, the flow suddenly ceased and we learned that the evacuation was to all intents and purposes finished. Most of the refugees were taken in Greek and British ships to Mytilene where a camp had been formed.[94]

On 15 September, in an article titled "Smyrna Burning — Massacre Fears," *The Times* reported that up to the outbreak of the fire one thousand persons were said to have been massacred, but that there was fear that the death toll had increased greatly since.[95] On 16 September, *The Times* printed the estimate of John Manola of the American Relief Committee who claimed that the victims of a fire-ravaged Smyrna numbered at least 120,000.[96] According to Richard Clogg, in his volume *A Short History of Modern Greece*, first published in 1979, some 30,000 Christians perished in a "full-scale massacre of the Christian population."[97] George Horton, the U.S. Consul at Smyrna, estimated that at least 100,000 Greeks died as a result of the Turkish campaign of extermination.[98] In fact, the Greek death toll is likely to stand significantly higher since comparisons of Smyrna's population before and after the disaster show at least 190,000 Christians unaccounted for.[99] So far as the Armenians are concerned, a telegram received by the Foreign Office records the

---

[94] Diary of Captain Swinley, 83/44/11, Department of Documents, Imperial War Museum, London.

[95] "Smyrna Burning - Massacre Feared," *The Times*, 15 September 1922, 10.

[96] "Destruction of Smyrna -120,000 Victims - Fire, Massacre, and Pillage - Refugees' Plight," *The Times*, 16 September 1922, 8; "120,000 Die in Turk Massacre," *The Ignacio Chieftain* (Colorado), 22 September 1922, 1.

[97] Richard Clogg, *A Short History of Modern Greece* (Cambridge: Cambridge University Press, 1979), 118.

[98] Horton, *Blight of Asia*, 173–75.

[99] Housepian, *The Smyrna Affair*, 190.

opinion of senior British officer of the 3rd Light Cruiser Squadron at the scene that "only 25 per cent of Armenians living in Smyrna have escaped."[100]

The burned area of Smyrna was nearly one square mile and included the Armenian, Greek and European Quarters. According to an official statement released in Paris a few days following the fire, the burned area was comprised within the following limits: On the West, the Quay from Bella-Vista Street as far as the Custom House; on the South, from the Custom House to Basmahane railway station; on the East, the line of the Aydın Railway northward, as far as the tobacco factory; and on the North, the Hacı Paşa, Massurdi, and Bella-Vista streets as far as the Quay.[101] It is estimated that some twenty to twenty-five thousand buildings were burned. The fire had stretched 3,200 metres along the shoreline and it had penetrated 5,000 metres inland.[102] The cost of the damage was estimated at 200 million dollars or over 40 million English pounds.[103] The American, British, French, Dutch, Danish, Belgian and Spanish consulates had all been destroyed as well as the Armenian Church, the French Cathedral, the Greek Cathedral, and the whole of Rue Franque.[104] Smyrna, except for the Jewish and Turkish quarters, had ceased to exist.

On 26 September the French Foreign Office issued an official statement attempting to exonerate the Turks for the burning Smyrna.[105]A telegram sent by British High Commissioner Rumbold to the British Foreign Office outlines why France might have issued such a statement:

> We [Italian High Commissioner and Rumbold] both agree that French High Commissioner has [...] gone to Smyrna to see Mustapha Kemal in order to extricate French government from embarrassing position in which they now necessarily find themselves. [...] The destruction of Smyrna, including burning of French consulate and material damage to French interests, have come as a great shock to French here. True facts getting out it will be more difficult for the French to support a nation, which commits such barbarities. [...] There

---

[100] Senior Officer, 3rd Light Cruiser Squadron to Admiralty, 19 September 1922: Copies of telegrams exchanged between Sir H. Rumbold, Constantinople, and the Foreign Office, The Lloyd George Papers, British Parliamentary Archives, LG/F/208/1.

[101] "The Burned Area," *The Times*, 22 September 1922, 10.

[102] Türkmen Parlak, *İşgal'den Kurtuluş'a 2: Yunan Ege'den Nasıl Gitti, Son Günler* [*From Occupation to Liberation: How the Greek Left the Aegean, The Last Days*] (İzmir: Vakfi Kültür Yayınları, 1983), 2: 478–79.

[103] Oeconomos, Lysimachos, *The Tragedy of the Christian Near East* (London: The Anglo-Hellenic League, 1923), 11, and Macartney, *Refugees*, 79.

[104] Ibid., 10–11. Details of the burnt Spanish and Belgian consulates obtained from British Foreign Office documents, British Foreign Office Archives, FO 141/580/1.

[105] "French Exonerate Turks: Foreign Office Denies Kemalists Set Fire to Smyrna," *The New York Times*, 27 September 1922, 2.

> seems no doubt that Turks deliberately massacred many Armenians and then burnt the Armenian and European quarters of the town.[106]

The eyewitness testimonies of genocide survivors, relief workers, missionaries, journalists, servicemen and consuls are well documented in international archives.[107] They corroborate Turkish responsibility for the atrocities perpetrated at Smyrna during the month of September 1922. However, to this day, there remains doubt amongst genocide scholars and historians alike as to who originally issued the orders for the city's burning and to what extent, if any, Mustafa Kemal participated in organizing the city's destruction. Turkish historian Süleyman Külçe, in his book *Mareşal Fevzi Çakmak: Askeri ve Hususi Hayatı*, concedes that General Nurettin Paşa "was responsible for the fire."[108] Falih Rıfkı Atay also felt that if it had not been for Nurettin the events at Smyrna would have turned out very differently.[109] General Nurettin Paşa is also said to be responsible for the death of Archbishop Chrysostomos, the Orthodox Metropolitan of Smyrna. The U.S. consul general at Smyrna claimed that it was Nurettin Paşa who turned over Chrysostomos to a Turkish mob, who tortured and tore him to pieces in front of the military headquarters of the Kemalist forces in Smyrna on September 9, the day of the Turkish entry.[110] Of Chrysostomos, Reverend Charles Dobson, the British chaplain of Smyrna, said,

> He was truly a martyr who died through staying at his post to reassure his people.[111]

A report from acting British Vice-Consul Robert W. Urquhart of Smyrna sent to Sir Horace Rumbold, the British High Commissioner in Constantinople, on

---

[106] Sir H. Rumbold, Constantinople, to Foreign Office 17 September 1922: Copies of telegrams exchanged between Sir H Rumbold, Constantinople, and the Foreign Office, The Lloyd George Papers, British Parliamentary Archives, LG/F/208/1.

[107] U.S. archival documentation has recently been compiled by Constantine G. Hatzidimitriou in *American Accounts Documenting the Destruction of Smyrna.* See also Marjorie Housepian Dobkin, *Smyrna 1922: The Destruction of a City* (Kent, OH: Kent State University Press, 1988). British documentation can be found in Oeconomos, *The Martyrdom of Smyrna and Eastern Christendom.* The Smyrna Holocaust has also inspired novels such as Dora Barford's *Greek Fire: A Tale of the Levant* (London, 1935). In recent years a number of Turkish academics have questioned the Turkish state's thesis on its genocidal era. I would like to draw attention to one such article on Smyrna, namely Prof. Biray Kolluoğlu Kırlı's study "Forgetting the Smyrna Fire."

[108] Süleyman Külçe, *Maresal Fevzi Çakmak* [*Field Marshal Fevzi Cakmak*] (İstanbul: Cumhuriyet Matbaası, 1953), 236 [translation mine].

[109] Atay, *Çankaya: Atatürk'ün Doğumundan*, 325.

[110] Senior Officer, 3rd Light Cruiser Squadron to Admiralty, 19 September 1922: Copies of telegrams exchanged between Sir H. Rumbold, Constantinople and the Foreign Office, The Lloyd George Papers, British Parliamentary Archives, LG/F/208/1.

[111] Dobson, *The Smyrna Holocaust*, 23.

10 October 1922 provides an account of conditions at Smyrna a month after the calamity began. Urquhart writes:

> Bodies have been collected and burnt [...] Greek churches are being systematically razed to the ground. A house-to-house search and the activities of informers have completely cleared the town of Greeks and Armenians [...] The Turks claim to have solved the problem of the minorities.[112]

On 13 October Vice-Consul Urquhart telegraphed Sir Rumbold again,

> This morning it was reported to me that the British cemetery at Bournabat had been entered and the graves defiled. In company with Rear-Admiral Nicholson I visited the cemetery this afternoon, and found that, without exception, the tombstones had been smashed and overthrown, several holes, about 1 foot deep, dug over graves and many defiled with filth of human beings and animals.[113]

The British Consul General in Smyrna, Sir Harry Harling Lamb (1857–1948), had sent Lord Curzon a full account of the destruction of Smyrna in the second week of September.[114] On reading Lamb's account Winston Churchill was horrified by all that happened in Smyrna. In a telegram to the Dominion Prime Ministers on 3 October, Churchill gave the following account of the events:

> The Turkish troops entered Smyrna under perfect restraint. No reprisals were allowed even when a Turkish officer was wounded by a bomb thrown by an Armenian. Three days later, however, when superior Turkish authorities had arrived and the matter had been maturely considered, the whole Armenian quarter was methodically delivered to rape, pillage and massacre. 20 corpses in 50 yards were counted by Sir Harry Lamb on one occasion when he penetrated this quarter during the infernal orgy. Out of 900 females who were rescued by a British destroyer, only 20 were between the ages of 15 and 35. In order to obliterate the horror, fires were started on the windward side of the Armenian quarter and restarted to windward as particular areas burned themselves out. These fires were also carried to the European quarter equally on the windward side, and the Turks even besprinkled with petrol the bundles of the refugees on the quay, according to the Consul General and lighted them up. The Turkish quarter was undamaged. 180,000 refugees have been taken off and dumped down in Greece mainly by British agency. According to the facts reported by the Consul General, Smyrna must, for a

[112] Report dated 10 October 1922 from R. W. Urquhart, acting vice-consul at Smyrna, to Sir Horace Rumbold, British High Commissioner at Constantinople, British Foreign Office Archives, FO 141/580/1.

[113] Report dated 13 October 1922 from R. W. Urquhart, acting vice-consul at Smyrna, to Sir Horace Rumbold, British High Commissioner at Constantinople, ibid.

[114] Gilbert, *Winston S. Churchill*, 853.

> deliberately planned and methodically executed atrocity, find few parallels in the history of human crime.[115]

In the telegram, which is presumably largely, if not wholly, based on information from the "impartial" report by Consul Lamb, Churchill alludes to Turkish responsibility for massacres by the implication that considerable planning by "superior Turkish authorities" had taken place.[116] Winston Churchill also wrote of Smyrna in his published memoirs on the Great War,

> Turkey became once again the sole master of Asia Minor, and Mustapha Kemal's Army, having celebrated their triumph by the burning of Smyrna to ashes and by a vast massacre of its Christian population, turned the heads of their columns hopefully towards Constantinople and the Straits.[117]

In September 1922 Kemalist troops entered the city of Smyrna, indulged in an orgy of pillaging, rape and massacre at the expense of the city's Christian majority and burnt the city to rubble. The term Smyrna Holocaust refers both to the extermination of the native Smyrnaeans and to the fire which expunged an entire city from the face of the Earth. Mustafa Kemal saw the fire as a sign that Turkey was

> purged of the traitors, the Christians, and of the foreigners, and that Turkey is for the Turks.[118]

Today, the Turkish city of İzmir stands in place of what was once the ancient city of Smyrna. The destruction of Smyrna and the annihilation of its Christian inhabitants, both Greek and Armenian, remain a haunting chapter in the genocide of Turkey's Greek and Armenian population.

Before the outbreak of the Great War, or World War I as it is now known, at least 2.5 million Greeks lived in the Ottoman Empire but following a decade of violence, the population diminished to a little over a million. Most of the surviving Greeks, except those residing in Constantinople, fled or were transported to Greece by the 1923 convention concerning the exchange of Greek and Turkish nationals in Greece and Turkey.[119] The Greek Genocide

---

[115] Winston Churchill to Dominion Prime Ministers, 3 October 1922: Copies of telegraphic correspondence with the Dominions, The Lloyd George Papers, British Parliamentary Archives, LG/F/209/2.

[116] Churchill presumably found the report to be "impartial" since it begins by mentioning the unruly Greek retreat: "Every village they could reach in their retreat was burnt by the Greek rearguard and many Turkish inhabitants were killed."

[117] Winston S. Churchill, *The World Crisis: The Aftermath* (London: Thornton Butterworth, 1929), 419.

[118] H. C. Armstrong, *Grey Wolf: An Intimate Study of a Dictator* (London: Arthur Barker, 1934), 203.

[119] According to the census of 1928 1,104,216 refugees, Greeks and others, had left Turkey for Greece. This number is not restricted to refugees transferred by the population

saw approximately one million perish.[120] The League of Nations estimated that

> of the total number of Greeks in Asia Minor, who before the war amounted to at least 2,000,000, scarcely half survived [...][121]

The Genocide was the systematic policy of physical annihilation orchestrated and perpetrated by the Ottoman Empire, the Republic of Turkey's predecessor, against the indigenous Greek minority of the Empire between 1914 and 1923 in order to secure an end to their collective existence as an ethnic group.

---

exchange but also includes those forcefully expelled from the Ottoman Empire as well as those that left "voluntarily." Only 190,000 Greeks are recorded as having been transferred to Greece under the convention.

120 In their study "Ethnic Survival, Nationalism and Forced Migration: The Historical Demography of the Greek Community of Asia Minor at the close of the Ottoman era," *Δελτίο Κέντρου Μικρασιατικών Σπουδών* [*Bulletin of the Center for Asia Minor Studies*] 5 (1984–1985) Paschalis Kitromilides and Alexis Alexandris claim that approximately 700,000 Asia Minor Greeks died. However, their study does not take into account deaths among other Ottoman Greeks. Some have placed the total Ottoman Greek death toll as high as 1,700,000. However, this excessive figure illustrates the need to consider a wider range of factors in order to reach a more accurate assessment for loss of life. Accepting the general consensus that the Greek population of Ottoman Turkey numbered at least 2.5 million and then taking reasonable deductions for, a) migration of Greeks from eastern Ottoman provinces into Russia, b) the refugee influx into Greece during the genocidal era (1914–1923), c) the subsequent population exchange and d) the existence of a Greek population in Constantinople, one can then conservatively surmise that loss of life among Ottoman Greeks during the Great War (1914–1918) and its aftermath (1919–1923) stands at approximately one million. While this figure is provisional, it does provide insight into the magnitude of the crime. For a more detailed study on this issue, see my forthcoming article "Loss of Life among Ottoman Greeks during the Genocide: a Quantitative Survey."

121 League of Nations, *Greek Refugee Settlement* (Geneva: Publications of the League of Nations, 1926), 12.

Two Notes on the Title and Subtitle of this Article

A. The term *holocaust* to define the burning of Smyrna was widely used at the time. Attention may be drawn to the 1923 Anglo-Hellenic League publication *The Smyrna Holocaust* by Rev. Charles Dobson, the British Chaplain of Smyrna, as well as press articles too numerous to cite here. Publications such as *The Young Turks and the Truth about the Holocaust at Adana in Asia Minor during April, 1909* (1913) testify that the term *holocaust* to characterise pogroms and massacres against Christians in Ottoman Turkey was not rare, or new to the Smyrna Holocaust. The first use of 'holocaust' so far as events in modern Ottoman Turkey are concerned, was by various American Protestant missionaries serving among Armenians in connection with the burning of Armenian churches. Subsequently, the term holocaust has been expropriated and elevated to *The Holocaust* by Jews in connection with the genocide perpetrated against them in Nazi Germany during World War II. Many seem to think that holocaust was peculiar to them (see Jon Petrie, "The secular word HOLOCAUST: scholarly myths, history, and 20th century meanings," *Journal of Genocide Research* 2/1 (March 2000): 31–63). The word holocaust originally meant "burnt in whole" and derives from the Greek *holokauston*: *holo,* "whole" and *kauston,* "burnt." Its usage is very appropriate in the context of Smyrna.

I do not hesitate to state that some may well interpret the views expressed here as unabashedly pro-Greek and/or pro-Armenian. Nevertheless, attempts have been made to read works of contrasting viewpoints in the interest of achieving a fair and accurate assessment of the Smyrna fire. For example, Stanford J. Shaw and Ezel Kural Shaw, *History of the Ottoman Empire and Modern Turkey, Volume II: Reform, Revolution, and Republic: The Rise of Modern Turkey, 1808–1975* (Cambridge and New York: Cambridge University Press, Cambridge, 1977); Heath W. Lowry, "Turkish History: On whose sources will it be based? A case study of İzmir," *Osmanlı Araştırmaları* [*The Journal of Ottoman Studies*] 9 (1988); and Justin McCarthy, *Death and Exile: The Ethnic Cleansing of Ottoman Muslims 1821–1922* (Princeton: Darwin Press, 1995). However, all of these works are replete with sophistry and platitudes and are characterized by serious defects so typical of the official Turkish point of view — ranging from gross inaccuracies to blatant and selective use of sources. Given that all these authors, students (Lowry and McCarthy) and teacher (Shaw) respectively, have been severely criticised for their failure to maintain accepted standards of scholarship they have compromised their right to be taken seriously. Regarding Stanford J. Shaw see Speros Vryonis' review essay on Shaw's alleged "archival" work in *Balkan Studies* 24/1 (1983): 163–286; regarding Justin McCarthy see James J. Reid, "Necrophilia and Alienation, or Death and Exile, A Review Essay," *Journal of the Society for Armenian Studies* 9 (1996, 1997 [1999]): 105–23; and regarding Lowry see "Professional Ethics and Denial of the Armenian Genocide," by Roger W. Smith, Eric Markusen and Robert J. Lifton in *Holocaust and Genocide Studies* 9 no. 1 (Spring 1995): 1–22. Constantine G. Hatzidimitriou, in his volume *American Accounts Documenting the Destruction of Smyrna by the Kemalist Turkish Forces, September 1922* (New York: Aristide D. Caratzas, 2005), highlights the irony of Lowry's paper on İzmir. As Hatzidimitriou points out, "Lowry claims that the American sources are too contradictory to be relied upon and appends one such source to his study in order to document his contention." For further details see pp. 5–7 of Hatzidimitriou's volume.

B. It is my understanding there is as yet no contemporary comprehensive scholarly study on the Greek Genocide in the English language. However, it is hoped that this distinguished compilation of papers will be a significant step towards facilitating the availability of scholarly material on the subject and providing directions towards its study. Regrettably, despite the wealth of archival documentation detailing the genocidal practices of the late Ottoman Empire, volumes such as the *Encyclopedia of Genocide and Crimes against Humanity* (Detroit: Thomson Gale, 2005), 303, refer to the suffering of Turkey's Greek population as merely an act of "ethnic cleansing." On the other hand, as Prof. Adam Jones points out in *Genocide: A Comprehensive Introduction* (London: Routledge, 2006), 106, "only now are these events beginning to attract meaningful scholarly interest."

In December 2007, the International Association of Genocide Scholars (IAGS), an organization of the world's foremost experts on genocide, passed a resolution affirming the Greek Genocide.

On a final note: This article was written, and the archival material sourced periodically, mostly between 2006 and 2007.

Acknowledgements

Firstly, I wish to acknowledge the helpful suggestions afforded to me during the writing of this paper by Abraham D. Krikorian, also a contributor in this volume. In addition, Abraham has assisted tremendously by generously providing reading materials that were otherwise inaccessible to me here in the United Kingdom.

I am also indebted to the following institutions and their staff: the Parliamentary Archives in the House of Lords, Westminster; the British National Archives, Kew; the Imperial War Museum Archives; the British Library; and University of London's Senate House Library. In the reading rooms of these institutions I was granted access to invaluable and often rare and unpublished material on the subject of this paper.

Finally, I would like to express my utmost gratitude to the editors and publisher of this publication for their patience and support throughout.

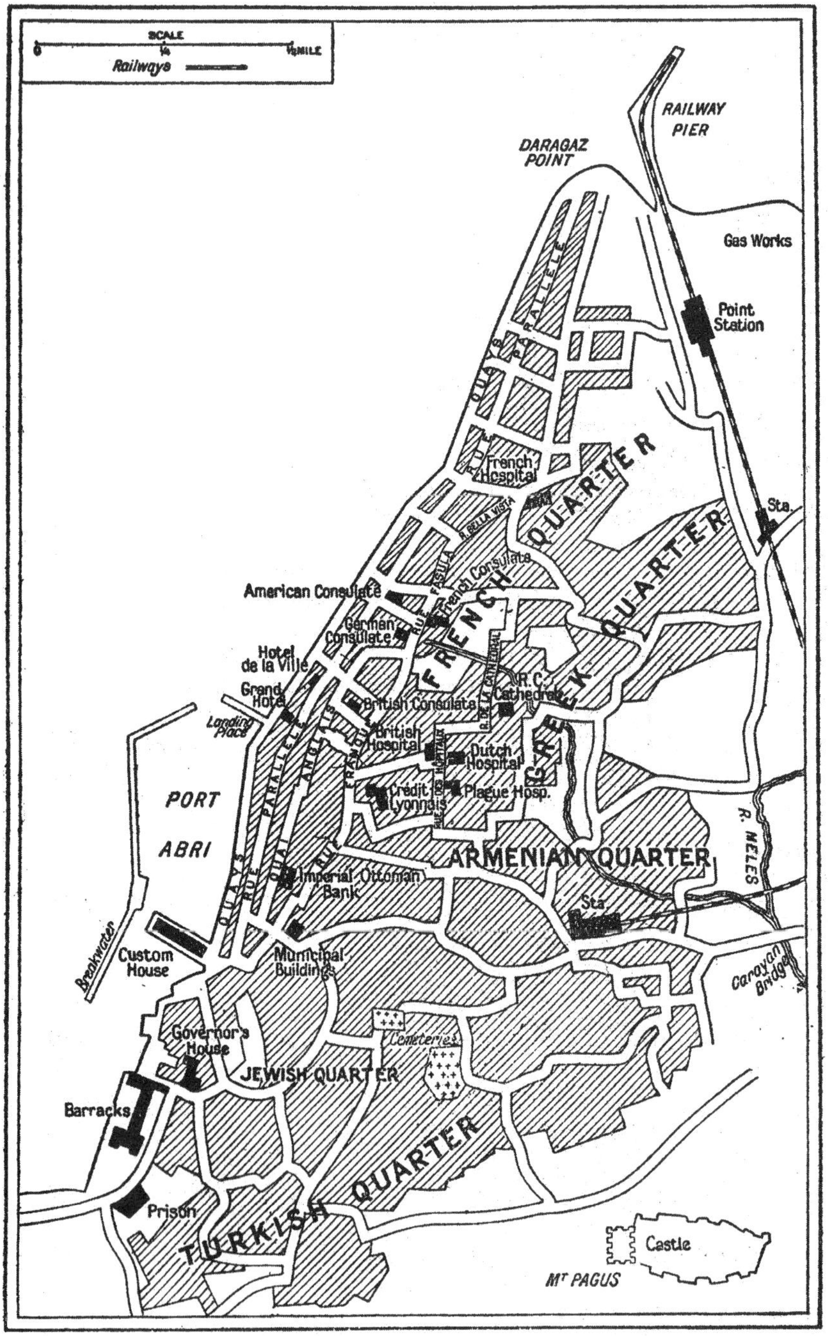

Smyrna Map
Source: *The Daily Telegraph*, 16 September 1922

APPENDIX: *Photographic Documentation*

All images in this Appendix (except the first [1]) are from the author's collection.

1. Turkish troops standing beside their hanged victim, a decapitated and mutilated Greek woman, in Nazilli, Aydin. The photograph was taken by N. Rigopoulos on 15 June 1920.

2. Massacred Greeks of western Anatolia laid out on stretchers; photograph by military photographer Evangelos Pappas (Greek: Ευάγγελος Παππάς)

3. Massacred Greek men, women and children of western Anatolia; photograph by military photographer Evangelos Pappas

4. Displaced Ottoman Greeks in western Anatolia.

5. (Above) and 6. (Below) The pitiful plight of Ottoman Greeks in western Anatolia

7. A Japanese commercial vessel picking up Greeks before the Kemalist entry into Smyrna, Friday, 8 September 1922;

8. Kemalist troops on Smyrna's quay moments after the Turkish entry, Saturday, 9 September 1922.

9. The start of the Smyrna fire, Wednesday, 13 September 1922.

10. Below the marked cross is a consulate's flag which remained there until the building collapsed and to the right of HMS *Trinidad's* mast is the undamaged Turkish Quarter, 13 September 1922.

11. Smyrna engulfed by fire;

12. Smyrna burning, as seen from the USS *Edsall*.

13. The HMS *Iron Duke* (right) at Smyrna, 14 September 1922

14. Smyrna burning as viewed from an Italian vessel, 14 September 1922.

15. (Above) and 16. (Below) In their haste to escape Smyrna refugees cause boat to overturn, while a sailor from the USS *Litchfield* tries to offer assistance, September 1922

17. American sailors from the USS *Litchfield* rescue a young women from the water.
18. Floating corpse in Smyrna's waters as photographed from an American vessel.
(Both images taken September 1922)

19. British sailors transferring Greek women and children to safety, September 1922.
20. Greek refugees boarding a British naval ship at Smyrna, September 1922 .

21. Greek men taking refuge aboard an Allied ship.
22. The Greek church of Saint John (Greek: Άγιος Ιωάννης), Smyrna, was first pillaged and then burnt.

23. The burnt-out Armenian Quarter of Smyrna.
24. The burnt-out Greek Quarter of Smyrna.

25. (above) and 26. (below) Scenes of the European section of Smyrna after the fire.

27. American sailors in the European section of Smyrna after the fire had died out.
28. Smyrna's quay after the fire.

29. Smyrna's quay after the fire.
30. Smyrna's rubble in the European section.

30. Two Greek refugee girls aboard the USS *Denebola* in Constantinople, 5 December 1922.

31. A refugee camp in Constantinople.

The Immediate Context of the Smyrna Catastrophe

The Peace Treaties and the Aftermath of the Greco-Turkish War of 1919–1922

MATTHEW STEWART

ON 15 SEPTEMBER 1922 THE FIRES of a raging holocaust began finally to burn themselves out.[1] Smyrna (İzmir), the gem-city of the Turkish Aegean had gone up in flames. Over breakfast that day, readers of the London *Morning Post* were informed that Turkish regular troops had set fire to the Greek, Armenian and European quarters of the city, while ensuring that no damage was done to Turkish neighborhoods. This assignment of guilt to the Turks has been disputed, of course, with charge and countercharge, accusation and denial hurled back and forth over the decades. What all witnesses could agree on was the magnitude of the fire.

> What I see as I stand on the deck of the *Iron Duke* [the British warship at anchor in the harbor], wrote the reporter Ward Price, is an unbroken wall of fire, two miles long, in which twenty distinct volcanoes of raging flames are throwing up jagged, writhing tongues to a height of a hundred feet.[2]

Future estimates would set the death toll as high as 100,000.[3] For two days while the fires burned and for some two weeks immediately thereafter, the citizens of this once lovely and essentially Greek city experienced brutality and neglect on a massive scale. George Horton, seasoned U.S. Consul and witness to these terrible days would later write:

---

[1] It is recognized that the word *holocaust* is highly charged. In this paper, the word is used in its primary sense of great destruction or devastation by fire.

[2] Quoted in David Walder, *The Chanak Affair* (New York: Macmillan, 1969), 176–77.

[3] Marjorie Housepian, concurring with the estimate of U.S. Consul George Horton, is among historians who have used the figure 100,000: *Smyrna Affair: The First Comprehensive Account of the Burning of the City and the Expulsion of the Christians from Turkey in 1922* (New York: Harcourt Brace Jovanovich, 1971), 190. Horton has been charged with anti-Turkish bias. However much Horton's impassioned rhetoric betrays a pro-Christian point of view, still he was a man of long experience in the Middle East when he witnessed the Smyrna catastrophe. Housepian's partisan point of view is buttressed with impressive research. U.S. Admiral Mark Bristol, a man with decidedly pro-Turkish leanings, may be taken as a representative of the other end of the spectrum, estimating 2,000 deaths, surely an underestimate given the known number of refugees, ibid. Biray Kolluoğlu Kırlı, has stated in a recent publication that, "we can estimate that the casualties were no less that 100,000." "Forgetting the Smyrna Fire," *History Workshop Journal* 60, no. 1 (Autumn 2005): 31.

> One of the keenest impressions which I brought away with me from Smyrna was a feeling of shame that I belonged to the human race.[4]

While the massacre received wide coverage in the western press in the immediately succeeding days, the affair is now virtually forgotten outside of the countries involved. One scholar has written that, "until 1927 when [U.S.] diplomatic relations with Turkey were fully restored, a flood of articles and books continued to review the Smyrna catastrophe."[5] Yet, by 1941 the American author Henry Miller wrote in his book of Greek travels *The Colossus of Marousi* that, "The Smyrna affair... has been somehow soft-pedaled and almost expunged from the memory of present-day man."[6] For the principal antagonists, on the other hand, the Smyrna catastrophe and the three-year war which led up to it continue to provoke bitter accusation and heated denial, and the affair lives on as the subject of continued propaganda and public relations efforts from both sides. Outside of Turkey, Greece and Armenia, a mention of the phrase "Greco-Turkish War" is more apt to elicit an exotic image from Lord Byron or Delacroix than an informed remark on David Lloyd George or Mustafa Kemal — that is if it elicits any response at all. This despite the scale of the immediate catastrophe, and the fact that the event triggered the largest European refugee problem prior to World War II. Some 1.5 million people were involved in a post-war "exchange of populations."[7]

Famously Hitler asked rhetorically, "Who remembers the annihilation of the Armenians today?" Subsequent to Hitler's cynical utterance, the Armenian catastrophe has become common knowledge, even as the terms used to describe it remain the subject of intense, emotionally charged public debate. During the early years of the twenty-first century in Europe, there has been significant public support for prohibiting the denial or even the trivialization of genocidal acts; laws prohibiting such claims have been proposed and to a more limited extent enacted. Armenian and Greek activists (and others)

---

[4] George Horton, *The Blight of Asia: An Account of the Systematic Extermination of Christian Populations by Mohammedans and of the Culpability of Certain Great Powers; with the True Story of the Burning of Smyrna* (Indianapolis: Bobbs-Merril, 1926; reprint, 1953), 153.

[5] Housepian, *The Smyrna Affair*, 218. As early as 1922 a collection of journalistic accounts was published in London: Lysimachos Oeconomos, *The Martyrdom of Smyrna and Eastern Christendom: A File of Overwhelming Evidence, Denouncing the Misdeeds of the Turks in Asia Minor and showing their responsibility for the Horrors of Smyrna* (London: Allen and Unwin, 1922).

[6] Quoted in Housepian, *The Smyrna Affair*, vii.

[7]Richard Clogg has written that 380,000 Muslims were brought to live in Turkey, while some 1,100,000 Greeks were removed from former Ottoman lands (many had left before the official enactment of the refugee conventions), see *A Short History of Modern Greece* (Cambridge: Cambridge University Press, 1979), 121. See also Michael Llewellyn Smith, *Ionian Vision: Greece in Asia Minor 1919-1922* (New York: St. Martin's, 1973), 319.

have pushed for these prohibitions to be applied to Turkish actions during World War I and its aftermath. As of this writing, Turkish admission of genocide seems a very distant prospect even while it has, in the minds of many, become a litmus test for that country's full acceptance into the European community. The Turkish Government continues to exert pressure on official bodies, including other governments, not to use the term "genocide" in relation to Armenians or Greeks. To read the web sites of Armenian or Greek advocacy groups and Turkish "self-defense" groups leads one to conclude that positions have not softened or moved towards the middle over the decades. Yet, even in light of such intense public debate and the re-energizing of raw sensibilities, it would seem that very few among the general public now remember the holocaust at Smyrna. Most certainly the convoluted Great Power diplomacy and the blundering war, which led up to it, have disappeared from public memory. This article, then, proposes to set the disaster at Smyrna in its immediate context.

Settlement with the Ottoman Empire was not at the top of the Great Powers' agenda when they convened at Versailles in 1919. Indeed the terms of peace between the victorious Allies and the Ottoman Empire were not determined during that long series of meetings, but rather awaited settlement in the Treaty of Sèvres (France) which was signed on 10 August 1920, nearly two years after the fighting had ceased. Its terms were never implemented. The length of deliberation was not matched by a commensurate amount of wisdom, foresight or good fortune. The document was produced in the wake of mutually exclusive, often secret, Allied wartime promises, and fabricated in the mold of nationalistic self-seeking and diplomatic intrigue that characterized such a large part of the victors' agenda. Charles Swallow has summarized the outcome by saying that Sèvres "came draped in the flags of Western imperialism."[8]

The treaty's salient stipulations provided that: (1) Smyrna and the adjacent regions of Anatolia would nominally remain Ottoman but would be administered by Greece for five years, after which a plebiscite would determine whether it would be Turkish or Greek; (2) virtually all of Thrace, both eastern and western, would be ceded to Greece; (3) Constantinople (present-day İstanbul) would remain under Ottoman control, but a substantial garri-

---

[8] Charles Swallow, *The Sick Man of Europe: Ottoman Empire to Turkish Republic 1789–1923* (London: Ernest Benn, 1973), 114. The Treaty of Sèvres is compactly outlined by Stanford J. and Ezel Kural Shaw, *History of the Ottoman Empire and Modern Turkey, Volume II: Reform, Revolution, and Republic: The Rise of Modern Turkey, 1808–1975* (Cambridge and New York: Cambridge University Press, 1977), 356. It can be read online at: http://net.lib.byu.edu/~rdh7/wwi/versa/sevres1.html.

son of former Entente powers would remain there. This prescription for confusion had already been preceded by the Greek military occupation of Smyrna, which had begun on 15 May 1919, and initially entailed 20,000 troops, a number that swelled in the ensuing months. This action was undertaken with the especial consent of Lloyd George's Government and achieved under the flags of the Allied warships positioned in Smyrna's harbor.

These events proved intolerable to the Turkish nationalists, whose political strength grew in proportion as the Greek forces pushed further eastward and as the surviving Ottoman power structure's capacity to rule authentically diminished. The ruling Sultan, Mehmet VI Vahdetinn, had ascended to the throne in July 1918, the closing days of the Great War, and lived in fear of losing the position he had only just gained. In the words of Efraim and Inari Karsh, he

> went out of his way to buy the Allies' benevolence: he dissolved Parliament ... [he] imprisoned members of the Unionist Government, together with scores of suspected political activists; ... and progressively disarmed and demobilized the Turkish army throughout the country, resigning himself to the idea that Asia Minor would be occupied by foreign powers.[9]

Mustafa Kemal and likeminded patriots had other ideas.

> To ordinary Turks the Greek invasion was anathema; to the sultan it was a personal affront by a former minor subject people. Kemal, in contrast, saw it as a lightning strike galvanizing the defeatist masses into a reinvigorated national effort.[10]

At first glance, the Greek military incursion presents itself as premature and entirely heavy-handed,[11] but it was in part the result of understandable Greek anxiety that Italy might gain regional control, for it emerged that Italy had been promised Smyrna in 1917 and had already inserted its own troops elsewhere in Asia Minor, claiming the necessity of maintaining order.[12] With their various, sometimes secret treaties made during the war, the Allies had cut the cake in eight, then invited twelve to tea afterwards. The Greek insertion must also be viewed as a result of the warm relations that had developed between Lloyd George and Greek Prime Minister Eleutherios Venizelos, who had taken a vigorously pro-Allied position within Greece during the war years and who charmed not only Lloyd George but seemingly the entire Allied entourage at Versailles, some in spite of themselves. "So anxious was

---

[9] Efraim and Inari Karsh, *Empires of the Sand: The Struggle for Mastery in the Middle East, 1789–1923* (Cambridge: Harvard University, 1999), 327.

[10] Ibid., 331.

[11] Winston S. Churchill, *The World Crisis: The Aftermath* (New York: Scribner's, 1929), 388–91. Peter Kincaid Jensen, "The Greco-Turkish War, 1920–1922," *International Journal of Middle East Studies* 10, no. 4 (Nov. 1979): 554.

[12] Paul C. Helmreich, *From Paris to Sèvres: The Partition of the Ottoman Empire at the Peace Conference of 1919–1920* (Columbus: Ohio State University Press, 1974), 94–97.

[U.S. President Woodrow] Wilson to see Greek forces land in Asia Minor that he told Venizelos that 'men did not keep in good condition on board ship'."[13]

Venizelos (a Cretan whose first name means "liberator") was a man to whom the now clichéed and Greek-derived epithet *charismatic* truly did apply. His wartime posture had put the Greek prime minister in direct opposition to King Constantine, whose official posture was neutral, but who was widely known to hold pro-German sentiments. Venizelos was also the principal force behind the so-called "Great Idea," an idealistic conception whereby Greece set out to regain its former power and prestige and to realize its unfulfilled potential. Sharing his aspirations for a Greek Constantinople only with Greek insiders, he nonetheless publicly pledged a Greece "on two continents, washed by five seas." This return to greatness was not to be confused with a merely vulgar, imperialistic land grab; nevertheless, it was to be achieved in the first instance by recovering territory perceived by the Greeks to be Greek, mostly at the expense of Ottoman territory. The ardent patriot and inveterate French power broker Raymond Poincaré offered an especially scathing and anti-British assessment of the goings-on prior to the final settlement at Sèvres:

> Mr. Lloyd George, in particular, and M. Venizelos, made up their minds to throw Greece into an adventure which had no other object than to serve the interests of British Imperialism in Asia Minor, and which was doomed from the outset to certain failure.[14]

This interpretation of events was proffered not only by British rivals and realpolitik cynics, but found essential agreement in the judgment of Winston Churchill:

> At last peace with Turkey: and to ratify it, War with Turkey! However, so far as the Great Allies were concerned the war was to be fought by proxy. Wars when fought thus by great nations are often very dangerous for the proxy.[15]

Churchill, however, could appreciate both Britain's dilemma and the effects it eventually had on both Turkey and Greece. Britain had been steadily demobilizing after four long years of war and the prospects were dim for rallying the public to renew hostilities with the same enemy that had recently defeated her in the disastrous Dardanelles campaign.[16] Yet British interests

---

[13] Karsh, *Empires of Sand*, 331.

[14] Poincaré letter to S. Cosmetatos dated 30 June 1926, see S. P. P. Cosmetatos, *The Tragedy of Greece*, transl. E. W. and A. Dickes (New York: Brentanos, 1928), 301.

[15] Churchill, *The World Crisis: The Aftermath*, 399.

[16] Churchill's championing of the Gallipoli invasion cost him politically and was not soon forgotten by his foes or by the electorate.

in this potentially oil-rich and strategically significant region needed protection, not least from the designs of her wartime Allies. Thus while Churchill joins Poincaré in acknowledging the core idea of Greek adventurism on behalf of Great Power interests, and shows Greece to have been induced primarily by Britain, he also apportions a measure of blame to all the Allies.

To these complicating facts on the ground it should be added that Lloyd George's philhellenism was quite sincere. And Britain's chief negotiator Lord Curzon, despite speaking out against the idea of Greek insertion into Ionia, was not motivated by any counterbalancing positive desire to support Turkey. His low opinion of Ottoman achievements was undisguised; he had been so blunt as to state openly that, "the presence of the Turks in Europe has been a source of unmitigated evil to everybody concerned. I am not aware of a single interest, Turkish or otherwise, that during nearly 500 years has benefitted by that presence." (Curzon also loathed Poincaré, referring to him as "that horrid little man.")

However, two specific items should be noted in defense of the Lloyd George Government. In the first place, as has been stated, Italy had already made landings elsewhere in the crumbling Ottoman territory, claiming rights under a secretive wartime treaty made with the French. Surely Greece had greater claim to Smyrna (which then had a larger Greek population than Athens) and to Ionia with its large Greek population, than did the suddenly threatening Italians. This first argument entails the second: Greek nationalistic sentiments in regards to the region could be buttressed by legitimate demographic arguments and socio-cultural claims (though Venizelos's propensity to exaggerate these claims should also be noted). If Turkey was not to be entirely entrusted to the Turks in the post-war scheme, surely history was on Greece's side as claimant.

The matter was complicated all the more by a quintessential Balkan can of worms: the definition of nationality. What constituted a Greek (or a Turk, or any other nationality) was not always clear when it came to actual cases. If one's family had come from Greece a hundred years or more before, had thus lived under Ottoman rule for several generations and no longer spoke Greek, was one still a Greek? In some cases, affiliation with the Orthodox Church might seem to be the only significant remaining tie to Greek culture. Was this sufficient to make one a Greek? Such were the realities bound to cause consternation to those who assumed the task of putting together a new order after the Great War.

The Sèvres terms naturally represented a spur to the Turkish nationalists, a party associated with the erstwhile Young Turks, the party of the war hero Mustafa Kemal Paşa, later Atatürk, the founder of modern Turkey. The Young Turks had gained power in 1908, forcing the exile of Sultan Abdülhamit II, but then lost it after leading Turkey to defeat in World War I.

They awaited the proper set of circumstances to reemerge preeminent and planned to construct a new, Turcocentric version of their country out of the Ottoman ruins. For Kemal and like-minded patriots, Constantinople — symbol of decay, defeat and decadence, a city too close to Europe — would be supplanted by a new capital rooted in Anatolia. Neither of Kemal's parents were Turks, yet he would center his operations, then his new Turkey, in the mud-brick town of Ankara, a locale just barely deserving to be called a regional center at the time of the war.

It may need reminding that the Turks were not synonymous with the Ottomans; nor was Turkey synonymous with the Ottoman Empire. Indeed the ruling Ottoman class, clinging precariously to power in the immediate aftermath of the Great War, tended to look down on the Turks as a lowly and inferior lot. Indeed, the very term "Turk" was deemed an insult by the Ottomans. That a Turk could harbor, let alone successfully act upon, patriotic aspirations for self-determination had struck the Ottoman elite with some surprise. The war of 1919-22 became for the nationalist Turks, then, a two-fold war for national liberation: first from invading foreign powers and their menacing Allies, and second from the last vestiges of Ottoman power. Indeed, while Mustafa Kemal fought the Greeks a price had been declared on his head in his own capital.[17]

Subsequent to landing at Smyrna, the Greeks pushed eastward into Anatolia, augmenting their forces. Their landing was accompanied by some 350 Turkish casualties, and instances of deliberate mistreatment of Turks by occupying Greek forces were documented. In the autumn of 1919 two official reports were issued drawing attention to problems created by the Greeks. The first was prepared by the Allied commander-in-chief in Asiatic Turkey, General Milne. Harsher and more censorious than the Milne report was one prepared by a group of Allied commissioners, which discredited the very idea of the landing in Smyrna and which stated that the Greek occupation "far from presenting itself as the carrying out of a civilizing mission, at once took the form of a conquest and crusade."[18] Turkish nationalists were not content to suffer indignities passively, least of all the insertion of Greek

---

[17] Philip Mansel, *Constantinople: City of the World's Desire, 1453-1924* (New York: St. Martin's, 1996), 393.

[18] Quoted in Michael L. Dockrill and J. Douglas Goold, *Peace Without Promise: Britain and the Peace Conferences, 1919-23* (Hamden, Conn.: Shoestring Press [Archon Books], 1981), 200. The authors go on to state that "the occupation had turned into an annexation, despite the fact that apart from the cities of Smyrna and Ayvalık (Kydoniai (Gr.)) the Turks were incontestably in a majority," ibid.

troops into the heart of their homeland. A cycle of uncongenial co-existence arose, consisting of non-cooperation and occasional hostile acts on the part of Turks and, too often, of heavy-handed re-assertion of authority on the part of Greece.

The understandable swelling of Turkish patriotic sentiment was turned to good use by the nationalist Turks. While the defeated official Ottoman Government had agreed to the Treaty of Sèvres, the nationalists used its unpalatable terms as the starting point of their rebirth. They would lead the fight against Greek occupation and Allied intrusiveness both militarily and politically. Lloyd George and the other Allied leaders had neither sought nor even foreseen the demise of the more compliant Ottoman remnant still installed in Constantinople, but that is what their actions precipitated.[19] As Biray Kolluoğlu Kırlı has reminded us,

> On 19 May 1919, immediately after the Greek army disembarked in Western Anatolia, Mustafa Kemal Pasha landed in the Black Sea port of Samsun under orders from Constantinople to disband the remaining Turkish forces in Anatolia. But he did just the opposite and began to organize a nationalist resistance army against the occupation of European powers and the Sultanate in Istanbul that had accepted their terms.[20]

Modern Turkey, molded by Atatürk, the former hero of Gallipoli (Kallipolis (Gr.), Gelibolu (Tur.)), was to be born once and for all out of the miscalculations surrounding Sèvres.

The Greco-Turkish war can be divided into four stages, with the already described Greek occupation of Smyrna in 1919 serving as the first phase. The Greek mistreatment of Turks was an outcome that might have been predicted (as was Turkish resistance and lack of cooperation), for it was consummate with the pattern of misdeed, revenge and reprisal that form an important aspect of regional history. As well as accelerating the Turkish nationalist cause, Greek conduct (both at this stage and later) pushed some in the Allied camp to become pro-Turkish, including the famous historian Arnold Toynbee, who published his observations in *The Western Question in Greece and Turkey: A Study in the Contact of Civilizations* (1922) shortly after

---

[19] Abe Attrep, "'A State of Wretchedness and Impotence:' A British View of Istanbul and Turkey, 1919." Churchill, *The World Crisis: The Aftermath*, 435–37.

[20] Biray Kolluoğlu Kırlı, "Forgetting the Smyrna Fire," *History Workshop Journal* 60, no. 1 (Autumn 2005): 30. Stanford J. and Ezel Kural Shaw, on the other hand, review the possibility that in the early stages of the Ottoman reaction to Allied (including Greek) presence in Anatolia, Kemal Paşa and other leaders were given such orders with the tacit understanding, or at least hope, that they would not obey them. The Shaws also remind the reader that it was not until the final stages of what they term the "Turkish War for Independence" with the Ottoman cabinet once again headed by the more compliant Damat Ferit Paşa that orders went out to shoot Kemal and certain of his comrades on the spot. Cf. *History of the Ottoman Empire*, 341–43, 349.

returning from service as an observer with the Red Crescent. Toynbee spoke with a dual authority, having already authored several historical studies of the Balkan states as well as volumes on the "German Terror (wartime crimes and abuses against civilians) in Belgium and France." He did not hesitate to testify about Greek outrages. Influenced narrowly by the particular phases of the war, which he had witnessed first hand, he returned to England fully sympathetic to Turkey.

British merchant Donald Whittall testified that in the days preceding the catastrophe there was anxiety over Turkish reprisals generated by Greek misdeeds:

> My manager, Mr. Parker, who lives about 100 miles from Smyrna, came to report that the retreating Greek army was committing terrible excesses, murdering women and children and generally destroying property. In fact, it is the opinion among the British in Smyrna that during the past two years no fewer than 100,000 non-combatants have been massacred by Greek soldiers. Mr. Parker was afraid lest the sight of the barbarities of the Greeks should inflame the otherwise orderly marching Turks and subsequent events would point to his surmises having been correct.[21]

The accuracy of this number can, of course, be disputed, but Whitall's testimony can be taken as representative of a general awareness that the Greek military presence had been inflammatory.

During 1920 the Greeks advanced from Smyrna's immediate environs into Anatolia (and also Rumelia) with relative ease, marking the second phase of the war. This militarily successful Greek stage ended ironically for Venizelos with his defeat for re-election. Nearly coincident with this electoral change, King Alexander died from having been bitten by his pet monkey, absurdly setting the stage for the return to power of his father Constantine, whose deposition had been engineered by the pro-Venizelos faction in 1917. Twenty-three year old American Ernest Hemingway, working as a special correspondent to the *Toronto Star*, revealed the militarily disastrous consequences of the changed political scene: "When Constantine came into power, all the officers in the field were suddenly scrapped, from the commander-in-chief down to platoon commanders." The incompetence subsequently displayed was stunning, and Hemingway epitomized the deterioration of the

---

[21] "Accuses Greek Army, Too. British Merchant Suggests Their Excesses Roused Turks," *New York Times*, 18 September 1922, 2.

Greek army by reporting that the new artillery officers "massacred their own infantry."[22]

Despite the dilution of military talent brought on by the shift in power, the Greeks managed to stage offensives of limited success in 1921, the third phase of the war. These offensives were launched under the apparent Greek belief that they still had British support; however, Richard Clogg has characterized Lloyd George as offering "ambivalent statements of encouragement" at this point.[23] These partial victories actually portended Greece's eventual loss, for the Greek lines had become overextended, and each offensive thrust was terminated by a decisive Turkish victory, including the battle at the Sakarya (Sangarios (Gr.)) river, where Atatürk commanded. Halide Edip Adıvar, point-woman for Kemal and symbol of the new Turkey, said of this grueling twenty-two day battle that, "it was fought as if by two giant dragons coiling around each other and around the curling banks of the great river."[24] The battle at the Sakarya indeed entailed "some of the most murderous fighting in history, lasted twenty-two days and nights. Entire units perished as rugged hills were lost, captured and lost again."[25]

The Greek occupation of the Ottoman territories continued to go badly. It seemed to some Allied observers not only to be undermined by lack of local support, but also to be under bad management. Western observers, often based in Smyrna, reported the general indiscipline and occasional brutality of Greek soldiers, many of whom were poorly trained and inexperienced recent draftees. As Turkish nationalism grew, Allied support for Greece faded correspondingly. The French and Italians chose sooner rather than later to begin dealing with Kemal, who convinced them to withdraw their forces from Turkish territories. Eventually even Britain would abandon her hopes in the Aegean.[26]

---

22 Hemingway's 3 November 1922 dispatch is quoted in Jeffrey Meyers, *Hemingway: A Biography* (New York: HarperCollins, 1985 [reprint, New York: Da Capo Press, 1999]), 99. The young writer was "furious about the murderous incompetence of the Greek officers," according to Meyers, ibid., 98. Indeed, although he did not witness the battles, they must have haunted his imagination, for he was still drawing on their imagery and on his fury with the tragic incompetence of the Greek officers as late at the mid-1930s, when he inserted them in his masterpiece short story "The Snows of Kilimanjaro" (1936).

23 Clogg, *A Short History*, 117.

24 Lord Kinross, *Ataturk: A Biography of Mustafa Kemal, Father of Modern Turkey* (New York: Morrow, 1992 [reprint of 1964 edition]), 316.

25 Jensen, "The Greco-Turkish War," 560.

26 David Fromkin, *A Peace to End All Peace: The Fall of the Ottoman Empire and the Creation of the Modern Middle East* (New York: Henry Holt, 1989; reprinted 2001), 536–48. Margaret MacMillan, *Paris 1919: Six Months that Changed the World* (New York: Random House, 2001), 447–45. Dockrill and Goold, *Peace Without Promise*, 199–227.

"By the summer of 1922," according to Michael Llewellyn Smith, "the Greek army was like an apple eaten out inside by insects or disease, superficially whole and apparently firm, but ready to disintegrate at the first sharp blow."[27]

In August of 1922 the Turks defined the fourth phase of the war by mounting a large-scale offensive westward. They moved with stunning rapidity, covering the distance from Ankara to Smyrna (some 550 kilometers) in just over three weeks, winning two major pitched battles en route, and breaking through the front under the command of İsmet Paşa on 26 August. From then on the war was a route. The Greek forces retreated westwards, burning Turkish villages as they went. "The Turkish population was subjected to horrible atrocities by the retreating troops and accompanying civilian Christian mobs," writes Peter Kincaid Jensen. "The pursuing Turkish cavalry did not hesitate in kind on the Christian populace; the road from Uşak to Smyrna lay littered with corpses."[28]

On September 9, the Turks entered Smyrna, having pushed the Greek forces back across the entire extent of the Turkish Anatolian homeland. Much of the Greek army managed to evacuate itself, but thousands of Greek civilians were left with no alternative but to await Turkish mercy or retribution.[29] Setting aside any consideration of the moral justification and political wisdom of Greek occupation of Asia Minor or the Allied encouragement that had spurred Greece to land at Smyrna and tolerated her march eastward to occupy large areas of a large Turkish-majority area, it is fair to say that the Greek military collapse had been rapid and colossal.

For several days before Smyrna blazed, the Turks had systematically hunted down and murdered Armenians in their enclave. If captured, Armenian men were likely to be sent on forced marches into the vast interior of Asia Minor.[30] The Turkish genocide against the Armenians begun in 1915 had been accomplished in great measure by just such forced marches and "deportation to the interior." This phrase, wrote the highly experienced international relief physician, Esther Pohl Lovejoy, "was regarded as a short life sentence

---

[27] Llewellyn Smith, *Ionian Vision*, 276.

[28] Jensen, "Greco-Turkish War," 563.

[29] Llewellyn Smith, *Ionian Vision*, 306.

[30] Contemporary sources are replete with references to the roundups and forced marches. Multiple newspaper accounts report on them; see, for example, the various articles reprinted in Oecenomos, 164–67. Likewise foreign residents of Smyrna can be consulted, including the American medical relief worker Esther Pohl Lovejoy, *Certain Samaritans* (New York: Macmillan, 1927), 150.

to slavery under brutal masters, ended by mysterious death."[31] In a memorandum dated 26 September 1922, American Consul in Smyrna George Horton describes the quickly degenerating behavior of Turkish soldiers towards Armenians. Downplaying the role of Armenian resistance, including allegations of sniping and bomb throwing, Horton speaks of murderous reprisal and then forced marches initiated by the Turks.[32]

Those men who managed to make it to the quay at Smyrna often found that they had only succeeded in postponing the inevitable, for no help was being offered there. Summarizing the events as of the evening of 9 September, Llewellyn Smith writes:

> Eventually order broke down and something like a massacre ensued, as batches of Armenians were rounded up, taken to the Karak and murdered. What made these scenes the more frightful was the impotence – in the case of officials, impotence as a matter of policy – of the foreigners. British marines stood by, deliberately idle, while Turkish troops goaded and chased their Armenian victims into the sea, then coolly shot them as they swam for safety. [Foreign] troops were clearly under instructions not to interfere with the course of events but to confine themselves to the protection of their nationals' lives and properties. [33]

On 16 September, after the fire had subsided and thousands were massed on the quays, Mustafa Kemal issued a proclamation that all Greek and Armenian men between the ages of eighteen and forty-five were to be considered prisoners of war, thus paving the way for further roundups and death marches. The Turks informed their captives of this decision by dropping leaflets onto the over-crammed waterfront from airplanes.[34]

But how did the fire begin in the first place? Not surprisingly, there is no agreement on the measure of Turkish culpability for setting and sustaining the fire. The position of Turkish officials and of most Turkish people is not hard to predict: the fire was either an accident or was started by the retreating Greeks themselves. It could not be contained or mitigated because the

---

[31] Lovejoy, *Certain Samaritans*, 150, 162–63.

[32] The memorandum has been declassified by the U.S. State Department and was published in 1979 under the title "Turkish Massacres in Smyrna in 1922: As They Appear from the Unpublished Secret Document of the American Consul in Smyrna to the American Secretary of State," by Petros Stylianou, *Kypriakos Logos* 11, no. 61–62 (1979): 7–8. Horton, and to a lesser extent Lovejoy, are open to criticism of religious bias against the Muslim Turks. In Horton's case his memorandum, like his later book on the Smyrna disaster, is given to impassioned rhetoric and one-sided, heavy-handed denunciations of Turkey. Nonetheless, he, like Lovejoy, had long experience in the Middle East. In neither case does biased rhetoric constitute sufficient grounds to dismiss the reportage of actual events in this case echoed by multiple journalists on the ground.

[33] Llewellyn Smith, *Ionian Vision*, 307.

[34] Housepian, *The Smyrna Affair*, 172.

local fire department was undermanned and inadequate to the task. In English-language works oriented to the study of Turkey or important Turkish figures such as Atatürk, it is common to encounter descriptions of the event that are brief, bland, passively voiced, sometimes described in terms fatalistic, sometimes distinctly evasive. "A fire raged through the city" would serve as a typical example, the questions about responsibility begged, but not addressed:[35]

Precisely how did the fire start? How did it grow to such immense proportions and rage for so long? What did the Turks do in response to the fire? In the end, so many testimonials exist (not only from victims, but also a substantial number from other European nationals and North Americans), that it would seem impossible to refute the evidence that the Turks deliberately staged the fire.[36]

If the Turks did not literally light the first spark, they almost certainly helped fuel the nascent blaze. Multiple witnesses report seeing Turks moving about with cans of fuel, soaking structures in the Greek and Armenian quarters.[37] There certainly was no effort made to put out the fire in these quarters, a fact that has been defended by citing the uncertain situation brought about by the war and the lack of an adequate fire department. Yet the Turks had controlled the city for several days, and the Turkish quarters of the city significantly remained intact after the two-day-long inferno. "A disagreeable incident," Atatürk opined indifferently. Others have judged the affair criminally wanton, an act of reprisal out of all proportion to Greek affronts and misdeeds, one deliberately calculated to go far towards driving

---

[35] In an extreme instance of looking the other way, Erik J. Zürcher's *Turkey: A Modern History* outlines the disputes about the Armenian genocide, but fails even to mention the razing of Smyrna.

[36] The two initial *New York Times* reports of the fire can serve as an example: "Smyrna Burning, 14 Americans Missing 1,000 Massacred as Turks Fire City; Kemal Threatens March on Capital : Our Consulate Destroyed. Fire Starting in Armenian and Greek Quarters Is Sweeping City. Believed a Turk Reprisal. 300,000 Starving Refugees in the City Are Thrown Into a Panic. Our Marines Fight Flames But Brigade of Allied Soldiers. Italy Rushes Ships." *New York Times* (1857–Current file), 15 September 1922; "City a Mass of Wreckage: Foreign Quarter Leveled but Turkish Section Untouched. Streets Strewn with Dead. 900 Armenians Were Driven Aboard a Lighter and Killed by Fusillade from Shore. Our Bluejackets Policing but the Host of Homeless Christians Are in a State of Terror." *New York Times* (1857–Current file), 16 September 1922.

[37] "Smyrna Burning," *New York Times*, 15 September 1922

Greeks out of Asia Minor once and for all and thus solidifying the Turkish identity of the new Turkish state.

While the city burned from 13 to 15 September, only a relative handful of refugees made their way onto the Allied ships which remained in the harbor throughout.[38] No systematic evacuation was undertaken prior to 24 September when the first Greek ships entered the harbor. During the interval, tens of thousands of victims crowded the waterfront, living not only under extreme deprivation, but also under the constant threat of deliberate brutality. Allied naval ships remained at anchor several hundred meters from the waterfront, their crews under orders not to intervene. In the words of Richard Clogg, "A quarter of a million people fled to the waterfront to escape the inferno, but the Allied troops and ships stationed in the port for the most part maintained an attitude of studied neutrality."[39] The Allies feared provoking an incident with the Turks, a fact which afterwards fueled bitter reproaches by witnesses and survivors. George Horton, whose impassioned book on Smyrna is unreservedly pro-Christian, but who nevertheless speaks with the authority of a thirty-year diplomatic career made in the Mediterranean-Aegean region, opines that,

> [a] united order from the commanders or from any two of them — one harmless shell thrown across the Turkish quarter — would have brought the Turks to their senses.[40]

Eventually, refugees were taken aboard ships, with, ironically, the Italians being perhaps the most generous in their relief efforts. But space was too limited to accommodate all. Scenes of chaotic scrambling and tussling naturally ensued on the quay, particularly after word went around that Turkish authorities had fixed a date by which all evacuation must be complete. Panicky crowds anticipated further slaughter for those unlucky enough to be left behind.[41]

It was now evident that the Greek occupation of Asia Minor had ended in a debacle and that a new Turkey would emerge triumphant in the region. The Great Powers, at odds with one another over the issue during the preceding months, could now all at least agree that there was no point in offending or provoking the victor. For one thing, there were oil interests to maintain, a

---

[38] Abraham Hartunian, an Armenian refugee present in Smyrna for the entire ordeal states that "more than forty European and American battleships and transport ships were anchored before Smyrna" as the fires were set. *Neither to Laugh Nor to Weep: A Memoir of the Armenian Genocide*, 3rd edition, Vartan Hartunian, trans. (Belmont, Mass.: Armenian Heritage Press, 1999), 195.

[39] Clogg, *A Short History*, 118.

[40] Horton, *Blight of Asia*, 153.

[41] Clare Sheridan, *Naked Truth* (New York: Harper Brothers, 1928), 309–10.

factor kept clearly in sight at the proceedings that issued in the Treaty of Lausanne that concluded the war. As the historians of the Standard Oil Company have written, "at Lausanne ... oil usurped the center of the stage."[42]

What exactly transpired in those long days and nights after the fire burned out when the quays were crammed with refugees? While the origins of the fire are outside the bounds of absolute and certain proof, on this question there can be little doubt. The Turks robbed, assaulted, brutalized, and murdered men, women and children alike. Women were raped and abducted as the spoils of war. "Here is the truth," wrote one British eyewitness, "think of all the old time torture, add to them modern appliances for the destruction of mankind, exaggerate as much as you like, and you will not realize half the horrors."[43] The nighttime screaming halted only when the battleships played their searchlights upon the masses, an image used by Hemingway in his masterfully condensed, fictionalized evocation of war-induced misery "On the Quai at Smyrna" (1930). The recollections of Melvin Johnson, an American seaman stationed to guard the YMCA, are both typical and noteworthy. Five hundred women and children had sought refuge there and were jammed inside the building. But beyond the predicament at hand, Johnson recalls the screaming on the docks that started as the sun fell and continued without cease all night. "And all the time those women, some of 'em giving birth from fright — you know, ahead of time," he reported, echoing a key image used in Hemingway's "On the Quai at Smyrna."[44] Prolonged states of intense anxiety are known to induce premature labor, a contributing factor, undoubtedly, in producing the improvised births and the dead babies clung to by their traumatized mothers.[45]

---

[42] George S. Gibb and Evelyn H. Knowlton. *History of the Standard Oil Company: The Resurgent Years* (New York: Harper and Row, 1956), 2: 295. It is beyond the scope of this article to pursue the issue of oil interests in any detail, but it has been raised by some historians. If the Ottomans (or their successors, the Nationalist Turks) were to control the gateway to oil-rich lands, as now seemed evident, then there was all the more reason to come to terms with them sooner rather than later. George Horton brought the charge early. Peter Balakian has pursued the theme in "The New U.S. Oil Policy in the Middle East and the Turnabout on the Armenian Question," a chapter in *The Burning Tigris: The Armenian Genocide and America's Response* (New York and London: Harper Collins, 2003), 363-72.

[43] Anonymous account written contemporaneously and handed to British seaman Henry Walter Shonfield. Published online in August 2004 by *History Today*, http://www.historytoday.com/ArticleComments.aspx?m+30401&amid=30206811.

[44] Quoted in Housepian, *The Smyrna Affair*, 123.

[45] "Many premature births" are also noted by the witness in the Shonfield account.

Confined to their ships, the sailors resorted to the feeble measure of searchlight sweeps in an effort to discourage predation. Esther Pohl Lovejoy has given this description:

> Night after night blood-curdling shrieks, such as Dante never imagined in Hell, swept along that ghastly waterfront ... When Turkish regulars or irregulars, under cover of darkness, came through the ruins to the quay for the purpose of robbing the refugees or abducting their girls, the women and children, a hundred thousand or more in concert, shrieked for light, until the warships in the harbor would throw their searchlights to and fro along the quay, and the robbers would slink back into the ruins.[46]

Though the stench of burned flesh and dead bodies that hovered over the harbor was surely impossible to ignore, some important international spectators labored to turn a blind eye and a deaf ear to the final results of their nations' political designs. Aboard ships sailors played records at full volume in an effort to drown out the nocturnal outcry. Survivors report hearing Caruso singing *Pagliacci* as men drowned or were shot while trying to swim out to the ships.[47] Likewise, on board the British flagship the *Iron Duke* the navy band played nightlong concerts. Atatürk's biographer Lord Kinross assures his readers that these military strains were merely the result of the band's compliance with "service routine at this hour," which merely emphasizes the question already begged: under such dire circumstances, why was the British navy merely following routine?[48]

The answer, in short, was that Britain had backed the wrong horse and now feared provoking a furtherance of the war that would directly involve its own forces. The so-called Chanak Crisis marks the final phase of the conflict for the Turks, one that no longer involved a Greek enemy, but rather the prospect of a British stand against them at Chanak (Çanakkale (Tur.)). The Turkish army swung north towards the Sea of Marmara after reaching the Aegean, and Lloyd George was urging a confrontation. British commanders on the spot advised otherwise and found their spokesman in Lord Curzon, who talked down the prime minister as he also began to back away from his collapsing coalition government.[49] Turkey had won, thus placing itself in a position to negotiate inexorably at Lausanne, where a new treaty would be drawn up to supplant the never-realized terms of Sèvres.[50] The old Sick Man of Europe, albeit considerably trimmed in size, fared better in the immediate

---

[46] Lovejoy, *Certain Samaritans*, 156.

[47] Housepian, *The Smyrna Affair*, 171.

[48] Kinross, *Ataturk: A Biography*, 371.

[49] In one striking incident, British soldiers, evidently desirous of avoiding a fight, helped their Turkish counterparts to string wire in front of their positions.

[50] Dockrill and Goold provide a cogent overview of the Chanak Crisis in *Peace Without Promise*, 228–36.

post-war world than did the once emergent German powerhouse or the shattered empire of the Hohenzollerns.

At Lausanne Great Power diplomacy staged its third act beginning in November 1922 and ending with the signing in July of the following year. Allied power brokers now had to accept the situation on the ground and recognize that (1) Greece was defeated in Thrace and Asia Minor, and (2) the nationalist Turks now comprised the power structure within Turkey, replacing the older, more compliant Ottoman holdovers. Modern Turkey had become a recognized sovereign nation, the only losing nation in the Great War able to significantly shape peace terms — with the delay of some four years — for itself. A separate treaty between Greece and Turkey formalized an "exchange of populations," a scheme headed by the Norwegian explorer and humanitarian Fridtjof Nansen.[51] Greeks living in Asia Minor or Eastern Thrace were required to move to the Greek homeland, while Muslims living in Greek territory were compelled to move to Turkish homelands. Greeks living in Constantinople were exempted from these provisions, as were Muslims living in Western Thrace.

Estimates vary somewhat, but approximately 375,000 Muslims, and 1.25 million Greeks were thus uprooted, with the Greek exodus already well underway long before the exchange program was formally enacted. The numbers bespeak human misery on a massive scale.[52] Ernest Hemingway witnessed the misery of those retreating through Thrace after the Greek collapse and recorded it in reportage and fiction alike:

> The carts were jammed for thirty miles along the Karagatch road.... No end and no beginning. Just carts loaded with everything they owned. The old men and women, soaked through, walked along keeping the cattle moving.[53]

It was a glimpse ahead to what would become a tragically commonplace European scene in the fallout from the next great war.[54] In the words of

---

[51] Nansen's reflections on the matter have been published in his *Armenia and the Near East* (New York: Duffield, 1928), see especially 20–26 and 314–24.

[52] These numbers represent averages from a variety of sources, which do not vary greatly from one another, cf. Clogg, *A Short History*, 121, Housepian, *The Smyrna Affair*, 207–208. Stephen P. Ladas, *The Exchange of Minorities: Bulgaria, Greece and Turkey* (New York: Macmillan, 1932), see especially 640ff.

[53] "Chapter II" of *In Our Time* (1925). Published in *The Complete Short Stories of Ernest Hemingway: The Finca Vigía Edition* (New York: Scribner Paperback Fiction, 1998), 71.

[54] This sort of scene had been limned as early as the Greek retreat towards Smyrna after the routs suffered in the summer of 1922. Here is a description of the (British) *Daily Telegraph* correspondent of that scene: "refugees and erstwhile fighting men were travel-

Efraim and Inari Karch, it was also "another indication of Kemal's determination to retreat from empire and to forge a new and homogenous Turkish nation, come what may."[55]

The enormity of the refugee problem for Greece can scarcely be exaggerated. A poor country with a population on the order of 4,000,000 was suddenly faced with an influx of people that amounted to roughly one-third of its population. Housing and lands abandoned by Muslims leaving Greece did not begin to approach the level necessary to accommodate the newly arriving Greeks, whose culture and manner of living were, in any case, more in line with Constantinople than Athens. Indeed, some fifty years after their transplantation, the anthropologist Renée Hirschon found the Asia Minor refugees and their offspring still maintaining a separate sense of identity from the people they called "locals," or "Old Greeks" or simply "Greeks."[56]

Looked at one way, the Treaty of Lausanne represents the signature to the Allied abandonment of Greece. Britain in particular had consistently encouraged Greece, only to step aside as she faltered and, finally, to drop her in her utter defeat. No Allied help was forthcoming as Greece crumbled in Asia Minor in 1922, no military aid, no significant diplomatic pressure, and, apart from belated and insufficient relief efforts, no purposefully organized humanitarian support in response to the Smyrna debacle.[57] Yet, it should be acknowledged that Greece played a significant role in her own failure. Arnold Toynbee is among those who concluded that while Greece had been dealt with badly by the Great Powers, she must also be seen as having vic-

---

ing in any sort of conveyance that came to hand. Wagons, carts, donkeys, mules, camels, and even prehistoric wooden wheeled bullock carts were pressed into service [...] The confusion was indescribable." (quoted in Oeconomos, *The Martyrdom of Smyrna and Eastern Christendom,* 53).

[55] Karsh, *Empires of Sand,* 340.

[56] Renée Hirschon, *Heirs of the Greek Catastrophe: The Social Life of Asia Minor Refugees in Piraeus* (Oxford: OUP/Clarendon Press, 1989), 4–5 and passim.

[57] On the more narrow point concerning humanitarian relief: some warships already in the harbor did allow a limited number of refugees on board. In what would seem to be an irony, the British, whose government had most vigorously backed the Greek adventure into Asia Minor, have been accused of putting forth the least effort towards impromptu rescues. On the larger issue of Anglo-Greek relationships, see Abe Attrep, "'A State of Wretchedness and Impotence:' A British View of Istanbul and Turkey, 1919," *International Journal of Middle Eastern Studies* 9, no. 1 (1978); Briton Cooper Busch, *Mudros to Lausanne: Britain's Frontier in West Asia, 1918–1923* (Albany: SUNY Press, 1976); Clogg, *A Short History*, 116–18; Dockrill and Goold, *Peace Without Promise*; Helmreich, *From Paris to Sèvres.* Llewellyn Smith, *Ionian Vision*, 282–83 discusses circumstances immediately prior to the Smyrna disaster. No doubt biased, Cosmetatos, *The Tragedy of Greece*, is scathing in his indictment of David Lloyd George as chief architect of the disaster.

timized herself by failing to predict the predictable military failure. He went on to ascribe a moral component to the disastrous results:

> Overborne by the pressure of the Entente Powers and the imperious personality of Mr. Venizelos ... [Greece] pushed into that foreign policy of reckless aggrandizement.[58]

By the winter of 1922, as thousands of Ionian Greek refugees streamed miserably westward through Thrace, Venizelos and Lloyd George alike were out of power, as was Wilson. In Athens a handful of blameless government ministers were publicly executed by way of scapegoating.[59] Atatürk and his nationalist party were clearly ascendant, and the Western Powers would be making their deals with his regime for a long while to come. It was surely unexpected, perhaps ironic, that the core state to emerge from the now defunct Ottoman Empire — the long-time sick man of Europe — would be the one defeated nation able to "defy the imposed peace settlement and pursue its own foreign and domestic policies" in the post-World War I years.[60]

---

[58] Arnold J. Toynbee, *The Western Question in Greece and Turkey: A Study in the Contact of Civilisations* (London: Constable, 1922 [reprint, New York: Howard Fertig, 1970]), 63. Elsewhere Toynbee praises Venizelos's noble statesmanship in maneuvering so as to avoid embarrassing the Allies "at a moment when any Greek had a right to feel bitter against... them," ibid. xix–xx.

[59] This incident was also seized upon by Hemingway as the subject of one of his intensely wrought vignettes, "Chapter V" of *In Our Time* (1925) published in *The Complete Short Stories*, 95.

[60] William L. Cleveland, *A History of the Modern Middle East* (Boulder: Westview Press, 1993), 161–62.

The American Near East Relief (NER) and the *Megale Katastrophe* in 1922[1]

HARRY J. PSOMIADES

The Destruction of Smyrna

THE LONG AWAITED TURKISH OFFENSIVE began on 26 August 1922 southwest of Afyon Karahişar at the most vulnerable point on the Greek front. Hopelessly outnumbered, the Greeks were overcome and within a few days the Turks succeeded in cutting the rail link to Smyrna (İzmir (Tur.)), occupying Afyon Karahişar and totally disrupting the principal Greek route of communications and supplies. The Greek forces were cut in two and in full retreat. While those in the northern sector, some three divisions, skillfully retreated to the Sea of Marmara and embarked for Greece, the larger concentration of forces, in the southern sector, was completely routed. Disoriented and in disarray, they fled to Smyrna and the coast, accompanied or followed by some 150,000 destitute and panic-stricken refugees from the interior, who, in search of security and sustenance, camped on the city's quay.

In an attempt to calm the population, the Allied consuls of Smyrna gave formal assurances to the Greeks and Armenians that they need not fear for their lives, although they were not prepared to take concrete steps to ensure the safety of the city's civilian population. Only the American Consul General, George William Horton, who was an old Near East hand, refused to give such assurances and indeed, on 4 September he cabled the U.S. High Commissioner in Constantinople, Admiral Bristol,

> [i]n the interest of humanity and for the sake of American interests to mediate with Mustapha Kemal [Atatürk] for an amnesty to permit the orderly withdrawal of Greek forces from Anatolia and possibly avoid the destruction of Smyrna.[2]

---

[1] This is a slightly revised version of the first version "The American Near East Relief (NER) and the *Megali Catastrophe* in 1922," *Journal of Modern Hellenism* 19–20 (Winter 2002–3): 135–50.

[2] Louis P. Cassimatis, *American Influence in Greece, 1917–1929* (Kent, OH: Kent State University Press, 1988), 111; Marjorie Housepian, *The Smyrna Affair: The First Comprehensive Account of the Burning of the City and the Expulsion of the Christians from Turkey in 1922* (New York: Harcourt Brace Jovanovich, 1971), 94–96; and George Horton, *The Blight of Asia: An Account of the Systematic Extermination of Christian Populations by Mohammedans and of the Culpability of Certain Great Powers; with a True Story of the Burning of*

His great concern was who would police the city between the time of the Greek withdrawal and the arrival of the Turks. His plea was essentially ignored by Washington, and instead, three destroyers were sent for the protection of American lives and property.

On September 8, the Greek army completed its evacuation from Smyrna. On the following day, the victorious Turks entered the city and the looting, armed robbery, rape and killings began. The situation worsened when fire broke out on September 13, and after three days, some two-thirds of Smyrna lay blackened and smoldering. The Armenian, Greek and European quarters were almost totally destroyed, and those that survived the holocaust were compelled to join the ranks of the refugees on the quay. Without food and water, some 300,000 hapless souls were now so pressed together that

> [o]ne could not lie down without being crushed to death — women gave birth to still-born babies and sheltered them against their dried-up breasts, for lack of a burial place ... waiting for a momentary pathway to open up for them to lay their burdens in the all-receiving sea.[3]

In the meantime, the Allied navies (some twenty-one warships — eleven British, five French, two Italian and three American) congregated in Smyrna harbor, unashamedly declared their strict neutrality, and stated that their mission was simply to observe the demise of Hellenism in Asia Minor and to protect the lives and properties of their nationals and consuls. None wanted to give even the appearance that they were siding with the enemy, thus encouraging the Turks to believe that whatever action they took against the Ottoman Greeks and Armenians, there would be no interference from the Great Powers.

By September 24, the situation got completely out of hand as Turkish handbills informed the displaced multitude that those not out of the city within a week's time would be deported to the interior.[4] There was also a report by British Foreign Secretary Lord Curzon that Sakallı Nurettin Paşa,[5] governor-general of Smyrna, had announced that any refugees remaining in the city after 30 September would be massacred.[6] The dramatic result of these an-

---

Smyrna (New York: Bobbs-Merrill, 1926).

[3] Melville Chater, "History's Greatest Trek," *The National Geographic Magazine,* XLVIII, 5 (November, 1925): 539.

[4] Ibid., 539–40; Housepian, *The Smyrna Affair,* 97; and Edward Hale Bierstadt, *The Great Betrayal* (New York: Robert M. McBride, 1924), 56–87.

[5] Sakallı Nurettin Paşa had a long record of atrocities committed against Ottoman Christians. As commandant of the 3rd Army (of the Kemalist Government at Amasya/Angora), he was responsible for the atrocities committed in Sivas 1921. Vartkes Yeghiayan, ed., *British Reports on Ethnic Cleansing in Anatolia, 1919–1922: The Armenian-Greek Section* (Glendale, CA: The Armenian Remembrance Center, 2007), 234.

[6] *British Secretary's Notes of a Conference between French President of the Council, the*

nouncements was a further stampede of thousands of people toward the harbor, desperately seeking passage to a safe haven. Shortly thereafter, given the refusal of Allied ships to provide passage for the refugees and in order to hasten their departure from Turkish soil, the Kemalist Angora (Ankara) authorities gave the American relief workers in Smyrna, and Asa Jennings in particular, assurances that Greek ships could come to Smyrna to take the refugees, provided the ships did not fly Greek colors and did not dock at the quay. The Athens Government at first feared to release its transports, concerned that the Turks would seize them and use them for an invasion of the Aegean islands, but it finally relented, and, on 24 September, Greek rescue vessels flying American colors and escorted by American destroyers entered Smyrna harbor. Thus, by 8 October, the evacuation of the entire Christian population of Smyrna was completed.[7] A week later the International Red Cross reported that a total of one half-million refugees had reached Greece in wretched condition and that more were on their way.[8] In the thirty days following the Turkish entry into Smyrna over at least 50,000 Greek and Armenian civilians lost their lives.[9]

Even though the newly established League of Nations (1919) had for the first time provided an international framework to meet the challenges of massive hardships, it was prevented by the Allied powers from playing a major political role which could have alleviated human suffering. They did not wish the League to make political decisions bearing upon their interests, although they were happy to use the League's machinery "for the gradual and orderly evacuation of the Greeks from Eastern Thrace and to examine the whole question of transfer of population."[10] While the League bolstered the limited scope and efforts of the International Committee of the Red Cross (ICRC), it was clearly the swift and positive response of American philanthropy, which saved the day.[11] American efforts to effect emergency relief surpassed all other efforts combined, excepting the Greek.[12]

British Secretary of State for Foreign Affairs, and the Italian Ambassador in Paris, held at the Quai d'Orsay, 22 September 1922. Doc. 48. [E 9843/27/44].

7 Chater, "History's Greatest Trek," 535–40; Michael Llewellyn Smith, *Ionian Vision: Greece in Asia Minor, 1919–1922* (London: Allen Lane, 1973), 306–11; Housepian, *The Smyrna Affair,* 175–85; and William T. Ellis, "Jennings of Smyrna," *Scribner's* (August 1928): 230–35.

8 *Nansen Papers*, R 1761 (1922), 48/24380/24357, 17 October 1922.

9 The American Consul-General George William Horton estimated the figure closer to 100,000. See Housepian, *The Smyrna Affair,* 258–59.

10 Rumbold, Constantinople, to Curzon, 16 October 1922, Doc. 126. [E 11167/27/44].

11 Cassimatis, *American Influence in Greece*, 110–17; Dimitra M. Giannuli, "American Philanthropy in the Near East: Relief to the Ottoman Greek Refugees, 1922–1923" (Ph.D. Dissertation, Kent State University, 1992); *Nansen Papers,* R 1761 48/24722/24357,

The American Near East Relief (NER)

Next to the American Red Cross (ARC), the American Near East Relief (NER) performed the largest service among the foreign relief agencies in rendering aid to the refugees. It was originally formed by a group of men in response to the "systematic oppression and destruction of the Armenian people in Anatolia" in 1915 and was called the American Committee for Armenian Relief. It had several name changes as it steadily expanded the scope of its work and achieved the transition from emergency services following the Armenian massacres in 1915 to a well-developed education and reconstruction program in the post-Lausanne period.[13] Granted a name change and a charter by an act of Congress in 1919, its expanded mission was,[14]

> To provide relief and to assist in the repatriation, rehabilitation, and reestablishment of suffering and dependent people of the Near East and adjacent areas; to provide for the care of orphans and widows; and to promote the social, economic, and industrial welfare of those who have been rendered destitute, or [made] dependent directly or indirectly by the vicissitudes of war, the cruelties of their mentors and by other causes beyond their control.

After the armistice of 1918, the NER undertook the care of refugees, particularly of the surviving Armenians who returned from the deportations only to find their homes destroyed and property looted, or their homes and land

---

"Nansen Report: Refugees in Greece and Asia Minor," Part II (Geneva), 18 November 1922, 4; and Areti Tounda-Fergadi, "L'histoire de l'emprunt accordé pour les réfugiés de 1924," *Balkan Studies* 21 (1983): 90–91.

[12] The American Red Cross (ARC) fed and cared for over 700,000 refugees in Greece from October 1922 to April 1923. The American Women's Hospital organized 33 medical stations and hospitals. Also active in Greek relief were the YMCA and YWCA, the American foreign Missions Board, the Anglo-American Committee of Thessalonica, and the Athens American Relief Committee. In addition to governments, the Greek Red Cross and private Greek initiatives, the European relief committees at work in Greece from October 1922 to June 1923 included the British Red Cross, the British Relief Committee, Save the Children Fund (UK) (which distributed over 50,000 rations to children and adults), Action Suisse, Union internationale de secours aux enfants, the League of Nations' Epidemic Commission, and others, including Swiss, Swedish and Dutch groups in Athens. See Apostolos Doxiadès, "La situation des réfugiés en Grèce," *RICR*, 6th year, no. 47 (August 1924): 724–34; Rodolphe de Reding-Biberegg, "Secours aux réfugiés," *R1CR*, 4th year, no. 47 (November 1922): 951–60; and Cassimatis, *American Influence in Greece*, 117–19, 126–34.

[13] NER had done its work under different names: The American Committee for Armenian Relief, 16 September 1915 to 20 November 1915; the American Committee for Armenian and Syrian Relief, 20 November 1915 to 27 June 1918; the American Committee for Relief in the Near East, 27 June 1918 to 6 August 1919; the Near East Relief, the name by which it was incorporated by Congress on 6 August 1919. In 1930, Near East Relief became the Near East Foundation.

[14] For the Act of the US Congress see, http://www.armeniangenocide.org/Affirmation.228/current_category.7/affirmation_detail.html

occupied by Muslims. Although legally bound to assist the Armenians and the Greeks after the armistice of 1918, the local Turkish authorities and the Allied representatives, who were to enforce the armistice agreements, provided very little, if any, aid to compel the Turks to relinquish the expropriated properties.[15] Thus, the returning Armenians found themselves in an inhospitable environment and were compelled to flee their villages for the security of the larger towns. Unable to support themselves in the urban centers, they became dependent upon American charity, namely, the NER.[16]

For almost three years prior to the Smyrna disaster, the NER developed extensive, life-saving relief projects in Anatolia, Syria, Palestine and the Caucasus.[17] Moreover, the NER workers had served for some time, along with American missionaries,[18] as the eyes and ears of the Western powers in the vast expanse of Anatolia, manning their soup kitchens, hospitals and orphanages. They witnessed and reported the horrors of the deportations. They were the first non-Greeks to report the systematic extermination and deportation of the Pontic Greeks in 1921 and consequently were placed under a great deal of pressure by the Kemalist authorities to close their orphanages and schools and leave Turkey. In May 1922 NER worker Dr. Ward upset the Kemalists by reporting Armenian massacres "and the death of hundreds of Greek deportees from starvation, thirst, cold, fatigue and ill-treatment." He also informed his superiors that the Turkish authorities in Harput had forced him to turn over to them some 500 girls who were above

---

[15] Consul Ralph F. Chesbrough, Trebizond, to the US Department of State (August 3, 1919), NA 867.00/00.923.

[16] The same problem occurred with the returning Greek deportees, especially those from Pontus, but they were cared for by local Greek philanthropy and to some extent by the Greek Red Cross in the towns of the Pontic coast from Samsun to Trebizond.

[17] *American Near East Relief Activities in Greece*, 1; James L. Barton, *Story of Near East Relief 1915-1930: An Interpretation* (New York: Macmillan, 1930); and Mark H. Ward, *The Deportations of Asia Minor: 1921-1922* (London: Anglo-Hellenic League & British Armenia Committee, 1922). See also the Reports of the Near East Relief for the years ending 1920-1927.

[18] During most of World War I, the United States was neutral and therefore the American missionaries were allowed to remain in Turkey and to provide relief to the Armenians. For their reports on the deportations and persecutions of the Christians, especially of the Armenian massacres of 1915, see The Archives of the American Board of Commissioners for Foreign Missions, Houghton Library, Harvard University. See also Suzanne Elizabeth Moranian, "Bearing Witness: The Missionary Archives as Evidence of the Armenian Genocide," in Richard G. Hovannisian, ed., *The Armenian Genocide: History, Politics, Ethics* (New York: Macmillan, 1992), 103-28; Zenovia Lithoxoou-Salata, "Παιδικές Αναμνήσεις" [Childhood memories], in *Ποντιακή Στοά (1972-1974)* (Athens: Παμποντιακή Ένωσις, 1974), 245-58. Many of the missionaries stayed on after the war or returned to Turkey to work with the Near East Relief organization.

the age limit (over fifteen years old) in the Christian orphanages under his care. He was soon expelled from Harput.[19]

Also in Spring 1922 NER worker Miss E. Wood wrote in her diary that during her two weeks journey to the coast she saw every day,

> [g]roups of deportees, mostly women and children, all starving, and a great number of bodies along the road [...] and the entire remaining population was being deported without food and clothing [...] Conditions at Malatia, where the deportees died at the rate of forty or fifty a day, were far worse than in Harpoot.[20]

At the time of the Smyrna tragedy, only the United States among the major powers gave thought to the refugees; the personnel of various American religious and educational institutions in the city, along with the local YMCA and YWCA, and the American consulate, organized relief committees and distributed food among the destitute. NER was the only organized relief agency in the Smyrna area. The American Red Cross, providing an initial $50,000 for relief supplies, soon followed with a U.S. Disaster Relief Committee from Constantinople arriving in Smyrna shortly before the Turkish nationalist forces entered the city.[21] The team also included a much needed medical team consisting of Esther Lovejoy, the only American and woman doctor, Dr. Wilfred Post, and a British naval surgeon. Their magnificent humanitarian work in caring for, feeding, and transporting the panic-stricken

---

19 Admiral Bristol vouched for the authenticity of his reporting in his diary, See Bristol's Diary entries for May 22 and 23, 1922, NA 867.00/1581; and Bristol, Constantinople, to Hughes, October 3, 1921, NA 967.00/1500. See also "Memorandum by Mr. Rendel on Turkish Atrocities between March to October 1922," Foreign Office, October 30, 1922, [E11885/10524/44] FO 371/7960], 2; and Ward, *The Deportations in Asia Minor.* For the Ottoman policy of the deportation of the Armenians, see Leslie A. Davis, *The Slaughterhouse Province: An American Diplomat's Report on the Armenian Genocide,* 1915–1917, Susan K. Blair, ed. (New Rochelle, New York: Aristide D. Caratzas, 1989). See further: Ara Sarafian, ed., *United States Official Records on the Armenian Genocide 1915–1917* (Princeton and London: Gomidas Institute 2004). This publication includes the Davis reports as well as many other reports on the subject.

20 "Memorandum by Mr. Rendel on Turkish Atrocities between March to October 1922," Foreign Office, 30 October 30, 1922 [E11885/10524/44] FO 371/7960], 2.

21 Both organizations were actively involved in relief efforts in Constantinople. From February 1919 they used that city as a base from which to feed most of the Caucasian and Armenian refugees. See Briton Cooper Busch, *Mudros to Lausanne: Britain's Frontier in West Asia, 1918–1923* (Albany: SUNY Press, 1976), 65. Conforming to a decision of President Harding of the United States and a resolution of the Central Committee of the ARC, the American Red Cross, on October 9, 1922, had taken complete charge of the American operations of relief in the Near East, in cooperation with the American Near East Relief. See the Red Cross Courier, 14 October 1922; the *Report of the Near East Relief for the Year Ending 31 December 1922*; and Charles B. Eddy, *Greece and the Greek Refugees* (London: George Allen and Unwin, 1931), 53–54.

refugees during the Smyrna fire was responsible for saving over 200,000 lives in the Smyrna region alone.[22] Soon after the Smyrna conflagration, NER sought to secure from the Kemalist, or nationalist, government assurances of safety for the children of its orphanages in Anatolia. Such assurances failing, NER was forced to leave the country and to remove all of the Christian orphans in its care from Asia Minor to Greece.[23] Thus, in October 1922, a systematic program of evacuation began. Under the care of NER workers, the orphans were brought out by way of the Mediterranean and Black Sea ports of Anatolia, mostly on American ships. The American workers suffered with their charges the privation of a journey of hundreds of miles in severe winter weather over vast stretches of mountains and open plains. By the end of December 1922, NER had transferred 15,644 orphans to Greece.[24] The widely publicized refusal of the Kemalists to provide security guarantees for the orphanages was one more indication that the presence of Greeks and Armenians in Turkey would no longer be tolerated, and that the Turkish movement toward "ethnic cleansing" was irreversible.[25]

In mid-October 1922, the NER reported that there were some 200,000 refugees left in Asia Minor and that they were under enormous pressure by the Turkish authorities, including force and the threat of the use of force, to leave.[26] Indeed, the rising tide of Turkish nationalism, fed by the Turkish victory in the Mudanya armistice negotiations in early October,[27] precipitated another severe refugee crisis by awarding Eastern Thrace to Turkey. It initiated the rapid exodus of almost 300,000 Christians from Eastern Thrace and Constantinople to Greece, and the renewal of the forced eviction of thousands of Greeks and Armenians from their homes in the interior of Ana-

---

[22] *Report for Near East Relief for the Year Ending December* 31, 1922, 4–6; and René Puaux, *La mort de Smyrne* (Paris: Edition de la Revue des Balkans, 1922), 30–35. American nationals involved in the relief effort were Admiral Bristol, Consul General Horton, the staff of the American College, and the local representatives of American relief organizations and commercial firms.

[23] *Report of Near East Relief for the Year Ending December 31, 1922,* 3.

[24] *Ibid.*, 21. It was also caring for another 14,000 orphans in Constantinople. See also *American Near East Relief Activities in Greece* (September 1922–December 1924), 2–13. Two American workers lost their lives in this movement of orphans – one died of pneumonia induced by exposure, the second was shot by bandits. The total number of children being cared for by NER exceeded 115,000. This figure includes orphans and children whose parents were unable to care for them. See *Report of Near East Relief for the Year Ending December 31, 1922,* 28–36.

[25] *Nansen Papers,* R 1761 (1922) 48/24722/24357, 18 November 1922.

[26] *RICR,* 4th year, no. 48 (December 1922), 920–24; and telegram Henderson, Constantinople, to the Foreign Office [E 13187], FO 371/7960, November 26, 1922.

[27] Harry J. Psomiades, "Thrace and the Armistice of Mudanya, October 3–11, 1922," *Bulletin of the Centre for Asia Minor Studies* 12 (1997–1998): 213–55.

tolia to the coast. The latter were in a particularly dangerous situation. Marooned at Turkish ports or aboard crowded ships, they had to be fed and cared for or left to perish. Since Turkey and, for the most part, the Allied high commissioners in Constantinople, refused to take any responsibility for these refugees, it is appalling to contemplate what would have happened to them if not for the swift response of the NER to provide relief and transportation to places of safety.[28]

The NER also reported that the Christians were told that they had permission or were free to leave Anatolia provided that they did so before November 30, 1922. As on previous occasions when Christians were told that they had permission to leave Turkey, the word "permission" was a euphemism for an order to leave, or else. The Christians were given to understand that by that date if they did not leave they would be deported to internment camps in the interior.[29] A similar order was announced to the surviving deportees, and to the Greek women and children of the Black Sea coast of Anatolia, who had not been exiled, that

> [w]ithin one month [...] starting on November 1, 1922 [...] they must exit the national boundaries of Turkey.[30]

Another order issued by the Turkish authorities to the deported Pontic Greeks interned in the Malatya region of Anatolia read that, "those refugees [it called those deported "refugees"] who went away from their homes [as if they left freely] are free under the condition that they leave the national boundaries."[31] Turkish methods of intimidation employed varied according to circumstances,

> [b]ut its methods are fully successful whether it's called expulsion or permission to depart, the object of the Turks end result is identical ... It is interesting to note that the Turks have been careful to avoid giving orders in writing ... except by mistake in Zungouldak.[32]

Thus, the surviving Greek population in Turkey, prior to the agreement on a population exchange in late January 1923, after the armistice of Mudanya in

---

[28] See the *Reports of the Near East Relief for the Years Ending 1923 and 1926.*

[29] Henderson, Constantinople, to Foreign Office, FO 371/7960, E 13187, November 26, 1922. Henderson was the British Acting High Commissioner in Constantinople.

[30] *Report of the Near East Relief for the Year Ending December 31, 1922*, 25–26. See also Ιορδάνης Ενεπεκίδης, *Ο Γολγοθάς των Ελλήνων του Πόντου* [Iordanes Enepekides, *The Golgotha of the Greeks of Pontus*] (Athens: Παμποντιακή Ένωσις, 1976), 121–30; and Γιάννης Καψής, *1922: Η Μαύρη Βίβλος* [*1922: The Black Book*] (Athens: Νέα Σμύρνη, 1992), 17–131.

[31] Σάββας Π. Ιωακειμίδης, *Συμβολή εις την Γενικήν Ιστορίαν του Πόντου, 1922–1924* [Savvas P. Ioakeimides, *Contribution to the General History of Pontus, 1922–1924*] (Athens, 1970), 186.

[32] Henderson, Constantinople, to Foreign Office, FO 371/7960, E 13187, November 26, 1922.

mid-October 1922, which presumably ended Greek-Turkish hostilities, continued to be expelled from Turkey, with the usual exception of the majority of the able-bodied men who, having been declared prisoners of war, were sent to the interior to join the infamous labor battalions (*amele taburları*) For many this spelled death.[33] The lifespan of a Greek or Armenian in a Turkish labor battalion was generally about two months.[34] Young women were also detained and carried off into captivity.[35]

A more widely flung call for the lifeline came with the new wave of mass expulsions following the Smyrna catastrophe. The service stations established by the NER along the routes to sustain the orphans in their flight to Greece and at the ports of embarkation were inevitably called upon to save the lives of adult refugees, who would have perished by the roadside without the nourishment, which these temporary kitchens provided. The following telegram urgently dispatched at that time to the New York head office of NER by one of its managing directors tells the sad story of countless thousands of refugees on a tortuous march to an uncertain future:

> Extreme cold, snow and storms aggravate the plight of Asia Minor refugees. Death is overtaking thousands of the children and the aged infirm on the frozen roads of Anatolia, aboard the tossing rescue ships in the Black Sea, and in the camps near Constantinople.
>
> Moving over the worst mud roads in the world, I saw a crowd of broken civilians more depressing than an army in hard-pressed retreat. Women about to become mothers tramped in snow up to their knees. Tired children dropped weary by the wayside, and girls of tender years bore men's burdens.[36]

To save these refugees, NER began to feed them at the Black Sea ports of embarkation of Samsun, Ordu (Kotyora), and Trebizond (Trabzon), as well as at the Mediterranean port of Mersin (Mersina). Although NER provided a

---

[33] Llewellyn Smith, *Ionian Vision*, 318–19; Δημήτριος Α. Φιλλίζης, *Οι Τελευταίες Ημέρες της Τραπεζούντας, 1918–1923* [Demetrios A. Phillizes, *The Last Days of Trebizond, 1918–1923*] (Thessalonica: Kyriakides, 1982), 56; "Memorandum bγ Mr. Rendel on the Situation of the Refugees in Greece," Foreign Office, 17 November 1922, No. 202 [E 12845/10524/44]; and Extracts from Col. Rawlinson's Diary: *Journey from Erzerum to Trebizond, 5– 14 October 1922,* in FO 371/7878, Y/P 9206.

[34] "Memorandum by Mr. Rendel on Turkish Atrocities between March and October 1922," 1; and Henry Morgenthau, *An International Drama* (London: Jarrolds, 1929), 29.

[35] *Nansen Papers,* R 1761 (1922) 48/24929/24357, 15 November 1922: "The Work of Doctor Nansen Concerning the Organization of Aide to Refugees in the Near East." Also, *The Daily Telegraph* (London), 10 October 1922.

[36] Jacquith, Constantinople, to Vickrey, New York, 16 December 1922, in *American Near East Relief Activities in Greece,* 2. See also H. C. Jacquith, "America's Aid to 1,000,000 Near East Refugees," *Current History,* 33:3 (1924): 403; and C. A. Macartney, *Refugees: The Work of the League* (London: League of Nations Union, 1930), 77.

minimum ration for them,[37] the death toll at these ports remained extremely high.[38] Moreover, many refugees also died of illness and disease onboard over-crowded rescue ships. In the refugee camps at Constantinople alone, particularly at the notorious Selimiye Barracks, which was the first stopover for most of the refugees from the Black Sea ports, between 40 and 300 people died daily. One observer described it as a veritable morgue.[39] Admiral Bristol, in his official report to Washington in July 1923, stated that, without NER activities in the Pontus and Constantinople an additional 100,000 refugees would undoubtedly have perished of hunger and disease.[40]

The Movement toward a Population Exchange

The mission of all the relief agencies in the refugee crisis was to save lives, not to extend relief indefinitely, nor to assume the primary burden of making the refugees self-sufficient. The latter was beyond their resources and mandate, and raised a critical political question — where should the refugees be settled permanently so that they could regain their ability to be self-supporting? Consequently, by the end of October, the relief agencies had informed the League of Nations and the three Allied high commissioners in Constantinople that relief could not be extended indefinitely to the refugees and that they should start thinking of a permanent solution for the refugee predicament. In the discussions that ensued they expressed the belief that, since Turkey would not allow the refugees to return to their homes in safety and no one was prepared to force them to do so, the most likely solution to the problem would be the permanent settlement of the refugees on Greek soil and/or some kind of a Greek-Turkish population exchange.[41] Any notion of the possibility of autonomous areas for minorities within the Turkish state, areas to which the exiles could return with some semblance of security, or other special provisions for the protection of minorities were com-

---

[37] *Nansen Papers,* R 1761 (1922) 48/149382/4938, 19 October 1923. Childs, Constantinople, to High Commission for Refugees, Geneva.

[38] Φιλλίζης, *Οι Τελευταίες Ημέρες,* 54–55; and, Βλάσης Αγτζίδης, *Ποντιακός Ελληνισμός: Από την Γενοκτονία και τον Σταλινισμό στην Περεστρόϊκα* [Vlases Agtzides, *Pontic Hellenism: From the Genocide and Stalinism to Perestroika*] (Thessalonica: Κυριακίδης, 1991), 26–30.

[39]Παύλος Χαιρόπουλος, *Εισαγωγικά Στοιχεία Ποντιακής Ιστορίας και Λαογραφίας* [Pavlos Chairopoulos, *Introductory Elements of Pontic History and Folklore*] (Thessalonica: Kyriakides, 1992), 91; *American Near East Relief Activities in Greece* (September, 1922–December, 1924), 1; and Chater, "History's Greatest Trek," 559. Also, for the ordeal in Pontus, see Fermanoğlu, Constantinople, to the Greek Ministry of Foreign Affairs, 31 October 1922, AYE/ 1922 /AAK (13) Pontus.

[40] *Near East Relief Activities in Greece,* 1.

[41] Ibid., 960, and *American Near East Relief Activities in Greece,* 3.

pletely unacceptable to the Turkish leadership,[42] and therefore to the Great Powers and the refugees themselves. The defeat of Greek arms in Anatolia, the procrastination, rivalry, and indifference of the Entente powers and the triumph of a Turkish nationalism bent on creating a homogeneous Turkish nation-state could not be ignored or denied. These facts were obviously on the minds of those whose task it was to find a solution to the refugee problem — a problem which threatened the peace and stability of the Balkan-Eastern Mediterranean region, and indeed, the very survival of an impoverished and politically turbulent Greek state.

In conclusion, the international relief agencies were a primary source of intelligence on conditions in Turkish-controlled territory. They often provided the Entente powers with the only reliable information on the treatment and displacement of the native Christian population in Anatolia. Their fundraising efforts for Near East relief and the many eyewitness media accounts of conditions in Turkey by relief workers also aroused international public opinion, particularly in the United States, where they were often an embarrassment to Washington, exerting additional pressure on governments to act expeditiously on behalf of the refugees. Yet, by taking the initiative in providing timely humanitarian assistance and saving many lives, the relief agencies unwittingly relieved the reluctant Allied powers of their responsibility toward the refugees, at least until after the bulk of the refugees had been evicted, or had fled from their homes in fear and were expelled or transferred to Greece. Indeed, Allied and American reluctance to interfere in the internal affairs of a resurgent Turkey in order to secure economic advantage along with the successful work of the international relief agencies encouraged the Turkish nationalists to expedite their plans for "ethnic cleansing" by minimizing the risk of international intervention, and by relieving the international community of any responsibility for the welfare of the refugees, in the unlikely event that they were so inclined. In other words, the international relief agencies became the unwilling accomplices of Turkey for ethnic cleansing. But the alternative was no less ghastly. One shudders to think what would have happened if American philanthropy and the foreign relief agencies had not provided timely humanitarian assistance.

---

[42] Llewellyn Smith, *Ionian Vision,* 302–303. As late as 7 September 1922, the Metropolitan of Smyrna Chrysostomos wished to establish an autonomous Christian state in the Smyrna region under the sovereignty of the Ottoman Sultan with Venizelos as High Commissioner. At that time, there was even a suggestion of some kind of an autonomous state under the League in Eastern Thrace for the protection of its Christian majority and to serve as a buffer between Greece and Turkey. See Doc. 48, "British Secretary's Notes of α Conference," 22 September 1922, [E 9843/27/44]. Nansen, the League's High Commissioner for Refugees, tried on several occasions, only to be adamantly rebuffed, to get the Nationalist Government to set up an autonomous district in eastern Anatolia for the few remaining Armenian survivors.

International Red Cross: A Mission to Nowhere

STAVROS T. STAVRIDIS

"Remembering"
Forget! Forget! Forget!
I close my eyes,
But cannot.
— Sofia Kontogeorge Kostos (2004)

FROM THE MIDDLE OF 1921 TO MAY 1922, Great Britain, France and Italy and the United States were receiving information from American relief workers that the Kemalists were deporting large numbers of Ottoman Greeks from the coastal regions of the Black Sea into the Anatolian interior. Nevertheless, the European Powers maintained their policy of neutrality in the Greco-Turkish conflict.

Lord Curzon, the British Foreign Secretary 1919–24, suggested to his counterparts in Paris, Rome and Washington that Allied officers should be dispatched to investigate these claims. The French tried to delay the setting up and sending of an inter-Allied mission to Asia Minor. In order to maintain Allied unity, Britain was able to win the support of the other Powers, whereby the International Red Cross (IRC) as an international organization was to be approached to conduct the investigation of the reported atrocities in Anatolia. The IRC wanted the European Powers and the U.S. to provide it with the funds so that it could discharge its duties.

This article will address several issues. The main one being that the Powers and the Unted States used the IRC as a convenient front in order to avoid the responsibility of protecting the Christian minorities from Turkish violence. The Great Powers thus assumed the role of the bystander, hence passive and indifferent to the plight and suffering of the Christian minorities. If the Great Powers were prepared to apply military force or threaten the use of force, then it is conceivable that the actions of the Turks against the Ottoman Christians may have been more restrained.

This study is divided into four parts that include, the British initiative and the reactions of the other powers; the approach to the IRC; the financial assistance to the IRC by the Great Powers and finally the involvement of the League of Nations.

1. *The British Initiative and the Reactions of Other Powers*

a) Curzon's initiative

The Turkish nationalists deported Greeks from along the Black Sea coast into the Anatolian interior in 1921–22. This information is based on the reports received from American relief workers in Sivas (Sevasteia (Gr.)). In early May 1922, Dr. Mark H. Ward of the American Near East Relief (NER) informed Sir Horace Rumbold, the British high commissioner in Constantinople, that the Turks continued their "deliberate plan to get rid of minorities" where the deportees were assembled at Amasya from the regions between Samsun (Amisos (Gr.)) and Trebizond (Trabzon, Trapezous (Gr.)).[1] They were then marched off to Erzurum (Theodosiopolis (Gr.)), Van, Bitlis and Sarıkamiş in eastern Anatolia to join the labor battalions, where many of them perished before reaching their final destination. Rumbold immediately passed this information on to Lord Curzon at the Foreign Office in London.[2]

Another eyewitness account given by F. Yowell, former Director of NER in Harput, added further weight to Ward's testimony. Yowell mentioned to the U.S. Secretary of State Charles E. Hughes that he was expelled from Turkey as the local Turkish administration had shown an antagonism towards the work of the NER. He stated that the Turks refused the Americans permission to travel "within the limits of the work on the Harput (Elaziğ (Tur.)) unit for the purpose of giving medical aid to the Armenians dangerously ill with typhus." Yowell cites the example of 1,000 men being taken by the Turks to work on the roads between Diyarbakır (Amida (Gr.)) and Harput. These men received no pay for their work and slept out in the open. When they became ill, they received no medical assistance. These poor wretched individuals would have quickly perished in the bitter cold winter of eastern Turkey. He concluded:

> I beg to state that I have endeavored to confine myself strictly to the facts as they are evidenced and to base my statistics on the most reliable data obtainable under abnormal conditions. I feel that as an American citizen I should emphatically protest against the treatment accorded American citi-

---

[1] Original place and ethnic names will be used as they appeared in the original documents cited in text of this paper. E.g. Trebizond (Trabzon) and Persians (Iranians).

[2] *Documents on British Foreign Policy 1919–1939*, first series, vol. 17, 817 n. 1. (Hereafter cited as *D.B.F.P*); *Records of the Department of State relating to Internal Affairs of 1910–1929 867.4016/459* British Embassy, Washington D.C., to Hon. Charles E. Hughes, May 15,1922; hereafter cited as *Turkey Internal*; *Turkey Internal 867.4016/588* Admiral Mark L Bristol, Constantinople, to Secretary of State, July 12, 1922 *Encl.1* Extracts from Diary of Dr. Mark Ward. It is interesting that Dr. Ward kept a diary from May 1921 – February 1922 which contains the information on the number of deportees passing through Harput on their way to Van, Bitlis or Diyarbakır, cf. Marjorie Housepian Dobkin, *Smyrna 1922: The Destruction of a City* (New York: Newmark Press, 1998), 96.

zens and more especially the treatment accorded the helpless Christian subjects of the Turkish Empire by the Turkish Nationalist Government.[3]

He hoped the major European powers and the United States would strongly pressure the Turkish nationalists to halt the deportations and that the Christians would receive better treatment.

On 12 May 1922, Curzon decided that an impartial team of Allied officers should be dispatched to Trebizond or other Black Sea ports to investigate the American accounts of Turkish deportations of Greeks. Curzon informed the British ambassadors Lord Harding, Sir R. Graham and Sir A. Geddes in Paris, Rome and Washington D.C., respectively, to request the cooperation of the governments to which they were accredited. Furthermore Curzon instructed Rumbold to seek the cooperation of the other high commissioners once their respective governments had given their high commissioners their official approval.[4]

On 18 May Rumbold informed Curzon that while the French and Italian high commissioners had yet to receive instructions from their governments, they nevertheless believed that two inter-Allied commissions should be dispatched, including into the Greek-occupied areas. It was envisioned that such a plan would not give the Kemalists the opportunity to reject the commission of enquiry on their territory.[5] It can be seen that Curzon was trying to elicit the support and collaboration of his Allied and associated partners for a united approach in investigating atrocity claims raised by the American relief workers.

On 18 May Admiral Bristol, the U.S. High Commissioner in Constantinople, reported to Secretary of State Hughes the instructions Rumbold had received from Curzon regarding the proposed dispatch of Allied officers. Bristol believed that Curzon's proposal should be rejected and was highly critical of the British action. Some of the reasons advanced for rejecting the British proposal were: (1) the British were using the Yowell report for anti-Turkish propaganda purposes in order to bolster their position in the Near East; (2) the publicity given to Curzon's telegram in the House of Commons and in the British press "clearly [pointed] to purpose of political propaganda." The

---

[3] *Turkey Internal 867.4016/882* F. D. Yowell to Sec of State, Washington, (marked strictly confidential not for publication).

[4] *D.B.F.P.i,* 17: 817–8 & fns. 2–3. Sir Eyre Crowe, the permanent Under-Secretary at the Foreign Office made representations to the French, Italian and American Ambassadors in London regarding Curzon's proposal: Dept of State, *Papers Relating to the Foreign Relations of the United States 1922* (Washington, D.C.: U.S. Government Printing Office, 1938), 2: 919–20; hereafter cited as *F.R.U.S. 1922*; Harry Tsirkinidis, *"At last we uprooted them...": The Genocide of Greeks of Pontos, Thrace and Asia Minor, through the French Archives* (Thessalonica: Kyriakidis Brothers, 1999), 257–58.

[5] *D.B.F.P.*, 17: 824.

French high commissioner in Constantinople, General Pelle, stated that Admiral Bristol had told him confidentially that Lord Curzon's telegram was intended for political propaganda purposes rather than humanitarian concerns. The Italian high commissioner, Garroni, revealed that assuming the Kemalists allowed the Allied investigation to take place on its territory, the Turks would probably judge that the Allies lacked the resources to uncover the truth regarding the persecution of Christian minorities. Pelle concluded that it was easy to blame only one side for all the atrocities in the Greco-Turkish war. Only the restoration of peace would end all violence in the Near East.[6]

Finally, the plight of minorities in Anatolia was known for a long time by the British, as full information had been provided by Lieutenant-Colonel A. Rawlinson, British military officer and also ex-prisoner of war in Kemalist Turkey. He stated:

> [when] we arrived without incident at Trebizond on October 14th [1921], the tenth day after leaving Erzeroum. I noted, however, that the coast range and its fertile valleys, hitherto intensively cultivated by the Greeks, was at this time everywhere deserted, the villages being abandoned and the crops unreaped. Also I had not failed to observe the many gangs of Greek prisoners which we had passed on their way to the interior under guard, so that it was evident the Greek population were being deported into the interior to replace the Armenian prisoners, of whom, by this time very few remained alive.[7]

Therefore Bristol believed that further examinations were not necessary.

Taking note of Bristol's comments, Allen W. Dulles, the director of Division of Near Eastern Affairs in the State Department, pointed out in his memorandum to Charles E. Hughes dated 20 May, that it was important for the United States to participate in the proposed commission of enquiry. Dulles mentioned that there might be repercussions it did not participate in the enquiry. Some consequences if the United States refused to participate could be:

1. It would be taken badly by the churches and missionary societies throughout the country and severely criticized. Telegrams had already started to flood in.

---

[6] *Turkey Internal* 867.4016/463 Admiral Bristol, Constantinople, to Secretary of State, May 18, 1922; This dispatch is also in *F.R.U.S. 1922,* 2: 920–1; Dobkin, *Smyrna 1922*, 96–97; Laurence Evans, *United States Policy and the Partition of Turkey 1914–1924* (Baltimore: Johns Hopkins University Press, 1965), 342; Tsikirnidis, *"At last we uprooted them...,"* 259–60.

[7] A. Rawlinson, *Adventures in the Near East* (London and New York: Andrew Melrose, 1924), 348.

2. The Allies might put the blame on the United States for being responsible for possible failure of the proposed commission and also to a certain extent for the consequences of such a failure for the Christians of Anatolia.

3. The Turks would interpret it as supporting their claim that atrocities had not been committed and as there being no reason for an investigation.[8]

Dulles believed that United States involvement would demonstrate that Washington was interested in the fate of Christian minorities, "but also in our trade and commerce and would put us on much firmer ground in insisting that the Allies give proper consideration to our interests in Turkey."[9] He concluded that "an impartial report was important for the State Department in terms of responding to the incessant church and missionary demand" in helping the Christians and could be useful in "directing the activities of the American relief societies in Turkey along really constructive lines."[10]

b) British parliamentary discussion, American, Turkish and Greek responses

In the meantime, Rumbold's information including Curzon's proposed action was raised in the British parliament. Furthermore the American, Turkish and Greek Governments responded to Curzon's proposal too. Austen Chamberlain, the Conservative leader in the House of Commons, answering a question in Parliament on 18 May 1922, admitted that Greek aspirations in establishing a Pontian republic were ill-conceived; but this did not excuse the actions of the Turks in carrying out the wholesale deportation of women and children into the Anatolian interior.[11]

U.S. President Warren Harding informed Hughes on 20 May 1922 that he did not wish to see U.S. troops becoming involved in the Near East, as this was opposed by American public opinion. Harding favored the appointment of General Harbord, an individual respected and trusted by the administration, to the commission of enquiry. The President left it to Hughes's discretion to come up with an official United States response to Curzon's proposal.[12] On 25 May, Hughes expressed his views to Harding regarding U.S. participation in the proposed commissions of enquiry to Anatolia. In many respects, Hughes's note resembled Dulles's memorandum of 20 May, which outlined the

---

[8] *Turkey Internal 867.4016/500* A.W Dulles, Division of Near Eastern Affairs, memorandum for the Secretary 20 May 1922.

[9] *Turkey Internal 867.4016/500*; Dobkin, *Smyrna 1922*, 97.

[10] *Turkey Internal 867.4016/500.*

[11] *Great Britain, House of Commons 5th Session Parliamentary Debates,* vol. 154 (1922), 538–39.

[12] *F.R.U.S. 1922*, 2: 921–2; Evans, *United States Policy and the Partition of Turkey,* 343.

consequences of United States refusal to participate in the enquiry. Hughes however saw advantages for American involvement in the enquiry.[13] Two such advantages were, (1) it "would give England courage to publish the facts to the world even in the face of the Indian Moslem opposition." (2) It would have,

> [a] salutary influence in France where there is a tendency to favor the Turks and to belittle reports of acts of injustice and cruelty. We cannot but believe that it would help bring about a better understanding among all the nations of Europe and furnish the basis in fact for a settlement of the Near Eastern question.[14]

The Kemalist authorities reacted by dismissing the atrocity reports as lies, distortions and fabrications that were intended to portray Turkey in a negative light. Angora (Ankara) used the press as part of its propaganda strategy to dismiss the claims of Ward and Yowell. The *Anatolian News Agency* published an article on 20 May trying to debunk Yowell's account of atrocities in Anatolia as lies. It continued,

> [t]he accusations against the Angora Government for mistreatment of Christians in Anatolia have proven to be baseless on investigation by Americans who travelled in Asia Minor.

In order to lend credibility to its news story, the *Anatolian News Agency* quoted Americans such as Florence Billings, an official of Near East Relief, and Harold C. Jaquith, the director of Near East Relief, who was visiting Angora at this time and who dismissed Yowell's statement as being baseless. It could be argued that the *Anatolian News Agency* may have deliberately distorted or misquoted Jaquith to show that he was angry with Yowell's version of events. Furthermore Jaquith may have been trying to protect American missionary interests in Turkey and at the same time ensure that the Christian minorities received every possible assistance from Near East Relief. The article in the *Anatolian News Agency* was also critical of Curzon's proposal to establish enquiry commissions to Anatolia. It concluded, "We are glad to hear that America has refused to participate in Curzon's plan."[15]

The Angora newspaper *Hakimiyet-İ-Milli's* editorial titled "England and Us" published on 22 May was strongly anti-British, accusing Britain of trying "to strangle [Turkey] and to [put] an end to our existence." It concluded, "We are said to have massacred the Christians in Anatolia. This new comedy is

---

13 *F.R.U.S. 1922*, 2: 922–6; Evans *United States Policy and the Partition of Turkey*, 343.

14 *F.R.U.S. 1922*, 2: 925; Evans, ibid., 343.

15 *Turkey Internal 867.4016/554 Enc. 4* Anatolian News Agency, Angora, 20 May 1922; Joseph L. Grabill, *Protestant Diplomacy and the Near East: Missionary Influence on American Policy, 1810–1927* (Minneapolis: University of Minnesota Press, 1971), 261–63.

put to scene by Lord Curzon."[16] The plight and suffering of deportees in Anatolia could hardly be described as a comical scene.

Even the so-called Turkish Orthodox Church and the Roman Catholic communities protested to Papa Eftim Efendi (whose real name was Efthymios Karachissaridis) and to the U.S. High Commission regarding Yowell's report of Christian persecution in Asia Minor. In the latter case, the Roman Catholic communities stated that they lived "in perfect security in the bosom of justice of the Anatolian Turk" and "the Orthodox Christians of Anatolia are treated with the greatest courtesy, their lives and securities are assured by the Angora Government."

The Turkish Orthodox Church described Yowell's report as "lies and slander against our national government." They argued that the "Pontus incident cannot be concealed. The uprisers went to the mountains, revolted against our government and pillaged our villages." Papa Eftim had very close links with members of the Turkish nationalist movement during the Greco-Turkish conflict 1919–1922. He founded the Turkish Orthodox Church in Kayseri (Kaisareia (Gr.)) in 1921 in opposition to the Ecumenical Patriarchate in Constantinople and was even quoted as saying "I shall turn off the lights of the Patriarch in the Phanar, and I shall do it very fast. Long live the victorious Turkish Army!"[17]

It is interesting to note that the Turkish news report does not state the ethnic origins of the Roman Catholic community as to whether they were Greek Catholic or Chaldean and in what region of Anatolia they lived. The Roman Catholic community was possibly very small in number.[18] There is no doubt that such public pronouncement on the part of the Turkish Christians was part of Angora's campaign of denial to deflect criticism away from itself by shifting the blame onto the victims.

Fethi Bey, the home minister in the Angora Government, explained to a correspondent of the *Anatolian News Agency* that Yowell and Ward were asked to leave because they "spread lies about Turkey." The minister's remarks

---

[16] *Turkey Internal 867.4016/554, Enclosure. 5, Hakimiyet-İ-Milli,* Angora, 22 May 1922; Dobkin, *Smyrna 1922*, 98.

[17] *Turkey Internal 867.4016/554* Admiral Mark L. Bristol U.S. High Commissioner, Constantinople, to Secretary of State, Washington D.C., 7 June 1922 *Enclosures 3 and 4*: Angora to Stanav, Constantinople, via Turkish telegraph Catholic Christian Communities signed by Dr Habib, Lata Oghlou, Agha Papa et al.; Anatolian Orthodox Churches Congress held in Kaisseri to Papa Eftim Efendi, Angora 23 May Anatolian Agency; Alexis Alexandris, *The Greek Minority of Istanbul and Greek-Turkish relations 1918–1974* (Athens: Center for Asia Minor Studies, 1983), 151–52; Racho Donef, "The political role of the Turkish Orthodox Patriarchate (so-called)," January 2003, available here:
http://www.atour.com/~aahgn/news/20040123b.html

[18] I would like to thank Dr. Racho Donef for providing me with this information.

were intended to create an impression in western capitals that Turkey was treating its minorities with kindness and justice. He cited a few examples:

- Christian men are never put to prison without legal cause. Prison registers refute lies of this kind.
- Christian women are not employed in Moslem houses against their will.
- These lies are spread about to picture the Turks as mean people.
- Greeks were deported into the interior in good order and have been freed.

He concluded that Yowell had a personal grudge against Turkey by helping to spread lies about the "persecution of the Christians."[19]

The Turkish press in the Allied-occupied Ottoman capital Constantinople responded differently to the atrocities, proposing a commission of enquiry to Anatolia. Rumbold informed Curzon that the position of the Turkish press varied in its coverage regarding the proposed commissions of enquiry. Some Turkish journalists believed that Angora had nothing to hide and would "welcome [an] enquiry provided it is properly conducted, and provided the same treatment is given to Turks and Greeks." There were others who considered the proposed Allied commission "an illegitimate interference with Turkey's internal affairs." The editor of the *Vakit* Newspaper stated that Turkey was at war with three of the powers and suggested that, "if any enquiry at all is necessary, it should be carried out by the Americans only."[20]

According to Rumbold, the French authorities in Constantinople gave greater latitude to the local Turkish press to attack Britain, at a time of strict press censorship in the Sultan's capital. Rumbold told General Pelle, that while the Turks were given some latitude, it would be fair if the Greek press in Constantinople too was offered the opportunity to respond to the Turkish press. Pelle acquiesced to Rumbold's views.[21]

On a visit to London, Greece's former premier, Eleutherios Venizelos, held a conversation with Sir Eyre Crowe, a British Foreign Office official, on 25 May 1922 regarding the situation in the Near East. The suggestion to dispatch a commission of enquiry into Greek and Turkish administered territory met with the approval of Venizelos. There were two issues that needed consideration before the commission began its mission.

---

[19] *Turkey Internal 867.4016/554 Encl. 6* Fethi Bey's statements.

[20] *National Archives of United Kingdom (formerly Public Record Office), London, FO406/41–50 series, Eastern Affairs 1918–22, FO406/49 no. 137* Sir H. Rumbold, Constantinople, to Curzon, 23 May 1922.

[21] *FO406/49 no. 137.*

Venizelos understood that in a war zone a retreating army might cause damage during its retreat. He therefore believed that nothing meaningful would be gained from such an enquiry. What really mattered was to compare the areas where Turks and Christian populations lived under Greek and Turkish administrations and which were not part of the war zone. He cited the example of Turks living under a Greek civil administration in Macedonia, Thrace and Smyrna. Venizelos was convinced that an enquiry conducted in Greek administered Smyrna "would receive the warmest praise from any impartial observer."[22]

The second problem cited by Venizelos was that the dispatching of two separate commissions would result in no communication between them and that they would be making separate reports. This problem could be solved by creating "only one commission, under the one supreme head which would then divide this commission into two sub-commissions, to go to the Turkish and Greek sides respectively."[23]

The interchange of officers between the two sub-commissions would greatly assist in the collection of information and attainment of firsthand knowledge as a means of cross-checking and verifying each sub-commission's report. Venizelos stated "it would be the head commissioner who would make the [final] report, on receiving the evidence submitted by the two sub-commissions," thus ensuring that impartiality was maintained.[24]

Curzon considered Venizelos' ideas to be theoretically sound. However, Curzon considered problems such as the inaccessibility of areas and the interchange of officers as impractical. Furthermore, the impartiality of the French and Italian delegates to this joint commission could not be trusted, in particular because both of them were close to the Kemalists. Curzon believed that the "Americans are suspicious and disloyal, like Admiral Bristol, or frightened of publicity." His solution was that "two sub-commissions report to the high commissioners in Constantinople or select someone like a Dr. Nansen to act as a liaison between the two sub-commissions."[25]

Another Greek response was that of Foreign Minister Georgios Baltazzis who addressed the Greek National Assembly on 31 May 1922. He outlined the Turkish atrocities committed in Asia Minor and Pontus and identified "Osman Agha for his cruelties and sanguinary instincts, [who had] assassinated a great many notable Greeks."[26] Baltazzis quotes Yowell as the indivi-

[22] *D.B.F.P.*, 17: 839.

[23] Ibid., 839-40.

[24] Ibid., 839-40.

[25] Ibid.., 841. n. 3.

[26] *The Turkish Atrocities in Asia Minor and in the Pontus: Speech Given before Greek Third National Assembly* by G. Baltazzis, the Minister for Foreign Affairs, 31 May 1922, 7.

dual who had witnessed the terrible cruelties against and sufferings of the Christians in Asia Minor and that the Turks had embarked on a deliberate policy "to exterminate all the Greek race."[27] He welcomed the commission to be conducted by the Allied powers "to the centers where the massacres and persecutions are taking place." It was important that the massacres during and after the First World War would not be overlooked or forgotten when implementing policy measures affording guarantees and protection to the Christian populations of Asia Minor.

Baltazzis emphasized that the Greek Government was "quite ready to open [its] doors wide to this commission [of enquiry]" and that an impartial commission would create a favorable impression of the Greek administration in Smyrna.[28] He raised an important point, solely aimed at the Great Powers, that Greece had done everything in her power to protect both Christians and Muslims under her administration "from the forced recruiting and the operations of Angora, and she had given them the means to live peacefully and continue their work."[29] Therefore, Athens felt it had nothing to hide from an impartial commission proceeding to areas under its authority.

The French, Italian and American Governments agreed on 17, 19 May and 3 June 1922, respectively, to the British proposal to appoint representatives to these commissions of enquiry. They all agreed that the commissions should proceed to investigate alleged outrages in both Greek and Turkish occupied areas of Thrace and Anatolia. Moreover the U.S. suggested that the two commissions should produce one joint and thorough report. This would permit the exchange of officers between the two commissions during their respective investigations and would "ensure impartial application of identical standards of judgment and comparison of like with like."[30] It is noteworthy that the American suggestion sounded similar to the one proffered by Venizelos.

On June 9, Hughes cabled Bristol in Constantinople outlining his reasons for the U.S. involvement in the proposed investigations in Asia Minor and Thrace. This was probably something that Bristol disliked, but he had no choice but obey the orders received from Washington.[31]

---

[27] Ibid., 17–19.

[28] Ibid., 20–21.

[29] Ibid., 21.

[30] *D.B.F.P.*, 17: 842–43.

[31] *Turkey Internal 867.4016/463* Charles E.Hughes, Washington, to Admiral Mark L. Bristol, U.S. High Commisssioner, Constantinople, 9 June 1922 with enclosures. Copy of note from British Embassy, 15 May 1922; Memorandum from British Embassy, 19 May 1922;

2. *The Approach to the International Red Cross*

On 11 June Caffery, the U.S. chargé d'affaires in Athens, notified Hughes that the Greek Government had accepted the commissions of enquiry. The British chargé d'affaires in Athens, Lindley, informed Caffery that Angora had not been officially approached regarding the proposed investigations and that the French and Italian high commissioners in Constantinople were suggesting that neutral officers be appointed to conduct the enquiry. The overall tone of Caffery's telegram indicates one of pessimism and the improbability of the enquiry being conducted.[32]

To complicate matters the Hellenic Navy bombarded the Black Sea port of Samsun on 7 June 1922 in an attempt to destroy Turkish ammunition dumps. Britain was furious with Athens over this incident, and Rumbold informed Lindley "to make strong representations to the Greek Government pointing out that bombardment [...] is quite useless." In fact Rumbold thought that the Greek action would make Angora unlikely to accept the commission of enquiry to the Pontus. Greece's action could be used by the Kemalists to,

> [l]end colour to Turkish contention that Pontic district is within zone of active hostilities and give fresh stimulus to persecution of minorities. H.M.G's earnestly hope that Greek Government will prohibit such bombardments in future.[33]

Lindley raised this issue with Greece's foreign minister who stated categorically that he knew nothing of the shelling of Samsun that had been reported in the Athenian press. Maybe Baltazzis did not read this news report. It is

---

Copy of reply of Department of State to British Embassy, 3 June 1922; Copy of Statement given to the press, 3 June 1922.

[32] *Turkey Internal 867.4016/532* Caffery, Athens, to Secretary of State, Washington D.C., 11 June 1922.

[33] *D.B.F.P.*, 17: 853–54 n. 1; Evans, *United States Policy and the Partition of Turkey*, 340. It is worth noting that there were fresh reports from American and British relief workers in late May 1922 who "reported to H.M. Consul General at Beirut that the Ottoman Greeks and Armenian deportees who passed through Arabkir came not only from Pontus but from Konya and South Western Asia Minor and even from Kars." Another report in early June 1922 by "American relief workers reported to Sir H. Rumbold that the deportees passing through Sivas district were clothed in verminous rags and ravaged by smallpox, typhus and dysentry. The men were formed into labour gangs to work on the roads without shelter." See National Archives of United Kingdom, FO371 Series, the General Political Correspondence of the Foreign Office, FO371/7955/E10952, "Notes on Turkish atrocities from February–September 1922" by Mr Rendel, Foreign Office, 10 October 1922, p. 3; in an interview given by Dr. Mark H. Ward, Near East Relief, to a journalist of the *Times* newspaper, he told of the deportations of Greeks and Armenians and that the Kemalists displayed hostility towards American relief measures; cf. "Kemalist war on Christians: Hostility to American Relief Work." *The Times* [London], 8 June 1922, 7.

hard to believe, however, that Greece's foreign minister did not know of the action taken by the Hellenic Navy in the Black Sea. In their ensuing discussion the foreign minister admitted that Athens "had positive information that large quantities of munitions of war were reaching the Kemalists via Mediterranean port." The Greek Government informed Paris and Rome that it wanted "a renewal request for right to visit and search" French and Italian ships carrying munitions to the Kemalists.[34]

The Angora Government protested through its representative Hamit Bey to the Allied High Commissioners in Constantinople over the Greek shelling of Samsun. In its note Angora protested Greece being permitted to use Constantinople as a naval base despite the Allied proclamation of neutrality in May 1921. The Kemalists argued that the Allied undertakings of impartiality and neutrality in the Greco–Turkish war could not be trusted if the Greek Navy was allowed to enter and leave the Black Sea with impunity. Angora blamed the Greek Government for creating "complications calculated to make peace impossible."[35]

A British Foreign Office memorandum submitted by Lancelot Oliphant, a British Foreign Office official, to Mr. Wakely at the India Office on 7 July 1922 regarding the Greek bombardment of Samsun raised some important issues. The shelling of Samsun may have been justified under Article 2 of the 9th Hague Convention, which "regulates bombardment by naval forces in time of war. It is further stated that a Kemalist battery replied to the Greek fire, so that town would not appear to have been undefended." British authorities in Constantinople were instructed to obtain a full report with respect to this incident.

This document also mentions that the Bolsheviks were supplying war material to the Kemalist ports along the Black Sea. The most important issue raised in this document was the importance of Samsun as a port:

> Samsoun is the port for one of the most important routes from the coast to the interior of Anatolia, and is natural landing place for shipments from Russia to Asia Minor and there is every reason that it should be used as a distributing base, as the Greeks allege.[36]

Bristol reported that the Greek naval shelling destroyed a municipal building, some fifty Greek and Turkish houses and that the number of casualties

---

[34] *D.B.F.P.*, 17: 853–54.

[35] Ibid., 861–62.

[36] National Archives of United Kingdom, *FO424 series Confidential Correspondence respecting Turkey Part. 1 'Further Correspondence respecting Eastern Affairs' July–September 1922, FO424/254 no. 13* Mr. Oliphant, Foreign Office, to Mr. Wakely, India Office, 7 July 1922, enclosure in No. 13 "Foreign Office memorandum respecting the neutrality of Constantinople and the Straits and Greek bombardment of Samsoun."

was very small. There was damage to American property owned by the Alston Tobacco Company and a garage rented by the Near East Relief. What really irked the Americans was that before the Greek bombardment, the Turks had prevented American citizens from leaving Samsun. Bristol interviewed Hamid Bey regarding the detention of American citizens by Turkish authorities. Hamid Bey replied "that Samsoun authorities had feared serious disturbance, if anybody were allowed to leave."[37] Obviously Washington would have been unhappy with the Angora Government pursuing such a policy towards its citizens.

On 30 June, Balfour, the acting British foreign secretary, informed Rumbold that the French Government had given Lord Harding, the British ambassador in Paris, a note on 26 June which mentioned that the enquiry commissions would be better served if instead neutral delegates or the IRC were approached to conduct the investigations. It would appear the French were trying to frustrate the British proposal by offering an alternative instead.[38] Lord Harding was instructed to inform the French Government that Britain would

> (1) agree that period to be covered by enquiry [...] should be limited to one year. (2) maintain objections to reinvestigation of previous excesses. (3) wish to point out that U.S. Government agreed to participate only on condition that commissions were confined to fact finding. (4) propose that commissions be appointed by four high commissioners at Constantinople acting in concert.[39]

Neville Henderson, the acting British High Commissioner in Constantinople, replied on 2 July to Balfour's note by stating that Rumbold objected to the French proposal on two grounds: firstly, the French approach was seen as another stalling tactic to assist the Kemalists; secondly, the Kemalists could use the French offer to their own advantage against Britain. However, Henderson believed that the appointment of selected neutral delegates "would carry as much conviction as that of enquiry by Allied and American commissions."[40]

On July 5, Saint-Aulaire, the French Consul in London, reported to the French Foreign Ministry his conversation with Lord Balfour and Sir Eyre Crowe regarding the proposed investigations on occupied Greek and Tur-

---

[37] *Records of the Department of State relating to Political relations between Turkey and other States 1910–1929 767.68/208* Bristol to Secretary of State, Washington D.C., 9 June 1922; *767.68/215* Bristol to Secretary of State, Washington D.C., 22 June 1922; hereafter cited as *Turkey Political*; *FO424/254 no. 12* Mr. Henderson, Constantinople, to Earl of Balfour, 4 July 1922; Evans, *United States Policy and the Partition of Turkey,* 340–41.

[38] *D.B.F.P.*, 17: 871–72.

[39] Ibid., 850–51.

[40] Ibid., 872. n. 4; *FO424/254 no. 6*, Mr. Henderson, Constantinople, to Earl of Balfour, 2 July 1922.

kish territory. Sir Eyre Crowe who is described as a confirmed Turcophobe was suspicious of French intentions that were designed to support the Turks. Crowe stated that the Allies had to pressure the Turks to accept Allied officers based in Constantinople. It was important for the Allies to display a united front for the investigations to proceed without a hitch. He believed that if the Allies lacked the resolve to impose their will on the Kemalists, then it would be better to invite neutral delegates or an organization like the IRC. According to Crowe, so that there would be no more delays, the committees of the Red Cross based at Constantinople should undertake the investigation.[41]

Britain changed its policy by replacing the Allied commissions with a neutral organization out of deference to its French ally. On 7 July Lancelot Oliphant approached the British Red Cross to explain that the four Great Powers had intended to dispatch two separate commissions of enquiry that would submit "one joint report on the facts for the information of Allied and associated governments." With the changed circumstances, the British Government requested that the British Red Cross approach the IRC in Geneva to see if it "would be in a position to undertake the proposed enquiry and to appoint suitable delegates in the immediate future to proceed to Smyrna and Kemalist Turkey."[42]

Chilton, the British chargé d'affaires in Washington D.C., was instructed to approach the U.S. Government regarding the IRC being invited to conduct the investigations. This was a much welcome opportunity for the Europeans and Americans to avoid their direct involvement in the actual enquiry. Charles E. Hughes and U.S. President Warren Harding agreed with the British on 20 and 21 July respectively, that the IRC was the best organization to conduct such an impartial investigation.[43] The French Government had approved the IRC conducting the investigations and the British, French, Italian and American high commissioners in Constantinople, in turn, were to be instructed to approach Athens and Angora for them to grant facilities by allowing the IRC to carry out its mission "especially in the Black Sea coastal regions, as well as in territory in occupation of Greek forces."[44]

3. *The Financial Assistance to the IRC by the Great Powers.*

The IRC would not undertake such a mission without the provision of financial assistance from the European Powers and the United States. On 3 Au-

---

[41] Tsirkinidis, *"At last we uprooted them...,"* 267–68.

[42] *FO424/254, no. 12* Foreign Office to British Red Cross Society, July 7, 1922; Dobkin, *Smyrna 1922,* 98.

[43] *F.R.U.S. 1922,* 2: 929–30; Evans, *United States Policy and the Partition of Turkey,* 343; Dobkin, ibid., 98.

[44] *D.B.F.P.,* 17: 901 and fns 1–3.

gust Chilton informed Charles E. Hughes about the conditions under which the IRC was willing to conduct the inquiries: (1) the two commissions were to be composed of three Red Cross and two neutral delegates each; (2) the IRC did not have sufficient funds to conduct the investigations and asked the four governments to advance it 1,000 pounds each to cover its expenses for a two month period. Chilton also stated that the IRC was "extremely anxious that no unnecessary publicity should be given to the proposed enquiry." Lord Balfour approached the British Treasury for it to advance the necessary funds for the IRC missions.[45] By August 23, William Phillips, the acting U.S. Secretary of State, notified Sir A. Geddes, the British ambassador in Washington, that the American legation in Berne had been "authorized to advance 1000 pounds to the [IRC] to contribute its share toward the expenses of the Commissions."[46]

The French, again, changed their position on the proposed enquiry. Poincaré, the French premier, objected to the appointment of neutral delegates to the Red Cross missions and raised difficulties over the French share of the expenses. Poincaré pointed out that any French expenses would require the approval of the French parliament. Curzon reminded the French premier that in May they had originally accepted the British proposal of sending commissions to investigate the alleged atrocities. The French employed their customary stalling tactics to slow down and frustrate the British initiative. Such a ploy on the part of the French could only benefit the Kemalists final military offensive against the Greeks in late August. It is possible that the French reasoned that the Red Cross might produce a report that would show France to be partial to the Turks and indifferent to the plight and suffering of Christian minorities. After all, the French supported and supplied the Kemalists with war material, and could have used the Franklin-Bouillon Agreement signed in October 1921 to influence Angora to moderate its harsh policy towards the Christian populations. It should be noted that in early September 1921, French Premier Aristide Briand dispatched Franklin Bouillon, a French journalist and Turcophile senator, empowered by the French Government to negotiate with Angora over French troop evacuation, the release of French prisoners and the protection of minorities in Cilicia (Kilikia (Gr.), Kilikya (Tur.), Çukurova (Tur.)).[47]

On 14 August 1922, the IRC was to approach Athens and Angora for both governments to grant it the necessary facilities for the investigations to take place in the Greek and Turkish occupied areas.[48] In a surprising deve-

[45] *F.R.U.S. 1922*, 2: 933–34; *D.B.F.P.*, 17: 922. n. 5; *Turkey Internal 867.4016/717 Annexes* FO to the President, IRC Society, Geneva, 2 August 1922.

[46] *F.R.U.S. 1922*, 2: 935.

[47] *D.B.F.P.*, 17: 464–65, 924–25 and 922, n. 6.

[48] *F.R.U.S. 1922*, 2: 935; *D.B.F.P.*, 17: 922.

lopment, Red Cross officials in Constantinople informed Rumbold that the Greek Government had yet to consent for the dispatch of an enquiry team to Thrace. As previously stated the Greek Foreign Minister Baltazzis and former Premier Venizelos saw no problem with an investigation taking place in Thrace. It was important for the Greek Government to approve a mission to Thrace, so as not to give Angora officials a pretext for delaying or refusing a commission for Asia Minor.[49]

Caffery reported on 6 September that an IRC representative in Athens had told him that Greek foreign office saw no purpose in including Thrace because "(it) is open for anyone who likes to come and go as he pleases." He also stated that the British chargé d'affaires informed Greek officials that the Red Cross believed "that Turkish authorities will insist in Thrace being included" and therefore "under these circumstances, Greek authorities had no opposition to the inclusion of Thrace."[50] If Greece had refused, the Turks could then argue that Athens had something to hide in Thrace.

On 24 August Raymond Schleirer, a delegate of the IRC, visited Bristol at the U.S. High Commission in Constantinople where the former raised the issue of an American being appointed to the commissions. Bristol was surprised by Schleirer's remark that America was a neutral party in this matter. Bristol explained that America could not be considered a neutral because its policy was "to stand with the Allies in the same way that we had been expected within the war."

In their conversation, Schleirer told Bristol that the British High Commissioner favored the appointment of an American as a neutral delegate for the IRC mission to Anatolia. Bristol believed that Britain was trying "to embroil America in the Near East mix-up and at the same time if possible break down the prestige that America has succeeded in establishing in this part of the world." Schleirer also stated the French and Italian high commissioners had raised "no objection to an American being on the committee." Bristol concluded that since no British, French or Italian delegates were to be appointed to these committees no American representative should be selected either.[51]

By early September, Britain, France and the U.S. Governments had undertaken to contribute their share of the funds towards the proposed atrocity enquiry. Eager to commence its task, the Red Cross sought the permission of the Angora and Greek Governments to proceed with the enquiry. Athens

---

[49] *D.B.F.P.*, 17: 932.

[50] *Turkey Internal 867.4016/662* J. Caffery, Athens, to Secretary of State, Washington D.C., 6 September 1922.

[51] *Turkey Internal 867.00/1542* Admiral Bristol, U.S. High Commissioner, Constantinople, to Secretary of State, Washington D.C., 31 August 1922.

replied, granting its permission, whereas Angora failed to respond to the Red Cross request. Italy promised on 24 September to contribute 25,000 gold francs as its contribution to the IRC investigations. The response of the Great Powers was pitiful in light of the fact that the evacuation of the Hellenic Army from Asia Minor in early September had left the surviving Christian minorities to fend for themselves. Angora, on the other hand, did not want the IRC to report atrocities committed against Ottoman Greeks in its area of control.[52]

4. *The Involvement of the League of Nations*

In order to deflect attention, the Turks blamed the Greek forces for excesses committed in Smyrna and Thrace and appealed to the League of Nations. On 9 September Reşat Nuri, the Turkish chargé d'affaires in Berne, in a letter to Mr. Edwards, the president of the third assembly of the League of Nations, outlined the destruction committed by the Hellenic Army in its evacuation of Asia Minor. He mentioned that "Systematic massacres of peaceful people, the burning of entire districts, ... such is the terrible toll of three years of Greek occupation in Anatolia and in Thrace" and protested,

> [m]ost emphatically against the savage methods used by our enemies. As soon as I receive precise details of the appalling havoc wrought by the Greek armies in their retreat, I shall hasten to forward them to the Secretariat of the League.[53]

The Persian delegation, acting on behalf of the Angora Government, raised a motion on 18 September 1922 that was duly adopted by the League assembly, urging the League council to send a commission of enquiry to investigate alleged atrocities in Thrace and Asia Minor. As far as the Greeks were concerned, they did not feel that they had anything to hide regarding the

---

[52] *D.B.F.P.*, 18**:** 64 and fns 1–5; *Turkey Internal 867.4016/717* Annexes Lancelot Oliphant, F.O., London, to President of IRC, Geneva, 14 September 1922 and to Sec, IRC, Geneva, 27 September 1922; *Turkey Internal 867/4016/691* Joseph C Grew, Legation of U.S. of America, Berne, to the Secretary of State, Washington D.C., 26 September 1922 with four enclosures: 1. The American Legation, Berne, to The International Red Cross. Geneva, 9 September 1922; 2. The American Legation, Berne, to The International Red Cross, Geneva, 22 September 1922; 3. The International Red Cross, Geneva, to The American Legation, Berne, 23 September 1922; 4. Translation of above note.

[53] *League of Nations C684.11.398.1922 V11* The Near East. Note by Sir Eric Drummond, Secretary–General of the League of Nations, Geneva, including letter from Rechad Noury, the Turkish Chargé d'Affaires, Berne, to Mr. Edwards, President of Third Assembly, 9 September 1922 (Held on microfilm at Deakin University Library Waurn Ponds, Geelong, Australia); *FO424/255, no. 516*, Director of Military Operations, War Office to Foreign Office, 14 November 1922 with enclosure on Greek and Turkish atrocities subsequent to the burning of Smyrna.

treatment of minorities and may even have welcomed the commission of enquiry to Thrace.[54]

On 19 September Georgios Streit, president of the Greek delegation to the assembly, sent a note to the secretary-general of the League questioning the Persian action on three grounds. In the first case, the Angora Government was not even recognized as a state by members of the League. Next, he questioned the admissibility of the procedure adopted by Persia to act on behalf of a non-member state. Finally, he pointed out that the enquiry over the alleged atrocities never took place owing to the intransigence of the Angora Government. Streit was correct in criticizing the actions of the Persian delegation, but this did not assist Greece in her hour of crisis. She was now facing the monumental task of accommodating hundreds of thousands of refugees from Asia Minor.[55]

The IRC mission, in the end, went nowhere. On 20 October Lucien Brunel, the secretary-general for mission service at IRC, thanked the U.S. State Department and the British, French and Italian Governments for entrusting the IRC with carrying out the proposed investigations, but it failed in its mission due to the refusal of the Angora Government.[56]

The Kemalists defeated the Hellenic Army and ejected it from Smyrna in early September with the Kingdom of Greece facing a huge influx of Ottoman Greek and Armenian refugees from Asia Minor. In early October, an armistice concluded at Mudanya between Greece and the Kemalists paved the way for the Lausanne Peace Conference, which commenced in November 1922.[57]

Conclusion

This article has attempted to show how the Great Powers tried, more or less seriously, to investigate such atrocities as mentioned above, and procrastinated as innocent men, women and children perished at the hands of the Kemalists in the Anatolian interior. In fact, the Powers did nothing to halt the deportations and massacres of the Ottoman Greeks. They simply used

---

[54] *League of Nations A88. 1922 V11* "The Situation in the Near East" signed by Prince Arfa-Ed-Dowleh & Emir Zoka-Ed-Dowleh, Geneva, 19 September 1922; League of Nations, Third Assembly of the League of Nations, "The situation in the Near East," motion proposed by the Persian delegation on 19 September 1922, Geneva, September 19 1922 (available on microfilm at Deakin University); *D.B.F.P.*, 18: 64 n. 1.

[55] *League of Nations, A98.1922.V11* "The situation in the Near East," signed by Georgios Streit, President of Greek Delegation, Geneva, 20 September 1922.

[56] *Turkey Internal 867.4016/717* Lucien Brunel, Secretary General of the Mission Service, International Committee of the Red Cross, Geneva, to Department of State, Washington D.C., 20 October 1922 (translation).

[57] *D.B.F.P.*, vol. 18, docs 124-26 & 129.

the commissions of enquiry as a smokescreen behind which to hide their inaction and passed responsibility on to the IRC. The European Powers and the United States were not interested in becoming involved in a war with Kemalist Turkey.

The Turks used the press both in Angora and Constantinople to deny the reports of Ward and Yowell. There is no doubt that Ward's and Yowell's reports attracted a fair bit of coverage in the western press and even inspired Lord Curzon to push ahead with the idea of establishing an inter-Allied commission of enquiry into the reported massacres of Ottoman Greeks. Even Curzon's inspired idea never garnered the support of France who along with Italy supported the Kemalist movement in Asia Minor. The stalling tactics of France and Kemalist Turkey were instrumental in the IRC mission going nowhere.

It is clear that the IRC lacked the financial resources and depended on the Powers to provide it with the necessary funds to conduct its investigations in Asia Minor and Thrace. Whether the IRC thought that western efforts regarding the proposed investigation were serious or that the investigation had a chance of succeeding is difficult to say. On the other hand, the IRC being an impartial organization it did not wish to become embroiled in the political and diplomatic games of the major parties involved in Asia Minor. If the IRC had conducted such an investigation, it would have been fair and impartial interviewing both Ottoman Greeks and Turks. This author did not find any evidence of the IRC conducting preliminary studies into massacres of Ottoman Greeks or interviewing survivors who managed to escape from the Kemalists. However, further research into the IRC archives held in Geneva might shed more light on the role and activity of the IRC in this tragic period of the Near East.

Genocide of Others: Raphael Lemkin, the Genocide of the Greeks, the Holocaust, and the Present Moment

Steven Leonard Jacobs

Introduction: Lemkin the Man

More and more, Raphael Lemkin (1900-1959) — émigré Polish lawyer; Jewish refugee from the carnage and devastation of Hitler's Europe; professor of law at both Duke University, Durham, NC, and Yale University, New Haven, CT; advisor to Justice Robert H. Jackson (1882-1954) at the International Military Tribunal at Nuremberg, Germany, at the close of World War II; author of our word "genocide;" and moving force behind the United Nations Convention on the Prevention and Punishment of the Crime of Genocide (1948) — is coming into his own as the growing interdisciplinary field of genocide studies is taking off.

Born in the Polish village Bezwodna in Czarist Russia (today Bezvodna in Belarus), an agricultural community away from the larger cities, he enjoyed a reasonably positive childhood interacting with his cousins and other Jewish children as well as the non-Jewish children of those who farmed the land. A chance encounter sometime during his teenage years with the book *Quo Vadis* by the (1904) Polish Nobel Laureate for Literature Henryk Sienkiewicz (1846-1916), telling the horrific story of the Roman Emperor Nero's near-genocidal destruction of the early Christians, so dramatically influenced him that it caused him (a) to investigate other instances throughout history of humanity's inhumanity to itself (e.g. the Armenian Genocide, Japan's treatment of Roman Catholic missionaries, French treatment of the Huguenots), and (b) affected his choice of a career in law, believing that only through international legal actions could such future tragedies be avoided and those who perpetrated such deeds be brought to justice.

Already a practicing attorney and secretary to the Polish Court of Appeals in Warsaw, he fully intended to present his arguments against "barbarity" (crimes against persons and groups) and "vandalism" (crimes against cultures) at the 1933 meeting of the League of Nations in Madrid, Spain, but was prevented from doing so by his supervisors who maintained that his position was too parochially Jewish to be of value and of substance, and forbade his attendance, as he himself states in his largely unpublished autobiography "Unofficial Man." He had not yet coined the word genocide, which was to appear in Chapter 9 of his *Axis Rule in Occupied Europe.*[1]

The start of World War II with Germany's invasion of Poland in September of 1939 found him active in both the military and the underground, but later fleeing first to Sweden and ultimately to the United States, never again to see the forty-nine members of his family, including his own parents, who perished in the Holocaust (with the exception of his brother and his sister-in-law). Working with U.S. Supreme Court Justice Robert H. Jackson (1892-1954), chief prosecutor at the Nuremberg War Crimes Trials of the top Nazi leadership in 1945 and 1946, he tried, unsuccessfully, to get the crime of genocide made part of the prosecution's case. For the remaining thirteen years of his life, he was to devote himself fully to pursuing his dream of the passage of international legislation outlawing genocide, dying largely unmourned in 1959. Somewhat ironically, forty years after his death, in 1988, his adopted country of the United States finally ratified the Genocide Convention.[2]

Lemkin the historian:
Lemkin's unpublished "History of Genocide: III.5. The Greeks"

Though initially scattered primarily in three locations — the 42nd Street Public Library, New York City; the American Jewish Archives, Cincinnati, Ohio; and the American Jewish Historical Society Archives, Waltham, Massachusetts — more than 20,000 pages of Lemkin's papers, including notes, correspondence, articles, interviews, unpublished manuscripts and the like remain a veritable treasure trove for scholars working in the field of genocide studies.[3]

Among those papers is an incomplete set of chapters for what was to be his magnum opus: his three-volume "History of Genocide" (I Ancient; II Medieval; III Modern).[4] According to his outline, Chapter Five of Book Three,

---

1 Raphael Lemkin, *Axis Rule in Occupied Europe: Laws of Occupation, Analysis of Government, Proposals for Redress* (Washington, DC: Carnegie Endowment for International Peace, 1944); see Steven Leonard Jacobs, "Genesis of the Concept of Genocide According to Its Author From the Original Sources," *Human Rights Review* 3 no. 2 (2002): 98-103.

2 Raphael Lemkin, "Totally Unofficial Man," in *Pioneers of Genocide Studies*, ed. Samuel Totten and Steven Leonard Jacobs (New Brunswick: Transaction Publishers, 2002), 365-399.

3 Steven L. Jacobs, "The papers of Raphael Lemkin: a First Look," *Journal of Genocide Research* 1 no. 1 (1999): 105-114.

4 As was the case with all of Lemkin's unpublished manuscripts, he does not affix any information whatsoever regarding the dating of his compositions prior to their publication. Methodologically speaking, however, Lemkin's apparently rigorous legal training, his voracious reading in a wide variety of historical sources, his ability to do so in a multiplicity of languages, and his own analytical and intellectual talents (coupled with his

entitled "Greeks" or Chapter Nine of Book Three, entitled "Greeks in Asia Minor," (different titles of same material) was to address the genocide of the Greeks by the Turks, and, relevant to this contribution, was evidently completed (no completion date given).

A third file entitled simply "Greeks in Asia Minor" consists of the same material but without chapter or book designation. Fifty-five pages long, with type-written material, oft-times on both front and back, it is divided into the following sub-sections: (1) Background (pages 1-11), (2) Technique (pages 12-37), (3) Who is guilty? (pages 38-43), (4) Psychological Reactions on both sides (pages 44-49), (5) Reaction of public opinion abroad (pages 50-52), (6) Cultural and other losses (pages 53-55), and (6) a two-page Bibliography consisting of 51 sources.

Thus, three separate copies of the same material are preserved among his papers, two with different titles and different chapter placements, with no additional explanations. What follows, then, are brief summaries of each section, replete with essential quotations, before my own analysis, thoughts and reflections.

Background

Lemkin begins his account:

> On the 29th of May, 1453 Constantinopel [sic] after a siege of 52 days, fell into the hands of the Ottomans. From this date is counted the osman [sic] sovereignty over Greece, although some regions succumbed earlier and some a little later.
>
> At this period, the national spirit of the Greeks had long ceased to exist. (Page 1)

He then goes on:

> The situation of the Greeks remained more or less unchanged for sixty years, until Selim I [1467-1520], grandson of Mohammed II [1429?-1481] ascended to the throne. He hated the Christians and was on the point of having them massacred to a man, when he was persuaded by his councellors [sic] *and the*

moral sense of integrity) well positioned him at the intersection between law and history, and foundationally as a central figure in the later-emerging field of "genocide studies," growing out of Holocaust studies. Whatever flaws later colleagues may find with either his use of sources, his approach to his material, and/or his judgments, he was the first to fully put the study of genocidal atrocities "on the map," so to speak, and his breakthrough work must be appreciated at that level. Later scholars (e.g. Leo Kuper, Helen Fein, Israel Charny), including the next generation (e.g. Ben Kiernan, Mark Levene, Adam Jones, etc.), and the establishment of now two international organizations — the International Association of Genocide Scholars (IAGS) and the European Network of Genocide Scholars (ENOGS) — together with their respective journals, *Journal of Genocide Studies and Prevention* and *Journal of Genocide Research* — must all ultimately attribute their work to that pioneered and begun by Lemkin.

> *Greek patriarch* to desist. But he had a number of churches converted into mosques.
>
> In 1656 the infamous "blood-tax" was suppressed which had been the worst suffering of the Greeks, namely the forcible recruiting of Christian children into the regiment of the Janissaries, where they were converted into Musulmans...
>
> The condition of the Greeks improved greatly under the administration of Koupuli-Zadè Moustafa, surnamed the virtuous ... *He was probably somewhat motivated by the reverses which Christian armies inflicted upon the Ottoman arms [should read "armies"] beyond the frontiers.* (Pages 2-3; emphases added)

Thus, early on, we see in Lemkin's writing two characteristic traits: good use of whatever historical sources were available to him as he tells the story, in this case the campaign against the Greeks of Ottoman Turkey, and an interweaving of his own assessments and analyses of historical materials. No apologist or propagandist, Lemkin's legal training as well as his moral commitment to truth enabled him to tell both the positive side of the story as well as the negative (at least in draft form, as this manuscript was never published).

Technique

After first discussing the heavy and oppressive taxation used by the Turks against their Greek subjects, and the capturing of children for service in the Janissary corps, he writes:

> In 1640 the question of exterminating the raiahs was again considered. It was the last year of the reign of Murad IV [1612-1640] and he also was prevailed upon to renounce his bloody plans.
>
> The Greeks of Asia, especially those of Asia Minor, were becoming so degenerate that it was a miracle that they still were Christians. Their very language seemed in danger of disappearing; many Orthodox Greeks spoke only Turkish. How they slowly rallied and founded schools, how they slowly managed to achieve quite a measure of independence and riches, has been told in the first part. On the whole, their situation became bearable after the "blood tax" was demolished in the 17th century, as far as their material existence was concerned. But, of course, spiritually they remained "in fetters," an alien element, considered with contempt. Hopes of regaining the lost territories never died down. They received considerable impetus when Greek independence was proclaimed in 1822 and this in turn increased the hatred and suspicion of their oppressors which culminated in the bloody happenings of the 19th century.
>
> The fall of the last sultan Abdul Hamid [II, 1842-1918; deposed 1909], was made possible through the cooperation of the Christians. But they were soon disappointed. (Pages 18-19)

Fully aware of the Turkish agenda against the Greeks, he continues:

> That the Young Turcs [sic] movement tried to strike a mortal blow against everything Christian and especially against everything Greek during the four years prior to the Balkan War can be proved by a look at the various laws which were passed and which were pictured in a memorial presented to the Turkish government by the Greek deputies to the Turkish parliament in 1910. (Pages 19-20)[5]

[A page and one-half of quotations from that document follow.]

> Moving on to Turkish participation on the side of the Great Powers during the First World War, Lemkin sees and understands it as marking "the beginning of a second period of persecution, incomparably fiercer and more effective than the first" (Page 22).

Lemkin concludes this section with the comment "The culmination of all these crushing measures was the burning of Smyrna on September 13, 1922" (page 36), and then goes on to detail some of these atrocities as well.

The Burning of Smyrna

The horrific destruction of the city of Smyrna equally captured Lemkin's attention as he wrote:

> The culmination of all these crushing measures was the burning of Smyrna on September 13, 1922. The Turks had entered the city four days before and after looting, raping and killing, a fire was started in the Armenian quarter and from there spread all over the city, reducing it to ashes, except the Turk-ish quarter which was spared by a favorable wind. The fire was described as "a wall of fire two miles long, in which several distinct volcanoes of raging flames were throwing up jagged writhing tongues to a height of a hundred feet." [Ward Rice in *London Daily Mail*, 16 September 1922] At the time there were 200,000 refugees in the city who had fled from the interior from the advancing Turkish troops.
>
> Three fifths of the city were destroyed, more than 300,000 persons were made homeless and the financial loss was estimated at close to 40 million sterling pounds. [*Daily Telegraph*, 16 September 1922] It was one of the biggest fires in the world's history. According to the *Daily Mail* correspondent, the Messina earthquake [1908] and the San Francisco fire [1906] were "merciful in comparison" [19 September 1922). "More than 125,000 of its inhabitants, mostly Greeks and Armenians, were massacred and burnt alive." [*Birmingham Post*, 21 October 1922]
>
> "The scenes of massacre amid the flames are described as horrible... Eye-witnesses narrate how a party of eight hundred Christians who took refuge in the Catholic Cathedral were horribly massacred, notwithstanding the presence of two French officers. Sometimes the slaughterers paused in their work to pick up money or valuable articles thrown to them by their victims,

[5] George Horton, *The Blight of Asia: An Account of the Systematic Extermination of Christian Populations by Mohammedans and of the Culpability of Certain Great Powers; with a True Story of the Burning of Smyrna* (Indianapolis: Bobbs-Merrill, 1926), 32.

but went immediately afterwards. A number of women and girls and brothers and husbands committed suicide so as not to survive dishonour." [*Daily Telegraph*, 18 September 1922] (Pages 36-37)

Who is Guilty?

Not one to hide behind diplomatic niceties in his writing — a far different characterization of him in contradistinction to his public persona of the passionately committed and caring person, sensitive yet driven, when dealing with international diplomats at the United Nations in Switzerland and New York in pursuit of the passage of the Genocide Convention — he begins this section with the comment:

> While the persecutions of the Greeks by the Turks in this century are the result of governmental intentions and planning, *those of the former centuries were in part due to the attitude of the Greeks themselves.*
>
> From the start, Mohammed II [1432-1481], after he took Constantinopel [sic] in 1453, tried to make accomplices out of the high ecclesiastics and get hold of the population through them. In this he was extremely successful.
>
> The head of the church paid big sums to the Porte. This had not been instituted by the sultan, but by intriguing Greeks who tried to get official support while trying to get the top posts in the church....
>
> The priests in the villages in turn were forced to raise big sums to pay to the bishop and when they were unable to do so, their superiors arrived and deposed them with the help of Turkish soldiers. (Page 38; emphasis added)

For Lemkin, then, in this terribly tragic case, guilt was to be shared by both the Turks and the Greeks:

> Comparable to these [ecclesiastics] were the Fanariotes. They made themselves indispensable to the Turcs [sic] by their intellectual superiority. Beginning as translators, secretaries, writers, and business men, they became in the 17th century part of the government. They finally became so rich, that they became a source of credit for the Turkish government, and so powerful that their own fortunes were bound up with the Ottoman Empire. And while the patriarch, for instance, threatened to excommunicate all Greeks who might rebel in 1821, so did the Fanariotes denounce plans of insurrection to the Turkish police. (Page 39)

His assessment, however, continues even stronger when he writes:

> From 1453 until 1821, therefore, the highly placed Greeks are just as guilty of oppressing their brothers, as were the Turks, because they lent themselves to be the instruments. But in 1821 the uprising in Greece provoked such feeling[s] of fear and hate, that all Greeks were attacked in massacres which were popular in origin and not ordered by the Governor.
>
> In the 20th century – finally – the guilty ones were to be looked for in Ankara. The Young Turk Committee decided to get rid of the Greek element. A general boycott was declared and posters, calling on the musulman to exterminate the Orthodox were posted in the schools and mosques. The Turkish newspa-

> pers were full of violent articles, exciting the readers to persecution and massacre. The procedures bore evidence of being systematic and ordered from above. (Page 40)

Lest the reader, however, reach the wrong unbalanced conclusions — blaming the Greek victims for their own genocide — Lemkin continues:

> Although instigated by the government, the Turkish population took willingly part in the persecutions...
>
> The terror subsided a little during the World War until 1916, but even then the government ordered crushing requisitions from the merchants and wholesale mobilizations into the labor battalions. The deportations into the interior commenced with great brutality afterwards, and increased until there were no more Greeks left in 1923.
>
> That the government was behind it all was not even denied by the instigators. Everything was done in broad daylight. (Page 41)

Finally, Lemkin does not exonerate the Turkish people themselves when he writes:

> Yet, even though the government tries to shift the guilt from its shoulders, history proves, that the Turkish people were quite capable of living peacefully side by side with Greeks until the government tried to excite them by all means in its power to plunder and massacre. (Pages 41-42)

Psychological reactions on both sides

Contained within this section is a strident critique of the Turks coupled with a very real and evident appreciation of Greek survival. After first commenting that

> the prime cause for the survival of the Christian communities [Greeks *and* Armenians] was the incompetence of the Turks for any pursuit other than that of soldiering." (Page 46),

and that after the Young Turks came to power

> it is interesting to note that the Turks, although they loudly proclaimed the Greeks as traitors and deserving of their harsh fate, felt compelled quite often to conceal their deeds." (Page 48)

Stepping back somewhat, Lemkin writes:

> As always, of course, a partial guilt can be found in the hysteria breaking out among the Greeks. Many villages packed up and left before they were actually forced to do so. Fear drove them away, fear which was easily awakened in a race whose mothers had for centuries dated events by having occurred so many years before or after a certain massacre. That the uneasy equilibrium in which they had finally managed to live with the Turks for so long should be violently upset by the introduction of the modern ideas of nationalism and liberalism of which they themselves had first become conscious, was probably clear to very few of them. (Page 49)

Reactions of public opinion abroad

Lemkin begins this section with the rather prescient comment that

> the outside world began to take an active interest in the affairs of Turkey in the 18th century" (Page 50),

and later

> the outside world became concerned for the Greeks only when the intensive persecutions began [in the early 1900s]." (Page 51)

Having already negatively critiqued the Turks and less so the Greeks, he is not above critiquing other nation-states as well:

> And although all these powers [Russia, Great Britain, France] were well aware of the "fifth column" possibilities of the Greek population in Turkey, they made only lame protests when thousands were then slaughtered in 1821. In fact, the ambassadors were even instructed not to give any longer refuge to fleeing Greeks, and the captains of boats were also advised not [to] take refugees on board. (Page 50)

Cultural and other losses

For Lemkin, as he developed his concept of genocide, such consequential devastation and destruction encompassed not only the physical destruction of life, but what we may characterize as "cultural genocide" as well. Thus, his final paragraphs of this chapter:

> The Greeks suffered from the conquest not only in numbers, but also in the quality of their population since so many learned people went into exile. It took almost two whole centuries before newly founded schools made up somewhat for the deficiencies in Greek education. And although these exiles awakened commiseration and interest in the foreign courts, this advantage was small compared to the loss at home, where the drain upon the population was most seriously felt.
>
> It was due to this exile of learned men that it took the Greeks so long to rise in the service of the Sultans. Only when the wealthy Fanariotes established schools and began sending their children to foreign universities, had the Greek race another crop of intellectuals who were able to rise to high posts.
>
> The loss of the total persecution in the 20th century is difficult to assess, but it [is] certainly tremendous. There were not only incalculable losses of life and property, but a nation deliberately got rid of intelligent, prosperous and progressive citizen[s] in order to achieve uniformity of creed and race. (Page 54)

Finally, it should also be noted that, on just about every page, there are quotations from Lemkin's various sources, all duly footnoted. These 51 sources are in English (26), French (18), and German (7).

Analysis

What Lemkin's writing on the genocide of the Greeks by the Turks and the involvement of some among their own leadership historically in creating an environment which fostered hostility between the two groups reveals is the complexities of addressing the topic of genocide in general, and specific genocides in particular. No victim group wants to look so closely at its own devastation that it realizes that, unwittingly or not, its own actions and behaviors may have played even a minor role in its own destruction. Thus, the Armenians' socio-economic successes may have been a source of resentment for the Turks.[6] Their Christianity may have been a contributing factor breeding resentment among the Muslim majority no matter how secularized.

The Jews, too, given perhaps their own naiveté as to their questionably successful assimilation into German society may have and did misread the results of 2,000 or more years of social, cultural, political antisemitism and disregarded their own warning signals prior to Hitler's ascension to power. Then, too, their own Judaism and communal cohesiveness perceived in Western Europe as strange, negatively exotic, and exclusive may have played directly into the hands of their enemies. This is not to fall into the trap of blaming the victims for their own destruction; it is simply to suggest that, if one is truly willing to examine this phenomenon of genocidal destruction, then one needs to do so "with the kid gloves off," striving for historical accuracy and supportive evidence all along the way, no matter where it ultima-tely leads.

Secondly, while scholars may fault Lemkin's use of this or that particular source as biased, less credible than another, or worse, his writing does suggest a serious attention to detail which was a hallmark of all of his work. His willingness to both identify and quote directly from his sources and his use of sources in several languages reveal not only a consistent familiarity with his sources, but, also, all the characteristics of good scholarly work.

Specifically, in the case of the genocide of the Greeks by the Turks, what comes through from a careful reading of this fifty-five-page chapter is both an historical excursus as well as an evaluative judgment of those responsible for the genocide. Where condemnation is necessary, Lemkin condemns;

---

[6] Non-Muslims (Greeks, Armenians, Jews in particular) had a position comparable to that of Jews in Medieval Europe. In both cases they prospered because they were largely excluded from military careers and civil service. At the same time, their high economic/ financial positions made them visible targets for social envy and envy's violent consequences. The genocide of the Ottoman Christians and the pogroms of Jews in pre-Modern Europe can be understood as a type of "economicide." [I thank Tessa Hofmann for this additionally insightful comment.]

where praise is necessary, Lemkin praises. In so doing, Lemkin, as in all other aspects, presents and represents himself not as an ivory-tower academic or office-bound lawyer, but as both the scholar-activist and lawyer on a mission. In so doing, he reminds us that this newer field of genocide studies, evolving out of and including the older field of Holocaust studies, is one which, by virtue of its focus, cannot simply be confined to either the classroom or the office.

Genocide studies requires knowledge of and the use of the very best investigatory tools from the best scholarly minds in their respective disciplines, be they history, political science, law, anthropology, sociology, psychology, biology, philosophy, religious studies, and the like. It also requires a moral passion and commitment that mandate involvement in matters political, governmental, economic, and social. It is not enough to read about and write about Rwanda if the opportunity presents itself to do something in the aftermath of that genocide for the victims of that horror. It is not enough to read about and write about the genocide in Bosnia-Herzegovina if similar opportunities come to the fore. It is not enough, as of this writing, to read about and write about the genocide in Sudan when others, and not necessarily the scholarly community, are addressing very real and ongoing humanitarian needs and challenging the international community of nation-states to bring this tragedy to its conclusion.

Having put the word genocide before the international community, and having striven mightily to have it understood and accepted as a legal instrumentality by the family of nations, Lemkin's legacy may very well be the refusal to remain silent and do nothing in the face of such horror. Though, perhaps, unfamiliar with the phrase which has resonated among Jews in the aftermath of the Holocaust, "Never Again!" — for we do not find it in his writings — there can be little doubt that, in the aftermath of that murderous moment which took his own family from him, Lemkin, the Jewish survivor, refused to acquiesce in silence or let his own grief overwhelm him, but allowed it to energize and motivate him even more in tribute to his own family.

Lemkin and the Genocide of Others

In the aftermath of the greatest tragedy to inflict itself upon the Jewish people — the wanton destruction of almost 6,000,000 Jewish children, women, and men — the Jewish people continues to nurse its wounds more than six decades after the end of World War II. Its overriding concern with the present and future survival of the State of Israel, the veritable flood of books, articles, speeches, literary and artistic creations which continue to address the Holocaust, not to mention the seemingly inexhaustible conversations and debates among those attempting to understand the meaning and implications of these events make one realize that the pain has not yet subsided and this tragedy has not yet ended.

But it is this latter quest for meaning that remains the most problematic. How are Jews to understand themselves, their present, and their future, in light of these events which defy description? How are others, both those whose nations were willingly complicitous in the Holocaust and those whose nations were, at best, neutral observers and/or bystanders to understand themselves?

Here, again, Lemkin provides the model. From the beginning, Lemkin's early investigations into what he would later label genocide were not parochial, either in origin or in reference. To know Jewish history, and there is no reason to suggest he did not know his own history as a the child of a learned mother well-read in several languages, was part of his increasing understanding of the worst that humanity can do to itself, not the sum total of that knowledge. As he experienced genocide, as it caught him, his family, and his people in its vice-like maw, it became a source that impelled him forward, but, importantly, not the only source. The genocidal tragedies of humanity were at issue, not solely the tragedy of his own people. For Lemkin, there was a shared suffering with others that mandated universal concern — which is as it should be.

While one must guard against the community of victims sliding into the trap of rank-ordering one people's suffering as superior to that of another, Lemkin's work on behalf of all victims, writing about the genocide of others, transcended any sense of parochialism. For one such as myself — the child of a survivor-escapee from the Holocaust who saw more than 150 members of his own large family murdered during the years 1939-1945, including his own parents, all his cousins except three, and all his aunts and uncles except four — Lemkin becomes the role model par excellence.[7] To work toward eradicating those evils which produced a Holocaust against the Jewish people, my own people, does not negate working to alleviate those conditions which become foundational to the genocide of others. In both scholarly and anti-genocide work, there is no "either-or," there is only "and."

---

7 Steven Leonard Jacobs, "From Holocaust to Genocide: The Journey Continues," in *Pioneers of Genocide Studies*, Totten and Jacobs, eds., 507-517.

APPENDIX: *Lemkin's Bibliography*

[Alphabetized by title in the original]

A History of Greece, George Finlay, 1877

A History of the Greek People, William Miller, 1922

Cantemir's Histoire Ottomane, [n.d.]

Carte Ethnographique de la Turquie d'Europe et denombrement de la population grecque, A. Synvet, 1877

Constantinople, Théophile Gautier, 1875

Consular reports contained in the Greek Ministerial Archives

Cours de Littérature Grecque Moderne, Rizos-Néroulos, [n.d.]

*Der Verfall des Griechentums in Kleinasien im 14 Jahrhunder*t, Albert H. Wachter, 1902

Die politische Vernichtung des Griechentums, Friedrich Münzer, 1925

Die Turken und das osmanische Reich, Eugen Oberhummer, 1917

Encyclopedia of Social Sciences, [n.d.]

Etat Historique sur l'etat des Grecs depuis la Conquête Musilmane, M. Villemain, 1827

Europe and the Young Turks, René Pinon, [n.d.]

Geschichte des Osmanischen Reiches in Europa, Johan W. Zinkeisen, 1854

Geschichte des osmanischen Reiches, Joseph von Hammer, 1925

Greece in Asia Minor, published by the Press Bureau of the Ministry for Foreign Affairs, 1921

Greece, C. W. Oman, 1907

Griechische Geschichte im 19 Jahrhundert, Robert Põhlman, 1902

Hellenism in Asia Minor, Dr. Karl Dieterich, 1918

Histoire de l'Empire Ottoman, Vicomte de la Jonquiére, 1914

Histoire de la Gréce, Francois Pouqueville, 1824

Histoire Diplomatique de la Grècs, Edouard Driault, 1925

History of the Ottoman Empire, Edward Upham, 1829

La Macédonie et sa population chrétienne, D. N. Brancoff, 1905

La Vérité sur un Drama Historique, E. Dourmoussis, 1922

Lascaris où les Grecs du quinziéme siècle, E. Villemain, 1827

Lascaris, M. Villemain, 1827

Les Grecs de l'Empire Ottoman, A. Synvet, 1878

Les Persécutions antihelléniques en Turquie, Rapport Officiel, 1918

Les Peuples Aryens d'Asia et d'Europe, M. S. Zaborowski-Moindren, 1908

Letters on Turkey, M. A. Ubicini, 1856

Mémoires du Baron de Tott sur les Turcs et les Tarares, 1784

Misericorde, Alfred Silbernagel, 1918

Persecution of the Greeks in Turkey before the European War, Alexander Papadopoulos, 1919

Persecution of the Greeks in Turkey before the European War, C. N. Brown, [n.d.]

Persecutions of the Greeks in Turkey since the beginning of the European War, Carroll N. Brown and Theodore P. Ion, 1918

Researches in Greece and the Levant, John Hartley, 1863

Schriften und Tagebücher, Jakob Phillipp Fallmerayer, 1913
The Balkans, a History of Bulgaria, Serbia, Greece, Rumania, Turkey, D. G. Hogarth, Nevill Forbes, Arnold J. Toynbee, D. Mitrany, 1915
The Blight of Asia, George Horton, 1926
The Foundation of the Ottoman Empire, Herbert Adams Gibbons, 1916
The Frontiers of Language and Nationality in Europe, Léon Dominian, 1917
The People of Turkey, Stanley Lane Poole, 1878
The Struggle for Power in Moslem Asia, E. Alexander Powell, 1923
The Sultan and his subjects, Richard Davey, 1897
The Turk and the Greek, Samuel G. W. Benjamin, 1867
The Turkish Atrocities in Asia Minor and in the Pontus. G Baltazzi, 192?
The Turkish Empire, Alfred de Bessé, 1854
The Western Question in Greece and Turkey, A. J. Toynbee, 1922
Turkey, Greece, and the Great Powers, G. F. Abbott, 1916.
Various Newspapers
Voyage an Morée, á Constantinople, en Albanie, Francois Pouqueville, 1805

The Ottoman Genocide of the Greeks and of the Other Christian Minorities

In Light of the Genocide Convention

ALFRED DE ZAYAS

On doit des égards aux vivants; on ne doit aux morts que la vérité.
[We owe respect to the living; to the dead we owe only truth.]
— François Marie Arouet (1694 - 1778), dit Voltaire[1]

General Introduction

GENOCIDE[2] AND CRIMES AGAINST HUMANITY[3] are the gravest international crimes and entail both civil and penal consequences. Because of the nature of the crimes, state responsibility for reparation to victims and descendants and individual criminal liability are not subject to prescription or statutes of limitation.

In the case of the Ottoman genocide against the Greeks and other Christian minorities during and after World War I, the perpetrators are dead and beyond the reach of criminal justice, but the Turkish State remains liable for the crimes committed by the Ottoman Empire.

Genocide and crimes against humanity also give rise to obligations of the perpetrating state toward the entire international community (*erga omnes* doctrine). Turkey's international obligations are thus not only those towards the victims — Greeks, Armenians and Assyrian/Aramaean Christians — but also toward the international community at large. Moreover, according to general principles of international law and international *ordre public*, states may not recognize as legitimate the consequences of *erga omnes* crimes. Thus, the international community must take appropriate measures to ensure adequate reparation to the victims and refrain from giving recognition to the consequences of genocide and crimes against humanity, includ-

[1] *Oedipe (Oeuvres completes)* (Paris: Société littéraire typographique, 1785) 1: 15n.

[2] William Schabas, *Genocide in International Law* (Cambridge: Cambridge University Press, 2000), 21. See also revised and updated report on the question of the prevention and punishment of the crime of genocide, prepared by Special Rapporteur Mr. Ben Whitaker (E/CN.4/Sub.2/1985/6).

[3] Egon Schwelb, "Crimes Against Humanity," *British Yearbook of International Law* (Oxford: The University Press, 1946), 23: 181.

ing the wrongful acquisition of land and of the personal property of the murdered victims.

The Genocide Convention of 1948 can be applied retroactively, because it is declarative of pre-existing international law. There are numerous precedents for the retroactive application of treaties, including the London Agreement of 8 August 1945 establishing the Nuremberg Tribunal, and the Convention on the Non-Applicability of Statutes of Limitations to War Crimes and Crimes against Humanity of 1968. It should be remembered that the Genocide Convention did not "create" the crime of genocide, but was intended to strengthen the pre-existing claims of victims of genocide, including the victims of the Armenian genocide and of the Holocaust.

According to Article 31 of the Vienna Convention on the Law of Treaties, the principal rule of interpretation is "the ordinary meaning given to the terms of the treaty in their context and in the light of its object and purpose." The retroactive application of the Genocide Convention is not only compatible with the ordinary meaning of the terms used in the convention, but also necessary in the light of the convention's object and purpose.

Indeed, such retroactive application advances the important goal of deterring future acts of genocide (prevention) by way of condemning acts of genocide (suppression) that occurred prior to its entry into force, and rejecting the consequences of said acts of genocide. This analysis supports the conclusion that the Genocide Convention can be applied retroactively to the genocide against the Greeks of Pontus and of Smyrna (İzmir (Tur.)). The General Assembly can, pursuant to Article 96 of the UN Charter, ask the International Court of Justice for an advisory opinion on the retroactive application of the Genocide Convention. In this connection, Greece and every state party to the Genocide Convention, can invoke Article VIII of the Convention and request the General Assembly "to take such action under the Charter of the United Nations as they consider appropriate."

Even without such an advisory opinion by the ICJ, the government of Greece or any other state party to the Genocide Convention, could invoke Article IX of the convention and submit a dispute to the ICJ, requesting a determination that the massacres against the Greeks and other Christian minorities constitute "genocide" within the meaning of the convention. States parties to the convention, including Turkey, are bound by Article IX which stipulates: "Disputes between the Contracting Parties relating to the interpretation, application, or fulfilment of the Present Convention, including those relating to the responsibility of a state for genocide or for any of the other acts enumerated in Article III, shall be submitted to the International Court of Justice at the request of any of the parties to the dispute."

The dispute is thus *prima facie* justiciable. A general challenge to the jurisdiction of the court would be subject to a determination by the ICJ of its own competence. Pursuant to Article 36, paragraph 6, of the ICJ statute, "in the event of a dispute as to whether the Court has jurisdiction, the matter shall be settled by the decision of the Court." With regard to a *ratione temporis* challenge to the court's jurisdiction, the ICJ may rely on the declaratory nature of the convention, and may also take into consideration the jurisprudence of the European Court of Human Rights and of the United Nations Human Rights Committee, concerning the issue of "continuing situations," bearing in mind that the substance of the Greek and Assyrian/Aramaean claims entails a continuing attack on the human dignity of the victims and their descendants through a continuing denial of their right to truth,[4] to their historical identity, and a denial of the restitution of centuries-old cultural heritage.

The continuation of the genocidal process is manifested by the İstanbul Pogrom[5] of 6–7 September 1955 and by the Turkish invasion of Cyprus[6] and the brutal expulsion of 180,000 Greek Cypriots from their homelands in 1974.

Logical consequences of the application of the Genocide Convention to the genocide against the Greeks and other Christian minorities should be the return of monasteries, churches and other assets of historic and cultural significance, as well as the granting of a measure of compensation to the descendants of the victims of the genocide. In this connection, the restitution and compensation schemes elaborated for the victims of the Holocaust provide a useful precedent. To the extent that any compensation may have been paid pursuant to the Treaty of Lausanne of 1923, this should be duly taken into consideration.

---

[4] On 20 April 2005 the United Nations Commission on Human Rights adopted a relevant resolution entitled the Right to Truth, UN Doc. E/CN.4/2005/66. See also Yasmin Naqvi, "The right to the truth in international law: fact or fiction?," *International Review of the Red Cross* 88 (June 2006): 245–73.

[5] Speros Vryonis, *The Mechanism of Catastrophe: The Turkish Pogrom of September 6–7, 1955* (New York: Greekworks.com, 2007); A. de Zayas, "The Istanbul Pogrom of 6–7 September 1955 in the Light of International Law," *Genocide Studies and Prevention* 2 no. 2 (August 2007): 137–55; *The Greeks of Turkey* (New York: Helsinki Watch, 1992).

[6] For a pro-Turkish point of view see Frank Hoffmeister, *Legal Aspects of the Cyprus Problem* (Leiden: Martinus Nijhoff, 2006), reviewed by A. de Zayas in *Zeitschrift für ausländisches öffentliches Recht und Völkerrecht* (2007): 987–91. See also Van Coufoudakis, *Cyprus, a Contemporary Problem in Historical Perspective* (Minneapolis: University of Minnesota Press, 2006); A. de Zayas, "Ethnic Cleansing: applicable norms, emerging jurisprudence, implementable remedies," *International Humanitarian Law: Origins, Challenges and Prospects*, John Carey and R. John Pritchard, eds. (New York: Transnational Press, 2003), 1: 283–313; A. de Zayas, "The Annan Plan and the Implantation of Turkish Settlers in the Occupied Territory of Cyprus," *Cyprus Yearbook of International Relations* I (2006): 163–179.

There is not only a legal but also a moral obligation on the part of the international community to take appropriate action in order to ensure that a measure of justice be done in respect of all victims of genocide and their descendants. A first step is the necessary recognition by Turkey of the historical reality of the genocide and of its responsibility as the successor state of the Ottoman Empire. For as long as Turkey persists on its policy of negationism,[7] it has no place in the community of European states.

1. *Historical and Legal Introduction*

For centuries, the Christian minorities of the Turkish Ottoman Empire were subjected to harassment and discrimination. Hundreds of thousands were forced to convert to Islam.[8] Non-converts had to pay higher taxes, were suspected of disloyalty by local and central authorities, and in times of armed conflict were conscripted into "labor battalions," the women, children and the elderly being deported[9] to severe weather conditions in the interior, to Kurdistan and Syria where they were decimated. Theirs has been the fate of many minorities throughout history. Following the adoption of the United Nations Convention on the Prevention and Punishment of the Crime of Genocide on 9 December 1948,[10] of the Universal Declaration of Human Rights

---

[7] Joseph Kéchichian, "The Armenian Genocide and an Updated Denial Initiative," *Genocide Studies and Prevention* 2 no. 2 (2007): 173–82.

[8] See generally Lord Kinross, *The Ottoman Centuries: The Rise and Fall of the Turkish Empire* (New York: Harper Collins Publishers, 2002); Norman Naimark, *Fires of Hatred, Ethnic Cleansing in Twentieth Century Europe* (Cambridge: Harvard University Press, 2001).

[9] "In January 1916, the Greek deportations from the Black Sea began. These Greeks came through the city of Marsovan by thousands, walking for the most part the three days' journey through the snow and mud and slush of the winter weather. Thousands fell by the wayside from exhaustion and others came into the city of Marsovan in groups of fifty, one hundred and five hundred, always under escort of Turkish gendarmes. Next morning these poor refugees were started on the road and destruction by this treatment was even more radical than a straight massacre such as the Armenians suffered before." George Horton, *The Blight of Asia, An Account of the Systematic Extermination of Christian Populations by Mohammedans and of the Culpability of Certain Great Powers; with the True Story of the Burning of Smyrna* (Indianapolis: Bobbs-Merrill Company, 1926), 194. "After leaving Samsoun on my return trip to Harpoot, I passed the old men of Samsoun, Greeks who were being deported. Many of these men were feeble with age, but in spite of that they were being pressed forward at a rate of thirty miles a day and there was no transport available for those who were weak or ill. There was no food allowance for them and any food they could obtain had to be procured by money or sale of small articles that they could carry with them. On this trip I passed many corpses of Greeks lying by the roadside where they had died from exposure. Many of these were the corpses of women and girls with their faces toward the sky, covered with flies." "Report by Stanley K. Hopkins of the Near East Relief, November 16, 1921," *Genocide*, 13: 219–20.

[10] G.A. Resolution 260 A (III) of 9 December 1948, entry into force 12 January 1951.

on 10 December 1948, of the International Covenant on Civil and Political Rights on 16 December 1966, and of the Statute of the International Criminal Court on 17 July 1998, it is to be hoped that minorities in the new millennium will be spared persecution and will be permitted to enjoy their human rights in equality with the majority populations.[11]

This paper focuses on the legal aspects of the massacres of the Greeks and Assyrians/Aramaeans living in the Ottoman Empire through the end of World War I in the light of the Genocide Convention. The same legal analysis applies to the mass killings of Greek civilians during the armed conflict that ended with the genocide of the Greeks of Pontus and of Smyrna, the expulsion of the Greek population of Anatolia, before and after the Treaty of Lausanne of 1923, the genocidal riots known as the İstanbul Pogrom of 6–7 September 1955,[12] and the 1974 Turkish invasion of Cyprus and brutal expulsion of 180,000 native Greek Cypriots from their homelands.[13] All of these events manifest a century-long genocidal process and evidence the Turkish "intent to destroy in whole or in part"[14] its non-Muslim populations. While

---

[11] Alfred de Zayas, "Minority Rights in the New Millennium," *Geneva Post Quarterly* 2 (May–June 2007): 155–208.

[12] Vryonis, *The Mechanism of Catastrophe,* 2007; Dimitris Kaloumenos, *The Crucifixion of Christianity,* fourth ed. (Athens: [n.p.], 2001).

[13] The European Commission of Human Rights and the European Court of Human Rights have repeatedly condemned the Turkish invasion of Cyprus as entailing a complex of violations of the European Convention on Human Rights, including the right to life, the right to home, family and the right to freedom of movement. See Cyprus v. Turkey, Applications Nos. 6780/74 and 6950/75, Report of 10 July 1976, application No. 8007/77, Report of 4 October 1983. In 1983 the European Commission again dealt with the issue and found that the displacement of persons, separation of families and discrimination violated the European Convention. See Christa Meindersma, "Population Transfers in Conflict Situations," *Netherlands International Law Review* (1994): 71–72. Article 1 of Protocol 1 provides, *inter alia*, that "every natural or legal person is entitled to the peaceful enjoyment of his possessions." *Loizidou v. Turkey* (Merits), No. 40/1993/ 435/514. In a Grand Chamber judgment delivered at Strasbourg on 10 May 2001 in the case of *Cyprus v. Turkey* (application no. 25781/94), the European Court of Human Rights held, by sixteen votes to one, that the matters complained of by Cyprus in its application entailed Turkey's responsibility under the European Convention on Human Rights. The Court held that there had been 14 violations of the Convention, including a continuing violation of Article 2 (right to life) of the Convention concerning the failure of the authorities of the respondent state to conduct an effective investigation into the whereabouts and fate of Greek-Cypriot missing persons who disappeared in life-threatening circumstances, and a continuing violation of Article 5 (right to liberty and security) concerning the failure of the Turkish authorities to conduct an effective investigation into the whereabouts and fate of the Greek-Cypriot missing persons in respect of whom there was an arguable claim that they were in Turkish custody at the time of their disappearance. See A. de Zayas, "The Annan Plan," *Cyprus Yearbook of International Relations* (Nicosia: KIMEDE, 2006): 163–79.

[14] Article II of the Convention on the Prevention and Punishment of the Crime of Genocide.

historical events are briefly dealt with, the reader is referred to other chapters in this book, which address the historical issues in greater detail.[15]

The punishment of the crime of genocide — whether called democide,[16] exterminations, mass atrocities, annihilation, liquidations or massacres — as well as the obligation to make restitution to the survivors of the victims were envisaged by the victorious Allies of the First World War and included in the text of the Peace Treaty of Sèvres of 10 August 1920 between the Allies and the Ottoman Empire.[17] This treaty contained not only a commitment to try Turkish officials for war crimes committed by Ottoman Turkey against Allied nationals,[18] but also for crimes committed by Turkish authorities against subjects of the Ottoman Empire of different ethnic origin, in particular the Armenians, the Greeks and the Assyrian/Aramaean Christians,[19] crimes which today would be termed genocide or crimes against humanity.

Pursuant to Article 230 of the Treaty of Sèvres:

> The Turkish Government undertakes to hand over to the Allied Powers the persons whose surrender may be required by the latter as being responsible for the massacres committed during the continuance of the state of war on territory which formed part of the Turkish Empire on 1st August 1914. The Allied Powers reserve to themselves the right to designate the Tribunal which shall try the persons so accused and the Turkish Government undertakes to recognize such Tribunal ...[20]

The principle of just restitution for the victims also existed, and was reflected in Article 144 of the Treaty of Sèvres:

> The Turkish Government recognizes the injustice of the law of 1915 relating to Abandoned Properties (Emval-I-Metruke), and of the supplementary pro-

---

[15] See also *Ethnic Cleansing in Twentieth Century Europe*, Steven Vardy and Hunt Tooley, eds. (Boulder: East European Monographs, 2003), in particular the chapters by Alfred de Zayas, "The Twentieth Century's First Genocide," 157–180, Ben Lieberman, "Ethnic Cleansing in the Greek–Turkish Conflicts from the Balkan Wars through the Treaty of Lausanne," 181–198 and Eleni Eleftheriou, "Consequences of Population Transfers: the 1923 Case of Greece and Turkey," 199–218.

[16] R. J. Rummel, *Death by Government* (Piscataway: Transaction Publishers 1994).

[17] [1920] UKTS 11, Martens, *Recueil général des traités* , 99, 3e série 12 (1924): 720.

[18] Particularly for violations of the Hague Regulations on Land Warfare, appended to the IV Hague Convention of 1907.

[19] "The Armenians are not the only subject people in Turkey which have suffered from the policy of making Turkey exclusively the country of the Turks. The story which I have told about the Armenians I could also tell with certain modifications about the Greeks and Syrians [Assyrians/Aramaeans]. Indeed the Greeks were the first victims of this nationalizing idea ...," Henry Morgenthau, *Ambassador Morgenthau's Story* (Chapter 24 "The Murder of a Nation,") (Ann Arbor: Gomidas Institute, 2000), 214.

[20] *American Journal of International Law* 15. Supplement, Official Documents (1921): 235.

visions thereof, and declares them to be null and void, in the past as in the future.

The Turkish Government solemnly undertakes to facilitate to the greatest possible extent the return to their homes and re-establishment in their businesses of the Turkish subjects of non-Turkish race who have been forcibly driven from their homes by fear of massacre or any other form of pressure since January 1, 1914. It recognizes that any immovable or movable property of the said Turkish subjects or of the communities to which they belong, which can be recovered, must be restored to them as soon as possible, in whatever hands it may be found [...] The Turkish Government agrees that arbitral commissions shall be appointed by the Council of the League of Nations wherever found necessary [...] These arbitral commissions shall hear all claims covered by this Article and decide them by summary procedure.[21]

Although Turkey signed the Treaty of Sèvres, formal ratification never followed, and the Allies did not ensure its implementation. Such failure was attributable to the growing international political disarray following the First World War, the rise of Soviet Russia, the withdrawal of British military presence from Turkey,[22] the isolationist policies of the United States, the demise of the Young Turk regime and the rise of Kemalism in Turkey. No international criminal tribunal as envisaged in Article 230 was ever established. No arbitral commissions as stipulated for in Article 144 were ever set up.

A new peace treaty eventually emerged between Kemalist Turkey and the Allies (British Empire, France, Italy, Japan, Greece, Romania, and the Serbo-Croat-Slovene state). The Treaty of Lausanne of 24 July 1923 abandoned the Allied demand for international trial and punishment of the Turks and the commitment to grant reparations to the survivors of the genocide. Instead, it approved the concept of a population "exchange" between Turkey and Greece.[23]

Notwithstanding the fact that the Treaty of Sèvres never entered into force, the text of the Treaty remains eloquent evidence of the international recognition of the crime of "massacres" against the Christian population of Turkey. And although the first tentative step toward the creation of an international criminal tribunal to punish genocide failed because of Turkish nationalism and Allied indifference, consensus on the reality of the genocide had been largely achieved.[24] Of all failures to punish the war criminals of the

---

[21] Ibid., 210.

[22] Paul Helmreich, *From Paris to Sèvres: The Partition of the Ottoman Empire at the Peace Conference of 1919-1920* (Columbus: Ohio State University Press, 1974), 131ff.

[23] G. Streit, *Der Lausanner Vertrag und der griechisch-türkische Bevölkerungsaustausch* (Berlin: Verlag von Georg Stilke, 1929).

[24] Courts martial did take place in İstanbul in 1919 in which conclusive evidence was proffered of the intent to destroy the Christian minorities of the Ottoman Empire. Several

First World War, this one was the most regrettable and it would have terrible consequences.[25]

2. *The Convention on the Prevention and Punishment of the Crime of Genocide Does Not Create a New Offense in International Criminal Law, But Is Declaratory of Pre-Existing International Law.*

As reflected in the relevant provisions of the Treaty of Sèvres, the doctrine of state responsibility for genocide and crimes against humanity already existed at the time of the Ottoman massacres against its Christian populations. Such state responsibility entailed both an obligation to provide restitution or compensation[26] and the personal criminal liability of the perpetra-

---

Turkish officials were convicted and three were executed. The proceedings have been published in Osman Selim Kocahanoğlu, *İttihat ve Terakki'nin Sorgulanması ve Yargılanması* (İstanbul: Temel Yayınları, 1998). For contemporary US press reports on these trials that relates to perpetrators of the Greek genocide, see e.g.,

http://www.greek-genocide.org/press/18031919.html;

http://www.greek-genocide.org/press/13071919.html;

http://www.greek-genocide.org/press/21011920.html.

At the Trial of the Armenian Soghomon Tehlirian in Berlin for the murder of former Minister Talât Paşa, Johannes Lepsius gave testimony concerning the statement of Count Metternich, the German Ambassador in Constantinople in 1918: "The Armenians are finished. The Young Turk gang is impatiently awaiting the moment when the Greeks will turn on Turkey. Hellenism is the cultural element of Turkey. It will be destroyed as the Armenian element was." Quoted in Merrill D. Peterson, *"Starving Armenians:" America and the Armenian Genocide, 1915–1930 and After* (Charlottesville and London: University of Virginia Press, 2004), 124. According to Tessa Hofmann, the full quote reads as follows in her translation: "Defense attorney Niemeyer: 'Is it not this way? The Armenians were the last oppressed Christian people, on whose territory and oppression Turkey could still count. All peoples of the Balkans and all others, previously oppressed by Turkey peoples had rebelled one after the other and freed themselves from Turkish rule. In order to prevent that the Armenians could do the same, their annihilations was decided. Is this view correct?' Expert Lepsius: 'Yes. Count Metternich, who was German Ambassador in Constantinople in 1918, wrote in a report of 30 June: The Armenians are finished. The Young Turkish pack now prepares with impatience for the moment, when Greece will turn against Turkey. The Greekhood [Griechentum] forms the cultural element of Turkey. In that case, it will be annihilated, as was the Armenian [element]. — That was the view of Count Metternich." *Der Völkermord an den Armeniern vor Gericht: Der Prozess Talaat Pascha*, new edition, Tessa Hofmann, ed. (Göttingen and Vienna: Gesellschaft für bedrohte Völker, 1985; reprint of the first edition, Berlin 1921), 61.

[25] James F. Willis, *Prologue to Nuremberg. The Politics and Diplomacy of Punishing War Criminals of the First World War* (Westport, Connecticut: Greenwood Press, 1982), 163.

[26] For instance, in the context of international armed conflict, Article III of the 1907 Hague Convention IV on Land Warfare stipulates: "A belligerent party which violates the provisions of the said Regulations shall, if the case demands, be liable to pay compensation. It shall be responsible for all acts committed by persons forming part of its armed forces."

tors. The norms were clear. Non-compliance with said norms by Turkey and its eventual impunity do not mean that the norms were meaningless. It only means that effective international enforcement machinery did not exist yet.

At the end of the Second World War, the victorious Allies, pursuant to the London Agreement of 8 August 1945,[27] adopted the Charter of the International Military Tribunal, which provided in Article 6(c) for the prosecution of the newly formulated "crimes against humanity," which encompassed "murder, extermination, enslavement, deportation and other inhumane acts committed against any civilian population."

In the *History of the United Nations War Crimes Commission*, we discover that the genocide against the Christian minorities in World War I was very much in the minds of the drafters of the London Agreement:

> The provisions of Article 230 of the Peace Treaty of Sèvres were obviously intended to cover, in conformity with the Allied note of 1915 [...] offences which had been committed on Turkish territory against persons of Turkish citizenship [...] This article constitutes, therefore, a precedent for Articles 6 (c) and 5 (c) of the Nuremberg and Tokyo Charters, and offers an example of one of the categories of 'crimes against humanity' as understood by these enactments.[28]

The term genocide itself was officially used in the Nuremberg indictment of 18 October 1945, charging under count 3 that the defendants had committed murder and ill-treatment of civilian populations, and, in particular:

> conducted deliberate and systematic genocide, viz., the extermination of racial and national groups, against the civilian populations of certain occupied territories in order to destroy particular races and classes of people and national, racial or religious groups ...[29]

In his concluding statement, the British prosecutor, Sir Hartley Shawcross, stated that:

> Genocide was not restricted to extermination of the Jewish people or of the Gypsies. It was applied in different forms to Yugoslavia, to the non-German inhabitants of Alsace-Lorraine, people of the Low Countries and of Norway. The techniques varied from nation to nation, from people to people. The long-term aim was the same in all cases ...[30]

By Resolution 95(1) of 11 December 1946, the General Assembly "affirms the principles of international law recognized by the Charter of the Nurem-

---

[27] 8 U.N.T.S. 279; Reprinted in 39 *American Journal of International Law*, 257 (1945) (Supp).

[28] United Nations, War Crimes Commission, *History of the United Nations War Crimes Commission and the Development of the Laws of War*, 45.

[29] *Trial of the Major War Criminals before the International Military Tribunal, Nuremberg, 14 November 1945 - 1 October 1946* (Nuremberg 1947), 1: 43-44.

[30] Ibid., 19: 497-98.

berg Tribunal and the judgment of the Tribunal," and in Resolution 96(1) of the same date, it confirmed "that genocide is a crime in international law, which the civilized world condemns, and for the commission of which principals and accomplices — whether private individuals, public officials or statesmen, and whether the crime is committed on religious, racial, political or any other grounds — are punishable."[31]

On 9 December 1948, the United Nations General Assembly adopted the Convention on the Prevention and Punishment of the Crime of Genocide, in which the parties "*confirm* that genocide, whether committed in time of peace or in time of war, is a crime under international law which they undertake to prevent and to punish." [*emphasis added*].

In the classic Oppenheim/Lauterpacht textbook on *International Law*, Professor Hersh Lauterpacht noted that the convention was not only forward-looking but that it had a primary retrospective significance:

> It is apparent that, to a considerable extent, the Convention amounts to a registration of protest against past misdeeds of individual or collective savagery rather than to an effective instrument of their prevention or repression. Thus, as the punishment of acts of genocide is entrusted primarily to the municipal courts of the countries concerned, it is clear that such acts, if perpetrated in obedience to national legislation, must remain unpunished unless penalized by way of retroactive laws. On the other hand, the Convention obliges the Parties to enact and keep in force legislation intended to prevent and suppress such acts, and any failure to measure up to that obligation is made subject to the jurisdiction of the International Court of Justice and of the United Nations. With regard to the latter, the result of the provision in question is that acts of commission or omission in respect of genocide are no longer, on any interpretation of the Charter, considered to be a matter exclusively within the domestic jurisdiction of the States concerned. For the Parties expressly concede to the United Nations the right of intervention in this sphere. This aspect of the situation constitutes a conspicuous feature of the Genocide Convention — a feature which probably outweighs, in its legal and moral significance, the gaps, artificialities and possible dangers of the Convention.[32]

In this context, it is useful to look once again at the language of the convention, which does not purport to create a new crime, but recognizes in the preamble "that at all periods of history genocide has inflicted great losses on humanity" and in Article 1 "The Contracting Parties confirm that genocide,

---

[31] Official Records of the First Session of the General Assembly, Fifty-fifth plenary meeting (11 December 1946), 188–89. See also Preamble of the Genocide Convention.

[32] Oppenheim/Lauterpacht, *International Law*, eighth ed. (1955), 1: 751. He adds: "It is clear that as a matter of law the Genocide Convention cannot impair the effectiveness of existing international obligations."

whether committed in time of peace or in time of war, is a crime under international law ..." It is important to note that the contracting parties do not "declare" or "proclaim" for the future, but "confirm" that genocide is an international crime.

Moreover, in the view of leading publicists in public international law, the Genocide Convention of 1948 was not constitutive of a new offense in international law termed "genocide," but was declaratory of the pre-existing crime;[33] in other words, the convention merely codified the prohibition of genocide, which was already binding international law. In this sense, the convention is necessarily both retrospective and future-oriented.

What the Genocide Convention added to the existing body of international law was a clearer definition of the elements of genocide, most importantly the "intent to destroy in whole or in part"[34] a given group. The convention also stipulated an affirmative obligation on states parties to make provision for effective penalties for all acts punishable under the convention (Article V), a duty to prosecute (Article VI) by a competent national tribunal or by an international criminal court to be established. The convention also creates a preventive mechanism by urging states to call upon organs of the United Nations to take appropriate measures (Article VIII), and confers jurisdiction on the International Court of Justice in all matters relating to the Genocide Convention, including determination of the responsibility of a state for genocide (Article IX).

In its 1951 advisory opinion, the International Court of Justice stated that "the principles underlying the Convention are principles which are recognized by civilized nations as binding on all states, even without any conven-

---

[33] Nehemiah Robinson, *The Genocide Convention: A Commentary* (New York: Institute of Jewish Affairs, 1960); Leo Kuper, *International Action Against Genocide* (London: Minority Rights Group, 1984); "Genocide," by Hans Heinrich Jescheck in *Encyclopaedia of Public International Law*, R. Bernhardt, ed. (New York: Elsevier Science Publishing, 2000). Dieter Blumenwitz, *Rechtsgutachten über die Verbrechen an den Deutschen in Jugoslawien 1944–48* (Munich: Juristische Studien, 2002), 26–27, where Professor Blumenwitz affirms the retroactive application of the Genocide Convention to the killing of some 200,000 civilians, members of the ethnic German minority in Yugoslavia, by Tito partisans and militia in 1944–45. Christian Tomuschat, "Die Vertreibung der Sudetendeutschen. Zur Frage des Bestehens von Rechtsansprüchen nach Völkerrecht und deutschem Recht," in *Zeitschrift für Ausländisches öffentliches Recht und Völkerrecht* 56 (1996): 1–69; Felix Ermacora, *Die Sudetendeutschen Fragen* (Munich: Langen-Müller Verlag, 1992), 178, where Professor Ermacora affirms the retroactive application of the Genocide Convention to the killing of some 250,000 civilians, members of the German ethnic minority of Czechoslovakia, in 1945–46.

[34] Article II of the Convention.

tional obligation."[35] Also in this sense, the UN Commission on Human Rights[36] noted in 1969 that "It is therefore taken for granted that as a codification of existing international law the Convention on the Prevention and Punishment of the Crime of Genocide did neither extend nor restrain the notion genocide, but that it only defined it more precisely."[37]

Even though the Genocide Convention has not been universally ratified, the prohibition of genocide must be deemed to be *jus cogens.*[38] As of April 2010, 141 of the 192 member states of the United Nations had ratified the convention. Moreover, as the International Court of Justice elaborated in the *Barcelona Traction Case* (second phase), there are distinctions to be drawn between state obligations arising *vis-à-vis* another state and obligations *erga omnes*, or "towards the international community as a whole." The court stated:

> By its very nature, the outlawing of genocide, aggression, slavery and racial discrimination are the concern of all states. In view of the importance of the rights involved, all states can be held to have a legal interest in their protection; they are obligations *erga omnes* ...[39]

It is precisely because of its *erga omnes* quality that the crime of genocide cannot be subject to prescription, and that state responsibility for the crime, i.e. the obligation of the genocidal state to make reparation, does not lapse with time. This is independent of a determination whether or not the Genocide Convention applies retroactively to the Holocaust or to the genocide against the Greeks and the Assyrian/Aramaean Christians.

3. *Non-Prescription of the Crime of Genocide*

When the United Nations drafted the Convention on the Non-Applicability of Statutory Limitations to War Crimes and Crimes Against Humanity (adopted 26 November 1968, in force 11 November 1970), it clearly and

---

[35] Reservations to the Convention on the Prevention and Punishment of the Crime of Genocide, Advisory Opinion, ICJ Reports (1951): 15–69. See Diane F. Orentlicher, "Genocide," *Crimes of War*, Roy Gutman and David Rieff, eds. (New York: W. W. Norton, 1999), 153–57. Joe Verhoeven, "Le Crime de Génocide," *Revue belge de droit international* 24 (1991): 13.

[36] Established by ECOSOC in 1946, held 62 sessions until its dissolution in 2006, predecessor of the new UN Human Rights Council.

[37] Report of the *ad hoc* working group of experts established under Resolution 2(XXIII) and 2(XXIV) of the Commission on Human Rights, Doc. E/CN.4/1984/Add. 18.

[38] Ian Brownlie, *Principles of Public International Law*, fourth ed. (Oxford: Clarendon Press, 1990), 513.

[39] *Barcelona Traction, Light and Power Co., Ltd (Belgium v. Spain),* ICJ Reports (1970) 3 at 32.

deliberately pronounced its retroactive application. In Article 1 it stipulated "No statutory limitation shall apply to the following crimes, *irrespective of the date of their commission...* the crime of genocide as defined in the 1948 Convention.... " [*emphasis added*].

The principle of *nullum crimen sine lege, nulla poena sine lege praevia* (no crime without law, no penalty without previous law), laid out in paragraph 1 of Article 15 of the International Covenant on Civil and Political Rights is conditioned as follows in paragraph 2: "Nothing in this article shall prejudice the trial and punishment of any person for any act or omission which, at the time when it was committed, was criminal according to the general principles of law recognized by the community of nations."

Similarly, Article 11, paragraph 2, of the Universal Declaration of Human Rights of 10 December 1948 stipulates that the prohibition of *ex post facto* penal sanctions does not apply if the offence was an offence under national or international law.

In this context it is relevant to recall the double vocation of the Genocide Convention, namely to prevent and to punish the crime of genocide. In order to prevent genocide, it is important to deter future offenders by ensuring the *punishment* of prior offenders. Indeed, the punishment of Nazi officials for participation in the crime of genocide has made the horrible reality of genocide visible and concrete, so that genocide can be perceived by all to be a heinous crime. One consequence of the universal recognition that genocide is a crime is that the criminal, besides being condemned and punished for the crime, is not allowed to keep the fruits of the crime. Confiscated Jewish properties have thus been returned to the survivors or to their heirs, or appropriate compensation has been paid. This illustrates the principle that, together with the recognition of genocide as a crime under international law there is also an international duty to undo its effects and to grant restitution and compensation to the victims and their heirs.

Although Turkey is not a state party to the Convention on the Non-Applicability of Statutory Limitations to War Crimes and Crimes Against Humanity, international law is clear on the subject: there is no prescription on the prosecution of the crime of genocide, regardless of when the genocide occurred, and the obligation of the responsible state to make restitution or pay compensation for properties obtained by means of genocide does not lapse with time.[40]

---

[40] General Assembly Resolutions 2538 (XXIV) of 15 December 1968; 2583/ (XXIV of 15 December 1969, 2712 (XXV) of 15 December 1970: 2840 (XXVI) of 18 December 1971, 3029 (XXVII) of 18 December 1972; 3074 (XXVIII) of 3 December 1973, etc.

In its judgment of 6 October 1983 in the case concerning Klaus Barbie, the French *Cour de Cassation* rejected the objections of the defense and stated that the prohibition on statutory limitations for crimes against humanity is now part of customary international law.[41] France also enacted a law on 26 December 1964 dealing with crimes against humanity as *"imprescriptibles"* by nature (Nouveau Code penal de 1994, Arts. 211-1 to 213-5).[42]

4. *International and National Prosecution of Genocide*

The crime of genocide was one of the charges against the accused in three of the twelve successor trials held at Nuremberg pursuant to Control Council Law No. 10, before U.S. military tribunals following the international military tribunal proceedings. In *United States v. Alstötter,* the Court made repeated reference to General Assembly Resolution 96(I):

> The General Assembly is not an international legislature, but it is the most authoritative organ in existence for the interpretation of world opinion. Its recognition of genocide as an international crime [in Resolution 96(I)] is persuasive evidence of the fact. We approve and adopt its conclusions... [We] find no injustice to persons tried for such crimes. They are chargeable with knowledge that such acts were wrong and were punishable when committed[43]

In the *Einsatzgruppen* trial, the defendants were charged with participation in a

> systematic program of genocide, aimed at the destruction of foreign nations and ethnic groups, in part by murderous extermination, and in part by elimination and suppression of national characteristics.[44]

The first national prosecutions specifically on the crime of genocide, but without reference to the Genocide Convention, which had not yet been adopted, were carried out by Polish courts. Thus, in July 1946, Artur Greiser was charged with and convicted of genocide.[45]

The leading prosecution by a national court, with reference to the Genocide Convention, was carried out by the State of Israel. In 1960 Adolf Eichmann, a Nazi official in World War II, was abducted from Argentina and taken to Is-

---

[41] *Fédération nationale des deportés et internés et patriots et al v. Barbie,* 78 *International Law Reports* 125: 135. See Nicholas R. Doman, "Aftermath of Nuremberg: The Trial of Klaus Barbie," *Colorado Law Review* 60 (1989): 449.

[42] Jacques Francillon, "Aspects juridiques des crimes contre l'humanité," in *L'actualité du Génocide des Arméniens* (Paris: Edipol, 1999), 398.

[43] *United States of America v. Alstötter et al.,* (1948) 6 LRTWC 1, 3TWC 1: 983.

[44] *United States of America v. Greifeldt et al.,* (1948) 13 LRTWC 1: 2.

[45] *Poland v. Greiser (1948)* 13 LRTWC 70 (Supreme National Tribunal of Poland).

rael for trial under Israeli law for his involvement in the genocide against the Jews during the war. Eichmann was prosecuted under the "Nazi and Nazi Collaborators (Punishment) law of 1951," which was modeled on the genocide provision of the 1948 Genocide Convention.[46] He was charged with four counts of genocide corresponding to the first four subparagraphs of Article II of the convention: killing Jews, causing serious physical and mental harm, placing Jews in living conditions calculated to bring about their physical destruction, and imposing measures intended to prevent births among Jews.[47]

Eichmann challenged the jurisdiction of the Israeli Court with reference to Article 6 of the Genocide Convention, which stipulates:

> Persons charged with genocide or any of the other acts enumerated in Article III shall be tried by a competent tribunal of the State in the territory of which the act was committed, or by such international penal tribunal as may have jurisdiction with respect to those Contracting Parties which shall have accepted its jurisdiction.

In rejecting Eichmann's objections, the district court held:

> We must... draw a clear distinction between the first part of Article 1, which lays down that "the Contracting Parties confirm that genocide, whether committed in time of peace or in time of war, is a crime under international law" — a general provision which confirms a principle of customary international law as "binding on States, even without any conventional obligation" — and Article 6, which comprises a special provision undertaken by the contracting parties with regard to the trial of crimes that may be committed in the future.

Specifically on the issue of retroactivity, the Supreme Court of Israel endorsed the view of the district court concerning the customary nature of the crime of genocide, and noted that "the enactment of the law was not from the point of view of international law a legislative act which conflicted with the principle *nulla poena* [no penalty without previous law] or the operation of which was retroactive, but rather one by which the Knesset gave effect to international law and its objectives."[48]

A number of courts in the United States have dealt with the question of *ex post facto* legislation by relying on the judgment of the International Military Tribunal at Nuremberg to the effect that the Nuremberg Charter was declarative of international law and was not new law. In allowing the extradition

---

[46] *A-G Israel v. Eichmann* (1968) 36 ILR 5 (District Court of Jerusalem), paragraphs 20–22. District Court Jerusalem, 11 December 1961 "*The Attorney General of the Government of Israël v. Eichmann* (case No. 40/61)" *American Journal of International Law* (1962): 814.

[47] Schabas, *Genocide in International Law*, 387.

[48] *Attorney-General v. Eichmann* , (1968) 36 ILR 277, paragraph 11.

to Israel of John Demjanjuk, the United States District Court for Ohio and the Circuit Court for the sixth Circuit held:

> The Nuremberg International Military Tribunal provided a new forum in which to prosecute persons accused of war crimes committed during World War II pursuant to an agreement of the wartime Allies, see The Nuremberg Tribunal, 6 F.R.D. 69. That tribunal consistently rejected defendants' claims that they were being tried under *ex post facto* laws. Id.... the statute is not retroactive because it is jurisdictional and does not create a new crime. Thus, Israel has not violated any prohibition against the *ex post facto* applications of criminal laws which may exist in international law.[49]

There are many other precedents of retrospective application of international law in other countries in matters concerning genocide. For instance, in the case of *Regina v. Imre Finta* in Canada, a trial for "crimes against humanity" was carried out on the basis of a 1987 Canadian statute that permits retrospective application of international law. In its judgment the court recognized the existence of "crimes against humanity" under international law before 1945.[50]

The practice of courts in other countries also vindicates the validity of the principles contained in the Genocide Convention. Although prosecution has not been based on the Genocide Convention itself but rather on German penal law, the Federal Republic of Germany has prosecuted more than sixty thousand Germans and other nationals for war crimes and complicity in the crime of genocide committed during World War II, prior to the entry into force of the Genocide Convention, and many judgments make reference to the Genocide Convention. The German Government has similarly recognized its international obligation to make restitution of property stolen from victims of genocide and to grant compensation to the survivors of the victims.[51]

It is important to note, moreover, that whether or not the Genocide Convention itself applies in a concrete situation, state practice and, in particular the Eichmann case, shows that the crime of genocide can be prosecuted on the basis of national law enacted following the commission of the offence. *A fortiori* civil liability for genocide can also be imposed on the basis of *ex post facto* legislation.

---

[49] *In the Matter of the Extradition of John Demjanjuk*, 612 F. Supp. 544 (DC Ohio 1985): 554–58.

[50] *Regina v. Finta*, 50 C.C.C. (3d) 247; 61 D.L.R. 85 (fourth ed., 1989). See also Green, *Canadian Law, War Crimes and Crimes Against Humanity*, 59; *British Yearbook of International Law*, (1988) 217; Cherif Bassiouni, *Crimes Against Humanity* (Dordrecht: Kluwer Academic Publishers, 1992), 144, 226–27.

[51] Schabas, *Genocide in International Law*, 443.

5. *The Doctrine of State Responsibility for Wrongful Acts*

A general principle of international law stipulates that a state is responsible for injuries caused by its wrongful acts and is bound to provide reparation for such injury.[52] The Permanent Court of International Justice enunciated this principle in the *Chorzow Factory Case* as follows: "it is a principle of international law, and even a general conception of law, that any breach of an engagement involves an obligation to make reparation." [53] It should be stressed that the wrong in question is not just a mere violation of international law engaging inter-state responsibility, but the gravest criminal violation of international law engaging, as the International Court of Justice has determined, international responsibility *erga omnes* — an obligation of the state toward the international community as a whole.

Thus, the international crime of genocide imposes obligations not only on the state that perpetrated the genocide, but also on the entire international community: (a) not to recognize as legal a situation created by an international crime, (b) not to assist the author of an international crime in maintaining the illegal situation, and (c) to assist other states in the implementation of the aforementioned obligations.[54] In a very real sense, the legal impact of the *erga omnes* nature of the crime of genocide goes far beyond the mere retroactivity of application of the Genocide Convention. It imposes an affirmative obligation on the international community not to recognize an illegal situation resulting from genocide. The mechanism of international mediation and conciliation can be called upon to design appropriate schemes to redress the wrong.

---

[52] Malcolm N. Shaw, *International Law* (Cambridge, Cambridge University Press, 2003), 481: "A breach of an international obligation gives rise to a requirement for reparation."; Wladyslaw Czaplinski, "State Succession and State Responsibility," *Canadian Yearbook of International Law* 339 (1991): "State responsibility is a legal relationship created through the violation of an international legal obligation by a State; that violation gives rise to the duty to compensate for any resulting damage, one of the oldest principles of international law and universally recognized in international practice." Karl Zemanek, "Responsibility of States: General Principles," in *Encyclopedia of Public International Law,* Bernhardt, ed., 4: 219–29; Mohammed Bedjaoui, "Responsibility of States: Fault and Strict Liability," *ibid.*, 212–16; Irwin Cotler, "Confiscated Jewish Property: The Holocaust, Thefticide and Restitution: A Legal Perspective," *Cardozo Law Review* 20 (December 1998): 601–24.

[53] *Chorzow Factory Case (Germany v. Poland)*, P.C.I.J. (ser. A) no. 17 (1928): 29. Ignaz Seidl-Hohenveldern, "German Interests in Polish Upper Silesia Cases," in *Encyclopedia of Public International Law*, R. Bernhardt, ed. (Max Planck Institute for Comparative Public Law and International Law, 1995), 2: 550–53.

[54] Zemanek, "Responsibility of States," 226.

6. *Doctrine of State Succession*

Turkey is responsible not only for the discrimination, persecution and killing of Greeks and Assyrians/Aramaeans that continued after the demise of the Ottoman Empire, but, as the successor state, it is also responsible for the crimes perpetrated by the empire. In the report of the independent expert on the right to restitution, compensation and rehabilitation for victims of grave violations of human rights, Professor M. Cherif Bassiouni reiterated a basic principle of state succession:

> In international law, the doctrine of legal continuity and principles of State responsibility make a successor Government liable in respect of claims arising from a former government's violations.[55]

This applies *a fortiori* in the case of genocide and its consequences for the survivors and their descendants, because state responsibility necessarily attaches to the state itself and does not allow for *tabula rasa*. Thus, it was consistent with international law for the Federal Republic of Germany to assume full responsibility for the crimes committed by the Third Reich. This has also been the case with regard to the responsibility of France to repair the wrongs committed by the Vichy Government during the German occupation, and of Norway to grant restitution for confiscations and other injuries perpetrated on Jewish persons during the Quisling regime.[56]

Article 36 of the Vienna Convention on Succession of States in Respect of State Property, Archives and Debts of 8 April 1983[57] provides that a succession of states does not "as such affect the rights and obligations of creditors." Thus, the claims of the Greek and Assyrian/Aramaean Christians for their wrongfully confiscated properties did not disappear with the change from the sultanate to the regime of Mustafa Kemal.[58]

The principle of responsibility of successor states has been held to apply even when the state and government that committed the wrong were not that of the successor state. This principle was formulated, *inter alia*, by the Permanent Court of Arbitration in the *Lighthouse Arbitration* case.[59] There

---

[55] UN Commission on Human Rights, Document E/CN.4/1999/65.

[56] Björn Westlie, *Coming to Terms with the Past: the Process of Restitution of Jewish Property in Norway*, Policy Forum, no. 12 (New York: Institute of the World Jewish Congress, 1996).

[57] UN Doc A/Conf.117/14.

[58] Cf. Kevork K. Baghdjian, *La confiscation, par le gouvernement turc, des biens arméniens... dits abandonnés* (Montréal: K.K. Baghdjian, 1987).

[59] *Lighthouses Arbitration between France and Greece*, 23 International Law Reports: 659–76. C. Rousseau, "L'affaire franco-hellénique des phares et la sentence arbitrale du 24 juillet 1956," *Révue Générale due Droit International Public* 63 (1959): 248–92. J. P. Mon-

France claimed that Greece was responsible for a breach of state concessions to its citizens by the autonomous State of Crete, committed before Greece's assumption of sovereignty over Crete. The PCA held that Greece was obligated to compensate for Crete's breaches, because Greece was the successor state.

The principle of state succession undoubtedly applies to the Eastern European states, and, in particular, to Serbia–Montenegro for the crimes committed by the Federal Republic of Yugoslavia.[60] State practice, decisions of international tribunals and decisions of domestic courts support this conclusion.

7. *The Remedy of Restitution Has Not Lapsed Because of Prescription*

Article 6 (Section IV) of the *United Nations Basic Principles and Guidelines on the Right to a Remedy and Reparation for Victims of Gross Violations of International Human Rights Law and Serious Violations of International Humanitarian Law*, adopted by the General Assembly on 16 December 2005, stipulates:

> [...] statutes of limitations shall not apply to gross violations of international human rights law and serious violations of international humanitarian law.[61]

Because of the continuing character of the crime of genocide in factual and legal terms, the remedy of restitution has not been foreclosed by the passage of time.[62] Thus the survivors of the genocide against the Greeks and Assyri-

---

nier, "La succession d'Etats en matière de responsabilité internationale," *AFDI* 8 (1962): 80–85.

[60] For the question of the Federal Republic of Yugoslavia's status *vis-à-vis* the Genocide Convention, see Matthew Craven, "The Genocide Case, the Law of Treaties and State Succession," *British Yearbook of International Law* (Oxford: University Press, 1997), 127–63. In its Judgment of 26 February 2007 in *Application of the Convention on the Prevention and Punishment of the Crime of Genocide (Bosnia and Herzegovina v. Serbia and Montenegro)*, the International Court of Justice affirmed the continuity between the State of Serbia and the former State of Serbia and Montenegro and between the State of Serbia and the former Socialist Federal Republic of Yugoslavia. In its judgment the ICJ found that Serbia had violated the obligation to prevent genocide in respect of the genocide that occurred in Srebrenica in July 1995, that it had violated its obligations under the Genocide Convention by failing to transfer Ratko Mladic, indicted for genocide and complicity in genocide, and for failing to cooperate with the International Criminal Tribunal, and that Serbia had violated its obligations to comply with the provisional measures ordered by the ICJ on 8 April and 13 September 1993.

[61] UN General Assembly Resolution 60/147, 16 December 2005.

[62] A leading international law expert in Europe, Professor Felix Ermacora, member of the UN Human Rights Committee, member of the European Commission on Human Rights, and Special Rapporteur for Afghanistan and Chile of the UN Commission on Human Rights, maintained this view. In a legal opinion on the continuing obligation to grant restitution to the expelled Germans from Czechoslovakia, some 250,000 of whom had per-

an/Aramaean Christians, both individually and collectively, have standing to advance a claim for restitution. This has been also the case with Jewish survivors of the Holocaust, who have successfully claimed restitution against many states where their property had been confiscated.[63] Whenever possible *restitutio in integrum* (complete restitution, restoration to the previous condition) should be granted, so as to re-establish the situation that existed before the violation occurred. But where *restitutio in integrum* is not possible, compensation may be substituted as a remedy.

Restitution remains a continuing state responsibility also because of Turkey's current human rights obligations under international treaty law, particularly the corpus of international human rights law.

The United Nations subcommission's earlier *Basic Principles and Guidelines on the Right to Reparation for Victims of Gross Violations of Human Rights and International Humanitarian Law* provide in part:

> Reparation may be claimed individually and where appropriate collectively, by the direct victims of violations of human rights and international humanitarian law, the immediate family, dependants or other persons or groups of persons closely connected with the direct victims.

Particularly important are Principle 9,

> Civil claims relating to reparations for gross violations of human rights and international humanitarian law shall not be subject to statutes of limitations.

and Principle 12,

> Restitution shall be provided to re-establish the situation that existed prior to the violations of human rights or international humanitarian law. Restitu-

---

ished in the course of their ethnic cleansing 1945–46, Ermacora wrote: "Ist die Konfiskation von Privatvermögen Teil eines Völkermordes, so ist auch ihre Rechtsnatur Teil eines Rechtsganzen. D.h. der Vermögensentzug hatte für sich selbst im vorliegenden Gesamtzusammenhang Völkermordcharakter. Er unterliegt auch der Beurteilung aufgrund der Völkeremordkonvention, deren Partner sowohl die BRD als auch die Tschechoslowakei ist. Entsprechend den Regeln internationalen Rechts sind die Akte des Völkermordes — so auch die Vernichtung von Lebensbedingungen, wie sie durch einen totalen Vermögensentzug stattgefunden haben und mit der Vertreibung kombiniert waren, zumindest nach der Konvention über die Nichtverjährbarkeit von Verbrechen gegen die Menschlichkeit nicht verjährbar." Ermacora, *Die Sudetendeutschen Fragen*, 178.

[63] Cotler, "Confiscated Jewish Property," 609. Sabine Thomsen, "Restitution," in *Encyclopedia of Public International Law*, Bernhardt, ed., 4: 229–32; Irwin Cotler, "Nuremberg 50 years later: The restitution of Jewish Property and Norwegian Justice," *Nordic Journal of International Law* 3 (1998): 275–87.

tion requires, *inter alia*, ... return to one's place of residence and restoration of... property.[64]

UN sub-commission member Mr. Louis Joinet presented two reports containing comparable language:

> Any human rights violation gives rise to a right to reparation on the part of the victim or his beneficiaries, implying a duty on the part of the state to make reparation and the possibility of seeking redress from the perpetrator.[65]

In 2002, the UN Sub-Commission for the Promotion and Protection of Human Rights appointed Paulo Sergio Pinheiro (Brazil) as the UN Special Rapporteur on Housing and Property Restitution. In 2005, Pinheiro released his report, now known as the "Pinheiro Principles," which reaffirms and strengthens the prior work of Louis Joinet, Theo van Boven and Cherif Bassiouni.[66]

Although the International Criminal Court, established in July 2002, does not have jurisdiction to examine instances of genocide having occurred prior to the entry into force of the Rome Statute, it does reaffirm the international law obligation of providing reparation to victims. Article 75, paragraph 1, of the statute stipulates that "The Court shall establish principles relating to reparations," which it defines as restitution, compensation and rehabilitation.

In the context of reparation for gross violations of human rights, two other general principles are relevant. The principle *ex injuria non oritur jus* (from a wrong no right arises), that no state should be allowed to profit from its own violations of law, and the principle of "unjust enrichment."[67] It is a general

---

[64] UN Commission on Human Rights, fifty-third session, Doc. E/CN.4/1997/104. Compare with the first report by Professor Theo van Boven C/CH.4/Sub.2/1993/8 of 2 July 1993, section IX, and the second report C/CN.4/Sub.2/1996/7 of 24 May 1996.

[65] Special Rapporteur Louis Joinet, Principle 36 in document E/CN.4/Sub.23/1997/20 of 26 June 1997 and Principle 33 in Document E/CN.4/Sub.2/1997/20/Rev.1 of 2 October 1997.

[66] U.N. Doc. E/CN.4/Sub.2/2005/17 (2005) ("Pinheiro Principles") *endorsed* Sub-Com. res. 2005/21, U.N. Doc. E/CN.4/2006/2 at 39 (2006).

http://domino.un.org/pdfs/ocha_pinheiro_principles.pdf.

See also OHCHR/FAO/IDMC/NRC/OCHA/UN-Habitat/UNHCR: *Housing and Property Restitution for Refugees and Displaced Persons: Implementing the 'Pinheiro Principles,'* 2007. See also the Report of Special Rapporteur Awn Shawkat Al Khasawneh on the Human Rights Dimensions of Population Transfers, UN Doc E/CN. 4/Sub. 2/1997/23, including the appended Declaration, which affirms the right to restitution, and the pertinent Sub-Commission Resolutions 2002/30 and 2005/21.

[67] Peter D. Maddaugh and John D. McCamus, *Law of Restitution* (Ontario: Aurora, 1990), 484–93. Even in the Old Testament we find an admonition against unjust enrichment, 1 Kings 21:19 (King James Version): "Thus saith the Lord, Hast thou killed, and also taken

principle of law that the criminal cannot keep the fruits of the crime.[68] The lands, buildings, bank accounts and other property of the Greek and Christian Assyrian/Aramaean communities in the former Ottoman Empire and in Kemalist Turkey were systematically confiscated. Should there be no restitution for this act of mass theft, accompanying, as it did, the ultimate crime of genocide? In denying the applicability of statutes of limitation to restitution claims by survivors of the Holocaust, Professor Irwin Cotler argues:

> The paradigm here is not that of restitution in a domestic civil action involving principles of civil and property law, or restitution in an international context involving state responsibility in matters of appropriation of property of aliens; rather, the paradigm — if there can be such a paradigm in so abhorrent a crime — is that of restitution for Nuremberg crimes, which is something dramatically different in precedent and principles ... Nuremberg crimes are *imprescribable*,[69] or Nuremberg law — or international laws anchored in Nuremberg Principles — does not recognize the applicability of statutes of limitations, as set forth in the Convention on the Non-Applicability of Statutory Limitations to War Crimes and Crimes Against Humanity.[70]

The same argument applies with respect to the survivors of the genocide against the Greeks and the Christian Assyrians/Aramaeans and their descendants. It is an enduring challenge to international morality that Turkey continues to benefit from the cultural heritage, the lands and buildings of the victims of genocide.

In this context it is important to recall the obligations of states parties under the International Covenant on Civil and Political Rights (ratified by Turkey on 23 September 2003, entry into force 23 December 2003), in particular the obligations that result from Article 1, which stipulates the rights of peo-

---

possession?" The story is that Naboth, a man from Jezreel, had a vineyard on the outskirts of the city near King Ahab's palace. The king coveted the land, because it was convenient to his palace, but Naboth did not want to sell, because the vineyard had been in his family for generations. Jezebel, Ahab's wife, persuaded the king to have Naboth falsely accused of blasphemy and stoned to death. When King Ahab went to take possession of the vineyard, Elijah came to him and admonished the king: "Isn't killing Naboth bad enough? Must you rob him, too? Because you have done this, dogs shall lick your blood outside the city just as they licked the blood of Naboth!," *The Living Bible* (new translation) (Wheaton, Illinois: Tyndale House Publishers, 1971).

[68] J. W. Wade, "Acquisition of Property by willfully killing another – A Statutory Solution," *Harvard Law Review* 49 (1936): 715ff; W. M. McGovern, "Homicide and Succession to Property," *Michigan Law Review* 68 (1969): 65ff. There is ample case law stating that "it is against public policy for a person who is guilty of feloniously killing another to take any benefit in that other person's estate." Re Johnson, (1950) 2 D.L.R. 69: 75–76 D.L.R., 1 W.W.R. 263.

[69] Sic: imprescriptible or indefeasible.

[70] Cotler, "Confiscated Jewish Property," 621.

ples to self-determination and their right to their natural wealth and resources, as well as the obligations resulting from Article 27, which provides for special treatment of ethnic and cultural minorities. It would follow that "historical inequities" should be redressed, and that the Greek, Assyrian/Aramaean and Armenian peoples are entitled, both under Articles 1 and 27 of the covenant, to the return of their cultural heritage. Pertinent in this context is the decision of the United Nations Human Rights Committee in case No. 167/1984, *Lubicon Lake Band v. Canada*, where the committee determined that there had been a violation of Article 27 and commented: "Historical inequities, to which the State party refers, and certain more recent developments threaten the way of life and culture of the Lubicon Lake Band, and constitute a violation of Article 27 so long as they continue."[71]

Article 11 (Section VII) of the 2005 UN Basic Principles and Guidelines stipulates the victims' right to remedies: "Remedies for gross violations of international human rights law and serious violations of international humanitarian law include the victim's right to the following as provided for under international law:

> (a) Equal and effective access to justice;
>
> (b) Adequate, effective and prompt reparation for harm suffered;
>
> (c) Access to relevant information concerning violations and reparation mechanisms."[72]

Articles 15–20 address in greater detail the reparation to which victims are entitled. Article 15 stipulates in part "Reparation should be proportional to the gravity of the violation and the harm suffered." Article 18 provides in part that,

> ... victims of gross violations of international human rights law and serious violations of international humanitarian law should, as appropriate and proportional to the gravity of the violation and the circumstances of each case, be provided with full and effective reparation, as laid out in principles 19 to 23, which include the following forms: restitution, compensation, rehabilitation, satisfaction and guarantees of non-repetition.[73]

8. *A Red Herring: The Genocide Convention and the Principle of Non-Retroactivity*

The international debate over the genocide committed by the Ottoman Empire on its Christian minorities has recently experienced a new variant: It is

---

[71] *Selected Decisions of the Human Rights Committee under the Optional Protocol*, 3:78. UN Doc CCPR/C/OP/3, New York and Geneva 2002.

[72] UN Doc. A/RES/60/147.

[73] Ibid.

argued that even if the Armenians, the Greeks, and the Assyrian/Aramaean Christians were subjected to genocide, there is little that can be done about it today, because the Genocide Convention cannot be applied retroactively.[74] This theory contains two fallacies: 1) that the claims of the victims are exclusively derived from the Genocide Convention, and 2) that the convention cannot be applied retroactively.

It is clear from the above that the claims originate in the doctrine of state responsibility for crimes against humanity, and that this international liability pre-dated the entry into force of the Genocide Convention. As shown above, the Turkish liability for genocide was confirmed in Articles 230 and 144 of the Treaty of Sèvres of 1920. The German liability for the Holocaust was reflected in the London Agreement of 1945, both predating the convention.

As to the general principle of non-retroactivity of treaties, however, it is important to note that this principle admits of many exceptions and, in any event, is not a peremptory norm of international law.[75] Admittedly, the positivist approach to international law relies on a presumption of non-retroactivity, as noted by Professor Charles Rousseau: "International law appears to be determined by the principle of non-retroactivity. This principle is the result of treaty, diplomatic and judicial practice."[76]

Moreover, Article 28 of the Vienna Convention on the Law of Treaties provides that,

> Unless a different intention appears from the treaty or is otherwise established, its provisions do not bind a party in relation to any act or fact which took place or any situation which ceased to exist before the date of the entry into force of the treaty with respect to that party.

---

[74] The doctrine of "continuing effects" trumps this attempt to deprive victims of compensation. Moreover, the İstanbul Pogrom of 6–7 September 1955 occurred long after the entry into force of the Genocide Convention for Turkey. The İstanbul Pogrom constitutes one of many events in the genocidal process of destroying "in whole or in part" the Greek minority under Turkish jurisdiction.

[75] Ian Sinclair, *The Vienna Convention on the Law of Treaties*, second ed. (1984), 85; Vahakn N. Dadrian, "The Armenian Genocide and the Legal and Political Issues in the Failure to Prevent or Punish the Crime," 29 *U. West. L.A. L. Rev.* 43 (1998); Vahakn N. Dadrian, "Genocide as a Problem of National and International Law: the World War I Armenian Case and its Contemporary Legal Ramifications," *Yale Journal of International Law* 14, no. 2 (Summer 1989): 221–334; John Shamsey, "Comment: 80 Years Too Late: The International Criminal Court and the 20th Century's First Genocide," *Journal of Transnational Law & Policy* 11 (Spring 2002): 327.

[76] Charles Rousseau, *Principes Généraux du droit international public*, 486, 1944.

Yet, in his commentary on the Vienna Convention on the Law of Treaties, Sir Ian Sinclair refers to the commentary of the International Law Commission on the opening phrase of Article 28, which explains that such language (instead of the more usual wording "unless the treaty otherwise provides") was used "in order to allow for cases where the very nature of the treaty rather than its specific provisions indicates that it is intended to have certain retroactive effects."[77] Sinclair goes on to refer to the famous *Mavrommatis Palestine Concessions* case, in which the United Kingdom had contested the jurisdiction of the Permanent Court of International Justice on the ground that the acts complained of had taken place before Protocol XII the Treaty of Lausanne had come into force. In rejecting this submission, the court stated:

> Protocol XII was drawn up in order to fix the conditions governing the recognition and treatment by the contracting parties of certain concessions granted by the Ottoman authorities before the conclusion of the Protocol. An essential characteristic therefore of Protocol XII is that its effects extend to legal situations dating from a time previous to its own existence. If provision were not made in the clauses of the Protocol for the protection of the rights recognized therein as against infringements before the coming into force of that instrument, the Protocol would be ineffective as regards the very period at which the rights in question are most in need of protection. The Court therefore considers that the Protocol guarantees the rights recognized in it against any violation regardless of the date at which it may have taken place.[78]

Sinclair also addressed the debate that accompanied the retention of the words "in relation to any ... situation which ceased to exist before the date of entry into force of the treaty". Whereas the United States delegation unsuccessfully argued for deletion, the majority of the delegations insisted that a treaty may well apply to "situations" that continued, even if the facts giving rise to the situation had punctually occurred prior to the entry into force of the treaty.[79]

Among the many exceptions known to the principle of non-retroactivity is the inclusion in the London Agreement of 8 August 1945 of the new "crime against peace", formulated *ex post facto*, and applied by the Nuremberg and Tokyo Tribunals. In this connection Professor Hans Kelsen commented:

> The rule against retroactive legislation is a principle of justice. Individual criminal responsibility represents certainly a higher degree of justice than collective responsibility, the typical technique of primitive law. Since the internationally illegal acts for which the London Agreement established indi-

---

[77] *Yearbook of the International Law Commission* (1966–II): 212–13.

[78] (1924) P.C.I.J., ser. A, No. 2, at 34.

[79] Sinclair, *The Vienna Convention on the Law of Treaties*, 86. The US proposal was defeated by a vote of 47 to 23, with seventeen abstentions.

vidual criminal responsibility were certainly also morally most objectionable, and the persons who committed these acts were certainly aware of their immoral character, the retroactivity of the law applied to them can hardly be considered as absolutely incompatible with justice. ... In case two postulates of justice are in conflict with each other, the higher one prevails; and to punish those who were morally responsible for the international crime of the Second World War may certainly be considered as more important than to comply with the rather relative rule against *ex post facto* laws, open to so many exceptions.[80]

The general rule of non-retroactivity of treaties and conventions, which was abandoned in Nuremberg in connection with the new concept of "crimes against peace,"[81] is not, however, of relevance in the context of the crime of genocide, which has always been a crime under national penal laws, as a manifestation of multiple murder, and which, moreover, must be seen as an international crime under "general principles of law."[82] Reference to the "general principles of law" is found, for instance, in the famous "Martens Clause," contained in the preamble of the 1899 and 1907 Hague Convention on Land Warfare:

> Until a more complete code of the laws of war has been issued, the High Contracting Parties deem it expedient to declare that, in cases not included in the Regulations adopted by them, the inhabitants and the belligerents remain under the protection and the rule of the principles of the law of nations as they result from the usages established among civilized peoples, from the laws of humanity, and the dictates of the public conscience.

Thus, the Genocide Convention of 1948 can be applied retroactively, because it is declarative of pre-existing international law. Among several precedents for the retroactive application of treaties, the following are particularly relevant in the context of genocide:

---

[80] Hans Kelsen, "Will the Judgment in the Nuremberg Trial Constitute a Precedent in International Law?," *International Law Quarterly* 29 (1947): 153, 164–65. See also Hans Kelsen, "The Rule Against *Ex post Facto* Law and the Prosecution of the Axis War Criminals," *The Judge Advocate Journal* 8 (1945): 2.

[81] Alfred de Zayas, "Aggression," in Dinah Shelton, *Encyclopedia of Genocide and Crimes Against Humanity* (New York: Macmillan, 2004), 1: 11–16.

[82] In his opening statement at the International Military Tribunal, the British Chief Prosecutor Lord Hartley Shawcross stated: "There is thus no substantial retroactivity in the provisions of the Charter. It merely fixes the responsibility for a crime already clearly established as such by positive law upon its actual perpetrators. It fills a gap in international criminal procedure. There is all the difference between saying to a man, 'You will now be punished for what was not a crime at all at the time you committed it,' and in saying to him 'You will now pay the penalty for conduct which was contrary to law and a crime when you executed it, although, owing to the imperfection of the international machinery, there was at that time no court competent to pronounce judgment against you.'"

* The London Agreement of 8 August 1945 (Charter of the Nuremberg Tribunal).
* The Convention on the Non-Applicability of Statutes of Limitation to War Crimes and Crimes Against Humanity of 1968.
* Similarly, there is precedent for the *ex post facto* drafting and adoption of international penal charters by the United Nations Security Council under its Chapter VII jurisdiction, such as the Statutes of the International Criminal Tribunal for the Former Yugoslavia,[83] the International Criminal Tribunal for Rwanda,[84] and the International Tribunal for Sierra Leone.

The language of the Genocide Convention neither excludes nor requires its retroactive application. In other words – there is nothing in the language of the convention that would prohibit its retroactive application. By contrast, there are numerous international treaties that specifically state that they will not apply retroactively. For example, Article 11 of the 1998 Statute of the International Criminal Court specifies that, "the Court has jurisdiction only with respect to crimes committed after the entry into force of this Statute."

And there are treaties that purportedly do not apply retrospectively, but in practice are so applied, as is the case with the Vienna Convention on the Law of Treaties of 1969, Article 4 of which stipulates: "the Convention applies only to treaties which are concluded by states after the entry into force of the present Convention." Ever since the adoption of the convention, however, international courts and tribunals have made reference to its provisions as being declarative of pre-existing law and practice, thus reflecting the customary international rules on treaties and the prevailing *opinio juris.*[85]

It is significant that the drafters of the Genocide Convention did not stipulate that it should apply only in the future, although they could easily have done so, had they intended to limit its scope of application. Thus, the question arises as to the object and purpose of the Genocide Convention.

Pursuant to Article 31 of the Vienna Convention on the Law of Treaties, the principal rule of interpretation is "the ordinary meaning given to the terms of the treaty in their context and in the light of its object and purpose." The retroactive application of the Genocide Convention is compatible with the ordinary meaning of terms in the light of the object and purpose of the con-

---

[83] William A. Schabas, "Sentencing by International Tribunals: A Human Rights Approach," *Duke Journal of Comparative and International Law* 7: 461.

[84] Raquel Cross, Case Western Reserve University School of Law, International War Crimes Project, International Criminal Tribunal for Rwanda, Memorandum for the Office of the Prosecutor. Issue I: The Relevance of the Eichmann, Barbie and Finta Trials for the ICTR, Spring 2003.

[85] Rudolf Bernhardt, "Treaties," in *Encyclopedia of Public International Law*, Bernhardt, ed., 4: 926–32.

vention. Further, such retroactive application appears necessary in order to serve the important object of deterring future acts of genocide (prevention) by way of establishing the precedent of punishing acts of genocide that occurred prior to its entry into force (suppression). According to Article 32 of the Vienna Convention on the Law of Treaties, the use of the *travaux préparatoires* of any treaty or convention is deemed only a supplementary means of interpretation. The *travaux préparatoires* of the Genocide Convention, however, are inconclusive with regard to the issue of retroactive application. Whereas several delegations were future-oriented, others saw the problem more broadly, in the light of the retroactive application of the London Charter of 8 August 1945 to the Nazi crimes of genocide that had preceded it, e.g. the Polish representative, Professor Manfred Lachs, and the United Kingdom Representative, Sir Hartley Shawcross.[86]

While non-retroactivity is a principle that has pragmatic value, it is frequently abandoned in international treaties and in national legislation concerning intellectual property, copyright and taxation. Bearing in mind that there exists a higher legal regime for human rights and a *jus cogens* obligation to refrain from genocide, retroactivity is not only appropriate but also just and necessary as a matter of international *ordre public*.

In regard to private property confiscated in the context of the Holocaust, United States jurisdictions have not hesitated to apply laws retroactively. Thus, for instance, in affirming its jurisdiction in *Altmann v. Republic of Austria*, the United States Court of Appeals for the Ninth Circuit decided on 12 December 2002 that the 1976 Foreign Sovereign Immunities Act (FSIA) applied retroactively to the events of the late 1930s and 1940s. The U.S. Court took jurisdiction and found that the property of Mrs. Altmann had been wrongfully and discriminatorily appropriated in violation of international law.[87]

Similarly, with regard to the restitution of Greek and Assyrian/Aramaean property, it is conceivable that in an action brought by Greek and Assyrians/Aramaeans against Turkey before a United States federal court, jurisdiction could be established pursuant to the United States Alien Tort Claims

---

[86] *Official Records of the Third Session of the General Assembly*, Sixth Committee, Sixty-fourth meeting, Palais de Chaillot, Paris (1 October 1948): 17–20, See also the statements of the Czechoslovak representative, Mr. Prochazka, stressing the need to connect the convention directly with the historical events which had proved the necessity for its existence, and to stress the relationship between genocide and the doctrines of nazism, fascism and Japanese imperialism, 66th meeting (4 October 1948): 29–30.

[87] United States Court of Appeals for the Ninth Circuit: *Altmann v. Republic of Austria*, No. 01-56003, 12 December 2002. Affirmed on writ of certiorari, 7 June 2004, United States Supreme Court, 541 U.S. 677.

Act,[88] which states that "the district courts shall have original jurisdiction of any civil action by an alien for a tort only, committed in violation of the law of nations or a treaty of the United States."[89]

9. *Conclusion: Bringing the Genocide against the Greeks and Assyrian/ Aramaean Christians before the International Court of Justice*

Since both Turkey (31 July 1950) and Greece (8 December 1954) are states parties to the Genocide Convention, it would be possible to invoke Article VIII, which provides that any contracting party may call upon the competent organs of the United Nations to take such action as they consider appropriate for the "suppression" of genocide. "Suppression" must mean more than just retributive justice. In order to suppress the crime, it is necessary to suppress, as far as possible, its consequences. This entails, besides punishing the guilty, providing restitution and compensation to the surviving generations. Greece may also invoke Article IX of the Convention, which provides that

"Disputes between the Contracting Parties relating to the interpretation, application, or fulfillment of the present Convention, including those relating to the responsibility of a state for genocide or for any of the other acts enumerated in Article III, shall be submitted to the International Court of Justice at the request of any of the parties to the dispute."

Admittedly, the criminal law aspects of the Genocide Convention are of lesser relevance in the Greek and Assyrian/Aramaean context, since none of the perpetrators of the genocide against them are still alive. On the other hand, the properties of Greek and Assyrian/Aramaean persons that were wrongfully confiscated have not been returned to the survivors of the genocide, to their descendants or to the Orthodox Church, nor has compensation been paid to the survivors of the genocide or to their descendants. In this context it is worth noting the important restitution of many churches and monasteries in the former Soviet republics including Armenia, restitution that was effected in the 1990's for confiscations that had occurred seventy years earlier, following the Bolshevik revolution.[90] Based on this precedent, restitu-

---

[88] 28 U.S.C. § 1350

[89] The Federal Alien Tort Claims Act (ATCA) of 1789 is now being used to sue governments and transnational corporations for violations of international law in countries outside the United States. See also Harold J. Berman, "The Alien Tort Claims Act and the Law of Nations," Emory International Law Review, Forthcoming available at:
http://ssrn.com/abstract=666146;
J. Romesch Weeramantry, "Time limitation under the United States Alien Tort Act," *ICRC Review* 85 (September 2003): 627–36.

[90] Dickran Kouymjian, "La confiscation des biens et la destruction des monuments historiques comme manifestations du processus génocidaire," in *L'actualité du Génocide des Arméniens*, 227.

tion of Greek and Assyrian/Aramaean churches and monasteries would appear not just morally mandated, but also entirely implementable in practice.

A determination of the crime of genocide by the International Court of Justice would facilitate the settlement of claims for restitution, including the identification of cultural and other properties confiscated and/or destroyed, such as churches, monasteries and other assets of historic and cultural significance to the Greek and Assyrian/Aramaean peoples that should be returned to their legal owners.

To the extent that any compensation was paid pursuant to the Treaty of Lausanne of 1923, this would have to be taken into consideration, drawing upon the vast experience of United Nations compensation commissions.

In a spirit of reconciliation, it would be highly desirable if Turkey would issue an apology to the Greek, Armenian, and Assyrian/Aramaean peoples who were the victims not only of discrimination and persecution, but also of genocide, perpetrated both by the Ottoman Empire and by the new Turkish State. In this context it is worth remembering that great nations have recognized mistakes committed by prior governments in the past, and have issued formal apologies to the victims and their survivors, including Germany, Austria, and more recently the United States[91] and Australia.[92]

---

[91] On 23 November 1993 US President Bill Clinton signed Public Law 103–150, the "Apology Resolution," a Congressional apology to the Hawaiian people because of the 1893 overthrow of the Hawaiian Kingdom: http://www.hawaii-nation.org/acknowledges.html,

[92] On 13 February 2008 Australian Prime Minister Kevin Rudd issued an apology to the Australian Aborigines: http://australianetwork.com/news/infocus/s2161253.htm.
The apology was well received by the Aborigines and by a majority of the Australian population. "Australia PM's popularity at record high after apology poll,"
http://afp.google.com/article/ALeqM5jdxkxSMtpSeI6P6YDDVg39R7bDSQ.

Teaching the Greek Genocide

RONALD LEVITSKY

ELIE WIESEL'S MEMOIRS *Night* (1955) begins with Moishe the Beadle returning to the village from which he had been deported by the Nazis. Moishe tells other Jewish villagers of the mass murders he had witnessed. "But people not only refused to believe his tales, they refused to listen. Some even insinuated that he only wanted their pity, that he was imagining things. Others flatly said that he had gone mad."[1]

In a sense, a teacher engaging in genocide education is like Moishe the Beadle. Many children have a great sense of justice - what they call fairness. How could something as horrible as genocide have occurred? It seems beyond belief. As Charlie Engelman, one of my eighth graders, said after studying the Armenian and Greek Genocides, "I didn't know that people could be that bad and do such horrible things. Sure, there are bad leaders out there, but who could order hundreds of thousands of people to walk through a desert until they starve and die? I mean, what's the point of that?"

Yet, other students have difficulty engaging in the subject, not because it is so exceptional, but because it has become all too familiar. As a high school student in the early 1960's, I was deeply disturbed by the Holocaust. The only comfort was my impression that this was an aberration — that genocide had never happened before and because the Holocaust was so evil, it could never happen again. Of course, I was wrong on both counts. I hadn't been taught that genocide had been perpetrated earlier in the twentieth century — including against the Armenians, Greeks, West and East Syriacs (Aramaeans, Assyrians) during 1914–1923. What seemed to me an aberration would become a pattern after the Holocaust — including as victims, among others, the Cambodians, Bosnians, and Tutsis of Rwanda. Not only is genocide occurring again, this time in Sudan, but by using the internet to track events in Darfur, people throughout the world can actually witness these crimes against humanity.

---

[1] Elie Wiesel, *Night* (New York: Hill and Wang, 2006), 7. Translated from the French by Marion Wiesel (Elie's wife). The first book in the trilogy (along with *Dawn* and *Day*), *Night* was first published in Buenos Aires, Argentina, in 1955, as *Un Di Velt Hot Geshvign* [*And the World Remained Silent*]. Wiesel rewrote a shorter version in French, *La Nuit* under the advice of French novelist, François Mauriac. Even with the latter's support, Wiesel had trouble finding a publisher for the book and initially sold very few copies.

When an aberration becomes a pattern and the world does little to stop it, what are children to think? How are they to distinguish genocide from other acts of violence, such as suicide bombings in the Middle East and school shootings that have become mass murder? What of movies and video games that celebrate violence, cheapen human life and, in the process, dehumanize those being "entertained"?

Educators who wish to teach about genocide face these problems, but they also face other pressures, often by the very governments that give lip service to the importance of genocide education. In my own state of Illinois, a mandate has been passed requiring teaching about genocide, yet no money is provided for training or purchasing materials. Pressured by the U.S. government that now requires annual testing of students in reading and mathematics, many schools have cut funding and time allotted for social studies (including history and geography), the very place in the curriculum where genocide education is taught.

Of course, many organizations publish excellent educational resources. The United States Holocaust Memorial Museum not only provides unit and lesson plans but also offers teacher training workshops. *Facing History and Ourselves* is another program with lessons and training on the Holocaust and the Armenian Genocide. The Armenian National Committee of America has an educational wing, and the Genocide Education Project has developed materials on the Armenian Genocide. The latter sponsors an annual contest for the best teacher-prepared lesson on the Armenian Genocide and disseminates this lesson on its website. The Center for Southeast Asian Studies at Northern Illinois University has developed lesson plans, teaching materials, lists of films and books, and links to other sources dealing with the Cambodian Genocide.

The *Choices for the 21st Century* education program of Brown University's Watson Institute for International Studies publishes what may be the single best curricular overview of the genocide issue, *Confronting Genocide: Never Again?* This unit discusses five historical case studies of genocide then presents a role play in which students are asked to debate how the United States should respond to a current crisis, such as the one in Darfur.

The above represents a sample of resources available on various genocides. Those who publish such materials realize that before a subject can be taught, teachers must understand the topic and curricular materials must be made available. Regrettably, no such organization yet exists that publishes extensive information or provides training on the Greek Genocide. Even the *Choices* unit mentioned above, which includes significant information on the Armenian Genocide, ignores that of the Greeks and the Syriacs. Thus those who advocate teaching about the Greeks not only struggle to gain a place for genocide education in a school's curriculum, but also have to compete with other genocide education organizations that are far better financed, organized, and connected politically.

How then can one advocate for the inclusion in a school's curriculum of the Greek Genocide? Instructional materials must be created that not only will educate the teacher on the background of this tragedy, but will offer him/her easy access to effective classroom materials. As a way of beginning this process, I worked with members of Xeniteas, the Pontian Greek Society of Chicago, to create a unit of study for middle and high school students (ages thirteen to eighteen). *The Greek Genocide: A Teaching Unit* includes such pedagogical strategies as analysis of primary sources, use of multiple intelligences, writing, questioning techniques (including asking both convergent and divergent questions), and higher order thinking based on Bloom's Taxonomy (including analysis and evaluation). Key to this unit is the intent to engage the student both intellectually and emotionally and to personalize this tragedy in a way that will truly connect the past to the present.

The following are examples of effective pedagogical strategies for teaching the Greek Genocide.

The Use of Narrative

It is common for history teachers to rely on a textbook as the major source of instruction. This may be why American students frequently rate history as their most boring subject. These textbooks are usually written by a committee, often simplified for the lowest-level reader, and purposefully bland to avoid offending any potential buyer. In contrast, journalist Frances Fitzgerald noted how an early American history text, even though it had many inaccuracies and stereotypes, was hugely popular in the United States because of its gripping narrative, such as blood-curling stories of the Indian wars.[2] In *Lies My Teacher Told Me*, James Loewen castigates the textbook industry, not only for ignoring the life and death struggles of American labor, but for not having the courage to defend establishment figures like John D. Rockefeller and Andrew Carnegie. Instead, coverage of American capitalism is uniformly bland.[3]

If American history texts deal with the topic of genocide, it is usually limited to the Holocaust as part of a chapter on World War II. Some of these treat-

---

[2] Frances Fitzgerald, *America Revised: History Schoolbooks in the Twentieth Century* (Boston: Little, Brown and Company, 1979), 89–93.

3 James W. Loewen, *Lies My Teacher Told Me: Everything Your American History Textbook Got Wrong* (New York: Touchstone, 1995), 212.

ments can be several pages[4] and include brief personal narratives. Genocide is not treated as a separate chapter or unit of study, and rarely, if ever, are the Armenian and Greek cases discussed. This is in spite of the fact that popular support for these Christian minorities of the Ottoman Empire was the first great international relief effort in American history.[5] Of course, even if textbooks did include such information, how meaningful would it be to students?

For over fifty years, what have gripped young people about the Holocaust are not the words of scholars in a textbook but the words of a thirteen-year old girl in her diary.

> Who has made us Jews different from other people? Who has allowed us to suffer so terribly up till now? It is God that has made us as we are, but it will be God, too, who will raise us up again.[6]

Anne Frank wrote of her life-and-death struggle that of her family and her people. Yet, she also wrote excitedly about her first kiss.

> He stroked my cheek and arm a bit awkwardly, played with my curls and our heads lay touching most of the time.[7]

What teenager can't relate to the emotions of fear, bewilderment, but also love?

Other personal testimony has been collected and utilized by various genocide groups to speak of the deaths of thousands, even millions, as singular experiences. The United States Holocaust Memorial Museum has catalogued many thousands of examples. In addition, the [Armenian] Genocide Education Project's Human Rights and Genocide Ten-Day Unit includes photographs of survivors and their personal testimony, such as that of Haig Baronian, who wrote,

> [...] he [a Turkish gendarme] pulled out his dagger and plunged it into my grandmother's back. The more he plunged his dagger, the more my beloved Nana asked for heaven's curses on him and his kind.[8]

Scholars and activists of the Greek Genocide should also collect and catalogue personal recollections of the genocide experience. Two non-fiction book length accounts relating the tragedy that befell Greek girls are George Andreadis's *Tamama, The Missing Girl of the Pontus*, and Thea Halo's *Not*

---

4 E.g., Gerald Danzer, et al., *The Americans* (Evanston, IL: McDougal Littell, 1998), 714–18.

5 Merrill D. Peterson, *"Starving Armenians" America and the Armenian Genocide, 1915–1930 and After* (Charlottesville and London: University of Virginia Press, 2004), 51–88.

6 Anne Frank, *The Diary of a Young Girl* (New York: Washington Square Press, 1952), 184.

7 Ibid., 187.

8 *Human Rights and Genocide: A Case Study of the First Modern Genocide of the 20th Century* (Genocide Education Project, 2005), 43.

Even My Name, the story of her mother Sano. In each case, the long deadly march through the desert into exile and death is recounted movingly. For example, as Sano Halo's mother discovers that her youngest child has died:

> "Move!" A soldier shouted as he trotted up to where we stood.
>
> "My baby," Mother said.
>
> She held out Maria for the soldier to see, as if her shock and grief could also be his.
>
> "My baby."
>
> "Throw it away if it's dead!" he shouted. "Move!"
>
> "Let me bury her," Mother pleaded, sobbing.
>
> "Throw it away!" he shouted again, raising his whip. "Throw it away!"[9]

From an unpublished family history, Ioannis Koktzoglou, who lived in a village near Samsun (Amisos (Gr.)), recounted his experiences in 1919 when he was fourteen years old:

> Those who survived the first round of killings were forced into three big houses.
>
> There were women, children, and older adults. The perpetrators poured fuel onto the houses and set them on fire. Those who attempted to escape were either shot, stabbed, or strangled using ropes. I was extremely fortunate because the day before the massacre I left the village and went to join my uncle and his 'Andartes' [irregulars; partisans; resistance group] ... No one escaped out of approximately 340 people who were in the village.[10]

First-hand accounts such as these, often written from the point-of-view of a child or adolescent, have a powerful impact on both the cognitive and affective learning of students who not only read what happened but vicariously share these experiences.

The Student as Historian

One reason why many students consider history boring is because they view the subject in an inevitable cause-and-effect sequence without controversy. Of course, historians and educators know better. For example, in his book, *How Can We Commit the Unthinkable? Genocide: The Human Cancer*, Professor Israel Charny investigates the possibility of "A Genocide Early Warning System" — ways to analyze and avoid such disasters.[11] Getting students to be active learners, including the ability to analyze and evaluate historical data, also can become a way of making history more interesting. This can

---

[9] Thea Halo, *Not Even My Name* (New York: Picador, 2001), 139.

[10] Ioannis Koktzoglou, "A Survivor's Testimony of the Pontian Greek Genocide" (Unpublished family document).

[11] Israel W. Charny, *How Can We Commit the Unthinkable? Genocide: The Human Cancer* (Boulder: Westview Press, 1982), chapter 13.

relate to a favorite literary genre of students — the mystery. Making historical research seem like a detective story adds to this interest.

When researching a topic, historians utilize several strategies. Instead of secondary sources, they use primary documentation. Instead of relying on one source, they use many, preferably given from multiple perspectives. Historians vet these sources, examining each for motivation and bias, and seek corroboration to prove a particular thesis. Even then, they realize that as new evidence unfolds, or new interpretations are suggested, any given thesis may need to be modified.

Although reputable historians accept as fact the Armenian, Greek, and Syriac Genocides, the government of Turkey disputes this. Instead of dismissing Turkish denial as propaganda, the teacher can use this as an opportunity for students, as "mini–historians," to investigate and substantiate genocide.

In *The Pontian and Anatolian Greek Genocide: A Teaching Unit* (Second Edition), students are presented with a lesson entitled, "Why Was What Happened to the Pontian and Anatolian Greeks a Genocide?" They read ten documents dealing with the genocide. These are primarily first–hand accounts, gathered from a variety of sources, and placed in chronological sequence. Among the witnesses, George Horton, U.S. Consul–General in the Near East, wrote of the deportations of Greeks, "these poor refugees" from the Black Sea in 1916. A Lieutenant Slade of the British navy reported, in 1919, on the forced conversion to Islam of kidnapped Christian women and children. Stanley Hopkins of the Near East Relief recounted, in 1921, how he had "... passed many corpses of Greeks lying by the roadside where they had died from exposure." Vasileios Anastasiades, who as a boy survived the genocide, witnessed how, "[...] When the Red Cross [...] came looking for us the Turks would move us around by night."

Using these selections, students first complete a worksheet entitled, "Historical Documents," to demonstrate a basic understanding of the sources. Next, they are presented with a worksheet that gives the United Nations definition of genocide, broken into sections, such as "Causing serious bodily or mental harm to members of the group" or "Forcibly transferring children of the group to another group." Spaces are left after each section of the definition for students to include examples from the documents. In the ensuing class discussion, it is easier for students to understand why the Greek tragedy was, indeed, genocide, because they themselves have used documentation to prove that the UN definition applies.

While dealing in specificity, historians frequently draw generalizations from their research. If the teacher chooses to go further, students can compare the Greek Genocide to others. While each genocide has unique circumstances, each also fits most or all of the United Nations definitions. For example, perpetrators of any large scale genocide commit mass murder and inflict "conditions of life calculated to bring about its physical destruction in whole or part."

Beyond this definition are other comparisons. For example, the Turks tried to hide their Greek captives from the Red Cross, just as the Nazis tried to deceive the Red Cross about conditions in concentration camps. Also, students come to realize that genocides don't simply happen; they are orchestrated by a government often utilizing technology (for example, the railroad). Students are more likely to remember these valuable lessons, because, rather than hearing a lecture, they are permitted to work with, and draw conclusions from, the sources.

Multiple Intelligence Theory

Howard Gardner, a psychologist from Harvard University, suggests that human beings possess many types of intelligences. Some educators have extrapolated his theory to warn against relying too heavily on the traditional "school intelligences" - verbal-linguistic (use of words) and logical-mathematical. Children weak in these areas may grow disinterested in school. Rather than lack of ability, their failure may be due to a lack of matching educational goals to varied intelligences. Like adults, children feel better about themselves and work harder when their success is rewarded. Schools with strong fine arts and physical education programs (musical, interpersonal, and bodily-kinesthetic intelligences) usually find that their academic programs benefit as well. Many classroom teachers routinely utilize multiple intelligences to interest and energize their students.

The Pontian/Anatolian Greek Genocide — A Teaching Unit also does this. A lesson entitled "The Destruction of Smyrna" includes three written accounts of this tragedy (including a selection from a short story by Ernest Hemingway), as well as two photographs, one showing the burning quay and the other depicting refugees fleeing the fire. Using their verbal-linguistic skills in a creative way, students write a poem about the burning of Smyrna. One of my eighth graders, Kristine Kim, wrote "A Hidden Hell:"

> Death...
> Consumes
> Lives, homes, and hope.
> Watch ...
> People drop to the ground
> Weak, limp and lifeless.
> Blackened corpses and burnt bones
> Left to decay with rotting flesh.
>
> "Light another fire!"
> I can't do this any longer.

What has the world become?
I, too
Fight for my life …
Along with the people of Smyrna.

Like all good poetry, this piece captures the emotions of its subject and leaves a more lasting impression than the words of a textbook.

Another lesson from the unit taps into students' artistic abilities. They are asked to create "A Memorial to the Greek Genocide." The teacher may wish to show examples of memorials, such as the Washington Monument, the Vietnam Memorial, and the one in Montgomery, Alabama dedicated to the civil rights movement. In planning their project, students are asked to consider mood, specific imagery, and materials to be used. This is a non–verbal way of reflecting on the effects of genocide that reinforces what they have learned from readings and discussions in class. For many students, this holistic approach strengthens learning.

Current Events

The government of Turkey continues to deny genocide of the Armenians, Syriacs, and Greeks. The teacher can use this denial as a current events topic to prompt critical thinking. For example, students might be asked to consider the following questions:

• What is the relationship between the United States and Turkey? Why is this relationship important? What issues, such as the Greek Genocide, may have an impact on this relationship?

• What is the relationship between Israel and Turkey? Why is this relationship important? How does the history of the Jewish people relate to the Greek Genocide? Why might Jewish history complicate Israeli–Turkish relations?

• Turkey continues to deny its genocide of the Greeks. Likewise, the Japanese government has never formally recognized its guilt in the massacre and enslavement of hundreds of thousands of Chinese and South Koreans during World War II. How have these denials affected the foreign relations of Turkey and Japan? Why is it important for a nation to come to grips with its past and to accept responsibility for its actions?

• How has the international community reacted to the massacre and displacement, by the Sudanese government and paramilitary forces, of hundreds of thousands of people in the Darfur region of western Sudan?

• Can connections be made between lessons learned/not learned from the Greek Genocide? If so, what are they?

The *Choices for the 21st Century* unit, "Confronting Genocide: Never Again?" challenges American students with a foreign policy simulation, putting them into the role of either the U.S. Senate Committee on Foreign Relations or advocates for four policy options regarding contemporary genocide:

- Lead the World in the Fight to Stop Genocide
- Stand with the International Community Against Genocide
- Speak Out, But Preserve State Sovereignty
- Intervene Only When U.S. Interests are Directly Threatened

In discussing these options, students refer to historical examples to support their arguments. While the Greek Genocide is not mentioned in the background readings, the Armenian Genocide is, and the teacher can add necessary materials to include the Greek experience.

Conclusion: Why Teach the Greek Genocide?

Despite student apathy and the government's emphasis on testing basic skills, good educators struggle to teach the very core of education — that which makes us more human. Understanding genocide — its causes and history, is only a first step in turning students into what Samantha Power, author of *A Problem From Hell*, calls "upstanders." By this she means those people who had the courage to stand up to genocide. According to Power, "upstanders" share two qualities — they have a personal connection to genocide (e.g., knowing a survivor or being the member of a group that suffered genocide) and they have a strong set of values.[12]

This latter quality is something teachers can help to instill in their students, whether or not their school has a formal character education program. By teaching about genocide, educators make a strong statement that this topic is important. The Holocaust and the Armenian Genocide, as well as those that have taken place in Rwanda and Cambodia, are powerful examples for study. But they are not the only ones.

It is a tragic commentary on education that because other genocides are currently being taught, the systematic murder of one to 1.5 million Greeks is not granted space in a school's curriculum. By choosing to teach about the Greek Genocide, as part of the greater genocide of Christians in the Ottoman Empire (the number of victims during the period between 1912–1923 totaled over 3.5 million Armenian, Greek and Syriac Christians), educators are telling their students that all those who suffered genocide deserve recognition. Indeed, in 1914, if the world had acted against this injustice, not only might the Greek Genocide have been avoided — along with those of the Armenians and Syriacs — but also there might have been no future genocides, and instead of students reading this anthology as terrible fact, it might only have been a work of the darkest fiction.

---

[12] Samantha Power, from a speech she gave at the National Council for the Social Studies (NCSS) Annual Conference in Baltimore, Maryland (November, 2004).

Memorial monument to the Greeks of the Pontus, Kallithea (Athens)

Remembering the Genocide and the "Unforgettable Homelands"

The Erection of Commemorative Monuments in Greece by Refugees from Asia Minor

MICHEL BRUNEAU AND KIRIAKOS PAPOULIDIS

THE PRIMARY FUNCTION OF MONUMENTS, erected by communities or social groups, is to solicit memory, to invite those who look upon them to "remember or help other generations remember people, events, sacrifices, rituals or beliefs."[1] Monuments strive to stir up emotion by appealing to memories kept alive in order to "contribute to maintaining and preserving the identity of an ethnic or religious, national, tribal or family community."[2] Contrary to historical monuments erected *a posteriori*, monuments such as those considered here are deliberately thought out and designed *a priori* to "bring the forgotten past alive again in the present moment."[3]

Although the Greek refugees of Asia Minor, who arrived in Greece in the wake of the First World War up until 1923, felt the need to build such commemorative monuments from the 1930s onwards, most of such projects were only realized between 1960 and the present day. Initially, the immigrants were pre-occupied with practical questions of survival. The Second World War and German occupation then froze the situation, while also allowing the refugees to improve their integration into Greek society, thanks to their active participation in the resistance movement. However, over the last two decades the movement for commemorating in the public spaces of the Greek towns, where those expatriated originally from Asia Minor now live, has become extremely active. The monuments give voice to a variety of different themes, but all of these are strongly rooted in the notion of identity, that of the territories or, more accurately, their ancestors' homelands; this is also associated with the notion of exile, expulsion, being uprooted or with the fact of being victims of genocide.

These "lost homelands," as they are sometimes called, are most often referred to as "unforgettable," in the sense of "that which must not be forgotten." The monuments embody the right to remember as well as the duty of

[1] Francoise Choay, *L'allégorie du patrimoine* (Paris: Editions du Seuil, 1992), 15.

[2] Ibid., 15.

[3] Ibid., 22.

remembrance, not least the duty to pass down to the third and fourth generations the memory of the massacres suffered, the genocide perpetrated, the lives and heroism of the victims who died.

Such "right to remember" was given belated recognition by the Greek state. The vast majority of such forms of remembrance only appeared some 40 to 80 years after the events they commemorate, which is somewhat surprising when compared with France's First and Second World War monuments to the dead and its commemorative plaques, most of which were put up within ten years of the historical events they commemorate.

A number of questions arise: Why such oblivion, and then such a renaissance of collective memory? How, over the last thirty years, were all these monuments put up and public spaces transformed into places of remembrance to honor the refugees of Asia Minor, and how did they develop? Who financed them? Which roles did the State and NGOs play? What meta-narrative, charged with reconstituting the unifying signs of community membership or refugee identity, do these monuments convey?

The present study focuses on monuments situated in the different districts of the Athens–Piraeus and Thessalonica urban centers, along with a range of small towns and market towns in Northern Greece. A survey was carried out among the town councils and associations to try and reconstruct the tale behind these monuments and their funding, and to determine who it was who initiated their construction and assumed the role of main contractor. What sort of stumbling blocks were encountered? Our aim was to shed light on these diverse factors and, as far as possible, to gauge the extent of the phenomenon.

A Population of Refugees Torn from their Native Lands

In the wake of the Treaty of Lausanne (1923), which set up the population exchange, about 1.2 million expatriated Greek Christians were forced to abandon their native lands, the lands of their ancestors, in Asia Minor (including Pontus and Cappadocia) and Eastern Thrace, on which they had lived for over three thousand years, to settle in Greece, the land of the Greek nation–state.

For over eighty years, while the first generation of expatriated *Mikrasiates* was passing away, there followed three more generations; these are perfectly well integrated nowadays into the Greek population, which initially, in 1923, numbered some 5 million. One part of this population then went on to emigrate further and farther away, joining the New World diaspora (North America, Australia) and that of Western Europe, where the percentage of Greeks from Asia Minor and their descendants was disproportionally high among the post–World War II emigrant laborers from Greece.

Some additional 200,000 refugees, trapped in the USSR until 1989 have, in part, just recently immigrated to Greece and Cyprus, frequently as the result of hostile attitudes by, or inter-ethnic conflict within, post-Soviet majority populations. In Greece, the integration and acceptance of these newcomers, often Russophone descendants of Asia Minor Greeks, are proving to be a challenge for the Greek state and its administration and for indigenous society.

For many decades, the Greek State kept silent about this aspect of its history, bent as it was on preserving relations with its neighbor Turkey (as exemplified by the İnönü-Venizelos Greco-Turkish Entente of 1931). In this way it managed to conceal the part played by different political and military agendas (Turkish, Greek and Western) in this disaster, and thereby avoided embarrassing the western powers, which needed the support of Turkey against the Eastern Bloc during the Cold War.

In Greece, up until the 1980s, those who survived the Great Catastrophe (*Μεγάλη Καταστροφή*, *Megale Katastrophe*) and the massacres had no choice but to erase from their memories what had happened in Turkey, from the start of the twentieth century until 1922 and, in the USSR, from 1937 to 1956 when the Greeks were deported to Central Asia by Stalin. The silence of Greek historiography was encouraged by a state whose attention, turned essentially to the situation in the Balkans, was more concerned with the Slav communist states to the north than with Turkish nationalism to the east, with Turkey being an inescapable partner within NATO.

Only from the 1970s, as Greece began to take off economically, did the refugee associations become increasingly active and their work of remembrance start to gather pace. The veil of silence imposed by national historiography on the events in Asia Minor and the fate of the refugees then began to lift, thanks to the publication of books on the subject and to the organization of Pan-Pontian international congresses (1985, 1988, 1993, 1997, 2002), in which several leading political figures took part. All of this, however, was but the first stage in the remembrance process being called for by the Greek Asia Minor NGOs.

During the 1980s, a debate started within Pontian associations and Greek political spheres as to the genocide, first of the Greeks of Pontus, and then that of the Greeks from all over Asia Minor between 1916 and 1923. The genocide had been organized by the highest Ottoman authorities, first under the war regime of the Young Turks and, in particular, by Interior Minister Talât, and since 1919 by Mustafa Kemal.

This debate started to rage as early as 1985, coinciding with the first Pan-Pontian Congress, thanks to the work of an Austrian historian of Greek Pontian descent, Polychrones Enepekides (1985 and 1996), using hitherto undiscovered documents from the Vienna and Berlin archives of the ministries of foreign affairs of two First World War allies of the Ottoman Empire. The massacres and deportations (by forced marches) caused the deaths of huge numbers of victims from 1916 to 1923: some 350,000 people are estimated to have died at the start of the twentieth century, out of a total Greek Pontian population of about 700,000.

The demand for international recognition of this genocide became a central theme in subsequent Pan-Pontian international congresses from 1988 onwards, the aim being to obtain a formal request for an apology from the Turkish state, similar to that obtained by the Jews from Germany. Until today (2010) however the Greek parliament remains the only national lawmaker that officially recognizes this genocide. Apart from Greece itself, those who fight most insistently for recognition, especially for that by the United Nations, are members of the diaspora in the United States and Canada.

Staging Remembrance in Specially-Dedicated Sites: the Monuments

One way of preserving the bond with national heritage and the memory of the "lost homelands" is to build within the host country new monuments whose sculptural forms allude to the original, now lost, monuments, thereby creating a substitute heritage for the one that has been lost.

Situated as they are in particularly central and visible public spaces, these monuments crystallize the affirmation and transmission of an identity which, too long denied, was threatened with extinction. They also contribute widely in helping to integrate this identity into the larger framework of the nation, which, instead of ignoring the identity or denying its existence, now recognizes it *per se,* incorporating it even into its collective memory as an integral part of its own history.

Between 1950 and 1980, the Pontians reconstructed their five main monasteries at great financial expense.[4] Monument construction then gained pace, paralleling the increasing politicization of the Pontian association movement, which was calling not only for the right to remember as well as the duty of remembrance, but also for recognition of the genocide of the Pontian Greeks (1916–1923) on the part of the international community. The remembrance process began to flourish, and a noticeable memorial commemoration momentum saw the light of day in Greek Pontian civil society during the second half of the twentieth century. This movement, which grew apace from the 1970s on, continues to gain new ground today in the first years of the twenty-first century.

---

[4] Michel Bruneau, "Les monastères pontiques en Macédoine, marqueurs territoriaux de la diaspora," in M. Bruneau, ed., *Les Grecs Pontiques* (Paris: CNRS-Éditions 1998), 213–28.

The expatriated Greeks of Asia Minor can be divided into four sub-groups according to their native region within Asia Minor — Pontians, Ionians or *Mikrasiates*, Cappadocians and Thracians. Each sub-group varies widely in terms of population size. There is no correlation between the demographic weight of each group and the number of memorials erected, since over half of the total number of monuments put up are dedicated to the Pontians (36, or 58%), while the refugees from the Ionian and Bithynian coasts of Asia Minor, by far the most numerous, have only erected 12 monuments (19%). There are also large numbers of Thracians, but they have only built three monuments (5%), and the Cappadocians just one (2%).

The Political and Legal Framework

The Greek parliament finally recognized the right to remember, as well as the duty of remembrance, by former Asia Minor refugees and their descendants, bowing to the pressure of NGOs and a number of members of parliament. The decision to submit 19 May to parliament as a remembrance day for the commemoration of the Greek Pontian genocide was taken by twenty-two PASOK (moderate socialist party) members of parliament of Pontian descent as early as 1991. The arrival of Kemal Atatürk in Samsun was 19 May 1919. That date that marked the beginning of an intensification of the massacres perpetrated against the Pontians, especially by Turkish militias led by Topal Osman.

In March 1994, a law was passed that established 19 May as "a day of remembrance of the genocide perpetrated against the Greek people of Pontus," and in October 1998 another law was issued by the Greek parliament fixing 14 September as "a day of national remembrance of the genocide perpetrated against the Greek people of Asia Minor by the Turkish State." September 14 was the first of the three days of the burning of Smyrna (İzmir (Tur.)) and of the massacres that came with the defeat of the Hellenic Army in Asia Minor. Although these two laws were passed unanimously by parliamentary members of all political hues, the official publication of the presidential decree recommending that each elected provincial head organize "remembrance services including a *Te Deum*, speeches and laying of wreaths at the central prefectural and regional buildings, with the participation of refugee and women's associations," was to suffer setbacks until September 2001. This simple fact alone shows that there is still a reluctance within the Greek state, which is linked to its relations with Turkey. It was to take fifteen years (1986–2001) to establish this legal framework and put a full stop to the "deaf ear politics" that had characterized the Greek State's attitude ever since 1920.

Setting Aside Sites and Then Building the Monuments

The construction of commemorative monuments is generally the result of a long process, one that may last as long as five to ten years on average. Funds have to be raised, the local, provincial and national authorities (such as ministries) have to be persuaded to set aside a suitable site and to provide financial support. Most often it is the associations and especially their presidents, who bear the brunt of the hard work involved.

A successful outcome depends very much on having developed a network of personal relations within local government and the ministries in Athens. The very first commemorative monument was inaugurated in 1936 in the square located behind the Athens Metropolis: "In memory of the Asia Minor Catastrophe victims from the holy metropoles of Asia Minor, Pontus and Thrace." The marble statue of Chrysostomos, the last metropolitan of Smyrna who was martyred in 1922, advancing towards the supreme sacrifice, his head lifted to the skies, one hand on his heart and the palm of the other turned to the sky, gives him emblematic status as victim (*see* page 358).

Five other memorials from among the first to be erected were put up in the 1960s (three under the regime of the colonels from 1967–1974). The others appeared principally during the 1980s and 1990s, and the first years of the twenty–first century, with a noticeable increase in recent years. It was, thus, some forty years after most of the expatriates had arrived in Greece, in the wake of the population exchange of 1923, that the memorial movement began, flourishing from the 1980s onwards; in other words when the first generation of refugees were reaching the end of their lives.

This phenomenon also resulted from the social advancement of the second generation, which had attained by then a relatively fair level of material comfort. The choice of the sites depends mainly on the municipalities of the concerned cities, and of course on the lobbying that allows the refugee associations to exercise an influence over this choice.

Most of the monuments are located in central squares, or more seldom within parks, of the different cities or next to churches or Pontian monasteries like Panagia Soumela. For instance, in Thessalonica, three monuments built at different periods have been erected in front of Agia Sophia in the town center. In Athens, on the other hand, they are located only in central squares of former refugee neighborhoods (Nea Smyrne, Kallithea, Menidi, among others), not alongside national symbols in the main squares or sites like Syntagma Square, the Greek Parliament, Zappeion or Omonoia Square.

Financing and Erecting the Monuments

The two main sources of financial support come from the state and NGOs. As contributions by individuals are somewhat marginal these have been included within the part represented by associations. In fact, as shown below, it is the state, which lies behind all financial backing, by:

• Playing an active role via a range of central governmental agencies (the ministries of foreign affairs, culture, commerce, finance, the interior, and those of Macedonia and Thrace), local governments and administrations (provinces, town halls, national archives), educational institutions (universities, institutes of science and technology) and financial institutions (national lottery, national bank).
• Subsidizing associations and refugee institutions (federations of refugee associations, public foundations like Community Center of Nea Smyrne (*Εστία Νέας Σμύρνης*) and Council of Pontian Studies (*Επιτροπή Ποντιακών Μελετών*), to make it look as though the latter are joint financiers of the construction work.

Another, indirect, source of funds is furnished by many architects and sculptors of Pontian descent working free of charge on such projects, with many private engineering companies that have been receiving political encouragement following suit.

Our survey shows that the state and the associations each contribute half of the financial means necessary for the construction of the monuments in 50% of the cases (31 out of 62). It should be noted however that behind this facade, it is the state and local governments, which, directly or indirectly, in reality finance these projects. This is of course a recent phenomenon dating mainly from the recognition of the genocide by the Greek parliament in the 1990s. Before, it depended only on the initiative of the towns where the refugees were influential and/or in a majority, like Nea Smyrne, Kallithea, Thessalonica and others.

Typology of the Monuments or Monumental Ensembles

The sixty–five monuments studied here can be classified according to their shape and central thematic import:

– Three cenotaphs referring to a region and a particular event: the Tripolitans, Sandetians, inhabitants of Pergamos and its region.

– Three other monuments, even though they are not cenotaphs, are also dedicated to a specific population and region: Kydonies and Aravissos (Cappadocia), the Thracians at Thessalonica.

– The Pontian heroes, either alone or shown with other figures and bas-reliefs (15).

– Monuments to the refugees from all of Asia Minor and Eastern Thrace, with allegorical figures (6).

– Iconic historical figures: Chrysostomos, Kourtides, Chrysanthos, Kapetanides, Anthopoulos and others (10)

The marble statue of Archbishop Chrysostomos, martyred in Smyrna in 1922, was erected behind the Metropolis (Cathedral) of Athens.

- Busts or statues of historical figures with no specific iconic status (14).
- Memorials to the genocide and Pontian Hellenism (14).

The Community Center of Nea Smyrne (Εστία Νέας Σμύρνης) and the Headquarters of the Council of Pontian Studies (Επιτροπή Ποντιακών Μελέτων)

Two monumental ensembles, which include a specific building to commemorate Asia Minor or Pontian Hellenism, stand out by the sheer wealth of objects and symbols they contain. They constitute memorials designed to preserve and promulgate remembrance of vast areas, which were once the native lands of the refugees. Each ensemble, with its own library and museum, is situated in Nea Smyrne, a part of the Athenian urban complex, where many former refugees and their descendents have settled.

The Community Center of Nea Smyrne *(Estia Neas Smyrnes)*, the largest monumental ensemble commemorating Hellenism across the whole of Asia Minor, is comprised of a marble palace (*Megaron*), and a multi–activity cultural center, set in a park, which in turn comprises fifteen monuments. The proclaimed aim of the ensemble was, in partnership with the Nea Smyrne municipality, to recreate the institutions and philanthropic foundations that had made Smyrna the main center of Ionian civilization. As early as 1938, the Nea Smyrne municipality had made provisions in its town planning projections for a large, centrally located site for the *Estia*.

The *Megaron* was inaugurated in April 1975. As soon as the first brick was ceremoniously laid in 1955, the term of remembrance was used in the speech proclaiming the twofold purpose of the center. On the one hand, the *Megaron* was to play a part in preserving the traditions and cultures of the lost homelands (Asia Minor, Pontus, Thrace and Constantinople), mainly through its library and museum. The other aim was to create an even more vibrant new culture in Greece and the Hellenic world generally, by developing workshops for young people and students, as well as a major scholarship program. This was designed to help refugees and their descendants preserve and develop both a specific identity and sense of memory that would differ from those of local Greeks.

This impressive monumental ensemble (18 different monuments) is almost entirely devoted to commemorating Smyrna and Ionia, with all of the project's patrons and main donors having come from both these places. The *Megaron* is unequalled, not only in terms of its size and architecture, but also in the variety and multiplicity of the activities it organizes each year through its association, in addition to the number of highly distinctive monuments in the memorial park. The bronze statue of Metropolitan Chrysostomos stands on a marble stele with a bas–relief depicting his murder and the exodus of the Greeks of Asia Minor; it was erected in 1965.

As the Pontians could not find a place for their specific identity within this ensemble, they created their own, somewhat smaller center, the Conservatory of Objects and Memories of Pontian Hellenism (*Στέγη Κειμηλίων του*

Ελληνισμού του Πόντου, Stege Keimelion tou Ellenismou tou Pontou), inaugurated in 1988, in another district of Nea Smyrne (Οδός Αγνώστων Μαρτύρων, i.e., The Unknown Martyrs' Street). Although this three-story building is less imposing than the *Megaron* of the *Estia*, it can lay claim to a library, a conference room and, since 1999, the Museum of Pontian Hellenism. The museum, which is ethnographic in nature, retraces ways of life in Pontus and the arts and crafts of this society that, in 1923, ceased to exist in its native land.

Monumental Ensembles or Monuments Dedicated to the "Unforgettable Homelands"

Two monumental ensembles, that of Nea Philadelphia (a part of the Athenian urban complex), and that of Xanthe (in Western Thrace), commemorate all the lost homelands. The first, inaugurated in 1994, is the monument park, situated within parklands planted with trees and flowerbeds in a public square in the town of Nea Philadelphia. The park commemorates the "Unforgettable Homelands of Asia Minor," as does the central part of its monument which depicts a priest with three women, surrounded by five children of varying ages, in the form of a group of stylized modern sculptures in bronze on a marble stele. Around this are a number of marble plinths with the names of twenty-four Asia Minor towns engraved vertically on them.

The second monument, called the *Monument to Refugee Hellenism*, inaugurated in 1997 in Xanthe and erected by the Pontian association of that town, bears witness to the battles fought and the sacrifices made by Hellenism, and underlines the responsibilities of the new generation in the pursuit of the ideals of virtue, courage and the freedom of all Greek people. Its aim is to be a place of remembrance and a pledge for the future in honor of those who have given or will not fear to give their lives. The marble plinth takes the form of the bow of a ship transporting refugees toward salvation in Greece. At the head of the prow, sculptor G. Tsaras placed a decapitated statue of the Winged Victory of Samothrace, symbolizing the renewal of hope among this throng of anonymous refugees who have played so important a part in the making of modern Greece. This monument to refugee Hellenism attains new heights in the sophistication in terms of its symbolism and themes it spans.

Three other, much simpler monuments also commemorate "the unforgettable homelands:" Nea Moudania (Chalkidike), Kalamaria (Thessalonica), Korydallos (Athens). These more recent monuments or monumental ensembles, erected over the last ten years, refer to a common memory and identity for all the refugees, from the Pontians to the Thracians. With their eyes turned resolutely towards the future, they celebrate the role the refugee population has played and can still play in the development of modern

Greece, its host country. Yet they also aim at showing that this part of the population has no intention of forgetting its eastern roots.

The Cenotaphs

Cenotaphs figure among the first monuments to have been erected to honor those who lost their lives in a particular region or place and thus allow the descendants of these victims to organize annual commemoration services. They refer to a specific massacre in a specific place and time and bear witness to the importance for the refugees of the specific homelands where their ancestors are buried. They represent the very first sites enabling the sense of their homeland identity and collective memory to be expressed.

The first such cenotaph was erected by the Tripolitans in 1968, in memory of the 10,000 Greeks from Tripolis and the surrounding villages (twelve villages according to the names engraved on the side of the stele) who died during deportation by forced marches across Anatolia (1916–18). It was the Fraternity of Tripolitans that erected this marble cenotaph at the entrance of the Kallithea cemetery in Athens. Another cenotaph was put up the same year, on the site of the Panagia Soumela monastery, to commemorate the holocaust that took place in seven villages of the Sanda region in September 1921. It is designed in the form of a tomb with an armed resistance fighter guarding its door on one side, and a female figure on the other. Seven fir trees, planted nearby, symbolize the seven hamlets of the Sanda Valley.

The Theme of the Pontian Hero Guarding the Frontiers

The iconic sculpted bronze figure, which appears most frequently on monuments, is that of the "Pontian Hero," often also called Akritas, the guard of the frontiers of the Byzantine Empire (Ακρίτας του Πόντου, *Akritas tou Pontou*), or Αντάρτης (*Antartes*), which means rebel or resistance fighter. The figures, which are life-size or larger (a height of 2.2 m. in Kozane, for example) and wear the traditional Pontian costume or *zipka*, symbolize the fierce resistance fighting led by the Pontian Greeks in the mountains of Pontus between 1916 and 1923; but also, more generally, they refer to the legendary hero, Digenis Akritas, who guarded the Byzantine frontiers. This serves to underline the territorial theme running through this form of memorial. Generally speaking, the hero stands alone, although he is sometimes shown accompanied by a female figure and two children, thus introducing the theme of the Pontian families who played a major role both in the armed resistance movement and in the life in exile of the refugees in Greece.

Sculptor Euthymios Kalevras designed this emblematic hero figure, in either classical or realistic style, using simple, understated and expressive forms to depict a warrior armed with a rifle, cartridge pouches slung across his chest, and a dagger at his belt. His facial expression confirms his determination and unambiguous bravery (Kallithea 1976, Veroia 2000, Drapetsona 1985, Kozane 1989, Therme 2002).

A variation of this heroic theme appears twice (Stauroupole 1980, Kavala 2001), with the same hero brandishing a spear held upright in his right hand, a sheath of wheat, and a scythe in his left hand. In this variation, stress is laid on the dual role of the country laborer or farmer in time of peace becoming an armed fighter in time of war.

The emblematic figure of the Pontian Hero has also been reworked by other sculptors, most often with the family group, at Naoussa (1998), Xanthe (1997), Kilkis (1992), Kalamaria (1997) and Aspropyrgos (1995). In only two of these monuments (Agia Sophia in Thessalonica and Florina), does the warlike theme of armed resistance give way to themes associated with education and a future life of peace.

The Theme of Genocide and Pontian Hellenism

Explicit use of the term "genocide" is very recent, officially recognized by the Greek Parliament in 1994. There are in fact six monuments, which explicitly commemorate the genocide: Kilkis (1993), Aspropyrgos (1995), Florina (1996), Therme (2002), Kastoria (2001), Thessalonica (2006). The genocide itself is rarely mentioned or depicted. More often than not, indirect mention of it is made through the image of a burning church, one or two corpses, or crosses in a cemetery (Therme and Euxinoupole). It is actually depicted only on the monument in Kastoria. This is the only bas-relief on which are represented scenes of massacred corpses, slaughtered with sabres wielded by Young Turks or Kemalist soldiers. A whole cross-section of the massacred population (women, children and the elderly) figures here, with only a small proportion being protected by the resistance fighters led by Metropolitan Germanos Karavangeles, who brandishes a cross and a flag. This explicit portrayal of events, the only one to be seen on a monument today, has led some to claim that it is the only monument which actually commemorates the genocide. Its inauguration by Kostes Stephanopoulos, the president of the republic, in November 2001 already constitutes a form of recognition, and plans for two other genocide memorials in Thessalonica and Athens are currently under way.

The Agia Varvara memorial, inaugurated in May 2002 on 19 May Square, alludes much more indirectly to the genocide of the Pontian Greeks. The means employed are quite different: there are no heroes, and no human figures; only the key symbols of Pontian history are used. A bronze arch on a marble base represents the entrance to the monastery of Panagia Soumela, a traditional place of pilgrimage for the Greeks of Pontus. A Byzantine cross and a text expressing its virtues is engraved in Byzantine characters, on the upper part. This reproduces the text painted on the stone walls of the original monastery. Under the arched doorway there is a candelabrum for candles to be inserted, as in a church; it also serves as a support for three iconic objects — a lyre, a sabre and a rifle. The monument has no surrounding enclosure but rather opens out at the front, as if welcoming in the future. At the back, the monument appears as if in ruins, with rough stonework and crushed building bricks symbolising the troubled past. This is, without the slightest doubt, the most original and creative work of its type.

At Xyrolimne, situated twelve kilometers from Kozane on the road to Kastoria, building work on the monument commemorating Pontian Hellenism was still in progress in 2004. Surrounded by railings it stands in half a hectare of land, its entrance is marked by a Byzantine great door: the grassy tumulus at its center symbolizes both the mass grave of the victims of genocide and the Pontian mountains. Three bas-reliefs in sculpted marble, representing everyday scenes from life in Pontus, are installed at the base of the tumulus, but no direct reference is made to the genocide. Most of the standard iconographic elements of Pontian culture are to be found — the single-headed eagle, the *Argo* (Jason's ship), armed resistance fighters, the Phrontistirio, schoolmaster or lyre. To the left, a chapel in honor of the Pontian saints is planned and, at the back, a group of fir trees has been planted to recall the wooded slopes of the Pontic mountains. The notion of being uprooted is also suggested by a group of resistance fighters dancing the *pyrrichios*, the ancient warrior dance, with their heads lowered, as they move off into the distance. When it reaches completion, the memorial will serve as a scale model of the Pontus region, the "lost and unforgettable homeland."

The monument on the square in the center of Euxinoupole (2001), in the outskirts of Thessalonica, also commemorates Pontian Hellenism and represents families forced to march down from the Pontic mountains. It symbolizes an unending life in exile, framed on one side by a Byzantine church with its door ajar and, on the other, by a female figure stooping over the dead or dying body of her son. This memorial was erected in a new district on the outskirts of Thessalonica in 2001 by refugees who had recently arrived from the former Soviet Republics. It celebrates all those Pontians who died at the hands of different regimes or during successive deportations. It is, to our knowledge, the only monument to have been erected in Greece by an association of refugees from the former Soviet Union, and it takes into account their own particular experiences, over and beyond the Pontian genocide *per se.* The theme of uprooting and exile outweigh that of genocide, which is only evoked here through the mother figure holding her dying child, while the church represents a point of stability for the marching population.

In May 2006, the mayor, the town council and representatives of Pontian associations of Thessalonica unveiled a monument in memory of the victims of the massacres in which many Greeks of Pontus lost their lives between 1915 and 1923. Known as the *Memorial to the Genocide of the Pontians*, the word genocide does not figure on it directly. The memorial takes the form of a female figure in bronze, set on a marble plinth, weeping disconsolately over the lost lives of her fellow countrymen and the bitterness of being forced into exile. She represents the refugee mother or grandmother.

So despite the official recognition of the Pontian Genocide by the Greek Parliament in 1994, hardly any mention of this can be found on the memorials themselves. Any mention of it tends to be indirect, and is always bound up with the exodus, exile and uprooting of this people. On the other hand, these memorials nowadays serve as an essential rallying point for the annual 19 May remembrance services which do pay homage to the memories of the victims of genocide, thereby constituting an integral part of the collective memory and identity of the Pontian refugees.

Inauguration and Commemorative Ceremonies

In accordance with the laws passed in 1994 and 1998, inauguration and commemorative ceremonies are generally held at the monuments on 14 September and 19 May. These ceremonies include the two essential ingredients provided for within the framework of the right of remembrance — "predetermined liturgy and participation according to pre-defined protocol."[5] Each commemoration service is based on the same procedure:

- An opening religious service, with a liturgy celebrated in honor of the victims in the nearest church; this is then followed by a procession to the site of the memorial with members of the army, police, church and other leaders of local government and administrations (municipal, provincial and regional governments), and elected representatives (members of parliament, ministers), where a second religious service is then held, such as a for example a *Te Deum*.

- Personal eyewitness accounts from elderly people having lived through the massacres, deportations and uprooting.

- Official speeches preceding the unveiling of a new memorial by the president of the republic, president or vice-president of parliament, and if not by these personages then by a local member of parliament, a mayor or provincial head.

---

[5] Serge Barcellini, "Les politiques de la mémoire, du droit au souvenir au devoir de mémoire," in *La mémoire entre histoire et politique*, Cahiers français, ed. Yves Léonard, no. 303 (Paris: La Documentation Française, 2001), 26.

– Wreaths are laid, a minute of silence observed in honor of the victims commemorated by the memorial, and the national anthem is played by a local military or brass band.

– A range of artistic activities, including the recitation of epic poems, singing accompanied by the lyre, and the performance of popular Pontian dances.

– Evening receptions with the political participants and members of the Pontian associations. This may include performances of Pontian dances or plays.

The major role played by (and the very presence of) the Orthodox Church in these remembrance services is directly linked to the identity of the refugees from Asia Minor, who often are more fervently observant Orthodox than their Helladic compatriots.

Monuments Bearing Pontian Iconography and History-Memory Narratives

Elements of Pontian iconography,[6] in addition to heroic figures or resistance fighters (*Antartes*), are common features on these memorials, which are usually made up of several elements in combination. Some monuments in remembrance of Pontian Hellenism (Xyrolimne-Kozane) or genocide (Kastoria), have most of the main symbols of Pontian iconography on their bas-reliefs: the single-headed eagle, Panagia Soumela, the Phrontisterio (lycée) of Trebizond (Trabzon), the *Argo*, a lyre, resistance fighters in *zipkas*, the profile of Mithridates the Great or of Alexius Comnenus on a coin.

In fact, these memorials should be considered as vectors of Pontian iconography and identity and, more generally, of the memory of the refugees, along with other means of transmission such as the premises of associations, cultural centers, museums, sanctuary-monasteries, and Pontian taverns. It is surprising to note that more than half of the monuments commemorate the victims and armed fighters of Pontus (35), while only a minority (five in all) are addressed to the memory of all the refugees of Asia Minor, irrespective of their specific origin.

The first memorials to be erected, exclusively in memory of the victims of genocide in Pontus, were the cenotaphs and steles (1961–1972). Although remembrance of the dead is a common theme in all these monuments, little direct reference is made to them thereafter in later edifices, with the exception of the monument at Nea Sanda in remembrance of Euklides Kourtides and the 141 victims identified in the Sanda massacres (memorial erected in 1994). The theme of the Pontian resistance hero was also a common feature

[6] Michel Bruneau, "De l'icône à l'iconographie, du religieux au politique, réflexions sur l'origine byzantine d'un concept gottmanien," *Annales de Géographie* 616 (2000): 563–79.

from the memorial in Kallithea (1977) to Kavala (2001). The theme of genocide, which figures in Kilkis (1993), appears on the most recent memorials, particularly those in Therme (2002) and Kastoria (2001). Very few memorials (only three to date) actually show scenes of violence linked to the genocide. On other memorials, the massacres are generally referred to in indirect fashion. However, the theme of being uprooted and torn away from the "unforgettable homeland," a notion often associated with the symbol of the *Argo*, is recurrent subject matter on bronze or marble bas-reliefs.

The family, especially the emblematic Pontian family, is also a recurrent theme in most monuments. The refugee mother, with one or several children, figures on both the Nea Moudania and Mytilene (Epano Skala) memorials in the name of all the Asia Minor refugees. Education is not a common theme *per se.* However, it does figure on some bas-reliefs, which show the Phrontisterio (lycée) of Trebizond.

The Orthodox Christian religion is a common theme, represented by the priest accompanying refugees or leading metropolitans (Chrysostomos, Chrysanthos, Germanos Karavangeles), or through the depiction of a church or monastery (Panagia Soumela). The "unforgettable homelands" figure on all these monuments with their lists of the regions, towns and, sometimes, villages concerned; a map of the Republic of Pontus (Panorama, Xanthe, Kastoria) may even appear, showing the border line claimed at the time modern Turkey defined her new frontiers.

The overall tone of some of the monuments (10%) is to reconcile the duty of remembrance of these lost homelands with a desire to lead the new generations towards a peaceful future rich with new aspirations in Greece, their host country. While the vast majority of memorials are uniquely concerned with the right to remember and the duty of remembrance, the frequent appearance of a distich on the rebirth of *Romania*, the homeland of the *Romans*, or of *Romiosyne* the inhabitants of the Eastern (Byzantine) part of the Roman Empire, does link remembrance with what is envisaged as the idea of a creative and prosperous future.

The three busts of Kapetanides and the maps of Pontus refer to the hope either of independence, or of joining with mainland Greece in the 1920s, and the political overtones of this are clear. Most monuments refer simply to resistance fighting in the mountains, sometimes to life in the countryside, the theme of being uprooted and/or genocide.

The bas-reliefs can be read as a narrative of Greek Pontian history, starting with the mythical adventures of the Argonauts in search of the Golden Fleece. The only monument to portray this tale in full, or rather its meta-narrative, with all the symbols of Pontian iconography displayed across a vast bas-relief sculpted fresco, is the memorial in Kastoria. It is also the most openly political monument, with its bust of Kapetanides above a map of the "claimed territory of Pontus (1918–1922)." The monument, which is quite recent (2001), stands out as an extreme example within the existing corpus.

Another recent monument in Agia Varvara (2002) provides a much more detached and non-nationalistic example of Pontian remembrance using symbolic elements alone, most of which are religious in tenor (Byzantine cross, the great door of Panagia Soumela, candelabras) or cultural (the lyre), with the rifle and sabre appearing as the sole symbols of armed resistance and combat. The great door opens up to the future with no reference to a possible return home. Two other monuments (Florina, Aspropyrgos) even show armed Pontian resistance fighters as belonging to a past that is over and done with, and the central theme is that of the future. Only eight monuments show clearly that what counts is the future, hope for a better life and new cultural roots in Greece.

Not one of the inscriptions or texts engraved on the monuments makes any explicit mention of the Ottomans or Turks, or uses words or expressions referring to them. This is quite surprising if we compare this with the plaques on memorials or in places of remembrance associated with the Second World War in France,[7] where explicit mention is made of the Germans, Nazis and members of the militia, often described in extremely negative terms as "barbarians, brutal hordes or traitors..." Any allusions to the barbaric acts committed by Kemalist troops only appear in the speeches delivered during commemoration ceremonies.

The monuments studied here represent, along with association periodicals, historical literature, and the stories told by those who lived through the events, one of the essential vectors of what Paul Ricœur calls "narrative identity."[8] These elements allow for the story of the Greek Pontian community and, more generally, that of all the Greeks of Asia Minor, to be expressed. However, it is the Pontians who undoubtedly possess the richest iconographic and cultural identity corpus, one that can be clearly distinguished from that of the other refugees. Based as it is on their collective memory, and in turn fuelled by it, this corpus allows a meta-narrative to be elaborated. The Pontians, even though they do not constitute the largest refugee group, certainly have their distinctive own cultural identity and collective memory. They were isolated from the other Greeks far away in the

[7] Serge Barcellini and Annette Wieviorka, *Passant, souviens-toi! Les lieux du souvenir de la Seconde Guerre mondiale en France* (Paris: Editions Plon, 1995).

[8] Paul Ricœur, *Temps et récit, Vol. 3: Le temps raconté: Points, Essais* (Paris: Editions du Seuil, 1985).

northeastern part of Asia Minor and were rooted in centuries of Byzantine history (the Trebizondine Empire of the Comnenans, 1204–1461). That may explain the resilience of their culture and their particularity.

Comparing these monuments with those of the Armenians referring to the same kind of events, we are impressed by the wide variety of the Greek ones as shown in our typology. Most of the Armenian monuments over the world are of the cenotaph type,[9] *khachkar* (cross-stones) or small Armenian churches, very few statues and bas-relief. The Greek refugees have used pictures to a much greater degree, representations, referring to events, to historical emblematic leaders or to the life and the history of their "lost homelands." This difference reflects probably a difference of culture[10] between these two people who were neighbours and had a similar fate in the Ottoman Empire.

---

[9] For comparison with the Armenian genocide memorials, see the Armenian website http://www.armenian-genocide.org/memorials.html. Political, financial and cultural circumstances were entirely different in the nearly mono-ethnic republic of (Soviet) Armenia, where a highly impressive memorial complex was completed in 1968, following massive demonstrations and protests of the Soviet Armenian population (including party and church leadership) against the further oppression by the Soviet government and party leadership of the commemoration of the genocide. In an attempt to counter this first massive demonstration in Soviet history, the central Soviet leadership hastened to give permission for the erection of the monument *Mets Yeghern*. It consists of a circle of nine pylons around an eternal flame, symbolizing the nine provinces (vilayets) of the Ottoman Empire where the bulk of Ottoman Armenians settled, and a split tower like structure, representing the separation of homeland and Diaspora. Annually, up to one million people visit this monument on the Yerevan hilltop Tsitsernakaberd on 24 April to lay down flowers and bow in commemoration.

[10] In this context, one has to recall the "iconoclastic" traditions in Armenian arts (with the exception of book illumination), in contrast to the veneration of icons in Greek and Byzantine traditions.

References Cited

Barcellini, Serge. "Les politiques de la mémoire, du droit au souvenir au devoir de mémoire," in *La mémoire entre histoire et politique*. Cahiers français, no. 303. Paris: La Documentation Française, 2001.

_____________ and Annette Wieviorka. *Passant, souviens-toi ! Les lieux du souvenir de la Seconde Guerre mondiale en France*. Paris: Editions Plon, 1995.

Bruneau, Michel. "Les monastères pontiques en Macédoine, marqueurs territoriaux de la diaspora," in *Les Grecs Pontiques*, ed. M. Bruneau. Paris: CNRS-Éditions, 1998.

___________. "De l'icône à l'iconographie, du religieux au politique, réflexions sur l'origine byzantine d'un concept gottmanien." *Annales de Géographie* (Paris) 616 (2000).

___________ and K. Papoulidis, "La mémoire des 'patries inoubliables:' la construction de monuments par les réfugiés d'Asie Mineure en Grèce." *Vingtième Siècle. Revue d'Histoire*. Paris: Presses de Sciences Po, 2003.

___________ and K. Papoulidis, *La mémoire de l'Hellénisme réfugié: les monuments commémoratifs en Grèce (1936–2004)*. Thessalonica: Kyriakidis, 2004 [Bilingual Greek-French edition].

Charalampidis, M. K. Fotiadis. *Πόντος, Δικαίωμα στην Μνήμη* [*Pontus, the Right to Memory*]. Thessalonica: Εκδόσεις Ηρόδοτος, 1987.

Choay, Francoise. *L'allégorie du patrimoine*. Paris: Editions du Seuil, 1992.

Enepekidis, P. "Το Ολοκαύτωμα του Μικρασιατικού Ελληνισμού" [The Holocaust of the Hellenism of Asia Minor]. In *A' Pankosmio Pontiako Synedrio*, 7–14 July 1985, Thessalonica.

___________. *Γενοκτονία στον Εύξεινο Πόντο* [Genocide in the Euxine Sea]. Thessalonica: Εύξεινος Λέσχη, 1996.

Fotiadis, Konstantinos. "Η Γενοκτονία των Ελλήνων του Πόντου" [The Genocide of the Greeks of the Pontus]. In *B' Pankosmio Synedrio tou Pontiakou Ellinismou*, 31 July–7 August 1988, Thessalonica 1988.

Hirschon, Renée. *Heirs of the Greek Catastrophe, the Social Life of Asia Minor Refugees in Piraeus*. Oxford: Clarendon Press 1989.

Ricœur, Paul. *Temps et récit, 3. Le temps raconté*. Paris: Editions du Seuil, 1985.

Sakka, G. I. *Το ιστορικό της ανεγέρσεως του Παμποντιακού ηρώου* [The Background of the Erection of the Panpontian Memorial]. Athens : [n.p.], 1979.

Wieviorka, Annette. *Déportation et génocide, entre la mémoire et l'oubli*. Paris: Editions Plon, 1992.

Λεύκωμα Εστίας Νέας Σμύρνης 1930–1980 [*The Album of the Community Center of Nea Smyrne*]. Athens.

The Eastern Question: Genocide in Support of Nationality

AKIS KALAITZIDIS AND DONALD WALLACE

GENOCIDE DENIERS HAVE FOR A LONG TIME used international crises as a shield to hide the perpetrators from international scrutiny. The international system is designed as an arbitrator of genocidal crimes, yet crisis within that system allows arbitration to break down and genocide to go unstopped. What are some of the conditions conducive to genocide?

We argue that transition systems, systems moving from multi-ethnicity to unitary nation state, are more likely to experience genocide, and in this sense, what happened after the collapse of the Ottoman Empire is an illustration.[1] To avoid the pitfalls of purely structural or utilitarian explanations of genocide, we attempt to include the concept of identity as a key factor in the formation of conditions that lead to genocide. As such, the transformation of the Ottoman Empire into a nation-state (Turkey) led to the primacy of ethno-religious identity as the key reorganizing principle of the new nation-state, what we would call ethno-nationalism as opposed to other categories such as civic nationalism. Once the decision was made for this reorganization, the move towards the creation of a single nation-state by employing the ideology of ethno-nationalism meant that the only options were the expulsion and extermination of non-Turkish populations. In the words of Reşat Kasaba,

> It was the political and intellectual elite who brought these three factors together [i.e., nationalism, institutional change, and the redrawing of borders]. They did this on the basis of their own visions of how transition should unfold. In doing so, they took advantage of the opportunities offered by the changes in the regional and international context and they also tapped the energies of the already mobilized groups and communities in the area.[2]

It is clear that the reinforcement of the ethno-political cleavages by the Ottoman Empire eventually led to ethno-nationalism (i.e., the longing for terri-

---

[1] Michael Mann argues along the same lines that genocide is a result of modernity in his seminal work *The Dark Side of Democracy* (Cambridge: Cambridge University Press, 2005).

[2] Reşat Kasaba, "Dreams of Empire, Dreams of Nations," *Empire to Nation: Historical Perspectives on the Making of the Modern World*, Joseph W. Esherick, ed. (Lanham, MD: Rowman and Littlefield, 2006), 221.

torial independence and control) and to the perpetration of not one, but three full-scale genocides (Armenians, Greeks and Syriacs) as a means of redefining itself. Even though the key principle of the genocides was ethno-politics (i.e. the political mobilization of ethnic groups), the leadership of the Ottoman Empire, and later of modern day Turkey, had a political opportunity that they used to perpetuate these genocides. One can also argue that the Turkish leadership's reaction to this political opportunity, i.e., the decision to commit genocide, keeps redefining the existing self view of modern Turkey; Turkish national identity is continually defined *vis-à-vis* its perceived enemies, and genocidal events appear to be a reference point for Turkish nationalism. A look at the recent murder of Hrant Dink, the chief editor of the Armenian newspaper *Agos,* founded in 1995 in İstanbul, by a young Turkish nationalist is just one illustrative point.

Genocide: A Definition

Predictably, part of the debate on genocide as a whole has focused on its very definition, and the difference between genocide and other forms of violence against people. Genocide is a compound word from the Greek words *genos* (race) and the Latin suffix *-cide* (killing). The intellectual father of the word itself is Raphael Lemkin, who in 1944 published his book, *Axis Rule in Occupied Europe,* in which he defines genocide as follows:

> Generally speaking, genocide does not necessarily mean the immediate destruction of a nation, except when accomplished by mass killings of all members of a nation. It is intended rather to signify a coordinated plan of different actions aiming at the destruction of essential foundations of life of national groups, with the aim of annihilating the groups themselves. The objectives of such [a] plan would be the disintegration of the political and social institutions, and the destruction of the personal security, liberty, health, dignity and even the lives of the individuals belonging to such groups.[3]

Lemkin was influential both in the Nuremberg trials and the Convention on the Prevention of the Crime of Genocide, which was adopted in 1948 and defines the act of genocide as:

> ... any of the following acts committed with intent to destroy, in whole or in part, a national, ethnical [sic], racial or religious group, as such:
> a) killing members of the group
> b) causing serious bodily or mental harm to members of the group;
> c) deliberately inflicting on the group conditions of life calculated to bring about its physical destruction in whole or in part;
> d) imposing measures intended to prevent births within the group;
> e) forcibly transferring children of the group to another group.

[3] Raphael Lemkin, *Axis Rule in Occupied Europe: Laws of Occupation, Analysis of Government, Proposals for Redress* (Washington, D.C.: Carnegie Endowment for International Peace, 1944), 3.

As Totten argues, it is precisely because of the vagueness of this statute that the definitional issues of the term genocide arise and have hampered the ability of researchers to move beyond the efforts of merely defining an act as genocide, not to mention whether or not anyone can use the term holocaust interchangeably with genocide when describing anything other than the destruction of the Jews in World War II.[4] The key to the UN definition is the words "intent" and "in whole or in part," which seems to add breadth to the definition of genocide. It is no longer necessarily as total and as disciplined as that perpetrated by the Nazis; instead, it could be scantily organized but ruthlessly executed, as in Darfur.

In her work, Helen Fein categorized genocides according to the perpetrators' motives, such as a) developmental genocide, one that is normally perpetrated by colonizers against indigenous peoples, b) despotic genocide, one that is perpetrated during a power struggle, c) retributive genocide, one that is perpetrated along different societal cleavages such as ethno-religious or linguistic ones, and d) ideological genocide, one that is perpetrated for reasons of ideology.[5]

Somewhat differently, Leo Kuper categorizes genocides according to the societal divisions existing in the country where the genocide takes place; they are a) genocides against indigenous peoples, b) genocide upon decolonization of a two tier system structure of domination, and c) genocide in the process of struggles by ethnic, or racial or religious groups, for power or secession, greater autonomy, or more equality.[6]

In this article we look at situations in which the state is using violence directly and by proxy simultaneously, in order to destroy populations that do not belong to the dominant group. In these instances, the genocide is retributive according to the typology used above. But we argue more radically that the specific killings took place during the process of the state's remodeling and the regrouping of smaller units into cohesive nation-states. The Greeks, the Armenians and the Syriacs (including Chaldeans, Nestorians and other groups of non-Muslims as defined by David Gaunt)[7] were targeted for destruction by the fathers of modern-day Turkey because of a) ethnic diffe-

---

[4] Samuel Totten, "To Deem or Not To Deem 'It' Genocide: A Double-Edged Sword," in *The Genocidal Temptation: Auschwitz, Hiroshima, Rwanda, and Beyond*, Robert Seitz Frey, ed. (Dallas: University Press of America, 2004), 41–55.

[5] As cited in *Genocide: A Critical Bibliographical Review*, Israel Charny, ed. (New York: Facts on File, 1988), 3.

[6] Leo Kuper, *The Prevention of Genocide* (New Haven: Yale University Press, 1985).

[7] David Gaunt, *Massacres, Resistance, Protectors: Muslim-Christian relations in Eastern Anatolia During World War I* (Piscataway, New Jersey: Gorgias Press 2006).

rences, b) religious differences, c) (alleged) wealth, and d) international reasons. However, the Greeks of Asia Minor were spared the fate of the Armenians, who were targeted for complete destruction, due to the existence of the sovereign, albeit small and poor, state of Greece that was willing to accept masses of expelled refugees.

As a result of the Treaty of Lausanne there was an exchange, or ethnic cleansing, of 900,000 Greeks from modern day Turkey and 300,000 Turks from Northern Greece. In addition, there had been massive killings of the Pontian Greeks, about half of the Greek population that lived in the area of the Black Sea, and the expulsion of the rest. This particular Greek subgroup was targeted for annihilation; in the pages that follow we will deal with this case as a subset of the larger Greek genocide, which was perpetrated between 1914 and 1922.

In the case of the Syriac victims, an analogous story unfolds, although the numbers were smaller because of the Syriacs' smaller communities. In *Massacres, Resistance, Protectors: Muslim–Christian Relations in Eastern Anatolia During World War I*, David Gaunt writes:

> The Assyrian, Chaldean, and Syriac victims were easy to single out because they belonged to a non–Muslim group and spoke non–Turkic languages. They were thus targeted for violent ethnic cleansing as religious and ethnic groups, but not as racial groups. Thus the reason for their extermination should be sought against the background of their religious and ethnic deviation from the political standards held by the ideologues in power.[8]

One thing remains clear: under the UN definition, this was the second genocide (one of several given the diverse peoples targeted) perpetrated in order to create modern–day Turkey. Of course, the first genocide is the best known one and was perpetrated against the Armenians, but other groups such as the Syriacs suffered the indignities of deportations, forced labor, starvation, and were finally massacred. Approximately 2.5 million people died in Anatolia between 1913 and 1920[9], the vast majority of whom were targeted for destruction by the Young Turks, CUP, and later on, the Kemalists. At least 1 million to 1.5 million Armenians, 350,000 Pontian Greeks (not including Greeks in western Turkey such as İzmir (Smyrna (Gr.)) and 250,000 Syriacs died in the years between 1914 and 1920.[10] It is our contention that ethno–politics in service of territorial nationalism can lead to genocide, and as such, all these groups mentioned above suffered one.

---

[8] Ibid., 303–304.

[9] Kasaba, "Dreams of Empire, Dreams of Nations," 215.

[10] Numbers compiled from different sources such as: Razmik Panossian, *The Armenians: From Kings and Priests to Merchants and Commissars* (New York: Columbia University Press, 2006), Gaunt, *Massacres, Resistance, Protectors* and Μιχάλης Χαραλαμπίδης & Κώστας Φωτιάδης, *Πόντιοι: Δικαίωμα στη Μνήμη* [Michales Charalampides & Kostas Fotiadis, *Pontians: The Right to Memory*](Thessalonica: Κυριακίδης, 1991).

Identity in a Nation-State

"What's in a name?" asks an author considering the implications of the naming of Former Yugoslav Republic of Macedonia, the last element of this designation being a name the Greeks consider their rightful inheritance.[11] Thea Halo highlights the impact of name changes on her historical homeland after the expulsion and genocide of the Greeks of Asia Minor in her famous book *Not Even My Name*.[12] The discussions are illustrative of the fact that names are important pieces of self-identification, of who we are and where we belong in the larger context of society.

This identity is extremely important in understanding genocide, more important than its tangible and material components, as Walker Connor would agree.[13] This is not to argue that tangible and material components of a group's identity, such as its way of life, its geographic location, and its understanding of history and kinship relations are not important. Contrary to relative deprivation theories, structural explanations of international relations, and economic utilitarian explanations of genocide, we argue that these are intervening variables in a larger explanatory framework, which begins with identity as the key causal variable for genocide. Invariably, the tangible elements of identity will manifest themselves once identity becomes the key cleavage along which society arranges itself both in peace and, most importantly, in conflict; thus, they will shape the logic behind the genocide.

How does ethnic identity relate to nationalism? It is understood that ethnic identity is a subset of a national identity if such a nation exists. If a nation does not exist, then this subset of people is called indigenous, tribal, regional, etc.[14] However the subsets are defined, they are mostly minority groups existing within a unit, but are not politicized. Essentially, for many centuries this was not a problem *per se*. Only in modern times do we see what Rothschild calls "ethno-politics," or the politicization of ethnic groups.[15] Ethno-politics can be considered a side effect of the modern political system, i.e. the Westphalian system. The famous peace of Westphalia established a new world order in Europe whose consequences among others were:

a) state sovereignty;
b) equality of states;

[11] Nikos Zahariadis, *Essence of Political Manipulation* (New York: Peter Lang, 2006).

[12] Thea Halo, *Not Even My Name* (New York: Picador, 2000).

[13] Walker Connor, *Ethnonationalism: A Quest for Understanding* (Princeton: Princeton University Press, 1994).

[14] Ibid., 100–11.

[15] Joseph Rothschild, *Ethnopolitics: A Conceptual Framework* (New York: Columbia University Press, 1981).

c) non–intervention;
d) the legitimization of realpolitik; and,
e) the demise of moral constraints in politics.[16]

In this type of system power and the use of force are the most important elements, so states "are only rewarded for being strong enough to do what is necessary."[17] This combination of consequences has proven deadly for many peoples around the world to this very day through the politicization of ethnicity. In Rothschild's words,

> [...] under contemporary conditions of rapid change, intrusive yet remote state apparatuses, weak functional interest groups, and diluted political consensus, people often cleave to, or rediscover, or even invent, their ethnicity — putatively rooted in primordial bonds — for personal identification, emotional security, and communal anchorage.[18]

However, the reason why ethnicity becomes politicized according to Rothschild is the societal cleavages that exist and reinforce some type of systemic ethnic inequality, which the elite attempts to support or destroy by using ethnicity as an instrument.[19] This explanation fits with other explanations, which see the politicization of ethnicity and its transformation into nationalism as an expression of the pressures of modernity and elite decision making.

In Kedourie's view, nationalism is an expression of the intellectual activities of elites.[20] In Gellner's famous works, especially his book *Nations and Nationalism*, nationalism is a reaction to the pressures of the modern post–industrial revolution society.[21] In his view, ethnicity becomes reinforced and politicized because of the homogenizing pressures of modernity. This complements the views expressed in other theses by contemporary writers who argue that nationalism is either a reaction to the modern state structure, such as the one advanced by Breuilly,[22] or a creation of the modern state structure such as the one advanced by Charles Tilly.[23] Finally, there are those who consider nationalism, as a societal expression, to be an invented

---

16 Charles Kegley and Gregory Raymond, *Exorcising the Ghost of Westphalia: Building World Order in the New Millennium* (Upper Saddle River: Prentice Hall, 2002).

17 Henry Kissinger, *Diplomacy* (New York: Simon and Schuster, 1994), 58.

18 Rothschild, *Ethnopolitics*, 247.

19 Ibid., 248.

20 Elia Kedourie, *Nationalism* (London: Hutchinson, 1966).

21 Ernest Gellner, *Nations and Nationalism* (Oxford: Blackwell, 1983).

22 John Breuilly, *Nationalism and the State* (Manchester: Manchester University Press, 1992).

23 Charles Tilly, *Coercion Capital and the European States AD 990–1992* (Cambridge: Basil Blackwell, 1990).

tradition based on a modern view of the past. An invented tradition, according to Hobsbawm,

> [...] is taken to mean a set of practices normally governed by overtly or tacitly accepted rules and of a ritual or symbolic nature, which seek to inculcate certain values and norms of behavior by repetition, which automatically implies continuity with the past. In fact, where possible, they normally attempt to establish continuity with a suitable historic past.[24]

As with Gellner and Hobsbawm, Benedict Anderson claims that the nation is an invented notion and became a popular feature of societal association with the invention of the printing press and the circulation of books and pamphlets.[25] Basically, once the public is educated, it begins grouping itself along ethnic and national lines.

There is, however, one aberrant case in point: Greece, in which, Hobsbawm explains, the ideals of republican France and middle class nationalism and the absence of any real authority in the Ottoman Empire produced a nation.[26] In his point of view, nationalism came before the nation. But because of French nationalism's success in Greece, it ceased to be an aberrant case, as other emerging national identities spawned new nations in the area.

Looking at the explanations for the development of the Armenian nation offered by Panossian, we see some similarities with the Greek case as well. Panossian writes,

> [t]he Armenian Case shows that eighteenth century Armenian merchants in India, or a religious brotherhood in Venice, played a similar role in the financing and directing endeavours of national identity creation as did states in Europe.[27]

Contrary to Hobsbawm's argument, Smith sees the emergence of nation states created after the collapse of the Ottoman Empire as products of the "scientific state," which "seeks to homogenize the population within its boundaries for administrative purposes by utilizing the latest scientific techniques and methods for the sake of efficiency."[28] The attempt by the Ottoman Empire to adapt new, successful European scientific and social elements failed and ultimately led to its dissolution. It failed because its leaders went through what Smith calls the "dual legitimization" process,

---

[24] Eric Hobsbawm and Terence Ranger, eds., *The Invention of Tradition* (Cambridge: Cambridge University Press, 1983), 1.

[25] Benedict Anderson, *Imagined Communities: Reflections on the Origin and the Spread of Nationalism* (London: Verso, 1991).

[26] Eric Hobsbawm, *The Age of Revolution 1789–1848* (New York: Mentor Books, 1962), 173.

[27] Panossian, *The Armenians*, 11.

[28] Anthony Smith, *Theories of Nationalism* (London: Holmes and Meier, 1983), 231.

which tends to shatter the old, traditional way in favor of the new (what we will call European, considering they came mostly from Europe) ways, creating a crisis of legitimacy for the Empire.[29]

One could claim however, that even though the Ottoman Empire lost the war and failed as an empire and a multicultural entity, the successive and interconnected CUP and Kemalist attempts to adapt European scientific and social elements were in both cases partially "successful," though to varying degrees. Firstly, the CUP was at least partially successful in "modernizing" what was considered the core of the empire by, among other things, Turkifying, cleansing, and exterminating non-Turkic nationalities. As Cevat Bey, Turkish minister to Copenhagen and *diplomate de carrière* with close connections to the Young Turk government, stated in a 1916 interview:

> We have now introduced the Turkish language in Turkey. This is the first result of a national awakening: Turkey for the Turks. [...] When we change old signs and street names, our enemies claim that we tear down the European inscriptions out of hatred and malice. There is no truth in that. We only do what all nations have done before us. They call us chauvinists and rebels. I assure you, we only want one thing: our economical and political independence. This we all agree upon. There are no longer both old and young Turks. There are only Turks. And during the war we are all young.[30]

The key to this passage is the sentence, "We only do what all nations have done before us." One could argue that the Kemalists built modern Turkey not just on a failure, but also on a) the radically modernizing ideological legacy of the CUP that had proved to be effective and, in the eyes of the Turkish nationalists, necessary, b) on many of the leading CUP members, and c) especially violent Turkification, the one big modernizing "success" of the CUP. They lost an empire, but gained a relatively secure, homogenous, and stable nation-state. They also idolized some of the same "heroes."[31] Hans-Lukas Kieser, discussing Reşid, the decidedly racist vali of Diyarbakır (Amida (Gr.)) the extermination of Armenians and Aramaeans in that region, writes,

> [t]he fact that the Unionist-Kemalist generation, which had founded the nation-state, counted Dr Reşid amongst its heroes instead of accepting the "universal" verdict, betrays a more general setting of the course of history.[32]

---

[29] Ibid., 238–41.

[30] UM, 2-0355, "Konstantinopel/Istanbul, diplomatisk repræsentation," "Noter og indberetninger om den politiske udvikling, 1914–1922," "Verdenskrigen. Rapporter fra Smyrna. Nov. 1914–Marts 1916," Van der Zee to Wandel, 17/7 1915.

[31] Hans-Lukas Kieser, "Dr. Mehmed Reshid (1873–1919): A Political Doctor," in Hans-Lukas Kieser & Dominik J. Schaller, eds., *Der Völkermord an den Armeniern und die Shoah* [*The Armenian Genocide and the Shoah*] (Zürich: Chronos, 2003), 273.

[32] We would like to thank Matthias Bjørnlund for his suggestions on this idea of success within the larger failure in the collapsing Ottoman Empire.

Another scholar agrees that,

> The CUP put its policies [of genocide, etc.] into practice for the sake of a thorough ethno-religious homogenization of the empire, resulting in the establishment of a Turkish nation-state in 1923. In subsequent decades, processes of social engineering went on, as many CUP potentates remained influential and continued to formulate and implement new policies of demographic engineering in the Turkish Republic.[33]

Therefore, we have a failing empire being transformed piecemeal into independent states, all of which trace their national identity to some pre-revolutionary roots. Whether or not these roots are imagined, invented or real, in the end, both the state and the intelligentsia that led the state to fruition had to adopt a new frame of reference for self-identity, and the most accessible one was the frame of reference that led to independence in the first place, ethno-nationalism. It is in this sense that atrocities such as massacres, genocides, ethnic cleansing, and the like have become part of our collective human experience.

Genocide is ultimately the ugliest expression of the difference between nation and state, and it starts with the notion of group allegiance. As Connor notes, it is difficult to pinpoint when the confusion between the two (nation and state) started, but it also led to the equation of nationalism with the allegiance to the state.[34] Such an equation, however, can become extremely dangerous for minorities, as it invites the titular nationality to question their allegiance to the state; it is one of the most destructive forces of nationalism.

Of course, it is not necessary that nationalism lead to genocide, or for that matter, even to the creation of a single nation-state. Consider that few states today can be characterized as nation-states.[35] In fact, Castells argues that nationalism is largely a reaction to global forces and should be treated as such.[36] No matter what, the demand for allegiance to the state can be detrimental to the existence of ethnic groups once such a concept becomes the key societal reference. Obviously, the Armenians, the Greeks, and the Syriacs in the Ottoman Empire are probably the best example of this, considering the changing conditions of the time such as the collapse of the Ottoman Empire and the creation of nation-states around titular nationalities. Although it is not our intent to provide answers to why the Ottoman Empire col-

---

[33] Uğur Ü. Üngor, "When Persecution Bleeds into Mass Murder: The Processive Nature of Genocide," *Genocide Studies & Prevention (GSP)* 1, no. 2 (Fall 2006): 173.

[34] Connor, *Ethnonationalism,* 98.

[35] Ibid., 96.

[36] Manuel Castells, *The Power of Identity, The Information Age: Economy Society and Culture* Vol. II (Malden, MA: Blackwell Publishers, 1997), 30.

lapsed, one needs to consider the impact of ethnic identities upon societal relations in order to understand the decision to perpetrate the crime of genocide.

Genocide and Political Opportunity Structure

Considering that not all state collapses lead to genocide and that some genocides do not come from the collapse of a state, one needs to consider the link between the political milieu and the process in which a decision is made to move forward with a genocide. Additionally, one must consider whether this decision is actually consciously taken or not, as the debate on the Holocaust underlines. As it is, extreme nationalism, international pressures, and domestic upheaval exist in several places in the world simultaneously, but they do not always result in genocidal action. If ethno-nationalism is the reason behind the genocide, what political conditions allow for it?

Manus Midlarsky developed a theory of the transformation of massacres into full-scale genocide in his influential book, *The Killing Trap*.[37] In Midlarsky's view, there is always a conscious decision to commit genocide, the roots of which are embedded in the win-lose perception of the perpetrators, i.e., the geographic, economic, and security losses of the perpetrator in his historical milieu weighed against the prospective gains of engaging in genocide. In his view, "the combination of risk minimization and loss compensation yields the genocidal outcome."[38] However, the perpetrator's "losses" are equally defined by his perceptions and ideas, such as his historical claims and his definition of "self" as opposed to "other."

Midlarsky prefers to take the rationalist prospect theory approach and claims that it is the coupling of the titular nationality's losses with the minority's advanced socioeconomic status, i.e. geographic location, economic, social, and political status, that leads to the titular nationality's decision to commit genocide.[39] Midlarksy takes a rather limited view of genocide and a very limited view of the impact of ethnicity. In fact, the interconnection of ethnicity and nationalism are hardly examined in favor of a rational socioeconomic explanation. This way, the author can fit his cases into his theory saliently and explain all three genocides, the Holocaust, the Armenian and the Rwandan genocides, leaving out cases such as the Greeks of the Ottoman Empire and present day Turkey as well as what precipitated from the collapse of Yugoslavia in Bosnia-Herzegovina and Kosovo, claiming that they were "mere" ethnic cleansing. In this he will find historians and internation-

---

37 Manus Midlarsky, *The Killing Trap: Genocide in the Twentieth Century* (Cambridge: Cambridge University Press, 2005).

38 Ibid., 85.

39 Ibid.

al organizations opposing him. Considering the recent decision of the International Court of Justice on a lawsuit brought by Bosnia–Herzegovina on the issue of genocide against Serbia, the court clearly found evidence of perpetrated genocide (in Srebrenica) without blaming the Serbian state (somewhat of a Solomonic solution to a sticky international problem).[40]

Similarly, Bloxham, in his seminal work *The Great Game of Genocide*, considers the scope of the massacres and ethnic deportations in Turkey as genocide (though he differentiates between the CUP and the Kemalist times as he should).[41] The distinguished Turkish scholar Taner Akçam, in his *From Empire to Republic: Turkish Nationalism and the Armenian Genocide*, suggests that more than the destruction of Armenians took place in Ottoman Turkey, i.e. the destruction of the Greeks and with an intent to follow with the Kurds soon after.[42] In his defense, Midlarsky refers to the destruction of the Greek ethnic communities of Ottoman Turkey as ethnic cleansing and contends that their total destruction was not decided due to the possibility of population exchanges.[43]

What is missing in Midlarsky's explanation is a discussion of ethno–nationalism and the politics of identity. By employing the ethno–political explanation, we are not necessarily disavowing rational choice explanations that include the same socioeconomic elements that Midlarsky employs. It seems a good case can be made for these explanations regarding colonial genocides (genocides perpetrated by organized states in search of material resources such as land).[44] It also seems that race was definitely an underlining issue, and though it is not our intention to treat the link between race and ethnic identity, one cannot dismiss the ethnic politicization process that preceded the massacres of Native Americans or Africans. Ethno–politics is the root of genocide, while the rest of the conditions act as independent variables, which shape the intervening socioeconomic explanations for genocide. It seems that psychologists argue that we, as humans, have a natural

---

[40] Accessed on 5 April 2007: http://www.icj-cij.org/icjwww/idocket/ibhy/ibhyframe.htm

[41] Donald Bloxham, *The Great Game of Genocide: Imperialism, Nationalism and the Destruction of the Ottoman Armenians* (Oxford and New York: Oxford University Press, 2005), 98 and 106. Although it is doubtful that the author believes the entire scope of ethnic persecution to be genocide, his work is used here as yet another indication of how genocide was used in support of the creation of the Turkish nation.

[42] Taner Akçam, *From Empire to Republic: Turkish Nationalism and the Armenian Genocide* (London: Zed Books, 2004).

[43] Midlarsky, *The Killing Trap*, 337–43.

[44] Robert Cribb, "Genocide in the Non–Western World: Implications for Holocaust Studies" in *Genocide: Case, Comparisons and Contemporary Debates* (Copenhagen: Danish Center for Holocaust and Genocide Studies, 2003), 123–40.

inclination (also shown by brain imaging research) to form identity groups and categorize other people in society.[45] Thus, issues of cooperation and conflict are affected by our process of cognition and grouping and can lead to prejudices. From prejudice to ethnic violence (if not genocide), there is an additional step that people must go through, though most people do not. Ethno-politics, the aforementioned step, as noted earlier in this paper, is an expression of mobilization along ethnic lines. We can successfully explore the extent of the impact of ethno-politics through the socioeconomic lens by employing the concept of political opportunity structure.

Political opportunity structure is a term that describes:

> ... exogenous factors [that] enhance or inhibit prospects for mobilization, for particular sorts of claims to be advanced rather than others, for particular strategies of influence to be exercised, and for movements to affect mainstream institutional politics and policy.[46]

The term "political opportunity structure" has been used variably by many social scientists looking at mass mobilization movements.[47] In the social mobilization literature, Kitschelt defined political opportunity structure as,

> comprised of specific configurations of resources, institutional arrangements, and historical precedents for social mobilization, which facilitate the development of protest movements in some instances and constrain them in others.[48]

Political opportunity can explain why ethno-politics become virulently violent and genocidal in some cases while in others, they do not. Using the same definition for genocide as today's international community and ethno-politics as the independent variable, we see how ethno-politics affect genocide. Because ethno-politics are necessarily defined by mobilization along ethnic lines, historians can trace the genesis of genocidal events to the decision to mobilize along ethnic lines. Thus, if mobilization takes place, what makes it genocidal or not?

In political opportunity literature, we have roughly the following schema:

---

[45] Mark Buchanan, "Born Prejudiced," *New Scientist* 193, no. 2595 (17 March 2007).

[46] David Meyer and Debra Minkoff, "Conceptualizing Political Opportunity," *Social Forces*, 82, no. 4 (June 2004): 1457–92.

[47] See the work of Herbert Kitschelt, "Political Opportunity structures and Political Protest: Anti-Nuclear Movements in Four Democracies," *British Journal of Political Science* 16, no. 1 (January 1986): 57–85, or Doug McAdam, *Political Process and the Development of Black Insurgency, 1930–1970* (Chicago: University of Chicago Press, 1995), or Charles Tilly, *From Mobilization to Revolution* (New York: McGraw Hill, 1978), or *Comparative Perspectives in Social Movements*, Doug McAdam, John D. McCarthy, Mayer N. Zald, eds. (Cambridge: Cambridge University Press, 1996), just to name a few.

[48] Kitschelt, "Political Opportunity structures and Political Protest," 58.

Antecedent conditions	→	Formation of political structures & institutions	→	Conflict/ mass mobilization

In our schema, this becomes:

		Ethnopolitics		
Collapsing empire or other multiethnic unit	→	Remaining institutions (Army, Church, Family)	→	Genocide

When the central authority is being radically transformed, and groups mobilize along ethno-political lines, whether religious, linguistic, ethnic, racial etc, conflict is inevitable. As Kuper would argue, domestic genocide is the result of the existence of such ethno-political cleavages in a multiethnic society.[49] Thus, genocide is the outcome of the interplay between mobilization and ethno-politics.

In the case of the annihilation of the Greeks, and also of the genocides in former Yugoslavia, the eminent collapse of the multiethnic unit allows for ethno-national mobilization, which in turn leads to conflict. In the case of Yugoslavia, it led to war between ethnic groups, which caused genocide, while in the case of the Greeks, war is an exogenous factor that only accelerated the process of extermination of the victim group.

Most theorists focus on the role of the state in perpetrating genocide, such as Dadrian in his comparison of the Armenian, Jewish, and Rwandan genocides. In the two of his three cases, the state is about to collapse and the ethno-political process is replacing state structures with ethnically mobilized groups that use remaining state institutions to perpetrate genocide, such as the army and the church.[50] In the third case, the state is captured by one ethno-political group via the democratic process.

The political opportunity structure of genocide is comprised of ethno-politics assisted by prospecting of the political milieu. Thus, if there is an eminent collapse of state structures, dominant sub-units may decide to take over, and when these units are solidly formed along ethno-political lines, the chances of genocide are advanced. In the case of Nazi Germany, an ideological group was ready to stand in at the end of the Weimar Republic, while in the case of Rwanda the Rwandan Patriotic Front (RPF) was the prospector. In the case of the Ottoman Greeks during 1919–1922, the group that perpetrated the mass killings was comprised of former Ottoman army units,

[49] Leo Kuper, *Genocide: Its Political Use in the Twentieth Century* (New Haven: Yale University Press, 1982).

[50] Vahakn Dadrian, "Patterns of Twentieth Century Genocide: the Armenian, the Jewish, and Rwandan cases," *Journal of Genocide Research* 6, no. 4 (2004): 487–522.

which later became the Turkish Army in search of a geopolitical nation-state for Turks alone.

Identity as a Source of Genocide

Having decided to employ the politics of ethno-nationalism in order to create a nation-state or to carve out a homeland, the perpetrators faced several options on how to proceed. The decisions were not absolutely in their own hands however, considering that the Ottoman Empire fell apart during World War I; Ülker argues that they faced the dissolution of the state, and thus they had to make tough choices.[51]

Most Turkish genocide deniers harp on the fact that during war, people die, and that modern historians fallaciously charge the Turkish state, which was only just born, with such heinous crimes.[52] The modern researcher, therefore, has to prove not only that the numerous deaths of civilians were not a direct result of the war (war casualties), but also that these civilian populations were largely targeted for extinction for specific reasons, and provide evidence of the executioners' plan. The debate on the Armenian Genocide is illustrative of the uphill battle the Greeks face to prove their claims of genocide, considering that nearly a century later, the Turkish state and politicians still deny the genocide and threaten the elite with severe punishments for insulting "Turkishness." Not all is lost, however, because the Greek populations that suffered in Turkey have partially preserved a large cache of documents, both Ottoman/Turkish and foreign, to defend the memory of those who lost their lives, and they are also assisted by the research done by the Armenians and a small but growing minority of Turkish scholars who are interested in shedding light on the events.

We posit that ethno-nationalism motivated the destruction both of the Armenians and of the Ottoman Greeks. Although the Armenians suffered proportionately greater losses than the Greeks (they were nearly eliminated as a result of the genocide), the Greeks also were *targeted* for destruction; thus, the intended perpetration against the Greeks clearly falls into the category of genocide. As Matthias Bjørnlund argues in his chapter, our main historical accounts come from westerners who were present in the Ottoman Empire at the time, and who saw the larger scale Armenian genocide. Therefore, historians have tended to focus more on it, rather than include the Greek genocide as part of the inheritance of the Turkish nation.

---

[51] Erol Ülker, "Contextualizing 'Turkification:' Nation-Building in the Late Ottoman Empire, 1908–18," *Nations and Nationalism* 11 no. 4 (2005): 613–36.

[52] See Israel Charny, "Innocent Denials of Known Genocides: a Further Contribution to a Psychology of Denial of Genocide," *Human Rights Review* 1, no. 3 (2000): 15–39. Also see, Yücel Güçlü, "Mislabeling Genocide?" *Middle East Quarterly* 8, no. 2 (Spring 2006): 67–68.

One thing is clear: the evident result of ethno-politics during the transformation and collapse of the Ottoman Empire is the complete destruction and expulsion of the Armenians and Syriacs from Anatolia, and the Pontian Greeks from the Black Sea. The ethno-politicization of Turkish identity, as opposed to minority identities, was Turkification; thus Turkification is inextricably linked to the genocides. To argue that Turkification was a mere nation-building exercise within a multiethnic empire[53] is tantamount to arguing that rape is a function of sexual compatibility.

What is more appropriate in this case is to examine how ethno-politics became the vehicle for genocide. Turkification is clearly one of the ways. Turkification, as Ulker notes, was the issue on the minds of all Ottoman minorities both in the pre-constitutional and the post-constitutional era, and leading all the way up to the beginning of the Armenian genocide in 1915–16 and the Greek genocide beginning in 1916.[54] The Hamidian regime used Islamization in an attempt to create a cohesive group of subjects, but only succeeded in dividing the empire into Muslim and non-Muslim populations, thus planting the seed for the arrival of Turkishness as an ethnic identity for the Muslim populations that were neither Arab nor Kurdish. While in power, the Young Turks then made Turkification an explicit policy and the creation of a nation-state their ultimate goal.

The late arrival of Turkishness is, according to Akçam, one of the main reasons why Turkish nationalism is so virulent.[55] In a study conducted by Bora İşyar, the emergence of Turkism as a dominant racial identity for the Muslim peoples of the Ottoman Empire is examined. He concludes that there were three alternative types of identity discourses dealing with,

a) the way Turks were mistreated in the outer parts of the Ottoman Empire and in the nation-states that resulted from its partial collapse;
b) the dehumanization of the "other," specifically the increasing racism, and especially against the Armenians and the Greeks; and
c) a sort of transference of nationalist ideas.[56]

He considers this encroachment of European, post-French revolutionary nationalism, which is evident in all the newly created states in the Balkans and the collapsing Ottoman Empire, to be the most influential on the Turks.[57] Akçam actually goes further in support of this concept by arguing

---

53 Ibid., 63.

54 Ibid., 68.

55 Akçam, *From Empire to Republic,* 62.

56 Bora İşyar, "The Origins of Turkish Republican Citizenship: The Birth of a Race," *Nations and Nationalism* 11, no. 3 (2005): 343–60.

57 Ibid., 346.

that there is a definitive psychological link between the collapse of the Ottoman Empire, the creation of the new nation-states around its base of titular nationalities, and the absence of a particular identity for the Muslims.[58] It is important, then, to understand the Young Turk and subsequent Kemalist movements for what they were, creators of the Turkish identity.

Mustafa Kemal, the first leader of modern day Turkey, epitomizes the Turkish nationalism that he inspired. Although not the most important commander to be directly involved in the killing in the Pontus, he arrived in Samsun (Amisos (Gr.)), on 19 May 1919, to head the eastern front, and his arrival marks the beginning of the end for the Greeks in the region.[59] His mission — which he did not fulfill — was to crush the armed nationalist bands. Instead, he became head of this movement.[60] He understood this to be the most significant assignment of his life, his rebirth so to speak, and chose that particular day to signify it.[61] As the founder of modern day Turkey, and honored by being referred to as the father of the Turks, his views on nationalities are very relevant to the development of Turkish identity and the implications for non-Turks living in the area. Mustafa Kemal understood this very well and insisted upon a post-Westphalian European order in which the nation-state is the cornerstone of organizational activity. As Dankwart Rustow notes in his profile of Kemal,

> He warned his listeners that "today the nations of the whole world recognize only one sovereignty: national sovereignty." Hence his basic goal was that the Turkish nation should live in dignity and honor. This goal could be achieved only by the possession of complete independence.[62]

His understanding of international relations and his world at the time of great upheaval was even more worrisome, and we would venture self-indicting on his role against the peoples of Anatolia. Rustow quotes him as saying,

> I confess that I, too, tried to define the national border somewhat according to the humanitarian purposes of Wilson's principles ... On the basis of these principles, I defended boundaries which Turkish bayonets had already defended and laid down. Poor Wilson, he did not understand that lines which cannot be defended by the bayonet, by force, by honor and dignity, cannot be defended on any other principle,

and more to the point,

---

[58] Akçam, *From Empire to Republic,* 30–107.

[59] Vamık Volkan and Norman Itzkowitz, *The Immortal Ataturk: A Psychobiography* (Chicago: University of Chicago Press, 1984), 121.

[60] Our thanks to Dr. Tessa Hofmann for highlighting this point.

[61] Volkan and Itzkowitz, *The Immortal Ataturk,* 132.

[62] Dankwart Rustow, "Ataturk as Founder of a State," in *Philosophers and Kings: Studies in Leadership,* Dankwart Rustow, ed. (New York: Braziller, 1970), 214.

> Before reorganizing Anatolia, I had to conquer its people.[63]

The reader will note the militarist understanding of both international relations and the concept of nation. This is to be expected, one may argue, since Kemal's time was one of extreme global bloodletting, but it is also fair to say that the statement is illustrative of the leadership's idea of the role of the Turkish nation in the modern world.

Kemal's views were by no means the most extreme, and in the context of the Ottoman Empire's collapse, one can argue that they represent simple modern-day realism in international relations. After all, realist thinkers tend to equate power with the military and the economy, and that was clearly part of the Kemalist programs for Turkey. There were, however, contemporary expressions of Turkish ethnicity in the form of writings by Tekin Alp and Ziya Gökalp, to name a few of the so-called nationalists. These writers did not define Turkishness along racial lines only, because their aim was Pan-Turkism. In his seminal study of Pan-Turkism, Jacob Landau argues that Gökalp was especially influential on the call for Pan-Turkism in his poem "Turan," in which he wrote,

> For Turks, Fatherland means neither Turkey, nor Turkestan; Fatherland is a large and eternal country — Turan![64]

The expression of Turkish nationalism reaches its climax at the time that Mustafa Kemal becomes leader of the nation, and even though it has some continuity to the present day, one can say that its ideological heyday was before its main leaders died in the 1930's. In fact, there is an evident racist undertone of the discourse before the genocides were perpetrated. The Turks established youth clubs that used the same biological and physical explanations of their superiority that were employed in genocides later on.[65] Anthropological studies explain how Turkish nationalism is racial in nature and include some of the same elements that both Hobsbawm and Anderson would find illustrative in their explanation of nationalism, mainly the invention of tradition.[66] Once the opportunity to create a nation-state for the Turks existed, they needed the assistance of a foundation discourse: a set of myths and axioms that reinforce ethno-political identity.

Finally, it seems that the development of Turkish national identity, from religious Ottoman to ethnic Turk, required a geopolitical space for Turks,

---

[63] Ibid., 215.

[64] Jacob Landau, *Pan-Turkism: From Irredentism to Cooperation* (Indianapolis: Indiana University Press, 1995), 37.

[65] İşyar, "The Origins of Turkish Republican Citizenship," 355.

[66] Nazan Maksudyan, "The Turkish Review of Anthropology and the Racist Face of Turkish Nationalism," *Cultural Dynamics* 17, no. 3: 291–322.

which was created through massacre, ethnic cleansing, and finally genocide of the populations existing in present day Turkey. The implementation of forced starvation, forced labor, and long marches has been described by Enepekides as a "rolling Auschwitz,"[67] in which forced relocations were essentially death marches. In this process, about 350,000 Pontian Greeks were exterminated, approximately half the population of Pontus, while the other half fled to the Soviet Union and Greece, which in earlier years had accepted nearly a quarter of its population in the form of refugees from Turkey.[68]

Conclusion

What makes states kill their own citizens? The answer that the Greek and other genocides point to is ethno-politics. Ethno-politics can lead to genocide, especially if there is an existing political opportunity structure. Political opportunity presents itself when there is radical transformation of the existing state, which may or may not lead to civil and ethnic conflict. Using identity as a solidarity-building mechanism, prospecting to accomplish the elites' expectations of a geopolitical nation-state and ethnic mobilization to gain momentum, different ethno-political groups attempt to "defend" themselves against the chaos and uncertainty of social and institutional transformation.

Since ethnic identity becomes the key variable, extreme expressions lead to calls for the elimination of "other" groups with equally legitimate claims. In the case of the Ottoman genocides, the radicalization and the creation of Turkish nationalism out of the remnants of the collapsing Ottoman Empire, the Balkan Wars and World War I, created an opportunity structure, of which nationalist leaders such as the Young Turks and Mustafa Kemal took advantage to create a sovereign state that could be "defended at the point of the bayonet."

The fusion of ethno-national and state boundaries (where admittedly the state has total control of the nation these days[69]) was the intended structure. The creation of a new structure, in which secular veto players are introduced in order to guarantee this domination, is not accidental. In this sense, the Ottoman Turks needed ethno-politics to build this system before they allowed the state to subjugate it. This meant that the creation of modern day Turkey was for Turks only, which led to the genocide of millions of Ottoman citizens.

---

[67] Πολυχρόνης Κ. Ενεπεκίδης, *Γενοκτονία στον Εύξεινο Πόντο* [Polychrones K. Enepekides, *Genocide in the Euxeinos Pontus*] (Thessalonica: Εύξεινος Λέσχη, 1996).

[68] Χαραλαμπίδης και Φωτιάδης, *Πόντιοι: Δικαίωμα στη Μνήμη.*

[69] As seen in more recent and previous military interventions ...

Achieving Ever–Greater Precision in Attestation and Attribution of Genocide Photographs

ABRAHAM D. KRIKORIAN & EUGENE L. TAYLOR

> [...] for it should be the duty of historians to be exact, truthful, and dispassionate, and neither interest nor fear nor rancor nor affection should swerve them from the path of truth, whose mother is history, rival of time, depository of deeds, witness of the past, and the future's counselor.[1]

Introduction

THE NEED TO LOCATE, IDENTIFY, ATTRIBUTE, PRESERVE AND CATALOG PHOTOGRAPHS and other images as they relate to the Armenian, Greek and Aramaean/Assyrian Genocides has been recognized for some time.[2]

One objective of this essay is to underscore this need and to encourage those who do chance upon photographs or deliberately seek them out, to recognize them first and foremost as assets of high value and significance for research. It cannot be overemphasized that the greater the detail that can be achieved, the more valuable they become for visual documentation purposes. Scholarly research dedicated to attaining ever greater detail in *attestation* (i.e., affirming the accuracy of what a photograph represents) and *attribution* (i.e., identifying a photo with a person, place and time) has so far been relatively sparse but has long been recognized as an ongoing need. It follows, of course, that correct interpretation of photographs depends on these two fundamental considerations.[3]

---

[1] From *The Ingenious Gentleman Don Quixote de la Mancha* by Miguel de Cervantes Saavedra, English translation by Samuel Putnam based on first edition of 1605 and 1615 (New York: Viking Press, 1958), 73.

NB: An Appendix of images referred to in this article follows on page 427.

[2] Tessa Hofmann and Gerayer Koutcharian, "Images that 'Horrify and Indict:' Pictorial Documents on the Persecution and Extermination of Armenians from 1877 to 1922," *Armenian Review* 45, no. 1 (1992): 53; Dzovinar Kévonian, "Photographie, genocide et transmission: l'exemple arménien," in Anne Grynberg, ed., *Enseigner et transmettre* (Paris: Les Belles Lettres, 2005), 119; Benedetta Guerzoni, "Il nemico armeno nell'impero ottomano," (2005): 17 http://www.storicamente.org/guerzoni.htm, last accessed January 2010.

[3] Some prefer the descriptor "provenance," but the connotation of that word usually suggests place of origin or of past ownership, and usually applies to an antique or work of art. For us, this nuance invokes still more questions and seems to impose yet other burdens of identification rather than to help clarify the case in point.

Although efforts in connection with the visual documentation of the broadly based campaign of genocide against the Greeks especially in the waning years of the Ottoman Empire and early Nationalist Turkey are generally more recent than, say, images dealing with the Armenian Genocide, considerable progress is steadily being made.[4] Similarly, details of the plight of the Aramaeans/Assyrians at the hands of the Ottoman Turks are also increasingly being reexamined and assessed after years of relative quietude and neglect.[5]

Another objective is to show that with steadfastness and no small degree of good fortune, many questions about photographs that may be well known, but which have been poorly or incompletely attested or attributed, can be resolved, either wholly or in part. Still another objective is to emphasize that this field of activity is still very immature but that any extraordinary efforts that may be made will be worth the effort.[6]

The several examples to be covered in this essay have been selected since they represent not only a category, but they typify a specific problem that required or still requires some degree of resolution from one perspective or another.

Finally, as Cervantes has admonished (see the quote introducing this essay) we have earnestly tried to be impartial, although some will adjudicate that we have done so, no doubt, vainly. To that we respond, "The truth shall make us all free!"

---

[4] Perhaps the Smyrna Holocaust has been, to date at least, more of a focal point for research than say, the Pontus, or other locales in Asia Minor and northern Syria. See e.g. the contribution of Nikolaos Hlamides in this volume.

[5] See e.g. Yonan H. Shabaz, *The Rage of Islam: An Account of the Massacre of Christians by Turks in Persia* (Piscataway: Gorgias Press, 2006 [facsimile reprint of 1918 edition]); Gabriele Yonan and Yvonne Bangert, *Ein vergessener Holocaust; die Vernichtung der christlichen Assyrer in der Türkei* (Göttingen: Gesellschaft für Bedrohte Völker, 1989); Sébastien de Courtois, *The Forgotten Genocide: Eastern Christians, the Last Aramaeans* (Piscataway, New Jersey: Gorgias Press, 2004).

[6] In the 28 August 2007 issue of *The Independent* (London), award-winning journalist Robert Fisk wrote of "The Forgotten Holocaust" and drew attention to a number of hitherto apparently unpublished photographs of the Armenian Genocide. Without doubt, and over time, many more photographs will surface, and they will apply to all the genocides of interest to us here. For example an online photographic collection depicting the work of Laurence Howland MacDaniels and his wife Frances Cochran MacDaniels for the American Committee for Relief in the Near East, 1919–1920, can be accessed at the following URL: www.oberlin.edu/archive/NearEast.html — "Near East Relief–MacDaniels Photo Album." Only a fraction of the album's photographs have been placed online. The authors of this article spent considerable time scanning and working on the photographs in that album. The MacDaniels were among the first group of ACRNE workers to be in the Harput region of Turkish Armenia after the end of the War.

Value of Imagery

What has been stated so far takes it as a given that imagery is very important. Humans are visual animals. One may go so far as to say that the Jewish Holocaust is in large measure so very well known by so many people *because* of the sheer volume and intensity of the visual documentation that accompanies the textual materials.

Outside the United States Holocaust Memorial Museum, Washington, D.C., the following statement is chiseled in stone:

> The things I saw beggar description. The visual evidence and the verbal testimony of starvation, cruelty and bestiality were so overpowering... I made the visit deliberately, in order to be in a position to give first hand evidence of these things if ever, in the future, there develops a tendency to charge these allegations to propaganda.

This is taken from a letter from General Dwight D. Eisenhower to General George Marshall, dated 15 April 1945 describing what he saw at the forced labor camp at Ohrdruf (a sub-camp of Buchenwald).[7] General Eisenhower thereafter ordered a thorough documentation of what the Allies encountered in the camps as they were liberated. This was done both in moving images and by still photography. It is due in no small measure to Eisenhower's foresight (and the penchant of the Nazi Germans for meticulous record keeping and prolixity) that The U.S. Holocaust Memorial Museum is so replete with imagery. Throughout the exhibits the visitor is constantly implored to "bear witness." Images and scenes such as those first shown at the Nuremberg Trials, and later in public in such works as the now classic and pioneering documentary motion picture by Alain Resnais entitled *Nuit et Brouillard* [*Night and Fog*], 1955 so stir the spirit and horrify the mind that viewers constantly ask, "How can humans be so inhuman?"[8]

As macabre and distressing as such images are, they seem today to have become something of a standard for any given individual's ability to relate to what genocide is all about. It is as if gruesome images are a *sine qua non* to impose, forcefully and relentlessly if need be, recognition of what genocide means. Unless there is an assault on the human senses through such images, genocide seems not to be "real." Remarkably, if the images do not horrify sufficiently, it cannot be genocide. Indeed, it has been repeatedly emphasized that the public increasingly receives its history through images.

---

[7] This letter was published in the series, Alfred Chandler, et al., *The Papers of Dwight David Eisenhower*: *The War Years* (Baltimore: Johns Hopkins Press, 1970), 4: 2615–16. The entire series may be accessed at www.eisenhowermemorial.org.

[8] See especially Richard Raskin, *Nuit et brouillard by Alain Resnais: On the Making, Reception and Functions of a Major Documentary Film, Including a New Interview with Alain Resnais and the Original Shooting Script* (Aarhus: Aarhus University Press, 1987), 184.

This is especially true in the United States of America, but one can be assured that this applies virtually everywhere. And it is certainly true of the public's experience with genocide, and even its identification.[9]

Some Case Histories

Images of Arrests and Deportations

A photograph that has become an icon of the Armenian genocide in its own right shows men under arrest or armed escort being led off to [the reader may fill in a location]. This picture is reproduced in different levels of quality, on many book covers of relatively recent vintage.[10] The one selected for reproduction here (see Appendix to this article, Fig. I,1) appears on the cover of a remarkable little volume that comprises many snapshot photographs taken in Syria by a truck driver with Armenian roots, who in the course of his work visited places that figured significantly in the wanderings forced on the Armenian "deportees."[11]

This photograph has been variously captioned in different publications as representing Armenian, Greek or sometimes, more generically, "Christian" men.[12] The location of the scene has usually been given as Harput, variously spelled Harpoot, Kharput, Kharpert, Kharberd, Kharpout etc. depending on the rendition of the name of that small city in eastern Turkey/historic western Armenia. In one case, it is asserted that the "Armenian" men were being taken out towards the city gates to be murdered. But Mezre, where as we shall soon see the photograph was taken, had no city gates. The town was of relatively recent development and lacked walls unlike some ancient cities like Diyarbakır (Amida (Gr.)), whose very old walls and gates were remarkably intact at the time of the genocides.

---

[9] Janina Struk, *Photographing the Holocaust: interpretations of the evidence* (London and New York: I.B. Tauris, 2005).

[10] See for example, Aram Antonean, *Mets ochire: haykakan verjin kotoratsnere ew Talead P'asha* [*The Great Crime: the last massacres of the Armenians and Talât Paşa*] (Beirut: Gh. Kharapetian, 1977 [second edition]), 299; Boghos Jafarian, *Farewell Kharpert, the Autobiography of Boghos Jafarian*, with supplementary chapters by Claire Mangasarian, Leon Mangasarian, ed. (Madison, WI; Privately printed, 1989), 258; Tessa Hofmann, ed., *Verfolgung, Vertreibung und Vernichtung der Christen im Osmanischen Reich 1912–1922* (Münster: Lit–Verlag, 2004), 261; Taner Akçam, *From Empire to Republic: Turkish Nationalism and the Armenian Genocide* (London and New York: Zed Books, 2004), 273.

[11] See Robert Jébéjian, *Routs* [read *Routes*] *and Centers of Annihilation of Armenian Deportees in 1915 within the Boundaries of Syria* (Aleppo: Violette Jébéjian Library, 1994). For the images cited see the appendix at the end of the article.

[12] Harry Tsirkinidis, *"At Last We Uprooted Them...": the Genocide of the Greeks of Pontos, Thrace and Asia Minor, through the French Archives* (Thessalonica: Kyriakidis Brothers, 1999), 301. Here the photograph is said to represent "Greeks of Pontos on the road to exile, leading to their extermination."

What follows here is a synthesis of the most relevant information so far available. It cannot be referred to as a model exercise on the path to a fuller attestation or attribution, because in our experience so far there is no orderly template that may be adopted. And, we hasten to add that identification at the level ultimately achieved here most likely could not have been pursued in any specific way beyond a certain point. Real progress was only achievable by access to photographs from a private collection given us.

There is no doubt whatever that the location of this scene is the small city of Mezre, officially named Mamuret-ul-Aziz, in the Ottoman vilayet of Mamuret-ul-Aziz, Turkey in Asia.[13] And, it is in no small measure the erudition and kindness of one of this volume's editors that enabled the perspective to be broadened considerably.

Mamuret-ul-Aziz was the provincial seat of the government and the residence of the vali or governor general. The United States consulate was located in Mezre as well, although it was officially listed as Harput by the U.S. Government in Washington, D.C. Many letters written on consulate stationery bore the return address Mezre (Mamuret-ul-Aziz/Harput) (personal knowledge from English language letters in our possession).

There is a sketch in a thin, small folio size German-language volume published without date but probably 1898 or 1899 dedicated to showcasing work carried out under the auspices of the Deutsches Hilfsbund für christliches Liebeswerk im Orient [German Relief Society for Christian Charitable Work in the Orient].[14] The sketch shows the "Turkish Post on the road from Mesereh [Mezre] to Baghdad" (see page forty-five, and the images reproduced in the appendix that follows this article). In the same volume there is a tinted reproduction of a drawing of the same street or roadway (Figs. I,2 and I,3).

A reproduction of a photograph in our hands will quickly convince the viewer that the street or road in question is indeed the same as in the infamous photograph of arrested men. This photograph (Fig. I,4) was taken in 1913/1914 by Louise Carroll Masterson, the wife of the Harput U.S. Consul, William Wesley Masterson, in Mezre.[15]

---

[13] A fair amount has been written about Harput. See for example volume III of Historic Armenian Cities and Provinces Series, University of California at Los Angeles. *Armenian Tsopk/Kharpert*, Richard G. Hovannisian, ed. (Costa Mesa: Mazda Publishers, 2002), passim.

[14] See Ernst Lohmann, *Skizzen & Bilder aus dem Orient* (Dinglingen, Baden: St. Johannis-Drückerei, 1899), passim.

[15] William W. Masterson was commissioned to Harput on 10 June 1908 and served there until 1914. He was succeeded by Leslie A. Davis who was commissioned to Harput 24

The Masterson snapshot is labeled on the back in her good handwriting "Camels passing through Mezreh from the South Coast." The perspective of the Masterson photograph permits establishment of the movement of the escorted men (southward) and allows clear-cut comparisons to be made between and among buildings along the street. The photograph was without doubt taken from a window in the American consulate building, and more than likely in spring/summer (note the trees in leaf). It is not certain from which window but one can be confident of the side of the Consulate from which it was taken. Another Masterson photograph (Fig. I,5) with a key on its back (Fig. I,6) to the rooms from the outside of the Consulate building shows number 1 as the Consul's office; number 11 on the same side of the building and one floor up, is a guest room.

In the U.S. National Archives in College Park, Maryland there are carefully executed ink drawings made in 1901 by Dr. Thomas H. Norton, the first U.S. consul in Harput, of the consulate building and its location in Mezre. It was on, what Consul Norton called in his drawings "Ambar Yiol Granary Street," and which he indicates to be some 27 feet wide. While the word *ambar* refers to "storehouse" in modern Turkish, we are given further insight into the street's name in late Ottoman times as a grain storehouse.

One can find the same infamous photograph published considerably later in the Armenian translation made from the original Danish of the diary Maria Jacobsen kept while she was in Harput 1907–1919 (Fig. I,7). The Danish caption written beneath the photograph of men under arrest in Maria's hand reads "Armenske Mænd føres ud af Byen for at dræbes 1915"[16] [Armenian men being led out of the city to be killed, 1915]. The Armenian caption, being a translation of the Danish, reveals no more insight of course.

Miss Maria Jacobsen, as a missionary nurse and subject of the neutral Kingdom of Denmark, was asked to look after the interests of Americans in Harput/Mezre when the Americans left in May 1917. She herself left Turkey in late summer of 1919 and that was well after the American Committee for Relief in the Near East volunteer workers arrived on the scene in mid-June 1919.[17]

April 1914 and served in Harput until 1917. See also "Mary C. Masterson, Daughter of Harput Consul William W. Masterson, Dead at Age 92," by Abraham D. Krikorian and Eugene L. Taylor, special to Groong; access e.g. via,
http://www.armeniangenocide.com/showthread.php?t=2700.

16 The caption in Armenian, in the Armenian translation of the diary from the Danish original "Armenian men being taken away out of the city to be killed, 1915." Maria Jacobsen, *Oragrut'iwn, 1907–1919: Kharberd* (Antelias, Lebanon: Catholicosate of the Great House of Cilicia, 1979), 214.

17 Maria Jacobsen, *Diaries of a Danish Missionary: Harpoot, 1907–1919,* Ara Sarafian, ed. (Princeton and London: Gomidas Institute Books, 2001), 248 and *passim.*

Some captions accompanying this important photograph in various reproductions assert that it was *taken by* Maria Jacobsen. Others cite the Red Cross. Still others say that it was taken by a German salesman or engineer (others assert that it was a military man) from a "hotel." There were no hotels in Harput/Mezre, but western visitors of any importance frequently did stay at the U.S. consulate. Whether German guests would have lodged at the U.S. consulate is a moot point, especially since there were various German facilities that could well have been available to ethnic Germans. Some captions state that the men were being led to their deaths — "eventual deaths" is considerably more precise.

Most archival evidence, period letters and reports indicate that arrests in the Harput region were first frequently accompanied by beatings and torture. Those arrested were subsequently moved out of town, usually under cover of darkness, and later savagely murdered. It is a minor detail whether their murder occurred in daylight or at night. Late afternoon before dusk seems to have been a popular time according to some eyewitness accounts by survivors who miraculously escaped.[18]

The men under armed guard appear well dressed and certainly do not look ragged by any stretch of the imagination. Neither do they appear road-weary and bedraggled. We can conclude from that fact alone that they were Armenians, not Greeks. One cannot say for sure whether or not there were a few Syriac Orthodox Christian men (referred to by the Armenians as *Hye Assoris*, i.e. Armenian-speaking Assyrians) in this particular group. Greeks violently uprooted from the Pontus or other parts of the Black Sea coast or other parts of eastern Turkey would not have been marched off through the roadway from Harput to Mezre looking so intact.[19] Besides, the presence of the photograph in the Maria Jacobsen diary and collection at the Armenian Catholicosate of Cilicia (Kilikia (Gr.), Çukurova (Tur.)) in Antelias, Lebanon (but not in another extensive collection of Jacobsen photographic miscellanea to which we have had access in the U.S.), suggests that perhaps she brought the photograph with her along with her other possessions when she left Turkey, i.e. before the main genocidal acts against the Greeks, especially those of the Pontian region, began in earnest.[20]

---

[18] James L. Barton, compiler, *"Turkish Atrocities": Statements of American Missionaries on the Destruction of Christian Communities in Ottoman Turkey, 1915–1917* (Ann Arbor: Gomidas Institute, 1998), 28–71 and *passim*.

[19] Mark H. Ward, *The Deportations in Asia Minor 1921–1922* (London: Anglo-Hellenic League & British Armenia Committee, 1922), 17 and *passim*); Herbert Adams Gibbons, "Near East Relief Prevented from Helping Greeks," *The Christian Science Monitor*, 13 July 1922, 1.

[20] A main region in eastern Turkey in which Greeks were concentrated for annihilation was Malatya Sancağı in the Province of Mamuret-ul-Aziz. Alternatively, Greek men would have been "dispatched" closer to home; or sent out to work in labor battalions. Primarily

If one accepts this stance, this further strengthens the position taken here that they were Armenian men. And, of course, Maria Jacobsen captioned the photograph as such in Danish. There remain other reasonable possibilities of course. For example, there is even a very remote possibility that the photograph was acquired in the U.S. when Maria came to lecture and fund-raise.

We will not provide here our detailed rationale for dating the photograph as probably early May/mid-June to certainly no later than mid-July 1915.[21] Suffice it to say that we have in our possession a *contemporary and authoritative unpublished report* of the early occurrences in Harput gives some details and dates of the arrests that justify our assertion.[22] The dimensions of an old print of the photograph suggest that it was taken by an American ca-

---

women and children would have been those most likely to have made it to Harput region. The Greek men who lasted long enough to reach Harput from the Black Sea coastal region were completely worn out. Cf. e.g. Ward, *The Deportations in Asia Minor 1921–1922* and Gibbons, "Near East Relief Prevented from Helping Greeks."

21 A period account in a private family archive available to us, typewritten in English entitled "Further Events at Harpoot during the Great War of 1914–1915," states that the arrests were initially of Armenian men, and as early as 1 May 1915:

"On the first day of May the cities of Harpoot and Mezereh were stirred as they had not been before. Rumors of sedition; mutterings about bombs and dynamite, were accompanied by general searching of Armenian houses and the arrest of a number of prominent Armenians." [page 38]

"Early in June it began to be reported that the prisoners, especially Prof. Tenekejian, were being subjected to various kinds of physical suffering to secure confessions from them. These reports were so gross and the tortures described so inhuman that the Americans were inclined not to believe in it."

The reports proved all too true ... [page 47]

"FIRST DEPORTATIONS

About this time the Armenians who had been serving in the army were separated out, those who had commissions were degraded and nearly all were sent out to work in the harvest fields. On July 16th these Armenians were recalled and placed in confinement in Mezereh, and the next day were started off on the road." [page 47]

See also Leslie A. Davis, *The Slaughterhouse Province: An American Diplomat's Report on the Armenian Genocide, 1915–1917,* Susan K. Blair, ed. (New Rochelle, New York: Aristide D. Caratzas, 1989), 200 and *passim.*

22 For other estimates, see Annette Schaefgen, *Schwieriges Erinnern: der Volkermord an den Armeniern* (Berlin: Metropol, 2006), 24, captions in translation, the photograph "Harput, May 1915: Leading Armenians of the City being deported under guard." She credits IDZA, Informations- und Dokumentationszentrum Armenien, Berlin as the source of the photograph. A reprint of a 1916 French translation *Les Massacres des Arméniens (1915–1916)* (Paris: Payot, 1987) [originally *Armenian Atrocities: Murder of a Nation* by Arnold Toynbee, 1915 without the photograph] has on its cover a copy of the photograph of arrested men. The back cover gives a quite good caption "Kharpout, May-June 1915. Armenian notables led away towards the Mezre prison. Rights reserved." As an aside, we question on what grounds rights are reserved to this photograph which has long been in the public domain.

mera.[23] Dare we even suggest that this is a photograph taken by U.S. Consul to Harput, Leslie A. Davis? Textual materials do not do violence to that possibility.[24] One of the editors of this volume, Danish historian Matthias Bjørnlund, has generously shared important information on this photograph that goes far to shed much additional light on the problem. (Simultaneously, it seems inevitably to raise and entail still new complexities of interpretation).

It has thus far been impossible to place a precise date as to when the photograph under consideration here first appeared in print. But Matthias Bjørnlund has tracked down a very early publication in the form of a small booklet by Amalia Lange entitled *Et Blad af Armeniens Historie: K.M.A. 1910–1920* [*A Page from Armenia's History: K.M.A. 1910–1920*]. In view of the fact that this 80-page booklet was printed in 1920, Bjørnlund ventures to say, and we certainly concur, that it seems likely it just might be Miss Karen Marie Petersen, or Jenny Jensen, or Hansine Marcher, the other Danish KMA [*Kvindelige Missions Arbejdere* — Female Missionary Workers] Missionaries in Harput/Mezre who might have given the photograph to KMA before leaving Denmark after World War I. Bjørnlund states that the 1920 Lange photograph is not cropped as much as that in the considerably later Armenian translation of the diary from Danish.[25] This is true, and there are yet other instances where the perspective of those being marched off is slightly altered, and thus gives emphasis to certain features that might otherwise appear rather mundane in the early printing. In a word, the dating of the print has been pushed back considerably, possibly even to the time of its first publication, but evidence is lacking to assert this with any degree of conviction.

Recently, British journalist Robert Fisk operating from Beirut has brought up an account which has been hitherto viewed by some as too difficult to confirm, and has thus been more or less relegated to the periphery of attestation and attribution until such time some detailed potential for confirmation emerges, states that a "German engineer in Kharput sent back a now famous photograph of Armenian men being led to their execution by armed

[23] Courtesy of George Eastman House, Rochester, NY.

[24] We were fortunate enough to visit with Harput Consul Leslie Davis' son, Caleb Davis and his wife Barbara. They graciously received us, and thereafter helped all they could before Caleb died in December 2003. One sad fact we learned was that after Consul Davis died, Caleb was left with the task of dealing with things that had been stored by his father in a barn on his property in Stockbridge, Massachusetts. The sheer volume of material was staggering. Caleb described his father affectionately as a "packrat." Given the pressure and responsibility on Caleb at the time, he was left with little alternative than to discard most, but happily not all of it. Of course Caleb regretted not being able to preserve it all. He was both surprised and pleased that his father's materials had generated such interest among the Armenian community.

[25] cf. Jacobsen, *Oragrut'iwn, 1907–1919,* 216 (Danish original and Armenian translation).

Turkish police officers."[26] Unfortunately there is, as yet, no confirmation of this assertion, so we are taking the considered position that until this can be done, we must for the time being adopt other avenues to glean details concerning this photograph.

Thus, lacking confirmation, and in consideration of the fact that Matthias Bjørnlund's research on the early publication history of the photograph raises many questions that cannot yet be resolved, we prefer to revise the caption as follows:

Reproduction of a photograph taken in Mezre, Mamuret-ul-Aziz Vilayet, Turkey, sometime in mid-June to mid-July 1915, from a window of the U.S. consulate building facing "Granary Street." The road, called Ambar Yol in Turkish, going south-southwest, but eventually to Baghdad, was a major thoroughfare used by the Turkish Post etc. These Armenians under armed guard were most likely some of the older men of the city of Harput and were most likely *en route* to the jail building or the government building, neither of which was very far away.[27]

The scene typifies what happened all over the Ottoman Empire during the period of the Armenian holocaust. Once under detention, the men frequently underwent torture, and more often than not, usually under cover of darkness they were taken out and slain. Miraculously, a few were able to escape with their lives by such means as feigning death under piles of dead bodies. They were later able to provide gruesome details. While some have asserted that the photograph was taken by a German engineer in Harput, it is equally plausible that American Consul Leslie A. Davis took the photograph, or even a visitor at the U.S. consulate. The earliest known publication of this photograph captioned in Danish and already mentioned above, is "A group of Armenian men being led out of town to be killed" [En Skare armeniske Mænd føres ud af Byen for at dræbes]. The photograph is in Amalia Lange's work published in Danish in Copenhagen, dated 1920 entitled in English translation as *A Page from Armenia's History: K. M. A. 1910–1920*. Clearly an extensive and detailed paper trail is associated with this photograph. There is much yet to learn from this and similar genre photographs.

Finally, after all is said and done, and having here gone through this not insignificant exercise, it should be stated that Armenian Project SAVE in Watertown, Massachusetts, on its website provides a good quality image of the men under arrest with the caption "Armenians are marched to a nearby

---

[26] Robert Fisk, "The Forgotten Holocaust," *The Independent* (London), 28 August 2007.

[27] It is not certain if the group shown here was taken to the jail, or to the government konak. There is evidence that both buildings were used for detention, cf. e.g. Hampartzoum Mardiros Chitjian, *A Hair's Breath from Death: the Memoirs of Hampartzoum Mardiros Chitjian: Memoirs of a Survivor of the Armenian Genocide* (London: Taderon Press, 2003), 152.

prison in Mezireh by armed Turkish soldiers. Kharpert, Armenia, Ottoman Empire — April 1915."[28] All in all, the Project SAVE caption is fairly accurate but we hope that readers will concur that we have just shown that even relatively good captions can profit considerably from refinement — a refinement that is frequently due to hard work, good fortune and cooperation.

A Photograph by Wilfred McIlvaine Post

In closing this section, attention may be drawn to a photograph of Armenian men under arrest with vastly fewer questions of attestation and attribution. Dr. Wilfred M. Post (1876–1966) an American physician and medical missionary in Turkey since 1903,[29] was working in Konya (Ikonion (Gr.)) at the time of the Armenian Genocide and took photographs, some of which are in the U.S. National Archives in Maryland.[30]

The caption on the photograph under discussion here (Fig. I,8) in Dr. Post's own hand states: "A company of men driven mostly on foot all the way from Constantinople — left 2 days and 2 nights in an open field without food or shelter (see my letter of September 21 [1915])."[31] An added note on the back of the photograph points out that there are "gendarmes with guns" near the wall in the background.

This photograph and Dr. Post's commentary make several points. It is often claimed by proponents of the official Turkish point of view, and others who choose to remain ignorant of the facts, that Armenian civilians only near the war zones were "relocated."[32] Although the majority of Armenians living in Constantinople were not "deported," many were. A few detailed accounts of

---

[28] http://www.projectsave.org/virtual.asp.

[29] Dr. Post's father was George Edward Post (1838–1909), an American medical missionary to Syria in the nineteenth century. He figures heavily in the history of the Syrian Protestant College, which became the American University of Beirut after the First World War. Wilfred Post served in American hospitals in Caesaria (Kaisareia (Gr.) Kayseri (Tur.)) and Konya, and was later director of the American Hospital in Constantinople. He was in Smyrna during the great fire and received a decoration from the Greek Government for work among refugees after the destruction of Smyrna. He was director of the Florence Nightingale Barracks orphanage at Scutari (Chrysopolis (Gr.) Üsküdar (Tur.)) during the typhus epidemic cf. Wilfred M. Post, "Stars and Stripes in the Near East," *Nassau Medical News* (Garden City, New York) 29, no. 9 (1957): 1, 14, 16.

[30] See Record Group 867.4016/213.

[31] Compare Wilfred M. Post, (Extracts from the Annual Report of the American Hospital at Konya, Turkey for the year 1917 with additional notes on the treatment of British prisoners in Konya) in Barton, *"Turkish Atrocities,"* 153–57.

[32] See e.g. Vahakn N. Dadrian, "Genocide as a Problem of National and International Law: the World War I Armenian Case and its Contemporary Legal Ramifications," *Yale Journal of International Law* 14, no. 2 (Summer 1989): 262 note 131 and refs. cited therein.

the events which began on 24 April 1915 have been published in English.[33] There is considerably more which still remains unpublished on the deportations from Constantinople.

Attention could be drawn to other examples of arrests, but one deserves special mention. It concerns a photograph of doomed Armenian men from Gesaria (Caesaria, today Kayseri). This sole photograph has been studied *in extenso* by Stephen Kurkjian, Pulitzer Prize-winning investigative reporter for the Boston Globe and is still being subjected to exhaustive analysis. For him, this photograph of Armenian men under arrest, posed as a group, and complete with identifications of most — probably made by a survivor(s) — tragically yet eloquently symbolizes and typifies a critical element in the Armenian Genocide. In a word, the Armenian community of Turkey was deprived of any possible leadership or effective organized resistance as a result of arrest, murder or deportation of its elite men.[34]

IMAGES OF ORPHANS EVACUATED FROM ASIA MINOR IN THE KEMALIST PERIOD

Having paid attention to a few photographs of arrests (to be followed by murder or "deportation") some attention may well be given to a genre of photograph that has mistakenly been described more than a few times as representing Christians being deported, and therefore in essence being sent to their possible deaths. One thing is certain, those in the photographs in question here are not being sent to their deaths — at least deliberately, although it should be added there were more than a few casualties among those being evacuated out of Turkey along the way. Hofmann and Koutcharian[35] have made a special plea that these photos be recognized not as death marches, and have re-emphasized whenever possible the need to correct such gross errors of attestation and attribution. Even so carefully compiled a work as *The Armenian Genocide: Documentation* (1987, see its photo entry II) includes the photograph with an incorrect caption.[36]

---

[33] A comment is in order on the significance of 24 April as day of commemoration for the onset of the Armenian Genocide. 24 April on the Gregorian calendar as now used over much of the world, was selected by Supreme Catholicos of All Armenians Gevorg V because many arrests of intellectuals in Constantinople began on that date. Because the Julian calendar differs by some 13 days, earlier accounts give 11 April as the date or, it is sometimes designated as 11/24 April to emphasize the calendric difference. Mik'ayel Shamtanchean, *Hay mtk`in harke eghernin: ak`sorakani mtatsumner ew zgayoghut`iwnner* [issued in English as *The Fatal Night*] (Toluca Lake, California: Manjikian, 2007).

[34] Stephen Kurkjian, "Kiss my children's eyes: a search for answers to the Armenian genocide through one remarkable photograph," *NAASR* (National Association for Armenian Studies and Research) *Newsletter* (Winter 2005–2006), 8–9.

[35] Hofmann and Koutcharian, "Images that Horrify and Indict," 180.

[36] Anonymous, *The Armenian Genocide: Documentation* (München: Institut für Armenische Fragen, 1987).

Any effort to present a detailed paper trail here on this kind of image incorrectly said to represent a death march will serve no useful purpose. We do, however, reproduce one here from the back cover [front cover in Arabic] of a small folio album dealing with the tracing of routes followed by Armenian deportees.[37] While the caption is more accurate than many, it still lacks precision (Fig. II,1). But one piece of the paper trail will suffice to underscore the point that it becomes very difficult to correct an error once it gets into the literature. As an example, the photograph appears in a "memorial re-publication" of *Ambassador Morgenthau's Story*, published in 1975.[38]

The caption opposite page 292 in that work states "The long line that leads to death. Deportation of the Armenians to the arid wastes to die. Many, particularly women, were violated on route." Each of these points is certainly true but has nothing to do directly with this photograph. The original 1918 publication of *Ambassador Morgenthau's Story* does not include the photograph.

One summary caption that accompanies a copy of this same photograph appears on the Pontus World website illustrating a poem by Nikolaos Hlamides. The latter advised us that the photograph did not originally accompany the text of his poem but that it was subsequently added by person(s) unknown.[39] The spurious caption reads,

> A group of refugees marched from Kharput to the Black Sea coast. Deportees on death marches would be forced to follow circuitous routes to their destinations in order to facilitate their destruction. Photograph by C. D. Morris.

The photographer is correctly identified as C. D. [Charles Dexter] Morris and the image derives from *the National Geographic Magazine* (issue of November 1925, page 537) where a longer caption is provided. The scene is described as,

> A section of a trekking train of 5,000 Christians who made their tragic way from Kharput to the sea. Although Kharput, in central Asia Minor, is only 160 miles by air from Trebizond, on the Black Sea, these unhappy refugees were forced to pursue a circuitous route which stretched to 500 miles (see text, p. 557).[40]

---

[37] See Jébéjian, *Routs* [read *Routes*] *and Centers of Annihilation.*

[38] The title page states "Memorial Edition. The copyright on *Ambassador Morgenthau's Story*, originally published in 1919 by Doubleday, Page & Co., has expired and the book is now in the public domain. This is the reprinted edition." On the next page it says "This Memorial Edition of 'Henry Morgenthau's Story' Honoring Henry Morgenthau friend and benefactor of the Armenian People is also designed to commemorate the 60th anniversary of the Armenian Genocide. New Age Publishers..."

[39] http://pontosworld.com/index.php?option=com_content&task=view&id=185&Itemid=54.

[40] Melville Chater, "History's Greatest Trek," *The National Geographic Magazine* 158/5 (November 1925), 537, 557.

The same photograph was published by James L. Barton in his *Story of Near East Relief*, published in 1930.[41] A much more generic caption as it applies to two photographs of orphan groups reads:

> In 1922–23 Near East Relief evacuated 22,000 children from orphanages in interior Turkey to Syria and Greece. These two pictures show part of the 5,000 children from Kharput en route on donkey back and foot.

A few points are in order. Charles Dexter Morris (1883–1954) was in Paris when he enlisted with the Near East Relief. He arrived in Constantinople 27 January 1922. Since he was news director of the Near East Relief Commission in Turkey, Asia Minor and Greece, he moved from one area to another gathering material. Apparently he did a good enough job to merit being decorated by King George of Greece in 1923, and by Russia, Montenegro and Romania.[42]

If one were limited only to Barton's caption, one would not have the more-detailed perspective provided by Melville Chater to accompany Morris' photograph. Whether Chater or Morris actually wrote the caption need not concern us here. Both served Near East Relief and did important work and both returned to the United States in 1923. This example, covered only superficially here, also demonstrates how a caption can become modified over time so that the author's orignal intent becomes distorted.

A still earlier publication of the photograph appears in *The New Near East* (December 1922), pages 10–11. The two-page spread is comprised of various images; the one under consideration here is printed as a mirror-image of the later versions. The associated text is not very detailed and reads, "Over desert sand and through mountain passes long lines of children wound their way."

Melville Chater (1878–1936), author of the *National Geographic Magazine* article certainly gave a more extensive caption since in the tradition of the magazine, coverage took the form of photo essays. To have a fuller picture of orphans being evacuated by the Near East Relief from Mustafa Kemal's nascent nationalist Turkey, it is important to appreciate that there were many trips made with Christian orphans from eastern Turkey — not just one, as might be mistakenly surmised from some of the writing.[43] Anyone not aware of the broad picture might get the idea that the orphans mentioned above in

---

[41] James L. Barton, *Story of Near East Relief 1915–1930: An Interpretation* (New York: Macmillan, 1930), the photograph facing page 152.

[42] "Charles Morris, newsman, is dead," *The New York Times*, 22 May 1954, 15.

[43] One case involving travel even by barge is reported in the 7 September 1922 issue of the *New York Times*. Mention is made on page four, that a hundred blind Armenian children age seven to fifteen years old were removed successfully from an orphanage for blind children to Aleppo from Harput, a journey of some 500 miles, lasting a full month. "For twenty miles the children floated down the Euphrates on barges."

reference to Harput were evacuated in one fell swoop. Not so; we shall turn our attention to that below.

Perhaps the best-known evacuations are those associated with the name of Jakob, a.k.a. "Papa," Kuenzler, the Swiss pharmacist, relief worker, orphanage director and indefatigable fighter for justice. He and his wife, a trained nurse, a.k.a. "Mama," became icons of heroic mercy on account of their work with Armenians, orphans and adults alike, after the genocide.[44] Indeed, there was a fair amount of publicity given by Near East Relief to the movement of Harput area orphans into Syria. A cover of *The Near East Relief: A Discussion Course for Students* shows a close-up of the moving column with the description,

> 5,000 Children Trek 500 Miles to Safety. The recent 500-mile pilgrimage of 5,000 children from Near East Relief Orphanages in Harpoot into Syria, to be distributed among the orphanages there or to be sent on further to Constantinople or Greece.[45]

Lester James Wright (1886–1922) is one Near East Relief worker who deserves special recognition by those working on, or interested in, orphans of Greek origin in eastern Turkey. Rev. Wright lost his life in service to orphans and was described as the first Near East Relief worker to meet a violent death[46] (more below). Wright had a degree in agriculture from the University of Wisconsin, had served on its faculty and was also a Theological Seminary graduate. He was appointed to Harput by the American Board as an agricultural missionary.

After reaching Constantinople in early 1921 and studying Arabic, the decision was made to second him, i.e. to associate him or loan him out, to the Near East Relief. He was appointed on 21 June 1921 to carry out relief work in Malatya (Melitene (Gr.)), not far from Harput. Near East Relief had two orphanages in Malatya with approximately 800 children, two hospitals (one general and one children's) with 60 persons each and was feeding another 1,700 people.

Lee Vrooman, who was his predecessor in Malatya,[47] had also told Rev. Wright that he would have to take charge of all activities pertaining to agri-

---

[44] A translation of Jakob Kuenzler, *Im Lande des Blutes und Tränen* was recently published in English under the title of *In the Land of Blood and Tears: Experiences in Mesopotamia during the World War* (Arlington: Armenian Cultural Association, 2007).

[45] Anonymous, *The Near East: A Discussion Course for Students* (New York: Student Volunteer Movement, 1923).

[46] Mabell S. C. Smith, et al., "Veteran's Number: A tribute and an appeal," *Team Work (Near East Relief)* vol. 3 no.6 (13 June 1924), 63.

[47] After his service with Near East Relief, Lee Vrooman and his wife Helen took courses at Hartford Theological Seminary and went to Turkey where he served for ten years as Dean of American College of Izmir [İzmir İnternasyonal Koleji]. The International College was

culture, in its broadest sense. Lester Wright ended up as director of the Malatya branch of the Harput unit of the Near East Relief. He was at the time the only American at Malatya for 60 miles in one direction and 150 in the other. He made three trips out of Turkey with orphans prior to his last fatal one, and on each trip he had in his charge from 214 to 400 children, over mountainous roads, some so rough that the little ones could not keep their seats on the mules that were to carry them and had to walk over the perilous trail. No vehicle with a wheel had ever been over these trails. The last group of children, whom Lester Wright called his "little family of 900," comprised children whom he had cared for over a year at Malatya. He got them safely across and was on a two days' vacation before going back to Harput. He had been to Antioch with friends and was on the return trip when he was killed by Turkish *chetes*.[48]

A letter, dated Aleppo 10 October 1922, was received by Lester Wright's family in Wisconsin after his death. It merits quoting in full:

> Dear Sister and Brother:
>
> I believe that the last time I wrote I was in Aintab. While there I received a telegram saying that permission had been granted by the government to

---

closed in 1934. In a letter dated 11 June 1934, he writes, "As you know, the International College has been working under very considerable restrictions during the last ten years, and during the last two or three years there has grown up considerable opposition to the College, on the ground that it was foreign and Protestant, and that it preached internationalism. This resulted in greatly reducing our student body, and in drawing a rather sharp line between students and foreign faculty. The Trustees have, therefore, after long and careful consideration, finally decided to close operations..." Vrooman goes on to state that "the [new] project is to subsidize Christian work among students at the University of Athens. The University of Athens is one of the largest institutions in the Near East, having in all its departments about 10,000 students. They have an able faculty, a book on the gold standard by one of their faculty was recently reviewed favorably in the Annals of the American Academy of Political and Social Science, but as far as I can learn the whole outfit is as pagan as one would expect. There is a splendid young Greek, a Robert College graduate who has been on the staff at Robert College, but who feels that because he is a Greek his future work should lay in Greece. I thought we might assist him with Maine–in–Turkey funds, to get in and see what he could do in a personal way among the students and faculty of the University to present Christ as a way out of the mess the Near East and the world is in today." Vrooman file, University of Maine, Special Collections.

[48] A good, succinct description as to who the *chetes* were is given by Florence F. Billings 1879–1959, of the Smith College unit doing relief work in Asia Minor for the Near East Relief. She served in Prussa (Bursa (Tur.)), Konya and Angora. From Angora she went to Greece in December, 1922, and came back to the U.S. in May, 1923. "After the Armistice, some of the Turkish army took to the mountains making a living for themselves. These men were called *chetes*. Later on they were organized into bands under certain leaders and offered their services to the revolutionist movement. During the Great War the Turkish Army was much neglected and these bands were used in guerilla warfare by the Nationalists against the invaders." Florence Billings Papers, Smith College Archives.

> move our Armenian children out of the country. I engaged a mule driver to furnish me an animal and accompany me back to Malatia. We traveled night and day. In two days we covered six days' journey over the mountains, rivers and valleys.
>
> When I got within two days' journey from Malatia I came down over one large mountain and found the Armenian children camped for the night on the plain. [See later commentary by Mr. McAfee which explains this circumstance. The children were obviously not alone.] We were all very glad to meet in this way. If I had been one day late they would have passed this point and I would have missed going with them. There were 214 of them and we had the customary hand-kissing ceremony. I then went with them for seven days until we got to Jeroblus where there is a railroad. The train will come next Wednesday and the children will wait there. That is French territory and there are wagon roads south of there. I came on to Aleppo with some of the sick children by auto from there.
>
> During the last two months I have been on the road about seven weeks and have traveled with about 1,300 children in all and today I start back via Jeroblus, Urfa, Diarbakir, Harpoot, to Malatia, a distance of about 360 miles. It is a round about way but there is an auto road and I can make it in about five days. *We have permission to move out Greek children so I will be busy with that for a while. About 700 of them at Malatia and 100 at Harpoot. We had many more at Malatia last fall but thousands died during the winter and we were not able to do much for some of them. You know they were all refugees that were driven from their homes a year ago or more. Some came to us without a stitch of cloth on their bodies. During the last winter we hired eleven men straight through the winter just to bury the dead. It cost about 8 cents each for funeral expenses. What we are sending out now is what is left* ... L. J. W. [italics for emphasis ours].[49]

This letter mentions several things that have special significance for us so far as photograph captions of orphans being moved out of the Harput region of Turkey are concerned. The first point that emerges is that Greek orphans were approved for removal from Turkey somewhat later than Armenian orphans.

The death of relief worker Rev. Lester J. Wright on 27 October 1922 occurred as a result of a gunshot from a party of Turkish bandits. According to the *New York Times* account,

> The attack occurred in French territory. The bandit party was composed of Turkish irregulars who fired a volley into the Near East Relief column without warning. In the column were *200 children, half Greek, half Armenian* [emphasis ours], who were being convoyed from Harput to Aleppo. They had already escaped unharmed through two attacks through Turkish territory. The children are now in safety having been handed over to the care of American representatives. The trip was a very difficult one owing to bad roads and

---

[49] From a news clipping without annotation in the [Waukesha County, Wisconsin] *Freeman* made available through the kindness of Lester Wright's relatives.

> three of the children died on the way as a result of the hardships of the journey. Wright was buried in the American cemetery in Beirut yesterday, an impressive funeral ceremony taking place in the American Church. The American College, the Consulate and other institutions observed official mourning, as did a large number of the local Armenian, Greek and Syrian population.[50]

The body was exhumed later and sent to the U.S. for final interment. He was buried alongside other relatives in Mt. Vernon Cemetery in Wisconsin, which the authors of this article have visited.

Howard B. McAfee wrote after Lester Wright's death that he had brought out four companies of children from Malatya.

> I was there when the first group (400 boys) started — all of them either on foot or on donkeys and pack animals. Wright had a horse and went through Jerablous on the Euphrates River with them. He returned immediately and took out the second group, taking them as far as Aintab over one of the worst mountain trails in Turkey. Before he had gotten back from this second trip we started the third group and sent a messenger to him on the road asking him to join and protect them on the way to the Euphrates ... when it came to the final wind–up at Malatia, Wright took charge of 130 weak delicate children. He brought them out with the tenderness of a mother, and got them all safely through to Aleppo ... Others were bringing the remainder of the children ...[51]

A photograph belonging to Lester Wright, now in the private family archive of Wright's relatives, captioned "Part of the 5000 orphans who marched over land from the Near East Orphanage in Harput, Turkish Armenia on their way out of Nationalist Turkey to safety in Syria" is reproduced here (Fig. II,2).

Photos showing similar scenes of Greek and Armenian youngsters are familiar to many, and various ones have been reproduced, including on book covers.[52] Hofmann and Koutcharian[53] reproduce a photograph from Ida Alamuddin's book published in 1970, *Papa Kuenzler and the Armenians* and state that it is a Near East Relief photograph. A copy of another similar pho-

---

[50] *The New York Times*, 3 November 1922, 6

[51] Rev. Edward C. Wicklein, "Lester James Wright: murdered missionary" (typescript). (Madison: Wisconsin State Historical Society Archives, 1983, 20); Edward C. Wicklein, "Lester James Wright, martyred missionary," *Landmark* (Waukesha [Wisconsin] County Historical Society) 26, no. 1 (Spring 1983): 9–23.

[52] Jébéjian, *Routs* [read *Routes*] *and Centers of Annihilation*; Jakob Künzler and Hans–Lukas Kieser, *Im Lande des Blutes und der Tranen: Erlebnisse in Mesopotamien während des Weltkrieges (1914–1918)* (Zürich: Chronos Verlag, 1999); Nora Arissian, *Asda' al-ibadah al-Armaniyah fi al-sihafa al-Suriyah: 1877–1930* [*Reflections of the Armenian Genocide in the Syrian press: 1877–1930*] (Beirut: al-Dhakirah lil-Nashr wa al-Tiba'ah wa al-Tawzi, 2004).

[53] Hofmann and Koutcharian, "Images that Horrify and Indict," fig. 115.

tograph which was among the effects of Jakob Kuenzler's daughter from the period in Urfa (Edessa (Gr.), Şanlıurfa (Tur.)) is provided here (Fig. II,3).

One could draw attention to many captions of "evacuation" photographs with varying degrees of precision and accuracy. For example, in an English-language edition of a book that initially appeared in German, we see that the caption to the photograph under consideration here states,

> Flight of 5000 children from Harput to Mersin [the port of Adana] (1922/23); they had to go 256 km [about 160 miles] to Trapezunt with big detours of 800 km [about 500 miles].[54]

We have been unable so far to establish whether each of the several orphan evacuation genre photographs known to us were taken on different trips or whether they were the culmination of different shots of the same group of orphans.[55] We speculate that some derive mainly from one or a few trips, but there are at least a few photographs of orphan evacuations that seem to derive from yet other journeys.

Based on various dates provided above it seems unlikely that the early photographs taken of evacuations into Syria included Greek children. Near East Relief worker Rev. Lester Wright would have been shot dead by the time a photograph of evacuation of Greek and Armenian children would have been taken, if indeed one ever was. [56]

A revised caption that best reflects the state of our present state of knowledge might read:

> Orphans, who had been removed from the Harput area, under escort of the Near East Relief into Syria in the early 1920s. A substantial number of orphans, Armenian and Greek were removed from Asia Minor under the auspices of the Near East Relief. No records have yet been located that permit identification of a specific group in a given timeframe. Suffice it to say that these evacuations should be viewed as positive events even though the hardships caused the loss of some orphans' lives. Those leading the orphans to safety were real heroes.

Some photographs showing orphan evacuations give an inkling of what was happening during the genocides. But we believe it would be near impossible to capture on camera film the kinds of cruelty endured, and the human tragedies that ensued before some of the victims were ultimately 'released' from their tortures through death. The survivor orphans that were taken into orphanages and sooner or later evacuated were "fortunate" if one can

---

[54] Wilhelm Baum, *The Christian Minorities in Turkey* (Klagenfurt: Kitab, 2006), 119.

[55] There were photographers in Aleppo, of course, and some were Armenian. It will hopefully emerge one day who did the photography.

[56] See, for instance, Künzler, *Im Lande des Blutes und der Tränen.*

justifiably use that word. Consider the following heart-wrenching picture related by Dr. Mark Ward to a Boston audience:

> Close your eyes and picture to yourself as I have seen them, a long line of them, [Greek] women and children, on the march, the march of death. At the rear[,] a few soldiers on horseback and on foot with whips in their hands. On their backs the women carry their beds [their bedding] and a bundle of clothes and what food they have saved[,] and even the little ones, five or six years old, stagger under a load. Some old lady with a stick for a cane, her eyesight poor, bent over with a little grandson trying to lead her by the hand, and carrying his little load. She seems very weak, hardly able to walk, she falls to the rear of the procession, her little grandson tries to encourage her. She seems to try, but it is too much; she stumbles and falls in the middle of the road. Her neighbors try to pick her up, but they also are too weak to give much assistance. The guard comes up and drives them on. The little fellow begs to remain, but the old lady is unable to walk, and she cannot last long. The guard drives him away with a curse. The old lady is left where she fell, the little fellow tries to return, but the soldier beats him and drives him on with the rest. The rest try to comfort him, but what can they say? It may be their turn next. But at night, when they camp by the roadside, the little fellow also is missing. An American coming along the road that night passes that same spot; the poor grandmother's body has been dragged to the side of the road, but she has been robbed of most of her clothes, one cotton shirt is left, her face is turned in the sky, and by that body sits the little grandson, crushed, forlorn, alone in the world, crying his heart out — and I had to pass on. There were thousands [of] others like him. Already we were feeding all we could; we had no more money to buy more. We could not take the little fellow into our orphanage. The Government would not permit us to help him, it was a crime in that country. It was a political matter. He would die a little later; no matter what we did to help him along that terrible road was just prolonging the agony. We left him there by the side of the road, under the stars. I pray to God that sweet death may claim him soon.[57]

In the 16 November 1922 issue of *Mid-Week Pictorial* (published by the New York Times Company) there is a double page spread entitled "Flight of orphan host from Turkish persecution; menacing developments in the Near eastern crisis." The feature of the story is to highlight Lester Wright's death and the wounding of his colleague, and the dangers associated with the successful evacuation of orphans from Asia Minor (Fig. II,4). The caption to the photograph states:

> Part of the 5,000 orphans who marched 500 miles overland from the Near East Orphanage in Harpoot, Turkish Armenia, on their way out of Nationalist Turkey to safety in Syria. The march was attended by intense privations. (Photos courtesy Near East Relief).

---

[57] Excerpted from Mark H. Ward, M.D., "Conditions in Asia Minor" (undated, typed document used for a talk in Boston on behalf of Near East Relief; courtesy of Ward family private archives. Brackets indicate minor editing by the authors of this article).

The photograph of the orphans appears in *The New Near East* (23 April 1923, 17) in a brief article entitled "The Last Convoy." The image is captioned "On the road to Harpoot."

Of considerable interest as well, is a photograph among Lester J. Wright's materials of "Greek and Armenian street children in Turkey, 1922."(Fig. II,5) There are no further details so one is left with the all too common situation of lack of, or partial at best, attestation or attribution. A close examination of the photograph shows the children under some sort of supervision of an adult woman (see background). Most of the children look as if they have been cared for after they had been perhaps gathered off the streets and placed in an orphanage. In other words, the children do not look extremely destitute. No doubt, however, a few that look as if they are in more dire straights are in evidence. The caption that they are "street children" is potentially confusing because, indeed, in some cases, orphans were only given some daily care in a feeding or so-called milk station situation. If, for instance, an orphanage was full and no more could be accommodated for lack of funds or other reasons, there might have been a rationale for performing a sort of triage, taking in only those who needed the most care, and merely feeding the others on an "out-patient" basis. Thus one cannot be absolutely certain what the term "street children" represents — former street children, street children under outpatient type supervision and/or partial care? As early as 1919 a message by Navy Radio received via Washington, 12 March 1919 stated: "Please forward to Armenian Syrian Relief New York from Constantinople." It gives a hint of what was happening all over Turkey, and what had happened to Armenians and Greeks by the time Lester Wright was on the scene:

> Many telegrams received from various parts of Turkey report thousands of Armenian women and children forcibly taken by Turks are being set adrift by command of high Turkish officers influenced by French and British authorities. Within few days 1300 children have been discharged in Constantinople and many more in interior. The situation demands immediate and comprehensive action upon a large scale as surviving Armenians while cooperating to their utmost are too depleted and impoverished to receive back all their own while the opportunity for rendering mighty humanitarian service has never been surpassed.[58]

Images of Murders Accomplished

Captions to a photograph that has been reproduced in more than one Greek language volume usually states that it represents a massacre of both Arme-

[58] Smith College Archives, War Service Collection, Box 30, Letters.

nians and Greeks. Another states in translation from the Greek "The massacre of Greeks and Armenians in Trebizond (28 February 1919)."[59]

It also happens to be reproduced on the cover, colorized at that, of Agampatian's *Η Αρμενία και τ' Αρμενικό Ζήτημα: Οι Τούρκοι, Δάσκαλοι της Γενοκτονίας* [*Armenia and the Armenian Question: the Turks, Teachers of Genocide*].[60] Hofmann and Koutcharian caption this photograph as,[61]

> Some of the Armenians who were killed and brought to the Armenian Relief Hospital, during the massacre of Feb. 28th 1919, at Aleppo. Phot. Najjarian Brothers.

They add that,

> The photograph shows some of the victims, who according to handwritten captions, were laid out in front of the Armenian Relief Hospital.

They prudently question the identification of the hospital as Armenian and query in brackets "American?"

This image, which has been related more than a few times to the Armenian Genocide of 1915, appeared in print at least as early as spring of 1919 in the Paris weekly *L'Illustration* (Fig. III,1). In the 5 April 1919 issue there is an article accompanied by two photographs, which are of quite good size and quality.[62] The author makes a point of stating: "Les documents photographiques que nous reproduisons suffisent á illustrer lugubrement ces scenes d'horreur" [The photographic documents which we reproduce here suffice to illustrate amply these scenes of horror].

Textual support for this carnage may be drawn from a memoir written by an Armenian eyewitness in Aleppo:

> That blow was the Friday morning, February 28, 1919 massacre. Savage wild *Arabs* [emphasis ours], led by their policemen, carried out the massacre against the poor, innocent and helpless Armenians, butchering some 100, and wounding another 150 who subsequently recovered almost completely. The same day, our defenseless barracks-shelter was besieged by the Arab mob. Death was hovering around us. A move in the next instant, and everything would be over for us. Many, particularly the women, were sobbing, wailing, praying, pulling their hair out, throwing themselves into each other's arms, thrashing about on the ground, and screeching. Some of them had turned as white as lime, others' eyes were swollen from tears. They all sought hiding

---

[59] Κωνταντίνος Φωτιάδης, *Η Γενοκτονία των Ελλήνων του Πόντου* [*Genocide of the Greeks of Pontus*] (Athens: Ίδρυμα της Βουλής των Ελλήνων, 2004), 604.

[60] Ochanes-Sarkis Agampatian, *Η Αρμενία και τ' Αρμενικό Ζήτημα: Οι Τούρκοι, Δάσκαλοι της Γενοκτονίας* [*Armenia and the Armenian Question: The Turks, Teachers of Genocide*], second ed. (Athens: Στοχαστής, 1988).

[61] Hofmann and Koutcharian, "Images that Horrify and Indict," fig. 111.

[62] Jules Chancel, "Les massacres du 28 Février 1919 en Syrie," *L'Illustration* (Paris), 5 April 1919, 377.

places deep in the recesses of the doorless and unenclosed cells [...] Fortunately, four British soldiers in the barracks held off the band of timid and indecisive hyenas for half an hour. Then Indian soldiers encamped on the outskirts of town came to help out and rescued us from a certain death [...] After the massacre, the barracks became overcrowded with the town's residents whose number reached 8,000 and who rushed there in panic. All the halls and corridors were full, and everybody waited for those massacrers to be punished severely by the British. But, alas, the British did nothing at all, even to the hundred Arabs they had arrested, finding them less guilty of shedding Armenian blood than engaging in upsetting the local administration.[63]

The photograph of the bodies laid out was also published in *Red Cross Magazine* by Melville Chater with the caption "Since the armistice, the Turks in the remote districts of Asia Minor have continued the slaughter of Armenian Christians. The massacres of these forty Armenians occurred in February, 1919."[64]

In a largely pictorial work, a "history in documentary photographs," on the end of the Ottoman Empire by the French intellectual, historian and journalist Jacques Benoist-Méchin, the same image is described as "Armenians massacred by Turks on 28th February 1919." None of the photographs in this interesting work seems to be seriously attested or attributed, and one is expected to accept them on faith, as it were.[65]

At a considerably later date, and in a carefully executed work entitled *The Armenian Genocide, News Accounts from the American Press 1915–1922* this very photograph is presented on the same page as an article written by U.S. Ambassador Henry Morgenthau entitled "Shall Armenia Perish?"[66] Placing Morgenthau's text and a photograph from a different article on the same page was simply done to conserve space. The "Source List of Photographs"

---

[63] These details of the event are published in an Armenian survivor memoir by Arnak entitled (in translation), *In the Claws of the Turks, 1916–1919* (Yerevan: Louysapats, 2007). Arnak was the pen name of Hampartzoom Zorthian (1885–1952). Zorthian was one of the few intellectuals who survived the genocide. See pp. 144–45 of the original Armenian edition published in 1936 and reprinted in 2007.

[64] Melville Chater, "Turkey's Wages of Sin," *Red Cross Magazine* 14, no. 8 (1919): 79.

[65] Jacques Bénoist-Méchin, *Turkey 1908–1938: The end of the Ottoman Empire (A history in documentary photographs)* (Zug, Switzerland: Swan Productions, 1989), 185.

[66] Richard D. Kloian, ed., *The Armenian Genocide, News Accounts from the American Press 1915–1922* (Richmond, California: ACC Books, 1992 [third edition]), 341; cf. Henry Morgenthau's commentary "Shall Armenia Perish?" *The Independent* (New York) 28 February 1920, 314.

in the *News Accounts* volume unambiguously states that the picture was published in *The Independent* (New York) vol. 101, 20 March 1920, 468.[67]

The contemporary caption of the photo of the results of the Aleppo pogrom situated beneath the reproduction of the Morgenthau article and included in the *News Accounts* by Richard D. Kloian reads: "So gruesome a picture as this would be taboo in *The Independent* if the seriousness of the situation in Armenia now did not demand forceful illustration. These victims of a Turkish massacre typify thousands of Christian Armenians slaughtered by the Turks since the signing of the Armistice" (Fig. III,2). The caption appears to have been given to the photograph by the editor or editorial staff of *The Independent* to accompany an article entitled "We are Desperate," by the Armenian general and hero Antranig. [68]

This same page from Kloian's edited work of newspaper accounts and other reports appears to have been selected, albeit innocently, to embellish an article attributed to Christopher Walker in a profusely illustrated issue in Greek, devoted to the Armenian genocide, published in a popularly written history magazine *Ιστορικά* [*Istorika*] (27 April 2000), which is now defunct.[69] Someone who was clearly not a serious enough reader to see that the image was taken from a different article in *The Independent* ended up reproducing an image that belonged to a different article — one with a caption that was very imprecise at that. Christopher Walker certainly did not select that image to embellish the article published under his name and translated into Greek and would not have approved that caption had his permission been sought (personal communication).

A double page spread of the photograph also appears in *The Great War and the Shaping of the 20th Century* by Jay Winter and Blaine Baggett. These serious scholars also erroneously state that the Armenians were slain by Turks in an otherwise perfectly legitimate caption. It was, however, undated as to when it might have happened. The source of the image is given as the well-known French picture resource Roger–Viollet in Paris.[70]

---

[67] Kloian, *The Armenian Genocide,* 342. The planned new edition of that work will redouble efforts to make clear the source of images so that any potential for errors by careless readers will be obviated.

[68] Hamilton Holt (1872–1951), journalist, internationalist and educator, was the editor and publisher of *The Independent* in New York from 1894–1922 and served on the Near East Relief board.

[69] See the image accompanying the article by Christopher J. Walker, 34–37.

[70] Jay Winter and Blaine Baggett, *The Great War and the Shaping of the 20th Century* (New York: Viking, 1996), 150–51. It is to be hoped that historically important newsphoto sources will soon enable workers to carry out attestation and attribution of photographs of the genre that are now frequently referred to as "file photos." For example, the Bett-

Finally, a glossy print in the U.S. National Archives is captioned,

> Some of the Armenians who were killed and brought to the *American* [*emphasis ours*] Relief Hospital, during the massacre of Feb. 28, 1919, at Aleppo.

Had it not been for a measure of serendipity at that point we would perforce have had to be satisfied. But we are able to go into considerably more detail than might have been anticipated from what we have thus far reported. Quite accidentally, and in a totally different context, we encountered a lengthy article by Francisan scholar Vincent Mistrih (1999) on the Aleppo "Incident" that came to be referred to as the Cuma Pazarı (Djouma Bazari in contemporary transliteration) [Friday Market] Massacre of February 1919.[71] This exquisitely detailed treatment using contemporary sources in Arabic etc. leaves few stones unturned. It substantiates, and considerably extends what we have said, and for that reason we include this important reference in our updated caption to the photograph.

In the article by Mistrih, reference is made to an account of the Cuma Pazarı Massacre by Monseigneur Jean Naslian, Catholic Bishop of Trebizond published in his *Memoirs*.[72] In that account it is specifically stated that a 35-bed hospital had been improvised earlier by the Archdiocese of Aleppo in the very large establishment of the École Arménienne Catholique. The Near East Relief had also taken over responsibility for some relief work with girls and children taken in by Muslims and Kurds, and who had been reclaimed and taken into custody. This may explain the confusion as to what kind of hospital it was, i.e. who supported it. It was clearly the sole courtyard of the École Arménienne Catholique, which served also as the hospital. [73] Efforts to identify the building by recent Armenian residents of Aleppo known to us have not been productive, however. But that may not be an intractable problem now that we have more to go on.

Taking all the above into consideration, a revised caption could read:

Photograph taken in Aleppo, Syria, of Armenian victims of the Sūq-al-Jum'a massacre, known in French as the Massacre du Marché du Vendredi, in English as the Friday Market Massacre. While usually incorrectly ascribed as the direct work of Turks, the massacre, which occurred on Friday 28 February

---

mann Archives, said to consist of some 11 million photographs and negatives, is part of Corbis, owned by Bill Gates of Microsoft fame. The plan is to digitize the entire collection. This is just one development which augurs well for locating and identifying photographs.

[71] V. Mistrih, "Un incident à Alep contre les Arméniens (Février 1919)," *Studia Orientalia Christiana Collectanea* 32 (1999): 277–348.

[72] See Jean Naslian, *Les Memoires de Mgr. Jean Naslian, Eveque de Trebizonde. Sur les événements politico-religieux en Proche-Orient de 1914 á 1928*, vol. 2 (Beirut: Éditeur Jean Naslian/Vienna: Imprimerie Méchthariste, 1958), 330–33.

[73] See Naslian, ibid., 2: 310–13.

1919, was perpetrated by Arabs encouraged and driven by Turkish propaganda, and mischief. One contemporary French commentator claimed that the pogrom was instigated by the Arab group Nadi al-Arab. While this group was mainly anti-Jewish, it supposedly had a Young Turk mentality, since its founder studied in Constantinople at the time of the Armenian Genocide, and was an officer in the Turkish Army. A *New York Times* article published 13 March 1919 (page 3), states,

> So much for the incidents of the last ten days. The significance of them is this: There is a Pan-Arabian movement under way in which the Arabs are now playing the old role of the Turks in terrorizing and persecuting the other races of Asia Minor. There is little difference, so far as European opinion is concerned, whether the massacre movements are inspired from Constantinople on the north or from Hedjaz in the south.

Whether this interpretation is sufficiently precise cannot be delved into here. Khoury in his *Syria and the French Mandate: The Politics of Arab Nationalism 1920–1945* provides substantial detail on how some Aleppine leaders turned to the Turkish nationalist leaders for support against the French.[74]

A contemporary photograph in the U.S. National Archives bears the label "Some of the Armenians who were killed and brought to the American Relief Hospital, during the massacre of Feb. 28, 1919, at Aleppo."[75] According to Mgr. Naslian, the photograph was taken in the sole courtyard of École Arménienne Catholique, the Armenian Catholic school, which served also as a hospital. He says that fifty-four dead were collected there. But the supposed death toll was between sixty-five and seventy victims, and a number were missing, as well as about ninety wounded.[76]

This example of the attestation of the photograph is of no little interest. The attribution to Najjarian Brothers photographers is of interest as well. Mgr. Naslian mentions that the bodies were photographed but does not add anything further. Neither does his memoir include the photograph. We have been unable to pursue further the photographer(s) aspect of the question.

---

[74] Philip S. Khoury, *Syria and the French Mandate: The Politics of Arab Nationalism 1920–1945* (Princeton: Princeton University Press, 1987), 104ff. For additional perspectives on the relationship of Arab Nationalists and Kemalists see also Fred H. Lawson, "The Northern Syrian Revolts of 1919–1921 and the Sharifian Regime: Congruence of Conflict and Ideologies?," in *From the Syrian Land to the States of Syria and Lebanon*, Thomas Phillipp and Christoph Schumann, eds. (Wurzburg: Ergon, 2004), 257–74.

[75] U.S. Archives 867.4016/417.

[76] See Mistrih, "Un incident à Alep contre les Arméniens (Février 1919)," 277–348, for an exhaustive treatment of this "incident." (The photograph shown was taken from *L'Illustration* (Paris), 5 April 1919, 377, and shows more of the building than some later cropped versions.)

Even so, all this underscores how a simple caption can quickly grow into a considerably fuller exposition.

A final comment is necessary at this point. The disappointment reflected by the statements of the Armenian eyewitness and author Arnak are borne out by Mgr. Naslian, who comments that the English were simply "being English" when they refused to act swiftly in quelling the massacre. They were having breakfast! (First things first?) Unlike what Arnak believed, there were some consequences, however, including some rather lenient fines for those having committed the murders.[77]

Conclusions

The examples represented here are only a few of the many that could have been selected and despite a significant amount of progress in refining their captions, they should be viewed as ongoing efforts of attestation and attribution. By no means should anything be taken as final. Its main objective has been to be informative and heuristic. Hopefully the day will come when the suggested captions can be shortened and literature citations can take the place of precisely crafted expanded text.

The Greek word *prolegomenon* (plural —*a*) comes to mind, since it is only a prelude of what must follow. Today, as intimated earlier, there are unprecedented opportunities for refinement and polishing as more information surfaces from hitherto obscure sources.

We have emphasized that photographs only have maximal value to the extent they can be accompanied with supporting textual evidence. Photographs do not speak for themselves. They can lie or tell the truth, and can thus be manipulated.[78]

Armenian Genocide denier (presumably also a denier of the Greek and Assyrian Genocides) Professor Justin McCarthy, now at the University of Louisville, states in the documentary film *An Armenian Journey* by Theodore Bogosian that photographs don't mean much.[79] For once we agree with him.[80]

---

[77] For details cf. Naslian, *Les Memoires de Mgr. Jean Naslian*, 2: 312.

[78] See for example the classic work by Allan Sekula, *Photography against the Grain: Essays and Photoworks* (Halifax: Nova Scotia College of Design, 1984).

[79] *An Armenian Journey* (1988), Bogosian Productions, initially shown on Public Broadcasting TV, WGBH, Boston; see also http://www.cstar.com/titles/all/d1ffc1dc-1c84-44a4-9376-71c13e1a113b; remastered DVD 2006, Theodore Bogosian Productions, running time 59 minutes.

[80] If one forces oneself to read McCarthy, or worse yet, to listen to him, one invariably recalls what Humpty Dumpty said in Lewis Carroll's, *Through the Looking Glass, and what*

That conclusion is certainly not original with McCarthy; it has long been a point of discussion by professionals in the field. *But* photographs can be useful, provided they are accurately attested, i.e. affirmed as correct, and better still, if they can be attributed, i.e. identified with a person, place and/or exact date and time. Combined with relevant and irrefutable textual or oral evidence, photographs, even drawings and paintings, with precise and detailed captions, can very nearly stand on their own.

This means that first and foremost, *evidence* is required to support any contention about a photograph or image or representation. Photographs with these qualities thus can, and should in our view, be used to supplement and complement more usual historical scholarship. The least they do is to help engage the imagination, and select and secure our memories. We have tried to follow what might be called, for lack of a better expression, a scientific method of finding out the political truth.

The overview presented here is necessarily only a glimpse of the challenges and unprecedented opportunities faced by workers interested in genocide images as they pertain to what happened in Ottoman, Ittihadist and early nationalist Turkey.[81]

We have seen that some photographs have been totally inaccurately attested or attributed. Even here, there is frequently a paper trail that gives some measure of explanation as to what may have led to an error, and equally importantly, its perpetuation.

There is no doubt in our minds that past efforts aimed at attestation and attribution, regardless of how excellent, good or incomplete or wrong the outcome, have been sincere in intent and driven by uncomplicated motives. There has been no malicious attempt to deceive.[82] Motivation has probably been no other than an attempt to seek the means to exorcize or ameliorate the pain and trauma experienced by self, parents or grandparents, or even great grandparents. Recall the truism "To know your past is to know yourself." What is nowadays being called "Trans-generational experience" is a

I found, namely, "When I use a word, Humpty Dumpty said, in a rather scornful tone, it means just what I choose it to mean, neither more nor less" (Chapter 6).

[81] Space considerations have prevented us from dealing with photographs which have been accurate as to what they depict, but have been attributed to the period of the First World War when, in fact, they represent people or events from the period of the Hamidian Massacres in the 1890s, or even later such as the pogroms in Baku in 1904, or in Adana and surrounding areas during the Cilician Massacres of 1909.

[82] *Honi soit qui mal y pense* [*Evil to him who thinks evil*].

very real thing and is being addressed by psychologists and psychiatrists. It takes time to resolve the many layers of hurt and pain.[83]

Some final considerations are in order. Many genocide-related images are in the public domain. But there are those, both individuals and governments, who see benefit in suppressing such images. And, one may be assured that they are not beyond using fatuous arguments and blatant, unmitigated, sophistry to cause mischief.[84]

One example of several that could be selected concerns a well-known photograph showing a female and two small children lying in what appears to be a background of garbage or rubble. This image had apparently been distributed by Getty Images/Hulton Archive in Britain to various newspapers over a number of years. A complaint from the Turkish Embassy in London objected to the caption that the dead were the victims of the Turkish massacres. The dead, according to the Turkish embassy official, had obviously *only* "starved to death." Hulton withdrew the (Armenian) genocide photos.[85] Journalist Robert Fisk, author of *The Independent* (London) articles referred to above, stated,

> According to a Hulton official, the [three] pictures were 'withdrawn' routinely after the complaint and — although the dead bodies were clearly the result of the Armenian holocaust — remained withdrawn after the copyright was found to belong to a German organization holding Wegner's pictures.[86]

What person knowledgeable about the specifics of the Genocides could have imagined that such a tumult could have erupted over a caption accompanying a photograph, which is so gruesome by any normal standard? Had the technicality of copyright not provided a convenient means to resolve the contentious issue for the Hulton Archive, one wonders if the political pressure from Turkey would have been ignored, or acceded to?

Could one argue that had the Getty Hulton Archives carried out a more careful job of attestation and attribution there would have been no issue at all?

---

[83] Some have called this "second- or third-generation of trauma." See e.g. Marc Nichanian, "Catastrophic mourning," in *Loss, The Politics of Mourning*, David L. Eng and David Kazanjian, eds. (Berkeley: University of California Press, 2003), 99–124.

[84] Kate McKenna, "Account of Armenian Massacre Provokes Diplomatic Storm," *New York Times*, 3 December 1989, LI1.

[85] See *The Independent* (London), 12 March 2001, 4. See another article on page 11 in the same issue of *The Independent*.

[86] The same image appears on page 80 of Richard D. Kloian's compilation of news accounts. See Kloian, *The Armenian Genocide*, 80. The caption of the picture there reads "These victims of Turkish cruelty were driven out to suffer extremes of hunger and hardship in their wanderings through the desert where so many thousands like them also died. Shown here is a mother and her two children found dead in the desert."

For example in the Fiftieth Anniversary Publications commemorating the Armenian genocide we read that the caption in Volumes 1 and 2 (1964 and 1965 respectively), "A starved Armenian mother and her two starved children."[87] Similarly, On the cover of the third edition of *Der Völkermord an den Armeniern vor Gericht, Der Prozeß Talaat Pascha* [*The Armenian Genocide before Judgement, The Trial of Talât Paşa*], edited by Tessa Hofmann, the picture occurs with the caption (in translation) "Turkish barbarity: Having been deported to the desert, a starved Armenian woman and her children." The image is also reproduced in the same volume following page 57 but with this caption (again in translation) "Death from starvation, the true aim of the Turk policy of mass deportation." And to quote one more level of refinement in captioning, we read what Hofmann and Koutcharian say in their 1992 pivotal paper on documentation and attribution as to Fig. 59, "Starved Armenian woman with two small children. Armin T. Wegner Collection."[88]

A perhaps still greater uproar that took place at a considerably earlier time over a photograph and its caption involved an image nominally representing a pyramid of skulls of Armenians who perished either through massacre or death by starvation in the deserts of Syria and Mesopotamia.[89] But the pyramid of skulls photograph was in fact not a photograph of a scene at all. It was a photo, perhaps even a photo of a photo, of an oil painting on canvas completed in 1871–72 by the Russian artist Vasily V. Vereshchagin. The painting, entitled in English translation *The Apotheosis of War*, hangs in the Tretiakov Gallery in Moscow.

One specific use of the image which seems to have started the tempest and elicited the fullsome wrath of a Turkish Professor Dr. Türkkaya Ataöv in Ankara involves its use on a softcover of an excellent book on the trial of Soghomon Tehlirian, complete with details of the trial testimony and proceedings. Tehlirian, it will be recalled, was the Armenian student who assassinated in Berlin one of the leading murderers of the Armenians Talât

---

[87] See photographs no. 9 of both Naim Bey, by Aram Antonean [Andonian], *The Genocide of the Armenians by Turks, The Memoirs of Naim Bey*, vol. 1 (Newton Square, PA: The Armenian Historical Research Association [AHRA], 1964) and also Josef Guttmann, Naim Bey, Aram Antonean [Andonian], compiled by Manasseh Giragos Sevag, *The Turkish Armenocide (The Genocide of Armenians by Turks). The Beginnings of Genocide, An Account of the Massacres in World War I by Joseph Guttmann; The Memoirs of Naim Bey by Aram Andonian*, vol. 2, compiled by M. G. Sevag (Newton Square, PA: The Armenian Historical Research Association [AHRA], 1965).

[88] We will not go into any detail here in this discussion and conclusions section as to whether it is a woman and her children or a girl with younger siblings etc. Armenian women in that period often married quite young.

[89] The use of "Arabian desert" sometimes appears on photographs like the one under discussion. The designation 'arabio' in Armenian connotes regions inhabited by Arabs.

Paşa.[90] The copy of the photograph used on the cover was apparently selected in belief of its authenticity by Dr. Tessa Hofmann and Dr. G. Koutcharian, both Genocide scholars of high repute. Whatever the reason for its selection, the image had not been adequately assessed as to attestation or attribution before use.

If one takes the wholly disproportionate reaction to this error as any measure, one may safely conclude that Professor Dr. Ataöv and those who support the official Turkish government denialist line, seem to have been both exhilarated — even re-inspired — by the error. Nevertheless, according to Hofmann and Koutcharian, it took the Turkish media many years to notice a mistaken and long-standing attestation.[91] And, we shall soon see below that the imprecise use was certainly not original to either of them.

It is of no little interest that the tirade over this photograph has yet to subside, and even seems to have taken on grander proportions — a life of its own so to speak, at least in some quarters, which are apparently ever desperate for new grist for the tired mill. The first detailed response to the error out of Turkey were heavily illustrated, but badly printed, 30-page booklets in English and in French, printed for foreign consumption in 1985. A new edition, again poorly printed, has appeared, this time so far only in Turkish[92] and is now some 157 pages long. Dr. Hofmann is still being accused of deliberately perpetrating "an Armenian falsification." This is so despite the fact that the first fresh edition of the trial's proceedings was purged of any reference to the Vereschwagin painting by Dr. Hofmann.[93]

The above is given as background.

Now, here are some minor details that seem to have passed through the fine sieve of Professor Dr. Ataöv's supposedly exhaustive research resulting in

---

[90] See e.g. Soghomon Tehlirean and Vartkes Yeghiayan, *The Case of Soghomon Tehlirian* (Los Angeles: A.R.F. Vartanian Gomideh, 1985); Edward Alexander, *A Crime of Vengeance* (New York: The Free Press, 1999).

[91] Hofmann and Koutcharian, "Images that Horrify and Indict," 60 n. 6.

[92] Türkkaya Ataöv, *Ermeni Belge Düzmeciliği* [*Armenian Document Forgery*] (İstanbul: İleri Yayinlari, 2006).

[93] It is, of course, unprofessional for Ataöv to hurl *ad hominem* insults at a distinguished scholar, who has been noted for her meticulous work. The motives are apparent. The only potential saving grace is that at the time of this writing there exists only one copy of Ataov's new edition in any institutional library in the U.S. The same tired imagery, ever more very badly reproduced, accompanied by persistent and relentless harping and gloating is still being used in recent Armenian Genocide revisionist denialist publications. See e.g. Cem Özgönül, *Der Mythos eines Volkermordes: eine kritische Betrachtung der Lepsiusdokumente sowie der deutschen Rolle in Geschichte und Gegenwart der "Armenischen Frage"* (Köln: Önel, 2006), 31–32.

his exposé of the "Armenian Falsification" using Vereshchagin's imagery of war, and specifically *The Apotheosis of War* in all its facets and varied ramifications.

The reader will see why the following excerpt from a letter containing an unambiguous reference made to Vereshchagin and the power of his brush *written in 1915* is worthy of notice for several reasons. It was written by Walter Rössler, the German Consul in Aleppo, and addressed to Hohenlohe-Langenburg, Ambassador on Extraordinary Mission in Constantinople, and is dated Aleppo, 27 September 1915:

> Regarding the deportation of the Armenians I am honored to continue reporting the following:
>
> 1) Individual events which presumably have otherwise taken place unnoticed, recently happened in Aleppo before the eyes of the population itself. Since then, the government has taken steps to ensure that, for the most part, the hordes of deported people rarely come through Aleppo any more.
>
> On both the 10th and the 12th of this month, a procession of about 2000 banished women and children arrived here on foot via Ras ul Ain in a completely exhausted state, a procession, *which could only have been depicted in its atrociousness by the brush of a Werechshagin* [Vereshchagin] [emphasis ours].[94]
>
> Using whips, the gendarmes drove the wretched emaciated creatures, many of whom had a death-look about them, through the streets of Aleppo to the train station without permitting them to drink or take a drop of water or to receive a piece of bread here in the town. The citizens of the town who wished to distribute bread and water were prevented from doing so. Two women fell down to give birth and were only protected from being whipped by the gendarmes of the town dwellers, who rushed to help them. Two German Borromeus Sisters witnessed an exhausted woman being pulled along by the hair by a gendarme. The Swiss chief operating officer of the Baghdad railway told me that he had experienced many things in his life, which had hardened him, but that he would never have thought that such a thing as this procession to be possible. It reminded him of pictures of Indian famines. Thus, it is understandable why Djemal Pasha issued a strict ban on photographing the exiles. In his report, a copy of which I obediently enclose and which he gave me to be used in strict confidence, he ordered that, to avoid punishment, *all of the Baghdad railway's engineers are to hand over prints, plates and films which they have. Photographing Armenians is to be considered the same as taking photographs of theatres of war without permission* [emphasis ours].[95]

---

[94] In the original German we read "... ein Zug der nur durch den Pinsel eines Wereschtschagin in seiner Grauenhaftigkeit hätte wiedergegeben werden können."

[95] See Wolfgang Gust, ed., *Der Völkermord an den Armeniern 1915/16. Dokumente aus dem Politischen Archiv des deutschen Auswärtigen Amts* (Springe: zu Klampen Verlag, 2005), 307 and www.armenocide.net Dok. Nummer 1915-09-27-DE-014.

Surely, what is quoted does not change the supposed attestation of the pyramid of skulls "photograph of a painting" used by many Armenians and by Dr. Hofmann three decades ago. Those ever-vigilant (and often professional) apologists of the official Turkish government denialist line conveniently ignore the fact that, as soon as it became possible, she admitted its erroneous use at least twice in writing and actively caused its removal in subsequent printings. There are certainly many detailed "word pictures" from eyewitnesses, especially of skulls and bones stuffed into wells. Pictures of "bones" that can be attested and attributed exist, and there are plenty of photographs of living skeletons of Armenians that could be selected if one were to wish to "horrify and to indict" today. All this lends poignant support to the appropriateness of invoking the imagery of Vereshchagin's works to describe what was happening to the Armenians. It seems that *The Apotheosis of War* was for educated Europeans and Armenians at least, a symbol of cruelty that was subsequently transferred to the genocidal events of World War I.

The paper trail connected with this image supposedly exhaustively investigated by Ataöv may be further expanded. *The Apotheosis of War* was described, albeit again incorrectly, and in English, in an early publication by an Armenian writer who was a survivor of the Genocide. He had been a student at Euphrates College in Harput and was fluent in English. The caption reads "All that remains of many caravans."[96] In another work republished through the efforts of Dr. Manasseh G. Sevag, an eminent Armenian biochemistry and microbiology professor at the University of Pennsylvania, the caption reads "A mound of skulls of murdered and starved Armenians in Deir al-Zor gathered from the desert at the end of World War I."[97]

A photograph of Vereshchagin's *The Apotheosis of War* is reproduced in a way that can hardly be distinguished from those of regular photographs in a volume by Rev. Aris Kalfaian titled *The Passion of the Armenians*, written in Armenian and published in Beirut.[98]

---

[96] Krikor M. Zahigian, *One Page of Armenia's Tragedy: a Story of the Years Wherein We Have Seen Evil; the Testimony of an Eye Witness* (Pacific Palisades, California: privately printed, 1923), 29.

[97] See penultimate unnumbered photograph of the edition edited by M. G. Sevag of *The Armenian Genocide by the Turks (The Turkish Armenocide)*. Armenian Historical Association, AHRA, Documentary Series volume 1, 1964 and in the 1965 expanded edition of the same work, the photograph appears as Fig. 17 with the same caption.

[98] See Aris Ter K. Galfaean, *Girk Elits Hayots* [*The Passion of the Armenians*] (Beirut: Tp. K. Tonikean, 1955), 651. Der (Rev.) Garabed III Kalfaian, died in Yettem, California in 1957, shortly after the publication of his book. He was an educator of considerable standing in Turkish Armenia.

One can also find essentially the same image captioned "A pyramid of skulls of a few of the Armenians who perished during the inhuman mass deportations."[99]

Further still, *The Apotheosis of War* also appears on the dedication page to "The Armenian Massacre," published as an excerpt from *The First Genocide of the 20th Century*, compiled and illustrated by James Nazer and advertised in 1970 as "Commemorating the 55th Anniversary of this great tragedy." The dedication page reads (with the image in a black frame), "Dedicated to the memory of 1,500,000 martyred Armenians who were massacred by the Turks." In the longer version of the book also published in 1968 the image is not presented, either on the dedicatory page or in the text proper.

Even as recently as 2004 the image of Vereshchagin's pyramid of skulls has been used on a dedicatory page albeit without describing it as a pyramid of Armenian skulls. "This booklet is dedicated to the immortal memory of the 1.5 million Armenians who were martyred by the Ottoman Turks (1915–1923)."[100] Many other places where this image has been reproduced could be cited.

We can conclude thus that no doubt errors have been made in both the attestation and attribution of this image. In the case of Dr. Hofmann, as a scholar with professional integrity, she saw to it that the imagery of the cover was changed in a new edition of her work.

It is easy to claim with the clarity of hindsight that *The Apotheosis of War* images published and reproduced without any qualifying statement that they were the Vereshchagin *painting* did not, and still do not, look like photographs under detailed analysis. Indeed, and as we have attempted to point out throughout this essay, the devil is in the details.

At the same time, it is readily arguable that some World War I period reproductions of Vereshchagin's "Apotheosis" do indeed look like photographs. Photographs of photographs frequently lose detail, of course, and take on a look of their own.[101] Sepia colored prints that we have seen of the painting

---

[99] James Kay Sutherland, *The Adventures of an Armenian Boy: an Autobiography and Historical Narrative Encompassing the Last Thirty Years of the Ottoman Empire* (Ann Arbor: Ann Arbor Press, 1964), 65.

[100] Gerard Pederian, *Armenian Massacres through the Centuries Culminating in the Genocide of 1915* (Toronto: Privately Printed, 2004), 5.

[101] Attention may be drawn to the many books and scientific papers published by Soviet bloc authors as late as the 1960s and even 1970s, and later still, wherein the photography and reproduction is so poor that the nominal photographs look like drawings or paintings! Examples are too many to give here.

can readily pass as poor quality photographs. Indeed they seem to have done just that.

It may also be added that we know of at least two immediate Post-World War I reproductions of *The Apotheosis of War* on postcard stock. One such postcard dated 15 May 1920 and sent from Constantinople to Glasgow says in a clear contemporary hand, "This is rather a unique photo of Skulls with Crows pecking at them. I believe that is part of some Massacre of Armenians by the Turks."

There is also, for the record, a photograph of the "Apotheosis" in an early twentieth century commemorative booklet in Armenian (and some Russian) published in Tiflis in 1907. The image clearly acknowledges that it is a picture of Vereshchagin's painting.[102]

We can thus readily conclude that the painting *The Apotheosis of War* was used on more than a few occasions in very early accounts to exemplify tragedy experienced by the Armenian nation at Turkish and Tartar hands. In what context and to what extent they were used for propagandistic purposes is something that needs much more research to disclose, much less assess. A revised caption might read:

Pyramid of skulls by the Russian painter and war artist Vasily Vereshchagin (1842–1904). He called the painting *The Apotheosis of War* and facetiously dedicated it "to all great conquerors, past, present, and future." The graphic imagery was intended to confront the viewer with the stark reality of war. It was Vereshchagin's hope that it would serve as his anti-war manifesto. This painting, completed in 1870–1871 reflected what he had witnessed during the so-called Turkestan War, a lengthy war fought by Russia in its imperial quest of expansion all the way to the borders of China. The "Apotheosis" was exhibited in 1874 along with several others of his paintings under the unified title "Barbarians." Available evidence suggests that photographs of this painting (not colorized) were adopted for anti-Turkish propaganda purposes at the end of World War I, especially as war crime trials were being launched in Constantinople. And, photo-reproductions of the painting without attribution to Vereshchagin appear in a number of Armenian works, the captions of which suggest or imply that the images are genuine photographs, and represent real events. Armenian skulls and bones were commonplace in Asiatic Turkey and Syria and Mesopotamia during the period of the Genocide, and long afterwards.

---

[102] *Artsunkner* [*Tears*] *Dedicated to the everlasting memory of the Armenian national heroes, 1905–1907* (St. Petersburg: Pushkinean Tparan). See the 'Art' part, page 4. This exceedingly rare work is dedicated to the victims of the Azeri Turkish/Tartar pogroms against Armenians in Baku.

Attention might also be drawn to a painting completed by Vereshchagin in 1878–79 that is considerably less exculpatory of the behavior of Turks on the battlefield. Vereshchagin was on the scene in the Russo-Turkish War of 1877–78. In a comprehensive volume entitled *Vereshchagin at War* by Vahan Barooshian, we read the following detailed analysis of a painting named "The Conquerors,"

> Vereshchagin also witnessed how the war had uprooted the Bulgarian population, whose property was plundered in the Turkish retreat and who required food, shelter, clothing, and medical care in the winter of 1877 after unspeakable Turkish atrocities. He saw the bodies of numerous Russian soldiers whose clothing had been stripped and whose ears, noses, heads and genitals had been severed by the Turkish troops. Vereshchagin re-creates this episode in "The Conquerors" (1878–1879) in which six soldiers dominate the center foreground, unify the picture, and shape the action of the remaining troops in the background. The figure in the center has stripped a Russian officer of his uniform and, with the aid of two companions, has donned it — however tight the fit — for the amusement of his fellow soldiers, all of whom seem insensitive to the slaughter they have committed. One Turkish soldier in a tan coat salutes the "officer," while the soldier sitting at the extreme right foreground has tucked a pair of Russian boots under his left arm and has flung an officer's coat over his right shoulder. The rest of the Turkish troops are scouring the battlefield to strip Russian bodies of their boots and uniforms, some are leaving with their bounty, while others are coming to join the search. The heads and decapitated bodies of Russian soldiers lie scattered in the field [103]

And, in the interest of casting a still wider net, attention may be drawn to yet another painting by Vereshchagin that shows a glimpse of some of the self-inflicted trials and tribulations at the Shiite Muslim commemoration of Muharrem in Susha, Karabagh in the Caucasus. Vereshchagin went to the Caucasus when he was 21 years old. An interesting sketch is provided on page 47.[104]

---

[103] Vahan D. Barooshian, *V. V. Vereshchagin: Artist at War* (Gainesville: University of Florida Press, 1993), 69 and plate 9.

[104] Ashura, the holiest date on the Shiite Muslim calendar, marks the end of the commemoration of the killing of Imam Hussein in 680 AD by the Sunni Caliph Yazid in Karbala. It is characterized by reliving the pain and suffering undergone by the Imam. An etching of a self-tormentor, after a drawing by the famous painter, is found In *Vassili Verestchagin, painter, soldier, traveler; autobiographical sketches*, trans. by F. H. Peters (London: R. Bently & Son, 1887), 47. See also pages 37–54, which deal with "A religious festival of the Shiites." An expanded version of the etching may be found in Frederick Davis Greene, *Armenian Massacres, or, the Sword of Mohammed:...* (Philadelphia and Chicago: International Publishing Co., 1896), 402. The caption, as wrong as wrong can possibly be, reads "Horribly tortured for their Christian faith." Justin McCarthy has alleged bias and even outright dishonesty on the part of missionaries and relief workers; see his "Missionaries

This seems to be an appropriate note on which to end. Truculent polemics, accusations of dishonesty and deliberate falsification are not worthy of rebuttal. Serious scholars feel that individuals who are guilty of this sort of behavior have, for the most part, disqualified themselves from being taken seriously.

The reality of the Genocides covered in this volume require no real photographic or visual confirmation. That is not to say that additional work and refinement and disclosure of nuances dealing with imagery need not be carefully assembled. Opinions may indeed be colored by personal bias, but carefully selected photographs without any modification cannot but show additional facts of the case.

There is a relevant quote excerpted from a work by the Armenian writer, critic, poet, and politician Avetis Aharonian (1866–1948) that appears in bronze on the plaque at the base of the Mount Davidson Cross in San Francisco that commemorates the Armenian Genocide. It reads,

> If evil of this magnitude can be ignored,
> if our own children forget,
> then we deserve oblivion and earn the world's scorn.

Those of Armenian, Greek and Aramaean/Assyrian ancestry should take heed.[105]

---

and the American Image of the Turk," in *Turkish-American Relations, Past Present and Future*, Mustafa Aydin and Çağrı Erhan, eds. (London & New York: Routlege, Taylor and Francis, 2003), 26–48. We concur that the inclusion of this totally inappropriate image in a serious book might otherwise lend some measure of credence of anti-Muslim bias. It is ironic that McCarthy's own publications contain arbitrary and unsubstantiated conclusions in the effort to deny the Armenian Genocide; for example, compare the attempt to discredit and dismiss the "Blue Book" as propaganda in his article "Wellington House and the Turks" in *The Turks* ed. Hasan Celal Güzel et al. (Ankara: Yeni Türkiye, 2002), 4: 457–67 to the richly documented treatment of the history of the Blue Book by David Miller in "The Treatment of the Armenians in the Ottoman Empire, a History of the Blue Book," *RUSI – Royal United Services Institute Journal* 150 no. 4 (August 2005): 36–43. In our opinion, what has been said of Julian the Apostate could be said of McCarthy "He tolerated no nonsense but his own." Besides, the use of what one would now refer to as poorly attested and attributed old "file photographs" cannot be expected to measure up with the rigorous standards of scholarship that we should seek to achieve today. That is, in fact, exactly one of the points that we are underscoring in this essay!

105 The poet Diana Der Hovanessian was responsible for the translation from the Armenian original (Personal communication).

Acknowledgments

First we wish to thank Nikolaos Hlamides for his intercession on our behalf and essentially arranging this essay to be included in this distinguished work. He has also kindly helped with Greek references and Turkish translations, and read drafts. Over the years many photo enthusiasts have kindly interacted with us and have shared information and viewpoints. They are too numerous to list individually but we would be remiss not to mention Missak Kelechian, Karekin Dickran, Dr. Eileen Hadidian and Ruth Thomasian (Armenian Project SAVE). The authors are especially grateful to Donna Sammis of the Interlibrary Loan Department of thc Stony Brook University Library for her expert help in obtaining for us many articles and books not available on this campus. We extend special thanks for access to family papers and photographs to the late Mary Carroll Masterson, and we offer thanks to Mrs. Jean Raht Cornille, Lester J. Wright's niece. We also thank Mrs. Cornille's son Dr. Thomas A. Cornille. We thank Pastor Edward Wicklein for his sharing information and materials from his research on Lester J. Wright. We are also grateful to Mr. Barry Zorthian for access to his father's rare book in Armenian. We thank a member of Jakob Kuenzler's family for permission to publish the image of the orphans being moved out of Turkey to Syria. We also thank Prof. Vahan Barooshian for permission to quote from his book and also the University of Florida Press. We also express our profound gratitude to The National Archives of the U.S., the Smith College Archives and the University of Maine Special Collections.

I,1 (above) **I,2** (below)

die Lasten des Lebens weiter. Bei den Kamelen muß der kleine Philosoph außerdem noch die Intelligenz vertreten. Man trifft wohl nie eine Kamelkarawane, der nicht ein kleines Eselein als

Die türkische Post auf dem Weg von Meserek nach Bagdad.

Pfadfinder vorangeht, und die übrigen Tiere folgen ihm in vollem

I,3 (above) **I,4** (below)

I,5 (above) **I,6** (*on the next page*) **I,7** (below)

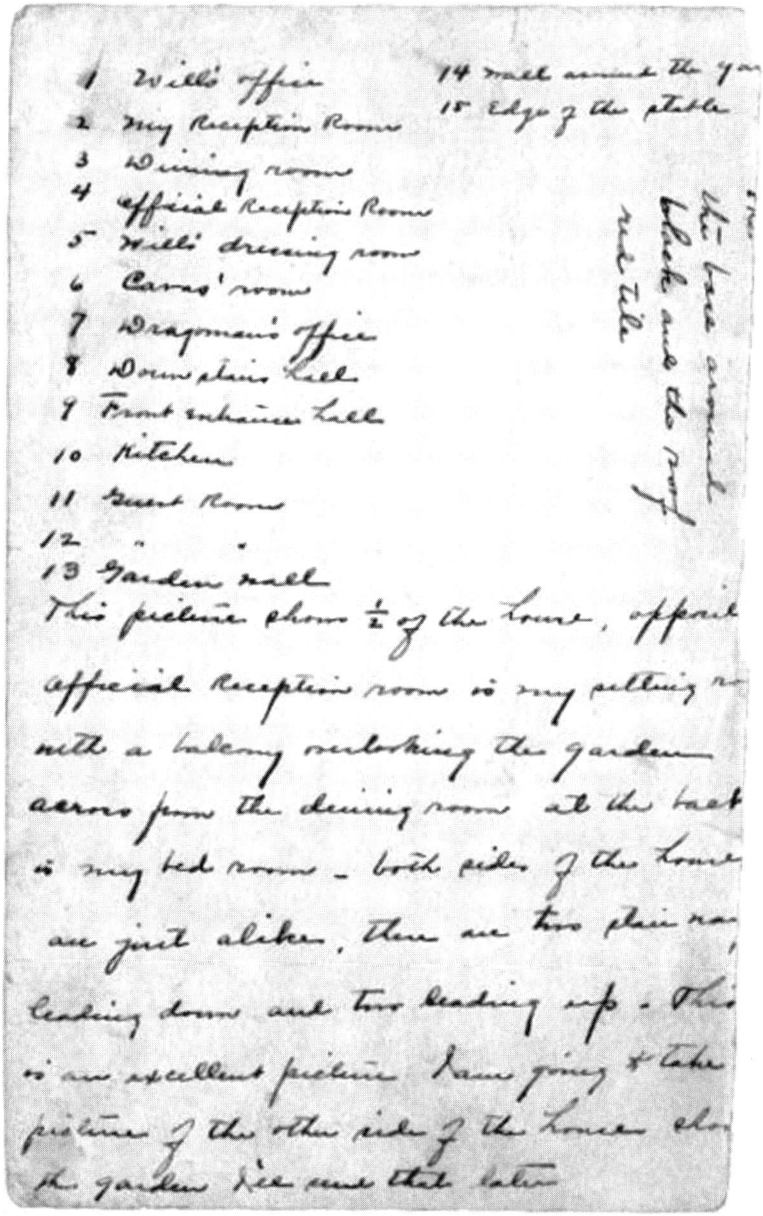

1 Will's office
2 My Reception Room
3 Dining room
4 Official Reception Room
5 Will's dressing room
6 Cavas' room
7 Dragoman's office
8 Down stairs hall
9 Front entrance hall
10 Kitchen
11 Guest Room
12 " "
13 Garden wall
14 wall around the yar
15 Edge of the stable

the base around
black and the roof
red tile

This picture shows ½ of the house, opposi
official Reception room is my sitting r
with a balcony overlooking the garden
across from the dining room at the back
is my bed room – both sides of the house
are just alike, there are two stair wa
leading down and two leading up – This
is an excellent picture I am going to take
picture of the other side of the house show
the garden I'll send that later

I,6

I,8 (above) **II,1** (below)

II,2 (above) **II,3** (below) **II,4** (facing page, above) **II,5** (Facing page, below)

Flight of Orphan Host From Turkish Persecution; Menacing Developments in the Near Eastern Crisis

THE group of Armenian orphans here pictured formed only part of a procession of more than 5,000 who, in order to escape from the massacre that threatened after the victory of the Turkish Nationalists, sought safety in Syria, to which they had to travel a distance of 500 miles. The hegira was carried on under the direction of Near East Relief workers, one of whom, Lester James Wright, formerly professor in the University of Wisconsin, was killed by bandits in the vicinity of Aleppo. Another American, Enoch R. Applegate of Jersey City, N. J., was wounded in the same attack, but escaped with his life.

The refugees here shown are only a small portion of the hundreds of thousands who thronged the roads of Asia Minor and later of Eastern Thrace, fleeing before the triumphant advance of the Turkish Nationalists. They knew too well what they had to expect from a lawless soldiery drunk with victory. How well founded were their fears is told in news dispatches giving detailed accounts of Turkish butcheries of the fleeing population.

Recrudescence of the Turkish power during the present year has completely changed the political situation in the Near East and seriously threatens the peace of Europe. Turkey had emerged from the war shorn of her fairest provinces, deprived of her control of the Dardanelles, ...

Part of the 5,000 orphans who marched 500 miles overland from the Near East Orphanage at Harpoot, Turkish Armenia, on their way out of Nationalist Turkey to safety in Syria. The march was attended by intense privations.

LESTER JAMES WRIGHT

ENOCH R. APPLEGATE

III,1 (above) **III,2** (below)

So gruesome a picture as this would be taboo in The Independent if the seriousness of the situation in Armenia now did not demand forceful illustration. These victims of a Turkish massacre typify thousands of Christian Armenians slaughtered by the Turks since the signing of the armistice. General Antranik's article does not overstate Armenia's need for immediate aid from America

Appendix I. *A Chronology of Major Events*

18 March 1821	Count Alexander Ypsilanti proclaims Greek independence.
21 January 1822	Proclamation of Greek independence in Epidauros.
22 February 1829	Russian-Ottoman Peace Treaty of Adrianople obliges the Ottoman government to improve the situation of Christian, Ottoman subjects.
1829–1876	*Tanzimat* (Reform) period.
7 May 1832	London Treaty: After the successful Sea Battle of Navarino (1827) and the Russian-Ottoman Peace of Adrianople (1829), Greece is internationally acknowledged as an independent kingdom; Otto I (son of king Ludwig of Bavaria) is made king of Greece with the consent of the Great Powers of Europe.
23 December 1876	Ottoman Constitution signed by Abdülhamit II (suspended on 5 February 1977).
24 April 1877– 31 January 1878	Russian-Turkish War, declared by Russia on the pretext of the Ottoman Christians' safety.
13 June– 13 July 1878	Berlin Congress and Treaty (13 July 1878), ruling and internationalizing the "Oriental" and the "Armenian Question."
1895-96	Armenian massacres in Asia Minor and North Mesopotamia turn into general anti-Christian persecution in some places.
1897	Greek-Turkish War ending with Greek defeat.
1897–1913	With the liberation of Crete from the Ottomans, the island becomes an autonomous state until its integration into the Greek Kingdom.
24 July 1908	Restoration of the Ottoman Constitution after the successful coup of the Young Turks (Macedonian Revolution).
April 1909	Attempted conservative counter-revolution in Adana province turns into massacre of Armenians.
18 October 1910– 10 March 1915	Eleutherios Venizelos serves as Greek prime minister.
29 September 1911– 18 October 1912	Italian-Turkish War (also "Libyan" or 'Tripolis War," in Turkish *Trablusgarp Savaşı*); Italy seizes the Dodecanese islands, which were (and are) inhabited by Greeks, including Rhodes.
5 October 1912– 5 May 1913	First Balkan War.
January 1913	After a military coup d'état, the *Ittihat ve Terakki Cemiyeti* returns to power.
17–27 June 1913	Second Balkan War.
Summer 1914	Ottoman Greeks conscripted into labor battalions.
29 October 1914	The Ottoman Empire's entry into World War I, after German battle-cruiser *Goeben* and light cruiser *Breslau*, operating under Turkish flag, shell the Russian Black Sea port of Odessa.
24 April 1915 (OS)	Massive arrests of members of the Armenian elite in Constantinople and subsequent deportation into the Ankara province and later to Diyarbakır; only few survive this "decapitation" of the Ottoman Armenians.
27 May 1915	Ottoman government decrees the deportation of "suspect persons," thus *a posteriori* sanctioning the already ongoing massive deportation of Ottoman Armenians to Mesopotamia.

23 August– 7 October 1915	Eleutherios Venizelos serves as Greek prime minister.
7 October 1915– December 1920	*Ethnikos Dichasmos* (National Schism) between royalists and liberals, led by Prime Minister Eleutherios Venizelos
April 1916– February 1917	Russian Imperial forces capture Trebizond/Trabzon (until the Russian revolution of 23 February 1917).
27 June 1917	Greece enters the World War I at the side of the Entente.
19 September 1916– 27 June 1917	Pro–Entente counter–government under Prime Minister Eleutherios Venizelos, controlling North Greece and Crete (recognized by Great Britain and France on 19 December 1916).
27 June– 18 November 1920	Government under Eleutherios Venizelos controls all Greece.
30 October 1918	Ottoman War capitulation (Armistice of Mudros).
2/15 May 1919	Greek forces occupy Smyrna in accordance to terms agreed with the Allies of World War I. The main intention of the latter was to balance the Italian expansion in Anatolia in anticipation of the Italian landing on the southern coast.
19 May 1919	Mustafa Kemal lands in Samsun (Pontus). Instead of disarming and dispersing armed Muslim bands resisting the Allied occupation of the Ottoman Empire, he became the leader of this liberation movement. Pontus Greeks therefore consider this date the beginning of the last and decisive phase of their genocidal destruction in their ancestral homeland.
21 May 1919– 8 September 1922	Greek administration of the occupied Smyrna district established.
27 November 1919	Treaty of Neuilly, as a victorious participant in World War I, Greece receives Western Thrace from Bulgaria.
1919-1921	Rebellion of Alevites (predominantly Kurds/Zaza) in Dersim, waged by the Kızılbaş Koçkiri tribe. In the aftermath of the rebellion there is talk in the new Grand National Assembly of Kemalist Turkey of some very limited forms of *Autonomous Administration* by the Kurds in a Kurdish region centred on Kurdistan. However, all this disappears with the Treaty of Lausanne (1923).
10 August 1920	Treaty of Sèvres between the Ottoman Empire and the Entente states; signed by four Ottoman representatives of the Sultan's government, but never sent to the Ottoman parliament for ratification, due to the Treaty's abolition by Great Britain. The Treaty accepts the Greek administration of the Smyrna enclave, while its sovereignty remained, nominally, with the Sultan. Smyrna is to be administered by a local parliament and, if within five years time this parliament for Smyrna to be incorporated into the Kingdom of Greece, the provision is made that the League of Nations is to hold a plebiscite to decide on such matters. The Treaty of Sèvres is neither ratified by the Ottoman Empire, nor by Greece that disagrees with the borders drawn in the Treaty.
1920-1922	Greek–Turkish War (Asia Minor War) between Kemalist forces and Greek occupation forces in Asia Minor.
23 September– 3 December 1920	Military intervention by Kemalist Turkey against the Republic of Armenia.

Summer 1920	Successful Greek offensives in the directions of Meander (Menderes) Valley, Peramos and Philadelphia. The overall strategic objective of these operations was to provide strategic depth to the defense of Smyrna. To that end, the Greek zone of occupation is extended over all of Western and most of North-Western Asia Minor.
25 October 1920	Death of Greek King Alexander after being bitten by his favorite monkey; after a crushing defeat in general elections of 1 November 1920, Venizelos went into exile (in Paris, until 1928). A plebiscite returned King Constantine to power; the Greek army in Asia Minor was purged of Venizelos supporters.
23 August – 13 September 1921	Battle of Sangarius (Σαγγάριος, Sakarya) stops the advance of the Greek forces towards Ankara.
March 1922	Mustafa Kemal rejects Allied proposals for negotiation and armistice with Greece.
26 August 1922	Launch of Turkish counterattack; fall of İzmit, Eskişehir (2 September), Aydın and Manisa (7 September).
26 August/ 8 September 1922	Greek forces disembark from Smyrna.
27 August/ 9 September 1922	Kemalist forces enter Smyrna.
31 August– 1 September/ 13–14 September 1922	Kemalists set fire to Christian (Armenian, Greek) quarters of Smyrna during the night of 31 August 1922 (OS).
3/16 September 1922	By order of commander Nurettin, male Ottoman Christians (age groups 18–45) in the Smyrna region are declared POWs. Women, children and other male Christians are expatriated.
14 October 1922	Greece accedes to the Allied-Kemalist Armistice of Mudanya (11 October 1922): Greece was to cede Eastern Thrace, after the local Greek population was evacuated, a process which began the next day.
30 January 1923	Greek–Turkish Convention of Lausanne on the obligatory population exchange of Ottoman Greek Orthodox Christians and Muslims of Greek nationality, was annexed under No. VI to the Peace Treaty of Lausanne of 24 July 1923.
24 July 1923	The signing of the multilateral Peace Treaty of Lausanne.

Appendix II. *A Glossary of Terms*

Amele taburlar-ı (Sg. Amele taburu) — Ottoman Turkish for "labor battalion(s);" unarmed units of the Ottoman forces used for road and public works; between 1914 and 1922, Christian Ottoman nationals were systematically conscripted to the *Amele taburlar-ı*, where they served under even harsher and more inhuman conditions than other units of the Ottoman forces, where living conditions were already known to be bad. During World War I, there existed a maximum of 120 such *Amele taburlar-ı*. Since the mortality rate in these units was extremely high, including due to the deliberate massacre of entire units after the completion of tasks, they can be seen as part of an annihilation scheme of the Ottoman Christians.

Anatolia — From Greek ἀνατολή *anatole* "East," or "Orient;" Turkish "Anadolu;" often used as a synonym for → Asia Minor. In Turkish, "Anadolu" had increasingly been used to replace older toponyms such as "Armenia" or "Armenian Highland," in particular since the Berlin Treaty (1878), which mentions "Armenian provinces" (Article 61). In linguistic usage as well as in geography, the Eastern border of Anatolia and → Asia Minor are not clearly defined against the Armenian Highland (Plateau) or South Caucasia.

Asia Minor — (Greek Μικρά Ἀσία, *Mikra Asia*; Latin: Asia Minor) or → Anatolia; in Greek usage, the term is frequently reduced to the littorals or Western part of the Asia Minor peninsula, without → Pontus.

Balkan Wars — 5 October 1912–5 May 1913; 17-27 June 1913; the two Balkan Wars were both the result of the emergence of competing and irredentist nation states in South-West Europe after the Berlin Congress (1878), and the disorganization of the Ottoman Empire, becoming evident during the Italo-Turkish War. In the course of the Balkan Wars, the loosely knit *Balkan League* (Bulgaria, Montenegro, Greece, and Serbia) first conquered Ottoman-held Macedonia, Albania and most of →Thrace and then fell out over the division of the spoils.

Following Italy's victory in its war against the Ottoman Empire (1911-1912), the Young Turks fell from power after a coup. The Balkan countries saw the weakening of Turkey as an opportunity to fulfil their desires of expansion and attacked at a time when Italy's war had not yet ended.

Initially under the encouragement of Russian agents, a series of agreements were concluded between Serbia and Bulgaria in March 1912. Since Greece was the only Balkan country with a navy powerful enough to deny use of the Aegean to the Ottomans, a treaty was signed between Greece and Serbia in May 1912. Serbia and Bulgaria had signed treaties to split between them the land of Vardar Macedonia, without Greece. After Greece vetoed the breakout of war several times in the summer, in order to better prepare her navy, the First Balkan War broke out in October 1912 following an impossible ultimatum given to the Porte.

No formal plan existed between the Balkan allies on how to wage the war that was practically four different wars fought against the same enemy, at the same time, and in the same region. Bulgaria attacked towards Eastern Thrace, being stopped only at the outskirts of Constantinople. Serbia attacked south towards Skopje and Bitola. After joining forces, Serbian and Hellenic forces turned west towards the Adriatic. Greece landed forces in the Chakidike peninsula while the main force of the army attacked from Thessaly into Macedonia. After the seizure of Thessalonica (26 Octo-

ber 1912, Julian calendar) the Hellenic forces linked up with the Serb forces to the north, subsequently turning west. Another Hellenic Army group had attacked into Epirus, and forces were deployed to that front.
Following the declaration of war the Ottoman Navy did not dare exit the safety of the Dardanelles. The Hellenic Navy was free to seize the islands of the Aegean. In January 1913, after a military coup that returned the Young Turks to power, the Ottoman Empire decided to continue the war. Bulgarian forces managed to capture Adrianople while Hellenic forces took Ioannina. The war was ended by the Treaty of London on 17 May 1913. Hostilities restarted, however, between Bulgaria and Greece, and later between Serbia and Bulgaria. Greece successfully cleared the areas it had seized in Macedonia of Bulgarian forces, but could not prevent that Bulgarian irregulars from razing Serres.
It is estimated that during both Balkan Wars 122,000 were killed in action, a further 20,000 died of wounds, and 82,000 died of disease. During and after the Balkan Wars (1912-1915), up to 560,000 Ottomans, Greeks and Bulgarians were expelled and "exchanged;" of those up to 200,000 Ottoman nationals, 160,000 Helladic Greeks, and 200,000 Bulgarians. The Balkan Wars, the expulsions in particular, left a lasting impression on the Turkish nationalists and are frequently quoted as a decisive factor for their decision to annihilate the Christian subjects of the Ottoman Empire.

Cappadocia — Greek *Καππαδοκία*, Turkish *Kapadokya*, derives from the Avesta toponym *Katpatuka* ("land of beautiful horses"); a region between the mountain ranges of Pontus and Taurus, interlinking with the Roman province of Armenia Minor. Politically situated between the *Imperium Romanum*, Iran (first under Parthian, than Persian rule) and the ancient kingdom of Pontus, Cappadocia was torn between contesting foreign influence. Its indigenous nobility managed to maintain its independence with many difficulties. In the year 17 AD Cappadocia became an imperial Roman province and since 395 a province of the Eastern Roman Empire. When its capital Masaka (renamed Caesaria by the Romans [Καισαρεία, *Kaisareia*; Turkish Kayseri]) became the seat of a bishop in the second century, Cappadocia developed into an outstanding stronghold of early and medieval Christian scholarship and spirituality during in the fourth and in the tenth and eleventh centuries.
After the conquest by the Seljuks (1074), the inhabitants were killed or assimilated. This process continued under Turkish rule (first of the Sultanate of Konya [Iconium], later the Ottomans). A center of this linguistic Turkification was Karamania, a successor state of the Rum Seljuks in the borderland of Cappadocia; its inhabitants - the *Karamanlides* - were Turkish speaking (*karamanlidika*) Greeks of Greek Orthodox religion; they used the Greek alphabet to write and print their form of Turkish.

Çete (Pl. çeteler) — Turkish for irregular armed units; bandits; often used as synonym for death squadrons of the → Teşkilat-ı Mahsusa (Special Organization)

Chronology → Julian/Gregorian calendar

Circassian(s) — Aboriginal inhabitants of the Northwest Caucasus; also collective term for all North Caucasian Muslim immigrants and refugees (→ muhaciler) to the Ottoman Empire (including Chechens, Abkhazians, Daghestanis). The brutal uprooting, expulsion, expatriation and deportation from the Tsarist Empire to the Ottoman Black Sea ports served as a negative model for subsequent Ottoman demographic engineering.

Committee for Union and Progress (CUP) — See → Ittihat (or Ittihad) ve Terakki Cemiyeti

Constantinople — See → Istanbul/ Stambul/ Constantinople

Deportation — In the Near East, compulsory resettlement of populations is a consistent tool of demographic policies since ancient times, subsequently applied by Assyrian and Iranian rulers of the Sassanide, Safavid and other dynasties, by Byzantine emperors, Ottoman sultans and Russian Tsars, as well as by rulers of less powerful states such as Armenia. The main aims of such policies were the reduction of unwanted ethnic or religious groups and likewise the increase or fostering of wanted ones.

As a punitive measure, individual and collective deportations were executed by Romans and in Byzantine times. Although the execution of collective deportations, in particular during war, was often inhumane, it was in modern times that deportation became a catchword for intended massive annihilation of collectives, or a synonym of death march - either in the sense that deportees were led to be massacred or destructed at other places, or that the march became a tool of destruction in itself.

The deportations of Christian and other ethno-religious groups conducted by Ottoman authorities before, during and after World War I, bore many elements of systematic and intended death marches: adult men selected, separated from their relatives and families, and often massacred; exhaustive forced marches of the deportees, no breaks to allow for rest; food and drink denied; compulsion to drink contaminated or poisonous water; exposure to extreme cold or hot climate; deliberate killings and violence against unprotected and undefended deportees. As a rule, the "destinations" of the convoys were desert or otherwise hostile areas or conditions that made survival of the deportees nearly impossible.

Because of the frequently close link of deportations with annihilation and genocide, contemporary international law restricts deportations (in times of peace under Articles 9 and 12 of the UN Charter, in war times by Article 49 of the Geneva Convention of 12 August 1949).

Dhimmi — From Arabic *dhimmi*, collectively *ahl al-dhimmah*, "the people of the *dhimmah*" or pact of protection, Ottoman Turkish *zimmi*: a non-Muslim subject of a state governed in accordance with → sharia law; originally synonym for "People of the Book" (see → millet). The term connotes an obligation of the state to protect the individual, including the individual's life, property, and freedom of religion and worship, in exchange for "subservience and loyalty to the Muslim order," and a poll tax known as the jizya.

Enosis — Ένωσις, Greek for "union" or "unification" with the Helladic Greek state; the irredenta of areas, predominantly inhabited by ethnic Greeks. The first case in history of a successful *Enosis* was that of Corfu (1864). More recently (1950s), *Enosis* relates also to the movement by the Greek majority population of Cyprus.

Ethnic "Cleansing"— Although the palliative term became widely popular during the 1990s wars in former Yugoslavia, examples and methods — terror and organized massive violence, expulsion, forced deportation and resettlement — date back to ancient times. Ethnic "cleansing" is not synonymous with genocide, but its methods can become part of it, if committed with the intention to destroy a group. The term itself derives from the language and thinking of perpetrators of crimes against humanity, including genocide. It suggests that an ethnic group or an ethnically heterogeneous society is 'dirty' and must therefore be cleansed. In this dehumanizing way, leaders and key figures of the CUP saw themselves as "social doctors" who healed the nation from "abscesses" (related to the Greeks of Asia Minor), from "bacteria" and "virus." Because of its palliative nature, ethnic "cleansing" conceals the criminal and destructive nature of the methods applied. For all these reasons, in Germany ethnic "cleansing" was declared the "un-word [Unwort] of the year 1992."

Ethnikos Dichasmos — Έθνικός Διχασμός, Greek for "National Schism." This developed between 1915-20 as a result of the clash between royalists and the Liberal Party, founded and led by Prime Minister Eleutherios Venizelos. A basically domestic conflict, nonetheless it had direct repercussions on Greece's foreign relations, in particular on her position towards the Entente and neutrality: Venizelos' alliance with Serbia and his mobilization order after Bulgaria (allied with the Central Powers) entered World War I, resulted in a conflict between King Constantine I and the prime minister on the issue of the country's neutrality. After being dismissed by the king despite his victory in the elections held in 1915, a year later Venizelos proclaimed a counter-government under the protection of the Entente. This resulted in the "National Schism," of Venizelists against royalists, with Venizelos controlling Crete, the Aegean Islands and the north of Greece, whereas the royalists controlled central and southern Greece. When in June 1917 the Entente forces compelled Constantine I to abdicate in favor of his second son Alexander, Venizelos returned to the capital (Athens) as prime minister and declared war against the Central Powers and their allies Bulgaria and the Ottoman Empire; at the same time he supressed his internal political opponents. As Greece was on the winning side in the war it received Western Thrace from Bulgaria as per the terms of the Treaty of Neuilly (1919), and Eastern Thrace and a large part of the Asian Minor littoral at Smyrna from the Ottoman Empire, per the terms of the Treaty of Sèvres (1920). The new northeastern border of post-war Greece was only few kilometres away from Constantinople/Istanbul.

After the death of King Alexander (25 October 1920) and early elections held in November 1920, Venizelos surprisingly lost and was ousted. In a plebiscite (December 1920) the new royalist government brought about the return of King Constantine. The Allies ceased to support Greece because of the Hellenic king's pro-German stance. Despite an unfavorable diplomatic situation, the royalist government launched a military offensive in Asia Minor in 1921 in order to seize Ankara (the seat of the opposition government, headed by Mustafa Kemal). The seizure of Constantinople in 1922 by the Hellenic forces occupying Asia Minor was prevented by British troops.

The repercussions of the Hellenic National Schism between liberals and monarchists were also disastrous for the Ottoman Greeks, because the internal situation in Greece led to her international isolation and the loss of support by the Allies.

Great Powers — The six signatories of the multilateral Treaty of Berlin (13 July 1878), i.e. Russia, Great Britain, France, Germany, Austria-Hungary, and Italy. The Congress of Berlin had been convened in order to revise the bilateral Ottoman-Russian Treaty of San Stefano (3 March 1878), resulting in the reduction of the influence of victorious Russia in Asia Minor. The Treaty of Berlin recognized the complete independence of the principalities of Romania, Serbia and Montenegro and the autonomy of Bulgaria, though the latter remained under formal Ottoman rule and was divided into three parts. The Treaty, though in vague terms, called for a border rectification between Greece and the Ottoman Empire, which occurred after protracted negotiations in 1881 with the transfer of Thessaly to Greece.

Paragraph 61 of the Treaty obliged the Ottoman government to introduce administrative autonomy in the "Armenian provinces," thus leading to an internationalization of the "Armenian Question." The discord and conflicting interests of the Great Powers — in particular the British-Russian antagonism over the "Eastern (Oriental) Question" (the integrity of the Ottoman Empire) and Russia's access to the "warm waters" of the Mediterranean — became a main reason for the deterioration of the situation of Christian minorities in the Ottoman Empire. While Russia followed a pan-Slavic and pro-Orthodox foreign policy, supporting Bulgaria and Serbia in particular, Britain wished to deny Russia access to the Mediterranean and supported the integrity of the Ottoman Empire, though it also supported a limited expansion of Greece as a backup plan in case the integrity of the Empire could not be maintained. France wished to strengthen her position in the region, especially in the Levant. Austria-Hungary and Germany wished for a continuation of the existence of the Ottoman Empire, although for different reasons.

Greeks/Hellenes — In this book, the term "Greek(s)" usually is used for Ottoman subjects belonging to the "Rum → millet-ı," that comprised not only ethnic Greeks or Hellenophones, but all of the followers of Greek Orthodox (Byzantine) doctrine and tradition (→ Romania/Romiosyne), while the nationals of the Hellenic state, i.e. the Helladic Greeks, are referred to as Hellenes in instances where confusion might arise.

İstanbul/ Stambul/ Constantinople — The original name of this Greek city on the Bosphorus, founded in antiquity by colonizers from Megara, was Byzantion. At the time of Emperor Constantine I it largely was rebuilt and was renamed *Konstantinoupolis* ("city of Konstantinos" — *Constantinople*, 324-330 AD). After the Ottoman conquest 1453, the new rulers adopted the Arabic version of *Konstantiniye*. Beside the official names, there were popular Greek as well as Turkish placenames, which at times obtained semi-official recognition: *Stin-poli(s)* or *Stin-bolis* [Greek for "into the city"], that developed into *[I]Stanbulin*, transformed by pious Muslims into *İslambol*. Since the 19th century, *Stambul* became the dominant vernacular version, while in official European and Western usage it remained *Constantinople*. After the conquest by Kemalist forces in 1922 and the foundation of the Republic of Turkey (October 1923), *Konstantiniye/Constantinople* was officially renamed Istanbul.

Ittihat (or Ittihad) ve Terakki Cemiyeti — *Committee for Union and Progress* (CUP); founded 1889 as a secret society of university students and military cadets that succeeded the oppositional constitutionalist movement; influential in the Third Ottoman Army (stationed in Selanik/Thessalonica, Macedonia), which began its march to the Sultan's Palace in Constantinople on 12 June 1908. About a month later, on 24 July the Ottoman Constitution that had been suspended since 1877 was restored. After its "Macedonian Revolution" in 1908, the CUP emerged as a dominant political party in the Ottoman parliament. After the military coup d'état of 1913, the CUP ruled supreme under the triumvirate of ministers ("the three Pashas") Mehmet Talat (Home Ministry), Ismail Enver (War Ministry) and Ahmet Cemal (Navy and Supreme Commander of the Fourth Ottoman Army, Syria). → Young Turks.

Julian/Gregorian calendar — As in the Russian Empire, the Ottoman Empire used the older Julian calendar/chronology in its communication with European states. In the early twentieth century the time difference between the calendars — "old" (OS) and "new style" (NS) — was 13 days, which was sometimes expressed by dual dating, with the earlier date being the one according to the Julian calendar; for example, the Russian October revolution took place on 25 October/7 November 1917, the latter date according to the Gregorian calendar.

Megale Idea — Greek "Μεγάλη Ἰδέα," or "Great Idea;" an irredentist concept that was first propagated in the late eighteenth century by the revolutionary Regas Velestinles or Pheraios (Ρήγας Βελεστινλής or Φεραίος; 1757-1798). The *Megale Idea* called for the liberation and unification of all areas predominantly settled by ethnic Greeks into one state that would comprise the territories of the Mediaeval Greek (Byzantine) Empire. The incorporation of Asia Minor and Constantinople were integral parts of this concept. A key figure of the *Megale Idea* policy was the leading political figure, and later prime minister, Eleutherios Venizelos, who became an ardent supporter of *Megale Idea* after the successful → *Enosis* of his home island Crete (1913) and who, after having sided with the victorious Entente during the World War, received its support for his irredentist ambitions. After the war, the abortive Treaty of Sèvres (1920) determined that Northern Epirus, the islands of Imbros and Tenedos and Thrace (but not Constantinople), would become incorporated into the Helladic Greek state. The *Megale Idea* also became popular among the Ottoman Greeks.

Millet — (Arabic-Turkish for "nation") In contrast to the modern European definition of a state or ethnic nation, *millet* defines a "nation" as an (ethno-)religious community possessing a book of revelation, such as the Bible. The legal/political position of "Peoples of the Book" was by far not equal to the Muslim faithful, but it secured life and property under Muslim rule. Compared to the entirely lawless "heathens" (followers of primaeval religions; polytheists), the "Peoples of the Book" were entitled to certain rights of internal autonomy with regards to their administration and jurisdiction, as long as no Muslims were involved or concerned. The Ottoman State would hold the religious heads of the acknowledged *millets* — the *millet-ı başı* — responsible for the conduct of their communities; these were the Christian patriarchs (Armenian Apostolic and Greek Orthodox) and the Supreme Rabbi of Constantinople for the [Jewish] *Yahudi Millet*. The heads of the *millets* depended on official approval by the Sultan when admitted to office, and it was he who concluded the treaties of protection for each *millet* community with their respective spiritual leaders.

In 1461, after the conquest of Constantinople, Sultan Mehmet II *Fatih* ("the Conqueror") founded an Armenian Apostolic Patriarchate in the new Ottoman capital with the intention of weakening the position of the Ecumenical Patriarch and better to control the Armenians under Ottoman rule. In this regard, the Armenian Apostolic Patriarchate of Constantinople countered both the existing Armenian Apostolic Catholicosate at Ejmiadzin (outside Ottoman rule) and to the Ecumenical Patriarchate. Mehmet II invested this new patriarchate with jurisdiction over all the other Oriental Orthodox (pre-Chalcedonian) Churches — including the Eastern and Western Syriac Churches.

Until the nineteenth century, there were only three *millets* acknowledged in the Ottoman Empire: the Jewish, the Greek-Orthodox (*Rum millet-ı*) and the Armenian-Apostolic (*Ermeni millet-ı*). During the *Tanzimat* period and until 1914, under pressure from European "protector states," in particular France and Austria, their number increased to seventeen. Those later *millets* included several Uniate Eastern

Churches. On 5 January 1831, the Ottoman government officially acknowledged the *Katolik millet-ı* (which also included Armenian Uniates), while Evangelical Christians gained the status of acknowledged *millet* in December 1850 (*Protestant millet-ı*).

Based on the inequality of religious communities, the *millet* system was by its very nature opposed to legal and societal equity and equality (emancipation); it was therefore a major obstacle to any profound reform and contained regulations on unequal taxation, exemption of Non-Muslims from national service, a lower or subordinate legal status etc.

Muhacir (*Pl.* **muhacilar**) — Turkish for (religious) refugee; exiled Muslims that immigrated into the Ottoman Empire (in particular from the Balkans and the Caucasus), where they at times systematically received land properties from dispossessed and/or deported Christian inhabitants.

Ottomanism — A political concept of the → *Tanzimat* period, in particular of the *Young* (or Neo) *Ottomans* (Turkish: *Yeni Osmanlilar*). Ottomanism promoted the equality of all Ottoman subjects before the law, including those of the → *millets*. Although the essence of the *millet* system was not dismantled, secular organizations and policies were applied. Primary education, conscription, head tax and military service were to be applied to non-Muslims and Muslims alike, the majority of the latter ("Old Ottomans") fearing for their traditional privileged status. The abolition of the Ottoman constitution (1877) by Sultan Abdülhamit ended the first phase of Ottomanism. A brief revival or second phase gained momentum after the "revolution" of the → Young Turks in 1908, but faded gradually by end of the Balkan Wars (1912–13).

Pan-Islamism — A political movement advocating the unity of Muslims under one Islamic state or a Caliphate. Late Ottoman Islamism attempted to avert the further collapse of Empire by neutralizing national secessionism by Muslim ethnic groups (Arabs, Kurds), to a large extent at the expense of the Ottoman Christians. A prominent key-figure of late Ottoman Pan-Islamism was Sultan Abdülhamit II (31 August 1876 - 27 April 1909).

(Pan)Turkism, (Pan)Turanism — The supra-national idea of the political, economical or cultural unity (and by extension, unification) of all Turkic speaking ethnic groups, which emerged in the nineteenth century among intellectuals of Turkic (Tatar and Azeri) nations under Tsarist rule, partly in opposition to, or after the model of Panslavism or Pan-Germanism. Key figures were the Crimean Tatar İsmail Gaspıralı or Gaspralı (Gasprinskyj; 1851—1914), the Tatar Yusuf Akçura (in Tatar: Yosıf Aqçura; 1876-1935), the Ottoman sociologist, author and leading CUP member Ziya Gökalp (born Mehmed Ziya; 1876—1924), the Azeris Dr. Ali Hüseyinzade ("Turkify, Islamicize, Europeanize") and Ahmet Ağaoğlu (Agayev; 1869-1935/9); the latter became a primary figure in the Turkish nationalist Hearth (Ocagi) movement and the president of its congress. As a first step towards the political unification of Turkic nations Pan-Turkists considered *Oghusianism*, the unification of Turks from Turkey, Azerbaijan, Crimea and Tatarstan, which belong to the southwestern (Oghuz) branch of the large Turkic language group.

Blended with the exclusive ethno-nationalism of the Ottoman Young Turks, Pan-Turkism developed into the expansionist idea of the political unification of Turkic nations into one state under Ottoman/Turkish leadership, stretching from Asia Minor to the Uygur areas of North China.

Often treated as a synonym of Pan-Turkism, (Pan-)Turanism is an even farther reaching concept of supra-nationalism, because it takes in not only Turkic, but all ethnic groups belonging not only to the Uralo-Altaic language group (including Mongols, Man (Manchu), but also Non-Altaic nations such as Japanese and the Finno-Ugric Hungarians). Turan was believed to be the mythic Central Asian homeland from where the grey mother wolf Asena originated.

Pontus (Pontos) — From the ancient Greek Πόντος Εὔξεινος, *Pontos Euxeinos* (the "Hospitable Sea"), the Black Sea and its mountainous Southern littoral. The original name of *Pontos Axeinos* (the "Inhospitable Sea") in Greek folk etymology is very likely derived from the Iranian-Avesta place-name "a-xsaena" — "black," that Greek seafarers learnt from Scythian or Sarmatian inhabitants. The Greek settlements of the Southern Black Sea littoral are a secondary colonization by Greeks from Ionia (predominantly from the city of Μίλητος, Miletos, in Latin Miletus, and in Turkish Milet), who founded their colonies in Σινώπη, Sinope (785 BC), Κερασούς, in later Greek, Κερασούντα (Kerasus, Keradus, Kerasunta, Giresunta; Turkish, Giresun) and Τραπεζούς, later Greek Τραπεζούντα (Trapezus, Trapezounta, in English and French, Trebizond, in Turkish, Trabzon) (756 BC).

Pontus became also the name of subsequent ancient and medieval kingdoms East of the Halys river, between the port cities Sinope and Trebizond; at times, the kingdom of Pontus included even areas of Κολχίς, Kolchis (Western Georgia) and Armenia. The Roman province "Bythinia and Pontus" comprised nearly the entire littoral of the Southern Black Sea and the Northern third of → Asia Minor (ca. 800 x 250 km), while during the Byzantine period (about 600 - 1143 AD) Pontus was located further to the east, with the inclusion of → Cappadocia as its hinterland.

The Fourth Crusade that weakened the Byzantine Empire in 1204, and the emergence of a powerful centralized Georgian kingdom under the rule of Bagrationi (originally from the Black Sea region of Tao/Tayk in Armenian) helped to establish the regional Pontian *Empire of Trebizond*, whose founders Alexios and David I Comnenus were closely related to Tamar(i) the Great, Empress of Georgia. For 250 years, this Pontian Empire, protected by the Pontus mountain range, prospered from intensive sea-trade, surviving the conquest of Constantinople (1453) until 15 August 1461.

Although Ottoman Greek plans at the time of the Paris Peace Conference to establish a Pontus republic with Trebizond as capital never came to fruition, this concept is frequently quoted by Turkish nationalist historiography to justify the increasingly brutal treatment of the entire Greek population after 1919 of the Pontus region.

Porte (Sublime Porte) — Also known as the Ottoman Porte or High Porte, in Ottoman Turkish Bab-ı Ali ("High Gate"); a term of contemporary Western diplomacy that refers to the Ottoman *Divan* (open court of the Sultan, led by the Grand Vizier), where government policies were established. The *Sublime Porte* was named after the gate to the headquarters of the Grand Vizier in Topkapı Palace, where the sultan held the greeting ceremony for foreign ambassadors.

After the "Macedonian Revolution" (1908) the functions of the Divan were replaced by the imperial government, and *Porte* came to refer to the Foreign Ministry. During this period "Grand Vizier" came to refer to the position of a president and viziers became the Ottoman Senate.

Raya(h), reaya — "Cattle" or "flock," in Ottoman Turkish; the tax-paying lower class of Ottoman society, in contrast to the elite class (*askeri*), to which the nobility, the military and the religious clergy belonged. Although the term originally included Muslim taxpayers as well, it was, in its later use, reduced to Non-Muslim taxpayers.

Romania, Romiosyne — Ρωμιοσύνη, Greek for the geographic space of the [Eastern] "Roman" Empire and of the [Eastern] "Romans," an expression signifying the consciousness of links with, and descent from mediaeval Greek [Byzantine] culture; a self-identifier by Ottoman → Greeks from Asia Minor (and other parts of the historic Greek world) and their descendants; Romania often appears as a synonym for Asia Minor.

Sharia(h) law — Arabic (transliterated sharī`ah — "Way or path to the water source;" the body of Islamic religious law on the public and some private aspects of life. Shariah deals with many aspects of day-to-day life, including politics, economics, banking, business, contracts, family, sexuality, hygiene, and social issues. There is no strictly static codified set of laws of shariah. Based on the Qur'an, *hadith* (sayings and doings of Muhammad and his companions), *Ijma* (consensus), *Qiyas* (reasoning by analogy) and centuries of debate, interpretation and precedent, the shariah does not separate the sacred and the secular, but suffuses law and religion.

Muslim theology considers shariah as the perfect order that generates peace and justice. Because shariah is believed to be divine, it is prohibited to replace it by human/secular law. This inflexibility is highly problematic since shariah regulates human behaviour in family and society (for example, in the marriage and penal laws), but also the way of venerating God. The practice of the daily ritual prayer and a contract of marriage are likewise not debatable by the individual. The largest discrepancies between Western secular law and shariah exist in the marriage and family law as well as in human rights.

Islamic penal law differentiates three kinds of crimes: "border crimes" (*hadd* crimes), "assessive (capital) crimes" (*tazir* crimes) and "retaliate crimes" (*qisas*). Whereas the first category is considered to be a violation of divine law (sexual offences such as prostitution, adultery, theft, robbery with murder, drinking of wine), whose punishment is regulated by the Qur'an or by Islamic law tradition, the *qisas* crimes are punished on the principle of "an eye for an eye," death for death etc., if the family of the victim insists on this form of satisfaction. It can otherwise be substituted by compensatory fines. All other crimes depend on the decision of a judge, with a range of punishment, including the death penalty.

Although shariah is at least theoretically the base of all the jurisdiction and legislation of Muslim states, in practices there is no state that fully applied the shariah. However, the extent to which it is applied and the five main schools of interpreting shariah differ considerably. Religious minorities in Muslim nations are generally governed under separate personal-status laws reflecting their own religious and/or legal traditions (see also →millet; →dhimmi).

Tanzimat — Turkish for "decree," often translated as "reform;" the era (1829-1876) of reorganization, characterized by various attempts to fight the increasing deficit of modernity in various areas of public administration, military, education, law and economy, in order to secure the territorial integrity of the Ottoman Empire against secessionist movements and internal corrosion. Partly under pressure from the European → Great Powers, the reforms included the emancipation of Non-Muslim ethno-religious groups (→ millet) and encouraged → Ottomanism among the diverse ethnic groups of the Empire, in the vain attempt to create a nation state. But the attempt to enhance civil liberties for Non-Muslims and to grant them equality throughout the Empire aroused the opposition first of conservative Muslims and later of Young Turkish nationalists, who used the term Ottomanism as a synonym for Turkism. The main achievement of the *Tanzimat* era was the first and only Ottoman constitution.

Teşkilat-ı Mahsusa — Turkish for "Special Organisation" (SO); its immediate predecessor was the paramilitary *Organization of Fidayin* (founded 1906 in Thessalonica), which served not only as a Turkish counter guerrilla force against Bulgarian partisans, but also as a death squad for the CUP Central Committee, which commissioned the executions of its extra-legal death sentences. Subsequently numerous Christian leaders disappeared or were found murdered in Macedonia and Serbia from 1909-1911. The CUP Central Committee reorganized the *Organization of Fidayin* into the SO in 1911; during the Italo-Turkish War the SO emerged as an intelligence and sabotage unit in the Ottoman struggle against regular Italian forces, and again in 1913, during the Balkan Wars in Eastern →Thrace. A secret meeting of the CUP Central Committee on 2 or 5 August 1914 led to another reorganization that brought the SO under the official supervision of the Ministry of War, where a Central Coordination Office was established; this now comprised a network of officials from various ministries, in particular the Home Ministry, and the CUP Central Committee (also known as the "Committee of the Three:" War Minister Enver, Home Minister Talat and CUP Central Committee Member Dr Behaettin Şakır, who assumed the main responsibility for recruiting the SO's irregular units in Eastern Anatolia.) The recruitment started in the second half of August 1914. While at this stage the functions of the SO were still twofold — sabotage beyond the Ottoman realms, in particular in Russian ruled areas, and promoting the cause of expansionist →Panturkism; domestic operations against the Christian population. In another secret meeting of the CUP Central Committee in late March 1915 it was decided that the SO should limit its activities to two domestic tasks: the deportation and destruction of the Armenian population. In 1915, the irregulars in the ranks of SO numbered 30,000.
After the Ottoman Armistice (Mudros, 30 October 1918), the SO was officially dissolved. Its immediate successor became the *Karakol Cemiyeti* i.e. "Precinct" or "Police Committee," founded by War Minister Enver in late October 1918 before his escape from the Ottoman Empire. *Karakol*'s mission became to assist CUP members prosecuted for their war crimes, the foundation of regional and local groups of armed resistance against the Allied occupation, preventing the return of surviving Ottoman Christians, and the destruction of those remaining. The current National Intelligence Service of Turkey (MIT) officially considers the *Special Organization* and the *Karakol* its predecessors.

Thrace — An oft-disputed area between the present-day states of Bulgaria, Greece and Turkey. In ancient times it encompassed the region east of Macedonia to the Black Sea, between the Danube in the north and the Aegean Sea in the south. Its Indo-European population (since the second millennium BC) was related to the Greeks, the Illyrians and the Phrygians. Under the name *Moesia* northern Thrace became a province of the Imperium Romanum ca. 9 AD, whereas the south was the Roman province *Thracia* (ca. 46 AD). In 395 *Thracia*, with its capital Philippoupolis (today Plovdiv in Bulgaria) was part of the Eastern Roman Empire; under Ottoman rule since the fifteenth century and part of the Ottoman province *Rumelia*, that comprised all European parts of the Ottoman Empire (Albania, Kosovo, Macedonia, western Thrace). Together with Bulgaria, *Eastern Rumelia* (including the north of *Thrace*) became an autonomous Ottoman administrative unit after the Congress of Berlin and Treaty (1878), whereas the remaining parts of *Rumelia* formed the new Ottoman provinces of Edirne, Salonika and Monastir. After the incorporation of *Eastern Rumelia* by Bulgaria in 1885, the term *Thrace* was applied to the still Ottoman ruled southern part of this ancient region. Since this time, the areas East and West of the Maritsa river (Meric in Turkish) were called *Eastern* and *Western Thrace.* As a result of the First → Balkan War (1912/13), the Ottoman Empire ceded the entire *Western Thrace* and half of the hinterland of *Eastern Thrace* (including Adrianople/Edirne) to Bulgaria. However, following her defeat in the Second → Balkan War (1913), Bulgaria had to return all previously Ottoman possessions of Thrace East of the Maritsa. As a result of WW1 and according the Treaty of Neuilly (1919), Bulgaria also had to cede the southern part of *Western Thrace* to Greece, thus losing her access to the Mediterranean Sea. With the Treaty of Sèvres (1920), Greece also gained the major part of *Eastern Thrace,* with the exception of Constantinople and the Dardanelles. However, the Armistice of Mudanya (1922) and the subsequent Treaty of Lausanne (1923) abolished this regulation at the expense of Greece. Subsequently, the entire area east of the Maritsa — *Eastern Thrace* — was returned to Turkey. During 1941-44, Bulgaria occupied the Greek part of *Western Thrace.* The Greek-Bulgarian border of 1919 and the Turkish-Greek border of 1923 were re-established after World War II.

Today, the historic region *Thrace* comprises the south of Bulgaria, the northeast of Greece (Western Thrace) and the European part of Turkey (Eastern Thrace), where, with the exception of Istanbul, no Greeks exist since 1923. In Western Thrace, the ca. 92,000 largely Turkic–speaking Muslims comprise the largest ethnic group among the Muslim minority population in this region.

Vali — Arabic-Ottoman Turkish for "governor" (head of a → Vilayet)

Vilayet — Arabic-Ottoman Turkish for "province," the highest administrative unit in the Ottoman Empire since 1864.

Young Turks — (Turkish "Jön Türkler" from French "Jeunes Turcs," also "Yeni Türkler" in translation; Greek "Νεότουρκοι," Russian "Mladoturki"); initially a political opposition movement succeeding secret organizations of Ottoman constitutionalists ("Neo-Ottomans," founded July 1865), that had been oppressed by Sultan Abdülhamit II in 1878. After the "Young Turk" or "Macedonian" military coup d'état of 1908, the previously ethnically and ideologically heterogeneous movement increasingly transformed into a nationalist movement, with the → *Ittihat ve Terakki Cemiyeti* as its politically most influential organization/party. The Young Turks had restored the Ottoman Constitution of 1876 — with the massive support of non-Muslim communities in the Ottoman Empire — even though constitutional/majority or even consensus democracy was not their aim. They also did not accept regional autonomy, as prescribed in Article 61 of the Treaty of Berlin (1878) for the "Armenian provinces" of the Ottoman Empire. The Young Turks followed the principle of developing an intellectual elite to govern the Empire, never envisioning popular participation in policy-making or administration. The political position of the ruling Young Turks can be best described as elitist, étatist, centralist, secular and → (Pan)Turkist. Ideologically, they were often adherents to the contemporary western European ideas of social Darwinism, biological materialism and positivism, which the Young Turks believed could easier be reconciled with Islam than other ideologies. Basically irreligious, they nevertheless understood the importance of Islam both as a tool for projecting influence (→ Panislamism) and a unifying principle. Since the CUP Congress of 1902, ethno-nationalism (Turkism) became the guiding idea of the Young Turkish movement. Combined with the other elements of their ideology, in particular Social Darwinism, it developed into an exclusivist chauvinism.

Appendix III. *A Select Bibliography*

This bibliography focuses on the genocide of Greek Orthodox subjects of the Ottoman Empire and related issues of general regional or national history such as the Greek foreign policy of the early twentieth century, the position of the Allies, or the asymmetric "population exchange" (deportation) of Ottoman Greek Orthodox and Greek Muslim citizens. In certain cases, the editors decided to include literature focusing on the genocide of the Ottoman Armenians that includes information on the Ottoman Greek Orthodox population.

The bibliography offers all genres of literature (monographs and periodicals), grouped by language (English, French, German, Greek), including contemporary newspaper articles in chronological order. It should be emphasized that this listing is nowhere near complete, but is intended to provide a first impression of the diversity and richness of the contemporary print media as sources of information. Furthermore, we provide some information on films and prose dedicated to the genocide of the Ottoman Greeks and the population exchange. As in all other aspects of this book, the editors thank the readers in advance for additional information and suggestions they may provide and that will be considered in future editions.

BOOKS and DISSERTATIONS

English

Abbott, George Frederick. *Greece and the Allies 1914-1922*. London: Methuen, 1922

_____ , *Turkey, Greece and the Great Powers: A Study in Friendship and Hate*. London: Robert Scott Roxburghe House, 1916.

Ahmad, Feroz. *The Young Turks*. Oxford: Clarendon Press, 1969.

Akçam, Taner. *A Shameful Act: The Armenian Genocide and the Question of Turkish Responsibility*. New York: Metropolitan Books, 2006

_____ , *From Empire to Republic: Turkish Nationalism and the Armenian Genocide*. London: Zed Books, 2004.

Alexandris, Alexis. *The Greek Minority of Istanbul and Greek Turkish Relations 1918-1974*. Athens: Centre for Asia Minor Studies, 1992.

[American National Red Cross]. *Reports of the American Red Cross Commissions upon their activities in Macedonia, Thrace, Bulgaria, the Aegean Islands and Greece*. New York: Oxford University Press/American-Hellenic Society, 1919

Anderson, Matthew S. *The Great Powers and the Near East 1774-1923*. London: Arnold, 1970.

_____ , *The Eastern Question 1774-1923: A Study in International Relations*. London: Macmillan, 1966. Reprinted with corrections, 1968.

Andrew, Prince of Greece and Denmark. *Towards Disaster: The Greek Army in Asia Minor in 1921*. London: Murray, 1930.

Armstrong, Harold Courtenay. *Grey Wolf*. London: Arthur Barker Ltd, 1932. Reprinted under the title, *Grey Wolf: Mustafa Kemal, an Intimate Study of a Dictator*. Harmondsworth: Penguin, 1937. German edition, Der *graue Wolf: Das Leben des Diktators Mustafa Kemal*. Berlin: S. Fischer, 1933).

Augustinos, Gerasimos. *The Greeks of Asia Minor: Confession, Community, and Ethnicity in the Nineteenth Century*. Kent, Ohio: Kent State University Press, 1992.

Barton, James Levi. *The Near East Relief 1915-1930: Administration of Relief Abroad, a Series of Occasional Papers*. New York: Russell Sage Foundation, 1943.

_____, *Story of the Near East Relief 1915-1930*. New York: Macmillan, 1930.

_____, *"Turkish Atrocities:" Statements of American Missionaries on the Destruction of Christian Communities in Ottoman Turkey, 1915-1917. Compiled by James L. Barton*. Ann Arbor, MI: Gomidas Institute, 1998

Bierstadt, Edward Hale. *The Great Betrayal: A Survey of the Near East Problem*. New York: Robert M. McBride, 1924.

Bourdon, Georges and others. *Hellas and Unredeemed Hellenism: The Policy of Victory in the East and Its Results*. New York: American-Hellenic Society, 1920.

Braude, Benjamin and Bernard Lewis, eds. *Christians and Jews in the Ottoman Empire: The Functioning of a Plural Society*. New York–London: Holmes and Meier Publishers, 1982.

Brown, Caroll N and Theodore P. Ion. *Persecutions of the Greeks in Turkey since the Beginning of the European War*. New York: Oxford University Press, 1918.

Bryce, James and Arnold Toynbee, eds. *The Treatment of the Armenians in the Ottoman Empire 1915-1916*. London: HMSO/Joseph Causton and Sons, 1916. Reprint, New Jersey: Taderon Press, 2000.

Can the Turks enter the League of Nations? [N.p.], 1919.

Childs, W. J. *Across Asia Minor on Foot*. London: Blackwood, 1917.

Clark, Bruce. *Twice A Stranger: Greece, Turkey and the Minorities They Expelled*. London: Granta Books 2007.

Compton, Carl C. *The Morning Cometh: 45 years with Anatolia College*. New Rochelle, NY: Aristide D. Caratzas, 1986.

Cosmetatos, S.P.P. *The Tragedy of Greece*. London: Stephen Austin and Sons, 1928

Couzinos, Efthimios N. *Twenty-Three Years in Asia Minor, 1899-1922*. New York: Vantage Press, 1969.

Daniel, Robert L. *American Philanthropy in the Near East, 1820-1960*. Athens, Ohio: Ohio University Press, 1970.

Davis, William Stearns. *A Short History of the Near East: From the Founding of Constantinople, 330 A.D. to 1922*. New York: Macmillan Co., 1922.

Diamadis, Panayiotis. *From Hearth to Holocaust: The Hellenic Holocaust of Pontos, Asia Minor and Thrace*. Sydney 1999.

Dieterich, Karl. *Hellenism in Asia Minor*. Transl. by Carroll N. Brown, Introduction and Preface by Th. P. Jon; a brief article on the Hellenic Pontus by D. H. Oeconomides Oxford: American-Hellenic Society, 1918

Dillon, Emile Joseph. *The Inside Story of the Peace Conference*. New York: Harper & Brothers, 1920.

Dobson, (Rev.) Charles. *The Smyrna Holocaust*. London: Anglo-Hellenic League, 1923.

Doukas, Stratis. *A Prisoner of War's Story.* Translated by Petro Alexiou. Birmingham: University of Birmingham, 1999

Economides, D. *The Pontus and the Right Claims of Its Greek Population: Topographical, Ethnographical and Historical Study.* Constantinople: Imprimérie française Léandre Mourkidès, 1920.

Einstein, Lewis. *Inside Constantinople: A Diplomatist's Diary during the Dardanelles Expedition, April-September, 1915.* London: John Murray, 1917.

Extract from the Black Book of Asia Minor, Persecution and Extermination of the Communities of Macri and Livissi (1914-1918). Paris, 1919.

Edib Adivar, Halidé. *Memoirs of Halide Edib.* London: John Murray, 1926; reprinted, Piscataway, NJ: Gorgias Press, 2005.

Foreign Office (UK). *Lausanne Conference on Near Eastern Affairs 1922-1923: Record of Proceedings and Draft Terms of Peace.* London: HMSO, 1923.

———, *Reports on Atrocities in the Districts of Yalova and Guemlek and in the Ismid Peninsula.* London: HMSO, 1921.

Fotiadis, Costas. *The Ethnic and Religious Consciousness of the Greeks of Pontos.* Thessalonica: Aristotle University, 1996.

Fromkin, David. *A Peace to End All Peace: The Fall of the Ottoman Empire and the Creation of the Modern Middle East.* New York: Henry Holt, 1989.

Gibbons, Herbert Adams. *The Blackest Page of Modern History: Events in Armenia in 1915, the Facts and the Responsibilities.* London: G. P. Putnam's Sons, 1916.

Germanos Archbishop of Amassia and Samsoun. *The Turkish Atrocities in the Black Sea Territories: Copy of Letter... Published by the Delegation of the Pan-Pontic Congress.* Manchester: Norbury/Natzio, 1919.

Greece and Great Britain during World War I: First Symposium organized in Thessaloniki (December 15-17, 1983) by the Institute of Balkan Studies and King's College. Thessalonica: Institute for Balkan Studies, 1985.

Greek [*sc.* Ecumenical] Patriarchate. *Persecution of the Greeks in Turkey 1914-1918.* Constantinople/London: Hesperia Press, 1919.

Halo, Thea. *Not Even My Name.* New York: Picador USA, 2000; revised edition, 2001.

Hanioğlu, M. Şükrü. *A Brief History of the Ottoman Empire.* Princeton, NJ: Princeton University Press, 2008.

_____, *Preparation for a Revolution: The Young Turks, 1902-1908.* Oxford/New York: Oxford University Press, 2001.

Hatzidimitriou, Constantine G. *American Accounts Documenting the Destruction of Smyrna by the Kemalist Turkish Forces, September 1922.* New Rochelle, NY: Aristide D. Caratzas, 2005.

Heinemann, Franz. *What Three Million Unreleased Greeks Hope of the League of Nations: A Swiss Plea.* Neuchatel: Attinger, 1919.

Hellenic Red Cross, *The Treatment of the Greek Prisoners in Turkey: Report of the International Commission of Inquiry appointed at the Request of the Greek Red Cross.* [London]: Anglo-Hellenic League, 1923.

Hidiroglou, Paul. *Turkish Conceptions of the Greeks of Asia Minor. Paper Delivered to the Academic Symposium on Aspects of the Asia Minor Question: A Historical Review and Implications... on October 1992.* Athens: Hellenic University Press, 1993

Hirschfeld, Magnus, *The Sexual History of the World War*. New York: Falstaff Press [1937].

Hirschon, René. *Heirs of the Greek Catastrophe: The Social Life of Asia Minor Refugees in Piraeus*. Oxford: Clarendon Press, 1989.

Horton, George. *The Blight of Asia: An Account of the Systematic Extermination of Christian Populations by Mohammedans and of the Culpability of Certain Great Powers; With a True Story of the Burning of Smyrna*. Indianapolis: Bobbs-Merrill, 1926; reprinted, 1953 (and subsequently).

_____ , *Report on Turkey: USA Consular Documents*. Athens: The Journalists' Union of the Athens Daily Newspapers, 1985.

Housepian, Marjorie Dobkin. *The Smyrna Affair: The First Comprehensive Account of the Burning of the City and the Expulsion of the Christians from Turkey in 1922*. New York: Harcourt Brace Jovanovich, 1971 (Later editions reprinted under the title *Smyrna 1922: The Destruction of a City*. London: Faber and Faber, 1972; reprinted by Newmark Press, 1998).

Ion, Theodore P. *Diplomatic Documents 1913-1917*. Translated from the original French & Greek texts by T. P. Ion; rev. ed. New York: The American-Hellenic Society, [nd].

Karagianis, Lydia. *Smoldering Smyrna*. New York: Carlton Press, 1996.

King, William H. *Turkish Atrocities in Asia Minor*. Washington, DC: U.S. Government Printing Office, 1922.

Kitromilides, Paschalis M., Ed. *Eleftherios Venizelos: The Trials of Statesmanship*. Edinburgh: Edinburgh University Press, 2006.

Kostos, Sofia Kontogeorge, Ed. *Before the Silence: Archival News Reports of the Christian Holocaust That Begs to be Remembered*. Piscataway, NJ: Gorgias Press, 2010.

Kyriakides, N.G. *The Tragedy of the Sea of Marmora: How the Greeks of Marmora Were Expelled from Their Homes and Scattered Among the Villages around Kermasti*. New York: Relief Committee for Greeks of Asia Minor, 1918.

Ladas, Stephen P. *The Exchange of Minorities, Bulgaria, Greece and Turkey*. New York: Macmillan, 1932.

Lewis, Bernard. *The Making of Modern Turkey*. London: Oxford University Press, 1961.

London Committee of Unredeemed Greeks. *Hellenism in Asia Minor*. London: London Committee of Unredeemed Greeks, 1919.

_____ , *Short Account of the Turkish Persecutions and Atrocities Committed Against the Greeks in Turkey*. London: London Committee of Unredeemed Greeks, 1919.

_____ , *The Anti-Hellenic Persecutions in Turkey: Pictures of the Atrocities Committed Against the Greeks in Turkey During the Early Months of 1914*. London: Hesperia Press, 1919.

_____ , *The Fall of the Empire of the Sultans and the Rights of Hellenism*. London: Hesperia Press, 1919.

_____ , *The Liberation of the Greek People in Turkey*. Manchester: Norbury, Natzio, 1919.

Lovejoy, Esther Pohl. *Certain Samaritans*. New York: Macmillan, 1933.

Manchester League of Unredeemed Hellenes. *Turkey's Crimes: Hellenism in Turkey.* Manchester: Norbury/Natzio, 1919.

Marriott, [Sir] J. A. R. *The Eastern Question: A Study in European Diplomacy.* Oxford: Clarendon Press, 1940.

The Martyrdom of the Pontus and International Public Opinion. Geneva: Hellenic League of Nations Union, 1922.

Memorandum Presented by the Greek Members of the Turkish Parliament to the American Commission on Mandates over Turkey. New York: American-Hellenic Society of Columbia University, 1919.

Midlarsky, Manus I. *The Killing Trap.* Cambridge: Cambridge University Press, 2005.

Miller, William. *A History of the Greek People (1821-1921).* London: Methuen; New York: E. P. Dutton, [1922].

Milton, Giles. *Paradise Lost: Smyrna 1922: The Destruction of a Christian City in the Islamic World.* New York: Basic Books, 2008.

Ministry of Foreign Affairs (Greece): *Persecutions of the Greek Population in Turkey since the Beginning of the European War: According to Official Reports of Hellenic Diplomatic and Consular Agents. London: Constable, 1918.*

_____ , *Persecutions of the Greeks in Turkey since the Beginning of the European War: Translated from Official Greek Documents by Carroll N. Brown and Theodore P. Ion.* New York: American-Hellenic Society by Oxford University Press, 1918

Morgenthau, Henry (I). *Ambassador Morgenthau's Story.* Garden City, NY: Doubleday, Page, 1918; first UK edition, *Secrets of the Bosphorus.* London: Hutchinson, 1918; first French édition, *Mémoires de l'Ambassadeur Morgenthau: Vingt-six mois en Turquie.* Paris: Payot, 1919; extracts of Chapter XXIX appeared since 1918 under the title, "The Murder of a Nation." Reprinted London: Sterndale Classics, 2003.

_____ , *The Greatest Horror in History. Red Cross Magazine*, March 1918 (UK reprint: *The Tragedy of Armenia.* London: Spottiswoode, Ballantyne, 1918; French edition: *Les Faits les plus horribles de l'Histoire.* Paris: Imprimerie M. Flinikowski, 1918).

_____ , *I was sent to Athens.* Garden City, NY: Doubleday, Doran, 1929. UK edition was published under the title *An International Drama*, London: Jarrolds, 1930.

[Moschonas, T. D.]. *Eight Letters from Turkey (1921-1922) with an Appendix.* Alexandria : Impr. du Commerce, 1935.

Murat, Jean de. *The Great Extirpation of Hellenism and Christianity in Asia Minor and the Historic and Systematic Deception of World Opinion Concerning the Hideous Christianity's Uprooting of 1922.* Miami, FL: 1999.

Oeconomos, Lysimachos. *The Martyrdom of Smyrna and Eastern Christendom: A File of Overwhelming Evidence, Denouncing the Misdeeds of the Turks in Asia Minor and Showing Their Responsibility for the Horrors of Smyrna.* London: George Allen & Unwin, 1922.

Oecumenical Patriarchate. *The Black Book of the Sufferings of the Greek People in Turkey from the Armistice to the End of 1920.* Constantinople: Press of the Patriarchate, 1920.

Pallis, Alexander Anastasius. *Greece's Anatolian Venture and After: A Survey of the Diplomatic and Political Aspects of the Greek Expedition to Asia Minor 1915-1922.* London: Methuen, 1937.

[Papadopoulos, Alexander]. *Persecutions of the Greeks in Turkey before the European War by Archimandrite Alexander Papadopoulos on the Basis of Official Documents, translated from the Greek by Carroll N. Brown.* Published for the Central Committee of the Unredeemed Greeks in Conjunction with the American-Hellenic Society. New York: Oxford University Press, 1919.

Papoutsy, Christos. *Ships of Mercy: The True Story of the Rescue of the Greeks – Smyrna September 1922.* Mermaid Waters (Australia): Zeus Publications, 2008.

Pentzopoulos, Dimitri. *The Balkan Exchange of Minorities and Its Impact on Greece.* London: Hurst, 2002.

Persecution and Extermination of the Communities of Macri and Livissi (1914-1918): Extract from the Black Book of Asia Minor. Paris: [n.p.], 1919

Petsalis–Diomidis, Nicholas. *Greece at the Paris Peace Conference, 1919.* Thessalonica: Institute for Balkan Studies, 1978.

Psomiades, Harry J. *The Eastern Question: The Last Phase.* Thessalonica: Institute for Balkan Studies, 1968.

Reeves, William Pember. *An Appeal for the Liberation and Union of the Hellenic Race: With an Ethnological Map of the Balkan Peninsula and Asia Minor.* London: Anglo-Hellenic League, 1918.

Reinhard, Richard. *The Ashes of Smyrna.* New York: Harper & Row, 1971.

Rendel, George William. *The Sword and the Olive: Recollections of Diplomacy and the Foreign Service, 1913-1954.* London: John Murray, 1957.

Ross, Frank Alexander. *The Near East and American Philanthropy: A Survey, Conducted under the Guidance of the General Committee of the Near East Survey.* New York: Columbia University Press, 1929.

Sakayan, Dora, ed. *An Armenian Doctor in Turkey: Garabed Hatcherian, My Smyrna Ordeal of 1922.* Montreal: Arod Books, 1997.

Smith, Michael Llewellyn. *Ionian Vision.* London: Allen Lane, 1973.

Solomonidis, Victoria. "The Greek Administration of the Vilayet of Aidin, 1919-1922." Ph.D. diss., King's College London, 1985.

Stephens, E. W. *Survival Against All Odds: The First 100 Years of Anatolia College.* New Rochelle, NY: Aristide D. Caratzas, 1986.

Stylianou, Petros. *Turkish Massacres in Smyrna in 1922: As They Appear from the Unpublished Secret Document of the American Consul in Smyrna to the American Secretary of State.* Cyprus: [n.p.], 1979.

Travis, Hannibal. *Genocide in the Middle East: The Ottoman Empire, Iraq, and Sudan.* Durham, NC: Carolina Academic Press, 2010.

Trumpener, Ulrich. *Germany and the Ottoman Empire, 1914-1918.* Princeton, NJ: Princeton University Press, 1968. Repr. Ann Arbor, MI: Caravan Books, 2000.

Tsirkinidis, Harry. *"At last we uprooted them...:" The Genocide of Greeks of Pontos, Thrace and Asia Minor, through the French Archives.* Thessalonica: Kyriakidis Brothers, 1999.

_____ , *The Red River: The Tragedy of Hellenism of Anatolia 1908-1923*. Thessalonica: Kyriakidis Brothers, 1999.

Toynbee, Arnold J. *The Western Question in Greece and Turkey: A Study in the Contact of Civilizations*. London: Constable, 1922.

Tsoukalas, Constantinos. *The Greek Tragedy*. London: Penguin, 1969

Turfan, Naim M. *The Rise of the Young Turks: Politics, the Military and Ottoman Collapse*. London: I. B. Tauris, 1999.

Ussher, Clarence D. *An American Physician in Turkey*. Boston, MA: Houghton Mifflin, 1917; reprinted London: Sterndale Classics, 2002.

Várdy, Steven Béla and T. Hunt Tooley, eds. *Ethnic Cleansing in Twentieth-Century Europe*. Eastern European Monographs Series. Boulder, CO: Columbia University Press, 2003.

Venizelos, Eleftherios. *Greece before the Peace Congress of 1919*. New York: Oxford, University Press, 1919.

Vryonis, Speros Jr. *The Mechanism of Catastrophe: The Turkish Pogrom of September 6-7, 1955, and the Destruction of the Greek Community of Istanbul*. New York: Greekworks, 2005.

_____ , *The Turkish State and History: Clio Meets the Grey Wolf*. New Rochelle, NY: Aristide D. Caratzas, 1991.

_____ , *The Decline of Medieval Hellenism in Asia Minor and the Process of Islamization from the Eleventh through the Fifteenth Century*. Berkeley and Los Angeles: University of California Press, 1971.

Ward, Mark H. *The Deportations in Asia Minor 1921-1922*. London: Anglo-Hellenic League & British Armenia Committee, 1922.

Waugh, [Sir] T. *Turkey, Yesterday, To-day and To-morrow*. London: Chapman & Hall, 1930.

Woodward, E. L. and Rohan Butler, eds. *British Documents on Foreign Policy, 1919-1939*. First Series, Vol. XIII. London: HMSO, 1963.

White, George F. *Adventuring with Anatolia College*. Grinnell, IA: Herald–Register Publishing Company, 1940.

Yeghiayan, Vartkes. *British Reports on Ethnic Cleansing in Anatolia, 1919-1922: The Armenian-Greek Section*. Glendale, CA: Center for Armenian Remembrance, 2007.

Zervos J. [A.]. *Hellenism in Pontos: A Paper Read in the Hall of the Philological Society "Parnassos" at Athens, on the 18th October 1919*. Athens: Hestia, 1920

French & Italian

Aaux, Louis-Paul and René Puaux. *Le déclin de l'Hellénisme*. Paris: Payot, 1916.

[Andréadès, A]. *La destruction de Smyrne et les dernières atrocités turques en Asie Mineure (Septembre-Novembre 1922): Conférence donnée par Mr. A Andréadès*. (Supplément au Bulletin N° 6 de la Ligue Hellénique pour la Société des Nations). Athènes : Imprimerie P. D. Sakellarios, 1923

Andréadès, A. *La Grèce devant le Congrès de la paix*. Paris: [n.p.], 1919

Antoniades, I. *La fin d'une civilisation ou la mort de Smyrne*. Paris, 1925.

Argyroglo, Georges, *L'Allemagne, ennemie de l'Hellénisme.* Avec une préface de Maurice Barrès et une lettre d'Alfred Croiset. Paris : Jouve & Cie, 1916

Asserin Marie-Louise, *La fin d'une civilisation ou la fin de Smyrne.* Paris, 1923

Les atrocités turques en Asie Mineure et dans le Pont devant la IIIe Assemblée Nationale des Hellènes (Séance du 18/31 Mai 1922). Athens: 1922. (English edition, *The Turkish Atrocities in Asia Minor and in the Pontus.* Athens : 1922).

Les atrocités turques au Pont-Euxin. Paris: Dubois et Bauer, 1919.

Bareilles, Bertrand. *Le drame Oriental; d'Athènes à Angora.* Paris: Bossard, 1923.

_____ , *Les Turcs: ce que fut leur empire, leurs comédies politiques.* Préf. J. de Morgan. Paris: Perrin, 1917.

Bérard, Victor. *La Mort de Stamboul : Considérations sur le gouvernement des Jeunes-Turcs.* Paris: Librairie Armand Colin, 1913.

_____ , *La politique du Sultan.* Paris: Éditions du Félin, 2005.

Botzaris, D.-Noti. *Les Hellènes et l'Asie Mineure.* Paris/Nancy: Berger-Levrault, 1919.

Bruneau, Michel, ed. *Les Grecs pontiques: Diaspora, Identité, Territoires.* Paris: Éditions CNRS, 1998.

Charmes, G. *L'avenir de la Turquie, le panislamisme.* Paris: Calmann Lévy, 1883.

Chrysostome de Smyrne [Kalaphates]. *Les persécutions des Chrétiens: Exposés authentiques et tableaux statistiques*, vol. I. [Smyrne]: 1910.

[Croix-Rouge hellénique], *Le traitement des prisonniers Grecs en Turquie : Rapport de la Commission Internationale d'Enquête Instituée sous les auspices de la Croix-Rouge Hellénique.* Paris: [n.p.], 1923.

Délégation du Dodécanèse à la Conférence de la paix. *Le Dodécanèse ensanglanté demande sa liberté : mémoires, résolutions, rapports, télégrammes, lettres, documents, soumis à la Conférence de la paix du 27 mai au 6 octobre 1919.* [Paris: Imp. F. A. Tourbier, 1919].

Délégation hellénique à la Conférence de la paix. *Responsabilité pour les crimes commis pendant la guerre: crimes commis par les Bulgares, les Turcs, et les Allemands contre des populations helléniques.* Paris: Imp. du journal Le Temps, J. Reiter, 1919.

Dieterich Karl, *L'Hellénisme en Asie Mineure, le témoignage d'un Allemand ; une étude du docteur Karl Dieterich..., avec une introduction critique de M. Théodore Ion.* Paris: Imprimerie de Chaix, 1919.

Dourmoussis, Evdokimos. *La Vérité sur un drame historique: La Catastrophe de Smyrne, Septembre 1922.* Paris: Impr. Lemaux, 1922.

Driault, Édouard. *La grande idée : la renaissance de l'hellénisme.* Paris : F. Alcan, 1920

_____ . *La question d'Orient (1918-1937): La paix de la Méditerranée.* Paris: Alcan, 1938.

_____ . *La question d'Orient depuis ses origines jusqu'à la Paix de Sèvres (1920)*, préf. G. Monod. Paris: Alcan, 1921.

_____ et Michel Lhéritier. *Histoire diplomatique de la Grèce de 1821 à nos jours.* Paris: Presses Universitaires, 1926.

_____ . *Histoire diplomatique de la Grèce.* Vol. 5. *La Grèce et la Grande Guerre: De la Révolution turque au traité de Lausanne (1908-1923).* Paris: Les Presses Universitaires de France, 1925.

Dufayard, C. *L'Asie Mineure et l'Hellénisme*. Paris: F. Alcan, 1919.

Efstratiades, G. *Les Alliés, La Grèce et la Crise orientale*. Paris: P. Thévos, 1922

L'Extermination des Chrétiens d'Orient: Faits, documents et témoignages anglais et américains. Paris: P. Thévoz, 1922.

Fattal, Antoine. *Le statut légal des non-musulmans en pays d'Islam*. Beyrouth: Imprimerie Catholique, 1958 (reprinted Beyrouth, 1995)

Faltaits, C. *Voilà les Turcs! : récits des massacres d'Ismidt*. Athènes : [Imprimerie française du "Progrès"], 1922.

Georgelin, Hervé. *La fin de Smyrne. Du cosmopolitisme aux nationalismes*. Paris: Éditions CNRS, 2005.

Georges-Gaulis, Berthe. *Le nationalisme turc*. Paris: Librairie Plon, 1921.

Gondrand, Richard. *La Tragedie de l'Asie Mineure et l'Anéantissement de Smyrne 1914-1922*. Marseille: Impr. Y. Armen, 1935.

Georgiadès, D. *Le nouveau régime en Turquie et l'œuvre néfaste du Comité Union et Progrès*. Paris : Leve, 1911.

[Germanos, Archevêque d-Amassia] *Les atrocités turques au Pont-Euxin: Copie d'une lettre de S.E l' Archevêque d'Amassia et Samsoun Germanos ; éditée par la Délégation du Congrès panpontique*. Paris: Dubois et Bauer, 1919.

Hadzipetros, Jean. *Appel à la conscience publique*. Lausanne: Ed. de la Ligue des Hellènes irrédimés, 1919.

L'Hellénisme de l'Asie Mineure et la Jeune Turquie; Protestation et Appel a l'humanité civilisée par un témoin oculaire des crimes Turcs. Paris: Imprimerie Chaix, 1918.

L'Hellénisme en Turquie: histoire complet des massacres, un plan diabolique. Paris: Imprimerie Chaix, 1919.

Kiazim, Omer. *Angora et Berlin: Le complot germano-kémaliste contre le traité des Versailles*. Paris: L'Édition Universelle, 1922.

_____, *L'Aventure Kémaliste : elle est un danger pour l'Orient, pour l'Europe, pour la Paix*. Paris : L'Édition Universelle, 1921.

Lichnowsky, Karl Max (Fürst von). *Le Mémoire Lichnowsky et les documents de Muehlon*. Préface de Joseph Reinach (Polybe). Paris, Nancy: Librairie Militaire Berger-Levrault, 1918

Luthringer, Emile. *Souvenirs de captivité en Turquie*. Paris: Édition-Impression P. Thévoz, 1920.

Lorieux, C. *Cristiani d'Oriente nelle terre dell'Islam*. Lecce: Argo, 2002.

Maccas, Léon. *L'Hellénisme de l'Asie Mineure: Son histoire, sa puissance, son sort*. Paris: Berger-Levrault, 1919.

_____, *Constantin Ier, Roi des Hellènes*. Paris: Bossard, 1917.

Missaelidis, Kostas. *En Bithynie: Par le Fer et par le Feu*. Athènes: Le Bureau de la Presse du Ministère des Affaires Étrangères, 1922.

Morgan, Jacques de. *Contre les barbares de l'Orient : Études sur la Turquie, ses félonies et ses crimes, sur la marche des Alliés dans l'Asie antérieure, sur la solution de la question d'Orient, renfermant de nombreux articles parus de 1915 à 1917 dans* L' Éclair de Montpellier *et dans la* Revue de Paris. Paris: Berger-Levrault, 1918.

Moschopoulos, Nicephore. *Les Turcs jugés... par leur Histoire. Une réponse à Damad Ferid pacha*. Paris: P. Thévoz, 1920

_____ . *La Turquie et l'Entente : Comment la Porte a repoussé les conseils et les faveurs des puissances de l'Entente*. Paris: L'Édition Universelle, 1922.

Nicol E., *Les alliés et la Crise Orientale*. Paris : L'Édition Universelle, 1922

Patriarcat Œcumènique. *Les Grecs de l'Empire Ottoman: Mémoire soumis à la conférence par le Patriarcat œcuménique*. Paris: Imprimerie Chaix, 1919.

Paillarès, Michel. *Le Kémalisme devant les Alliés: L'Entrée en scène du Kémalisme, le Traité de Sèvres, l'Accord d'Angora, vers la paix d'Orient*. Constantinople: Bosphore, 1922.

Les Persécutions anti-hellénique en Turquie depuis le début de la Guerre européenne d'après les rapports officiels des agents diplomatiques et consulaires. Paris: Librairie Bernard Grasset, 1918.

Philippson Alfred. *L'Hellénisme de l'Asie Mineure d'après le témoignage d'un savant allemand*. Paris: (np), 1919

Pinon, René. *L'Europe et la jeune Turquie: Les aspects nouveaux de la question d'Orient*. Paris: Perrin, 1911.

Puaux, René: *Les derniers jours de Smyrne*. Paris: Éd. de la Revue des Balkans, 1923.

_____ . *La Mort de Smyrne*. Paris: Édition de la Révue des Balkans, 1922.

_____ . *Constantinople et la Question d'Orient*. Constantinople: L'Auteur, 1920.

_____ . *La Déportation et le Rapatriement des Grecs en Turquie*. Paris: Éditions du bulletin hellénique, 1919.

_____ . *La malheureuse Épire*. Paris: Perrin et Cie, 1914.

Quelques témoignages sur l'Hellénisme de la Thrace. Geneva: Imprimerie Jent, 1919

Rapport du Comité américain de New-York sur les atrocités commises en Arménie, traduit de l'anglais. Paris: Henri Durville, 1915.

Relation de la fuite des carmélites de Smyrne lors de l'incendie du 14 septembre 1922, de leurs 23 jours de voyage et de leur retour en France. Aire-sur-Adour : Impr. J. Labrouche, 1922.

Sartiaux, Félix. *Les civilisations anciennes de l'Asie Mineure*. Paris: Rieder, 1928.

_____ . *L'Asie-Mineure Grecque*. Paris: Chaix, 1919.

_____ . *La Grèce devant le Congres*. Paris: Boivin, 1919.

_____ . *Le sac de Phocée et l'expulsion des Grecs ottomans d'Asie Mineure en juin 1914*. Paris: Renouard, 1914.

Schneider, Edmond, ed. *Les persécutions anti-helléniques en Turquie, depuis le début de la Guerre européenne, d'après les rapports des agents diplomatiques et consulaires*. Paris: Bernard Grasset, 1918

Seignobosc, H. [Capitaine]. *Turcs et Turquie: La vieille Turquie, les jeunes Turcs, l'armée ottomane, le rôle de la France en Orient, la Turquie et la guerre, les Dardanelles, l'Arménie martyre, l'avenir*. Paris: Payot, 1920.

Smyrnelis, Marie-Carmen, ed. *Smyrne, la ville oubliée ? 1830-1930. Mémoires d'un grand port Ottoman*. Mémoires, no. 121. Paris: Autrement, 2006.

_____ . "Une société hors de soi: Identités et relations sociales á Smyrne aux XVIII et XIX Siècles." Ph.D. diss., Paris 2000.

Traglia, Gustavo. *I Turchi tornano in Europa! Dai selvaggi massacri turchi di Smirne al tragico esodo della Tracia*. Roma: Società Anonima Poligrafica Italiana, 1922.

Vellay, C. *Smyrne ville grecque*. Paris: Librairie Chapelot, 1919.

German

Albrecht, Richard. "'Dies hätte nie geschehen dürfen' Das Smyrna–Tagebuch von Garabed Hatscherian als Primärquelle zum Holocaustos von 1922." 2006. http://www.hausarbeiten.de/faecher/vorschau/110255.html

Baum, Wilhelm. *Die christlichen Minderheiten der Türkei in den Pariser Friedensverhandlungen (1919-1923): Kemal Atatürk und der Genozid*. Klagenfurt: Kitab Verlag 2007.

_____. *Türkei und ihre christlichen Minderheiten: Geschichte, Völkermord, Gegenwart*. Klagenfurt: Kitab Verlag, 2005 (US ed., *The Christian Minorities in Turkey*, 2006).

Dieterich, Karl. *Das Griechentum Kleinasiens*. Länder und Völker der Türkei, Schriften des Deutschen Vorderasienskomitees, 9. Leipzig: Veit, 1915. English edition, *Hellenism in Asia Minor*. New York: Oxford University Press, 1918. (With an introduction by Theodore P. Ion, and a brief article on the Hellenic Pontus by D. H. Oeconomides).

Fotiadis, Konstantinos. "Die Islamisierung Kleinasiens und die Kryptochristen des Pontos." Ph.D. diss., Tübingen 1985.

Grulich, Rudolf. *"Ethnische Säuberung" und Vertreibung als Mittel der Politik im 20. Jahrhundert*. 2. Aufl. München: Institut für Nationalitätenrecht und Regionalismus, 1999.

Helfferich, Karl. *Die deutsche Türkenpolitik*. Berlin: Vossische Buchhandlung, 1921.

Hofmann, Tessa, ed. *Verfolgung, Vertreibung und Vernichtung der Christen im Osmanischen Reich 1912-1922*. Mit einem Geleitwort von Bischof Dr. Wolfgang Huber. Münster: LIT Verlag, 2004; second, revised edition 2007.

Leosius, Johannes. *Bericht über die Lage des armenischen Volkes in der Türkei*. Berlin 1916 (an enlarged Post-War edition appeared under the title: *Der Todesgang des armenischen Volkes in der Türkei während des Weltkrieges*; French edition: *Le Rapport secret du Dr Johannes Lepsius sur les massacres d'Arménie*. Paris, 1918).

_____ ed. *Deutschland und Armenien 1914-1918: Sammlung diplomatischer Aktenstükke*. Potsdam: Tempelverlag, 1919 (French ed., *Archives du génocide des Arméniens*. Paris: Fayard, 1986).

Pomiankowski, Joseph. *Der Zusammenbruch des Ottomanischen Reiches: Erinnerungen an die Türkei aus der Zeit des Weltkrieges*. Wien: Amalthea, 1928.

Sanders, Otto Liman von: *Fünf Jahre Türkei*. Berlin: Scherl, 1920 (US edition: *Five Years in Turkey*. Annapolis: United States Naval Institute, 1927).

Schätzel, Walter: *Die Welt der Pariser Friedensschlüsse*. Berlin: Verlag von Georg Stilke, 1921.

Schmitt, Oliver Jens. *Levantiner: Lebenswelten und Identitäten einer ethnokonfessionellen Gruppe im Osmanischen Reich im "langen 19. Jahrhundert."* München: Oldenbourg Wissenschaftsverlag, 2005. (Südosteuropäische Arbeiten, 122).

Stürmer, Harry. *Zwei Kriegsjahre in Konstantinopel: Skizzen deutsch-jungtürkischer Moral und Politik.* [*Two war years in Constantinople: Sketches of German-Young Turkish Ethics and Policies.*] Lausanne 1917, pp. 150-151.

Greek

Αβραμίδης, Αρίσταρχος Α. *Ο Βενιζέλος και ο εν Τουρκία ελληνισμός ήτοι τα μαρτύρια του ελληνισμού και αι προσπάθειαι του αρχηγού της φυλής περί σωτηρίας αυτού.* [Avramides, Aristarchos A. *Venizelos and Hellenism in Turkey, That Is the Martyrdom of Hellenism and the Efforts of the Nation's Leader Relating to Its Salvation*]. Constantinople: [n.p.], 1919

Αγγελίδης, Κ. Χ. & Ελευθέριος Θ. Κασιάνης, *Τούρκοι πέρασαν... χαλασμός!* [Angelides, K. C. & Eleutherios T. Kasianes, *The Turks Passed Through... Destruction!*]. Αθήναι: Εκδόσεις Ροδάκη, 1955.

Αγγελομάτης, Χρήστος Ε. *Χρονικόν Μεγάλης Τραγωδίας: Το Έπος της Μικράς Ασίας* [Angelomates, Chrestos E. *The Chronicle of the Great Tragedy: The Epic of Asia Minor*]. Athens: Εστία, 1971.

Αγτζίδης, Βλάσης. *Έλληνες του Πόντου: Η Γενοκτονία από τον Τουρκικό Εθνικισμό* [Agtzides, Vlases. *The Greeks of the Pontus: The Genocide by Turkish Nationalism*]. Athens: Ελληνικές Εκδόσεις, 2005.

[Αιγίδης, Α. Ι.] *Η ελληνικότης της Μικράς Ασίας και το μύθευμα των τουρκορθοδόξων: Διάλεξις γενομένη εν τη αιθούση της Φιλοπτώχου Αφελφότητος Ταταούλων τη 6η Μαρτίου 1922 υπό Αρ. Ι. Αιγίδη* [Aigides, A. I. *The Hellenicity of Asia Minor and the Myth of the Turkish Orthodox: A Lecture Delivered in the Hall of the Philoptochus Brotherhood of Tataula on 6 March 1922 by A. I. Aigides*]. Athens: Τυπ. Δημητριάδου, 1922.

Αικατερίνης, Γιάννης Δ. *Χαμένες Πατρίδες. Το χωριό μας η Αγία Παρασκευή του Τσεσμέ (Το Κιοστέ) 1760-1922* [Aikaterines, Giannes D. *Lost Homelands. Our Village Saint Paraskeve of Cesme (Kioste) 1760-1922*]. Skiathos: (Self published), 1984.

Αιλιανός, Μιχαήλ Χ. *Το έργον της ελληνικής περιθάλψεως* [Ailianos, Michael C. *The Work of the Hellenic Relief*]. Athens: Έκδοσις Γραφείου Τύπου Υπουργείου Εξωτερικών, 1921

Ακτσόγλου, Ιάκωβος Ζ. *Χρονικό Μικρασιατικού Πολέμου* [Aktsoglou, Iakovos Z. *Chronicle of the War in Asia Minor*]. Athens: Εκδόσεις Τροχαλία, 1998

_____. *Η Εξόντωση του μισητού Λιονταριού: Ο Ελληνισμός της καθ' ημάς Ανατολής και οι Επάλληλοι Κύκλοι του αφανισμού του* [*The Extermination of the Hated Lion: The Hellenism of the Greek East and the Consecutive Cycles of its Annihilation*]. Athens: Εκδόσεις Τσουκάτου, 2005.

Αμερικανική Περίθαλψις της Εγγύς Ανατολής. *Έκθεσις πεπραγμένων της Αμερικανικής Περιθάλψεως της Εγγύς Ανατολής εν Ελλάδι κατά το έτος 1925* [American Near East Relief. *Activity Report of the American Near East Relief in Greece during the Year 1925*]. Athens: [n.p.], 1926

_____. *Το έργον της Αμερικανικής Περιθάλψεως της Εγγύς Ανατολής εν Ελλάδι: Σεπτέμβριος 1922 – Δεκέμβριος 1924* [*The Work of the American Near East Relief in Greece: September 1922–December 1924*]. Athens: Τύποις Φοίνικος, 1925

Andler, Charles. *Ο παγγερμανισμός και τα κατακτητικά του σχέδια* [Andler, Charles. *Pan-Germanism and Its Plans of Conquest*]. Athens : Τυπ. Π. Α. Πετράκου, 1916.

Ανδρεάδης, Γεώργιος. *Φουρτούνα ήταν... Η Γενοκτονία του Ποντιακού Ελληνισμού μέσα από τα απομνημονεύματα του Παπα-Προδρόμου Ηλιάδη* [Andreades, Georgios. *"It was a tempest..." The Genocide of Pontian Hellenism in the Memoirs of Papa-Prodromos Eliades*]. [Thessalonica]: Ερωδιός, 2002.

Ανδρεάδης, Κώστας. *Η Θρακική τραγωδία του 1922* [Andreades, Kostas. *The Thracian Tragedy of 1922*]. Athens : [n.p.], 1933.

Αξιωτάκης, Ανδρέας Σ. *Ημέρα Μνήμης του Ελληνισμού της Μικράς Ασίας* [Axiotakes, Andreas S. *Memorial Day of Asia Minor Hellenism*]. Athens: Μορφωτικός Σύνδεσμος Βαρβασίου Χίου, 1979.

Αποστολίδης, Δημήτριος Γ. *Η μεγάλη τραγωδία του Πόντου* [Apostolides, Demetrios G. *The Great Tragedy of the Pontus*]. Athens: [n.p.], 1919.

_____. *Συνοπτική ιστορία του Ελληνισμού του Πόντου* [*A Brief History of the Hellenism of the Pontus*]. Thessalonica: Τύποις Σπύρου Σύρου, [1934]; reprinted Thessalonica : [n.p.], 1996.

[no author] *Από την μικρασιατική καταστροφή: Οι Έλληνες αιχμάλωτοι εις τον κεμαλικόν στρατόν. Αι αφηγήσεις των απελευθερωθέντων [από τας εφημερίδας εκείνης της εποχής]. Ανάτυπον εκ της εφημερίδος "Σκριπ" του έτους 1922* [*From the Asia Minor Catastrophe: Greek Prisoners in Kemal's Army. Narratives of Those Released (from the Newspapers of that Period). Offprint from the Newspaper Skrip of the year 1922*]. [Athens]: [n.p.], [1972]

Αραβαντινός, Ιωάννης Δ. *Βίαιοι ακρωτηριασμοί διαπραχθέντες υπό των Τούρκων: Ανακοίνωσις γενομένη ενώπιον της Ιατροχειρουργικής Εταιρείας κατά την συνεδρίαν της 24 Μαΐου εν τη Σιναία Ακαδημία* [Aravantinos, Ioannes D. *Forced Mutilations Committed by the Turks: An Announcement Presented before the Medical-Chirurgical Society at the Sinaea Academy during the 24 May Session*]. Athens: Δ. Τρεμπέλα, 1923

Αργυρόπουλος, Μιχαήλ. *(Ρήγα Ραγιά): Τ' ανιστόρητα (1922-1924)* [Argyropoulos, Michael. *(Regas Ragias): Things Unrecorded (1922-1924)*]. Athens: [n.p.], 1925

_____. *Χρονικά της Ανατολής: Χωρίς Ναόν και Χωρίς Τάφον* (*Chronicles of the East: Without a Church and Without a Grave*) Athens: [n.p.], 1933

Αρχιγένης, Δημήτρης Ι. *Μαρτυρίες από τη Μικρασιατική καταστροφή* [Archigenes, Demetres I. *Testimonies from the Asia Minor Catastrophe*]. Athens: [n.p.], 1973

Ασλανίδης, Σάββας. *Η Ωραία Κερασούς: Η αλησμόνητη νύμφη του Ευξείνου Πόντου* [Aslanidēs, Savvas. *The Beautiful Kerasous: The Unforgetable Bride of the Euxine Pontus*]. Athens: [n.p.], 1976

Ατέσης, Βασίλειος (Μητροπολίτης Λήμνου). *Εθνομάρτυρες Αρχιερείς των καθ' ημάς χρόνων* [Ateses, Vasileios (Metropolitan Bishop of Lemnos). *Ethnomartyr Bishops of Our Times*]. Athens: Αποστολική Διακονία της Εκκλησίας της Ελλάδος, 1972.

Βακαλόπουλος, Κωνσταντίνος Α. *Διωγμοί και Γενοκτονία του Θρακικού Ελληνισμού– Ο Πρώτος Ξεριζωμός (1908-1917)* [Vakalopoulos, Konstantinos A. *Persecutions and Genocide of the Thracian Hellenism – The First Uprooting (1908-1917)*]. Thessalonica: Ηρόδοτος, 1998.

_____. *Η Θρακική έξοδος (1918-1922): Από τη γενοκτονία, την παλιννόστηση, το ταγιαρικό καθεστώς και την απελευθέρωση στο δεύτερο ξεριζωμό* [*The Thracian Exodus (1918-1922): From the Genocide, the Return, the Tagiaric Regime and the Liberation to the Second Uprooting*]. Thessalonica: Ηρόδοτος, 1999; Thessalonica: Σταμούλης, 2003.

_____. Αριστείδης Κεσόπουλος & Νίκος, Κ. Μουτσόπουλος, *Η Γενοκτονία και η Προσφυγιά του Ελληνισμού* [Vakalopoulos, Konstantinos A., Aristeides Kesopoulos, & Nikos K. Moutsopoulos. *The Genocide and the Refugeeship*]. Thessalonica: Τζιαμπίρης-Πυραμίδα, 2006.

Βαλαβάνης, Γεώργιος Κ. *Σύγχρονος Γενική Ιστορία του Πόντου* [Valavanes, Georgios K. *Contemporary General History of the Pontus*]. Athens: Έκδοσις "Παμπροσφυγικής," 1925; reprinted, Thessalonica: Αδελφοί Κυριακίδη, 1985, 1995.

Βαλβαζάνης, Μιχάλης. *Πώς έζησα την καταστροφή της Σμύρνης*, επιμ. Γ. Παπαστάμος & Π. Κερασιώτου [Valvazanes, Michales. *How I Experienced the Catastrophe of Smyrna*, ed. G. Papastamos and P. Kerasiotou]. Chalkis: Κωστόγιαννος, 1998.

Βαλέτας, Γιώργος Μ. *Αιολική βιβλιογραφία: Λέσβος – Αδραμυτικός κόλπος 1566-1939* [Valetas, Giorgos. *Æolian Bibliography: Lesbos – The Gulf of Adramyttion 1566-1939*. Mytilene: [n.p.][n.d.]; Athens: Γεώργιος Π. Ξένος, [1939].

Βαλιούλης, Παντελής Χ.. *Σελίδες εκ της συμφοράς του Πόντου 1921-1924* [Valioules, Panteles C. *Pages from the Disaster of the Pontus*]. Athens: [n.p.], 1957; reprinted, Thessalonica: Αδελφοί Κυριακίδη, 2005.

Βαλσαμάκης, Πάνος. *Η πολιτεία δίχως κάστρα: Αϊβαλί 1914-1918* [Valsamakes, Panos. *The City without Forts: Aivali/[Ayvalik] 1914-1918*]. Athens: [n.p.], 1978.

Βασιλείου, Βενετία (Βαΐτσα Βένιου). *Γεννήθηκα στη Μικρασία* [Vasileiou, Venetia (Vaitsa Veniou). *I Was Born in Asia Minor*]. [Athens]: Εκδόσεις Γραμμή, 1984.

Βατίδου, Φιλή. *Εικόνες που δε σβύνουν* [Vatidou, Phile. *Images That Do Not Fade*]. Athens: Τυπογραφείον Ηλιάδη, 1943.

Βενέζης, Ηλίας. *Αιολική γη: Μυθιστόρημα* [Venezes Elias. *Æolian Land: A Novel*]. Athens: Άλφα, 1944; revised edition, *Αιολική γη: Μυθιστόστημα*, πρόλογος Άγγελου Σικελιανού [*Æolian Land: A Novel*, Foreword by Angelos Sikelianos [Athens]: Εστία, 1953.

_____. *Το Νούμερο 31328: Σκλάβοι στα εργατικά τάγματα της Ανατολής* [*Number 31328: Slaves in the Labor Battalions of the East*]. Mytilene: [n.p.], 1931. (Subsequent editions: *Το Νούμερο 31328: Το Βιβλίο της Σκλαβιάς* [*Number 31328: The Book of Slavery*], Athens: Οι Φίλοι του Βιβλίου, [1945]; reprinted, Athens: Άλφα, 1952).

_____. *Μικρασία, χαίρε* (*Διήγησις συμβάντων*) [*Hail, Asia Minor* (*Narration of Events*)]. [Athens]: Εστία, 1974

Βερβερίδης, Νικόλαος Ι. *Η έξοδος των Κιζδερβενιωτών της Μικράς Ασίας* [Ververides, Nikolaos I. *The Exodus of Kisderveni Inhabitants of Asia Minor*]. Siderokastron: [n.p.], 2001.

Βογιατζόγλου, Βάσος Η. *Η Πισιδία της Μικράς Ασίας: Η διαδρομή του ελληνισμού της από τους προϊστορικούς χρόνους έως τη Μικρασιατική καταστροφή* [Vogiatzoglou, Vasos E. *Pisidia of Asia Minor: The Course of Its Hellenism from*

Prehistorical Times to the Asia Minor Catastrophe]. Athens: Ένωση Σπάρτης Πισιδίας, 1978

_____. *Οι γειτονιές των απίστων: Τουρκία* [*The Neighborhoods of the Infidels: Turkey*]. Athens: Ένωση Σπάρτης Μικράς Ασίας, 1981; reprinted as, *Οι γειτονιές των απίστων: Οδοιπορικό στη Μικρά Ασία* [*The Neighborhoods of the Infidels: A Tour of Asia Minor*]. Athens: Φιλιππότης, 1995

Γαβριηλίδης, Αντώνιος Ι. *Σελίδες εκ της μαύρης εθνικής συμφοράς του Πόντου: 1914-1922* [Gabrielides, Antonios I. *Pages from the National Disaster of the Pontus: 1914-1922*]. Athens [n.p.], 1924; reprinted Thessalonica: Αδελφοί Κυριακίδη, 2002.

Γεραγάς, Κώστας. *Αναμνήσεις εκ Θράκης* 1920-1922 [Geragas, Kostas. *Remembrances from Thrace, 1920-1922*]. Athens: Εστία, 1925; reprinted Katerine: Εκδόσεις Μάτι, 2005.

Γεωργανόπουλος, Ευριπίδης. *Το νεοτουρκικό κίνημα και οι επιπτώσεις του στον ελληνισμό του Πόντου 1908-1914* [Georganopoulos, Euripides. *The Young Turk Movement and Its Impact on the Hellenism of the Pontus 1908-1914*]. [Thessalonica]: Αδελφοί Κυριακίδη, 2001.

Γεωργιάδης, Μαργαρίτης. *Ανατολική Θράκη–Μήδεια: Γεωγραφία, Ιστορία, πολιτισμός και διωγμοί 1914-1922* [Georgiades, Margarites. *Eastern Thrace–Medeia: Geography, History, Culture and Persecutions 1914-1922*]. Serres: Αδελφοί Χαραλαμπίδη, 2005.

Γιάμαλη-Χατζηιωάννου, Ευαγγελία. *Μικρασιατικός Ελληνισμός : Οδοιπορικό θανάτου και ανάστασης* [Giamale-Chatzeioannou, Evangelia. *Asia Minor Hellenism: An Itinerary of Death and Resurrection*]. Nicaea: Δήμος, 2001

Γιαννακάκης, Γεώργιος Ι. *Περιπέτειαι του Θρακικού Ελληνισμού από του 1904-1922* [Giannakakes, Georgios I. *The Adventures of Thracian Hellenism from 1904-1922*]. Athens: Εταιρεία Θρακικών Μελετών, 1955.

Γιαννακόπουλος, Γιώργος Α. *Ο τελευταίος Ελληνισμός του Ρένκιοϊ (Οφρυνίου)* [*The Last Hellenism of Erenköy (Ophrynion)*]. Asprovalta: Κοινότητα και Μορφωτικός Πολιτιστικός Σύλλογος, 1995.

Γιαννόπουλος, Λάζαρος. *Η εθνική τραγωδία Θράκης και Μικράς Ασίας* [Giannopoulos, Lazaros. *The National Tragedy of Thrace and Asia Minor*]. Athens: Μπλαζουδάκης, 1915.

Γκρίτση-Μιλλιέξ, Τατιάνα. *Η Τρίπολη του Πόντου. Ιστορική Μονογραφία* [Gritse-Milliex, Tatiana. *Tripolis* [Terebolu] *of the Pontus: Historical Monograph*. Athens: Εκδόσεις Κέδρος, 1976, reprinted 1981.

Γλεντής, Κωνσταντίνος Α. *Αναμνήσεις από την μικρασιατικήν εκστρατείαν*. [Glentes, Konstantinos A. *Remembrances from the Asia Minor Campaign*]. Athens: Εκδόσεις "Χαρτοβιβλιοεκδοτική," 1971.

[no author]. *Ο γολγοθάς του εν Τουρκία Ελληνισμού* [*The Golgotha of the Hellenism of Turkey*]. Constantinople: [n.p.], 1919.

Γρηγοριάδου-Σουρελή, Γαλάτεια. *Καυτές μνήμες από τη Σμύρνη: Διηγήματα* [Gregoriadou-Sourele, Galateia. *Burning Memories from Smyrna: Narratives*]. Athens: Εκδόσεις Φιλιππότη, 1985.

Δεληγιάννης, Βασίλειος Ν. *Τα Κουβούκλια: (Μία εγκαταλειφθείσα ελληνική κωμόπολις της Μικράς Ασίας)* [Delegiannes, Vasileios N. *Kouvouklia: (An Abandoned Greek Town of Asia Minor)*. Serres: [n.p.], 1956.

Δεληγιάννης, Γιώργος. *Η αιχμαλωσία–έξοδος από τη Σμύρνη: Μαρτυρίες* [Delegiannes, Giorgos, *Captivity–Exodus from Smyrna: Testimonies*]. Athens: Εκδόσεις Ίδμων, 1997.

Δεληγιαννίδης, Θεοφάνης. *Αντάρτης στα ποντιακά βουνά: Απομνημονεύματα* [Delegiannides, Theophanes. *Guerrilla in the Pontic Mountains: Memoirs*]. Katerine: Τέρτιος, 2001.

Διαμαντόπουλος, Βασίλης Γεώργιος. *Αιχμάλωτος των Τούρκων (1922-1923)* [Diamantopoulos, Vasiles Georgios. *Prisoner of the Turks (1922-1923)*]. Athens: [n.p.], 1977

[Δ.Ι.Π.]. *Η κατά του Ελληνισμού συνωμοσία του Γερμανισμού* [D.I.P. *The Conspiracy of Germanism Against Hellenism*]. Athens: Τυπ. Π. Α. Πετράκου, 1916

(Ο) *Διωγμός του ελληνικού στοιχείου εν τη Νομαρχία Σμύρνης* [*The Persecution of the Greek Element in the Smyrna Prefecture*] [no publication information is noted]

[Δομουχτσής, Σταύρος Δ.] *Σελίδες εκστρατείας και προσφυγιάς: Το ημερολόγιο του στρατιώτη στη μικρασιατική εκστρατεία Σταύρου Δομουχτσή. Εισαγωγή, επιμέλεια, σχόλια Απόστολος Γ. Καρύδας* [Domouchtses Stauros D. *Pages of Expedition and Refugeeship: The Diary of Domouchtses Stauros, Private in the Asia Minor Campaign.* Introduced, edited and with a commentary by Apostolos G. Karydas. Thessalonica: Αδελφοί Κυριακίδη, 2008.

Δούκας, Στρατής. *Ιστορία ενός αιχμαλώτου* [Doukas, Stratεs. *The Story of a Prisoner*]. Athens: Τυπ. Γανιάρη, 1929; reprinted, [Athens]: Εστία, 1958.

Δούλης, Πλούταρχος Ε. *Από τα Θείρα και τη Σμύρνη στη Ρόδο.* [Doules, Ploutarchos E. *From Theira and Smyrna to Rhodes*]. Athens: [n.p.], 1976

Δρόσος, Άγγελος. Ανάμεσα στους πεθαμένους: Το βιβλίο του χαλασμού [Drosos, Angelos. *Among the Dead: The Book of Destruction*]. Athens: Εκδόσεις "Αστήρ" – Παπαδημητρίου, 1933; reprinted, Athens: Ύψιλον/Βιβλία, 2005

[Δ.Φ.Π.] *Σαλπίσματα του παγγερμανισμού προς τον νεοτουρκισμόν κατά του Μικρασιατικού Ελληνισμού.* [D. P. P. *Trumpet Calls by Pan-Germanism to Neo-Turkism Against Asia Minor Hellenism*]. Athens: Τυπ. Π. Α. Πετράκου, 1916.

_____ . *Τό μέλλον του Ελληνισμού εν τη τριπλή συμμαχία των Γερμανοαυστριακών, Τούρκων και Βουλγάρων.* [*The Future of Hellenism in the Triple Alliance of the Germano-Austrians, the Turks and the Bulgarians*]. Athens: Τυπ. Πετράκου, 1916.

Εθνικόν Συμβούλιον Ελληνίδων. *Διαμαρτυρία Γυναικών Θράκης και Μικράς Ασίας* [National Council of Greek Women. *Appeal of the Women of Thrace and of Asia Minor*]. Athens: Έκδοσις Εθνικού Συμβουλίου Ελληνίδων [Publication of the National Council of Greek Women], 1922.

[Ελληνικός Ερυθρός Σταυρός]. *Αιχμάλωτοι Έλληνες εν Τουρκία, Πώς μεταχειρίσθηκαν αυτούς οι Τούρκοι. Έκθεσις, τη μερίμνη του Ελληνικού Ερυθρού Σταυρού καταρτισθείσης διεθνούς ανακριτικής επιτροπής* [*Greek Prisoners in Turkey: How the Turks Treated Them. Report of the International Commission of Inquiry Appointed at the Request of the Hellenic Red Cross*]. Athens: [Τυπογραφείον της Βασιλικής Αυλής Α. Ραφτάνη], 1923.

Εμμανουηλίδης, Εμμανουήλ Χ. *Τα τελευταία έτη της οθωμανικής αυτοκρατορίας* [Emmanouelides, Emmanuel Ch. *The Last Years of the Ottoman Empire*]. Athens: Τύποις Γ. Καλλέργη, 1924.

Ενεπεκίδης, Ιορδάνης. *Ο Γολγοθάς των Ελλήνων του Πόντου* [Enepekides, Iordanes. *The Golgotha of the Greeks of the Pontus*]. Athens: Πανποντιακή Ένωσις, 1976.

Ενεπεκίδης, Πολυχρόνης Κ. *Οι διωγμοί των Ελλήνων του Πόντου, 1908-1918 βάσει των ανεκδότων εγγράφων των κρατικών αρχείων της Αυστροουγγαρίας* [Enepekides, Polychrones K. *The Persecutions of the Greeks of the Pontus, 1908-1918: Based on Unpublished Documents of the State Archives of Austria-Hungary*]. Athens: Εκδόσεις Συλλόγου Ποντίων Αργοναύται-Κομνηνοί, 1962.

_____. *Γενοκτονία στον Εύξεινο Πόντο: Διπλωματικά Έγγραφα από τη Βιέννη 1909-1918* [*Genocide in the Euxine Pontus: Diplomatic Documents from Vienna 1909-1918*]. Thessalonica: Εύξεινος Λέσχη, 1996.

_____. *Τραπεζούντα, Κωνσταντινούπολη, Σμύρνη 1800-1923: Γερμανοί, Αυστριακοί και Ελβετοί πολιτικοί, διπλωμάτες, λόγιοι και συγγραφείς γράφουν για την άνθηση και την καταστροφή πόλεων του Μικρασιατικού Ελληνισμού* [*Trebizond, Constantinople, Smyrna 1800-1923: German, Austrian and Swiss Politicians, Diplomats, Intellectuals and Authors Write on the Bloom and the Destruction of Cities of Asia Minor Hellenism*]. Athens: Ωκεανίδα, 1989.

Επιτροπαί των εν Μυτιλήνη Μικρασιατών Προσφύγων. *Οι Διωγμοί των Ελλήνων εν Θράκη και Μικρασία: Αυθεντικαί εκθέσεις και επίσημα κείμενα: Έκκλησις προς το ελληνικόν γένος και την δημοσίαν Γνώμην του πεπολιτισμένου κόσμου* [Committees of the Asia Minor Refugees in Mytilene. *Persecutions of the Greeks in Thrace and Asia Minor: Authentic Reports and Official Documents: Appeal to the Greek Nation and to the Public Opinion of the Civilized World*]. Athens: Τύποις "Πανελληνίου Κράτους," 1915.

Ευαγγελίδης, Μαργαρίτης. *Οι διωγμοί των Ελλήνων εν Θράκη και Μικρά Ασία* [Evangelides, Margarites. *The Persecutions of Greeks in Thrace and Asia Minor*]. Athens: [n.p.], 1915.

_____. *Υπόμνημα περί των δικαιωμάτων και παθημάτων των εστιών του πολιτισμού Μικράς Ασίας και Θράκης* [*Memorandum Concerning the Rights and the Misfortunes of Centers of Civilization in Asia Minor and Thrace*]. Athens: [n.p.], 1918; reprinted Katerine: Μάτι, 1999.

_____. *Τα αίτια της εις Ελλάδα μεταναστεύσεως των εν Καυκάσω Ελλήνων του Πόντου και η ιστορία των παθημάτων αυτών* [*The Causes of the Immigration to Greece of the Greeks of the Pontus in Caucasus and the History of their Ordeals*]. Athens: [n.p.], 1900.

Ευαγγελίδης, Τρύφων Ε. *Βρύλλειον-Τρίγλεια: Ιστορική και Γεωγραφική Μελέτη από του ε΄ αιώνος π.Χ. μέχρι των καθ' ημάς* [Evangelides, Tryphon E. *Brylleion-Triglia* [Zeytinbağı]*: A Historical and Geographical Study from the Fifth Century BC until Our Times*]. Athens: Τύποις Ε. Ι. Χατζηϊωάννου, 1934.

Εφραιμίδης, Αναστάσιος Ι. *Μνήμες Μικρασιατικής Τραγωδίας* [Ephraimides, Anastasios I. *Memories of the Asia Minor Tragedy*]. Thessalonica: [n.p.], 1983.

Εφραιμίδης, Σάββας Σ. *Ιστορία–Λαογραφία του Κοτυαίου (Κιουταχείας) πόλεως της Κεντρικής Μ. Ασίας* [Ephraimidēs, Savvas S. *History–Folklore of Cotyæum/ Ko-*

tyaion (Kütahya)], a City of Central Asia Minor]. Thessalonica: Μερίμνη Επιτροπής Εκδόσεως και Φιλοπρόοδων Πατριωτών, 1960.

Εφραιμίδης-Σανταίος, Ιωάννης Χ. *Ο εκτοπισμός των κατοίκων της ηρωϊκής Σάντας και η καταστροφή αυτής* [Ephraimides-Santaios, Ioannes C. *The Deportation of the Inhabitants of Heroic Santa and its Destruction*]. Athens: Εκδόσεις Παμποντιακής Ενώσεως Αθηνών, 1974 (Offprint from "Ποντιακή Στοά," 1972-1974, p. 271-281).

Ζαμπαθάς, Ευστράτιος Χ. *Οι εκ Μικράς Ασίας Ελληνορθόδοξοι πρόσφυγες* [Zampathas, Eustratios C. *The Greek-Orthodox Refugees from Asia Minor*]. Athens: Τυπ. "Φιλικής Εταιρείας," 1969.

Ζερβός, Ιωάννης Α. *Ο Ελληνισμός του Πόντου: Διάλεξις* [Zervos, Ioannes A. *The Hellenism of the Pontus: A Lecture*]. Athens : Υπουργείον Περιθάλψεως, 1919.

Ζώρας, Γεώργιος Θ. *Μαρτυρίες τινές περί το παιδομάζωμα* [Zoras, Georgios T. *Some Testimonies Regarding the Abduction of Children*]. Athens : [n.p.], 1962

[no author]. *Η Ελλάς εις την Μικράν Ασίαν* [*Greece in Asia Minor*]. Athens: Έκδοσις Γραφείου Τύπου Υπουργείου Εξωτερικών [Press Office of the Ministry of Foreign Affairs], 1921,

[no author]. *Η Ελληνική εν Μικρά Ασία εκστρατεία κατά το 1921: Τηλεγραφήματα ανταποκριτών του παγκοσμίου τύπου* [*The Greek Expedition in Asia Minor during 1921: Cables by Correspondents of the International Press*]. Athens: Γραφείου Τύπου Υπουργείου Εξωτερικών, 1921.

[no author] *Η εν Ανατολή γερμανική πολιτική, η Ελλάς και ο Ελληνισμός* [*German Policy in the East, Greece and Hellenism*]. Athens : Τυπογραφείον της Βασιλικής Αυλής Α. Ραφτάνη, 1915.

Ηλιάδης, Χρήστος. *Πόντος Γενοκτονία: Όσα ενθυμούμαι από την περιπετειώδη ζωή μου* [Eliades, Chrestos. *Pontus Genocide: What I Recall from My Adventurous Life*]. Athens: Γόρδιος, 2002.

Θαβωρίτης, Μωϋσής. *Παύλος Ι. Παυλίδης (1876-1921): Ένας νεομάρτυρας της Μικρασιατικής τραγωδίας* [Thavorites, Moyses. *Paulos I. Paulides (1876-1921): A Neomartyr of the Asia Minor Tragedy*]. Athens: [n.p.], 1985.

_____ . *Οδοιπορικό Μικράς Ασίας: Αναζητώντας τις έπτά εκκλησίες της Αποκάλυψης* [*An Itinerary Across Asia Minor: Searching for the Seven Churches of the Apocalypse*]. Athens: [n.p.], 1994.

Θεοτοκάς, Μιχαήλ Γ. *Νομικά και ιστορικά μελετήματα* [Theotokas, Michael G. *Legal and Historical Studies*]. [Athens]: Εκδόσεις Ίκαρος, [1947].

Θεοφυλάκτου, Θεοφύλακτος. *Γύρω στην άσβεστη φλόγα: (Αυτοβιογραφία, αναμνήσεις, στοχασμοί, περιλήψεις πρακτικών Εθνοσυνελεύσεων, πολιτικόν αρχείον Εθνικού Συμβουλίου, αγώνες για την ανεξαρτησία του Πόντου)* [Theophylaktou, Theophylaktos. *Around the Inextinguishable Flame: (Autobiography, Recollections, Reflections, Summaries of Transcripts from National Assemblies, the Political Archive of the National Council, Struggles for the Independence of the Pontus)*]. Thessalonica: [n.p.], 1958; reprinted as, *Γύρω στην άσβεστη φλόγα: Βιογραφικές Αναμνήσεις: Αγώνες για την Ανεξαρτησία του Πόντου* [*Around the Inextinguishable Flame: Biographical Memories: Struggles for the Independence of the Pontus*]. Thessalonica: Αδελφοί Κυριακίδη, 1997.

Ινστιτούτο Ιστορικών Μελετών. *Ο Ξεριζωμός: Η επεκτατική πολιτική της Τουρκίας και οι Διωγμοί των Ελλήνων από τους Τούρκους στον 20ο αιώνα* [Institute of Historical Studies. *The Uprooting: The Expansionist Policy of Turkey and the Persecutions of Greeks by the Turks in the 20th Century*]. Athens: Ινστιτούτο Ιστορικών Μελετών, 1972.

Ιωακειμίδης, Σάββας Π. *Συμβολή εις την Γενικήν Ιστορίαν του Πόντου. Τα δεινοπαθήματα του ποντιακού λαού κατά το πρώτον τέταρτον του Κ΄ αιώνος (Από όσα ήκουσα, από όσα είδον και από όσα έπαθον κατά τα δεινοπαθήματα του Ελληνισμού και δη των Ποντίων προ της ανταλλαγής του 1922-1924)* [Ioakeimides, Savvas P. *Contribution to the General History of the Pontus: The Sufferings of the Pontic People during the First Quarter of the XXth Century: From What I Heard, from What I Saw and from What I Suffered during the Trials of Hellenism, Especially of the Pontians, before the Exchange of 1922-1924*]. Athens: [n.p.], 1970.

Καζταρίδης, Ιωάννης Φ. *Η "έξοδος" των Ελλήνων του Κάρς της Αρμενίας (1919-1921)* [Kaztarides, Ioannes P. *The "Exodus" of the Greeks of Kars in Armenia (1919-1921)*]. Thessalonica: Αδελφοί Κυριακίδη, 1996.

Καλαφάτης, Χρυσόστομος, Μητροπολίτης Σμύρνης. *Το αρχείον του εθνομάρτυρος Σμύρνης Χρυσοστόμου όπως διεσώθη από τον μητροπολίτη Αυστρίας Χρυσόστομο Τσίτερ*, Εισαγωγή–Σημειώσεις Αλέξη Αλεξανδρή [Kalaphates, Chrysostomos, Metropolitan of Smyrna. *The Archive of Ethnomartyr Chrysostom of Smyrna as It Was Preserved by Chrysostom Tsiter, Metropolitan of Austria*, Introduction and notes by Alexes Alexandres]. Athens: Μορφωτικό Ίδρυμα Εθνικής Τραπέζης, 2000.

Καλφέλης, Πέτρος Ι. *Αναμνήσεις από την αξέχαστη Πατρίδα* [Kalpheles, P. *Memories from the Unforgetable Homeland*]. Athens: [n.p.], 1980.

Καμέρη-Τσουκαλά, Ευτυχία. *Το χρονικό της Ευτυχώς : Οι διωγμοί της Σμύρνης 1912-1922* [Kamere-Tsoukala, Eutychia. *The Chronicle of Eutycho: The Persecutions of Smyrna 1912-1922*]. Leukosia: [n.p.], 1989.

Κανδηλάπτης-Κάνις, Γεώργιος Θ. *Τα επίχειρα της κακίας ή το τέλος του Κερασούντιου κακούργου Τοπάλ Οσμάν (Ιστορικόν δοκίμιον)* [Kandelaptes-Kanis, Georgios T. *The Just Deserts of Malice or the End of the Criminal Topal Osman of Kerasous (An Historical Essay)*]. Alexandroupolis: Γ. Σακελλαρίδης, 1956; reprinted, Thessalonica: Αδελφοί Κυριακίδη, 2000.

_____ . *Οι Μάρτυρες του Χριστιανισμού ή περί Κρυπτοχριστιανών του Πόντου* [*The Martyrs of Christianity or on the Crypto-Christians of the Pontus*]. Thessalonica: Αδελφοί Κυριακίδη, 2005.

Καραγεωργίου, Νικόλαος Ε. *Μάκρη και Λιβίσι Μικράς Ασίας: Τόποι, ήθη, έθιμα, ενθυμήματα, εξορίες*, Πρόλογος, επιμέλεια Μ. Π. Δελησάββα [Karageorgiou, Nikolaos E. *Makre and Livisi of Asia Minor: Places, Mores, Customs, Memories, Exile*, Foreword and ed. by M. P. Delesavva]. Athens: [n.p.] [n.d.]; Athens: Δ. Κασιούμης, 1986.

Καραγιαννίδης Ιωάννης. *Ο γολγοθάς του Πόντου: Το ξερίζωμα, τα πάθη και τα εγκλήματα εις βάρος του Ποντιακού Ελληνισμού* [Karagiannides, Ioannes. *The Golgotha of the Pontus: The Uprooting, the Sufferings and the Crimes Against Pontic Hellenism*]. Thessalonica: [n.p.], 1978.

Καραθανάσης, Αθανάσιος Ε. *Περί την Θράκην* [Karathanases, Athanasios E. *On Thrace*]. Thessalonica: Αδελφοί Κυριακίδη, 1996.

_____. *Σε λένε Σμύρνη, Φώκαια, Σερέκιοϊ, Μαινεμένη, Σαγγάριο: Στην ιστορία και τον χαλασμό* [*You Are Called Smyrna, Phocaea, Serekoy, Mainemene, Sangarius: In History and in Destruction*]. Thessalonica: Αδελφοί Κυριακίδη, 2007.

Καραμπλιάς, Ιωάννης Ν. *Ιστορία των Κυδωνιών: Από της ιδρύσεώς των μέχρι της αποκαταστάσεως των προσφύγων εις το ελεύθερον ελληνικόν κράτος* [Karamplias, Ioannes N. *The History of Cydoniæ* [Ayvalik]: *From Its Foundation to the Restoration of the Refugees into the Free Hellenic State*], 2 vols. Athens: [n.p.], 1949–1950.

_____. *Το δράμα της Σμύρνης* [*The Drama of Smyrna*]. [n.p.]: [n.p], [n.d.]

Καρανικόλας, Παντελεήμων Κ., Μητροπολίτης Κορίνθου. *Ο Άγιος Χρυσόστομος, ο άγγελος της εν Σμύρνη Εκκλησίας Ιερομάρτυς, οι σύγχρονοι αυτώ Ιερομάρτυρες... υπό των αλλοπίστων βαρβάρων εν τη Αποστολική Μικρά Ασία* [Karanikolas, Panteleemon K., Metropolitan of Corinth. *Saint Chrysostom, the Angel of the Church in Smyrna, Martyr of the Faith, His Contemporary Martyrs of the Faith... by the Infidel Barbarians in Apostolic Asia Minor*]. Corinth: Πνοή, 1992.

_____. *Ακολουθίαι Τρεις: Αγίου Χρυσοστόμου Σμύρνης, των πολυπληθών κληρικών και λαϊκών νεομαρτύρων κατά την αυτή εποχήν μαρτυρησάντων εν Μικρά Ασία και του Αγίου Ιερομάρτυρος Ευθυμίου Επισκόπου Ζήλων* [*Three Holy Offices: Of Saint Chrysostom of Smyrna, of the Numberous Clerical and Lay Neomartyrs Who Were Martyred at the Same Period in Asia Minor, and of Saint Euthymius, Bishop of Zela*]. Corinth: Πνοή, 1992

Καρζής, Θόδωρος. *Οι χαμένες πατρίδες των Ελλήνων: Μικρά Ασία, Κωνσταντινούπολη, Ανατ. Θράκη, Ανατ. Ρωμυλία, Πελαγονία, Βορ. Ήπειρος* [Karzes, Thodoros. *The Lost Homelands of the Greeks: Asia Minor, Constantinople, Eastern Thrace, Eastern Rumelia, Pelagonia, Northern Epirus*]. Athens: Βιβλιομεταφραστική, 1973.

Καρολίδης, Παύλος. *Σύγχρονος Ιστορία των Ελλήνων και των λοιπών λαών της Ανατολής από 1821 μέχρι 1921* [Karolides, Paulos. *The Contemporary History of the Greeks and of the Other Peoples of the East, from 1821 until 1921*]. 7 vols. Athens: Τυπογραφείον "Ερμής" Αλ. Βιτσικουνάκη, 1922-1929.

_____. *Ιστορία του Ελληνικού Έθνους (Κωνστ[αντίνου] Παπαρρηγοπούλου), Τόμος ΣΤ' – Συμπλήρωμα: Από της μετά του Ελληνικού Βασιλείου Ενώσεως Θεσσαλίας και Ηπείρου (1881) μέχρι του 1930* [*The History of the Hellenic Ethnos (by Konstantinos Paparregopoulos), Vol. VI – A Supplement: From the Union of Thessaly and Epirus (1881) with the Hellenic Kingdom until 1930*]. Athens: Ελευθερουδάκης, 1932.

Καρυοφυλλάκης, Δημήτριος. *Απομνημονεύματα αιχμαλωσίας στην Τουρκία*, επιμ. Αποστόλου Φωτούδη [Karyophyllakes, Demetrios, *Memoirs of Captivity in Turkey*, edited by Apostolos Photoudes]. Komotene: [n.p.], 1973.

Κασιάνης, Ελευθέριος Θ. *Τα Θυάτειρα (το Αξάρι): Η ιστορική πολιτεία της Μικράς Ασίας από τα αρχαία χρόνια ως τη Μικρασιατική καταστροφή* [Kasianes, Eleutherios T. *Thyateira (Axari)* [Akhisar]*: The Historic City of Asia Minor from Ancient Times until the Asia Minor Catastrophe*]. Athens: Εκδόσεις Ενώσεως Σμυρναίων, 1981.

Κασσιανίδου, Σταυρούλα. *Θυμούμαι από τότε: Ντοκουμέντο* [Kassianidou, Stauroula. *I Remember Since That Time: A Document*]. [Athens]: Νόμπελ, 1983.

[no author]. *Η καταστραφείσα Πέργαμος: Από την Μικρασιατικήν τραγωδίαν του 1922* [*Destroyed Pergamos: From the Tragedy of Asia Minor of 1922*]. Mytilene: Σύνδεσμος Περγαμηνών "Ο Άτταλος," 1926.

Καψής, Π. *Πως επήγαμε στη Σμύρνη και πως εφύγαμε* [Kapses, P. *How We Went to Smyrna and How We Left*]. Athens: [n.p.], 1934.

Καψής, Γιάννης Π. *Χαμένες πατρίδες: Από την απελευθέρωση μέχρι την καταστροφή* [Kapses, Giannes P. *Lost Homelands: From Liberation to Catastrophe*]. Athens: [n.p.], 1962;

_____. *Χαμένες πατρίδες: Από την απελευθέρωση στην καταστροφή της Σμύρνης* [*Lost Homelands: From Liberation to the Destruction of Smyrna*]. Athens: Νέα Σύνορα, 1989.

_____. *1922 Η Μαύρη Βίβλος* [*1922 The Black Book*]. Athens: Λιβάνης, 1992

[Κέντρο Μικρασιατικών Σπουδών]. *Η Έξοδος – Τόμος Α΄: Μαρτυρίες από τις επαρχίες των δυτικών Παραλίων της Μικρασίας.* Επιλογή κειμένων & επιμέλεια Φ. Δ. Αποστολόπουλου. [Centre for Asia Minor Studies. *Exodus – Volume I: Testimonies from the Districts of the Western Coast of Asia Minor.* Text Selection & ed. by P. D. Apostolopoulos]. Athens: Centre for Asia Minor Studies, 1980

_____. *Η Έξοδος – Τόμος Β΄: Μαρτυρίες από της επαρχίες της Κεντρικής και Νότιας Μικρασίας.* Επιμέλεια Γιάννη Μουρέλου [*Exodus – Volume II: Testimonies from the Districts of Central and Southern Asia Minor.* Edited by Giannes Mourelos]. Athens: Centre for Asia Minor Studies, 1982 (reprinted, 2004).

Κιτρομηλίδης, Πασχάλης Μ. *Συμβολή στη μελέτη της Μικρασιατικής τραγωδίας* [Kitromelides, Paschales M. A *Contribution to the Study of the Asia Minor Tragedy*]. Athens : [n.p.], 1972.

_____. *Ο εξισλαμισμός της Μικράς Ασίας και οι ιστορικές καταβολές των Ελληνοτουρκικών σχέσεων* [*The Islamization of Asia Minor and the Historical Roots of the Greco-Turkish Relations*]. Athens: [n.p.], 1975.

Κλεάνθης, Φάνης. Ν. *Ο φριχτός μήνας Σεπτέμβρης: Αναμνήσεις από τις στερνές στιγμές του Ελληνισμού της Μικρασίας, χρονικά και μαρτυρίες* [Kleanthes, Phanes. N. *The Horrific Month of September: Recollections from the Last Moments of Asia Minor Hellenism, Chronicles and Testimonies*]. Athens: [n.p.], 1973.

_____. *Έτσι χάσαμε τη Μικρασία: Ιστορική έρευνα* [*Thus We Lost Asia Minor: An Historical Investigation*]. Athens: Εστία, 1983.

_____. *Αλάτσατα: Η χαμένη πατρίδα μου: Ιστορία, λαογραφία, αναμνήσεις* [*Alatsata: My Lost Homeland: History, Folklore, Memories*]. Athens: [n.p.], 1987; reprinted, Athens: Σύλλογος Αλατσατιανών, 2003.

_____. *Η ελληνική Σμύρνη: Σελίδες από την ιστορία της, εικόνες από την ζωής της, και πλήρης εξιστόρηση της τραγωδίας του 1922* [*Greek Smyrna: Pages from Its History, Images from Its Life, and Complete Account of the Tragedy of 1922*]. Athens: Εστία, [1996].

Κλεομβρότου Ιάκωβος, Μητροπολίτης Σισανίου και Σιατίστης. *Ο Εθνομάρτυς Μητροπολίτης Κυδωνιών Γρηγόριος ο από Στρωμνίτσης* [*Iakovos Kleomvrotou. Metropolitan of Sisanion and Siatista. The Ethnomartyr Metropolitan of Cydoniæ Gregory, Formerly of Stromnitsa*]. Athens : [n.p.], 1956.

Κονόμου-Μαρδίκη, Γεωργία. *Τα μαύρα χρόνια της προσφυγιάς 1919-1923 και η βοήθεια από την Αμερική* [Konomou-Mardike, Georgia. *The Black Years of Refugeeship 1919-1923 and the Assistance from America*]. Athens: Τυπ. Β. Καρύδη, 1973.

Κοντογιάννης, Παντελής Μ. *Η ελληνικότης των νομών Προύσης και Σμύρνης* [Kontogiannes, Panteles M. *The Hellenicity of the Districts of Prousa and Smyrna*]. Athens: Σύλλογος προς Διάδοσιν Ωφελίμων Βιβλίων, 1919.

_____. *Γεωγραφία της Μικράς Ασίας: Φυσική σύστασις της χώρας, πολιτική γεωγραφία, φυσικός πλούτος* [*The Geography of Asia Minor: Natural Composition of the Country, Political Geography, Natural Resources*]. Athens: Τύποις Π. Α. Πετράκου, 1921; reprinted, Athens: Σύλλογος προς Διάδοσιν Ωφελίμων Βιβλίων, 1995.

_____. *Τουρκία και Τούρκοι* [*Turkey and the Turks*]. Athens: Ελευθερουδάκης, 1924.

Κοτρώτσος, Κ. *Από την αιχμαλωσίαν* [Kotrotsos, K. *From Captivity*]. Athens: [n.p.] 1923.

Κούλιγκας, Βασίλης. *Κίος 1912-1922: Αναμνήσεις ενός Μικρασιάτη* [Koulingas, Vasiles. *Kios 1912-1922: Memories of an Asia Minor* (*sc.* survivor)]. Athens/Ioannina: Δωδώνη, 1988.

_____. *Κίος 1912-1922: Σκόρπιες μνήμες* [*Kios 1912-1922: Scattered Memories*]. Athens: Δωδώνη, 1993.

_____. *Κίος η αλησμόνητη: Απ' όσα ακόμη θυμάμαι* [*Kios, the Unforgettable: From Whatever I still Remember*]. Athens/Giannina: Δωδώνη, 1995.

Κουλοχέρης, Ιάκωβος. Η Αμισός και τα πάθη της: Αναμνήσεις Ποντίου Δασκάλου [Koulocheres, Iakovos. *Amissos and Its Sufferings: Memories of a Pontian Teacher*]. Thessalonica: Αδελφοί Κυριακίδη, 1991.

Κουρτίδης, Θεόδωρος Π. *Η επαρχία Μελανθίας του Πόντου. Ιστορικά ενθυμήματα.* [Kourtidεs, Theodoros P. *The District of Melanthia* [Melet] *of the Pontus. Historical Recollections*]. Thessalonica: Έκδοσις «Παναγίας Σουμελά», 1975.

Κουτσογιαννόπουλος, Δημήτριος Σ. *Ανάμεσα στους αντάρτες του Πόντου* [Koutsogiannopoulos. Demetrios S. *Among the Guerrillas of the Pontus*]. Thessalonica: Μ. Τριανταφύλλου, 1936.

Κοφινάς, Γεώργιος Ν. *Περί του διωγμού των εν Τουρκία Ελλήνων κατά τον πόλεμον* [Kophinas, Georgios N. *On the Persecution of the Greeks in Turkey during the War*]. Athens: Εθνικόν Τυπογραφείον, 1919

Κράχτογλους, Δ. Κ. *Αι εν τη κωμοπόλει Καβάρνη και τοις πέριξ ελληνικοίς χωρίοις υπό των Κιρκασίων σφαγαί* [Krachtoglous, D. K. *The Massacres* (*sc.* Committed) *by the Circassians in the Town of Kabarne and in the Surrounding Greek Villages*]. Athens: Παπαλεξανδρή, 1878.

Κυνηγόπουλος, Νικόλαος Λ. *Η Πάφρα του Πόντου. Η Χώρα των Γενναίων. Ιστορική αναδρομή στις ρίζες των Παφραίων του Πόντου, τα σημαντικότερα γεγονότα που σημάδεψαν τη ζωή τους, μια μεγαλειώδης πορεία αίματος και θριάμβου* [Kynegopoulos, Nikolaos L. *Paphra* [Bafra] *of the Pontus, the Land of the Brave: Historical Retrospection into the Roots of the Paphraeans of the Pontus, the Most Significant Events That Marked Their Life, a Magnificent Journey of Blood and Triumph*]. Thessalonica: [n.p.], 1991.

Κυνηγόπουλος, Πολύκαρπος Κ. *Εκθέσεις περί των καταστροφών και σφαγών της επαρχίας Κολωνίας της Νικοπόλεως (Πόντου)* [Kynegopoulos, Polykarpos K. *Reports on the Destruction and Massacres in the Diocese of Kolonia of Nikopolis (of Pontus)*]. Constantinople: Τυπογραφείον Ε. Βασιλειάδου, 1919.

Κωνσταντίνου, Ιωάννης. *Η Μικρασιατική Καταστροφή κατά τον Αύγουστον του 1922* [Konstantinou, Ioannes. *The Asia Minor Catastrophe during August of 1922*]. Athens: Τυπογραφείον Ρυθμός, 1934.

Λακίδης, Σάββας. *Ιστορία των δεινοπαθημάτων των εν Θράκη ομογενών υπό των Νεοτούρκων* [Lakides, Savvas. *History of the Sufferings of the Greeks in Thrace* [inflicted] *by the Young Turks*]. Athens: Τυπογραφείον "Πατρίς," 1921.

Λαμέρας, Κωνσταντίνος Γ. *Η περί Μικράς Ασίας και των εν αυτή Κρυπτοχριστιανών διάλεξις* [Lameras, Konstantinos G. A *Discourse on Asia Minor and Crypto-Christians There*]. Athens: Γ. Η. Καλέργης, 1921; reprinted, Athens: Ελεύθερη Σκέψις, 1992.

_____ . *Το Μικρασιατικόν πρόβλημα* [*The Asia Minor Problem*]. Athens: Π. Α. Πετράκος, 1918.

_____ . *Η περί του χαρακτήρος των εν Τουρκία διωγμών διάλεξις... γενομένη εν τη αιθούση του Φιλολογικού Συλλόγου "Παρνασσού" τη 2α Ιουνίου 1921* [*Lecture on the Nature of the Persecutions in Turkey, Delivered in the Hall of the Philological Society "Parnassos" on 2 June 1921*]. Athens: Γ. Η. Καλέργης, 1921.

_____ . *Πόσοι και ποιοί οι κάτοικοι της Μικράς Ασίας μετά την ανταλλαγήν [How Many and Who Are the Inhabitants of Asia Minor after the Exchange* (sc. of Populations)]. Athens: [n.p.], 1929.

Λαμψίδης, Γεώργιος Ν. *Τοπάλ Οσμάν. Ένα χρονικό μιας άγνωστης ελληνικής τραγωδίας (1914-1924)* [Lampsides, Georgios N. *Topal Osman: The Chronicle of an Unknown Greek Tragedy (1914-1924)*]. Athens: Εκδόσεις Γ. Λαδιά, 1976.

Λαμψίδης, Οδυσσεύς. *Οι Έλληνες του Πόντου υπό τους Τούρκους (1461-1922) Α΄ Πολιτική Ιστορία* [Lampsides, Odysseus. *The Greeks of the Pontus under the Turks (1461-1922) I. Political History*]. Athens: [n.p.], 1957.

Λεονταρίτης, Απόλλων. *Το ιστορικόν μια ολεθρίας πλάνης: Χρονικόν των ομογενών του Αξαρίου κατά την Μικρασιατικήν συμφοράν του 1922* [Leontarites, Apollon. *The Record of a Disastrous Error: A Chronicle of the Greeks of Axarion* [Akhisar] *during the Asia Minor Disaster*]. Athens: Εκδόσεις Εστίας Νέας Σμύρνης, 1972.

_____ . *Τα Θυάτειρα: Το Αξάρι και το Ολοκαύτωμα αυτού – Ιστορική Μονογραφία* [*Thyateira: Axarion* [Akhisar] *and its Holocaust: A Historical Monograph*]. Athens: [n.p.], 1975.

Λοβέρδος, Σπυρίδων. *Ο Μητροπολίτης Σμύρνης Χρυσόστομος* [Loverdos, Spyridon. *Chrysostomos, the Metropolitan of Smyrna*]. Athens, [n.p.], 1929.

Λοϊζίδου-Γαληνού, Γλυκερία. *Ποντίων πάθη: Όσα έζησα και άκουσα* [Loizidou-Galenou, Glykeria. *The Sufferings of the Pontians: What I Lived Through and What I Heard*]. [Thessalonica]: Αδελφοί Κυριακίδη, 2005.

Μαζαράκης-Αινιάν, Αλέξανδρος. *Απομνημονεύματα* [Mazarakes-Ainian, Alexandros. *Memoirs*]. [Athens]: Εκδόσεις Ίκαρος, [1948].

Μαζαράκης-Αινιάν Ιωάννης Κ., Ed. *Η Σμύρνη καίγεται: Λεύκωμα με 53 φωτογραφίες* [Mazarakes-Ainian, Ioannεs K. *Smyrna Burning: Photo Album with 53 Photos*]. Athens : Ερμής, 1983.

Μαϊχός, Φίλιππας. *Φλόγες στη Μικρά Ασία: «Τραγωδία του Ελληνισμού», χρονικό* [Maichos, Philippas. *Flames in Asia Minor: "Tragedy of Hellenism," a Chronicle.* [Athens]: Ελληνικό Βιβλίο, [1978].

Μακκάς, Λέων Δ. *Η Γαλλία και η Γερμανία ενώπιον του Ελληνισμού* [Makkas, Leon D. *France and Germany Facing Hellenism*]. Athens: Α. Παπακωνσταντίνου, 1915.

Μακρίδης, Δημήτρης Α. Γ. *Από το μεγάλον εθνικόν δράμα: Μετά την Καταστροφήν* [Makrides, Demetres A. G. *From the Great National Drama: After the Catastrophe*]. Piraeus: Ζάννειο Ορφανοτροφείο, 1926.

Μακρίδης, Ν. Γ. *Ο αλύτρωτος Ελληνισμός και η Αγία Σοφία* [Makrides, N. G. *Unredeemed Hellenism and Hagia Sophia*]. Athens : [n.p.], 1922.

Μαθιώτη, Κυριακή. *Αϊδίνι. Μια πόλη – Μια ιστορία* [Mathiote, Kyriake. *Aidini* [Aydin]*: A City – A History*]. Thessalonica: Εκδόσεις Κώδικας, 1995.

Μαλλιαρός, Ιάκωβος, Μητροπολίτης Μηθύμνης. *Από το διωγμό του 1922: Ζωντανές σκηνές από τη δραματική περιπέτεια δύο παιδιών: Για τα 60 χρόνια από τότε 1922-1982* [Malliaros, Iakovos, Metropolitan of Methymne. *From the Persecution of 1922: Live Scenes from the Dramatic Adventure of Two Children: On the Occasion of the Sixty-Year Anniversary 1922-1982*]. Mytilene: Ευστράτιος Κ. Μυκονιάτης, 1982.

Μανωλεδάκης, Ιωάννης Ε. *Το παιδομάζωμα κατά τους χρόνους της δουλείας: Το σύγχρονον και η γενοκτονία ως μέσον επικρατήσεως δια της παρόδου των αιώνων* [Manoledakes, Ioannes E. *Child-Abduction* (sc. Devshirme) *during the Years of Slavery: Its Contemporary* (Form) *and Genocide as Means of Domination through the Ages*]. Thessalonica: Εταιρεία Μακεδονικών Σπουδών, 1953

Μαρουδής, Γιώργος Δ. *Η πορεία* [Maroudes, Giorgos D. *The March*]. Athens: Τυπ. Β. Καρύδη, [1976].

Ματαράγκας, Α. *Μαύραι ημέραι των Ελληνικωτάτων επαρχιών Κυδωνιών και Μοσχονησίων: Ακριβής εξιστόρηση των διωγμών, εκτοπισμών και λοιπών δεινοπαθημάτων αυτών από του 1914-1919 εξ αυθεντικών πηγών, αυτόπτων μαρτύρων και επισήμων εκθέσεων* [Matarangas, A. *The Dark Days of the Most Greek of Dioceses of Cydoniae and Moschonesia: An Accurate Narrative of the Persecutions, Deportations and Ordeals between 1914-1919* [Drawn] *from Authentic Sources, Eyewitnesses and Official Reports*]. Smyrna: [n.p.], 1919.

Μεγαλοκονόμος, Μανόλης. *Η Σμύρνη από το αρχείο ενός φωτορεπόρτερ* [Megalokonomos, Manoles. *Smyrna from the Archives of a Photojournalist*]. Athens: Ερμής, 1992.

Μέντορος του Πρωτέως. *Μαύρον ημερονύκτιον. Η φρικαλέα τραγωδία της Παλαιάς Φωκαίας Μαΐου 30-31, 1914* [Mentor of Proteus. *The Black Journal. The Horrific Tragedy of Old Phocaea, May 30-31, 1914*]. Athens: Τυπ. Φραντζεσκάκη, 1915.

Μεταξάς Ιωάννης. *Η Ιστορία του Εθνικού Διχασμού (και της Μικρασιατικής Καταστροφής)* [Metaxas, Ioannes. *The History of the National Schism (and of the Asia Minor Catastrophe)*], Athens: Εκδόσεις Καθημερινής, 1935.

Μηλιώρης, Νίκος Ε. *Τα Βούρλα της Μικράς Ασίας: Μέρος Α΄: Ιστορικά* [Meliores, Nikos E. *Vourla of Asia Minor: Part I: History*]. Athens: [n.p], 1957.

_____. *Οι κρυπτοχριστιανοί: Μελέτη* [*The Crypto-Christians: A Study*]. Athens: Εκδόσεις Ενώσεως Σμυρναίων, 1962.

_____. *Η μικρασιατική τραγωδία στη λογοτεχνία και στην τέχνη* [*The Asia Minor Tragedy in Literature and the Arts*]. Athens: [n.p.], 1967.

Μικρασιανός Γ. *Πώς η Γερμανία κατέστρεψε τον Ελληνισμό της* Τουρκίας [Mikrasianos, G. *How Germany Destroyed the Hellenism of Turkey*]. Athens: Γ. Α. Πετράκου, 1918.

Miller, William. *Ιστορία του ελληνικού λαού 1821-1921,* μετάφρασις Κώστα Καιροφύλλα [Miller, William. *History of the Greek People 1821-1921,* translated by Kostas Kairophyllas]. Athens: Εκδόσεις "Τύπος," 1924.

Μισαηλίδης, Κώστας. *Η καταστροφή και οι τελευταίες μέρες της Σμύρνης* [Misaelides, K. *The Catastrophe and the Last Days of Smyrna*]. Athens: [n.p.], 1923.

Μησίου, Σοφία. *Κίος, Οδησσός, Αθήνα: Πορεία ζωής μιας οικογένειας Ελλήνων της Μ. Ασίας* [Mesiou, Sophia. *Kios, Odessa, Athens: The Course of Life of a Family of Greeks from Asia Minor*]. Athens: Δωδώνη, 2005.

Μιχαηλίδου, Ανθούλα. *Για όσους ζήσανε* [Michaelidou, Anthoula. *For Those Who Survived*]. Athens: [n.p.], 1929.

Μοσχονήσιος, Π. Ι. Η Ωραία Σμύρνη νεκρόπολις: Η μεγάλη Ελλάς θρηνεί τα Μικρασιατικά θύματα της Κωνσταντινικής προδοσίας [Moschonesios, P. I. *The Beautiful Smyrna Necropolis: Greater Hellas Mourns the Asia Minor Victims of the Constantinian Betrayal*]. Athens: [n.p.], 1922.

Μοσχόπουλος, Νικηφόρος. *Το Αρμενικόν ζήτημα: Συμβολή εις την διπλωματική ιστορίαν* [Moschopoulos, Nikephoros. *The Armenian Question: A Contribution to Diplomatic History*]. Athens: Α. Βιτσικουνάκη, 1924.

_____. *Αι νέαι τουρκικαί ιστορικαί και εθνολογικαί θεωρίαι* [*The New Turkish Historical and Ethnological Theories*]. Athens: Εθνικόν Τυπογραφείον, 1935.

Μουμτζής, Τάσος Ι. *Αναμνήσεις απ' το Αϊβαλί* [Moumtzes, Tasos I. *Memories from Aivali* (Ayvalik)]. Thessalonica: [n.p.], 1978.

Μουράτ, Τζον [Murat, John]. *Ανατομία στην Αιτία και στην Αφορμή για την Μικρασιατική Καταστροφή του 1922* [*Anatomy of the Reason and the Cause of the Asia Minor Catastrophe of 1922*]. Miami: M. P. Academus, 1993.

Μπέλλου-Θρεψιάδη, Αντιγόνη. Μορφές *Μακεδονομάχων και τα Ποντιακά του Γερμανού Καραβαγγέλη* [Bellou-Threpsiade, Antigone. *Portraits of Macedonomachs and the Pontiaca of Germanos Karavangeles* [Metropolitan of Amasia in the Pontus]. Athens: Μαυρίδης, 1983; reprinted, Athens: Εκδόσεις Τροχαλία 1992.

Μπότσαρης, Δημήτριος Νότης Τ. *Η Μικρά Ασία και ο Ελληνισμός* [Botsares, Demetrios Notes T. *Asia Minor and Hellenism*]. Athens: Μαντζεβελάκης, 1919.

_____. *Οι νεκροί ήρωες* [*The Dead Heroes*]. Smyrna [n.p.], 1920.

Μπουλαλάς, Κλεάνθης Κ. *Η μικρασιατική εκστρατεία 1919-1922 (με τον φακόν της ιστορικής αληθείας). Αίτια και αφορμαί της Εθνικής Συμφοράς - Μεγαλεία και Αθλιότητες - Σφάλματα και διαφυγούσαι ευκαιρίαι* [Boulalas, Kleanthes K. *The Asia Minor Campaign 1919-1922 (Under the Lens of Historical Truth). Reasons and Causes of the National Disaster - Splendor and Misery - Errors and Lost Opportunities*]. Athens: [n.p.], 1959.

Nicol, E. *Οι σύμμαχοι και η κρίση στην Ανατολή: Ο ρόλος των συμμάχων έξι μήνες πριν από την καταστροφή ή γιατί πρέπει να καταστραφεί ο Μικρασιατικός Ελληνισμός* [*The Allies and the Crisis in the East: The Role of the Allies Six Months before the Catastrophe, or Why Asia Minor Hellenism Must Be Destroyed*. Athens: Ειρμός, 1990.

Νοταράς, Μιχάλης Ι. *Εις την Ιωνίαν, Αιολίαν και Λυδίαν, πριν πενήντα χρόνια: Αι ελληνικαί κοινότητες της περιοχής της Συνθήκης των Σεβρών και η εθνολογική σύνθεσις του πληθυσμού: Συμβάντα και αναμνήσεις της εποχής εκείνης* [Notaras, Michales I. *In Ionia, Æolia and Lydia, Fifty Years Ago: The Greek Communities of the Region of the Treaty of Sevres and the Ethnological Composition of the Population: Events and Recollections from that Period*]. Athens: Τυπ. Κωνσταντινίδη και Κ. Μιχαλά, 1972.

Ντάμπος, Κωνσταντίνος. Μικρά Ασία 1914-1922: *Το Χρονικό του ανθυπασπιστή Κωνσταντίνου Ντάμπου* [Dampos, Konstantinos. *Asia Minor 1914-1922: The Chronicle of Warrant Officer Konstantinos Dampos*]. Chios: Εκδόσεις Πελινναίο, 2005.

Οικονομίδης, Δημήτριος Η. *Ο Πόντος και τα δίκαια του εν αυτώ Ελληνισμού από χωρογραφικής, εθνογραφικής και ιστορικής απόψεως* [Oikonomides, Demetrios E. *Pontus and the Rights of Local Hellenism from a Geographic, Ethnographic and Historical Point of View*]. Athens: Σιδέρης, 1920.

[Οικουμενικόν Πατριαρχείον Κωνσταντινουπόλεως]. *Τακρίρια τινά του Οικουμενικού Πατριαρχείου προς την Υψηλήν Πύλην περί του Ζητήματος των Σταυριωτών και περί εξισλαμίσεων* [(Ecumenical Patriarchate of Constantinople). *Some Reports by the Ecumenical Patriarchate to the Sublime Porte about the Issue of the Staurioton and about Islamizations*]. Constantinople: Εκ του Πατριαρχικού Τυπογραφείου, 1909.

Παγτζίλογλου, Μίλτος. *Η γενοκτονία των Ελλήνων και των Αρμενίων της Μικράς Ασίας* [Pagtziloglou, Miltos. *The Genocide of the Greeks and of the Armenians of Asia Minor*]. Athens: [Self published], 1988.

Παντελιάς, Δημήτριος Γ. *Αίμα και πύρ: Οι τελευταίες μέρες της Σμύρνης* [Pantelias, Demetrios G. *Blood and Fire: The Last Days of Smyrna*]. Athens: [n.p.], 1976.

Παπαγιαννάκης, Ελευθέριος Ν. *Η τραγωδία του Ελληνισμού της Εγγύς Ανατολής 1908-1922* [Papagiannakes, Eleutherios N. *The Tragedy of Near Eastern Hellenism 1908-1922*]. Athens: [n.p.], 2001.

Παπαγρηγοριάδης, Σάββας. *Η φωνή της τέφρας και του αίματος της Ασιατικής Ελλάδος* [Papagregoriades, Savvas. *The Voice of the Ashes and of the Blood of the Asian Greece*]. Athens: Τυπ. Ι. Βάρτσου, 1923.

Παπαδόπουλος, Άνθιμος Α. *Ο υπόδουλος Ελληνισμός της Ασιατικής Ελλαδος εθνικώς και γλωσσικώς εξεταζόμενος* [Papadopoulos, Anthimos A. *The Enslaved Hellenism of Asiatic Greece Ethnically and Linguistically Examined*]. Athens: Ι. Ν. Σιδέρης, 1919.

_____. *Χρύσανθος Αρχιεπίσκοπος Αθηνών ο από Τραπεζούντος (1881-1949)* [*Chrysanthos Archbishop of Athens, formerly* [Metropolitan] *of Trebizond (1881-1949)*]. Athens: Απατσίδης, 1950.

Παπαδόπουλος, Γιάννης Κ. *Ανταλλάξιμοι Καππαδόκες: Οδοιπορικό μέσα στα χρόνια της Μικρασιατικής καταστροφής* [Papadopoulos, Giannes K. *Exchangeable Cappadocians: An Itinerary during the Time of the Asia Minor Catastrophe*]. [Volos]: [n.p.], [2008].

Παπαδόπουλος, Νικόλας. *Τουρκικά Ντοκουμέντα για τη Μικρασιατική Καταστροφή: Η Αλήθεια από το στόμα των Τούρκων* [Papadopoulos, Nikolas. *Turkish Documents about the Asia Minor Catastrophe: The Truth from the Mouth of the Turks*]. Athens: Μαυρίδης, 1985.

Παπαευγενίου, Αθανάσιος. *Η Ελληνική Εκκλησία εν Θράκη: Τούρκοι – Βούλγαροι: Καταστροφαί Ναών και Μονών, Φόνοι, Εξορίαι και Κακοποιήσεις Κληρικών 1912-1920* [Papaeugeniou, Athanasios. *The Greek Church in Thrace: Turks – Bulgarians: Destruction of Churches and Monasteries, Murders, Exiles and Mistreatment of Clergy 1912-1920*]. Thessalonica: Μ. Τριανταφύλλου, [1926].

Παπαζώης, Τριαντάφυλλος Δ. *Το αρχαίο Πάνιο (Πάνιδο) Ανατ. Θράκης* [Papazoes, Triantaphyllos D. *Ancient Panio[n] (Panido) in Eastern Thrace*]. Thessalonica: [n.p.], 1988.

Παπαθεοδωρίδης, Θ. *Μαρτυρολόγιον του εν Πόντω Ελληνισμού* [Papatheodorides, T. *A Martyrology of Pontian Hellenism*]. Constantinople: [n.p.], 1920.

Παπακυριακόπουλος, Ι. Π., Επιμ. *Αφηγήσεις ενός ναυτικού αιχμαλώτου* [Papakyriakopoulos, I. P., Ed. Accounts of a Naval Prisoner of War]. Athens: Υπουργείον Ναυτικών, 1923.

Παπαπαναγιώτου, Γερμανός. *Μικρασιατική Καταστροφή* [Papapanagiotou, Germanos.*The Asia Minor Catastrophe*]. Chicago: G. D. Clougher, 1924.

Παπάς, Νεόφυτος. *Εθνική συμφορά: Ήτοι θρήνοι Ποντίων, Σμυρναίων και εν γένει πάντων των ανταλλαξίμων προσφύγων* [Papas, Neophytos. National Disaster: That Is the Laments of the Pontians, the Smyrnaeans and Generally of All the Exchanged Refugees]. Thessalonica: Μ. Τριανταφύλλου, (1924).

Παραρά, Ελένη Α. *Η καταστροφή του 1922 όπως την έζησα: Αναμνήσεις απ' τα Βουρλά* [Parara, Elene A. *The Catastrophe of 1922 as I Experienced It: Recollections from Vourla*]. Athens: [n.p.], 1966.

Παραρά-Ευτυχίδου, Νίτσα. *Ένας Βουρλιώτης αιχμάλωτος των Τούρκων 1922-1923* [Parara-Eutychidou, Nitsa. *An* [Inhabitant of] *Vourla, Prisoner of the Turks 1922-1923*]. Athens : [n.p.], 1979; reprinted, Athens : [n.p.], 1986.

Παρασκευόπουλος, Λεωνίδας. *Αναμνήσεις 1896-1920* [Paraskeuopoulos, Leonidas. *Recollections 1896-1920*]. 2 vols. Athens: Πυρσός, 1933.

Παντελιάς, Δημήτριος Γ. *Αίμα και πύρ : Οι τελευταίες μέρες της Σμύρνης* [Pantelias, Demetrios G. *Blood and Fire: The Last Days of Smyrna*]. Athens: [n.p.], 1976.

Πατριαρχείον [Οικουμενικόν] Κωνσταντινουπόλεως. *Μαύρη Βίβλος διωγμών και μαρτυρίων του εν Τουρκία Ελληνισμού (1914-1918).* [Patriarchate (Ecumenical) of Constantinople. *The Black Book of Persecutions and Martyrdoms of the Greeks of Turkey (1914-1918)*]. Constantinople: Πατριαρχικόν Τυπογραφείον, 1919; reprinted, Athens: Αρσενίδης, 1996.

Παυλίδης, Ελευθέριος Δ. *Πώς και διατί εματαιώθη η δημοκρατία του Πόντου* [Paulides, Eleutherios D. *How and Why the Republic of Pontus was Thwarted*]. Athens: Νικόλαος Απατσίδης, 1956.

Παυλίδης Ι., *Σελίδες ιστορίας αίματος και θυσίας Πόντου και Μικράς Ασίας* [Paulides, I. *History Pages of Blood and Sacrifice of the Pontus and Asia Minor*]. Thessalonica, 1979.

Πεγιάδης, Λεωνίδας. *Οι διωγμοί της Θράκης και η διάσωσις της Γέννης* [Pegiades, Leonidas. *The Persecutions of Thrace and the Saving of Genna*]. Constantinople: Πατριαρχικόν Τυπογραφείον, 1920.

Περαντώνης, Γιάννης. *Λεξικόν των Νεομαρτύρων* [Perantones, Giannes. *Dictionary of the Neomartyrs*], 3 vols. Athens: Εκκλησία της Ελλάδος, 1972.

_____. *Τα αίτια και αι αφορμαί του μαρτυρίου των νεομαρτύρων [The Reasons and the Causes of the Martyrdom of the Neomartyrs*]. Athens: [n.p.], 1971.

[Η] Περίθαλψις των Προσφύγων 1917-1920– Δυτική Θράκη, Ανατολική Θράκη, Μικρά Ασία, Βόρειος Ήπειρος, Ανατολ. Μακεδονία, Νότιος Ρωσσία, Πόντος, Ρουμανία, Δωδεκάνησα [*Refugee Relief 1917-1920– Western Thrace, Eastern Thrace, Asia Minor, Northern Epirus, Eastern Macedonia, Southern Russia, Pontus, Romania, the Dodecanese (Islands)*]. Athens: Τυπογραφείον Κ. Θεοδωρόπουλου, 1920.

Πισσάνος, Αντώνης Β. *Αιχμάλωτοι του Κεμάλ: Πρωτοφανή μαρτύρια και ανελέητες σφαγές. Το καταπληκτικόν ημερολόγιον του υπό των τούρκων αιχμαλωτισθέντος συγγραφέως* [Pissanos, Antones, V. *Prisoners of Kemal: Unprecedented Tortures and Merciless Massacres: The Amazing Diary of the Author, Prisoner of War of the Turks*]. Athens: Πρόοδος, 1978.

Πληζιώτης, Χαράλαμπος. *Αναμνήσεις του μετώπου, 1920-1921: Μικρά Ασία και Θράκη*, επιμ. Μ. Ρίζου-Κουρουπού [Pleziotes, Charalampos. *Recollections from the Front, 1920-1921: Asia Minor and Thrace*, ed. by M. Rizou-Kouroupou]. Athens: Κέντρο Μικρασιατικών Σπουδών, 1991.

Πολίτης, Κοσμάς. *Χρυσόστομος ο Σμύρνης* [Polites, Kosmas. *Chrysostom of Smyrna*]. Athens: Εφημ. *Πατρίς*, 1934.

Πουρτσουκλής, Δανιήλ, Μητροπολίτης Καισαριανής, Βύρωνος και Υμηττού *Οι εσφαγμένοι δια τον λόγον του Θεού και δια την μαρτυρίαν του Αρνίου* [Pourtsoukles, Daniel, Metropolitan of Kaisariane, Byron and Hymettus. Those Slaughtered for the Word of God and as Witness of the Lamb]. Athens: Μητρόπολις Καισαριανής, Βύρωνος και Υμητού, 2008.

Πρινιωτάκης, Παντελής. *Ατομικόν ημερολόγιον: Μικρά Ασία, 1919-1922*, επιμέλεια Ν. Α. Καβαδδίας [Priniotakes, Panteles. *Personal Diary: Asia Minor, 1919-1922*, edited by N. A. Kavvadias]. Athens: Εστία, 1998.

Προκοπίου, Σωκράτης Α. *Σαν ψέμματα και σαν αλήθεια; Τα τελευταία χρόνια: Μικρασιατικόν ιστορικόν μυθιστόρημα με εικόνας* [Prokopiou, Sokrates, *Lies or Truth? The Last Years: Historical Novel with Images from Asia Minor*]. Athens: Μέλισσα, 1928; Reprinted, [Athens]: Δαμιανός, [2003].

Πρωτονοτάριος, Στυλιανός Β. *Η προδοθείσα Ελλάς: Τα αίτια της καταστροφής της Μικράς Ασίας και της Αν. Θράκης επί τη βάσει επισήμων εγγράφων και αναμφισβητήτων γεγονότων* [Protonotarios, Stylianos B. *Greece Betrayed: The Causes of the Catastrophe in Asia Minor and Eastern Thrace based on Official Documents and Undisputed Events*]. Athens: Τύποις "Κοινωνίας," 1922.

Πώρος, Σπύρος Δ. *Σμυρναϊκή τραγωδία: Έμμετρο προσφυγικό δράμα εις πράξεις τρεις* [Poros, Spyros. Smyrnaean Tragedy: Drama on Refugees in Three Acts]. Athens: [n.p.] 1926.

Ravand, A. *Ιδού, διατί, πότε...: Τι μου είπαν εις την Σμύρνην* [Ravand A. *Behold, Why, When! What They Told Me in Smyrna*]. Constantinople: [n.p.], 1922.

Ρακιτζής, Σταύρος Ι. *Στα ίχνη των μαρτύρων* [Rakitzes, Stauros I. *In the Traces of the Martyrs*]. Thessalonica: [n.p.], 1984.

Ράλλη, Βασιλική. *Πατρίδα αξέχαστη Μικρά Ασία: Η τραγωδία του μικρασιατικού ελληνισμού μέσα από την ιστορία μιας μοσχονησιώτικης οικογένειας* [Ralle, Vasilike. *Asia Minor, Unforgetable Homeland: The Tragedy of Asia Minor Hellenism through the Story of a Family from Moschonesia*]. Athens: Ακρίτας, 1995.

_____. *Μνήμες από τη Μικρά Ασία* [*Memories from Asia Minor*]. Athens: Ίνδικτος, 2004.

_____. *Ο Γολγοθάς του Ελληνισμού της Ανατολής: Αληθινές ιστορίες από την καταστροφή* [*The Golgotha of Hellenism of the East: True Stories from the Catastrophe*]. [Vatopaidion of Chalkidike]: Μονή Οσίου Αρσενίου του Καππαδόκη, 2007.

Ροδάκης, Περικλής Δ. *Ο τουρκικός εθνικισμός, η γενοκτονία των Αρμενίων και το ξερίζωμα του ελληνισμού της Μικράς Ασίας* [Rodakes, Perikles. *Turkish Nationalism, the Armenian Genocide and the Uprooting of Asia Minor Hellenism*]. Athens: Λαϊκό Αρμενικό Κίνημα, 1986.

_____, *Η ιστορία του Πόντου: από την τουρκική κατάκτηση ως την γενοκτονία και τον ξεριζωμό* [Rodakes, Perikles. *The History of the Pontus: From the Turkish Conquest to the Genocide and the Uprooting*]. Athens: Γόρδιος, 2004.

Ροδάς, Μιχαήλ. *Πώς η Γερμανία κατέστρεψε τον Ελληνισμό της Τουρκίας* [Rodas, Michael. *How Germany Destroyed Hellenism in Turkey*]. Athens: Π. Α. Πετράκος, 1916.

_____. *Η Σμύρνη, οι νεκροί και η ιστορία μας* [*Smyrna, the Dead and Our History*]. Athens: Σύνδεσμος Εθνικής Σωτηρίας, 1923.

_____. *Η Ελλάδα στη Μικρασία: Απομνημονεύματα* [*Greece in Asia Minor: Memoirs*]. Athens: [n.p.], 1950.

Ρωνάς, Σωκράτης. *Γκιαούρ Σμύρνη* [Ronas, Sokrates. *Giavur Smyrna* (Izmir)]. Athens: [n.p.], 1952.

Σακκάς, Γεώργιος Η. *Η Ιστορία των Ελλήνων της Τριπόλεως του Πόντου: Ιστορική αφήγηση* [Sakkas, Georgios E. *The History of the Greeks of Tripolis* (Terebolu) *of the Pontus: An Historical Account*]. Athens-Nicaea: Νικόλαος Απατσίδης, 1957; reprinted, Athens-Nicaea: [n.p.], 1979, and Athens: Έκδοσις Αδελφότητος Τριπολιτών του Πόντου και Περιχώρων "Ο Αρχιστράτηγος Μιχαήλ," 1990.

Σακκάρης, Γεώργιος. *Ιστορία των Κυδωνιών* [Sakkares, Georgios. *The History of Kydoniai* (Ayvalik)]. Athens: Α. Βιτσικουνάκης, 1920; reprinted, Athens: Έκδοση της Ένωσης Κυδωνιατών, 1982.

[Σ.Κ.]. *Σκηναί φρίκης από την Μικρασιατικήν τραγωδίαν* [S.K. *Scenes of Horror from the Asia Minor Tragedy*]. Athens: [n.p.], 1930.

Σακελλαρόπουλος, Κωνσταντίνος Μ. *Η σκιά της Δύσεως: Ιστορία μιας καταστροφής* [Sakellaropoulos, Konstantinos M. *The Shadow of the West: The History of a Catastrophe*]. Athens: Εκδόσεις Αετός, 1954; reprinted, second edition with supplements, Athens: [n.p.], 1961.

Σαμουηλίδης, Χρήστος Σ. *Μαύρη Θάλασσα (Χρονικό από την τραγωδία του Πόντου)* [Samouelides, Chrestos S. *The Black Sea (A Chronicle from the Tragedy of the Pontus)*]. Athens: Ιωλκός, 1970; reprinted, Athens: Εστία, 1976, 1994.

_____. *Ακριτική γενιά: Χρονικό της αντίστασης του Πόντου* [*Acritic Generation: A Chronicle from the Resistance in the Pontus*]. Thessalonica: Αδελφοί Κυριακίδη, 1992; reprinted, new edition, *Ακριτική γενιά: Στο φλεγόμενο Πόντο* [*Acritic Generation: In the Burning Pontus*]. Athens: Νέα Σύνορα, 1999.

_____. *Ιστορία του Ποντιακού Ελληνισμού* [*History of the Pontic Hellenism*]. Athens: Αλκύων, [1986]; reprinted, Thessalonica: Αδελφοί Κυριακίδη, 1991; reprinted a new, expanded edition, Athens: Α. Α. Λιβάνης, 2002.

_____. *Το Χρονικό του Καρς* [*The Chronicle of Kars*]. Athens: Γκοβόστης, [1988]; second, expanded edition, *Το Χρονικό του Καρς και η Ματωμένη Δημοκρατία του Πόντου* [*The Chronicle of Kars and the Bloodied Republic of the Pontus*] Thessalonica: Αδελφοί Κυριακίδη, 2010.

_____. *Η Αμισός (Σαμψούντα) και η περιφέρειά της* [*Amisos (Samsoun) and its Surrounding Area*]. Thessalonica: Αδελφοί Κυριακίδη, 2004.

Σαράντης, Σαράντης Γ. *Η Πατρίδα μου η Λάμψακος. Μνήμες που δεν χάνονται, επιμ. Γιάννη Κορίδη* [Sarantes, Sarantes Γ. *My Homeland Lampsacus. Indelible Memories*, ed. by Giannes Korides]. [Athens]: Ιωλκός, [1987].

Σβολόπουλος, Δημήτριος Κ. *Η Θράκη υπό την Ελληνικήν Διοίκησιν* [Svolopoulos, Demetrios K. *Thrace under Hellenic Administration*]. Constantinople: [n.p.], 1922.

Σγόντζος, Γιάννης Χ. *Στα χέρια του Κεμάλ* [Sgontzos, Giannεs C. *In the Hands of Kemal]. Athens*: [n.p.], 1933.

_____. *Πορεία μαρτύρων: Χρονικό από τη μικρασιατική αιχμαλωσία του 1922* [*The March of Martyrs: A Chronicle from the Asia Minor Captivity of 1922*]. Athens: [n.p.], 1966.

Σιανλόγλους Ι.Χ. *Από την τραγωδίαν του Πόντου, ήτοι σύντομος περιγραφή της γενικής θλιβεράς του εν Πόντω ομογενούς ελληνικού πληθυσμού καταστάσεως κατά τον διεξαχθέντα τελευταίον άχαριν ελληνοτουρκικόν πόλεμον* [Sianloglous I. C. *From the Tragedy of the Pontus, or a Short Description of the General Tragic Situation of the Greek Population in the Pontus during the Last Unfortunate Greco-Turkish War*]. 1923; reprinted, Thessalonica: Αδελφοί Κυριακίδη, 2007.

Σκαλιέρης Γεώργιος, Κ. *Τα δίκαια των εθνοτήτων εν Τουρκία (1453-1921). Πολιτικαί Σελίδες* [Skalieres, Georgios K. *The Rights of Nationalities in Turkey (1453-1921). Political Pages*]. Athens: Κίμων Ι. Θεοδωρόπουλος, 1921; reprinted (with an Introduction by K. Σβολόπουλος), Athens: Τροχαλία, 1997.

_____, *Λαοί καί φυλαί της Μικράς: Μετά Πινάκων και Χαρτών* [*Peoples and Races of Asia Minor: Including Tables and Maps*]. Athens: Τυπογραφείον "Τύπος," 1922; reprinted Athens: Ρήσος, 1990.

_____, *Πόσοι και ποιοί οι κάτοικοι της Μικράς Ασίας μετά την ανταλλαγήν* [*How Many and Who Are the Inhabitants of Asia Minor after the Exchange* [of populations]. Athens: Μικρασιατικός Σύλλογος "Ανατολή," 1929.

Σκιαδάς, Στέργιος. *Σμύρνη: Ποιήματα* [Skiadas, Stergios. *Smyrna: Poems*]. Athens: Τυπ. Κωνσταντινίδη και Μιχαλά, 1953; reprinted Athens: Το Ελληνικό Βιβλίο, 1962.

Σκίπης, Σωτήριος. *Προσφυγικοί καημοί: 1923* [Skipes, Soterios. *Refugee Suffering*]. Athens: [n.p.], 1924.

[Σκουλούδης, Α. Γ.] *Έρημες Χώρες, Νεκρές Πολιτείες ανά τον Ελληνικόν Πόντον 1919: Σημειώσεις του ειδικού απεσταλμένου της "Πατρίδος" των Αθηνών κ. Α. Γ. Σκουλούδη από ένα ταξίδι εις τους τόπους των διωγμών* [Skouloudes, A. G. *Deserted Lands, Dead Cities across the Hellenic Pontus: Notes of the Special Correspondent of "Patris" of Athens Mr. A. G. Skouloudes of a Voyage to the Places of Persecution*]. Athens: [n.p.], 1919; Reprinted, Thessalonica: Αδελφοί Κυριακίδη, 1987.

Σολομωνίδης, Χρήστος Σ. *Ύμνος και Θρήνος της Σμύρνης* [Solomonides C.S. *Ode and Plaint of Smyrna*]. Athens: Αρ. Μαυρίδη, 1956.

_____, *Χρυσόστομος Σμύρνης* [*Chrysostom of Smyrna*] 2 vols. Athens: Εθνική Μνημοσύνη, [196-?] and 1971; reprinted, Athens: Ειρμός, 1993.

_____, *Ο αφανισμός της Σμύρνης. Η θυσία του Χρυσοστόμου. Για τα 50 χρόνια της Καταστροφής* [*The Extermination of Smyrna: The Sacrifice of* [Metropolitan] *Chrysostom.* [In Memoriam] *of the 50 Years Since the Catastrophe*]. Athens: Έκδοσις Συλλόγου Φοιτησάντων εις την Ευαγγελικήν Σχολήν Σμύρνης, 1972.

_____, *Η Εκκλησίας της Σμύρνης* [*The Church of Smyrna*]. Athens: Τυπ. Μαυρίδη, 1960.

Σπανομανώλης, Χρήστος. *Αιχμάλωτοι των Τούρκων: Αύγουστος 1922–Αύγουστος 1923* [Spanomanoles, Chrestos. *Prisoners of the Turks: August 1922–August 1923*]. Athens: Εστία, 1969.

Σταμούλης, Μ. Α. *Φύρδην Μίγδην: Σελίδες ημερολογίου από την Σηλυβρίαν: Αναμνήσεις απ' όσα ενθυμούμαι* [Stamoules, M. A. *Here and There: Pages from a Diary from Selybria: Recollections from What I Remember*]. Athens: [n. p.], 1959.

Στούρνας, Κώστας. *Σμύρνη: Χρονικό του 1922* [Stournas, Kostas. *Smyrna: A Chronicle of 1922*]. Athens: [n.p.], [1963].

Στυλιανού, Πέτρος. *Οι τουρκικές σφαγές στη Σμύρνη στα 1922* [Stylianou, Petros. *The Turkish Massacres in Smyrna in 1922*]. Leukosia: [n.p.],[n.d.]; reprinted Leukosia: Θεοπρές, 1984.

[no author]. *Συνοπτική Έκθεσις των Διωγμών και Σφαγών του Πόντου 1914-1922: Έκθεσις του Κεντρικού Συμβουλίου των Επαρχιών του Πόντου* [*Summary Report of the Persecutions and the Massacres of the Pontus 1914-1922: A Report of the Central Council of the Provinces of the Pontus*]. Constantinople: Τύποις Π. Αγγελίδου, 1922.

Σχινάς, Αντώνης. *Η Σμύρνη στις φλόγες* [Schinas, Antones. *Smyrna in Flames*]. Athens: [n.p.], 1971.

_____, Από την τραγωδία της Σμύρνης [*From the Tragedy of Smyrna*]. Athens: [n.p.], 1973.

[no author] *Τακρίριον περί των κατά των Χριστιανών διαφόρων βιαιοπραγιών και κακώσεων* [*Report Concerning Various Acts of Violence and Injuries Against Christians*]. [n.p.]: [n.p.], [1911].

[no author] *Οι τελευταίες μέρες της Χριστιανικής Καισάρειας: Εικόνες από μακρινό ταξίδι* [*The Last Days of Christian Caesarea: Images from a Distant Journey*]. Athens: Τυπογραφείον Α. Ραφτάνη, [19x?].

Τζιμοπούλου, Μαρκησία. *Πρόσφυγες στην Κέρκυρα: Χρονικό 1922-1923* [Tzimopoulou, Markesia. *Refugees in Corfu: A Chronicle 1922-1923*]. Athens: [n.p.], 1973.

[Τζιώτης, Νίκος (Επιμ.)]. *Τα Πενηντάχρονα του Ξερριζωμού 1922-1972* [Tziotes, Nikos. Fifty *Years since the Uprooting 1922-1972*]. Athens: Έκδοσις της Ενώσεως Κάτω Παναγιάς, [1972].

Τοπαλίδης, Πανάρετος Κ. *Ο Πόντος ανά τους αιώνας* [Topalides, Panaretos K. *Pontus Through the Ages*]. Drama: [n.p.], 1929.

[no author], *Τα Τουρκικά εγκλήματα της Κωνσταντινουπόλεως την 6ην και 7ην Σεπτεμβρίου 1955: ή χρονικόν της 3ης αλώσεως της Κωνσταντινουπόλεως και της καταστροφής του εν αυτή Ελληνισμού/[υπό] ανωνύμου αυτόπτου μάρτυρος.*[*The Turkish Crimes of Constantinople on 6 and 7 September 1955: or a Chronicle of the Third Sack of Constantinople and of the Destruction of Its Hellenism, by an Anonymous Eyewitness*]. Athens: Εταιρεία Θρακικών Μελετών, 1956.

Τρεχαντζάκης-Κουτέλης, Γιάγκος Χ. *Σμύρνη – Χίος: Μνήμες φωτιά* [Trechantzakes-Kouteles, Giangos C., Ed. *Smyrna – Chios: Memories of Fire*]. Athens: [n.p.], [n.d.]; reprinted, (Athens: Ρεπάνης), 2007.

Τριανταφύλλου, Κώστας Ν. *Μικρασιατική Καταστροφή: Εισαγωγή εις την ιστοριογραφικήν θεώρησιν του θέματος* [Triantaphyllou, Kostas, N. *The Asia Minor Catastrophe: Introduction into the Historiographic Consideration of the Subject*]. [Patras]: [n.p.], 1962.

Τροβάς, Διονύσιος Α. *Εκεί που δε χτυπούν πια οι καμπάνες: Κρήνη (Τσεσμές)* [Trovas, Dionysios A. *There Where Bells No Longer Ring: Krene (Tsesmes)*]. Athens: Τυπ. Θεοδώρου Ματαφιά, 1976 .

Τσαϊλακόπουλος, Νικόλαος. *Η νοσταλγική γενέτειρά μου το Φουλατζίκι Νικομηδείας Μ. Ασίας* [Tsailakopoulos Nikolaos. *My Nostalgic Birthplace Phoulatziki* [Fulacik] *of Nicomedia Asia Minor*]. Europos: Έκδοσις Μορφωτικού Συλλόγου Ευρωπού, 1987.

Τσακιρίδης, Λάζαρος Χ. *Τόπτσαμ: Το ποντιακό αντάρτικο με τον καπετάν Γοτσάναστας: Αντίσταση στην ποντιακή Γενοκτονία* [Tsakirides, Lazaros C. Toptsam: *The Pontic Rebellion with Captain Gotsanastas: Resistance to the Pontic Genocide*]. Katerine: Εκδόσεις Τέρτιος, 2005.

Τσακόγλου, Βασιλική. *Ο Πρώτος Διωγμός των Ελλήνων στην Ανατολική Θράκη (1913-1918)* [Tsakoglou, Vasilike. *The First Persecution of the Greeks in Eastern Thrace (1913-1918*). Thessalonica: [self published], 2010.

Τσανακτσίδης, Θεόδωρος Β. *Πορεία προς τη λύτρωση: 1853-1923: Ιστορικό ντοκουμέντο* [Tsanaktsides, Theodoros V. *A March Towards Redemption: 1853-1923: An Historical Document*]. Thessalonica: [n.p.], 1997.

Τσαούσης, Αγαθάγγελος Π. *Η ιστορία του εν Πόντω χωριού Χόψα και η καταστροφή αυτής* [Tsaouses, Agathangelos P. *The History of the Village of Chopsa in the Pontus and Its Destruction*]. Athens: [n.p.], 1960; reprinted, Thessalonica: Αδελφοί Κυριακίδη, 2002.

Τσέρτικ, Χριστοφόρου. *Φλόγες στον Πόντο: Χρονικό μιας εποχής [Tsertik, Christophoros. Flames in the Pontus: A Chronicle of an Era].* Athens: [n.p.], 1956.

Τσιρκινίδης, Χάρης. *Συνοπτική Ιστορία της Γενοκτονίας των Ελλήνων της Ανατολής: Ντοκουμέντα Ξένων Διπλωματικών Αρχείων* [Tsirkinides, Chares. *Outline History of the Genocide of the Anatolian Greeks: Documents of Foreign Diplomatic Archives*]. Thessalonica: Αδελφοί Κυριακίδη, 2009.

_____. *Έχω όπλο την αγχόνη: Το ντοκουμέντο της Μεγάλης Καταστροφής υπό το φως των Ξένων Απορρήτων αρχείων 1908-1925 [I have gallows as weapon: The Documents of the Great Catastrophe Illuminated by Foreign Secret Archives 1908-1925*]. Thessalonica: Ερωδιός, 2005.

_____. *Επιτέλους τους ξεριζώσαμε... Η γενοκτονία των Ελλήνων του Πόντου, της Θράκης και της Μικράς Ασίας μέσα από τα γαλλικά αρχεία* [*'At Last We Uprooted Them' The Genocide of the Greeks of Pontus, Thrace and Asia Minor, through the French Archives*]. Thessalonica: Αδελφοί Κυριακίδη, 1995 (multiple printings/editions).

[Τσίτερ, Ηρακλής.] *Διάφορα: Σημειώσεις του Ηρακλή Α. Τσίτερ: Κωνσταντινούπολη–Τρίγλια–Σμύρνη*, επιμ. Εριφύλη Κοντοπούλου. [Tsiter, Herakles. *Varia: The Notes of Herakles A. Tsiter: Constantinople–Triglia–Smyrna*, ed. by Eriphyle Kontopoulou] Xanthe: Πολιτιστικό Αναπτυξιακό Κέντρο Θράκης, 2006.

Υπουργείον Εξωτερικών, *Οι ανθελληνικοί διωγμοί εν Τουρκία από της κηρύξεως του Ευρωπαϊκού πολέμου κατά τας επισήμους εκθέσεις των πρεσβειών και προξενικών Αρχών* [Ministry of Foreign Affairs. *The Anti-Greek Persecutions in Turkey from the Declaration of the European War According to the Official Reports of Embassies and Consular Authorities*]. Athens: Ministry of Foreign Affairs], 1917.

Φαλτάϊτς, Κώστας. *Αυτοί είναι οι Τούρκοι: Αφηγήματα των Σφαγών της Νικομηδείας* [Phaltaits, Kostas. *These Are the Turks: Narratives of the Massacres of Nicomedia*]. Athens: Τυπ. Μ. Δελή, 1921.

Φυλλίζης, Δημήτριος. *Αι τελευταίαι ημέραι της Τραπεζούντος, 1918-1923* [Phyllizes, D. *The Last Days of Trebizond, 1918-1923*]. Thessalonica: Ποντιακή Εστία, 1954; reprinted as *Οι τελευταίες μέρες της Τραπεζούντας 1918-1923*. Thessalonica: Αδελφοί Κυριακίδη, 1998.

Φυτόπουλος, (Παπα-)Βασίλης. *Δεινοπαθήματα των προγόνων μου στον Πόντο* [Phytopoulos, (Father) Vasiles. *The Sufferings of My Ancestrors in the Pontus*]. Xanthe: [n.p.], 1959.

Φουρνιάδης, Παντελής (Επιμ.). *Σελίδες από την ιστορίαν της Κερασούντος και τα τερατουργήματα του αιμοσταγούς Τοπάλ Οσμάν καθ' όλην την περιφέρειαν του Πόντου* [Phourniades, Panteles. *Pages from the History of Kerasous and the Monstrosities of the Bloodthirsty Topal Osman Across the Entire Region of the Pontus*]. Kavala: Έκδοσις Ιωάννου Παπαδοπούλου, 1965.

Φωτεινός, Νικόλαος Γ. *Αναμνήσεις και ιστορήματα από τη Σμύρνη* [Photeinos, Nikolaos G. *Recollections and Stories from Smyrna*]. Athens: Ένωσις Σμυρναίων, 1986.

Φωτιάδης, Κωνσταντίνος. *Η Γενοκτονία των Ελλήνων του Πόντου* [Fotiadis, Konstantinos. *The Genocide of the Greeks of the Pontus*]. Athens: Ίδρυμα της Βουλής των Ελλήνων, 2004.

_____. *Η Γενοκτονία των Ελλήνων του Πόντου Α' (1ος τόμος)* [*The Genocide of the Greeks of the Pontus*, vol. 1]. Thessalonica: Ηρόδοτος, 2004.

_____. *Η Γενοκτονία των Ελλήνων του Πόντου Β' (2ος τόμος)* [*The Genocide of the Greeks of the Pontus*, vol. 2]. Thessalonica: Ηρόδοτος, 2004.

_____. *Η Γενοκτονία των Ελλήνων του Πόντου Γ'(3ος τόμος)* [*The Genocide of the Greeks of the Pontus*, vol. 3]. Thessalonica: Ηρόδοτος, 2004.

_____. *Η Γενοκτονία των Ελλήνων του Πόντου, (4ος τόμος): Αρχεία Υπουργείου Εξωτερικών Ελλάδας (α) 1905-1919* [*The Genocide of the Greeks of the Pontus*, vol. 4. *Archives of the Ministry of Foreign Affairs of Greece (a) 1905-1919*]. Thessalonica: Ηρόδοτος, 2004.

_____. *Η Γενοκτονία των Ελλήνων του Πόντου (5ος τόμος): Αρχεία Υπουργείου Εξωτερικών Ελλάδας (β) 1920-1925* [*The Genocide of the Greeks of the Pontus*, vol. 5. *Archives of the Ministry of Foreign Affairs of Greece (b) 1920-1925*]. Thessalonica: Ηρόδοτος, 2004.

_____. *Η Γενοκτονία των Ελλήνων του Πόντου (6ος τόμος): Πρακτικά Κοινοβουλίων, Αρχεία Ιστορικών Κέντρων, Ερευνητικών Ιδρυμάτων, Προσφυγικών Σωματείων και Ιδιωτών* [*The Genocide of the Greeks of the Pontus*, vol. 6. *Proceedings of Parliaments, Archives of Historical Centers, Research Institutes, Refugee Associations and Individuals*]. Thessalonica: Ηρόδοτος, 2004.

_____. *Η Γενοκτονία των Ελλήνων του Πόντου (7ος τόμος): Αρχεία Υπουργείου Εξωτερικών Γερμανίας, Αυστρίας, Ιταλίας, Βατικανού: Μεταφρασμένα έγγραφα* [*The Genocide of the Greeks of the Pontus*, vol. 7. *Archives of the Ministry of Foreign Affairs of Germany, Austria, Italy, The Vatican: Translated Documents*]. Thessalonica: Ηρόδοτος, 2004.

_____. *Η Γενοκτονία των Ελλήνων του Πόντου (8ος τόμος): Αρχεία Υπουργείου Εξωτερικών Μ. Βρεταννίας, Γαλλίας, Κοινωνίας των Εθνών και S.H.A.T.* [*The Genocide of the Greeks of the Pontus*, vol. 8. *Archives of the Ministry of Foreign Affairs of Great Britain, France, the League of Nations and S.H.A.T.*]. Thessalonica: Ηρόδοτος, 2004.

_____. *Η Γενοκτονία των Ελλήνων του Πόντου (9ος τόμος): Αρχεία Υπουργείου Εξωτερικών Ρωσσίας και Σοβιετικής Ένωσης: Μεταφρασμένα έγγραφα* [*The Genocide of the Greeks of the Pontus*, vol. 9. *Archives of the Ministry of Foreign Affairs of Russia and the Soviet Union (Translated documents)*]. Thessalonica: Ηρόδοτος [Herodotus], 2004.

_____. *Η Γενοκτονία των Ελλήνων του Πόντου (10ος τόμος): Δημοσιεύματα ελληνικού και κυπριακού τύπου* [*The Genocide of the Greeks of the Pontus*, vol. 10. *Articles of the Hellenic and the Cypriot Press*]. Thessalonica: Ηρόδοτος, 2004.

_____. *Η Γενοκτονία των Ελλήνων του Πόντου (11ος τόμος): Ελληνικά και ξενόγλωσσα άρθρα και δημοσιεύσεις ιστορικών αφηγήσεων* [*The Genocide of the Greeks of the Pontus*, vol. 11. *Greek and Foreign Articles and Publications of Historical Narratives*]. Thessalonica: Ηρόδοτος, 2004.

_____. *Η Γενοκτονία των Ελλήνων του Πόντου (12ος τόμος): Αρχεία Υπουργείου Εξωτερικών Γερμανίας, Αυστρίας, Ιταλίας, Βατικανού: Πρωτότυπα έγγραφα* [*The Genocide of the Greeks of the Pontus*, vol. 12. *Archives of the Ministry of Foreign Affairs of Germany, Austria, Italy, The Vatican: Original Documents*]. Thessalonica: Ηρόδοτος, 2004.

_____. *Η Γενοκτονία των Ελλήνων του Πόντου (13ος τόμος): Αρχεία Υπουργείου Εξωτερικών Μ. Βρεταννίας, Γαλλίας, Κοινωνίας των Εθνών και S.H.A.T.: Πρωτότυπα έγγραφα* [*The Genocide of the Greeks of the Pontus*, vol. 13. *Archives of the Ministry of Foreign Affairs of Great Britain, France, the League of Nations and S.H.A.T.: Original Documents*]. Thessalonica: Ηρόδοτος, 2004.

_____. *Η Γενοκτονία των Ελλήνων του Πόντου (14ος τόμος): Αρχεία Υπουργείου Εξωτερικών Ρωσσίας και Σοβιετικής Ένωσης: Πρωτότυπα έγγραφα* [*The Gen-*

ocide of the Greeks of the Pontus, vol. 14. *Archives of the Ministry of Foreign Affairs of Russia and the Soviet Union: Original Documents*]. Thessalonica: Ηρόδοτος, 2004.

_____. *Η Μικρασιατική Καταστροφή: Αφηγήσεις, Ντοκουμέντα, Μελετήματα* [*The Asia Minor Catastrophe: Narratives, Documents, Studies*]. 2 vols. Pella: Εκδόσεις Καλοκάθη [in Athens], 2000.

_____. *Πηγές της Ιστορίας του Κρυπτοχριστιανικού Προβλήματος*. [*Sources on the History of the Problem of Crypto-Christianity*]. Thessalonica: Εκδοτικός Οίκος Αδελφών Κυριακίδη, 1997.

_____. *Οι Εξισλαμισμοί της Μικράς Ασίας και οι Κρυπτοχριστιανοί*. [*The Islamizations in Asia Minor and the Crypto-Christians of the Pontus*]. Thessalonica: Αδελφοί Κυριακίδη, 1988.

_____. (Επιμ.). *Μικρασιατική Καταστροφή : Αφηγήσεις–Ντοκουμέντα–Μελετήματα* [Fotiadis, K. ed. *The Asia Minor Catastrophe: Narratives–Documents–Studies*]. Athens: Εκδόσεις Καλοκάθη, 2008.

Φωτιάδης, Κ. & Μ. Χαραλαμπίδης. *Πόντιοι: Δικαίωμα στην Μνήμη* [Fotiadis, K. and M. Charalampides. *Pontians: The Right to Memory*]. Thessalonica: Κέντρο Ποντιακών Μελετών, 1987.

Χαϊδεμένου, Φιλιώ. *Τρεις αιώνες, μια ζωή: Γιαγιά Φιλιώ η Μικρασιάτισσα* [Chaidemenou, Philio. *Three Centuries, One Life: Granny Philio from Asia Minor*]. Athens: Λιβάνης, 2005.

Χαμουδόπουλος, Α., *Από το ημερολόγιον ενός δημοσιογράφου 1908-1948* [Chamoudopoulos, A. *From the Diary of a Journalist*]. Thessalonica: [n.p.], 1948.

Χατζηγεωργίου, Χρήστος. *Το Ορτάκιοϊ Βιθυνίας: Αι σφαγαί και η ξεθεμελίωσις αυτών* [sic] [Chatzegeorgiou, Chrestos. *Ortaköy of Bithynia: The Massacres and Their Extermination* (sic)]. Athens: [self published], 1965.

Χατζημωϋσής, Παύλος. *Βιβλιογραφία 1919-1978: Μικρασιατική εκστρατεία–ήττα, προσφυγιά*. [Chatzemoyses, Paulos. *Bibliography 1919-1978: Asia Minor Expedition–Defeat-Refugeeship*]. Athens: Ερμής, 1981.

Χιονίδης, Κ. *Ο Ελληνικός Πόντος* [Chionides, K. *Hellenic Pontus*]. Thessalonica: (Επιμέλεια Έκδοσης Εφημερίδα) *Ένωση Ποντίων* , 1983.

Χόρμπος, Νικόλαος Α. *Παλαιά Φωκαία Μικράς Ασίας* [Chormpos, Nikolaos A. *Old Phocaea of Asia Minor*]. Thessalonica: Εκδόσεις +γραμμα, 1988.

Χρηματόπουλος, Γεώργιος Θ. *Η πένθιμος ηχώ της δορυλικής σάλπιγγος περιλαμβάνουσα τα από του έτους 1916-1924 δεινοπαθήματατων ομογενών του Δορυλαίου (Δορούλ) νομού Τραπεζούντος* [Chrematopoulos, Georgios T. *The Mourning Sound of the Dorylaean Trumpet Containing the Sufferings of the Greeks of Dorylaion (Dorul) of the District of Trebizond*]. Drama: Αναστασόπουλος, 1927; reprinted as *Η Άρδασσα του Πόντου 1916-24: Τα δεινοπαθήματα των ομογενών του Δορυλαίου (Δορούλ) νομού Τραπεζούντος* [*Ardassa of the Pontus: 1916-24: The Sufferings of the Greeks of Dorylaion (Dorul) of the District of Trebizond*]. Thessalonica: Αδελφοί Κυριακίδη, 1996.

Χρύσανθος, Μητροπολίτης Τραπεζούντος *Βιογραφικαί αναμνήσεις του Αρχιεπισκόπου Αθηνών Χρυσάνθου του από Τραπεζούντος 1881-1949*. Επιμ. Γεωργ[ίου].

N. Τασούδη [Chrysanthos, Metropolitan of Trebizond. *(Auto)-Biographic Recollections of the Archbishop of Athens Chrysanthos, formerly Metropolitan of Trebizond, 1881-1949*. Ed. by Georgios. N. Tasoudes]. Athens: [n.p.], 1970.

Χρυσόστομος, Μητροπολίτης Σμύρνης. *Το αρχείον του εθνομάρτυρος Σμύρνης Χρυσοστόμου*. [Chrysostom, Metropolitan of Smyrna. *The Archive of Ethnomartyr Chrysostom of Smyrna*]. Athens: Μορφωτικό Ίδρυμα Εθνικής Τραπέζης, 2000.

Χρυσοχόου, Ιφιγένεια. *Πυρπολημένη Γη* [Chrysochoou, Iphigeneia. *Scorched Earth*]. Thessalonica: Εκδόσεις Αλέξανδρος, 1999.

_____. *Μαρτυρική Πορεία: Το Χρονικό της Ομηρίας 1922-1924* [*The Martyrical March: The Chronicle of Captivity 1922-1924*]. Athens: Εκδόσεις Ζαχόπουλος 1974; reprinted, Athens: Εκδόσεις Φιλιππότη, 1982.

Ψαθάς, Δημήτρης. *Γή του Πόντου: Χρονικό* [Psathas, Demetres. *The Pontian Land: A Chronicle*]. Athens: Φυτράκης, 1966 (and multiple subsequent reprintings).

ARTICLES

Alexandris, A. "Pontic Greek Refugees in Constantinople 1922-1923: The Human Cost of the Exchange of Populations." *Archeion Pontou* 37 (1982).

Bjørnlund, Matthias. "The 1914 Cleansing of Aegean Greeks as a Case of Violent Turkification." *Journal of Genocide Research* 10, no. 1 (March 2008): 41-58.

_____. "'When the Cannons Talk, the Diplomats Must Be Silent:' A Danish Diplomat in Constantinople during the Armenian Genocide." *Genocide Studies & Prevention (GSP)* 1, no. 2 (Fall 2006): 197-223.

Chapuisat, Edouard. "L'opinion genevoise contre les persécutions anti-grecques." *Les Études Franco-Grecques* (July 1918).

Clogg, Richard. "London and Greece, 1915-1922." In *Greece and Great Britain during World War I: First Symposium Organized in Thessaloniki (December 15-17, 1983) by the Institute of Balkan Studies and King's College*, 193-210. Thessalonica: Institute of Balkan Studies, 1985.

Eleftheriou, Eleni. "Ethnic Heterogeneity, Cultural Homogenization, and State Policy in the Interwar Balkans." In *Ethnic Cleansing in Twentieth-Century Europe*, edited by Steven Béla Váry and T. Hunt Tooley, 122-134. Boulder: Columbia University Press, 2003.

Glasgow, George. "The Greeks in Smyrna." *New Europe* (25 March 1920).

Gehri, Maurice. "Mission d'enquête en Anatolie, 12-22 May, 1921. " *Revue Internationale de la Croix-Rouge* (Geneva) 31 (1921).

Gust, Wolfgang. "Verständnislose Auswüchse des Militarismus." *Historicum: Zeitschrift für Geschichte* (Herbst 2007): 19-25.

Hassiotis, Ioannis K. "Shared Illusions: Greek-Armenian Cooperation in Asia Minor and the Caucasus 1919-22." In *Greece and Great Britain during World War I: First Symposium Organized in Thessaloniki (December 15-17, 1983) by the Institute of Balkan Studies and King's College*, 139-192. Thessalonica: Institute of Balkan Studies, 1985.

Hasluck, W. "The Crypto-Christians of Trebizond." *Journal of Hellenic Studies* 41 no. 2 (1921)

Hildebrand, Émile. "Kemal Promises More Hangings of Political Antagonists in Turkey." *Los Angeles Examiner* (Sunday Edition), 1 August 1926, sec. 6.

Hlamides, Nikolaos. "The Greek Relief Committee: America's Response to the Greek Genocide." *Genocide Studies and Prevention* 3, no. 3 (2008).

Housepian, Marjorie Dobkin. "George Horton and Mark L. Bristol: Opposing Forces in the U.S. Domestic Policy, 1919-1923." *Deltio: Bulletin of the Centre for Asia Minor Studies* (Athens) 4 (1983).

Janin, R. "Musulmans malgré eux: Les Stavriotes." *Échos d'Orient* 15 (1912).

King, William C. "1,500,000 Greek Christians Massacred or Deported by Turks." In *King's Complete History of the World War: Visualizing the Great Conflict in all Theaters of Action 1914-1918*. Boston: The History Associates, 1922

Kitromilides, Paschalis M. "Greek Irredentism in Asia Minor and Cyprus." *Middle Eastern Studies* 26, no. 1 (1990).

Levene, Mark. "Creating a Modern 'Zone of Genocide:' The Impact of Nation– and State–Formation on Eastern Anatolia, 1878-1923." *Holocaust and Genocide Studies* 12 (1998).

Lieberman, Ben. "Consequences of Population Transfers: The 1923 Case of Greece and Turkey." In *Ethnic Cleansing in Twentieth-Century Europe*, edited by Steven Béla Váry and T. Hunt Tooley. Boulder: Columbia University Press, 2003.

Lloyd, W. A. "More Turkish Massacres in Asia Minor." *Review of Reviews* (December 1919).

"L'oeuvre germano-turque d'extermination en Asie Mineure." *Les Études Franco-Grecques* (April 1920).

Macfie, A. L. "British Views of the Turkish Nationalist Movement in Anatolia, 1919-1922." *Middle Eastern Studies* 38, no. 3 (July 2002).

"Massacre of the Greeks in Turkey." *The New York Times Current History: The European War.* Vol. 18. New York: The New York Times Company, 1919

Sartiaux, Félix. "Turks and Greeks in Asia Minor." *New Europe* (19 February 1920)

Schaller, Dominik J. and Jürgen Zimmerer. "Late Ottoman Genocides: The Dissolution of the Ottoman Empire and Young Turkish Population and Extermination Policies." *Journal of Genocide Research* 10, no. 1 (March 2008): 7-14

"'Smyrna' oder nochmals Türken und die christlichen Völker Kleinasiens." *Der Orient* 4, no. 5 (1925).

Travis, Hannibal B. "'Native Christians Massacred': The Ottoman Genocide of the Assyrians during World War I." *Genocide Studies and Prevention* 1 no. 3 (December 2006).

Üngör, Uğur Ü. "When Persecution Bleeds into Mass Murder: The Processive Nature of Genocide." *Genocide Studies & Prevention (GSP)* 1, no. 2 (Fall 2006): 173-95.

[Uregian, Hovakim and Krikor Baghdjian]. "Two Unpublished Eyewitness Accounts of the Holocaust of Smyrna." *Armenian Review* (1982): 362-89

Vryonis, Speros. "Greek Labor Battalions in Asia Minor." *In* Richard Hovannisian, ed. *The Armenian Genocide: Cultural and Ethical Legacies*, 270-290. New Brunswick, NJ: Transaction Publishers, 2007.

Zayas, Alfred de. "Ethnic Cleansing in the Greek-Turkish Conflicts from the Balkan Wars through the Treaty of Lausanne: Identifying and Defining Ethnic Cleansing." In *Ethnic Cleansing in Twentieth-Century Europe*, edited by Steven Béla Váry and T. Hunt Tooley. Boulder: Columbia University Press, 2003.

REPORTS AND ARTICLES FROM CONTEMPORARY PRESS

[1909]

"Meaning of the Massacres of Christians," *The New York Times*, 25 July 1909

[1912]

"Panic in Constantinople," *The New York Times*, 2 November 1912

"Peril of Massacre in Constantinople," *The New York Times*, 8 November 1912

[1913]

"Turks Massacre Greeks in Thrace," *The New York Times*, 28 July 1913

[1914]

"Turkish Persecution of Greeks," *The Times*, 18 April 1914

"Persecution of Greeks," *The Times*, 28 April 1914

"Massacre of Greeks Feared at Nitilene,"(sic!) *The Wichita Daily Times*, 12 June 1914

"Greece Tells Turks to Stop Expulsions," *The New York Times*, 13 June 1914

"Massacre of Greeks Charged to the Turks," *The Atlanta Constitution*, 17 June 1914

"Turks Slay 100 Greeks," *The New York Times*, 17 June 1914

"Turkish Atrocities against Greeks," *The Scotsman*, 19 June 1914

"Plight of Greek Refugees," *The Times*, 9 July 1914

"Turks to War on Christians," *The Cook County Herald*, 28 August 1914

"Report Christians in Peril in Turkey," *The New York Times*, 12 November 1914

"Turks Massacre Greeks," *The Denton Journal*, 19 December 1914

[1915]

"Greeks in Asia Minor," *The Scotsman*, 11 January 1915

"Says Turks Advise Christians to Flee," *The New York Times*, 11 January 1915

"Christians in Great Peril," *The New York Times*, 13 January 1915

"Peril of the Christians in Turkey Never So Great." *The Washington Post*, 12 July 1915

"Persecution of Greeks." *The Scotsman*, 15 July 1915

"Greek Population of Turkey." *The Scotsman*, 20 July 1915

"Women Massacred by Turks." *The Fitchburg Daily Sentinel*, 22 July 1915

"Turkish Cabinet Split." *The Washington Post*, 27 August 1915

"A Byzantine Remnant." *The Times* (London), 10 September 1915

[1916]

"Massacres of Greeks in Turkey Reported," *The New York Times*, 20 April 1916

"Turks Deporting Greeks," *The New York Times*, 21 August 1916

"Turks in a Wholesale Massacre of Greeks," *The Chillicothe Constitution*, 2 October 1916

[1917]

"Deportations of Greeks." *The Scotsman*, 22 May 1917

"Deportation of Greeks in Asia Minor." *The Scotsman*, 23 May 1917

"Persecution of the Greeks." *The Scotsman*, 9August 1917

"Extermination of Greeks in Turkey." *The Times*," 23 August 1917

"Greek Deportations; The Needs of the Latest Victims of Turkish Cruelty." *The New York Times*, 8 October 1917

"Turks are Backed by Germany." *The Warren Evening Mirror*, 17 October 1917

"Turks Slaughter Christian Greeks." *The Lincoln Daily Star*, 19 October 1917

"Germans Help Turks in Deportation of Greeks." *The Lincoln Daily Star*, 28 October 1917
"Greek Persecution in Turkey." *The Scotsman*, 6 November 1917
"Hope America will Aid Greeks in Asia Minor." *The New York Times*, 19 November 1917
"The Need Colossal." *The Colorado Transcript*, 13 December 1917

[1918]
"1,000,000 Greeks Killed?" *The New York Times*, 1 January 1918
"1,000,000 Greeks Are Put to Death." *The Washington Post*, 1 January 1918
"Greek Massacres." *The Coshocton Tribune*, 9 January 1918
"Turkish Atrocities Continue." *The Newark Daily Advocate*, 27 March 1918
"Bombarding Ships Rescue 2,000 Greeks." *The New York Times*, 7 April 1918
"Turks Slaughter Greeks, Sell Women to Slavery." *The Los Angeles Times*, 9 June 1918
"Turkish Cruelty Bared by Greeks." *The New York Times*, 16 June 1918
"250,000 Exiled by Turks." *The Washington Post*, 3 August 1918
"Tells of Turkish Cruelty to Greeks." *The New York Times*, 26 August 1918
"Christians To Die Under German Edict." *The Syracuse Herald*, 4 September 1918
"Germans Inspired Turkish Atrocities Against Asiatic Greeks." *The New York Times*, 29 September 1918
"Proves German Guilt." *The Daily Northwestern*, 28 October 1918
"Greece." *The Syracuse Herald*, 1 November 1918
"900,000 Greeks Killed." *The New York Times*, 3 December 1918
"Turks Organizing New Massacres." *The New York Times*, 8 December 1918
"Turks Massacred 700,000 Greeks – 200,000 More Died of Suffering." *The Japan Times & Mail*, 8 December 1918
"Deputies Ask Turkish Government What Steps Will Be Taken." *The Elyria Evening Telegram*, 13 December 1918.

[1919]
"The Greatest Tragedy of the Great War." *The Littleton Independent*, 10 January 1919
"First Hun Held for Atrocities." *The Reno Evening Gazette*, 18 March 1919
"Extermination of Greeks." *The Times* (London), 21 March 1919
"Turks Massacre Greeks." *The New York Times*, 21 March 1919
"Greeks Persecuted by Young Turks." *The Syracuse Herald*, 30 March 1919
"Urge Turks to Massacre All Greeks in Thrace." *The New York Times*, 5 June 1919
"Tells How Turks Tortured Greeks." *The New York Times*, 5 July 1919
"Turkey Condemns Its War Leaders." *The New York Times*, 13 July 1919
"Turkish Bath Weapon." *The Stevens Point Journal*, 11 September 1919
"Reported Turkish Atrocities in Asia Minor." *The Scotsman*, 22 September 1919
"Turks Murdering Greeks." *The New York Times*, 23 September 1919

[1920]
"Turks Sentence Two Leaders For Organizing Massacres," *The New York Times*, 21 January 1920.
"Report Turks Killed Many In Rodosto," *The New York Times*, 4 March 1920.
"Kendallville Woman is Returning From Turkey," *The Fort Wayne News and Sentinel*, 1 April 1920
"Mild Greek Rule Prevails in Smyrna," *The New York Times*, 14 June 1920.
"Turkey Deporting Greeks," *The Ignacio Chieftain*, 5 November 1920.
"Turks Expel Greeks," *The Reno Evening Gazette*, 23 December 1920.

[1921]
"Massacre of Greeks Rages," *The Oakland Tribune*, 3 June 1921.
"Massacre of Christians Reported in Western Asia," *The Chronicle Telegram*, 3 June 1921
"Reported Massacre of Greeks," *The Argus*," 6 June 1921
"700,000 Greeks Victims of Turks," *The New York Times*, 10 July 1921
"Woeful Plight of Black Sea Greeks," *The Lincoln State Journal*, 9 August 1921
"Extermination Plan Alleged," *The Los Angeles Times*, 9 August 1921
"Church is Made Turks Have Plan of Extermination," *The Fort Collins Courier*, 10 August 1921
"Near East Aid Asked by Greek Patriarch," The Christian Science Monitor, 13 August 1921
"Villages Fired by Kemalists," *The Scotsman*, 18 August 1921
"Aidin a Vast Sepulchre," *The New York Times*, 29 August 1921
"Alleged Turkish Atrocities," *The Scotsman*, 12 September 1921
"Alleged Turkish Crime," *The Scotsman*, 7 October 1921
"The Turk at Work," *The Times*, 26 October 1921
"Reports Massacres of Greeks in Pontus," *The New York Times*, 6 November 1921
"Turks Persecute Christians Again," *The New York Times*, 2 December 1921
"Bill Condemns Turk Brutality," *The Reno Evening Gazette*, 14 December 1921
"Harding Urged to Intervene Against Turkish Atrocities," *The New York Times*, 15 December 1921

[1922]
"300 Greeks Massacred." *The New York Times*, 1 February 1922
"Slaughter By Turks Reported Going On Just As Formerly." *The Fort Collins Courier*, 2 February 1922
"Turks Burn 24 Greek Villages." *The New York Times*, 30 March 1922
"Turks Massacre Greek Christians." *The Record Journal of Douglas County*, 21 April1922
"Turks' Insane Savagery." *The Times*, 5 May 1922
"Killing by Turks has been Renewed." *The New York Times*, 6 May 1922
"Turkey Renews Persecutions Against Greeks." *The Syracuse Herald*, 14 May 1922
"Turkish Deportations." *The Times*, 16 May 1922
"The Unspeakable Turk." *The Irish Times*, 16 May 1922
"Turkish Atrocities Stir Britain to Act." *The New York Times*, 16 May 1922
"New Style of Atrocities Youths Permitted to Starve in Compounds." The Charleston Daily Mail, 31 May 1922
"303,238 Massacred, Greek Minister Says." *The New York Times*, 2 June 1922
"Quick Action Urged To Get Atrocity Proof." *The New York Times*, 6 June 1922
"Says 22,000 Greeks Died on the March." *The New York Times*, 7 June 1922
"Kemalist War on Christians." *The Times*, 8 June 1922
"Massacres Up In Commons." *The New York Times*, 16 June 1922
"Greeks Are Beheaded in Asia Minor." *The Sheboygan Press Telegram*, 21 June 1922
"Starve Christians; Lay it to Allah." *The New York Times*, 25 June 1922
"Greeks, Assyrians and Armenians to Protest." *The Fitchburg Sentinel*, 30 June 1922
"Near East Relief Prevented from Helping Greeks," *The Christian Science Monitor*, 13 July 1922
"Greeks Demand Action By World Against The Turk," *The Christian Science Monitor*, 17 July 1922
"Tells of Deporting Greeks and Others," *The Nevada State Journal*, 27 July 1922

"Kemal Won't Insure Against Massacres," *The New York Times*, 11 September 1922
"Bishop Would Use Navy Against Turks, Cannon Calls for, if Necessary, to Avert More Massacres," *The New York Times*, 14 September 1922
"Smyrna Burning," *The New York Times*, 15 September 1922
"Wholesale Massacre," *The Mexia Evening News*, 15 September 1922
"City A Mass of Wreckage," *The New York Times*, 16 September 1922
"Boston Greeks Pledge Help," *The Boston Daily Globe*, 18 September 1922
"120,000 Die in Turk Massacre," *The Ignacio Chieftain*, 22 September 1922
"Slain Archbishop Foresaw Massacre." *The New York Times*, 24 September 1922
"Report That 900 Christians Were Massacred in Bigha." *The New York Times*, 27 September 1922
"Thracian Deputies Appeal To Harding." *The New York Times*, 8 October 1922
"Woman Pictures Smyrna Horrors." *The New York Times*, 9 October 1922
"Greek Priests Burned When Scorn Islam." *The Fort Collins Courier*, 2 November 1922
"Expulsion of Christians." *The Times*, 3 November 1922
"Driving Greeks From Pontus." *The New York Times*, November 13th 1922
"Turks Declare Banishment Edict." The New York Times, 2 December 1922
"Turks Torture Greek Refugees." *The Los Angeles Times*, 31 December 1922

[1923]
"Uprooting of Greeks in Turkey." *The New York Times*, 21 January 1923
"Turks Resume Their Deportations Despite Raging Epidemics." *The Fort Collins Courier*, 27 January 1923
"Turks' Blow at Relief Work." *The Times* (London), 6 April 1923
"Christians Driven Out of Anatolia." *The New York Times*, 21 August 1923
"Turkey Deporting Greeks, Armenians." *The Indianapolis Star*, 21 August 1923

THE GENOCIDE OF THE OTTOMAN GREEKS AND THE "POPULATION EXCHANGE" IN FACTIONAL AND FICTIONAL PROSE

Andreadis, Giorgios. *Tamama: The Missing Girl of Pontus.* Athens: Gordios, 1993

Barford, Dora: *Greek Fire: A Tale of the Levant.* London: George G. Harrap, 1935

Eugenides, Jeffrey. *Middlesex.* New York: Farrar Straus & Giroux, 2002 (German ed., Reinbek: Rowohlt, 2003).

Hemingway, Ernest. *In Our Time.* New York: Boni & Liveright, 1925 (The chapter titled "On the Quai at Smyrna" was first published as the introduction to the 1930 edition).

_____, *The Wild Years.* Ed. Gene Z. Hanrahan. New York, 1962

Kemal, Yaşar [= Göğceli, Kemal Sadık]. *Fırat Suyu Kan Akıyor Baksana* [*Look, Blood is Flowing in the Euphrates*]. Istanbul: Adam Yayınları, 1998. German edition, *Die Ameiseninsel.* Zürich: Unionsverlag, 2001)

Βενέζης, Ηλίας. *Το Νούμερο 31328* [Venezis, Elias (= Mellos, Elias). *Number 31328*]. Athens: Βιβλιοπωλείον της Εστίας, 2004 (first published 1931).

_____, *Μικρασία, Χαίρε: Διήγησις συμβάντων* [*Asia Minor, Goodbye: A Narration of Events*]. Athens: Βιβλιοπωλείον της Εστίας, 1995 (first published 1974, many reprintings)

Σωτηρίου, Διδώ (Soteriou, Dido). *Farewell Anatolia.* Athens: Kedros, 1991.

Προκοπίου, Σωκράτης. *Ψέμματα και σαν Αλήθεια. Τα τελευταία χρόνια. Μικρασιατικόν ιστορικόν μυθιστόρημα* [Prokopiou, Sokrates. *Like Lies and Like Truth. The Later Years. An Asia Minor Historical Novel*]. Athens: [n.p.],1928.

GENOCIDE AND "POPULATION EXCHANGE" IN FILMS

- *Seeing is Believing* or *Uncle America Sees It Through* (USA c. 1920)

- *America, America* [also: *The Anatolian Smile*] (USA 1963); directed by Elia Kazan

- *1922* (Greece 1978); directed by Nikos Koundouros (based on Elias Venezis, *Number 31328* – see above)

- *Παιδιά Είμαστε Τότε... οι Μικρασιάτες Θυμούνται* [We Were Children Then... Reminiscences of Asia Minor Refugees] (Greece 1999); produced by the Foundation of the Hellenic World [FHW]

- *Το Ταξίδι* [The Journey]; directed by Maria Mavrikou (Greece n.d.), produced by FHW

- *Η Μικρασιατική Καταστροφή* [The Catastrophe in Asia Minor]; (Greece 2006), 3 vols., produced by Leon Films

- *Bulutları betlerken* [Waiting for the Clouds] (Turkey 2003); directed by Yeşim Ustaoğlu after the novel "Tamama" by Georgios Andreadis

- *A Touch of Spice* (Greece/Turkey 2003), directed by Tassos Boulmetis with George Corraface and Ieroklis Michailidis

- *Voices* (USA 2007), Aramai Films; directed by Apo Torosyan

- *The Morgenthau Story* (USA 2008), Aramai Films; directed by Apo Torosyan

STATE & OTHER ARCHIVAL SOURCES

Austria: Österreichisches Staatsarchiv, Wien
Belgium: Ministère des Affaires étrangères, Archives diplomatiques, Bruxelles
France: Ministère des Affaires étrangères: Direction des Archives, Quai d'Orsay, Paris
France: Ministère de la Défense: Service historique de la Défense (Centre historique des archives), Château des Vincennes, Vincennes, Paris
France: Assemblée nationale: Archives de l'Assemblée nationale, Paris
France : Sénat français : Service des archives du Sénat, Paris
Germany: Politisches Archiv des Auswärtigen Amtes [Political Archives of the Foreign Office], Berlin
Great Britain: Foreign Office Archives, Kew
Great Britain: Parliamentary Archives, Westminster
Great Britain: Imperial War Museum Archives, London
Greece: Ministry of Foreign Affairs Historical Archive, Athens
Greece: Centre for Asia Minor Studies Archive, Athens
Italy: Ministero degli Affari esteri, Archivio Storico Diplomatico, Farnesina, Roma
Switzerland: League of Nations, United Nations Office at Geneva (UNOG) Library, Geneva
Turkey: Ottoman Government's official gazette (Takvim-i Vekayi) in which the proceedings of the Turkish Military Tribunal are recorded
United States: National Archives, Records of the Department of States
United States: American Board of Commissioners for Foreign Missions (Originals housed at Harvard's Houghton Library but a microfilm copy of the collection is housed at a number of institutions)
United States: Records of the Department of State Relating to Political Relations between Turkey and Other States, 1910-29 (Microfilm collection)
The Vatican: Archivio Segreto Vaticano, The Vatican City-State

PHOTOGRAPHIC ARCHIVES

Benaki Museum (Μουσείο Μπενάκη), Athens, Greece
Hlamides, Nikolaos: private collection located in the United Kingdom (A selection of this collection has been reproduced in this volume)
Imperial War Museum Archive, London, Great Britain
Library of Congress Prints & Photographs, Washington, D.C., United States
War Museum (Πολεμικό Μουσείο), Athens, Greece
Union of Smyrneans (Ένωση Σμυρναίων), Athens, Greece
Hellenic Literary and Historical Archives (Ελληνικό Λογοτεχνικό και Ιστορικό Αρχείο, also known as ΕΛΙΑ), Athens, Greece

Index